ADVERTISING MANAGEMENT IN CANADA

-

ADVERTISING MANAGEMENT
in Canada

René Y. Darmon
Faculty of Management
McGill University
Montreal, Quebec

Michel Laroche
Department of Marketing
Concordia University
Montreal, Quebec

JOHN WILEY & SONS
TORONTO   NEW YORK   CHICHESTER   BRISBANE   SINGAPORE

CANADIAN CATALOGUING IN PUBLICATION DATA

Darmon, René Y.
   Advertising management in Canada

Includes bibliographical references and indexes.
ISBN 0-471-79794-4

1. Advertising—Canada—Management.   I. Laroche,
Michel.   II. Title.

HF5823.D37   659.1'11'0971   C82-094067-7

Cover illustrations courtesy of General Motors of Canada Ltd.,
General Foods Ltd., Mary Kay Cosmetics, Inc., Tourism British Columbia,
Robin Hood Multifoods Inc., IBM Canada Ltd.

DESIGN: Brant Cowie/Artplus Ltd.
TYPESETTING: Linotext Inc.

Printed and bound in Canada
10 9 8 7 6 5 4 3 2 1

To Nicole and Anne

Contents

Preface

Advertising has always played a major role in the Canadian way of life. This country, in turn, has contributed substantially to the growth of modern advertising. As early as 1890, concepts of advertising were being developed and refined in Canada. In that year, a former member of the Royal Canadian Mounted Police, John E. Kennedy, formulated the modern definition of advertising as "salesmanship in print".

This book looks at advertising mostly from management's point of view. Canadian advertisers, advertising agencies, and media face unique problems because of the special nature of Canada's market environment, and *Advertising Management in Canada* provides its readers with the theoretical knowledge and practical skills required to make advertising decisions within this environment. Since the advertising management function includes many different kinds of decision making, methods relevant to each kind are discussed and assessed here.

Based on input from all major Canadian sources, this text has been written to meet the needs of several groups of people:

- Business majors and other students of courses in advertising management at Canadian universities and colleges
- Users of mass communication, including marketing and advertising managers in firms, government agencies, and other institutions; advertising agencies; and media personnel
- Public relations managers in nonprofit organizations
- Anyone in this country or abroad who needs to

have a good grasp of what makes advertising different in Canada.

The text consists of five parts:

1. *The role and functions of advertising* within the marketing plan. This part places particular emphasis on interactions and co-ordination with the other marketing mix variables. It assumes a minimal knowledge of marketing.

2. *The structure and role of advertising organizations* in Canada. Examining these organizations from the manager's viewpoint, the four chapters in this part answer questions about selecting (or firing) an agency, and evaluating each medium.

3. *Opportunity analysis.* Drawing heavily on the behavioural sciences and communication theory, these four chapters discuss buyers' motivations and perceptions, attitudes, decision processes, purchase behaviour, and market behaviour. The theories are related to the development of advertising campaigns in the Canadian environment.

4. *Management of advertising programs.* This part describes the main decision areas and stages of the advertising campaign, including:
- the development of sound advertising objectives
- the process of developing an advertising budget
- the creation of an effective message
- the development of a media plan
- how to find the information relevant to a particular advertising program.

5. The concluding part of this book discusses the *economic and social effects of advertising* on Canadian society.

At the end of all chapters, there are summaries, questions for study, and problems to solve. Each part is followed by "Campaign Histories", which may be used to discuss some of the material developed in that part. Since they are summaries of actual Canadian campaigns, these campaign histories may raise other points nor directly related to the part after which they appear. They may be used to focus attention on various topics such as objectives, creative, and media selection. The discussions should help the reader in understanding the material, integrating various concepts, and applying it to his or her own campaign.

Appendices on broadcasting regulations and advertising production appear at the back of the book, along with a comprehensive glossary of advertising terms, including equivalent French terms.

The development of this text has generated an unusual amount of enthusiasm on the part of many individuals and organizations, and we are fortunate to have benefitted from their cooperation and encouragement. First, we would like to express our gratitude to M. Dale Beckman (University of Manitoba), Gord McLeod (Sheridan College), Robert G. Wyckham (Simon Fraser University), and H. Clifton Young (University of Alberta) for their thorough and thoughtful reviews of an early draft of manuscript. In addition, Harold Simpkins, Robert E. Oliver (President, Advertising Advisory Board), Nancy Church (SUNY, Plattsburg), and Christopher Ross (Concordia University) provided valuable comments on various portions of the manuscript.

We would also like to thank all the firms that gave us permission to reproduce their advertisements and/or storyboards. Their contribution is acknowledged throughout the book. We are also particularly grateful to the following individuals, who took a deep interest in our undertaking and gave us valuable comments: Eric C. Riordan, Pierre Pelland, and Nora Frechette (Publicité Foster); F. W. Convery and H. J. Scandrett (F. H. Hayhurst); Ross Hulme and David Saunders; Leon Burger (J. Walter Thompson); Keith B. McKerracher (Institute of Canadian Advertisers); Charles Laws (Atlas Copco); Kenneth Chan and Nancy Cunningham (Bureau of Broadcast Measurement); Gordon Steventon (Cadbury Schweppes Powell); Janis Chilcott (A. C. Nielsen of Canada); Janet M. Roger (Newspaper Marketing Bureau): P. W. Hunter and Bill Kitching; and Alan J. Waters (CARD).

In developing this text, we received complete support from John Wiley and Sons Canada Limited, particularly from Wendy Jacobs, Kathryn Dean, and Susan Marshall. In addition, Henri Darmon provided useful assistance. Our secretaries, Pina Vicario, Lyne Renaud, and Nancy Brennan deserve all our gratitude for their patience, attention to detail, and competent typing of a long manuscript, a task that they claim to have enjoyed!

Finally, we are thankful to our families for their support and understanding during the extensive process of developing an original manuscript. Without it, our task would have been more difficult to accomplish.

This is the first original textbook on advertising management in Canada. We hope that you will enjoy reading it and using it as much as we have enjoyed researching and writing it.

René Darmon
Michel Laroche
September 1983

THE ROLE AND
FUNCTIONS
OF ADVERTISING

Advertising is one of the most visible phenomena of modern times. No one can avoid being exposed to and, to some extent, influenced by advertising messages and commercials. At the same time, advertising is one of the least understood modern institutions, not only by the general public but also by many experts.

This text undertakes a systematic analysis of advertising in the Canadian context. Although the managerial perspective is favoured, advertising is also considered from the institutional, behavioural, economic, and social points of view. First, the role and functions of advertising in general and in Canadian society are examined. Then, the role and functions of advertising in a firm's marketing mix and in the promotional mix are discussed.

Advertising: Its Nature and Functions

Wherever they live, Canadians are exposed to advertising material. As they walk or drive through the streets, listen to the radio at home or in the car, watch television, read newspapers or magazines, attend a sports event, go shopping, read mail, Canadians are exposed to advertisements for products, services, and ideas. All these advertisements are vying for the generally limited number of dollars they can spend, for their political votes, or for their involvement in or commitment to engage in some desirable social action. Advertising messages may be in the form of flashy, luminous posters or billboards, broadcast advertisements on local or national radio and television networks, full-page colour advertisements in national magazines, or small black-and-white advertisements in the local newspapers, advertising at the point-of-purchase at their usual retailer, or leaflets mailed to their homes—and this list is by no means exhaustive. It has been estimated that an American consumer is exposed to a daily average of 1500 commercials, and this figure might be only slightly lower for Canadians.[1]

Because of advertising's continuous presence in daily life, everyone has some knowledge, beliefs, and often strongly held attitudes about it. Advertising is the most visible facet of marketing to many consumers; thus, not surprisingly, it has been attacked on social as well as on economic grounds. For some, advertising is a mischievous tool that marketers use to create needs, make consumers buy unwanted goods, and in general direct society toward the "false" values of mass consumption.

From another point of view, advertising is seen as a necessary mechanism through which Canadian society has been able to achieve its present high standard of living. Whichever position is taken, the controversy over advertising does not leave anyone indifferent, and unfortunately all too often emotions are involved in the debate.

Therefore, unless the nature and functions of advertising are studied objectively, its mechanisms, possibilities, and limitations cannot be understood and assessed properly. One objective of this book is to provide a framework in which to evaluate the institution of advertising. Thus a detailed study is made of advertising's influence on human behaviour and of the role and functions of advertising management.

Before this task is undertaken, the nature of advertising is discussed and a definition of the advertising function is proposed. Then the historical background of Canadian advertising is outlined in order to explain the role that advertising presently plays in the Canadian economy and in business.

The Nature of Advertising

The Raison d'être of Advertising

Why is so much money spent on advertising? Is advertising necessary? The answer to these questions is that no purchase can take place without some form of communication between the seller and a potential buyer. The exchange of money for some product or service materializes when all the participants in such a trading activity have been informed of and have accepted the terms and conditions of the exchange. That is, a consumer or industrial purchase takes place when each participant in the transaction finds or expects to find the fulfillment of some need or satisfaction. In a free market society, consumers buy goods and services because they hope to obtain satisfaction through their usage and consumption. In the same way, people give financial support to charitable organizations because they obtain some reward (if only psychological) by doing so.

Traditionally, sellers have attempted to show prospective customers the advantages and satisfaction that the advertised goods are likely to bring. Even past forms of buying and selling, for example, barter, involved persuasive discussions between merchants and prospective customers. At one time craftsmen showed the merits of their products and services to prospective clients. Today's salespersons, who are trained to perceive which arguments are likely to be most effective in selling goods to different categories of customers, are the craftsmen of marketing communications.

At the end of the nineteenth century, with the advent of the Industrial Revolution, marketing communications took on a new character. Entrepreneurs introduced mass production of goods as a new mode of operations. The problem now shifted from selling a custom-made product, manufactured according to the requirements of a specific client, to selling items produced on a large scale to a mass market. As a logical consequence of this trend, personal communications began to be replaced by mass communications. Rather than talking to one buyer at a time, manufacturers' problem was how to communicate effectively with large and sometimes remote markets. Thus, mass production led to mass marketing.

In order to build a communication link between mass production and mass markets, a mass communication tool was needed, and the device was advertising. Of course, the characteristics and functions of advertising have evolved since the Industrial Revolution, but the roots and raison d'être of modern advertising can be traced to that period.

Advertising Defined

Most definitions of advertising stress three basic elements—that advertising is *communication* aimed at a *mass audience* and that it has a *socio-economic function.* For instance, the definition given by the American Marketing Association is:

> Advertising is any *paid* form of *non-personal presentation and promotion of ideas, goods or services* by *an identified sponsor.*[2] [Emphasis added]

Thus the first element in the definition is that advertising is a set of *communications* originating from a sponsor. The flow of information is unidirectional and is directed at the advertiser's *customers* and *prospects*. The advertiser may be a business organization, a person, a firm, or a group of firms. It may be a manufacturing or a marketing organization, a producer, a middleman, or a retailer. The advertiser may also be a social organization, such as the Red Cross, or a religious organization, a political party, a government agency, or any organized group. The customers may be the final consumers of the product, other industrial firms, middlemen, or retailers. Consequently, advertising involves many kinds of communications, of which consumer advertising is only one type.

The second element is that advertising is *mass* communication, because it is directed at an entire market. It is different from such business communications as internal communication flows within a single firm or from marketing communications that a firm has with clients and that involves personal contact, for example, personal selling through a sales force.

TABLE 1.1   Comparison of Four Current Types of Communication

	Advertising	Personal Selling	Publicity	Propaganda
Scope	Mass	Personal	Mass	Mass
Function	Communication	Communication	Communication	Communication
Purpose	Socio-economic	Economic	Socio-economic	Political

Third, advertising has a *socio-economic function,* which results from its long-run objective of convincing customers and potential buyers to buy a firm's advertised products and services or to adopt the advertised idea or behaviour. The economic nature of advertising is a result of advertising's high cost, since it is expensive to communicate with mass markets.

Table 1.1 shows how advertising can be differentiated from three other types of communications: personal selling, where a salesperson directly addresses potential customers, publicity, and propaganda. Although all fulfill a communication function, their differences lie in the scope and/or purpose of the communication. *Personal selling* differs in scope from advertising in that it is a personal rather than a mass communication. *Publicity* departs from advertising in that it is not paid for by the beneficiary of the communication; it has more of a social than an economic purpose. Publicity often takes the form of editorial articles about a firm's performance or products and services and is published without charge by the media. Its purpose is to inform consumers and its role is essentially social, although it does have an underlying economic purpose. *Propaganda* is significantly different from advertising. It is a type of mass communication, but its source is not identified and it generally has a political rather than an economic purpose.

History of Advertising in Canada

The history of advertising in Canada is one of a fledgling industry that, in the space of forty years, grew to become a major force in the Canadian economy. Although it closely parallels the evolution of advertising in the United States (where modern advertising originated), its development in Canada differs in many respects. Canadian advertising operates in a specific cultural and geographic environment, and the imprint left by a few individuals lends it a distinct national flavour.

Beyond purely economic considerations, advertising has been instrumental in bringing about a revolution in Canadian lifestyles, outlook, and institutions. With its greatly increased sophistication and with sophisticated tools at its disposal, advertising now fulfills an essential role in the Canadian economy.

Early Advertising: 1752-1890

One could almost say that advertising is as old as Canada, since its presence in this country can be traced as far back as March 23, 1752. On this date was published the first issue of *The Halifax Gazette*, which contained three advertisements.[3] Advertising was present, although in an embryonic form, in Canadian life throughout the 1800s. In the latter half of the nineteenth century, economic trends paved the way for a growth of advertising as Canada started to industrialize.

After Confederation in 1867, newspapers multiplied and flourished, but their use of advertising was unsystematic and somewhat inefficient:

Advertising became an increasing source of revenue and the newspapers began to encourage and foster it. But even at the end of the eighties, advertising in Canada remained a more or less underdeveloped tool. Canadian advertising was still formless and haphazard, and what came to Canadian papers from "across the line" had scarcely more style or consistency.[4]

The 1890s, however, marked a radical departure from the concepts that had until then guided advertising. This last decade of the nineteenth century also marked the birth of modern Canadian advertising.

Evolution of Advertising Tools and Techniques: After 1890

The coming of age of advertising was closely related to the development of modern communications and mass production techniques. Without these, advertising would not have found a favourable environment in which to flourish.

Evolution of the Media

The first important factor that gave rise to modern advertising was the development of the modern mass media. After publication of *The Halifax Gazette*, Canadian newspapers steadily increased in numbers and circulation, but the 1890s was a period of great expansion. By 1891, Canada had a total of 1033 periodical publications—double the amount nine years earlier. Advertising was still infrequent, however, and printing techniques left much to be desired in the way of attractive illustration and copy presentation. At best, advertisements displayed simple line drawings or a few hand-lettered decorative headings.

But the giant technical leaps made by the printing industry, with such innovations as electrotyping, stereotyping, the rotary press, and the typesetting machine, made possible the expansion of printed media and the development of sophisticated advertising.

During the early twentieth century, newspaper coverage increased steadily, although the number of dailies fluctuated. As the newspaper industry was becoming increasingly complex and required large investments, a more competitive economic environment made it difficult for marginal publications to survive. In the first half of the twentieth century, the number of newspapers declined at the same time as ownership became more concentrated. This concentration resulted in increased coverage but made it difficult for advertisers to reach specific market segments, since newspapers became more standardized. This trend was compensated, however, by a steady gain in the number, variety, and circulation of more specialized periodicals that catered to limited but well-defined social or professional groups. These magazines and periodicals were a powerful outlet for advertising. This early use of print media may account for the popularity of print media as a source for advertising, even though print has had to compete with the more recent media of radio and television. The growth of audiovisual media irrevocably changed the nature of advertising. Advertisers now had a new and promising terrain in which to operate. The Canadian Broadcasting Corporation (CBC) rapidly extended its dominion beyond radio to television.

Economic Factors

The prominent place of advertising in Canada's economy is due in no minor fashion to the nature of the country's economic evolution. Such developments as standardization and mass production resulted in a more widely felt need for effective advertising. The generalization of branding and packaging during the 1890s, the development of manufacturing, the birth of the consumer society, and the expansion of the third sector were all instrumental in making advertising into what it is today. As we have seen, advertising is essentially a product of the industrial revolution, and it has accelerated and been a key factor in the advent of the modern consumer society. With the orientation of the Canadian economy toward greater reliance on services and on the third sector, which has been more apparent during the past decade, it appears that advertising will play an even more important and constructive role in the future.

The Evolution of Advertising Concepts and Institutions

Once a favourable environment for advertising was created, its potential still remained to be tapped. The evolution of concepts encouraging and fostering a more sophisticated and scientific approach to advertising also played an essential role. At the beginning of the 1890s, advertising was still a crude affair. Most printed ads merely exhibited a brand name, and possibly a price. The real efficiency of such advertising was far from established and elicited much skepticism in the business community. Furthermore, there was a widespread notion that it was somehow undignified for manufacturers to flaunt their merchandise. The sole function of advertising was therefore to maintain public awareness of a brand name.

Moreover, the persons who created advertisements tended to have little or no formal training in advertising techniques and were not trained to communicate very effectively with mass markets. Advertisers did not try to translate their own experience into the language of the average consumer. As a result, advertisements were, more often than not, clever and humorous, but their wit was lost on most people; consequently they lacked real selling power.

This was further aggravated by the low quality of advertising design. The notion that an advertisement would be more attractive and attention-grabbing if it combined a half dozen different typestyles in copy that was hopelessly overcrowded seemed to prevail among early advertisers. See, for instance, the advertisement for Bissell's carpet sweepers in Figure 1.1.

The first advertising agency appeared in Canada in 1889, with the founding of the McKim agency. Its sole function, however, was to sell newspaper space to advertisers. Most early advertising agencies served mainly as

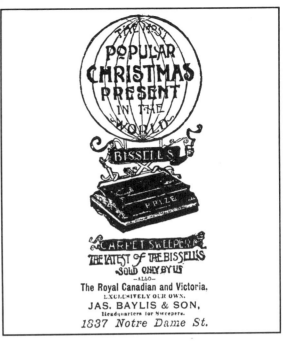

FIGURE 1.1 Bissell's Carpet Sweepers
SOURCE: H.E. Stephenson and C. McNaught, *The Story of Advertising in Canada* (Toronto: Ryerson Press, 1940).

brokers of media space and had little to do with the content of the ads. The adoption of a more systematic approach to advertising was largely the work of a few individuals, whose accomplishments therefore merit some recollection.

The Canadian who probably did the most to bring about the birth of modern advertising was John E. Kennedy.[5] A former Mountie, he had a successful career in the garment industry by advocating what was then a revolutionary idea. Dividing consumers into nine broad categories, he produced large quantities of ready-made suits that could fit any standard build and were much less expensive than custom-made suits. The success of his clothing was due in no small part to advertising. Indeed, Kennedy used advertising to great effect and had a gift for communicating persuasively with mass markets. His experience with clothing convinced him that advertising could and should play a fundamental role in any selling strategy. He therefore decided to test some of his theories in the United States.

7

In 1904, he went to the offices of Lord & Thomas, a major advertising agency of the time. While waiting in the lobby, he sent a note to two of the agency's top executives, Ambrose Thomas and Albert Lasker. The note read: "I am downstairs in the saloon, and I can tell you what advertising is. I know that you don't know. It will mean much to me to have you know what it is and it will mean much to you. If you wish to know what advertising is, send the word 'yes' down by messenger." Intrigued by this unusual communication, Lasker sent for Kennedy. What Kennedy told Lasker was disarmingly simple: "Advertising is salesmanship in print."

This seemingly obvious truth landed Kennedy a job with Lord & Thomas for the unprecedented salary of $28,000 a year. His concept revolutionized the nature of advertising for he had discovered the true function and driving force behind advertising—persuasion.

From then on, the role of advertising became more than exhibiting a brand name and keeping it in the public eye; it was extended to that of a salesperson who used persuasive powers and argumentation to bring about a purchase. Although advertising concepts and techniques have been modified over the years, the underlying rationale—persuasion—remains basically unchanged. Building upon this firm theoretical ground, Kennedy devised a wholly novel approach toward advertising and was one of the first advocates of what is called "reason-why" copy. "Conviction is not produced by bare affirmation, but by proof, by inference, by argument—in short, by 'reason-why talk'."[6]

Summing up Kennedy's achievements, one writer on the history of American advertising said:

It was not until his [Kennedy's] time that any appreciable number of advertisers got away from the old publicity theory of advertising effect as the sole end and aim of the art. While he doesn't by any means deserve all the credit, he had more to do with it than anybody else.[7]

With the ideas introduced by John E. Kennedy, traditional advertising agencies underwent profound change. At the turn of the century, agencies specializing in ad creation were established. This type of organization was short-lived, however, and soon merged with the traditional advertising agency. Such mergers were the forerunners of modern advertising agencies.

In the 1910s, advertising agencies became more sophisticated. From a small personal enterprise in 1889, the McKim advertising agency mushroomed to a full-fledged corporation, providing a comprehensive range of advertising-related services, including ad creation, production, and media planning. Modern advertising agencies are an outgrowth of the phenomenal expansion of advertising in the 1900s, and without this growth, advertising would not be the dynamic and vital institution it now is.

Advertising in the Canadian Environment

Environmental factors were instrumental in giving advertising the role it plays in the Canadian economy. Indeed, certain particular aspects of the Canadian scene led to the development of unique features in advertising in this country. The most relevant environmental factors include Canada's unique demography, its biculturalism, strong economic and cultural ties with its southern neighbour, highly developed communication channels, a tradition of high advertising spending, and a high degree of advertising sophistication.

Canada has approximately 24 million people scattered over a territory substantially larger than the United States and unequally distributed. For example, the southern fringe, the St. Lawrence valley, the Great Lakes area and the West Coast are highly populated areas, while the northern part of the country is sparsely populated. As will be seen, this unequal population distribution makes it difficult to reach isolated market segments effectively through the mass media.

Language differences have proven another obstacle to effective mass communication. Quebec has a majority of francophones, and there are sizeable francophone minorities in other provinces—Ontario, New Brunswick, or Manitoba. The problem for advertisers has been reaching the two major language groups of this country through the proper media and in their own language. Other sizeable ethnic groups, for example, the Portuguese, Italians, and Chinese, should not be overlooked by advertisers who want to address these market segments and must therefore account for these groups' language, culture, and media habits.

A major environmental factor is Canada's strong economic ties with the United States, which have made it especially vulnerable to changes in the American economy. In recent years, the economic recession, inflationary pressures, and a general slowdown in real income growth have been shared by both countries.

From an advertising point of view, this strong link between the Canadian and the U.S. economies and cultures results in a substantial spillover of advertising from the United States into Canada. Canadians receive American television through cable or through American border stations, and they buy American magazines. As American advertising conveyed by these media reaches Canadians, the spillover is likely to play in favour of large American advertisers who also operate in Canada and sell approximately the same product in both countries. Thus, this spillover of American advertising, which is caused by the substantial coverage of the Canadian market by American media, creates a unique problem for Canadian advertisers, who must compete with American firms and are at a disadvantage even in their own country. In spite of attempts by the Canadian government to take corrective action, it has not been possible to change this situation substantially.

The strong ties between the American and the Canadian economies also have definite advantages. It can be argued, for instance, that Canada would probably not have reached its present high level of economic development were it not for the close ties with the United States. For the same reason, Canadian advertising might not have been able to achieve its present high level of spending and sophistication.

Tables 1.2 and 1.3 give some indications of the position advertising enjoys in Canada's economy. From Table 1.2 it can be seen that the amount spent on advertising in the past twenty years has increased steadily and is now more than four billion dollars. This increase is the result of a number of factors, such as the generally increasing gross national product and inflated dollars. On a per capita basis, advertising expenditures have grown from $33.40 in 1961 to $185.25 in 1982.

Table 1.3 gives a breakdown of Canadian advertising expenditures for each type of media.

TABLE 1.2 Total Advertising Expenditures in Canada, 1961-1982

Year	Total Advertising Expenditures ($ millions)	Year	Total Advertising Expenditures ($ millions)
1961	609	1972	1,303
1962	643	1973	1,479
1963	674	1974	1,721
1964	724	1975	1,938
1965	798	1976	2,244
1966	812	1977	2,458
1967	873	1978	2,790
1968	914	1979	3,219
1969	1,014	1980	3,763
1970	1,060	1981	4,231
1971	1,144	1982	4,446

SOURCE: Statistics Canada.

TABLE 1.3 Net Advertising Revenues by Media (in millions of dollars)

	1977	1978	1979	1980	1981	1982
Radio	269	305	352	392	439	458
Television	376	442	527	610	692	779
Newspapers	848	930	1029	1224	1452	1422
Periodicals	331	387	454	554	589	615
Other Print	472	544	646	742	806	892
Outdoor	162	182	211	241	255	280
Total	2458	2790	3219	3763	4231	4446

SOURCES: 1977-1980, Statistics Canada actuals; 1981-1982, estimated by Maclean Hunter Research Bureau and published in *CARD*, March 1983, p. 154.

Direct mail (22.0 per cent), newspapers (19.4 per cent), followed by television (18.2 per cent) and radio (11.5 per cent) account for about 71.1 per cent of total advertising expenditures.

Table 1.4 lists the twelve top advertisers in Canada in 1982. The first major advertiser by far is the federal government, and the government of Ontario is among the first ten major advertisers. Also on the list are five Canadian subsidiaries of multinational corporations.

TABLE 1.4 The Twelve Top Advertisers in Canada in 1982

1. Government of Canada	$54,539,989
2. Procter & Gamble Inc.	35,393,574
3. John Labatt Limited	26,894,597
4. General Foods Inc.	25,078,304
5. Rothmans of Canada Inc.	24,704,858
6. Ontario Government	23,221,527
7. Nabisco Brands	23,188,457
8. General Motors of Canada Ltd.	22,864,244
9. Dart & Kraft Ltd.	21,396,951
10. The Molson Companies	18,445,783
11. Imasco Holdings Canada Inc.	15,928,876
12. Unilever Inc.	15,571,674

SOURCE: Media Measurement Services Inc.

To sum up, Canadian advertising is characterized by a high level of expenditure and sophistication and is much influenced by the demographic, cultural, and geographic environment in which it operates. Although Canada's long history of close relations with the United States has had a profound impact on advertising, a number of unique features give Canadian advertising a particular flavour and originality.

Advertising as Communication

The definition of advertising given previously has several implications about the distinctiveness of advertising. First, because it is a type of communication, advertising therefore plays a specific role in the complex communication network of an industrial or commercial firm. Second, as a communication device, advertising draws upon the theories and findings of communication theory and social psychology. Third, because of the wide audience addressed, advertisers must have a comprehensive knowledge of their markets in order to deliver an efficient message. This is why advertisers must use research and apply the principles of scientific method. Fourth, because it is a type of mass communication, advertising plays a role in a firm's marketing program that is markedly different from personal selling, which is the other major marketing communication tool. Fifth, because of its socio-economic function, advertising is assigned very precise objectives. In a marketing program, advertising's role should be consistent with the other elements of the marketing mix.

Advertising within a Firm's Communication Network

Advertising has been defined as a communication channel through which information flows from a firm to its markets. An industrial firm can be considered as being made up of two closely interrelated sub-systems: the production and the communication subsystems. The first includes the facilities, equipment, and resources that a firm uses to manufacture the products it markets. In commercial firms (those which do not manufacture products) or in service enterprises there is no production sub-system, and the whole firm can be viewed as one large communication network.

The information–communication sub-system can be subdivided into two main types of communication: internal and external (Figure 1.2). Internal communications include all the

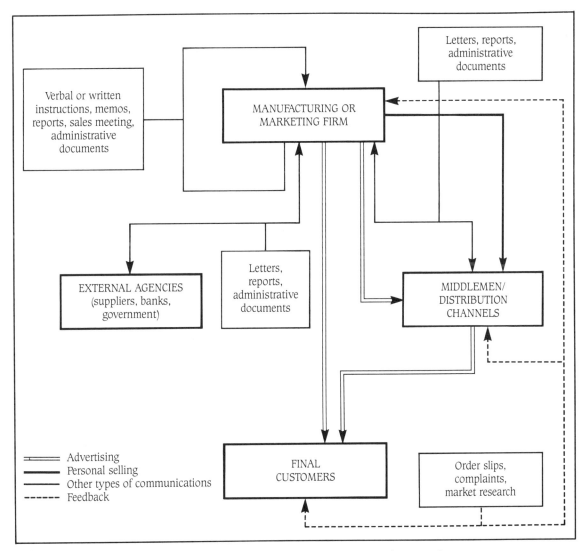

FIGURE 1.2   Typical Information Flows within a Consumer Product Market

information flowing among employees, workers, executives, departments, and functions of the firm. Verbal or written instructions, administrative memos and documents, meetings, minutes of meetings, reports, and organization charts are examples of internal communications.

External communications are directed or are received from people or organizations outside the firm. They include the communications a firm has with suppliers, bankers, the government, or advertising agencies. From a firm's point of view, external communications involve the financial, purchasing, or marketing functions of the firm. There is also a large and intensive information–communication network between a firm, its markets, and its distribution channels. Responsibility for these communications belongs to the marketing department.

All the communications that a firm has with its customers and the members of its distribution channels are bidirectional. In the direction from the firm toward the market or the middlemen, three types of communication are used: advertising, personal selling, and sales promotion. In the other direction, a firm receives information from markets and from distribution channels through order slips, sales reports, and customer complaints or suggestions. More formally, a firm receives information through its market research department, when specific marketing research studies are undertaken on the distribution channels or on the needs, desires, or behaviour of consumers.

Within a firm's information–communication network, advertising is the mode of communication the firm uses to address markets and/or distribution channels. This role is shared to some extent by personal selling, but advertising has a purpose that only it can fulfill because it is a mass communication. Thus advertising supplements and must be consistent with other communications and, more generally, with the other elements in a marketing program.

Advertising and the Social Sciences

The Communication Process

Because advertising is a special type of communication, the general model of communication theory is applicable. This model (see Figure 1.3) is comprised of six elements: the communicator (or the source), the message, the channels, the audience, the intended effect, and the feedback.

The *communicator* or *source* is the individual or the organization initiating the communication. In an advertising context, the communicator is the firm advertising its products or services.

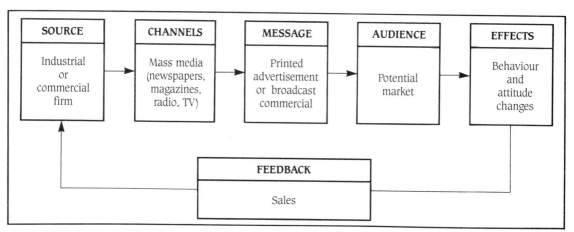

FIGURE 1.3   **Theoretical Process of Advertising Communication**

The *message* includes the set of words, sounds, and images used by the communicator to convey an idea to the audience. In advertising, the message is a printed or broadcast piece of information. The communication *channels* are the media used to convey the message to the audience. In advertising, these channels are the mass media. The *audience* of the communication is an individual or group of individuals for whom the message is intended. In advertising, the audience is the potential market for the firm's products or services.

Any message has a precise objective or *intended effect*. For example, its purpose may be to inform an audience. When the additional information triggers a response from the audience, the intended effect is persuasive.

An advertiser gives consumers information about products or services in order to influence consumers' attitudes. The final objective is to obtain a behavioural response, that is, the purchase of a product or service, or the adoption of an idea.

In Figure 1.3 the arrows indicate the direction of the information flow. Advertisers translate information into a specific message; the information is coded. Subsequently, the message is delivered through a communication channel to a target audience. Individuals in the audience decode the message; they attribute a meaning to the message and interpret the information it contains. Obviously, a communicator must make sure the message has been properly deciphered, understood, and interpreted, and thus produced the intended response. This process constitutes the *feedback*.

In advertising, the feedback is the effect of the advertising message on the consumer. It can be observed as a change in a consumer's attitude toward an advertised product, service, or idea or as a change in the consumer's behaviour pattern (i.e., a sales volume increase).

The Advertising Communications Process
The communications model suggests that for a communication to be effective, the same code must be used by the communicator and the receiver (Figure 1.4).[8]

In this diagram, the lines surrounding the communicator and the audience represent what is called their *field of experience* at the time of the communication. Communicators can only code a message in terms of their experience. For instance, a mathematical equation can be decoded (understood) by a scientist because mathematics is part of a scientist's field of experience. It could not be decoded by an individual who has not had some training or

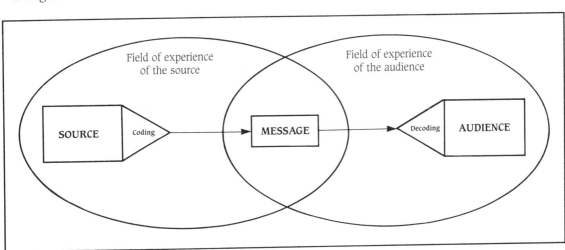

FIGURE 1.4 **Theoretical Process of a Communication**

experience in mathematics. Consequently, a successful communication cannot take place without two conditions being fulfilled: first, the communicator and the audience must share at least part of their field of experience; they should at least be able to speak and understand a common language. Second, the message must be expressed in terms of their shared experience—their common language.

Classifications of Advertising

This concept of the communication process can be used to describe different types of advertising and advertising classifications. Advertising may be classified according to the communication element it emphasizes, as shown in Figure 1.5.

Thus, advertising may be classified according to the source of the communication, between *business advertising* and *non-profit advertising*. Business advertising can be further subdivided into *manufacturer, wholesaler*, or *retailer advertising*. Non-profit advertising may be sponsored by government, by a social organization, or by a political party. Advertising may also be classified according to the content and/or format of the message. For instance, *product advertising* is intended to help sell a product, *service advertising*, a service, and *idea advertising* "sells" an idea. *Institutional advertising* promotes a corporation, rather than its products or services.

A classification according to the approach selected to deliver the message differentiates

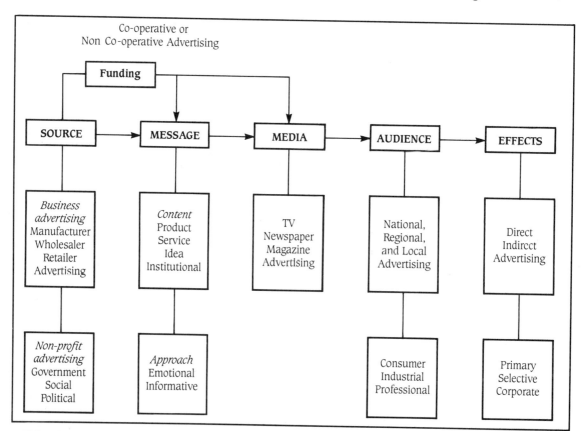

FIGURE 1.5   Current Classifications of Advertising

14

between what may be called *emotional advertising*, because it appeals to consumers' conscious and abstract motivations, and *informative advertising*, which emphasizes the physical characteristics of products. This classification is based on the type of message, because an advertiser who gives factual information about a product or appeals directly to consumers' motivations creates the advertising message so as to influence consumers' motivation. (This subject is discussed further in Chapter 7).

Advertising may be classified according to the type of medium used, for instance, *television, newspapers*, or *direct mail* advertising, or according to the nature or geographical spread of a target audience. *Consumer advertising* is directed at final consumers; *industrial advertising* is targeted at industrial firms. *Professional advertising*'s main objective is to reach professionals who are likely to influence the purchases of final consumers (for instance, doctors who prescribe certain drugs to their patients). *Middleman advertising* is intended for members of a distribution channel. In a classification according to the geographical dispersion of audience, advertising is called *national advertising* when it is directed at the whole country, *regional advertising* if concentrated in a specific area, and *local advertising*, if it is limited to a city or a smaller locality.

Advertising is also characterized by its intended immediate effects. Thus, it may be primary or selective, direct or indirect. *Primary advertising* promotes the consumption of a generic product category. An example is an advertising campaign aimed at convincing consumers to drink more milk. *Selective advertising* promotes the sale of a specific brand, for instance, a campaign for drinking Sealtest milk. *Direct advertising* tries to get an immediate response from the consumer (such as advertising for a specific offer). *Indirect advertising* tries to build a favourable image which, in the long run, would enhance a company's sales and profits.

Finally, advertising may be classified according to its source of funding. *Co-operative advertising* is partly paid for by a manufacturer and partly by a member of the distribution channel, for example, a retailer. Thus, a retailer who wants to advertise a certain brand might seek the support of the brand's manufacturer because such advertising is likely to benefit both of them.

Of course, these classifications of advertising are not mutually exclusive, since an advertising campaign might be initiated by a manufacturer, be informative, and be a television national campaign for industrial products.

Advertising as Mass Communication

Application to the Mass Communication Process

The Production and Consumption Worlds

As we have seen, many concepts from communication theory can be applied to advertising.[9] The experience gained by a firm and the experience acquired by a potential consumer of an advertised product are generally quite different. For example, a manufacturing firm evolves in a technical world. It has technical and scientific knowledge of its products and can code different information about its products in technical language. A firm also evolves in a professional world: to manufacture and market a product is the day-to-day task of the firm's officers and employees. In contrast, the product or service is part of consumers' private world. Consumers buy the product or service in order to experience some personal, familial, or social satisfaction. Therefore, their field of experience in relation to this product has more to do with product usage than with technical knowledge.

Because of these differences, a common language between a firm and its consumers does not develop either naturally or spontaneously. It must be worked out by the firm. This is why a firm must enlarge its experience in order to include in it consumers' experience of the product.

A Firm's Advertising Philosophy

The evolution of the prevailing advertising philosophies can be best explained in terms of these concepts. When craftspeople had to produce and communicate with clients on a large scale, they lost personal contact with their clients. The gap between producers' experience and that of consumers widened. Firms no longer knew their consumers and lacked the desire to know them. Figure 1.6a illustrates this phenomenon.

At one time, consumers needed the products and bought the goods available on the market without paying too much attention to quality.

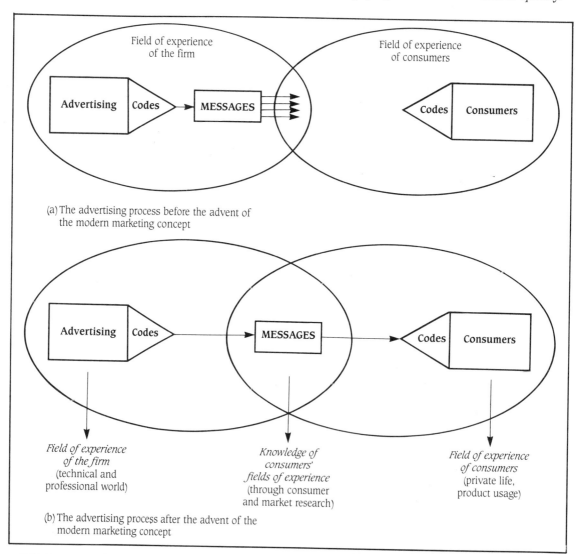

(a) The advertising process before the advent of the modern marketing concept

(b) The advertising process after the advent of the modern marketing concept

FIGURE 1.6   The Advertising Process before and after the Advent of the Modern Marketing Concept

Hence, advertising played only a minor role in a firm's marketing plans.

As mass production enabled basic consumer demands for goods to be met, consumers became increasingly difficult to satisfy and firms had to improve communications with their markets. Unfortunately, most firms knew very little about the reasons why consumers bought their products. Moreover, firms communicated with their clients in a language that the consumers hardly understood. Advertisers often coded a message that was not expressed in terms of the consumer's experience, and thus the large amounts of money spent on advertising were for the most part wasted. This may explain the origin of the public's negative image of advertising as "persuasion at all costs".

With the advent of the modern marketing concept, manufacturers rediscovered consumers. They inquired about consumers' tastes, needs, and wants. So companies' communications with their markets are based on consumers' deepest motivations for buying a product and on sometimes hidden satisfactions consumers seek. Consequently, through consumer motivation and marketing research advertisers must discover what motivates consumers.

The modern marketing concept holds that the language of advertising must be adapted to its target. A manufacturer and a marketer must be able to predict clients' probable reactions. Advertising uses much the same selling techniques as last century's merchants, who presented their arguments in the manner which they were likely to be best appreciated by their customers. In the past, craftspeople relied on intuition to understand clients' psychology. Today this role is accomplished by market surveys and motivation research, which help advertisers provide their mass communication with the content and format that best suit their market. This is shown in Figure 1.6b; the message is located in the middle where both fields of experience overlap.

Advertising in the Canadian Bicultural Environment

Advertising campaigns must be adapted when they are used for a market segment other than the one they have been originally designed for. If a domestic firm uses commercials created for a national market in its international operations, the cost of advertising is reduced significantly. However, consumers' field of experience is deeply influenced by the culture to which they belong, and the same message can be very differently interpreted depending on consumers' culture or sub-culture.

In Canada a classic example is the Quebec market.[10] Ever since advertising appeared in Quebec, advertising campaigns were mere French translations of English advertising campaigns originated by New York or Toronto advertising agencies. For example, the Canadian Security Company's[11] Ontario advertising slogan was: "The Canadian Security Company suggests, environment protection is everybody's business. Financial protection is our business." For the Quebec market, the slogan was given a literal translation: *"La Canadian Security Company fait valoir que la préservation de notre environnement est l'affaire de tous et que la protection financière est la sienne propre."* In this case the meaning of the slogan is the same in either language. The danger of such an approach, however, is that very often what is suitable for English Canada may, for cultural and linguistic reasons, be unsuitable for Quebec.

In the 1960s, advertising messages for the Quebec market were more or less successful adaptations of English commercials.[12] For example, the Bank of Commerce used the theme "Commerce 'O Canada' cheques make cheque writing a beautiful Canadian experience," in English Canada. But for Quebec, the theme was changed to: *"Les chèques Commerce illustrés de paysages canadiens sont agréables à remplir"* (Commerce cheques with Canadian landscapes are nice to fill out). Therefore,

17

Quebecers' allegiance to Canada was played down. But the problem with such an approach is that the advertising campaign may lack unity and consistency. In the Bank of Commerce advertisement, the illustration accompanying the printed slogan was, in both the English and French versions, a Canadian saluting the new cheques hung on a flagpole to simulate a national flag. Obviously, the advertisement's wording in French did not match the illustration, resulting in a poor adaptation of the advertising message.

More recently, advertisements aimed at Quebec's francophone population have changed greatly.[13] In order to account for special characteristics of the Quebec market, advertising campaigns are generally conceived and designed by Montreal advertising agencies. Although this trend makes advertising creation more costly, it has the merit of recognizing that French and English Canadians have different cultural fields of experience.[14]

Advertising Research: A Consequence of Mass Communication

Advertising communications, like the other elements of the marketing mix, is elaborated from a precise knowledge of consumer needs, motivations, attitudes and opinions, behaviour, and purchasing habits. However, because of the high costs involved, advertising communications must not be inefficient. Thus, the various elements of an advertising communication program are the subject of formal research by advertisers and advertising agencies. (See Chapter 15 for a description of the research techniques used in advertising.[15])

What is important to keep in mind here is that the scientific method and systematic approach play a major role in an area that traditionally relied upon art and intuition. This does not mean that creativity and art have no part to play in advertising. An architect can design a masterpiece and still meet the functional constraints of the building. In the same way, advertisers must reconcile art and marketing communications. Their responsibility is to translate raw selling arguments into the words and images that are likely to induce consumers to buy what the economy has produced for them.

Personal vs. Mass Communications

Personal communications through sales representatives and advertising communications have a common objective: both are directed at potential customers to increase a firm's sales and profits. However, the two types of communication differ in their nature and effectiveness because of two essentially different characteristics they possess: the type of medium they use and their cost structure.

The Medium of Personal Communications

Advertising communications are transmitted through the mass media—newspapers, magazines, television, and radio. In contrast, sales force communications take place between a salesperson and a customer, a prospect, or at most a small group of potential customers.

Figure 1.7 shows the difference between personal selling communications and advertising communications. A firm communicates formally with its sales force through training or retraining programs, which are formal communication systems. Sales meetings and directives that a sales manager periodically sends to sales personnel are examples of the more usual and recurrent formal communications. During sales calls a sales representative communicates information to customers and prospects. Unlike advertising, however, these communications do not occur only once nor are they unidirectional; the information flows back and forth between the sales representative and customers and prospects. For instance, a sales representative inquires about a customer's needs. To do so, the representative gives information about the products and services for sale and answers the questions and objections of prospective buyers.

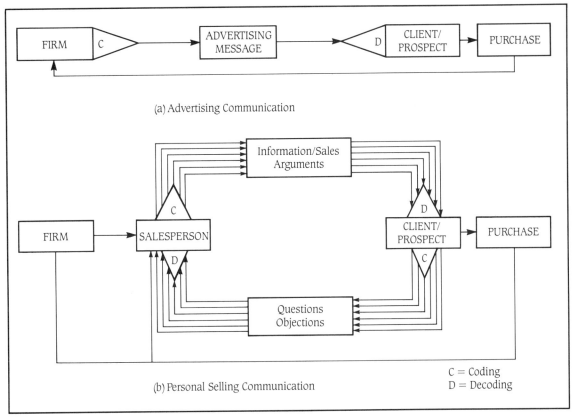

(a) Advertising Communication

(b) Personal Selling Communication

C = Coding
D = Decoding

FIGURE 1.7   Difference between Advertising and Personal Selling Communications

This information goes back and forth between the sales representative and the customer in a continuous and two-directional communication flow. Information is exchanged until a customer response eventually terminates the process by the signing of an order or by a change of attitude.

These attitudinal or behavioural changes constitute the feedback on the effect of personal selling communications. Another important difference between personal communications and advertising is that during a sales call a sales representative can observe the effect of the sales pitch on potential customers. Consequently, the representative can adjust or give a different orientation to the message depending on the feedback received from the client. The sales manager can directly assess the quality and effectiveness of a sales communication by observing the customer's behavioural responses, that is, whether a customer places an order or is satisfied with the product or service.

Consequences of the
Type of Communication Used

The use of personal or mass communications has several implications for the quality and efficiency of marketing communications. A comparison of the advantages and drawbacks of personal or mass communications and advertising is shown in Table 1.5.

DIFFERENCES AFFECTING THE COMMUNICATOR.   The communicator of advertising messages generally has only a global knowledge of a market, that is, an "average profile" of a "typical" consumer in a target segment. Advertising messages are directed toward this average individual, who

TABLE 1.5   Comparison of the Advantages and Drawbacks of Advertising and Personal Selling as Communication Tools

	VALUE	PERSONAL SELLING	VALUE	ADVERTISING
SOURCE	+	Direct knowledge of the audience	−	Knowledge of only the audience average profile
MESSAGE	+	Message can be adapted according to audience feedback	−	Inflexible message in the short run
	+	Possibility of using a range of selling arguments	−	Possibility of using only one or two selling arguments
	−	The message content and format cannot be controlled by the firm	+	Message content and format can be controlled by the firm
MEDIUM	+	Human and personal contacts	−	Lack of personal contact
	−	Possibility of communicating with only a few clients over a certain period of time	+	Possibility of communicating with many consumers in a short period of time
AUDIENCE	+	Coding errors affect only one client	−	Coding errors affect the whole market
	+	Attracting customers' attention is easier	−	Difficulty of attracting and holding consumers' attention
	+	Communication generally takes place during working hours	−	Communication generally takes place during leisure time
EFFECTS	+	Possibility of completing the purchase immediately	−	A behavioural response from the consumer cannot be obtained immediately

+ Advantage   − Drawback

may resemble to a greater or lesser degree any of the actual individuals in the target market. A sales representative, however, communicates personally with customers and prospects and thus can learn a lot about them. Through intuition and observation (two important assets of a successful sales person) the motives and interests of customers can be detected and the communication adjusted accordingly. In marketing communications, sales representatives are to advertisers what craftspeople are to mass producers.

DIFFERENCES AFFECTING THE MESSAGE.   Once an advertising communication has taken place, a sales manager must wait for the effects, if any, to become evident. In contrast, personal selling messages are adaptive: depending upon the feedback received during a sales presentation, a salesperson can adjust the message or leave it unchanged. Arguments that seem to satisfy potential customers' important concerns can be emphasized or sales points that seem irrelevant to the customers' decision-making processes can be played down.

A salesperson can also use several arguments during a presentation. In the media, an advertiser can emphasize at most one or two reasons for buying a product. This is not the case for salespersons, who can stress many persuasive selling points during a single sales call.

An advertiser can, however, have some control over the sales message's content and presentation. Advertisers carefully select—often after formal research—the theme, copy, and layout of their advertisements. They make sure that the message can be properly understood by prospective buyers and can influence their target audience.

Sales managers can also test sales arguments and train the sales force to make effective presentations. However, a firm has no direct control over the exact content and wording of the message each salesperson will actually deliver; there is little a sales manager can do to prevent salespeople from delivering poor presentations or being rude to customers.

DIFFERENCES AFFECTING THE MEDIA. Personal and advertising communications have both advantages and drawbacks with regard to the effectiveness of the media through which a message is delivered. A sales representative has the advantage of establishing personal and often lively communication with a customer or prospect, while advertising, and especially print advertising, can be perceived by consumers as an impersonal way to communicate. Advertising has an important advantage over personal selling: through the mass media, it can reach a large number of people in a short period of time, whereas a sales representative can make only a limited number of calls in a day.

DIFFERENCES AFFECTING THE AUDIENCE. This latter advantage of advertising over personal selling has a negative counterpart in its effects on the audience of the communication. Any blunder that a sales representative makes during a sales call affects only that customer or prospect. At worst, an inadequate salesperson affects sales negatively during the time he or she is part of the sales force and only in a limited territory. But an advertisement in poor taste has more damaging effects because it reaches an entire market simultaneously.

A salesperson also gets some attention from a client once the sales pitch has started. In contrast, the attention given to the mass media and to the advertising messages they convey cannot be controlled. Commercials often reach consumers during their leisure time, when they are watching television or reading newspapers or magazines. In contrast, a salesperson usually calls on customers during working hours; meeting sales representatives is often a part of the duties of the individuals on whom a sales representative calls. Thus, the audience is more favourably disposed toward listening to a sales pitch.

DIFFERENCES AFFECTING THE EFFECTS. As far as communication effects are concerned, personal selling has a distinct advantage over advertising because it produces immediate responses. After a salesperson has succeeded in proving to a customer that the offer is superior to that of competitors, the selling process can be ended by persuading the customer to sign an order. In contrast, even when a commercial has been convincing enough to trigger the act of purchasing, this behavioural response cannot be immediate. There is always a time lag between the moment a commercial is seen or heard by a consumer and the moment the purchase is completed. This lag is the time necessary for the consumer to drive to a neighbourhood store or, more realistically, to wait for the next purchase occasion. Of course, during this time, the consumer may be subjected to other commercials from competitive products or may decide not to buy the product.

A Cost-Benefit Comparison of
Both Types of Communication
From the comparison of the various aspects

of advertising and personal selling, it can be seen that personal selling is a more effective and powerful communication tool than advertising. This does not mean that only personal selling should be used as a marketing tool and that advertising should have only a marginal role in a firm's marketing program. Contacting an individual through a sales representative costs about a hundred times more than an advertisement. Consequently, unless the personal element of a selling communication is essential to a firm, marketing managers will find that advertising is more time and cost efficient.

Advertising as a Socio-economic Communication

The Economics of Advertising Communications

The various socio-economic aspects of advertising are discussed more thoroughly in subsequent chapters. Here it is important to emphasize that commercial advertising has a precise economic objective. This objective is, in the long run, to contribute to the firm's sales and profits. To meet this objective, advertising is assigned short-run objectives that contribute to a firm's wider objectives.

To be justified from an economic point of view, advertising, along with the other elements of the marketing program, must help generate a firm's gross profits (long run, and discounted at their present value, but excluding the direct costs of advertising). A marketer's task is to ensure that a firm's gross profits are greater than the costs of advertising, which include the costs of media, the costs of creating and producing the advertisement, and the research costs so that the firm retains a flow of net profits. Figure 1.8 outlines the economics of advertising, but similar charts could be designed for all the elements of the marketing program.

The Social Objectives of Advertising

Increasingly, advertising is used by non-profit organizations. For instance, an advertising campaign to raise funds for a cancer research institute, the Red Cross, or some charitable organization, does not result in sales and profits. An advertising campaign to induce Canadians to adopt better health habits or to use safety belts in their cars, or advertising messages sponsored by a political party to gain citizens' votes for the next election do not result in dollar-measurable effects. Whenever advertising is used, however, certain social benefits are anticipated by the sponsors. Whether the social gains warrant the advertising expenditures is a far more difficult question to answer, because the effects are not quantifiable as for business advertising. Nevertheless, no advertising campaign is likely to be run unless the sponsors feel that the social and/or economic gains warrant the advertising expenditures.

A Prospective View of Canadian Advertising

The direction advertising is likely to take in Canada over the next decades may be determined by considering how present trends may influence in the future the various elements involved in advertising.[16] Because it is a mass communication tool, advertising will be affected by research in communications and in the behavioural sciences. Thus, advertising probably will become more efficient in the presentation of messages and in its diffusion processes, thanks to such technical innovations as communication by satellites, visual presentations by telephone, and other improvements in telecommunications. The use of scientific tools and techniques in advertising is likely to increase.

As a marketing tool, advertising will be linked to evolution of the modern marketing concept. If, as predicted by Philip Kotler,[17] marketing philosophy is applied to many other

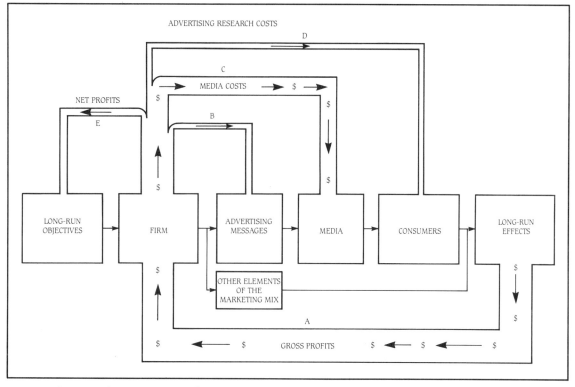

FIGURE 1.8   The Economics of Advertising Communications

kinds of institutions, such as government agencies, educational institutions, and political parties, advertising will increase in scope to include what has so far been the domain of public relations. On the other hand, as a result of increased market demand, a large number of products are likely to cater to smaller and specific market segments. Consequently, advertising appeals will have to become more specific and will have to find new media vehicles for communicating with smaller market segments.

As for the future role of advertising research, new research techniques will undoubtedly be developed and at an accelerated pace. Because advertisers always need to reduce the uncertainty of their decisions, they will rely more systematically on advertising research. Advertising research will then take a larger share of the advertising dollar. The economic and social effects of advertising will likely lead consumers to exert tighter control over marketing activities

and especially over advertising, which is the communications link between manufacturers and consumers.

Two major trends can be predicted: the further evolution of the modern marketing concept will decrease the amount of misleading advertising and limit the use of exaggerated advertising claims. This trend should lead to a general acceptance of the ethical standards (discussed in Chapter 16) to which the largest advertisers have subscribed.

The other trend is toward more legislation to control advertising activities. Under the increasing pressure of consumer-related movements, legislators will have to exert more control over and restrict some activities of advertisers.

All these changes will affect the day-to-day decision-making tasks of advertisers. They will probably obtain increasing help from operational decision tools and, with the use of computers, will concentrate on more delicate problems. Advertisers will also be subject to new constraints from consumers, consumer groups, and legislators. At the same time, their potential for action will increase as new research methods and decision tools become available and as knowledge from the social sciences increases. Far from having their freedom to act curtailed, Canadian advertisers will face new challenges and tasks in the future.

Summary

Advertising plays an important role in the Canadian economy. It can be defined as a mass communication tool with an economic purpose. There are several implications of this definition, and any study of advertising should include an analysis of communication theory and the role of advertising in a firm's communication system. Advertisers also need to understand the importance of advertising research as well as the role advertising and personal selling play in the marketing program.

From these analyses can be drawn some important conclusions. First, because advertising is a mass communication, it tends to lose contact with its audience and is efficient only if it is based on research initiated by the advertiser. Second, advertising is not an isolated phenomenon in a firm's activities. It is but one part of a firm's communication network and must be a consistent and integrated part of that network. Third, advertising is only one tool at the disposal of a marketer and therefore is subject to a firm's overall objectives. Therefore, it must be integrated with the other marketing elements into a coherent marketing program.

Questions for Study

1. Canadian advertising expenditures reached a peak in 1982. The yearly increase of advertising expenditures is the result of several factors. Identify some of these factors, and show how each one contributes to the increase of advertising expenditure volume.

2. Explain how the modern marketing concept changed the nature of and approach to advertising.

3. After having been banned for some time, advertising has been reintroduced in the USSR. What reasons do you think made this move necessary? Is there any economic system that could do without advertising? Explain.

4. Describe the differences in advertising for consumer products, industrial products, services, and charitable organizations.

5. Taking the buyer's point of view, contrast the quality and effectiveness of the information received from a sales representative and from an advertisement. Explain in what ways the concept of "salesmanship in print" was such an innovation at the time it was first proposed by John E. Kennedy.

6. What are the main differences between an advertising campaign run by a retailer (such as Canadian Tire) and an advertising campaign for a consumer product (such as one run by Nabisco)? What are the main factors responsible for these differences?

7. Go through some magazine and newspaper ads. Find examples of
   • manufacturer advertisements
   • retailer advertisements
   • product advertising
   • institutional advertising
   • emotional advertising
   • informative advertising

- primary advertising
- selective advertising
- direct advertising
- indirect advertising

8. Why would an advertiser want to do primary advertising? Give examples. Why would an advertiser want to combine primary and selective advertising campaigns? What important differences are likely to be found in both types of campaign? (Use Figure 1.3 to answer this question.)

Problems

1. Assume that you head the advertising department of a large electronic equipment manufacturer. Over the past years, the firm's main line of products has been computers, and until recently the firm's only clients have been important medium-sized organizations and businesses. In 1980, following trends in the data processing equipment industry, the firm introduced a new line of personal computers especially designed for consumer markets.

(a) What kind of adjustments to your advertising approach, advertising programs, and strategies do you think you would have to make in order to advertise this new line of products effectively?

(b) How could the concepts of fields of experience described in Figure 1.4 help you make the necessary adjustments?

2. As a successful advertiser for a major detergent manufacturer in Canada, you have been recently approached by one of the major federal political parties to design their advertising strategy and campaign for a forthcoming election.

(a) Draw up a list of the relevant factors that you would like to account for before you would specify such a strategy.

(b) Are these factors different from those that you would consider if you were a consumer product advertiser?

(c) In what ways (if any) could the concept of the field of experience help you to carry out your assignment?

Notes

1. Raymond A. Bauer and Stephen A. Greyser, *Advertising in America: The Consumer View* (Boston: Division of Research, Graduate School of Business Administration, Harvard University, 1968).
2. Ralph S. Alexander and the Committee on Definitions, *Marketing Definitions* (Chicago, Ill.: American Marketing Association, 1963), p. 9.
3. H.E. Stephenson and Carlton McNaught, *The Story of Advertising in Canada* (Toronto: The Ryerson Press, 1940), p. 1.
4. Ibid., p. 8.
5. See John O'Toole, *The Trouble with Advertising* (New York: Chelsea House Publishers, 1981).
6. Stephenson and McNaught, p. 101.
7. Ibid., pp. 101-2.
8. Wilbur Schramm, "How Communication Works," *The Process and Effects of Mass Communication*, ed. Wilbur Schramm (Urbana, Ill.: University of Illinois Press, 1965).
9. Henri Joannis, *De l'Etude de Motivation à la Création Publicitaire et à la Promotion des Ventes* (Paris: Dunod, 1967), pp. 8-9.
10. See, for example, Serge Proulx, "Pour une Pratique de la Publicité au Québec," *Communications*, No. 14 (CECMAS, 1971).
11. Example given in Claude Cossette, *Communication de Masse, Consommation de Masse* (Sillery, Qué.: Boréal Express, 1975), p. 261.
12. Ibid., pp. 262-3.
13. Robert MacGregor, "The Utilization of Originally Conceived French Language Advertisements in Parallel Canadian Magazines," *Marketing*, ed. Robert G. Wyckham (Montreal: Administrative

Sciences Association of Canada, 1981), pp. 186-95.

14. Michel J. Bergier and Jerry Rosenblatt, "A Critical View of the Past and Current Methodologies for Classifying English and French Canadians, *Marketing*, ed. Michel Laroche (Montreal: Administrative Sciences Association of Canada, 1982), pp 11-20.

15. M. Lucas Darell and Steward H. Britt, *Measuring Advertising Effectiveness* (New York: McGraw-Hill, 1963); see also Paul Green and Donald S. Tull, *Research for Marketing Decisions*, 3rd ed. (Englewood Cliffs, N.J.: Prentice-Hall, 1975).

16. J.R.G. Jenkins, "The Canadian Advertising Industry in the 1980's," *ASAC Proceedings* (1975), pp. 4-125.

17. Philip Kotler and Sidney J. Levy, "Broadening the Concept of Marketing," *Journal of Marketing*, 33 (January 1969), 10-15.

Advertising and the Marketing Mix

A properly developed advertising strategy is conceived and designed within the framework of the general marketing strategy. This is why an advertising campaign must be fully integrated into an overall marketing program. In the same way, an advertising plan should always be viewed as a part of the broader marketing plan. Thus to design an effective advertising campaign, advertisers must understand the role and function of advertising in the overall marketing program and its contribution to the global marketing strategy.

This chapter analyzes how an advertising strategy can be derived from a marketing strategy and be made consistent with all the other elements of the marketing program. Then it is shown how advertising can be co-ordinated with the other dimensions of the promotional mix—personal selling and sales promotion.

From Marketing to Advertising Strategy

Development of a Marketing Strategy

Generally, a single firm cannot supply all the consumers who experience a broad generic need. For instance, no one firm is able to satisfy all the transportation needs in Canada. Therefore, a firm must select which part(s) of a market it wants to and/or can supply. To make such a decision, a firm must identify one or several consumer groups whose needs and behaviour patterns are *sufficiently alike* to enable them to receive satisfaction from the

product or service being offered. Such a group of consumers is called a *market segment*. The program that is set up to fulfill some needs of a selected market segment is generally called the *marketing program*.

A marketing strategy is developed by selecting one or several market segments and designing marketing programs that result in effective market supply and consumer satisfaction. The strategy can be defined once a firm can identify a group of consumers (or market segments) who have similar patterns of unsatisfied needs or wants and can develop a marketing program that is likely to satisfy these needs and wants, at the same time as it meets the firm's objectives and constraints.

The marketing plan describes in detail the marketing program that a firm intends to follow. A short-term marketing plan usually covers a six-month to one-year period. Medium-term plans run from one to three years. When the marketing plan covers a three-to ten-year period, it is called a long-term plan.

We have said that the marketing program must also account for various constraints, for example, the need to reach a sufficient profit level. Since profits are essential to a firm's survival, the search for market opportunities must aim toward increasing profits. Advertisers must also ensure that the marketing program benefits both the firm and its customers; the firm should be able to make a satisfactory level of profit to increase its resources at the same time as consumers should be able to satisfy some of their needs and wants.

In order to develop effective marketing and, consequently, advertising strategies, it is essential to have an understanding of the key concepts advertisers use: market segmentation, marketing environment, marketing mix, product positioning, and product life-cycle.

The Concept of Market Segmentation[1]

WHAT IS MARKET SEGMENTATION? There are two types of definitions of market segmentation. One defines market segmentation as a *disag-gregative* process, while the other views segmentation as an *aggregative* process.

The first type of definition is borrowed from economic theory, and its application to marketing was originally proposed by Wendell Smith.[2] The concept of market segmentation was put forth to explain how a firm that sells a homogeneous product in markets with heterogeneous demand schedules could charge different prices to maximize profits. Wendell Smith defined market segmentation as the strategy that takes account of varying intensities of demand within

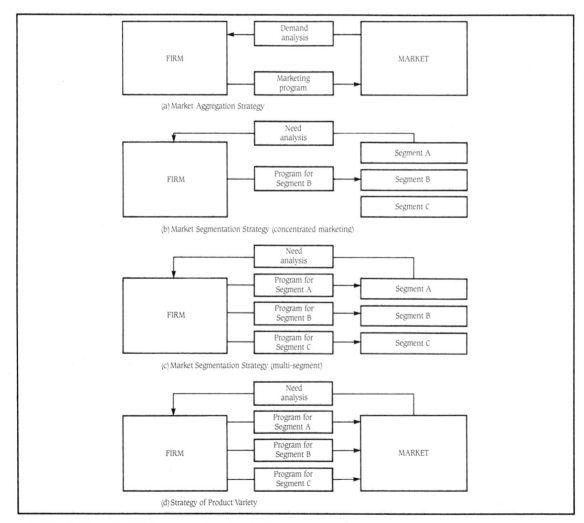

FIGURE 2.1　Market Segmentation Strategies

a particular market. Consequently, the strategy consists of adjusting the product and the marketing program to satisfy the demand. A similar definition was proposed by Ronald Frank.[3]

These disaggregative definitions recognize that an overall market exists, that there are various demand schedules or demand functions within this market as various groups of consumers experience different needs and wants, and that these consumer groups should have differential treatment.

Thus according to the disaggregative definition of market segmentation, markets are split into sub-markets according to consumers' reactions to a firm's product. With the second definition, however, the process is just the reverse. According to Steven Brandt[4] and Claycamp and Massy,[5] market segmentation is an aggregative process of grouping together consumers whose expected reactions to a marketing effort will be similar over a given period.

Before the marketing concept was widely accepted, many firms followed a strategy of *market aggregation.* Market aggregation (or product differentiation) is the strategy by which a firm sells its products to as many customers as possible through a single marketing program. The basic idea is to control, to some extent, the demand for the product through the emphasis of its differences from competitive products. For example, until recently Coca-Cola had only one bottle size, a unique selling price, and a single advertising appeal as a selling proposition. With this approach, a firm builds its marketing program on the similarities of its potential customers, not on their differences. This strategy is not as popular as it once was, because "it is seldom possible for a product or brand to be everything for everybody at the same time" (Figure 2.1a).[6]

The concept of market segmentation is a corollary of the modern marketing concept. Because any marketing process starts from an analysis of consumer needs, one of the first findings of marketers was that needs differ from one customer to another. However, recognizing the heterogeneity of consumer needs would not have helped much if technological change had not allowed marketers to take this fact into account. One of the reasons market segmentation is now possible is that the minimum size of production series in most industries has decreased considerably. Thus, for a manufacturer, the additional profit to be earned through market segmentation should be higher than the cost of economy of scale in production runs. Thus a strategy of market segmentation should be followed as long as certain consumer groups react differently to a firm's marketing program. Taking into account the costs of supplying each market segment, a firm can always transfer some resources from the least profitable segments to the most profitable until the profit margins generated in each market segment are equal.

Of course, a firm may cultivate only one market segment, a strategy which is called *concentrated marketing* (Figure 2.1b). If it is profitable, a firm may decide to go after several or even all the defined market segments. This strategy is called *multi-segment marketing* (Figure 2.1c).

IMPLEMENTING A SEGMENTATION STRATEGY. The market segmentation concept may be simple, but its practical implementation is fraught with difficulties. The major problem is that segmentation is a two-way process; it goes from the market to the company (for the design of the marketing program) and then from the company to the segment (for actual implementation of the marketing program). Therefore, several steps are required to implement a market segmentation strategy effectively. The first step is to define the global market toward which the firm's activities shall be directed as a function of consumer needs.

A second step is to identify sufficiently homogeneous and well-differentiated consumer groups. Here is needed a *conceptual segmentation criterion:* the various groups must be defined on the basis of consumers' needs and desires. This means that the segments thus defined must be *significant* and that the demand elasticities in the various segments, with regard to changes in some elements of the marketing program, must be different for each segment.

Then, once the segments have been identified, the advertiser must evaluate their profit potential. To do so, the environmental forces affecting each segment should be evaluated and the marketing and advertising methods chosen. For a segmentation strategy to be worthwhile for a firm, the defined segments must be large enough to generate sufficient revenue and profits. Unfortunately, segments defined on the basis of consumer needs or likely behavioural responses to elements of the marketing program are usually not directly measurable; this is one of the major difficulties of a segmentation strategy. More often than not, one must therefore define consumers in each segment by more practical criteria, for instance, demographic characteristics. It is easier to estimate the number of Vancouver residents between the ages of 18 and 65 than the number of people who buy toothpaste mainly to prevent cavities. It is necessary to define one or several criteria that can directly or indirectly evaluate the size of a market segment.

Next, a marketing mix that can respond to the specific needs of each target market segment must be determined. Once this is done, sales and revenue forecasts as well as cost estimates can be established. These combined estimates must give an acceptable profit level for the company. The economic analysis of each segment indicates whether a segment constitutes a market opportunity for the company.

Finally, the marketing program must be able to reach the target market segments. To establish clear communication and distribution channels that can reach consumers in each segment, an advertiser must identify the consumers in terms of geographic or socio-demographic variables. (As will be shown later, advertising media usually describe their audiences' profiles along such characteristics.)

THE CHOICE OF SEGMENTATION CRITERIA.   Market segments should ideally be identified by two sets of criteria: specific needs and behaviour of consumers, and socio-demographic variables (Table 2.1). Unfortunately, segments defined in terms of needs and/or behaviour generally do not coincide with socio-economic classifications. That is why the choice of a segmentation criterion is so important. When marketers use a definition based on consumer needs and behaviour, they can make better decisions about the product or service mix that best suits the segment's needs. On the other hand, it becomes more difficult to evaluate the size of the segment and to develop the other elements of the marketing program, especially the distribution and media plans. Conversely, if marketers use socio-economic variables as segmentation criteria, they may define segments that are easier to reach but less homogeneous in needs and behaviour. Keeping this dilemma in mind, advertisers must often rely on judgment and on formal market research in order to select the best possible segmentation criterion.

Because of the inherent drawbacks of any segmentation strategy, William M. Reynolds[7] has advocated a strategy of *product variety* (Figure 2.1d), which is a compromise between product differentiation and segmentation strategies.

Instead of marketing different products designed for specific market segments, Reynolds suggested that a variety of products be put on the market. Among Reynold's reasons for such a strategy were:

1. Customers are not always different;

2. Competition among the products of a same company is sometimes a good marketing practice;

3. Directing a series of specific marketing propositions to various market segments may be a better strategy than directing several propositions to an entire market (the costs, however, of reaching consumers in an entire market are generally much higher);

TABLE 2.1 Choice of Segmentation Criterion

Desirable Features for Each Segment	Significant Segments	Measurable Segments	Segments That Can Be Reached
Objectives	Determination of product/service mix and prices	Determination of sales potential and profitability	Determination of the promotion and distribution programs
Types of desirable segmentation criteria	Needs/desires, behaviour, psychographic variables	Socio-economic variables	Socio-economic variables

4. It is often difficult to classify consumers into preference groups for products and brands;

5. What seems to be market segmentation is often the result of random purchases made by many consumers buying a variety of products.

Traditionally, various segmentation criteria have been proposed or used in marketing. The most widely used criteria are the following:

Consumers' reactions to various elements of the marketing program.[8] Different treatment of consumers through certain elements of the marketing program should be a consequence and not a cause of market segmentation.

Purchase characteristics, such as sales volume, purchase rate, brand loyalty.[9] The advantage of using this criterion rather than socio-economic variables has been frequently challenged.[10]

Consumer characteristics. This set of criteria includes socio-economic and demographic variables (age, sex, geographical location, income, social class).[11] Many studies have shown, however, that these variables were very weak in explaining and predicting consumer behaviour.[12]

Psychographic variables. These include lifestyle and buyer personality variables.[13] For instance, the "backward" segmentation strategy proposed by William D. Wells[14] consists in uncovering "natural" consumer segments characterized by similar needs and consumption habits and by homogeneous lifestyles. Similarly, Russell I.

Haley suggests grouping consumers according to the benefits they may derive from consuming a product.[15]

Psychological variables. Consumer motivations, attitudes, preferences[16] and perceptions fall into this category. For instance, the product segmentation strategy proposed by Norman L. Barnett[17] holds that consumers differentiate among brands according to their perceptions of real or imaginary attributes and then choose the brand whose attributes they prefer. Thus, the starting point of a marketing program should not be the characteristics of various consumers in a market segment but rather the product features as perceived by the consumers in the segment. Unlike the market segmentation strategy, product segmentation designs a product according to consumers' perceptions.

The Marketing Environment Concept
The marketing process starts with an analysis of consumer needs and market behaviour so that the goods and services produced are wanted by consumers and likely to be accepted. This marketing philosophy has implications for the definition of a marketing strategy and for the tools marketers use to achieve their goals. A marketer's role can be compared to that of a marine officer. The officer's responsibility is to bring a ship safely back to harbour. The harbour that marketing managers must reach represents the marketing objectives.

The marine officer must allow for various forces that cannot be controlled, for example, storms, winds, currents, and the routes of other ships. In the same way, marketing managers are also affected by and must adjust to external constraints over which they have no control. Although they cannot control these elements, marketers must identify and, insofar as possible, predict them in the same way as marine officers cannot control the winds or the currents but can inquire about meteorological forecasts and consult ocean maps.

Thus, marketing actions are affected by the market environment at two different levels. On one level are the uncontrollable forces influencing a market: the socio-economic, competitive, institutional, technological, and legal environments. This is called the marketing macro-environment. At the second level are environmental forces over which marketers have no direct control but which can be manipulated through promotional activities. This is called the marketing micro-environment. Such forces are, for instance, the consumers in the various target market segments. Marketers want to be able to affect the attitudes and the behaviour of these consumers and have some tools at their disposal to do so.

THE MARKETING MACRO-ENVIRONMENT. A market can be characterized by descriptive factors: size, population concentration, demographic trends, the average annual income of consumers or households, growth areas, and immigration or emigration trends. These basic factors are used to assess the importance of a particular market. For example, analysis of consumers' age group distribution in a given market indicates the important changes that will likely occur in consumer patterns for different product and service categories. Such other factors as ethnic origin, religious beliefs, education, income levels and sources, occupation, and language are also relevant market characteristics.

Competitive market structures. The competitive environment in which a firm operates is one of the most constraining factors when selecting a marketing strategy. A market of perfect competition is characterized by a very large number of small-size firms competing in an industry. No one firm can dominate the market, and no marketer can profitably make the marketing program different from that of competitors. The product is essentially the same for all the firms in the market. The product's price is determined by the forces of supply and demand and not by any one firm. Promotion and advertising are useless tools because consumers are supposed to have complete and free information in a homogeneous market in which the same product is sold.

At the other extreme is a monopoly market, in which only one firm supplies a certain kind of service or product. In this situation a firm can set any price for a product and can decide on the level of all the other variables in the marketing mix. Marketing efforts and advertising can be profitably increased as long as the total demand for the product is sufficient to warrant the increase.

When a market has an oligopolistic structure, it is dominated by a small number of firms (the petroleum industry is one example). In this case, the marketing strategy of each firm is likely to affect competitors' market share significantly. Thus when one firm takes an aggressive marketing action, competitors usually react immediately to protect their market positions. The harshest competition typically takes place in markets with an oligopolistic structure. Since in this market structure, a price decrease is likely to be immediately matched by competitors, price is not a very effective marketing weapon. Marketing efforts are more likely to hinge on advertising and sales promotion.

Finally, a market characterized by an imperfect competition structure has a certain number of firms manufacturing products that differ only slightly from one another. This is a common market structure, especially for such products as television sets and automobiles. In this type of market, each firm tries to cater to a specific market segment with a product and marketing program designed to meet that segment's needs, while trying to avoid any possible confusion between its products and those of competitors. In some ways, each firm has a quasi-monopoly in a very limited market segment.

Institutional market structure. In addition to its competitive structure, a market is also characterized by its institutional structure. Various organizations, for instance, wholesalers, brokers, retailers, selling organizations, and advertising agencies, specialize in distributing and promoting products. Moreover, certain relationships among these organizations have become a tradition in most markets. These relationships have evolved into their present form as the result of market forces and power structures within marketing channels. Thus the institutional structure of a market usually cannot be modified by a single firm.

The technological environment. Each industry is characterized by various degrees of technological evolution. Certain industries, such as electronics and aeronautics, have experienced dramatic change in the past few decades. Technological change compels the firms in these industries not only to keep abreast of, but also to promote technological development. In order to benefit from technological breakthroughs, a firm must constantly look for new market opportunities and for innovations that are desired by various market segments.

The legal environment. Marketing managers and advertisers need to be aware of the laws designed to keep competition active or to protect consumers against unfair practices and abuse. In Canada, the Combines Investigation Act is intended to discourage practices that might lessen competition. These practices include collusion among competitors, mergers, monopolies, discriminating practices, price fixing, illegal discounts, and false or misleading advertising.

THE MARKETING MICRO-ENVIRONMENT. The second category of environmental variables includes the factors that induce consumers to buy certain kinds of products (a given brand, at a specific point of purchase, at a certain time); in other words, how and why consumers behave in a certain way. To apply the modern marketing concept is to examine consumers' lives, to understand their needs, motivations, perceptions, attitudes, purchasing habits, and to be aware of the changes they want or are ready to accept.

The Marketing Mix Concept
Let us return to the comparison between a marketer's and a marine officer's tasks. Taking environmental constraints into account, the officer plans a route to take advantage of the wind and the current in order to reach a destination quickly and safely. Similarly, a marketing manager takes account of controllable marketing variables, and plans a marketing program. When the marketing manager makes a decision about all the controllable variables, he or she defines what is usually called the marketing mix. These controllable variables of the marketing program have been classified by Jerome C. McCarthy into a scheme that has gained much acceptance in marketing: the 4 Ps,[18] which are *P*roduct, *P*lace (distribution), *P*romotion (advertising and personal selling), and *P*rice (Table 2.2) They can be considered a marketing manager's "steering wheel" (Figure 2.2).

PRODUCT. An advertiser must make decisions that directly or indirectly affect a firm's products. These decisions include the quality level of the product or service to be marketed and the number and variety of product versions, styles, and sizes. Physical products are typically wrapped up in a package with a label. Directions for use and other relevant information are generally written on the labels. More important, a name or brand name is prominently displayed on the label or on the package. This

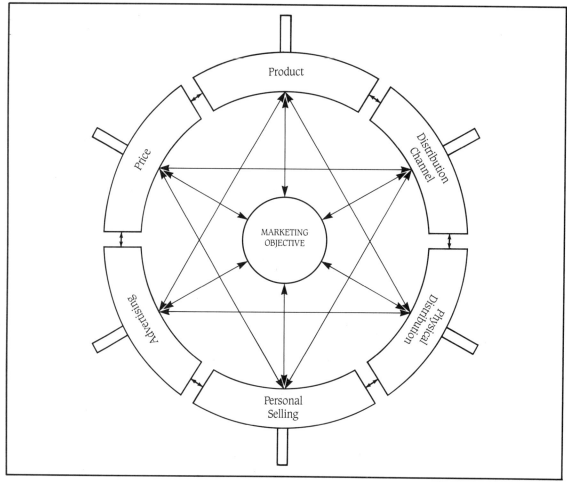

FIGURE 2.2   The Marketing Manager's "Steering Wheel"

name may be the same name for all products sold by the firm. Alternatively, it may be specific to a given product within the product line. The services included with the purchase of a product, such as the warranty, product maintenance, or service allowances, are considered part of the product offer. Advertisers must also establish policies for introducing, researching, and developing new products.

PLACE.   Advertisers must determine the distribution channels through which products should flow from the producer to the final consumers. The decisions about distribution channels are complex. For instance, products may be sold

directly to the final consumers (through mail or catalogue sales), or through retailers or wholesalers. Whatever the method, marketers must ensure co-operation from the middlemen in the distribution channel selected and that all the tasks to be performed in the process of distributing goods from the factory to the final consumers are carried out in the most efficient way. These tasks include the transporting, handling, storing, and financing of the goods.

PROMOTION.   Advertisers must establish communication channels with their markets. Mass communication, especially advertising, is typically directed toward the final consumer or sometimes to the middlemen in the firm's distribution channels or even to the entire community. Several types of marketing decisions are involved: what amount should be spent on advertising to do an effective communication job? Which ideas should be communicated to the target audience? Which media are most efficient for reaching the right people, at the right time and at the least possible cost? Communications through sales representatives are very often a vital part of a firm's marketing communication program. Sales promotion activities, which are the marketing actions designed to move products into distribution channels to the final consumers or middlemen, also require communication decisions. The *promotional mix* is the selected blend of advertising, personal selling, and sales promotions efforts.

PRICE.   The fourth area of marketing decisions includes all the aspects of the marketing program dealing with the price of the transaction. Once the general price level of a product is determined, an advertiser must decide which specific figure(s) will be used as a price; for instance, should an even or an odd price be used; should a product be priced at 99¢ or $1? In competitive markets, pricing policies must be flexible so that a firm can act quickly to counteract competitive actions. The credit terms and payment procedures for final consumers or middlemen should also be carefully designed. These variables of the marketing mix are presented in Table 2.2.

Marketers first set objectives and then define an appropriate marketing program to meet the objectives. To do so, allowances must be made for predictions of the future marketing environment. Even if these predictions of market conditions are reasonably accurate, they will differ at least slightly from what actually happens. Thus actual marketing performance in terms of sales, profits, or market penetration will depart from the targeted objectives. If there is not too wide a gap between the objectives

TABLE 2.2   The Four Ps and Their Related Decision Areas

The 4 Ps	DECISION AREA
Product	Product line decisions (quality, type, sizes)
	Packaging and labelling decisions
	Brand name decisions (individual or family brand names)
	Product-related service decisions (trade-ins, maintenance and repair facilities)
	New product introduction decisions
	New product research and development decisions
Place	Selection of the distribution channels toward the final consumers
	Selection of the appropriate means to ensure channel members' co-operation
	Decisions about the distribution channel task allocation (transportation, handling, storage)
Promotion	Advertising decisions (advertising budget, advertising copy). Advertising directed at —consumers —middlemen —the community
	Personal selling decisions
	Sales promotion decisions (couponing, cents-off)
Price	Pricing decisions (price level, specific prices—odd vs even price)
	Price change policies
	Credit terms, payment procedures

and the actual performance, one or more elements of the marketing mix may be adjusted slightly, e.g., by making tactical adjustments. If the gap is too wide, the objectives may be modified, or major changes made in the marketing program, or both.

The Concept of Product Positioning

A product can be defined according to a reference point (the target market); physical, psychological, and sociological dimensions; and the time elapsed since the product was introduced. At a given moment, advertisers define their product strategy by deciding what the level of a product's attributes should be. The attributes may be weighted according to the perceived importance of each choice criterion. Thus, advertisers are said to decide the position of a product in the space defined by the attributes important to the firm's target market.[19] The product strategy must also be adjusted according to the age of the product. The history of a product, from its introduction to its decline, is called the product life-cycle. The position of a product in its life-cycle is determined by market dynamics.

The objective of product positioning is to identify the means of reducing the distance between the company's brand and the target market's ideal. There are three general types of strategies for positioning a product.

One strategy is to try to shift the position of a brand toward the ideal point by improving the product and communicating this improvement to the target market. Another possibility is to improve consumers' perceptions of the company's brand. Pepsi-Cola pursued this strategy with the campaign, "More than half of Coke drinkers prefer Pepsi to Coke," by proposing a test in which blindfolded consumers chose the drink they preferred after tasting each one.[20]

A second product positioning strategy is for advertisers to shift the ideal point of the target market toward their brand. This can be achieved by inducing consumers to use new choice criteria or by conducting an information campaign on the product or the product class in order to change consumers' perceptions of the importance of some criteria.

This strategy may be successful only if the product is in one of the first stages of its life-cycle. As soon as consumers know the characteristics of a product class, it may be difficult to change their ideal point.

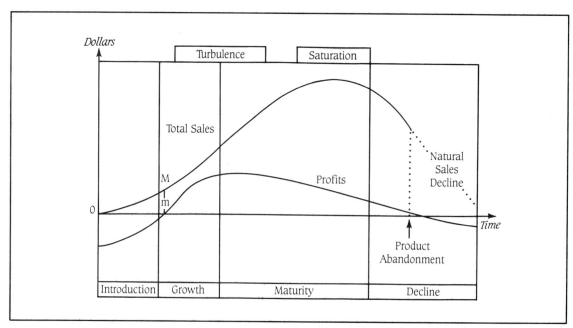

FIGURE 2.3   The Stages in a Product Life-Cycle

A third strategy is to shift the brand and the ideal point simultaneously toward a new intermediate position. This solution, which is a compromise between the first two strategies, may be easier and less costly to implement.

To conclude, the concept of product positioning is pertinent only at a given moment in a product's life-cycle. Most markets change constantly, with brand images shifting and new brands being introduced. As a result, advertisers must adjust the marketing mix according to changes in market situations.

The Concept of Product Life-Cycle

The concept of product life-cycle is the recognition of market dynamics. The conditions that cause a product to be adopted by a market at various stages change according to a firm's actions and that of its competitors.

This concept is useful in planning an advertising program because different market conditions may prevail at each phase of a product's life-cycle, and the survival of a product in a given market may be constantly threatened by those market conditions. All decisions required by the marketing program must fall between two important levels of product management: the long-term planning of product strategy and the adjustments or tactics dictated by a particular situation.

STAGES OF THE PRODUCT LIFE-CYCLE. There are four stages in a product's life-cycle: introduction, growth, maturity, and decline (Figure 2.3). The stage in which a product may be at a given time can be determined by the evolution of the market's total sales for this product.

Introduction. During the introduction stage of a new product, sales rise at a slow pace. At first, the company can only activate this process with a small number of consumers. These may be consumers who have been in contact with one of the levels within the distribution channel or who have been exposed to a promotional message. Since the product is new, the objective of promotional efforts is to make potential consumers aware of and understand the new product. Therefore the advertising message must primarily be informative and secondarily mention the product's brand. It is not necessary to allocate larger sums to support the brand, since the latter is usually the only one on the market, but it is important to induce acceptance of this product. In addition to being aimed at potential consumers, product promotion must also be directed toward the various members of the distribution channel, to convince them of the product's profitability and induce them to stock and distribute it.

A firm may incur considerable expense in developing a new product: for the research on a new product that satisfies a specific market need; for the purchase of special tools and use of the firm's productive capacity; and for intensive product promotion. Because a firm may have incurred significant investment and losses during the introduction stage, it might adopt a high price policy in order to minimize losses. This policy is feasible, since an innovative company has a temporary monopoly for the product. On the other hand, a market for the product must be developed and a penetration pricing policy (setting a low price in order to capture a large part of a market) may be indicated.

Growth. During the growth stage, sales increase at an accelerated pace if the product is successful. If the contrary arises, the product is taken off the market and the company suffers considerable losses. During growth, the success of the product is largely due to the culmination of a large number of consumers having made extensive information searches, in order to decide whether to buy or at least try the product. In turn these new users act as information sources and convince other consumers to adopt or try this product. This process then goes on at an accelerated pace.

During the growth in sales, the firm's revenue increases rapidly and profits begin to appear. These profits may encourage other companies to offer products that are more or less improved imitations of the original product. Competition then forces the innovative company to promote its brand aggressively and to try to keep its leadership in product quality. At this stage, the company may realize important reductions in manufacturing costs, since the process has been streamlined and "debugged", and in promotion costs, since spending is spread over a larger volume of sales.

As more firms penetrate the market, the original company's profits may reach a peak and begin to decline. Perceptible improvements may then be made to the product. At this point, conflicts usually emerge among institutions competing in a channel. This part of the growth stage, which also marks the beginning of the maturity phase, has been defined as the turbulence stage.[21] Promotional expenses are usually high and the product advertising emphasizes the superiority of the brand and its attributes. The methods of product positioning discussed previously may be used to develop marketing strategies.

The growth stage has a great influence on market share and profits, since during this phase it is relatively cheaper to build a strong market share and brand loyalty occurs. For these reasons companies with specific market share objectives must maintain an intensive promotion effort and steady sales growth.

Maturity. The maturity stage corresponds to the natural sales ceiling of the target market, taking into account all the needs that the product satisfies. During this stage competing brands tend to have the same attributes. This convergence toward the same product quality is due to competing advertisers' increased knowledge of the market ideal.

Pressure on prices is generally strong during the maturity stage, and market profits gradually decline. The erosion of profits is also due to promotional efforts required to maintain market share by firms whose efforts are aimed at both the consumer and at the various distribution channels. During the maturity stage, each firm in an industry may have a promotional budget that is a fixed percentage of total sales, especially when sales are stable. Even so, some firms may spend more on advertising in order to maintain their market share. Others may spend a larger part of their budget on special offers in order to reduce inventories, stimulate consumer trials, strengthen consumer loyalty through repeat purchases, or attempt to get greater shelf space for their brand at the retail level.

Early in the maturity stage and toward the end of the turbulence stage, the number of competing brands on the market is probably at a maximum. At this point, inefficient firms may withdraw from the market. When all potential buyers have tried a product and sales become only replacement sales, which is called the saturation phase,[22] only the efficient firms remain. The competitive situation is then extremely stable, and each company is content to maintain its market share. An aggressive advertising campaign at this stage would probably not be profitable.

Decline. The decline stage starts when regular consumers of a product stop using it because the needs it satisfies have become less important or because the needs are better satisfied by a new product.

Competing firms have a choice between withdrawing the product from the market or supporting it because profits are still good. Generally, fewer companies compete in this market, and those that remain try to lower their production, promotion, and distribution costs. In particular, there may be a shortening of product lines, and advertising campaigns may aim simply at reminding consumers that the product is still available.

STRATEGIC OPTIONS FOR ADVERTISING DURING A PRODUCT'S LIFE-CYCLE. The strategy of *market penetration* for a brand consists of attempting to increase the use of the brand and to reach new customers for the brand. Traditionally, this strategy is used by a company during the growth and maturity stages of its product. The total demand for a product generally follows the life-cycle evolution, and a company may increase its market share by taking sales from the natural growth of demand and/or from competitors.

The strategy of *product development* represents, with the next two strategies, a modification of the product's life-cycle. This strategy consists of developing a product with new characteristics aimed at the present target market. For example, the introduction of sweetened cereal and those with high nutritive value have raised the ceiling on total sales for cereals by about forty per cent. By the same token, milk has been at the maturity phase for a long time; most people stop drinking it after a certain age. The introduction of a new milk-based drink that would be appreciated by people of all age groups could raise the present sales ceiling considerably. Another example is the introduction of colour television, which represented an improved product for families already owning a black and white television set. To families already owning a colour television set, new black and white portable sets may be offered for use in the bedroom, the basement, or the summer cottage.

The strategy of *market development* consists of adapting a product to other consumers or to other markets.[23] For example, the adaptation to the feminine market of such male products as attaché cases, pants, and suits has lengthened the life-cycle of these products. It also works the other way: more men use cologne, skin cosmetics, and wear clothes made out of "feminine" fabrics.

Development of an Advertising Strategy

The strategy for the advertising component of the marketing mix is generally developed at the same time as the marketing strategy and is based on the communication objectives defined in the marketing plan.

An *advertising strategy* is developed by taking the market segment defined in the marketing strategy statement and designing an advertising program for achieving the communication objectives within a specified budget and time period. The *advertising plan* describes the advertising program that is to be followed over a specific period. The program may describe one advertising campaign or a series of consistent campaigns.

In order to design an advertising campaign, an advertiser must make decisions in five key areas:
• setting the advertising campaign objectives
• setting the advertising budget
• designing the advertising messages
• determining the media to be used in conveying the message, as well as the advertising media schedule
• setting the mechanisms to control the effectiveness of the advertising campaign.

The decisions made in these areas are interrelated, as shown in Figure 2.4.

As has been pointed out, an advertising campaign should be designed to achieve precise marketing objectives. The means to achieve these objectives are the advertising message content and format and the media selected to convey the message to the relevant market segments. Decisions about the structure and format of the message depend on the types of media selected. These advertising tools involve costs that indicate what size budget is necessary in order to meet the marketing objectives.

This approach to determining an advertising budget is the objective and task method. For an advertising campaign to be effective and profitable, an advertiser must select objectives in such a way that the costs involved still warrant their pursuit. It is always necessary to reassess the objectives in the light of costs whenever the difference between expected returns and costs are too great. Procedures for measuring an advertising campaign's effectiveness are designed to control the advertising process; advertising objectives can be reassessed for the

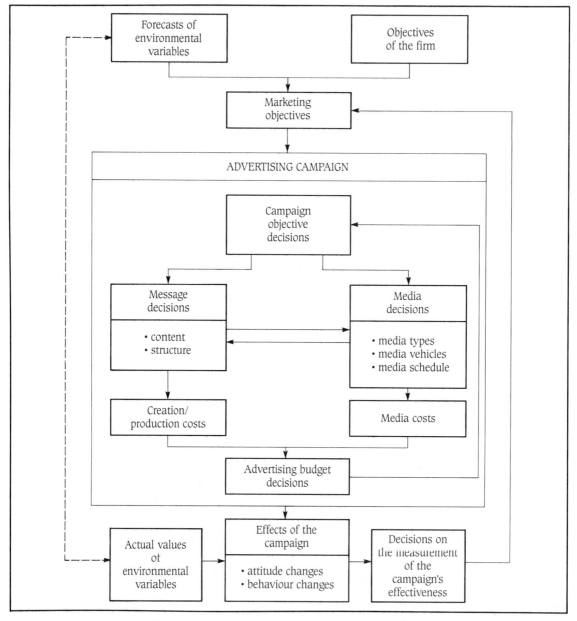

FIGURE 2.4   Relationships among the Various Decision Areas in Advertising

following period because market penetration, the level of consumer awareness, or consumer attitudes achieved at the end of the campaign can be measured. These measurements affect the marketing objectives and consequently the advertising goals.

Advertising as Part of the Promotional Mix

Advertising campaigns are not independent of a firm's other marketing activities, since all the elements of the marketing mix should fit into a homogeneous plan that can achieve the marketing objectives. In the same way, advertising must be co-ordinated with the other elements of the promotional mix—personal selling, publicity, and sales promotion.

Co-ordination with the Sales Force

Selecting the best possible mix between the two major communication tools—personal communication through sales representatives and mass communication through advertising—has strategic importance.

Figure 2.5 shows a common distribution channel that makes use of two different strategies: a manufacturer sells to wholesalers who in turn sell to retailers; retailers then sell to the final consumers. This distribution channel is used to distribute small ticket items in the consumer market.

How does communication flow through this distribution channel? The communication system first takes into account a basic constraint, which is the cost of a communication. Studies have shown that the average cost of a

sales call in 1982 was \$137.[24] In contrast, the cost of reaching a potential customer through the mass media was a fraction of a cent.[25] Personal contact is, however, sometimes more effective despite the greater cost; for example, when it is important to have immediate knowledge of customers' reactions, or to interact between buyers and sellers, or to maintain personal ties with middlemen. If personal contact is not essential, a marketing manager may reduce expenses by using advertising.

Pull and Push Strategies

With communication through advertising, a marketing manager attempts to stimulate market demand for a product. The objective is to create positive attitudes among consumers toward a brand, to give information about the positive attributes of a product or service, and eventually to induce consumers to buy the product. Through stimulation of market demand, goods flow through the distribution channel, and the final consumers play the role of a pump in keeping goods moving in the distribution

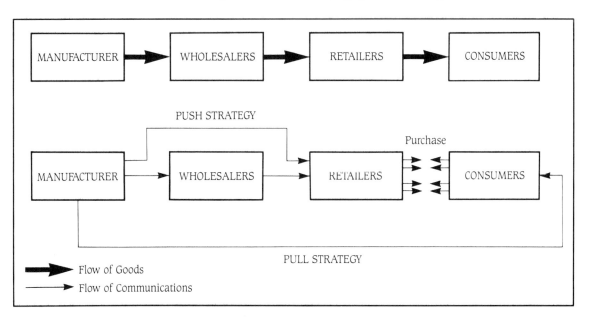

FIGURE 2.5   Equilibrium between Pull and Push Strategies

Courtesy Colour Scripts Ltd.   *Courtesy* Broadcast Monitoring Services Ltd.

FIGURE 2.6   Storyboards such as the ones advertised here show the television commercial on a single sheet of photographic paper.

channel. This strategy is known as the *pull strategy*.

With communication through personal selling, a marketing manager tries to make a product flow through the channel by persuading middlemen to keep inventories of the product and by making sure that the product gets enough shelf space. A strategy that pushes products into a distribution channel is the *push strategy*.

Figure 2.5 shows that the purchase of a certain brand takes place only when a consumer is ready to buy the product (knows of it, wants it, or insists on it) and can find it at a retail store.

If a consumer is ready to buy a certain product brand following some advertising pressure exerted within the framework of a pull strategy, and if the retailers do not carry this

brand, the consumer will likely purchase a competitive brand. Conversely, if the brand has reached retailers' shelves but the consumer is not ready to buy it or try it due to a lack of information about the brand's attributes, the purchase will probably not take place. The two types of strategy should therefore complement each other so that an informed consumer can buy the brand from a retailer who can supply it.

Although a marketing manager has some latitude in emphasizing one strategy over the other, the two strategies should be mixed to reach a harmonious equilibrium. To do so, the communication task should be properly allocated to the two communication channels so as to meet this objective. For instance, Procter & Gamble launches most of its new products by using a pull strategy. The advertising campaign directed at the final consumers only starts once the product has achieved a high level of distribution among retailers. This objective can be met because Procter & Gamble sales personnel are able to convince retailers that the product will be backed by major advertising efforts and that they should be well stocked in order to meet the expected demand. With Procter & Gamble brand names, retailers are likely to co-operate. A firm less well known would probably have more difficulty achieving a high level of distribution before starting its pull effort; many retailers would want to make sure that the manufacturer's pull strategy was creating sufficient demand for the product to warrant keeping it in stock.

Other Factors Affecting the Advertising–Personal Selling Mix

Other factors likely to influence the advertising–personal selling mix are the type of product and the type of market. For instance, Cash and Crissy have noted that the mix between advertising and personal selling is affected by the phase in which a market is.[26] According to these authors, a market goes through three phases: pretransactional, transactional, and post-transactional. Advertising plays a major part in the pretransactional phase (for cultivating the market) and in the post-transactional phase (for providing a rationalization to the buyer). Only in rare instances can advertising accomplish the transaction by itself; this role is best fulfilled by personal selling. In a sense, advertising can be considered as readying a market for a salesperson's personal effort.

Co-ordination Techniques

The sales force should be fully briefed and informed about the advertising campaign in order to reassure distributors and retailers about the promotional effort in support of the brand. The following are some of the techniques that may be used in co-operation with the sales force:
- The agency may prepare a film describing the product features, as well as the advertising campaign designed to support the brand. This film may be shown by the sales force to intermediaries.
- The agency may organize a sales meeting at which the new campaign is presented. This meeting may take place at a desirable location (e.g., a resort hotel), and use entertainers for impact. The objective of such meetings is to get the sales force enthusiastic about the product and the campaign.
- The sales force may be given copies of the print advertisement or the television commercial to show or distribute to intermediaries. The television commercials are often presented in the form of coloured storyboards with six to ten frames reproduced on photographic paper (Figure 2.6).

Co-ordination with Publicity

Activities related to *publicity* aim at realizing a firm's marketing objectives by obtaining free media space or time for articles, editorials, press releases, and photographs that provide information free of charge about products, services, or the firm itself. In general, the firm prepares the text of the message, which is given to the media by the public relations department. Since the message appears as editorial matter, it is more credible to an audience and thus is a more efficient communication form than a commercial message of similar size and repetition. This is because the medium is viewed by the public as objective and independent of the firm.[27] Publicity is also a relatively inexpensive form of promotion since the only costs involved are those related to preparing the message and finding the media that are willing to use it. The time or space the media allocates to such items is limited and is often given to a medium's best clients. The content of the message must be consistent with the advertising strategy in order to reinforce the campaign's effectiveness. Ideally, the message should be prepared by or in co-operation with the advertising agency.

Editorial matter that reports on problems with a product, a service, or a company is called

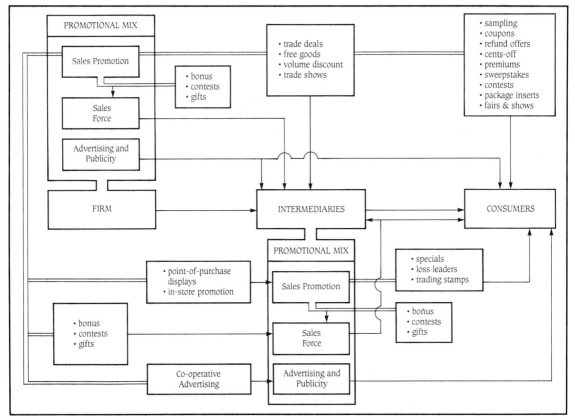

FIGURE 2.7   Sales Promotion Activities in the Context of the Overall Promotional Effort

negative publicity.[28] Examples of negative publicity are product recalls that are announced in the media. If sustained over a long period, such publicity may be damaging. As with other forms of promotion, however, negative publicity may be forgotten over time if it is not reinforced by the media. The rate of forgetting depends on the seriousness of the problem, consumers' experience with the problem, and the amount of negative publicity.

Co-ordination with Sales Promotion

Sales promotion activities are the activities other than publicity, advertising, and personal selling that promote the products and/or services of a firm or intermediary. These activities support, assist, or reinforce the other elements of the promotional mix (Figure 2.7).

Within the distribution channel, the firm and each intermediary develop a promotional mix with a proper balance among advertising, publicity, sales force, and sales promotion activities. Consumers may be exposed to advertising and publicity about products originating from the firm or from intermediaries, for example, retailers. Distributors may be exposed to the firm's advertising and publicity campaigns and be called upon by its sales force.

Based on their objectives within the mix, sales promotion activities fall into one of five categories:

1. *Firm—consumers sales promotion activities* encourage brand trial or brand loyalty through sampling, coupons, refund offers, cents-off, premiums, sweepstakes, contests, package inserts, or trade fairs and shows.

Sampling is effective for introducing a new or improved product and for increasing product trial of an existing product. The cost of a sampling campaign can be reduced by proper identification of the target market. Samples can be sent directly to households separately or by co-operative direct mailing, which distributes the sample along with coupons or other direct mail pieces. Sampling may also be done in-store with product demonstration or by including the sample with other products.

Couponing is the most widely used sales promotion technique in Canada. In 1980, more than two billion coupons were distributed, and 128 million were redeemed by consumers.[29] This figure reached 2.8 billion in 1982[30] and is expected to continue to rise. Coupons are most often used to generate brand trial or to introduce new products. Some advertisers use couponing to increase market share or to defend the brand against competitors. Coupons may be in or on the package, or they may be delivered to selected consumers. This former method of distribution is economical and effective because the coupon may help attract new users to the brand and provide an incentive for buying it again. This method also stimulates the retailers to stock the brand. However, non-users of the product category are not reached, and the direct delivery of coupons to potential users is the preferred method. Coupons may be sent directly to potential users, often by using co-operative mailing, which is more economical than a separate mailing, or by including them in a magazine or newspaper advertisement. A couponing campaign must be based on several factors affecting the cost of the campaign: the face value, the cost of redemption, the redemption rate, the expiration date, the method of redemption, and the nature of the advertising campaign. On the other hand, many advertisers are very concerned about the risk of misredemption by dishonest dealers.[31]

Refund offers is a technique used to promote sales of a brand. Cash refunds are offered to consumers who buy a given number of items, and the refund amounts to a price reduction based on *actual* purchase of the brand. The value of the refund must be high enough to encourage consumers to write in for it. Refund offers are used for a variety of products, from cereals to cars.

Cents-off offers a temporary price reduction to encourage consumers to try or repurchase a brand. Consumers may stock up on the product, and if the product is satisfactory, the consumer may purchase it at the regular price. The promotion should not run too long or be repeated too often, because consumers then consider the reduced price as the maximum amount they should pay.

Premiums give consumers a product "bonus". The premium may be unrelated to the product, like a beach towel for a detergent brand, or related to the product, like a razor with a package of razor blades. It may be free, like a small plastic toy in a cereal box or sold at or below cost with proof of purchase. Some premiums may be included in the package, while with others the consumer must write the manufacturer and include proof of purchase and a payment for the premium. Premiums may be used to attract attention to a package or to enhance interest in advertisements for the brand. Since it is a rather complicated technique, premiums are not as popular as couponing or refund offers.

Sweepstakes ask consumers to fill out contest entry forms. At a fixed date, the winners are selected by random drawing from all entries. Because the prizes are often spectacular, sweepstakes generate high interest from consumers and from the trade. This interest in turn may translate into additional trade support and increased consumer awareness of the brand. Sweepstakes must be co-ordinated closely with the advertising campaign to generate excitement about the product and to ensure that the product's image is not compromised.

Contests is a technique similar to sweepstakes, except that consumers must demonstrate some skill. As with sweepstakes, "instant-win" contests help generate excitement about a brand, encourage multiple product purchases, and increase brand loyalty. This type of contest is often used by soft drink companies and fast food chains.

Package inserts include in a package a promotional piece about a product, a line of products, or a related product.

Fairs and shows for consumers help manufacturers promote their products to highly interested audiences. Examples of consumer fairs are book fairs, antique fairs, auto shows, and video shows. For industrial marketing, trade shows are an economical means of contacting customers; in 1981, the cost of a personal contact at a trade show was estimated at about $57.[32]

2. *Firm–sales promotion activities to intermediaries* include trade deals, free goods, volume discounts, and trade shows. These techniques encourage intermediaries to stock a brand and promote it to other intermediaries.

Trade deals reduce prices to the intermediary for a limited time and are an incentive to carry the brand being promoted.

Free goods are an alternative to trade deals. A firm offers free goods for the purchase of a quantity of a brand, e.g., "Buy twelve cases, get one free."

Volume discounts encourage an intermediary to carry large stocks of a brand in anticipation of heavy demand spurred by the advertising campaign. The discount rate may increase as the volume ordered increases.

Trade shows are an economical means of contacting distributors and getting their support for a brand. Examples of trade shows are fashion shows.

3. *Intermediary–sales promotion activities to consumers* include specials, loss leaders, and trading stamps. These activities stimulate traffic in the premises of the distributor or retailer.

Specials are products a distributor sells at a discount for a limited time. The distributor temporarily lowers the profit margins on that item or passes on to the consumer the manufacturer's discounts. Specials are an effective tool for distributors to build traffic and increase store loyalty.

Loss leaders are items sold at or below cost and are used to attract attention to the store and/or its advertisements. The products are used regularly and are often perishable, e.g., milk, eggs, bread, or meats.

Trading stamps increase loyalty to the retail store by providing some merchandise according to the cumulative value of goods purchased. The consumer is given stamps in proportion to the amount purchased, and these may be exchanged for goods once a certain volume has been reached. This technique is not as popular now as it was twenty years ago. One version of the technique offers consumers a set of products in exchange for receipts totalling a given amount; for example, a set of glasses for receipts of $100 per glass.

4. *Assistance to the intermediary's promotion program* may be offered by a firm at all levels in the promotional program. The firm may

provide the distributor with point of purchase (POP) display materials, posters, flyers, in-store demonstrations, or other forms of in-store promotion. It may provide incentives to the distributor's sales force by giving them bonuses (often called push money or spiffs), gifts, or participation in a contest. The firm may also finance some of the distributor's costs of advertising to consumers. This is called a co-operative advertising allowance, and the distributor is often required to use in the advertisement illustrations provided by the firm.

5. *Stimulation of the firm or intermediary's sales force* ties sales objectives to a short-term incentive program that uses bonuses, gifts, and contests. These activities are non-recurring and separate from the normal remuneration the sales force receives. They are used to increase the momentum of the promotional plan and to ensure that the sales force pushes the brand when the advertising campaign is attempting to build strong demand.

Summary

Advertising plays a role both in the marketing mix in general and the promotion mix in particular. Marketing and advertising strategies are developed by taking into account various factors, in particular the market's environmental forces. The important concepts an advertiser uses to derive an advertising strategy from the overall marketing strategy are market segmentation, product positioning, and the product life cycle. Advertising is but one part of a marketing program and should be integrated with the other elements of the marketing mix into a consistent and logical program.

Advertising is integrated into the overall marketing plan by planning and co-ordinating advertising actions with the other elements of the promotional mix, especially the sales force communication program, publicity, and sales promotion activities.

Questions for Study

1. Marketing and advertising strategies should follow from an analysis of consumer needs and wants. Why then is it necessary to segment a market? How is the definition of a market segment likely to affect the definition of an advertising strategy?

2. How does a firm's decision to pursue a strategy of market aggregation, or concentrated marketing, or multi-segment marketing, or product variety, affect the corresponding advertising strategy? Give specific examples.

3. Select a company with which you are fairly familiar. Describe its marketing strategy as best you can, including all the elements of its marketing mix. What is its advertising strategy? Is it consistent with the other elements of the marketing mix? Why?

4. Describe and contrast the use of advertising during the four phases of a product's life-cycle for: (*a*) package goods, (*b*) hard goods, and (*c*) a service.

5. Discuss the concept of product positioning and its importance in the development of an advertising strategy.

6. Select three different products, one from a grocery store, one from a department store, and one from a specialty store. Describe the marketing strategy for each and recommend an advertising strategy.

7. Assume that you are a product manager reviewing the details of your advertising plan before starting an important campaign. How would you try to get the most out of your advertising effort even before the campaign reaches final consumers?

8. Discuss the promotional mix (advertising vs. personal selling) typically followed by firms

selling
• life insurance
• beauty care products
• household detergents
• electronic equipment
As much as possible, refer to actual examples.

Problems

1. A manufacturer of electronic watches has developed a new concept for a digital watch that can be manufactured at a relatively low cost and that has unusual lasting characteristics in comparison with most similar products on the market. The firm's marketing manager is considering two possible product positioning and marketing strategies for this new product:

1. Market the product to the price-conscious market segment.

2. Market the product to the high-income market segment, which wants expensive and lasting watches.

(*a*) As an advertiser, show how these two marketing strategies are likely to affect your advertising program.

(*b*) For both alternatives, outline an advertising strategy and the major elements of the campaign (the objectives, budget, message, media plan).

(*c*) In both cases, show how the decisions on the other elements of the marketing mix and of the promotional mix are likely to affect your advertising decisions.

2. A brand manager for a leading biscuit manufacturer is in charge of the launching of a new brand of biscuits on the Canadian market. The brand manager must make consumers aware of and try the brand. At the same time, trade acceptance and co-operation for launching and distributing the new brand must be ensured. Design the promotional mix for the launching of the new brand. Emphasize the co-ordination of the launch advertising campaigns, the sales promotion program, and the sales force communication effort.

Notes

1. For a thorough analysis of the segmentation concept, see Ronald E. Frank, William F. Massy, and Yoram Wind, *Market Segmentation* (Englewood Cliffs, N.J.: Prentice-Hall, 1971); see also Yoram Wind, "Issues and Advances in Segmentation Research," *Journal of Marketing Research*, 15 (August 1978), 317-37.

2. Wendell R. Smith, "Product Differentiation and Market Segmentation as Alternative Marketing Strategies,"*Journal of Marketing*, 21 (July 1956), 3-8.

3. Ronald E. Frank, "Market Segmentation Research: Findings and Implications," *Applications of the Sciences in Marketing Management,* ed. F. Bass et al. (New York: John Wiley and Sons, 1968).

4. Steven C. Brandt, "Dissecting the Segmentation Syndrome," *Journal of Marketing*, 30 (October 1966), 22-7.

5. Henry J. Claycamp and William F. Massy, "A Theory of Market Segmentation," *Journal of Marketing Research*, 5 (November 1968), 388-94.

6. Burleigh Gardner and Sidney Levy, "The Product and the Brand," *Harvard Business Review* (March-April 1955), p. 37.

7.William M. Reynolds, "More Sense about Market Segmentation," *Harvard Business Review* (September-October 1965), pp. 107-14.

8. See, for instance, Alan A. Roberts, "Applying the Strategy of Market Segmentation," *Business Horizons*, 4 (Fall 1961), 65-72; Ronald E. Frank, Paul E. Green, and Henry F. Sieber, "Household Correlates of Purchase Price for Grocery Products,"*Journal of Marketing Research*, 4 (February 1967); Ronald E. Frank, Susan P. Douglas, and Rollando P. Polli, "Household Correlates of Package Size Proneness for Grocery Products," *Journal*

of Marketing Research, 4 (November 1967), 381-84.

9. Johan Arndt, "Profiling Consumer Innovators," *Insights Into Consumer Behavior*, ed. Johan Arndt (Boston: Allyn and Bacon, 1968), pp. 71-83; see also Frank, (Boston: Allyn and Bacon, 1968), pp. 71-83; also see Frank "Market Segmentation," in Bass et al.

10. Ronald E. Frank, William F. Massy, and Harper W. Boyd, Jr., "Correlates of Grocery Products' Consumption Rate," *Journal of Marketing Research*, 4 (May 1967), 184-90.

11. Pierre Martineau, "Social Class and Spending Behavior,"*Journal of Marketing*, 23 (October 1953), 121-30; see also Richard P. Coleman, "The Significance of Social Stratification in Selling," *Marketing: A Mature Discipline,* ed. Martin L. Bell (Chicago: American Marketing Association, 1961), pp. 171-84.

12. See Frank, "Market Segmentation."

13. J.A. Lunn, "Psychological Classification Commentary," *Journal of the British Market Research Society* (July 1966), pp. 161-73.

14. William D. Wells, "Backward Segmentation," *Insights Into Consumer Behavior,* pp. 85-100.

15. Russell I. Haley, "Benefit Segmentation: A Decision-Oriented Research Tool," *Journal of Marketing,* 3 (July 1968), 30-35.

16. Daniel Yankelovich, "New Criteria for Market Segmentation," *Harvard Business Review* (March-April 1964), pp. 83-90.

17. Norman L. Barnett, "Beyond Market Segmentation," *Harvard Business Review,* (January-February 1969), pp. 152-66.

18. Jerome E. McCarthy and Stanley S. Shapiro, *Basic Marketing* (Georgetown, Ont.: Irwin-Dorsey, Ltd., 1975), pp. 75-80.

19. See, for example, Y. Allaire, "The Measurement of Heterogeneous Semantic, Perceptual and Preference Structures" (Ph.D. diss., M.I.T., August 1972); R.M. Johnson, "Market Segmentation: A Strategic Management Tool," *Journal of Marketing Research*, 9 (February 1971), 13-8; R.Y. Darmon, "Multiple Joint Space Analysis for Improved Advertising Strategy,"*The Canadian Marketer*, 10, no. 1 (1979), 10-4; J.E. Brisoux, "Le Phénomène des Ensembles Evoqués: Une Etude Empirique des Dimensions Contenu et Taille" (Ph.D. diss., Université Laval, 1979).

20. "Coke–Pepsi Slugfest," *Time*, 4 July 1976, pp. 51-52.

21. Thomas A. Staudt and Donald A. Taylor, *A Managerial Introduction to Marketing* (Englewood Cliffs, N.J.: Prentice-Hall, 1970), chapter 10.

22. *Management of New Products*, 4th ed. (New York: Booz, Allen & Hamilton, 1965), p. 4.

23. Theodore Levitt, "Exploit the Product Life-Cycle," *Harvard Business Review* (November-December 1965), pp. 81-94.

24. "Industrial Sales Call Tops $137, But New 'Cost to Close' Hits $589," *Marketing News*, 14, no. 22 (May 1981), 1.

25. Kenneth A. Longman, *Advertising* (New York: Harcourt Brace Jovanovich, 1971), p. 18.

26. Harold C. Cash and W.J.E. Crissy, "Comparison of Advertising and Selling," *The Salesman's Role in Marketing: The Psychology of Selling*, 12 (1965), 56-75.

27. Emmanuel J. Cheron and Jean Perrien, "An Experimental Study of the Effects of Commercial TV Advertising and Pro-Consumer Product Test-Results on TV," *Advances in Consumer Research*, vol. 8, ed. Kent B. Monroe (Association for Consumer Research, 1981), 423-27.

28. Carol A. Scott and Alice M. Tybout, "Theoretical Perspective on the Impact of Negative Information," *Advances in Consumer Research*, 8, ed. Kent B. Monroe (1981), pp. 408-9.

29. W. Mouland, "The Marketer's Viewpoint," A Special Research Report on Consumer Promotion (Don Mills, Ont.: Nielsen Clearing House Canada 1982), p. 6.

30. "Coupon Distribution Reaches Record High of 2.5 Billion," *Canadian Premiums & Incentives* (February 1982), p. 7; "It Was a Record Year for Couponing," *Marketing* (17 January 1983), p. 13.

31. Mouland, p. 9; see also W. Mouland, "Coupons Are The Most Important Consumer Promotion Method," *Canadian Premiums & Incentives* (August 1982), pp. 11-14.

32. "The Trade Shows Story: It's a Value-For-Money," *Marketing* (22 March 1982), pp. TS6-7.

CAMPAIGN HISTORIES FOR PART 1

1. Montreal Trust Corporate Campaign

2. Kraft Cheese Slices

CAMPAIGN HISTORY 1

MONTREAL TRUST CORPORATE CAMPAIGN
Advertising the Services of a Trust Company

ADVERTISER: Montreal Trust
AGENCY: J. Walter Thompson

Montreal Trust has a wide network of branches, but only one or two in each city. Therefore, when it comes to personal banking or trust business, it is usually more convenient to go to a closer bank or trust company.

In the absence of any great difference in products or services, it was decided to take a stance telling consumers that Montreal Trust could help them through the complex maze of trust company services. This would give people a reason to go out of their way, perhaps even across town, to their local Montreal Trust branch.

From this overall positioning came the "Money Talk" campaign—an ongoing series of small space black and white newspaper ads that answer people's questions. In addition to giving helpful information, this campaign succeeds because it makes Montreal Trust *look* helpful, even to the casual reader. Also, by using local newspapers, the ads can be localized to support individual branches.

Results have been highly satisfactory in terms of consumer communication and internal relations.

Money Talk

A series in which Montreal Trust answers your questions.

"Free chequing– is it really free?"

"You advertise a chequing account that offers free cheques and no service charges. Is this true, or are there any hidden costs?"

There are no hidden costs. A Montreal Trust Personal Chequing Account really does offer you free unlimited chequing and no service charges whatsoever.

This, of course, includes all the other benefits. For example, your cheques are personalized with your name and there's a wallet for your chequebook.

Each month, a statement is mailed to you outlining what you've spent, and to help you keep track, your used cheques are returned, too.

Overdraft protection avoids embarrassment.

"I was recently embarrassed when a cheque I wrote was returned because of a lack of funds in the chequing account at my bank. The annoying thing is that I had enough in my savings account at the same branch to cover the amount. Wouldn't you think they'd have had the courtesy to check?"

That kind of situation can be irritating, but it's one we at Montreal Trust help our clients avoid by offering an overdraft protection service.

If you open a Montreal Trust Personal Chequing Account together with one of our savings accounts (either our Plus Savings or 60-Plus), we will, if you ask us, automatically cover any overdraft with funds from your savings account.

Many of our clients find this a useful service, and it has saved many an awkward situation.

Talk to us about any of these services

Personal Chequing Accounts.
Plus Savings.
60-Plus Savings.
Guaranteed Investment Certificates (GIC).
Registered Retirement Savings Plans (RRSP).
Registered Home Ownership Savings Plans (RHOSP).
Mortgage Fund.
Investment Funds.
Wills and Estate Planning.
Executor Services.
Mortgages.
Real Estate.

If you have any questions about our services, write, call, or come in and see us at the address below.

Montreal Trust
Well worth talking to.

Money Talk

A series in which Montreal Trust answers your questions.

"RRSP's–what are the options?"

"I understand the basics of Registered Retirement Savings Plans (RRSP's), but I'm not sure about all the options you have available. Could you enlighten me, please?"

At Montreal Trust we have six RRSP options available. You can deposit all or a portion of your contribution to any option. Here is a brief description of each. Note that the first two sections (a and b) are **guaranteed,** but all others are liable to **fluctuate.**

a) Guaranteed Investment Certificate Section.

Here, contributions are applied to the purchase of a certificate whose principal and high interest rate is fixed and guaranteed for a 5 year period. Interest is compounded annually.

This section is for people who want a safe investment and who won't transfer or deregister this portion for 5 years. The plan cannot be redeemed prior to maturity.

b) Guaranteed Savings Section.

Contributions are placed in secured investments and income is compounded quarterly. The interest rate is established monthly.

This section is designed for individuals who are perhaps close to retirement, or who want a guarantee that their RRSP investment will not fluctuate.

c) Mortgage Section.

Contributions to this section are invested in quality first mortgages. Income is credited monthly.

It's designed to fulfill the need for a fund offering a dependable rate of return based on a diversified mortgage portfolio.

d) Income Section.

Contributions are invested in government bonds, corporate bonds and debentures, and other fixed income securities. There are no guarantees on the principal or interest. The holdings in this section are valued each month and fluctuate according to the economy and interest rates.

This section is for investors looking for long term yields with moderate fluctuations.

e) Equity Section.

Contributions are invested in quality common stocks. This section is designed for the investor who is looking for gains in the longer term and can accept the ups and downs of the stock market in the short term.

It provides for no guarantees on capital or interest.

f) Self-Directed Plan.

This is a plan set up to hold securities selected by you or your investment advisor. In this case, we act as trustee handling administrative and reporting procedures.

If you have any questions about our services, write, call, or come in and see us at the address below.

Montreal Trust
Well worth talking to.

EXHIBIT 1 Sample advertisements from the "Money Talk" campaign, in which long copy is used to discuss free chequing and RRSPs.

CAMPAIGN HISTORY 2

KRAFT CHEESE SLICES
Advertising a Consumer Food Product

ADVERTISER: Kraft
AGENCY: J. Walter Thompson

It was Kraft who first developed cheese slices, but in recent years store brands and generics have been challenging Kraft's traditional dominance by offering cheaper alternatives.

After trying and testing several more aggressive concepts, a campaign was developed that takes a warm, nostalgic stance, recalling the early days of J.L. Kraft, who started business in Canada around the turn of the century. The basic promise is that Kraft now uses only the best cheddar in making cheese slices, as ol' J.L. did.

The result has been to firmly position Kraft Slices as the premium quality brand, worthy of the few extra cents. The campaign is doing very well in the marketplace.

EXHIBIT 1 A still from the television commercial for Kraft cheese slices that uses the nostalgic approach. It recalls the early days of J.L. Kraft, around the turn of the century.

THE STRUCTURE
AND ROLE OF
ADVERTISING
ORGANIZATIONS
IN CANADA

The development of an advertising program requires the co-operation of many individuals and organizations. Chapter 3 explains and demystifies the agency business in Canada. The different types of Canadian advertisers and their approaches to the advertising function are described in Chapter 4. Chapter 5 analyzes the print media available to Canadian advertisers, while Chapter 6 covers broadcast media.

Advertisers, agencies, and the media rely on countless outside suppliers that perform highly specialized tasks at all phases in the planning, execution, and control of the advertising campaign. These suppliers include freelance artists, art studios, production companies, and market research firms. The role of these suppliers is mentioned throughout Part 2.

Advertising Agencies in Canada

Nearly everyone has heard or read something about advertising agencies, but what they actually do and how they operate is unclear to many business people, who often wonder whether or not to hire an agency or replace or fire their present agency. This chapter will discuss the advertising agency business in Canada, a business which has undergone many important changes in this century and will probably evolve even more quickly in the future.

Evolution of the Role of the Advertising Agency in Canada

The evolution of the modern advertising agency was the result of the merging of two functions: the older function of "placing" advertisements for the advertiser in various media, and that of assisting the advertiser in preparing the advertising copy.

Space Brokers for Newspapers

Until 1889, advertising agents working on a 15 per cent commission acted as intermediaries between advertisers and newspapers, selling space to advertisers for a commission. These agents helped advertisers deal with several newspapers while providing information on circulation and negotiating rates for the space.

In 1878 Ansom McKim, a space broker who represented a Toronto newspaper, *The Mail*, was sent to Montreal to open an office and solicit business. McKim soon found that Montreal businessmen wanted information

about and placement services for other Ontario newspapers. Since this information would help sell space in *The Mail*, the rates and circulation figures were collected in Toronto and sent to McKim's Montreal office. This office came to be called The Mail Advertising Agency.[1]

Since the agency was primarily doing business for *The Mail*, McKim realized that he could be more effective if he were independent of any newspaper and could eliminate any conflicts of interest with advertisers and other newspapers. In January 1889, he created the first Canadian advertising agency, A. McKim & Company, Newspaper Advertising Agency. The agency was established to obtain the most accurate information on newspaper circulation, to negotiate fair rates for advertisers, and to handle the negotiations between the two groups, including specifications for placing an advertisement, verifying the execution, and billing. This information was published in 1892 in the *Canadian Newspaper Directory*, which rapidly became the standard reference book on Canadian publications (Figure 3.1).[2]

Birth of the Modern Advertising Agency

Initially, most advertisers wrote their own advertisements. They would then provide the manuscript with or without illustrations to the newspaper to have it set in type. Gradually, a new kind of specialist emerged who helped advertisers write copy. These people were often called "ad-smiths", since many were freelance

THE CANADIAN NEWSPAPER DIRECTORY

CONTAINING:

A HISTORY OF THE RISE AND PROGRESS OF JOURNALISM IN EACH PROVINCE, WITH A FACSIMILE OF THE FIRST PAPER PRINTED IN CANADA; STATISTICS AND TABLES SHOWING THE INCREASE IN CANADIAN NEWSPAPERS SINCE THE PERIOD OF CONFEDERATION; TABLES OF THE IMPORTS AND EXPORTS OF MATERIALS IN THE PRINTING AND PUBLISHING TRADES; THE CUSTOMS TARIFF AFFECTING THESE TRADES; OFFICERS OF THE VARIOUS PRESS ASSOCIATIONS OF CANADA. ETC.

A GAZETTEER

OF ALL CANADIAN AND NEWFOUNDLAND NEWSPAPERS AND PERIODICALS, IN WHICH IS GIVEN THE NAME OF EACH PAPER, ITS EDITOR AND PUBLISHERS, DATE OF ESTABLISHMENT; POLITICS OR CLASS; FREQUENCY OF ISSUE; SUBSCRIPTION PRICE, NUMBER AND SIZE OF PAGES, AND ITS ESTIMATED CIRCULATION; TOGETHER WITH A STATEMENT OF THE CHIEF INDUSTRIES AND EXPORTS OF EACH NEWSPAPER TOWN, ITS LOCAL FEATURES, ITS BANKING, TELEGRAPH, TELEPHONE AND TRANSPORTATION FACILITIES, ITS POPULATION, IN WHAT COUNTY SITUATED, ETC, AND A PARTIAL LIST OF SURROUNDING TOWNS AND VILLAGES IN WHICH NO NEWSPAPER IS PUBLISHED.

CLASSIFIED LIST

INCLUDING A CONDENSED LIST OF ALL CANADIAN AND NEWFOUNDLAND NEWSPAPERS ALPHABETICALLY ARRANGED FOR READY REFERENCE; A LIST OF ALL THE NEWSPAPERS BY COUNTIES; OF PAPERS PUBLISHED IN LANGUAGES OTHER THAN ENGLISH; OF RELIGIOUS PAPERS AND OF PAPERS PUBLISHED IN THE SPECIAL INTERESTS OF VARIOUS ORGANIZATIONS, SCIENCES, TRADES AND INDUSTRIES WITH A SHORT DESCRIPTION OF EACH CANADIAN PROVINCE AND OF NEWFOUNDLAND.

PRICE - - - $2.00.

MONTREAL.
A. McKIM & CO., PUBLISHERS.
1892.

FIGURE 3.1 Title Page of the First McKim Canadian Newspaper Directory (1892)

SOURCE: H. E. Stephenson and C. McNaught, *The Story of Advertising in Canada* (Toronto: Ryerson Press, 1940), p. 31.

FIGURE 3.2 Advertisement for Peter Rutherford, one of the first freelance copy writers in Canada, offering to write "four advertisements for a dollar."

SOURCE: H. E. Stephenson and C. McNaught, *The Story of Advertising in Canada* (Toronto: Ryerson Press, (1940), p. 102.

writers offering their services to advertisers and to agencies. One of the first freelance copywriters was Peter Rutherford, who worked in Toronto and promoted his services in advertisements (Figure 3.2).[3]

It was not until about 1910 that the two types of services—advertisement placement and copywriting—merged to form the modern advertising agency, and by this date most Canadian advertising agencies had permanent copy staffs.

The work of the copywriter originally included producing simple line illustrations. The layout and design of an advertisement eventually involved more than simple illustration and was integrated more closely with the advertising message. The need for more sophisticated art work gave rise to a new kind of expertise, that of the creative department. The copywriter evolved from a person clever with words to a specialist who could communicate effectively with the market by using the market's language in talking about a product. This evolution marked the birth of the modern advertising agency, which grew by expanding its range of services and clients. After World War I, emphasis was put on research and merchandising, and most large agencies gradually became full-service agencies.

Nature and Role of a Full-Service Agency

The full-service advertising agency developed in response to advertisers' increasing needs, not only in terms of media placement and

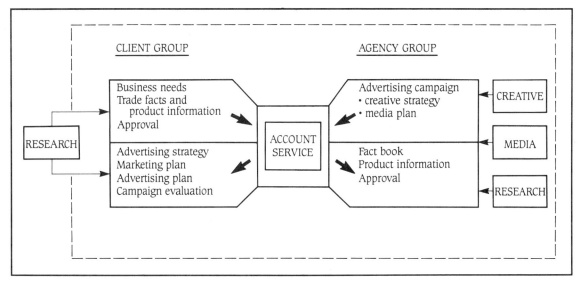

FIGURE 3.3   Role of the Account Service Group in Managing the Relationship between the Client Group and the Agency Staff Assigned to the Client

creative services but also in terms of marketing services. A full-service agency provides a complete range of marketing services, except for personal selling. Some agencies also organize sales conventions for the launching of a new product or service.

Types of Services

Full-service advertising agencies offer advertisers three broad types of services: account, creative, and media services. These services are covered by the commissions the agency receives.

Account Services

The account service group of the advertising agency is responsible for managing the relationship between the client group and the agency staff assigned to this client. In cooperation with the client, the account service group manages the whole advertising process, from marketing strategy to advertising execution (Figure 3.3).

The account service group works closely with the advertiser to ensure that the flow of information between them is as efficient as possible. It obtains from the client all relevant trade facts and product information as well as a thorough understanding of the client's business needs. In addition to day-to-day consultation with the client, the account service group must obtain the client's approval for the work done by various agency departments.

The account service group also provides the client with the marketing plan, the advertising plan, the creative strategy, and the campaign evaluation report.

Account service may also act as a marketing consultant to the client, particularly in the following areas:
• new product introduction (concept testing, branding);
• product strategies (packaging, repositioning);
• pricing (price deals, coupons);
• distribution (in-store displays, demonstrations).

In its relationship with various agency departments the account service group must ensure the client's needs and requirements are fully understood. It provides agency personnel with a compilation of the relevant information on the client's product, called the fact book, as well as any other additional information requested by agency personnel.

With the creative and media departments, the account service group co-ordinates media advertising, corporate graphics, point of sales material, packaging, and the planning and buying of media space or time.

Once the advertising campaign has been presented to and approved by the client, the account service group expedites the execution of the campaign and develops procedures to evaluate the campaign's effectiveness.

Creative Services

The creative services group provides the advertiser with the creative ideas and concepts for executing the campaign. This function is crucial, since agencies are often evaluated and compared on the basis of their creative talent. The reason is that this is the most visible part of the agency's work. The creative services group performs three main functions: copywriting, art direction, and print and broadcast production.

Copywriters transform the creative strategy into effective verbal or written communications that integrate illustrations, radio sound effects, and television. The copywriter works closely with the art director in developing the main idea for the campaign and then writes the headlines, subheads, and body copy for the print advertisement or the broadcast commercial.

Art directors translate the creative strategy into an effective visual communication that is integrated with the copy. They design the basic visual elements of the communication and work closely with copywriters, graphics specialists, art studios, and photographers in producing the final print advertisement or broadcast commercial. Detailed illustrations and most finished artwork is usually subcontracted to freelance artists or commercial art studios for final rendering.

Print and broadcast production managers prepare the print advertisements or broadcast commercials for production. In print production, the functions of typesetters, printers, and other graphic art suppliers must be co-ordinated

and completed in time for publication. In broadcast production, the script or storyboard is developed into a radio or television commercial. Typically, this involves actors, film directors, music directors, cameramen, and other specialists. A commercial may be shot several times until the creative or art director is satisfied that the commercial effectively executes the creative concept. It is the responsibility of the production manager to ensure that all technical aspects in producing the commercial are successfully completed well before air date.

In some large agencies, a *traffic manager* is responsible for verifying that the final print advertisement and broadcast commercial have reached the selected media.

Media services

The media services group provides the advertiser with a media plan based on the marketing strategy and the creative strategy (Figure 3.4). First is developed a media strategy, which includes the decisions on the media selected and the size, length, and timing of the media placements. Then, based on the media strategy, this group buys the selected time and space at the best possible price. Media research is often used to evaluate different media according to costs and suitability for the target market.

Media services are extremely important to the advertiser for several reasons:

1. Although it does not have the glamour of creative services, media services represent the traditional strength of an advertising agency.

2. It is essential that media planning be efficient, since a very large percentage of the advertising budget, usually more than 80 per cent, is spent on media placements. In 1981, more than $1 billion was spent for *national* advertising alone.[4]

3. Media planning is a complicated task because a large volume of data is available on the various media and it is difficult to evaluate the effectiveness of each

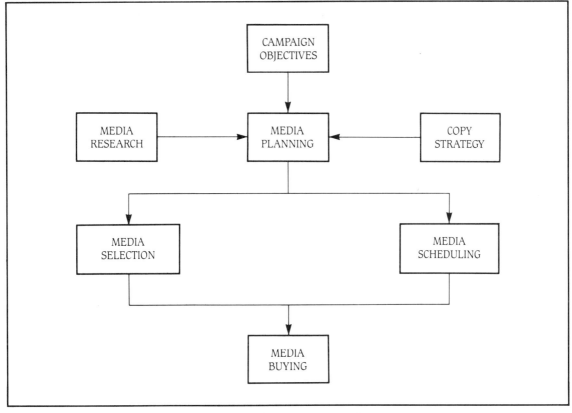

FIGURE 3.4   Media Services Offered by Advertising Agencies

medium in relation to the others. Thus media planning requires well-trained specialists as well as computing services to carry out the large amount of analytical work involved.

Complementary Services

As the need for more sophisticated marketing advice arose, some agencies set up specialized marketing services groups. Some of the most important are advertising and marketing research, sales promotion and merchandising, packaging and new product development, and publicity/public relations.

Advertising and marketing researchers provide the client and agency groups with planning information on all phases of a campaign: defining market segments, developing marketing plans, testing product concepts and creative executions, and measuring the effects of the campaign. Depending on the problem, they may use a variety of research instruments, from focus-group interviewing to large-scale mail surveys. They may draw heavily from outside research firms and organizations that supply such services as market research, copy testing, and media data as well as computer software for evaluating broadcast media plans. Examples of such outside sources are A.C. Nielsen, the Print Measurement Bureau, the Bureau of Broadcast Measurement, and private research firms. The role of these outside suppliers is to provide agencies with the most accurate information on the market and its reaction to messages and media selections. This will be explained further in Chapter 15.

Sales promotion or merchandising special-ists are most important to packaged goods accounts. They have specialized knowledge of the sales promotion industry and advise the other agency groups on developing marketing strategies and implementing such promotional activities as sampling, couponing, premiums, sweepstakes, and contests. Also, they provide counsel on co-operative advertising, point-of-purchase displays, and direct-mail advertising.

Packaging and new product development specialists help the client improve an existing package or design a new package for an existing product. Usually, they work in conjunction with the creative group. For new products, they may assist the client in many of the steps involved in new product development, from concept testing to the selection of a brand name, sales forecasting, pricing, and test marketing.

Publicity/public relations specialists respond to client needs and integrate public relations and advertising. To be effective, publicity about

company products must be consistent with claims made in advertising and vice versa.

Organization of a Full-Service Advertising Agency

Although the organization of a full-service advertising agency may vary, the basic structure is shaped by the functions described previously. Thus, most full-service agencies have an organizational chart that is a variation on Figure 3.5. Such titles as chairman, chief executive officer, and vice-president establish comparable levels with those of the client group and designate department head status.

An organizational chart is merely an administrative tool to establish an agency's broad functional areas and services. Often, in small and medium-sized agencies, the same person may perform several functions and work on several accounts. As an agency becomes larger, there is a greater degree of specialization, with

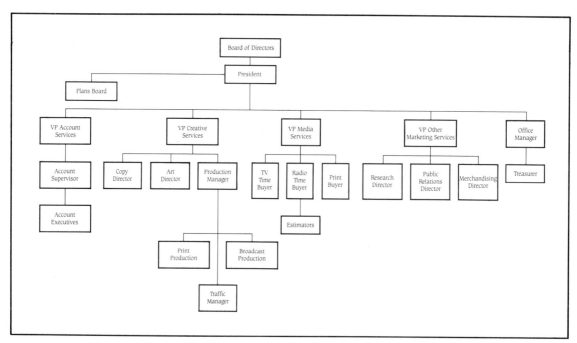

FIGURE 3.5   A Typical Advertising Agency Organization Chart Organized along the Major Advertising Functions

personnel assigned to one or two accounts. The various functional tasks may be organized by department or by group, depending on the size of the agency and the size of the account.

In a *departmental organization*, which is a functional type of structure, each account executive initiates work to be done with the various departments. Each department works on all accounts and is responsible for allocating the tasks among its specialists and for meeting the deadlines prescribed by the account executive. This type of organization is often found in small agencies or for small accounts in large agencies.

In a *group organization*, which is a modular type of structure, a complete team including service, creative, and media personnel is responsible for a specific account or a line of products. Each group is responsible for developing a complete campaign for the client, and its tasks may include formulating a marketing plan, an advertising strategy, creating and testing several advertisements, and executing and controlling the campaign as approved by the client. This type of structure is most often used for large clients, whose complex businesses are more effectively handled by the personal attention afforded by the group system. Group members are completely responsible for all advertising activity on the account.

To ensure that an agency's output is of sufficient and consistent quality, a *plans board* may be set up. This board, usually composed of senior executives representing the various agency disciplines, is responsible for approving the advertising strategy developed before it is shown to the client. The board acts as a quality control mechanism, and in this role it can help improve the quality of the agency's presentation to the client.

Finally, agencies have the personnel common to most businesses: an office manager, a treasurer, secretaries, and switchboard operators. In addition, because of the numerous laws and regulations in force in Canada and its provinces, a lawyer may be retained by the agency. Since the agency is legally responsible for the advertising it creates, it could be convicted, if found guilty, for false or misleading advertising.[5] Thus the role of the lawyer is to make sure that copy claims prepared by the agency are fully supported by facts.

Other Types of Agencies

Alternatives to the complete package offered by full-service advertising agencies arose from advertisers' desire to improve the value received for their commissions or fees. Advertisers' concern that full-service agencies did not give them the best possible counsel in all areas of advertising encouraged the creation of *à-la-carte agencies, creative boutiques, media buying services* and *in-house agencies.*

À-la-Carte Agencies

À-la-carte agencies provide the services of a full-service agency, but they allow the clients to choose, for a specified or negotiated fee, the services to be performed. This unbundling of services allows advertisers to organize an ad hoc group by selecting the best talents in various à-la-carte agencies.

Creative Boutiques

A creative boutique is a special type of à-la-carte agency that became popular in the late 1960s and 1970s. Intense competition in several markets led advertisers to depend on the creativity of their advertising to give them an advantage over competitors. Competition for the best creative talent led many art directors and copy writers to leave full-service agencies and set up their own creative shops, which became known as creative boutiques. The term "boutique" was initially used by full-service agency people as a derogatory term conveying the idea of narrowness, but its other connotation—that of personal attention and unique creative styles—led to its adoption to describe the new shops. The popularity of creative boutiques waned as advertisers realized they needed a whole range of services not provided by the boutiques. On the other hand, some boutiques added other types of services and became full-service agencies or à-la-carte agencies. In general, creative boutiques provide only creative services to advertisers, for a negotiated fee.

Media Buying Services

Media buying services sprang from the dramatic increase in media costs, particularly in spot television, and the willingness of certain media to negotiate prices on the basis of dollar volume. The independent media buying service looks for special buys priced at lower than regular advertising rates. In turn, they sell broadcast time or print space to clients and agencies at a rate lower than the one that could be obtained by the agency. The difference between these two rates represents the service's gross profit. They have forced advertising agencies to improve their media buying procedures, thus encouraging the industry to provide advertisers better value for their media dollars.

In-House Agencies

Some advertisers own and operate an advertising agency under their supervision. This in-house agency is entitled to all media commissions and usually works on the company's products or product lines. If solicited, they may handle outside accounts. They provide the same services performed by the traditional full-service advertising agency but at a total cost that is usually lower than the commissions from media buying. This is the economic rationale for establishing such an agency.[6] For campaigns with a straightforward creative approach or that are lifted from the U.S., this arrangement may work reasonably well, particularly with heavy television advertisers. Critics point out that by working on the same product line, the creative group of in-house

agencies becomes stale and cannot attract top talent. In addition, the advertiser loses the point of view and experience of outside agencies. Despite these drawbacks, this form of arrangement appears to be most popular with large U.S.-based consumer packaged-goods companies.

Structure of the Canadian Agency Business

Accurate statistics on the Canadian agency business are scarce, because in 1977 Statistics Canada discontinued its annual surveys of advertising agencies.[7] Nonetheless, the *patterns* apparent in the 1973-77 surveys are reasonably indicative of the industry in the 1980s.

Size Distribution of Canadian Advertising Agencies

The precise number of advertising agencies in Canada is difficult to determine since there is no complete list of Canadian agencies. In 1977, there were approximately 300 agencies in Canada; today the actual number is between 300 and 450. A partial list of agencies, their addresses, and the names of their personnel can be found in the monthly publication *Canadian Advertising Rates and Data* (CARD).

There is a wide disparity in size among Canadian agencies. Most of the largest ones belong to the Institute of Canadian Advertising, which has about seventy members accounting for about 85 per cent of national advertising. Thus, one finds the traditional 80-20 rule, i.e., 20 per cent of advertising agencies account for about 80 per cent of total billings.

Table 3.1 presents a list of the top twenty Canadian advertising agencies that was compiled on the basis of the amount of advertising business handled by each advertising agency, including all branch offices but excluding subsidiary companies or satellite agencies.[8] Based on this definition of total billings, the largest advertising agency in Canada is J. Walter Thompson, with billings of $127.5 million in 1982. A close contender for first place is McKim Advertising Limited.[9]

Based on the last survey done by Statistics Canada in 1977, one may draw a picture of the financial structure of the agency business. The average advertising billings per firm between 1973 and 1977 fluctuated around $3 million. The net profit before taxes amounted to about $46,000, which represents a little less than 9 per cent of gross revenues.[10] Total gross operating revenues as a percentage of total billings have declined to around 16 per cent, reflecting heavy competition among agencies. It is likely that this figure has declined since. More than half of gross revenues goes to salaries and wages. Research and other services have seen their share fluctuate around 3 per cent of total billings.[11]

A further analysis can be made by considering the size of the agency. Very small agencies (those billing less than $0.5 million in 1977) have about three employees. As an agency grows larger, the number of employees, average salaries, and net profit (before taxes) per employee tend to increase.

Distribution of Billings among Advertising Functions and Media Types

In order to understand the agency business, it is useful to know how the money received from clients is spent. As mentioned before, about three per cent of total billings is spent on market surveys, research, and other services. The remaining 97 per cent of total billings is divided into 81 per cent for media billings and 16 per cent for production charges. The actual breakdown of the advertising budget among media, production, and other services may deviate somewhat from the 81-16-3 per cent distribution according to the nature and size of the client or the size of the agency. In most

TABLE 3.1   The Top Twenty Canadian Advertising Agencies (in billings)

PARTICIPATING AGENCIES	$ Millions
1. J. Walter Thompson Co. Ltd.	$127.5
2. Baker Lovick Ltd.	$85.0
3. Hayhurst Advertising	$84.0
4. Ogilvy and Mather (Canada) Ltd.	$84.0
5. Vickers & Benson Companies	$76.0
6. Cockfield Brown Inc.	$70.0
7. Ronalds-Reynolds & Company Inc.	$68.0
8. McCann-Erickson Advertising of Canada	$60.0
9. Saffer Cravit & Freedman Advertising	$60.0
10. Leo Burnett Company Ltd.	$52.0
11. Cossette Communication-Marketing	$51.7
12. Young & Rubicam Ltd.	$42.06
13. Ted Bates Advertising Ltd.	$35.75
14. Grey Advertising Ltd.	$35.0
15. Publicité BCP Ltée.	$33.0
16. Foote Cone and Belding Advertising Ltd.	$31.18
17. R.T. Kelley Inc.	$28.0
Agencies not Participating in survey	
Foster Advertising Limited	
MacLaren Advertising Limited	
McKim Advertising Limited	

SOURCE: *Marketing* (13 December 1982), p. 21.

cases, however, this distribution is fairly accurate.

It is also useful to look at the relative importance of media billings and production charges according to media types (Table 3.2). The lowest percentage of production charges is for radio and the highest is for the other print

TABLE 3.2   Distribution of Advertising Billings between Media and Production Charges according to Various Media Types

Media Types	Per cent of advertising billings		Total (%)
	Media billings	Production charges	
Print	83.9	16.1	100
Television	86.7	13.3	100
Radio	91.6	8.4	100
Outdoor and transportation	87.5	12.5	100
Other print (direct mail, point of purchase, and others)	0.0	100.0	100
Total	*83.2*	*16.8*	*100*

SOURCE: Adapted from Statistics Canada, *Advertising Agencies, 1977,* Cat. 63-201, p. 6.

TABLE 3.3   Distribution of Advertising Billings according to Media Type and Agency Size

Advertising billings	Distribution of firms (%)	Distribution of advertising billings (%)	Distribution of advertising billings (%)					
			Print	Television	Radio	Outdoor and transportation	Other[1]	Total (%)
less than $0.5 M	41	3	61.2	11.0	15.5	3.2	9.1	100
$0.5 to $2.5 M	38	13	51.5	23.2	16.3	2.9	6.1	100
$2.5 to $ 5 M	10	10	46.1	28.0	17.8	3.3	4.8	100
$5 M to $10 M	3	7	40.6	33.8	14.2	5.6	5.8	100
More than $10 M	8	67	31.2	52.0	11.0	3.3	2.5	100
Total	*100*	*100*	*36.9*	*43.3*	*12.7*	*3.4*	*3.7*	*100*

[1]Direct mail, point of purchase, brochures, catalogues, contests, and others.
SOURCE: Adapted from Statistics Canada, *Advertising Agencies, 1977,* Cat. 63-201, p. 6.

media (direct mail and sales promotion). In relation to media billings, print has a higher percentage of production charges than television, although the absolute cost of a television commercial is much higher.

An analysis can also be made by comparing the size of the agency with the distribution of advertising billings among media types (Table 3.3).

Very small advertising agencies tend to allocate about 60 per cent of their billings to print, 11 per cent to television, and 9 per cent to other media. Large agencies represent about 8 per cent of all agencies, but they employ 58 per cent of all advertising personnel and account for almost two-thirds of all advertising billings. Large agencies allocated more than half of their billings to television, 31 per cent to print, and 11 per cent to radio.

Between these extremes are the medium-sized agencies, which tend to use all media. They allocate roughly 44 per cent to print, 30 per cent to television, and 16 per cent to radio.

TABLE 3.4   Agency Salaries in 1982

Agency Salaries

The following chart was compiled after talks with more than a dozen senior ad agency executives. The figures represent the lower and upper level annual salary ranges found in the creative, account management, and media departments of agencies with $25 million in billings and up. Also, the figures reflect total remuneration packages, but they do not include money earned from equity participation.

Creative	Account Management	Media
The creative director and vice-president $45,000 to $100,000+*	Director of client services and vice-president $35,000 to $85,000	Media director $30,000 to $100,000+**
Assistant creative director or senior writer/art director $35,000 to $80,000	Account group supervisor $30,000 to $60,000	Associate media director $25,000 to $55,000
Intermediate writer or art director $20,000 to $35,000	Senior account executive $25,000 to $55,000	Media supervisor $20,000 to $35,000
Junior writer or art director $12,500 to $20,000	Junior account executive $11,000 to $25,000	Media estimator, trainee $10,000 to $25,000

* There are probably between five and ten big-name creative directors earning more than $100,000.
** Traditionally the lowest salaries have been in the media department. But recently overall salaries have increased throughout agency media departments and several of the most prominent media directors are now in the $100,000+ category.

SOURCE: Mark Smyka, "JWT Takes the Lead in Training Recruits," *Marketing* (13 December 1982), p. 39.

These differences reflect a number of factors, including the size of their clients' advertising budgets, the availability of creative talent, and agencies' attempts to develop specific areas of expertise.

Salaries of Agency Personnel

Although salaries of agency personnel are a result of the supply and demand for qualified individuals, they tend to fall within ranges. The 1982 salary ranges are indicated in Table 3.4 for twelve agency positions. Although these figures were compiled for large agency personnel, they may also apply to other types of agencies. Entry-level positions in account services, creative, and media tend to receive similar salaries, somewhere between $10,000 and $25,000. Personnel in the creative group have, in the last twenty years, received some of the highest salaries, reflecting a strong demand for creative talent. Recently, competition be-

tween full-service agencies and media buying services has increased demand for experienced media personnel, and their salaries have increased faster than the other groups. Future changes in agency salaries will depend on the supply of and demand for qualified personnel.[12]

Geographic Distribution of Agencies

In terms of geographical location, most large agencies are in Toronto and Montreal, near the head offices of major corporations. Other major cities have local or regional agencies, as well as branches of major national agencies. Montreal has the additional characteristic that most agencies have personnel specializing in French creative and thus often handle the French component of a national advertising campaign that may have been developed in Toronto or Vancouver. As the need for original French creative arose,[13] several advertising agencies with strong creative talent in French grew in size and volume. This in turn forced some of them to open branches in Toronto in order to become truly *national* agencies.[14]

How Advertising Agencies Are Compensated

The method of compensation for most agencies is still based on the 15 per cent commission system of the nineteenth century newspaper space brokers. As agencies added services, the charges billed to the client were determined in a manner consistent with the standard 15 per cent commission. Other revenues come from fees for use of agency personnel. The three main sources of revenue for agencies are commissions, charges, and fees.

Commissions

A bona fide agency receives a commission from the medium in recognition of its traditional role as an agent. Advertisers are *not* entitled to a commission and thus do not bear any cost in media placement.

For example, suppose an agency places a contract with one television station for $100,000 (Figure 3.6). If the rate is $1,000 for each 30-second prime time slot, the client receives 100 prime time slots. The station allows the agency to *deduct* from the total buy a 15 per cent commission. This means the agency revenue would be $15,000 in order to cover salaries, overhead, and make a profit. If the bill is paid within ten days, the agency may also deduct 2 per cent of the net amount ($85,000) to be paid to the station. The agency may in turn pass this cash discount on to its client for prompt payment.

Technically, the commission of $15,000 is paid by the television station to the agency. In turn, the agency plans and executes the advertiser's campaign and assumes full responsibility for contractual dealings with the media. It is estimated that more than 80 per cent of all advertising agency revenues are derived from the 15 per cent commission from the media.

Charges

Additional costs the agency incurs in developing the advertising campaign are charged to the client. For example, the costs of using outside services to produce an advertisment are charged to the client, and this amount is usually marked up by 17.65 per cent. This percentage on costs leads to the same amount as the 15 per cent on the amount billed to the client. For example,

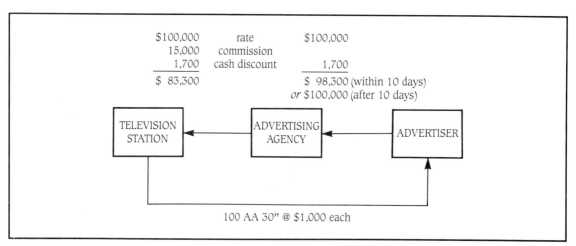

FIGURE 3.6 **The Commission System of Compensation**

suppose in producing a television commercial an agency uses an outside television studio, for the amount of $8,500. In billing the client, the agency would add $1,500, for a total of $10,000. The mark-up of $1,500 represents either 17.65 per cent of $8,500 or 15 per cent of $10,000. Thus the charge system is consistent with the commission system.

Fees

Fees are negotiated between the agency and the client whenever the commission or charge systems provide inadequate compensation, either because the agency feels it is receiving too little compensation, or the advertiser feels that the agency is not providing enough value for its commission.

Under the fee system, the advertiser and the agency negotiate a total fee for services rendered. Often, this is done on a project basis. The agency usually agrees to rebate all commissions to the client and to absorb all charges. The agreed-upon total fee may be higher or lower than the sum of the commissions and the charges, but the essential point is that both sides agree that the compensation is fair for the services rendered. In developing the agreed-upon fee, the agency often uses a multiple of the hourly rate of its personnel. This multiple may vary between 2.5 and 3, with 2.75 often selected. It is used to cover overhead costs and a reasonable profit in addition to the time agency personnel spend on the account. According to agency personnel, less than 10 per cent of advertising agency revenues are derived from fees.

Guaranteed Revenue System

A variant of the fee system, the guaranteed revenue system calls for the client to guarantee a minimum profit target for the agency. For example, the costs incurred by the agency in developing a campaign for a client may generate insufficient profit or a loss after all media commissions have been collected. Under this system, the client agrees to reimburse the agency the difference between the costs plus the profit target and the revenues. The advantage of this system is that the agency can make a satisfactory profit, while the client obtains the best service the agency can offer. The client has no guarantee, however, that the agency will be cost efficient.

Advantages and Disadvantages of the Commission and Fee Systems

There has been much debate over the advantages and disadvantages of both the commission system and the fee system.

The commission system has been criticized on the grounds that agencies are tempted to suggest excessive advertising budgets, relatively expensive media, or media that minimize the agency input and costs. In addition, the system leads to heavy competition for large accounts, often to the detriment of smaller or medium-sized accounts. Proponents of the commission system argue that it is very simple to administer and has been working reasonably well for more than a century. As we have seen, agency profit margins tend to be low, which indicates that agencies provide some value for their revenues.

The fee system has been criticized on the grounds that agencies may try to compete on the basis of price, rather than on quality of services. Also, the client may try to cut costs by eliminating such services as research; conversely, the agency may be tempted to add services in order to increase its fee. Proponents of the fee system claim that the bias toward commissionable media is removed and that the agency is more likely to provide non-commissionable services. Also, an agency receives a more stable income; it is not affected greatly by budget changes. The agency makes a fair profit on all accounts. An advertiser is more likely to receive good value for the agreed-upon services to be performed.

Although each system has advantages and disadvantages, the problem lies in the exchange relationship between the agency and the advertiser and the concept of "value" provided by the agency to the advertiser in exchange for a certain sum. Ultimately, the key to this relationship lies in the objectives the advertiser assigns to the advertising function and the cost of reaching these objectives. Thus, proper determination of the advertising objectives and budget is critical, and some form of *objective* or *incentive system* may be more appropriate. With an objective system both the advertiser and the agency agree on some precise objective and result for the advertising campaign (see Chapter 11). The incentive system bases compensation on the results achieved by the campaign.[15]

Agency Recognition

Because newspapers paid agencies a commission for their services, newspapers needed assurance that an agency was solvent. A credit system instituted and managed by the Canadian Daily Newspaper Publishers Association (CDNPA) was founded in 1925. Its roots can be traced to the Canadian Press Association founded in 1859 and incorporated under federal law in 1913.[16] The credit system of the CDNPA is revised periodically to allow for inflation and growth of the overall economy. In April 1982 the credit ratings of the CDNPA were:[17]

• *AA rating:* for agencies showing a current surplus of liquid assets over liabilities of at least $100,000. A portion of that excess may be a letter of credit from a Canadian chartered bank.

• *A rating:* for agencies showing a current surplus of liquid assets over liabilities of at least $50,000.

• *B rating:* for agencies showing a current surplus of liquid assets over liabilities on a two-to-one ratio of at least $15,000, or a letter of credit in the amount of $15,000.

• *C rating:* for agencies without one of the above ratings providing a cheque with the insertion order.

When an agency satisfies one of these requirements, it is said to be "enfranchised" or "recognized" and thus entitled to the 15 per cent commission. Recognition from the CDNPA only indicates an agency's credit worthiness; it does not confer any recognition or implication in terms of creative or marketing ability.

Four other associations grant recognition to agencies: the Periodical Press Association, the Canadian Community Newspapers Association, the Canadian Association of Broadcasters, and the Outdoor Advertising Association of Canada.

Growth in Agency Business

In the highly competitive advertising business, agencies must make sure that their revenues grow from year to year. Agencies may ensure continued growth in profits by keeping present clients satisfied, acquiring other agencies, and by obtaining new business.

Keeping Present Clients Satisfied

This is probably the most important objective, since it is harder to obtain new clients than to retain existing ones. The average client–agency relationship is probably between three and five years and in 1980 more than $100 million in billings changed agencies.[18] The main reasons for these changes are:

Lack of Proper Communication
Communication between the advertiser and the agency may be poor because of neglect, the advertiser's failure to understand clients' needs and expectations, or clients' unreasonable expectations. It is the responsibility of the account service personnel to ensure a complete understanding of client needs and to communicate to the client what the agency can and cannot do.

Lack of Chemistry or Trust

A client may feel uneasy about the agency, its personnel, and the advertising campaign's effects on the target market. The role of the agency's president is to make sure that clients are properly matched with agency personnel.

New Management

A change of management on the client side may lead to a change of agencies, since a new manager may want to renew previous ties with other agencies or may want to change the company's creative approach.

Changes in Market Performance

Positive or negative changes in clients' sales growth may cause an agency to lose an account, either because the company has grown larger and management feels that they need a bigger or different agency or the advertising agency may be the scapegoat for the company's financial setbacks.

Account Conflict

In principle, an agency cannot handle two competing accounts in the same market. But what about non-competing products from competing companies? Should the agency handle both accounts? To minimize potential problems, some agencies have set up or acquired separate advertising agencies to handle one of these two accounts and to ensure that both clients are satisfied.

Acquiring Other Agencies

By acquiring other agencies, an agency can obtain new accounts that may or may not conflict with its present accounts.[19] Acquisitions of or mergers with other agencies are quite frequent, and may be the result of account changes or losses of qualified personnel.

Obtaining Additional Business from Present Clients

This method stems from good performance on the client's business and soliciting business on

new product launching or proposing a change of positioning for an existing product. The idea is to be knowledgeable in the client's business and to assume marketing leadership and partnership with the client. New product ideas, market segments, uses of existing products, and channels of distribution may be proposed to the client by the account service or creative personnel. If adopted, these would lead to increased business for the agency.

Obtaining New Business

It is a challenge but essential for a growth-oriented agency to obtain new business. Most "good" accounts already have an agency and must be won over aggressively. Three methods are often used, singly or in combination:

Advertising the Agency

The reputation and name awareness of the agency is often important in deciding which agencies the client should contact. These agencies often advertise in order to keep their name in the public eye. The approach varies from listing services, describing their personnel, giving examples of successful campaigns, or mentioning important changes in personnel. Examples of agency advertisements are shown in Figure 3.7.

Calling on Selected Companies

This may be done by suggesting to the appropriate advertising manager that the agency make a presentation on the agency's strengths and demonstrate how these may benefit the company. If the manager is somewhat dissatisfied with the company's present agency, the presentation may lead to a switch of agencies.

Contacting Companies Openly Dissatisfied with Their Agencies

Contrary to the preceding method, this is a highly competitive game, since the information on these companies appears in such advertising trade magazines as *Marketing* or in such

"WE'RE DESPERATELY LOOKING FOR AN ART DIRECT(

Call for appointment.

The Nathan Fraser Agency

185 Bloor Street East, Suite 550,
Toronto, Ontario, Canada M4W 1C8 (416) 968-9472

CREATIVE DIRECTOR: Robert Monk
ART DIRECTOR: Liam McDonnell

The advertisement for the Nathan Fraser Agency uses a humorous approach, and in 1982 it won the Gold Award for the business press. The Cossette advertisement emphasizes the growth of this French agency in moving to Toronto.
Courtesy Cossette Communication/Marketing and The Nathan Fraser Agency

THIS IS THE HOUSE THAT COSSETTE IS BUILDING.

106 Avenue Road, Toronto

Cossette has been building for over 15 years. In Quebec City, and in Montreal. What has evolved, through careful planning and hard work, is an agency with fully integrated marketing, research, advertising, production, sales promotion and public relations departments, and an annual billing figure of over $40 million dollars. That places us, with considerable pride, among the top ten agencies in Canada.

That also places us, quite logically and with great pleasure, in Toronto. At 106 Avenue Road. In a charmingly renovated Victorian house, with an atmosphere that is highly conducive to bringing out the best in the best creative minds we can find in Toronto. Ambitious, professional, senior creative minds, interested in joining the already substantial Cossette family and our partnership with a loyal and widely varied clientele that spans both the private and public service sectors, as well as private manufacturers and food industries.
106 Avenue Road, Toronto.
This is, indeed, the house that Cossette is building.
Astute writers, art directors and account persons who would like to move in are invited to contact Mrs. Castonguay in the Montreal office at (514) 844-3011.

TORONTO, WE'RE PROUD TO BE HERE.

Cossette

Cossette Associates Communication · Marketing

FIGURE 3.7   Advertisements for Advertising Agencies

newsletters as *Adnews*, and many other agencies are probably soliciting the dissatisfied company. Often the company may ask four or five agencies to do a "speculative presentation," that is, a campaign proposal on their product. The company then reimburses the agency for the cost of preparing the proposal. Some agencies refuse to participate in speculative presentations, on the grounds that it is an excuse for a company to obtain free advice. Other agencies consider such presentations as part of the cost of doing business. For the client, this method is a means of selecting the best agency for its product when it is difficult to choose an agency on the basis of its past record or its "standard" promotional presentation.

Summary

Advertising agencies were born of newspaper publishers' need to sell space and collect bills. They evolved into independent businesses filling the needs of both media owners and advertisers for marketing and advertising counsel.

A full-service advertising agency offers clients three basic types of services; account management, creative services, and media planning. Complementary services include research, publicity, and sales promotion.

Advertisers who want to cut costs may use à-la-carte agencies, creative boutiques, or media buying services. Large advertisers may also set up in-house agencies.

The Canadian agency business is influenced strongly by the size of the agency. A few large agencies representing about 20 per cent of all agencies are responsible for about 80 per cent of the billings. They use television heavily and tend to attract the best talent. Small agencies use proportionally more print than large ones because their clients' budgets are smaller.

Advertising agencies derive their income from a combination of the 15 per cent media commission, charges, and fees. They may also negotiate a guaranteed profit target with clients. Although there is much criticism of the commission system, it is still the preferred method of compensation. In order to receive the 15 per cent commission from the media, an advertising agency must be recognized by the various media associations. This recognition merely indicates an agency's credit worthiness.

In order to survive, agencies must maintain or increase their billings. The first rule is to keep present clients satisfied. Growth in billings may come from acquiring or merging with another agency, obtaining additional business from existing clients, or attracting new clients.

With an understanding of the nature, role, structure, and functioning of advertising agencies in Canada, their contribution to the growth of an industry, firm, or organization can be evaluated.

Questions for Study

1. Explain under what conditions creative boutiques can be viable in the long run.

2. Explain under what conditions media buying services can be viable in the long run.

3. Discuss the advantages and disadvantages of using a full-service agency versus à-la-carte agencies, creative boutiques, and media buying services.

4. Under what conditions does it make sense for an advertiser to set up an in-house agency?

5. Read the last five issues of *Marketing*. Make a list of account changes and give the reasons why.

6. Discuss the pros and cons of speculative presentations. Under what conditions should an advertising agency agree to do such a presentation? When does it make sense for an advertiser to request four or five agencies to develop speculative presentations?

7. Should an advertising agency handle competing accounts? Explain your answer.

8. Why is the 15 per cent commission system still the preferred method of compensation? Does it favour the large advertiser to the detriment of the small one?

9. Do you think that conflict may arise between agency personnel in two different functional groups?

10. It has been said that an agency's inventory or assets go down the elevator every night at five o'clock. What does this mean, and what are the implications for an agency's top management ?

Problems

1. Assume that you are the owner of OEM Ltd., a small advertising agency billing about $1 million a year with about ten clients of similar sizes. You have one creative and one media person, and one secretary.

   (a) Analyze your overall situation and identify the main problem(s) that you will be facing in the next five years. Be sure to define clearly your business objective (mission).

   (b) Evaluate the different options that are open to you.

   (c) Develop a plan of action for OEM Ltd.

2. Select an advertising agency in your town and develop a complete picture of that agency in terms of its services, types of clients, organization, and method of compensation. If possible, interview key people in the agency, e.g., one or two account executives, the media director, and the creative director.

   If an agency is not available, write to one agency in a large metropolitan area and ask for their promotional package. Work from there.

Notes

1. H.E. Stephenson and C. McNaught, *The Story of Advertising in Canada* (Toronto: The Ryerson Press, 1940), pp. 20-24.
2. Ibid., pp. 28-32.
3. Ibid., pp. 99-109.
4. "The Feds Outspend Everyone," *Marketing* (19 April 1982), p. 1.
5. "The Canadian Media Directors' Council Media Digest, 1982/83," *Marketing*, pp. 20-21.
6. Robert G. Wyckham and Frank Anfield, "In-House Advertising Agencies—A Trend?" *The Canadian Marketer* (Fall 1974), pp. 25-27.
7. Statistics Canada, *Advertising Agencies, 1977*, Cat. 62-201, p. 6.
8. "Canada's Top 50 Advertising Agencies," *Marketing* (13 December 1982), p. 21.
9. Ibid., p. 37.
10. Statistics Canada, *Advertising Agencies, 1977*, p. 4. Advertising billings are defined as the sum of media billings and production charges.
11. Ibid.
12. Mark Smyka, "JWT Takes the Lead in Training Recruits," *Marketing* (13 December 1982), p. 39.
13. M. Saint-Jacques and Bruce Mallen, "The French Market under the Microscope," *Marketing* (11 May 1981), p. 14.
14. Rob Wilson, "The Anglo Connection: Taking a Nibble from the 'Big Apple'," *Marketing* (13 December 1982), pp. 42-44.
15. Roger G. Calantone and Donald H. Drury, "Advertising Agency Compensation: A Model for Incentive and Control," *Management Science* (July 1979), pp. 632-42.
16. Stephenson and McNaught, p. 264.
17. "CDNPA Adds 'AA' Agency Rating," *Marketing* (31 May 1982), p. 2.
18. Mark Smyka, "More Than $100 Million in Billings Moved in 1980," *Marketing* (5 January 1981), p. 1.
19. Gail Chiasson, "Marriage Quebec Style: For Some Agencies, Two Can Live Better as One," *Marketing* (13 December 1982), pp. 45-47, 52-53.

Canadian
Advertisers

The first large-scale advertisers in Canada were patent medicine men, who used direct mail to advertise their products. The patent medicine almanac contained jokes, stories, and general interest articles, and may be considered the forerunner of today's magazines.

These modest beginnings contrast sharply with the $4 billion that was spent on advertising in Canada in 1982. The variety of media available to advertisers includes 118 daily newspapers, 395 magazines, 588 radio stations, and 96 commercial television stations.[1]

The amount spent on advertising varies according to the nature of the industry and the organizations within one industry or one sector of economic activity.

Who Are the Main Canadian Advertisers?

Advertisers are classified according to the type of product, the type of marketing organization, and the size and nature of the firm.

Type of Product

The nature of the advertising effort varies according to the type of product being advertised. The most important distinctions in product classifications are between industrial and consumer products and between durable and non-durable goods.

Industrial vs. Consumer Advertising

Industrial advertising is directed toward a professional who is responsible for evaluating competitive products for use by an industrial firm. The copy in such advertisements is usually lengthy, and the approach tends to be rational and informative. The aim of industrial advertising is to create awareness of a company's name, to improve its image, and to open the door to sales representatives. Figure 4.1 shows an example of industrial advertising.

First, industrial advertising helps a firm increase the awareness of its name among potential customers. Since the selection process for an industrial product may be involved, industrial advertising increases the chances for the firm to be considered as a supplier. Second, industrial advertising is often used to supply specific information about an advertiser's products or services to some of the key individuals involved in a firm's purchasing decision. The copy usually conveys technical information about the product. Thus, such advertising prepares a potential customer for a visit from the advertiser's sales representative. This is important, considering that in 1982, the average cost of *one* industrial sales call was estimated at $134.[2] Third, industrial advertising is used to create a highly favourable image of a firm among its present customers, which reinforces their loyalty to the firm's products. Finally, since the advertising complements the sales effort, the advertising budget is a relatively small portion of the total promotional budget.

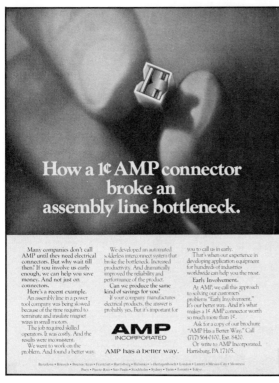

In this advertisement the judicious use of a headline and an illustration related to a common industrial problem leads into the long copy explaining the advertiser's "early involvement" approach.

Courtesy AMP of Canada Ltd.

FIGURE 4.1   An Example of Industrial Advertising

Industrial customers are often concentrated and highly specialized. Thus, industrial advertisers may use print media such as trade publications or direct mail. Nevertheless, the media decision may be complicated by the customer's purchase decision process, as well as by the number of people involved in the customer's organization.

In contrast, *consumer advertising* is directed toward groups of individuals during their leisure time. Thus it must be more intrusive, entertaining, and rather short. The role of consumer advertising is to create awareness of a brand name, increase consumers' interest, and create desire for the product. Most large advertisers are in this category since advertising is their main promotional tool. Unlike industrial advertising, consumer advertising has to fully convince its audience that the firm's products or services are the best available, since retail salespersons may not provide sales support for a particular item or since there may be no salesperson, as in self-service operations. However, consumer advertising may also be used by an advertiser's sales force to persuade the distributors to carry the firm's products.

Durable Goods vs.
Non-Durable Goods vs. Services
Another important distinction in product classifications is made among durable (or hard) goods, non-durable (packaged and soft) goods, and services. Table 4.1 lists the top 50 brands in 1981.[3]

Durable or *hard goods* are products that are rather expensive and require a long search process by the consumer. Examples are automobiles, appliances, stereo systems, and sophisticated cameras. Since consumers rely rather heavily on advertisements when considering whether to purchase durable goods, ads must be attractive, informative, and properly targeted. Figure 4.2 is a good example of this type of advertising.

The advertising campaign must also be coordinated with the personal selling effort, since the retail salesperson plays an important role in the customer's decision process. For example, in 1981, five of the 50 national advertisers were automobile manufacturers, who spent more than $44 million on national advertising alone (Table 4.2). More than $28 million was spent advertising eighteen makes of automobile. One objective of these campaigns was to draw traffic into the showrooms and induce customers to trade up. To accomplish this objective, the package offered by the advertiser had to be attractive to the target market and the salespeople sensitive to consumers' needs.[4]

Non-durable goods are of two types, packaged goods and soft goods. *Packaged goods* are

TABLE 4.1 The Fifty Top Brands, 1981 (in thousands $)

Brand	Total Media	TV
1. Coke	4800	2984
2. Loto Quebec	4310	2502
3. Eveready	3869	3821
4. Provincial Lottery	3832	2120
5. Super Loto	3428	2197
6. Western Canada Lottery	2885	1254
7. Colgate Toothpaste	2854	2854
8. Pepsi	2635	2316
9. Anacin	2351	2317
10. K-Tel	2339	2339
11. Crest	2307	1941
12. Head & Shoulders	2248	1524
13. Cavalier	2236	1111
14. Wintario	2181	114
15. 7-Up	2173	2057
16. Polaroid Camera	2158	1894
17. Esprit	2114	1922
18. Cash for Life	2094	1164
19. Michelin Tires	2084	2079
20. Fleischman's Sunflower Oil Margarine	2071	1619
21. Corolla	2068	1165
22. Sanka	2064	1624
23. Midas	2003	1696
24. Rothman's Light	1989	–
25. Tide	1976	1515
26. Pampers	1953	1733
27. Dristan	1942	1942
28. Kraft Cheese	1938	1375
29. J 2000	1930	1421
30. Corn Flakes	1927	1861
31. Seiko Watches	1880	1774
32. Timex Watches	1862	1555
33. Speedy Muffler	1838	1557
34. Craven A	1825	–
35. Philips Shavers	1795	1456
36. Maxwell House	1756	1382
37. Atari Games	1744	1657
38. Planters	1737	1038
39. Smirnoff	1715	–
40. Robin Hood Flour	1667	1431
41. Ford Trucks	1659	924
42. Mazola	1651	1651
43. Heinz Ketchup	1640	1640
44. Kraft Cheese Slices	1637	1270
45. Minute Maid	1628	1625
46. Hostess Potato Chips	1620	113
47. Dumaurier	1605	–
48. Vantage Lights	1590	–
49. Catelli Pasta	1588	1055
50. Trident Gum	1571	1184

SOURCE: Adapted from "Coke Tops List of Brand Advertisers," *Marketing* (5 July 1982), p. 19.
Courtesy Media Measurement Services Inc.

This advertisement for the new Kodak Carousel projectors makes good use of different types of lettering and composition to communicate how the new models can solve real consumer problems with other types of slide projectors.

Courtesy Eastman Kodak Company

FIGURE 4.2 An Example of Hard Good Advertising

convenience items, frequently purchased, low-priced, and distributed widely. Packaged goods advertisers tend to be among the largest users of advertising, as evidenced by their presence among the top 50 national advertisers (Table 4.2). Since for packaged goods, a brand is promoted to the consumer solely through advertising, packaging, and sales promotion, advertising is critical to a brand's success. Figure 4.3 gives an example of packaged goods advertising.

Soft goods are shopping good items, moderately priced, and distributed selectively. Thus,

TABLE 4.2   Top Fifty National Advertisers, 1981

Advertiser	Expenditures[1] ($000s)	by sales	net income[2] ($000s)	A/S Ratio (%)
1. Government of Canada	53,724	–	–	–
2. Procter & Gamble	27,336	98	728,575	3.8
3. John Labatt	24,557	57	1,296,934	1.9
4. General Foods	24,444	115	601,683	4.1
5. Rothmans of Canada	20,954	117	589,589	3.6
6. Ontario Government	18,615	–	–	–
7. Dart and Kraft	18,580	106	660,519	2.8
8. General Motors of Canada	15,479	2	10,416,050	0.1
9. Standard Brands	15,181	135	511,603	3.0
10. The Molson Companies	14,975	52	1,409,743	1.1
11. American Home Products	13,466	N.A.	N.A.	N.A.
12. Kellogg Salada	12,614	267	204,142	6.2
13. Unilever	12,492	N.A.	N.A.	N.A.
14. Imasco	12,189	82	965,464	1.3
15. Quebec Government	12,048	–	–	–
16. CP Enterprises	11,889	(S)	8,558,759	0.1
17. Ford Motor of Canada	10,973	6	7,206,600	0.2
18. Warner-Lambert Canada	10,837	N.A.	N.A.	N.A.
19. Bristol-Myers Canada	10,418	237	239,273	4.4
20. Canada Packers	8,877	22	2,943,099	0.3
21. Dairy Bureau of Canada	8,806	–	–	–
22. Hudsons Bay	8,593	12	4,172,442	0.2
23. Coca-Cola	8,189	187	348,856	2.3
24. Union Carbide Canada	7,965	91	827,306	1.0
25. The Seagram Co.	7,925	39	2,127,279	0.4
26. Nestle Canada	7,836	N.A.	N.A.	N.A.
27. Colgate-Palmolive Canada	7,824	N.A.	N.A.	N.A.
28. McDonalds Restaurants Canada	7,611	114	603,000	1.3
29. Dominion Stores	7,535	29	2,594,337	0.3
30. Imperial Oil	7,518	3	8,185,000	0.1
31. Chrysler Canada	7,499	31	2,480,600	0.3
32. S.C. Johnson and Son	7,489	N.A.	N.A.	N.A.
33. Nabisco	7,486	N.A.	N.A.	N.A.
34. Gillette Canada	7,161	N.A.	N.A.	N.A.
35. Ralston Purina Canada	6,733	224	259,116	2.6
36. General Mills Canada	6,712	287	1,982,579	3.5
37. RJR	6,544	N.A.	N.A.	N.A.
38. Hiram Walker Resources	6,535	21	2,945,344	0.2
39. Bank of Montreal	6,459	(B3)	358,533	1.8
40. Royal Bank of Canada	6,446	(B1)	492,520	1.3
41. Cadbury, Shweppes, Powell	6,304	347	133,466	4.7
42. George Weston	6,123	4	7,428,609	0.1
43. Johnson & Johnson	6,035	388	107,166	5.6
44. Toyota Canada	5,371	120	576,600	0.9
45. Canadian Imperial Bank of Commerce	5,317	(B2)	310,185	1.7
46. Gulf Canada	5,149	9	4,583,000	0.1
47. Simpsons-Sears	4,864	18	3,129,625	0.2
48. Canadian Honda Motor	4,848	N.A.	N.A.	N.A.
49. Benson & Hedges Canada	4,839	379	113,387	4.3
50. Gilbey Canada	4,733	N.A.	N.A.	N.A.

[1] These expenditures are for space and time only in the following media: daily newspapers, consumer magazines (does not include "special interest"), farm papers, radio, television. Radio and TV do not include direct buys.
[2] Sales or revenue figures include services or rental revenues, but exclude investment income. Net income (for banks) is after-tax profit, before extraordinary items.
SOURCES: "The Feds Outspend Everyone," *Marketing* (19 April 1982), p. 22; "The Financial Post 500", *The Financial Post* (June 1982), p. 65. *Courtesy* Media Measurement Services Inc.

FIGURE 4.3   An Example of Packaged Goods Advertising

In this advertisement no copy is used. The message is communicated by a handsome picture of the package and the product.
Courtesy Chanel

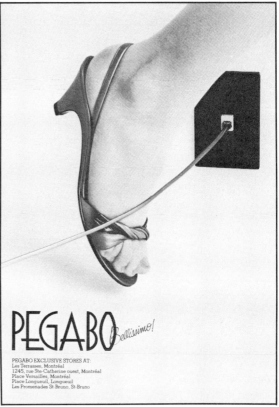

FIGURE 4.4   An Example of Soft Goods Advertising

This example of soft good advertising uses a clever device to call readers' attention to the product and the signature.
Courtesy Pegabo Shoes Inc.

the retailer is important to the success of a brand, since consumers often need help when purchasing the product. Examples of soft goods are clothing, carpeting and linens; such retailers as Hudson's Bay, Simpsons, and Sears are among the 1981 top 50 national advertisers.[5] In addition to using co-operative advertising, manufacturers advertise directly to consumers to reinforce an image of quality, as with designer clothes. Figure 4.4 illustrates soft goods advertising.

Services are more difficult to advertise than products, since they are intangibles.[6] However, there is much opportunity for creativity in promotional activities, for example, painting airplanes, decorating banks or hotel lobbies. Hotels often provide "extras", such as free drinks or a complimentary towel. Figure 4.5 is an example of service advertising.

Services are also well represented in the 1981 top 50 national advertisers, particularly governments and banks. Since they have adopted the marketing concept, banks have been advertising heavily to inform their target market about their new or improved services.[7] Advertising is also used to promote hotels, car rental companies, and airlines.

Types of Marketing Organization

Advertisers may be either *producers* of products or services or they may be *intermediaries*

Iberia Reservations. Electronics is just part of the game, not the game.

MORE THAN 50 YEARS MAKING FRIENDS.

FIGURE 4.5   An Example of Service Advertising

This advertisement for Iberia uses several devices to reinforce an image of quality. The "I" shape of the layout, the use of white space, the integration of headline and illustration, and the composition of the signature make the advertisement visually interesting.
Courtesy Iberia Airlines of Spain

between producers and customers. The nature and extent of the advertising depends in large part on the location of the target market.

Producers

Most major manufacturers of goods and services advertise on a national or regional basis, using mass media to reach a large number of people with one campaign. Some campaigns may have very large budgets, and thus it may be critical for an advertiser to use an advertising agency with a proven track record.

Intermediaries

Intermediaries and, in particular, retailers tend to advertise on a local basis and to run a series of small campaigns. A retailer's objectives are to offer selected merchandise for sale based on the target market's needs. Over the long run, the retailer's advertising should be designed to strengthen the retailer's image as a reliable buying agent for the consumer. Since retailers are not entitled to commissions from the media and have very tight schedules, the planning of the campaign tends to be done by the firm's advertising department with the assistance of manufacturers, other retailers, and the media.

Manufacturers provide retailers with matrices and co-operative advertising funds. *Matrices* are papier maché moulds of the manufacturer's product or package designs, and they are used by newspapers in making stereotypes to be included in the retailer's advertisement. In *co-operative advertising*, the manufacturer provides the retailer with an advertising allowance that usually covers half of the costs of advertising the brand in the retailer's advertising program. Since local advertising is cheaper than national advertising, both parties benefit from this type of arrangement.

Retailers in the same product category, such as hardware stores or realtors, may join forces in some form of co-operative advertising. This allows a bigger budget, the use of professional services, access to mass media, and extension of the retailer's audiences.

Most media have in-house personnel whose role is to assist retailers in developing their creative approach and their media schedules. These *copy service* departments may also call on outside freelance artists, stock shops that sell photographs to be used in the layout of the retailer's advertisement, or *advertising service companies* that sell prepackaged advertisements, called "idea service". The media provide these services free of charge to the retailer to make it easier for small retailers to advertise in their media.

In planning their advertising activities, some retailers may use the services of an advertising agency. The main role of the agency is to develop an *image campaign* for the retailer. In turn, the retailer would use the agency's work to design in-house campaigns based on *event advertising*, which involves special sales and promotions that may be timed to coincide with holidays and seasons.

In addition, retail advertising is affected strongly by seasonal factors or broad market trends and is designed to respond quickly to change. The retailer is mostly interested in building traffic and, thus, in maximizing the number of people reached by the advertisement. Consequently, repetition is not important. The advertisement has a short-term effect (in terms of the "event" advertised), and in-store promotions should be co-ordinated with the advertising campaign to maximize its effect.

The Size and Nature of the Advertiser

The size of a company's sales as well as the industry in which it operates may influence the amount of advertising it does. A distinction can be made between large and small businesses in order to explain the influence of company size on the advertising effort.[8]

Large Advertisers
Large advertisers are generally national advertisers. National advertisers use mass media to advertise their products or services throughout Canada. Overall, national advertising spending reached the $1 billion mark for the first time in 1981, which is almost double the total for 1977. Table 4.2 shows that the largest national advertiser in 1981 was the Government of Canada, and its expenditures were up 28 per cent from 1980. The largest private advertiser was Procter & Gamble, which increased its spending by 33 per cent over 1980. Among other large advertisers are the following categories:
- breweries and distillers: Labatt, Molson, Seagram
- cigarette manufacturers: Rothmans, Benson & Hedges
- car manufacturers: GM, Ford, Chrysler, Toyota
- banks: Bank of Montreal, Royal Bank

- retailers: Hudson's Bay, McDonalds, Dominion Stores
- packaged-goods manufacturers: Procter & Gamble, General Foods, Colgate-Palmolive, Coca-Cola
- oil companies: Imperial Oil, Gulf Oil
- conglomerates: Unilever, Imasco, CP Enterprises

In addition, there are wide variations in advertising efforts compared to a company's sales. The advertising to sales ratio (A/S) in Table 4.2 has been calculated by using the 1981 advertiser's sales or net income. A comparison of these ratios across the categories of advertisers (Table 4.2) indicates that the nature of the industry influences advertising efforts. For example, car manufacturers, large department stores, and oil companies spend a fraction of one per cent on advertising, while cigarette manufacturers and packaged-good companies spend a much higher proportion of their sales, from three per cent for Standard Brands to 6.2 per cent for Kellogg Salada. In the latter group, advertising is more important for promoting products or services than for the first group, where personal selling has a dominant role or where distribution is more important than promotion.

Small Advertisers
Although large advertisers may use a variety of mass media to reach a national audience with a high level of repetition, small advertisers may use only one medium and concentrate on exposure rather than on repetition. Small advertisers fall into several categories or industries. Retailers and industrial firms have been discussed; this section concentrates on other types of small advertisers.

Because their budgets are more limited, small advertisers must be resourceful. They must look for low-cost, not heavily used media or for low-cost special space units or time periods. Since they are not able to use large advertisements or long commercials, the creative approach must attract attention, especially if position in the medium cannot be controlled. In addition, small advertisers often cannot afford to advertise nationally, so they must carefully select the regions in which to concentrate their advertising effort. In this case, advertising may be a part of a phased penetration on a region-by-region basis.

Many small advertisers cannot afford to hire an advertising agency, because agencies are often reluctant to take these advertisers' accounts on a commission basis and they request additional fees or a guaranteed revenue to cover costs. Their limited budgets also prevent small advertisers from receiving from agency personnel the attention given to large advertisers. Sometimes an advertising agency will take on a promising client in the hope that today's small account may be tomorrow's large account. Otherwise, it is better for small advertisers to have a consistent planning approach with well-defined basic marketing objectives and strategies, and then to use the services of outside suppliers. Small advertisers who cannot afford an advertising manager may use the services of an outside consultant who acts as a part-time advertising manager.[9]

Factors Influencing the Organization of the Advertising Function

Since advertising must be co-ordinated with other marketing functions and because it receives public attention, it is conducted through a variety of organizational structures at three levels: the position of the advertising function in the overall organization, the responsibilities of the advertising manager, and the structure of the advertising department. The actual structures may depend on many other factors, such as size of the company, the nature of the industry, and top management philosophy. The principle behind these structures is described below.

Position of the Advertising Function in a Firm's Overall Structure

As mentioned previously, it is desirable to have the advertising manager report directly to the marketing manager, since the latter is responsible for the marketing plan and is trained to evaluate the quality of the advertising effort. This reporting arrangement is particularly important in the case of packaged goods manufacturers, for whom the advertising effort is the most important promotional ingredient.

Product or Brand Manager
In many large packaged goods companies with numerous brands, the advertising function is the responsibility of *product* or *brand managers*. A product or brand manager is responsible for planning, executing, and controlling the advertising campaign for one or several brands and for co-ordinating the advertising effort with the outside agency and the firm's in-house marketing specialists.

Advertising Department
In some companies, a separate advertising department is added to the brand management structure in order to assist and advise the product managers. The advertising department also may co-ordinate the brand managers' and their agencies' media buying in order to obtain the greatest media discount. This function may be the responsibility of one selected advertising agency, called the *agency of record*.

Under the Sales Manager
Some companies place the advertising function under the responsibility of the sales or marketing services manager, because the main promotional tool is personal selling and advertising is used to complement this effort by creating awareness of the company name, generating inquiries, or opening doors for the sales force.

Under the President or CEO
Corporate advertising may be used to enhance a

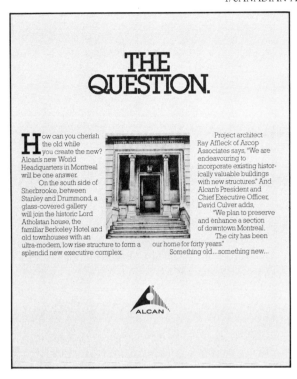

THE QUESTION.

How can you cherish the old while you create the new? Alcan's new World Headquarters in Montreal will be one answer.
On the south side of Sherbrooke, between Stanley and Drummond, a glass-covered gallery will join the historic Lord Atholstan house, the familiar Berkeley Hotel and old townhouses with an ultra-modern, low rise structure to form a splendid new executive complex.

our home for forty years"
Something old...something new...

Project architect Ray Affleck of Arcop Associates says, "We are endeavouring to incorporate existing historically valuable buildings with new structures" And Alcan's President and Chief Executive Officer, David Culver adds,
"We plan to preserve and enhance a section of downtown Montreal.
The city has been

ALCAN

FIGURE 4.6   An Example of Corporate Advertising

In this black and white advertisement for Alcan, the company explains to the public that its new world headquarters were designed to preserve and enhance the appearance of a section of downtown Montreal.
Courtesy Alcan Aluminum Limited

company's image among selected target groups, e.g., businesspersons, politicians, employees, investors, or the public. With corporate advertising, the advertising manager reports directly to the company's president or chief executive officer. An example of corporate advertising is presented in Figure 4.6.

Level of Centralization

With a centralized advertising function, scale economies may be realized, particularly in media buying. The centralized department usually reports to the president and may be staffed with specialists in research, public relations, and merchandising. It can often control the total advertising effort better. Centralizing

the co-ordination of advertising campaigns for dissimilar products may, however, create major planning problems.

With a decentralized advertising function, each operating division has its own advertising department. Advantages of this structure are that the department can focus on its specific needs and is better able to make its objectives consistent with other marketing decisions for a product. Disadvantages are the loss of scale economies in media buying and a possible lack of support from specialists.

To obtain the advantages of both types of structure, some companies adopt a mixed structure. A large firm with decentralized advertising departments may also set up a centralized advertising department in order to take advantage of scale economies in media buying and to co-ordinate advertising planning and execution.

Responsibilities of the Advertising Manager

The advertising manager's major responsibilities are analyzing, planning, executing, and controlling the advertising campaign. These functions involve co-ordination with the advertising agency, marketing specialists, and top management.

Analysis

The advertising manager must have all pertinent information on the product and the trade. The manager must also communicate to the advertising agency the company's business needs and corporate objectives.

Planning

Together with the agency's account service group, the advertising manager develops the advertising plan, which is based on the marketing plan's objectives and strategy. This process includes preliminary approval of the creative and media recommendations and the advertising budget, before these matters are presented to top management for final approval.

Execution

The advertising manager monitors the execution of the approved advertising plan and co-ordinates the execution with the department's other functions and with the activities of the firm's marketing specialists.

Control

The advertising manager also evaluates the campaign's effectiveness in terms of its stated objectives. In doing so, the manager constantly evaluates the agency's performance and reports the findings to top management. If the agency's performance is considered unsatisfactory, it is the manager's responsibility to take appropriate action with the account service group. Firing the agency should be a decision made when everything else has failed, since the search and breaking-in period for a new agency can take up to twelve months, during which time the company can lose momentum and continuity in its advertising.

Structure of the Advertising Department

Companies with a large marketing department may have one of the following five basic structures for the advertising department:

1. *According to advertising functions.* With this type of structure, individual employees are responsible for the various advertising functions. This structure is justified if the advertising department actually handles some of these functions or has to co-ordinate them among several agencies. An in-house advertising agency is a department with this type of structure.

2. *According to media types.* A firm may have different specialists whose job is to co-ordinate the various media budgets in order to take advantage of volume discounts.

3. *According to product lines or brands.* Each product or brand manager is in effect an advertising manager. Co-ordination may be carried out by an advertising director with or without additional staff members.

4. *According to customer types.* The advertising effort may be given to different specialists. For example, one manager may be responsible for industrial advertising, while another may handle consumer advertising.

5. *According to geographical or international markets.* The advertising effort may be decentralized, with responsibilities divided among divisional advertising managers. This structure is particularly important for international markets, where cultural and market-related factors usually require a different form of advertising. In some cases, control and/or co-ordination may be carried out by a centralized advertising department servicing all divisional departments.

Selecting an Advertising Agency

A thorough analysis of advertising's role within a firm's marketing effort can help the marketing manager decide whether an advertising agency is necessary, and if one is, what kind of services are needed and what kind of agency best suits the firm's needs.

Is an Advertising Agency Necessary?

The *advantages* of using an advertising agency are:

- Standard services are generally provided to the advertiser without charge, since agencies are compensated by the commission they receive from the media.

- Agencies often have some of the best resources and professionals, and they spread their costs over several accounts.

- Agencies can provide marketing assistance to small or medium-sized firms, which often do not have a marketing department. They also provide advertisers with an objective point of view and experience in specific industries.

- Agencies have considerable experience in all phases of campaign planning.

Thus, whether an advertiser is small or large, the services of an advertising agency are recommended unless the advertiser is able to handle all phases of campaign planning at a lower cost. For the advertiser who does not qualify for retail rates *and* who has a medium-size advertising budget, it is often more expensive to handle the advertising internally than through an advertising agency.

The *disadvantages* of using an advertising agency are:
• Local advertising is non-commissionable, thus agency services tend to be expensive for small- or medium-sized local businesses.
• Agencies are generally not organized to provide services on very short notice. For example, retail campaigns are often planned to respond to competitive moves or to take advantage of special environmental conditions, so it may be more efficient to handle the advertising internally.
• The main strength of advertising agencies is in advertising requiring broadcast media or special colour printing. Many small or medium-size advertisers make heavy use of newspaper advertising, which is relatively simple to undertake in-house.

Thus, the services of an advertising agency are generally not recommended when timing is important, the advertiser qualifies for retail rates, and the types of services needed can be easily obtained from outside suppliers or from the media. For some retailers or advertisers with small budgets, it may be more economical to handle the advertising function internally than through an advertising agency.

Choosing the Advertising Services Needed

The advertising manager should state clearly and in writing the kind of services the firm needs most and should evaluate how the agency can meet the firm's needs.

Agency Business Philosophy
The advertising manager must ensure that the agency's business philosophy and attitudes toward advertising and marketing are compatible with those of the firm. This factor is important because it permeates all exchanges between the two groups and affects the quality of their relationship.

The advertising manager must also make decisions in the following areas:

Account Services
How much marketing input is needed? What type of marketing counsel is required?

Creative Services
What are the creative styles of the agency's personnel? What is their past experience with similar products? What is their success record? Can it be documented?

Media Service
What is the ability, background, and level of experience of the media personnel? Do they have any clout with the media?

Other Marketing Services
Does the agency provide merchandising, sales promotion, research, and publicity/public relations services?

Other Selection Criteria

Additional criteria used to select an advertising agency are:

Size of the agency in relation to the size of the account: This criterion relates to the attention the agency can be expected to give to the account. A medium-size advertiser may get more attention from a small agency than from a large one, where it is competing with other large accounts.

Method of compensation: The advertiser evaluates the compensation system required by the agency in relation to the services to be provided.

Location of the agency: This is an important criterion for firms operating in several markets and particularly in international markets, where they may choose among agencies with foreign branches. Within Canada, most large agencies have offices in Toronto and Montreal as well as in other major metropolitan areas.

In conclusion, selecting an advertising agency is an important task for the advertising manager and a critical decision for the firm. Some firms and organizations consider the selection of an advertising agency so important that they use the services of a consultant, who acts as an intermediary between the two groups.[10]

Advertisers may find it helpful to consult an Institute of Canadian Advertising publication entitled *How to Select an Advertising Agency*, which provides a set of guidelines and recommendations as well as a sample questionnaire (Figure 4.7).

Advertising Needs and Problems in Other Areas

Although most principles developed in this book are general in nature, different areas have specific problems and require more specialized advertising objectives and strategies. Three such areas are institutional, non-profit, and multicultural advertising.

Institutional Advertising

Institutional advertising is undertaken by either a profit or a non-profit organization. Its purpose is to change an organization's image. There are three main types of institutional advertising:

The Organization as a Good Corporate Citizen
This kind of advertising aims to enhance an organization's reputation or image and is handled in various ways. For example, the campaign may convey the impression that the organization is concerned about the well-being of consumers or the public (see Figure 4.6). Another example of this type of advertising is sponsorship of a cultural event or a sports event.

The Organization as a Good Employer
This kind of advertising tries to create positive feelings among employees about the organization in order to improve loyalty, morale, or productivity over the long term. The organization's employees may be called upon to execute the campaign.

Advocacy Advertising
Through this type of advertising an organization advocates a particular position or course of action on a controversial issue, such as the effects of acid rain or the construction of nuclear power plants. Since the organization would benefit from the advocated course of action, the problem here is to make the advertiser seem credible. The organization can better assert its credibility to the target audience by designing its communication in accordance with the basic principles of persuasion.[11]

Non-Profit Advertising

Through non-profit advertising an organization seeks to encourage behaviour that benefits society in general or a particular community. The organization may be a government, a non-profit organization such as the Red Cross, or a political candidate.

With this kind of advertising it is difficult to design effective messages, since the "product"[12] may be an *organization*, such as a university that advertises courses and programs to increase or maintain enrolment.[13] The product may also be a *place*, such as a city that advertises its attractions to increase tourism. Or it may be a *person*, such as an incumbent running for re-election or a political candidate conducting

HOW TO SELECT AN ADVERTISING AGENCY

Introduction.

Selecting a new advertising agency is a major decision for any company. The choice of the right agency can have a significant effect on the company's long term sales and profit performance. The new agency will not only be responsible for making significant purchases on behalf of the company but also, and more importantly, for the care and maintenance of the company's most important asset: — its reputation with the consumer.

Selecting a new agency is also a bewildering decision. Very few marketing executives, even senior ones, have had much experience in selecting agencies. Despite the industry's reputation, account shifts are not common. Probably fewer than 10% of all Canadian accounts shift in a year. Thus many advertisers simply do not know how to go about an agency search, because it has been so many years since their company has done one.

There is no universally accepted approach to the best way to select an agency. How do I even know if I need a new agency? How do I screen the vast array of alternatives? What is the value of a screening questionnaire? What are the best questions to ask? How many agencies should I look at? How do I evaluate them? And many more.

Since the Institute of Canadian Advertising is the national association of advertising agencies, we thought it appropriate to produce a guide to help answer these questions. A committee of senior agency people, all of whom have been involved in new business efforts, went through a great deal of material that has been published on the subject. They sifted out what they thought was most relevant, added some of their own ideas, and this outline is the result.

We hope that this booklet will take some of the mystery out of selecting an agency. How to do it effectively and efficiently. And most importantly, to conduct your search in a professional way that will bring credit to you and your company from all the agencies you contact during the search process, even the ones that are unsuccessful candidates.

Defining your needs.

Selection of an advertising agency is perhaps best approached in the same manner in which a new staff member is employed. Indeed, when an advertising agency is hired, the advertiser has in reality employed a group of individuals to work with him.

Just as a precise job description is a sound basis for a successful employee acquisition, the same ground work is essential to the advertising agency selection process.

A specific definition of needs (i.e. job description) is essential to enable the advertisers to more easily sort through the wide variety of services offered by agencies. It helps each of the agencies under consideration to respond more precisely to the advertiser's requirements.

Most advertising agencies have a variety of talent available. The more clearly an agency can understand the advertiser's expectations, the better able it is to select the most appropriate people from its staff to work with him.

The consulting firm of Booz, Allen & Hamilton, in its report entitled "Management and Advertising Problems"

classified advertisers into five broad categories which illustrate the range of services that might be required from an advertising agency.

1. Companies where advertising is of limited importance. These companies are reasonably self-sufficient in other key marketing areas, such as marketing research, new product planning and sales promotion. Examples might be industrial companies or insurance companies. Because of the specialized technical nature of these companies, agencies can make only a limited contribution. All that companies in this first category want from their agencies, therefore, is *advertising help* — copy and media.

2. Companies where advertising is of limited importance, but which are not self-sufficient in some other key marketing areas. Examples might be an industrial company that needs agency help in developing trade exhibits and promotional material, or some consumer packaged goods companies that have decided to do part of their marketing work internally. Companies in this second category, therefore, want *advertising help plus certain selected services* (such as market research and sales promotion).

3. Companies where advertising is important and which have fully developed capabilities in all key marketing areas. Examples might be a large manufacturer of consumer durable goods or a large industrial company that wants to advertise past its customers to the ultimate consumer. Companies in this third category want not only advertising help, but objective and sound *marketing counsel* of the broadest sort.

4. Companies where advertising is of critical importance and which have fully developed capabilities in key marketing areas. Large, multi-agency consumer packaged goods companies frequently fall into this category. These companies want agencies that can offer in-depth, specialized talents and can share responsibility with the company for total marketing results — a *full marketing partnership*, in other words.

5. Companies where advertising is critically important, but which do not have fully developed capabilities in other key marketing areas. Many smaller consumer goods fall into this category. Companies in this fifth category look to their agencies for *marketing leadership*.

This review clearly indicates that the kinds of service needed by an advertiser can vary widely. It also explains why an advertiser must define these needs very clearly before the agency selection process is begun.

A comprehensive written check list of requirements which takes into account both present and possible future needs is essential to the selection process. It will help the advertiser sort through any broad claims by advertising agencies that they "do everything". Just as important, it helps prevent vulnerability to an emotional appeal on a personality basis. Having matched services from competing agencies against the list of requirements in an unemotional way, the advertiser can then weigh in the "chemistry" aspect, i.e. "would I enjoy working with these people?"

FIGURE 4.7
Courtesy The Institute of Canadian Advertising

Here's a list of needs you might consider:

Development of
— Marketing Plans
— Product Strategies
— New Products
— Advertising Strategies

Marketing Counsel on
— Product Mix
— Pricing
— Sales Targets

Creative Work on
— Media Advertising
— Brochures, Catalogues
— Point of Sale
— Packaging

Distribution Analysis
Marketing Research
Media
— Planning
— Buying
Public Relations

If you already have an agency.

If you already have an agency, before you search for another you should be very sure that a change is what you really want. You have invested a great deal of time and money in your agency, and in turn, they have learned a great deal about your business, about your people, and about the way you like to work. Before dissolving the relationship then, you should sit down with your agency to see if they can modify their operation to suit you. Perhaps a change of personnel on your account is indicated, or there may be other steps that will result in the very improvement you hope to find in a new agency (but always risk failing to find). Thus the list of needs you have prepared to help define your agency search should be analyzed in order to set down where your current agency is not performing. Then discuss the list with your agency. Ask your agency if it is a fair list. Does it match their understanding? Why have the shortfalls occurred?

You are urged to proceed very carefully through these steps. Changing an agency is a difficult, time consuming and expensive process. The expense is not just involved in the time demands and costs your management team will incur, but in the disruption of your advertising and other parts of your marketing mix, both during the search period and while your new agency is "getting up to speed" in your business.

If you have satisfied yourself that you have been fair with your agency, given them ample time to correct their shortcomings, and that there is no way to make a new beginning with your current relationship, then you should proceed with a search for a new agency. Only you and your executives can determine whether your present agency will stay on the "short list". If you feel that they have already been given every chance, perhaps it would be fairest to be frank, and have a mutually-agreed termination.

If you are choosing an agency for the first time.

If this is your first agency search, you should still go through the analysis of services you are searching for. This will help define the kind of agency you need, how involved in your business it will be, and therefore, in the end, how much you should be prepared to pay for its services.

Involvement of key executives in the entire process.

Your firm must be prepared to devote a substantial amount of time of key executives to the entire process. The selection of an advertising agency should be like selecting a new partner in your business. In order to make the partnership

a real success, each executive must feel comfortable with the selection, not only in order to have confidence in the advice the agency will give, but also to feel comfortable in sharing the confidential information the agency must have to do its complete job.

Getting a "feel" of the market.

Ultimately, you will probably want to send a questionnaire to a list of 10 to 15 agencies that seem to fit roughly into the requirements you have determined. This will help you prepare your "short list" of 3 to 5 from whom you will elicit presentations.

If you have no "feel" for the market, you should go through several steps to develop ideas to help you develop this first list. Here are some suggestions:

Ask ICA for a list of its members, who together account for about 85% of the advertising agency business done in Canada. Membership in ICA is a sign that an agency has joined with its colleagues in supporting the building of a more professional, and more effective industry. ICA will also be able to supply some details of size and type of operation for those of its members who submit such data to it.

Examine the agency listings in Canadian Advertising Rates and Data, a Maclean-Hunter publication most likely in your library. It lists most of the senior personnel of each agency. Since agencies usually employ between 3 and 5 persons per million dollars of billing, this is a good way to get an idea of relative sizes.

Read the National List, an annual publication of Maclean-Hunter that sets forth the accounts that each agency has. Here you will be able to exclude agencies on the basis that they already have accounts that conflict with yours.

Talk to people in other companies to get their help in preparing a list. You will most often find that people whom you scarcely know are very glad to be of help.

Visit a few agencies of different sizes. You will be welcomed and this may help you more than any other way of getting a feel of the market.

The questionnaire.

A recommended questionnaire is provided at the end of this booklet. It elicits all of the information you should need in order to narrow the replies down to a short list. Agencies don't mind answering questions that require factual answers. Some advertisers seem to like to add questions that require philosophical dissertations. Try to avoid this, because most replies will be so general (because the respondent won't know what you are looking for, and tries to give a bland answer to avoid being washed out at this point) they will not be helpful to you. The time to search for answers to your deeper questions is during the presentation stage.

Set a reasonable time, at least 3 to 4 weeks for receipt of replies.

If you stick to the questions recommended in the questionnaire, agencies can respond quickly and factually and allow you to get on with the really important part of the work, listening to the presentations of the agencies who have made it to the short list.

Your agency briefing document.

Your questionnaire will be most helpful to you if you send out a detailed briefing document with it. It will help the respondent agencies better determine whether they can serve you, and also give them common information on which to base their replies.

FIGURE 4.7 (continued)

Your briefing document should describe your company, product lines and involvement with other agencies, as well as provide as much history on the product or service category in question as you can release. It is at this point that your own work, or evaluating what type of agency services you require, will be most valuable.

Evaluating the replies.

Some of your questionnaires will come back with more material than you asked for. You may even find content that leads you to expand your "needs" list.

Remember that some agencies may have more insight into your product or service because of past associations, but that does not mean that they can serve you better. You should therefore, consider amending your briefing document in order to give all the "first wave" agencies a chance to reply before proceeding with the next step.

When all the replies are in, you are ready to proceed to the next step — preparing your short list. Review the replies against the "needs" that you set forth for yourself at the beginning of the process, and aim to get down to a list of not more than 3 or 4 agencies.

We recommend that you judge any contacts you get from agencies who were not on your list against these same criteria. As word gets out that you're looking, you will be contacted, and these contacts can lead to an enormous time investment on your part if they are not carefully controlled.

Some thoughts on agency presentations.

Your final agency selection will likely be based on presentations made by each of the contenders on your short list.

This means that you will be depending on about a two hour presentation from each agency to guide you to the right choice. It is, therefore, extremely important that the presentations be meaningful to your business, and that they permit an honest comparison among the agencies.

To achieve these objectives, we recommend that you supply an identical presentation outline to each of the prospects. The outline should include the criteria that you feel are essential. For example, if research is an important subject to you, then you want to be sure that each agency fully discusses their research capabilities.

The standard outline is not intended to restrict individual presentations. Beyond the areas you want covered, there should be ample scope for the agency to discuss its particular strengths, and other factors they feel will be of interest to you.

There are normally 3 types or levels of agency new business presentations:

1. Capabilities — limited to the agency's experience, service facilities, and people.

2. Strategic — thoughts on your company's marketing situation and strategy alternatives.

3. Creative Project — development of actual advertising creative, in response to objectives supplied by you; may also include media planning recommendations.

Usually, Levels 1 and 2 will provide sufficient information on which to base an agency selection decision. Level 3 requires extensive briefing of the agencies, and considerable time and effort. You should also be prepared to pay a reasonable amount of money for this degree of presentation. Keep in mind that a reliable assessment of an agency's strategic thinking and creative ability can be made on the strength of the work they have done for other clients.

Perhaps the single most important aspect of the presentation is your opportunity to meet the people who will work on your account. You should insist on having in the presentation the key account service, creative and media people who will form your team. They should each take an active part, so that you can judge their ability and compatibility to your business and people. Remember that personal chemistry is a very valid criterion for selection.

Finally, ask to have the presentations at the agencies' offices. This will ensure that you are not interrupted and it will give you a good opportunity to size up each agency in its own environment. In fact, you may want to visit the office, and/or have lunch with some of the people in each agency before making up your mind.

It is also at this point that you "get into people's heads" before making up your mind. As well you can resolve any unclear issues such as staffing, compensation, new personnel and so on.

Making the decision.

Make the decision and let everyone know right away. This is a business decision and prolonged speculation will only affect the attitude with which the new agency enters the partnership.

Welcome your new agency as a partner in your business. Agency people respond to contact. A note of optimism and high expectations can prove to be excellent motivation.

An agency agreement.

ICA recommends that you make a formal agreement with your new agency. It is at this point that many future misunderstandings can be avoided if each party sets down those business details that either have been or should be decided. Matters such as method of compensation, how commissions and trade discounts are to be handled, details of billing and payment should be covered. If compensation is by a commission arrangement, a detailed list of services to be expected as part of the arrangement should be outlined.

Details of how new product assignments or other projects which may come up from time to time can simply be covered under a "fee to be negotiated" category.

Remember that the best time to work out all of the details of the business arrangement is at the beginning of the relationship. ICA can supply an agreement format, if you're interested.

Letting the trade press know.

The trade press loves to know when an advertiser is beginning to look around. Often an advertiser, wanting not to disrupt the relationship with his current agency, will try to quietly look around to see if a new relationship should be investigated. In spite of the best efforts to keep the secret, the trade press often finds out, and the current agency finds out it's in trouble by reading the story.

The result of these leaks most often is an agreement to part when usually the advertiser had not formed that intention.

The best solution, then, if you've decided that you are unhappy enough to begin to look around, is to level with your agency. Discuss the reasons for your dissatisfaction as set forth in the section "If you already have an agency". It is at this time that you may decide that there is no point in continuing your relationship. If so, give the agency a chance to resign gracefully. Whether you decide to part company or keep your current agency in the running, work out a mutually satisfactory statement for the press.

After you've completed your search, there are again some ideas you should follow if you are to be seen as a thoughtful and gentlemanly advertiser.
• Obviously you'll want to build up the winner with praise and good wishes for the future. You can do much at this point to creating the healthy harmony and respect that is the basis for good work from any agency.
• Don't name the losers, for it cannot possibly help them to do so. Remember that they've put in a lot of work to try to get your account, so reward them all by making some graceful general statements about the quality of the competition.

• A thoughtful letter to each of the losing agencies can both thank them for their efforts, and may give them some help in assessing why they lost.
At both the beginning of the search and at its end, you will find many opportunities to do some excellent public relations for both yourself and your company by careful planning and management of the publicity which will surround your search, whether you want it or not.

Agency selection questionnaire.

SECTION I—BASIC FACTS

1. AGENCY NAME

2. ADDRESSES

TOTAL NUMBER OF EMPLOYEES

Head Office:

Branches:

3a. OWNERSHIP

□ Public Company □ Limited Partnership □ Private Company □ Chartered Federally □ Provincially

3b. NAMES AND TITLES OF PRINCIPAL SHAREHOLDERS/PARTNERS

4a. PRINCIPAL CLIENT LIST	YEAR ACQUIRED	SENIOR CLIENT PERSON DEALT WITH	MAY WE CONTACT? YES NO
1.			□ □
2.			□ □
3.			□ □
4.			□ □
5.			□ □
6.			□ □
7.			□ □
8.			□ □
9.			□ □
10.			□ □

FIGURE 4.7 (continued)

88

Reviewing operations with your new agency.

You should document your decision and the criteria you used to make it, both for the successful agency and those who were not successful.

You should review the expectations you had with the management of your new agency within 3 to 6 months and periodically after that. This will help you to keep the relationship at its most productive level.

You will have invested a lot of time in choosing an agency, and a lot more time and money in bringing them to the full understanding of your business and how you operate it. By working on the relationship to keep it happy and productive no one will want to conduct another search for a long time.

Period of notice with your old agency.

Any agency will arrange to hand over all production elements and documentation. Make sure this happens as quickly as possible.

4b. SPECIFIC NUMBER OF CLIENTS IN EACH SIZE CATEGORY

UNDER $100,000 _____ $100,000 to $500,000 _____ $500,000 to $1 Million _____

$1 Million to $3 Million _____ Over $3 Million _____

5a. LIST CLIENTS GAINED OVER PAST 24 MONTHS

_____

_____

_____

_____

_____

_____

_____

5b. LIST CLIENTS LOST OVER PAST 24 MONTHS	YEAR ACCOUNT ACQUIRED	REASON FOR LOSS (Attach longer explanation if desired)

6a. APPROXIMATE AGENCY BILLINGS

This year (estimated) $_____ Last year $_____ Year before $_____

6b. WHAT PERCENTAGE OF YOUR BILLINGS ARE:		6c. HOW DO YOUR BILLINGS BREAK DOWN BY THE VARIOUS MEDIA?	
Consumer packaged goods	____ %	Newspapers	____ %
Consumer durables	____ %	Consumer Magazines	____ %
Industrial products	____ %	TV	____ %
Office and commercial products	____ %	Radio	____ %
Retail advertising	____ %	Outdoor	____ %
Service organizations	____ %	Business & Financial Press	____ %
Agency of Record	____ %	Sales promotion/Collateral Materials	____ %
Other	____ %	PR/Publicity	____ %
		Other (specify)	____ %

6d. WHAT PERCENTAGE OF YOUR BILLINGS ARE FOR:

English language advertising _____ %

French language advertising _____ %

All outstanding billing and projects should be resolved at this time.

You might note at this time also that it could have been helpful to have an agreement with your agency that was, in effect, a divorce agreement. This may convince you to add such a section to the agreement with your new agency.

Although there is no "standard" practice for a termination notice for an agency, 90 days is considered to be a fair period during which the new agency will be selected and be ready to take over.

This booklet was produced by The Institute of Canadian Advertising (ICA), the national association of advertising agencies in Canada. It has been created to help you with what can be two different tasks.

First, not all advertising agency listings contain just full-service advertising agencies. Your Yellow Pages directory will list dozens, sometimes hundreds, of advertising agencies, but many are printers, photographers or others whose main business is not of a full-service advertising agency. There is no source that lists all of the advertising agencies in Canada, but there are believed to be somewhere between 300 and 450.

Your second task will be to determine which of the bona fide agencies you should select. ICA has about 70 members who together account for approximately 85% of all the national

---

SECTION II—FACILITIES, EXPERIENCE AND OPERATING METHODS

7. NUMBER OF PEOPLE BY DEPARTMENT

	Head Office	Branch	Branch	Branch	Branch	Branch
Account Management						
Creative — Copy						
— Art						
Media — Planning						
— Buying						
Production						
Research and Planning						
Billing and Checking						

8a. WHICH TYPE OF COMPENSATION ARRANGEMENT DO YOU PREFER?

☐ Commission ☐ Fee ☐ Combination

8b. IF "COMBINATION", PLEASE COMMENT ON WHICH SERVICES YOU FEEL MERIT SPECIAL FEES:

_____

_____

_____

_____

_____

_____

_____

_____

_____

_____

9a. DO YOU HAVE A FORMAL COST ACCOUNTING SYSTEM, WHEREBY YOU KNOW THE PROFIT PICTURE ON EACH ACCOUNT?

☐ Yes ☐ No

9b. IF "YES", DO YOU REVIEW ACCOUNT PROFITABILITY WITH YOUR CLIENTS?

☐ Yes ☐ No

Comment _____

_____

FIGURE 4.7 (continued)

advertising done in Canada. They vary in size from 4 employees to several hundred. Among its members can be found an agency that can look after the needs of almost any client, regardless of size of budget or type of business.

In order to join ICA, an agency has to meet a series of professional standards, including a test of financial competence. Thus, membership in this national association is one way to measure the stability and worthiness of an agency to meet your needs.

10. PLEASE COMMENT ON THOSE ACCOUNTS ON WHICH YOU FEEL YOU HAVE MADE A SIGNIFICANT CONTRIBUTION TO THE CLIENT'S SUCCESS.

11. PLEASE COMMENT ON BOTH THE OPERATING AND THE CREATIVE PHILOSOPHY OF YOUR COMPANY.

12. COMMENT ON THE PROCEDURES THAT YOUR AGENCY FOLLOWS TO EVALUATE QUALITY OF WORK SPECIFICALLY WITH REGARD TO:

Development of Advertising Strategy:

Development of The Creative Product:

DATE THIS QUESTIONNAIRE COMPLETED:

BY:

Name   Title

an election campaign.[14] Finally, the advertised product may be an *idea*, such as the need to wear seat belts, help cancer research, fight crime, or foster energy conservation.[15]

Multicultural Advertising

Most Canadian advertisers operate in multicultural markets both within and outside the country. Quebec represents 26 per cent of the Canadian population, 24 per cent of its disposable income, and 24 per cent of its retail sales.[16] Because of its French population, the Quebec market presents to the advertiser major cultural and linguistic problems.[17] Should a campaign designed for an English Canadian market have minor adaptations made for the French Canadian market? A similar question may be raised with respect to other Canadian ethnic and cultural groups that represent large, identifiable, and geographically concentrated markets. Furthermore, some authors argue that *regional* differences in Canada may call for differentiated marketing and communication strategies.[18]

Canadian advertisers also operate in other countries, since international transactions play a very important part in the Canadian economy. In fact, Canadian exports of goods and services account for more than 20 per cent of Canada's GNP.

Canadian marketers must devise appropriate promotion policies for foreign markets. Different external constraints influence the pull and push strategies adopted for each foreign market. In particular, the types of distribution system available in each country determine whether personal communication or advertising are more desirable. The availability and costs of reaching consumers through mass media[19] also determine the degree of reliance on a pull strategy. For instance, in countries where several languages are spoken (e.g., India), it is difficult to develop an efficient promotional strategy.

The relative costs of the two types of communication have a great effect on the promotional mix. In developing nations, where labour is cheaper, the promotional mix is based more on personal selling than in industrialized countries. Also, cultural differences must be accounted for in any international promotion program. The problems familiar to Canadian firms that deal with two cultures at home are compounded abroad.

For these reasons, it is important to examine the arguments both for and against standardized multicultural campaigns.

Arguments for Standardized Multicultural Campaigns

It is feasible to standardize a multicultural campaign when consumers' similarities are greater than their differences, and when evolutionary trends in various societies point toward increasing similarities and uniformities rather than to increasing differences.[20] One author states that with a universal appeal such as "better life for people and families," "to be beautiful," or "mother and child," a standardized campaign can be effective in any market. Nationalistic tendencies cannot be ignored but improved international communications, travel and work mobility, and the simultaneous launching of new products make standardized advertising more feasible and desirable.[21]

In his discussion about standardization in European Economic Community (EEC) advertising, Elinder states that different advertisements for the same product cannot be justified because trends in consumption habits across countries are more important than truly "national" trends. These trends in consumption habits are: (1) differences in habits are decreasing due to changes in the possession and availability of goods and services are decreasing; (2) Europeans live in increasingly similar conditions; (3) as trade barriers drop, convergence of consumption habits is favoured by individuals. Furthermore, increased international communication (especially television) and mobility in work and travel make it more desirable to repeat a consistent advertising theme.[22] Elinder also points out that company mergers and product standardization lead the way to advertising standardization, that nonstandardization in advertising contradicts the philosophy of a united European market, and that in the arts, national boundaries are less important, pointing to a convergent world style. "If there is no belief in advertising that can pass over all boundaries, then neither should we manufacture goods which pass over all boundaries."[23]

Buzzell mentions other market and environmental factors that favour standardization, while warning that "the question of advertising approaches cannot be considered realistically in isolation from other elements of a company's marketing 'mix' in each market, including its product line, packaging, pricing, distribution system, sales force, and other methods of promotion."[24] Significant cost savings create pressures for standardization, especially in product design. These savings may be so great that although sales may decrease in some markets, profits will increase. Some companies can save millions of dollars by standardizing their advertising.

The second factor that favours standardization is the advisability of consistent dealings with customers. Aside from the increasing cross-border flow of tourists, business, and communications, many companies sell to such multinational customers as industrial users and wholesalers, who either buy centrally or co-ordinate buying. Also, professional and technical groups are homogeneous enough to warrant a standardized approach. The third factor, improved planning and control, is particularly important in the context of increasing social and economic convergence and decreasing trade barriers. Finally, Buzzell points out that good ideas are hard to find and, once found, usually have universal appeal, for example, Avis's "We Try Harder" theme.[25]

Plummer analyzed lifestyles in twelve countries according to five dimensions (activities, interests, opinions, basic characteristics, and demographics), as well as media usage, product use, and orientation toward promotion. He found a high correlation between the level of product usage, which was used as the common element cross-nationally, and various lifestyle characteristics. For example, heavy beer drinkers in Canada, the U.S., and Mexico are similar enough so that a common campaign could be developed. Attitudes, interests, opinions, and values may also be universal, regardless of social class, occupation, product usage, or culture.[26]

Arguments against the Standardization of Multicultural Campaigns

One argument against standardization holds that cross-national or cross-cultural differences are too great to allow the development of effective standardized campaigns.[27]

The most obvious barriers to transferring an effective advertisement to another country are the legal restrictions on advertising. In some countries, comparison advertising is illegal (Table 4.3), as are certain forms of promotion. Regulations involving free samples, contests, and sweepstakes (some countries forbid straight lotteries), and two-for-one or other reduced-price deals vary from nation to nation. Even if regulations are standardized, however, administration of the laws may vary. In Germany, for example, comparative claims are legal, with major restrictions requiring proof of claims. *Interpretation* of the laws is very strict, however. A statement that "Brand X is better for your dog" can be interpreted as a comparative claim even if no other brand is mentioned.[28] In general, relatively poor countries such as Spain have fewer and less strictly enforced controls, while relatively rich countries have more controls and stricter interpretations.

In addition to legal controls, many countries have self-regulatory bodies. Most of these bodies have adopted at least the statement of basic principles and the rules (Articles 1 to 18) of the International Code of Advertising Practice (revised 1973), which has also been accepted by the International Chamber of Commerce. One study found that countries with a central

TABLE 4.3 The Legality of Comparison Advertising in 30 Major Countries, 1977-1982

Essentially Illegal		Relatively Minor Legal Restrictions		Relatively Major Legal Restrictions	
		with relatively minor self-regulatory restrictions	with relatively major self-regulatory restrictions	with relatively minor self-regulatory restrictions	with relatively major self-regulatory restrictions
Belgium	NU/O	Canada	SU/O	Australia	MU/−	Austria	NU/O	Agentina	NU/O
France	NU/O	Ireland	MU/+	Denmark	SU/−	Brazil	MU/O	Japan	NU/O
Italy	NU/O	Sweden	MU/O	Hong Kong	MU/O	Chile	MU/+	Korea	NU/−
		United Kingdom	SU/O	India	MU/+	Germany	MU/O	Mexico	MU/O
		United States	SU/O	Philippines	NU/−	Finland	MU/O	Switzerland	MU/O
				South Africa	MU/O	Greece	NU/O	Trinidad & Tobago	MU/+
				Spain	MU/+	Malaysia	MU/O		
						Netherlands	MU/+		
						Norway	MU/O		
Total	*3*		*5*		*7*		*9*		*6*

SU = significant use (4)   NU = no use (9)   MU = minor use (17)   O = no change (20)
+   = change favouring CA (6)
−   = change hampering CA (4)

SOURCES: J. J. Boddewyn, "Comparison Advertising: Regulation and Self-Regulation in 55 Countries," International Advertising Association, New York (January 1983), p. 8; J. J. Boddewyn and Katherin Morton, *Comparison Advertising: A Worldwide Study* (New York: Hastings House, 1978), p. 120.

self-regulatory body generally have a relatively high level of advertising expenditures, active consumer groups, and government controls on advertising.[29]

In addition to legal and self-regulatory codes, advertising practices are restricted by unwritten codes. In Japan, direct confrontation is discouraged by traditional values, and decorum in competitive behaviour is preferred. As a result, Japanese advertising refrains from comparative claims, open attack, and aggressive advertising. In Switzerland comparative advertising is considered a kind of in-fighting, and business people tend to unite against foreign competition.

Another barrier to cross-cultural advertising is "the silent language".[30] This refers to differences in cultural frames of reference, which enable the receiver of a communication to determine what is significant and/or relevant. Some of these differences are:
• the conception of time;

• the language of "personal space", or the meaning of the distance people maintain between themselves when speaking to each other (this distance may be greater with Northern Europeans than with North Americans);

• the language of things (since possessions have different meanings);

• friendship (in some countries friendships form more slowly, last longer, and involve real obligations, in contrast to North America);

• the language of agreements (for example, unstated, unwritten agreements may be the norm in some countries).

In a study comparing the British and the Americans, one author states that the manner of communication in advertising "is firmly anchored to cultural norms and often says more about a society's psyche than the more obvious stereotypes of content."[31]

Culture may affect perceptions of colours and sounds, cognitive and affective processes, evaluative behaviour, and learned motives. Lipton and Garza, in a study of the *attribution of responsibility* (i.e., under which conditions are people responsible for an event) involving Mexican-American, Black, and Anglo subjects, found the cultural factor highly significant.[32]

These results may contradict the assumption that there is a common appeal in the philosophy that "everyone wants a better life for oneself and one's family". What people want may be universal but what people perceive they can control or get may not be universal. It is the latter that determines whether "wants" are translated into behaviour.

Culture also affects the criteria consumers use to evaluate products.[33] One Canadian study found significant differences in the effectiveness of English advertisements dubbed into French and English advertisements adapted as to presenter, working, setting, and/or structures. The study did conclude, however, that with these significant adaptations, the campaign could be transferred.[34]

Other arguments against the standardization of advertising relate to market factors. Newell states that effective commercials offer a vital promise that fits the needs and desires of the audience. He distinguishes three categories of commercials: those that establish product benefits (overcome unfamiliarity, doubt or create primary demand by emphasizing a product, not a brand); those that establish brand superiority; and those that promote unique features. Newell claims that these categories are stages related to the degree of market development.[35] One could conclude, then, that markets at different levels of development (as measured, for example, in terms of a product's life cycle) need different advertising strategies that correspond to differing levels of awareness, knowledge, liking, preference, and/or conviction.

In addition, differences in the level of economic and industrial development may necessitate the development of separate campaigns.

Underdeveloped countries have relatively low literacy rates and low per capita income. Low literacy rates make a campaign based on visuals preferable or even necessary. Low per capita income may mean that the relative cost of a given product is higher than in North America. This may change the way a product is evaluated by consumers and make a purchase more risky. It is more difficult to influence consumers with a campaign suitable for countries where the *relative* cost is lower.

Standardization? It Depends

Several criteria determine whether uniform advertising is appropriate.[36] One is the type of product. A standardized appeal is effective with products that have a universal selling point and that are sold primarily on an objective basis (according to physical characteristics).

The homogeneity (or heterogeneity) of markets, the characteristics and availability of media, and the types of advertising agency service available should also be considered. For example, if only very poor agency service is available, standardized advertising developed elsewhere may be the most attractive alternative. Government restrictions, trade codes, industry agreements, and ethical practices may preclude standardization. Tariffs on artwork and printed matter may eliminate the cost advantages of centralized production.

The organization of a multinational firm determines whether the implementation of a standardized campaign is possible. For example, tight central control makes implementation easier, while a firm operating through independent, non-exclusive agents, or through licenses may have more difficulties. Implementation is the important element. The question is not only whether an effective cross-national or cross-cultural campaign can be developed, but also whether the firm is capable of imposing such a campaign.[37]

The standardization of product and communication strategies depends on three key factors.[38] The first is the *product* itself, defined in terms of

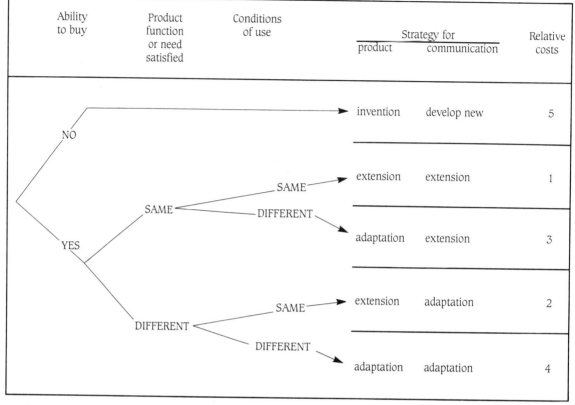

FIGURE 4.8   Product/Communication Alternatives in International Markets
SOURCE: Warren J. Keegan, "Multinational Product Planning: Strategic Alternatives," *Journal of Marketing*, 33:1 (January 1969), pp. 58-62.
Courtesy American Marketing Association

consumer needs satisfied. The second is the *circumstances* under which the product is used (including consumers' ability to buy and their preferences). The third is the *cost* of any changes should nonstandardization be necessary. The strategic product/communication alternatives are represented in Figure 4.8.

Summary

Canadian advertisers are a heterogeneous group with different needs, problems, and resources.

Industrial advertising is directed toward professionals. Its goals are to increase awareness of a firm as a suitable supplier, to provide information to individuals involved in the decision process, and to help salespersons gain entry, improve the selling effort, and reduce selling costs.

The nature of the advertising message and the type of media used also depend on the type of products advertised. In advertising for durable goods, the goals are to provide information and to draw traffic into the stores. For packaged goods, the goal is to pre-sell the brand before the consumer reaches the self-service retail establishment. For soft goods, advertising attempts to create a favourable brand image and assist retail salesclerks. The advertising of services requires a great deal of creativity to communicate the intangible benefits of the "product."

Retailers develop an advertising effort with two main goals. First, long-term development of the store image is the guiding principle of all retail advertising, and an advertising agency may be helpful. Second, retailers increase store traffic through in-house campaigns based on event advertising. Retailers receive free assistance from producers and media, and they use the services of outside suppliers.

In contrast to the large advertiser, the small advertiser is forced to use fewer media and to concentrate on increased exposure rather than frequent repetition of the message. Small advertisers may not be able to afford an advertising agency or have an advertising manager. Thus, the advertising campaign is often done in-house with the help of outside suppliers.

The main factors influencing the organization of the advertising function are the position of the advertising function within a firm's overall structure, the responsibilities of the advertising manager, and the structure of the advertising department.

The important questions in hiring an advertising agency are whether an agency is necessary, and if it is, what kind of services are needed.

There are three additional areas with special advertising needs and problems. Institutional advertising is directed to the general public or to the organization's employees, with the objective of improving its image or advocating a particular course of action. Advertising is used by non-profit organizations to promote an organization, a place, a person, or an idea. In advertising to different cultures, one of the main issues is whether a campaign designed for one culture may be transferred to another one and whether it is possible to standardize multicultural advertising campaigns.

Questions for Study

1. Describe the role of advertising for the largest department store in your town. Try to find out how the entire campaign is planned.

2. Select a small- or medium-sized business and describe the process of choosing an advertising agency for the company.

3. Explain in detail how advertising may be designed to appeal to the two main cultural groups in Canada and to other Canadian cultural groups (Italian, German, etc.).

4. What are the main differences between an advertising campaign run by a retailer (e.g., Sears) and the advertising campaign of a consumer product (e.g., Coca-Cola)? What are the main factors responsible for these differences?

5. Find three examples of institutional advertisements. Analyze them in detail, paying particular attention to the advertisements' objectives, their target audience(s), and the media selected.

6. Describe the differences in the decision process between a "typical" consumer buying a home computer and the purchase of a computer for use by a small business. What does this imply for the advertising to these two groups?

7. Assume that you are an exporter of furs to the United States, Great Britain, and Japan, and that you need to advertise in all of these countries. Explain the kind of problems that you are likely to encounter and how you would proceed in resolving them, in terms of (*a*) agency selection, (*b*) creative strategy, and (*c*) media strategy.

8. Select a recent advertising campaign done by a non-profit organization and analyze its objectives, the target audience(s), and the media selected.

9. Why are services difficult to advertise? Give three examples to illustrate your answer.

10. Select an advertisement for one durable good, one packaged good, one soft good, and one service. Explain for each one how the nature of the "product" has influenced the advertising strategy, the creative execution, and the media selection.

Problems

1. Assume that you are POCHI, a manufacturer of potato chips, and that your market is the province in which you live. You have determined that you can spend $100,000 for your advertising and you think that an advertising agency could help you with the marketing and advertising program. 1. Analyze your needs to select the best agency available. Try to interview as many agencies as possible, using the questionnaire, in Figure 4.7. If a personal interview is not possible, try to fill in the questionnaire basing your answers on the promotional brochures distributed by the agencies. 2. Justify your final choice.

2. Assume that you are the same manufacturer as in Problem no. 1. You have decided that you do not need an advertising agency, and that you should handle the advertising campaign yourself with the help of the media and outside suppliers. Based on the information in Chapters 1-4, develop an advertising campaign for your product, paying particular attention to the following elements: marketing strategy; advertising objective; advertising strategy; the message; media selection.

Notes

1. *Canadian Media Directors' Council Media Digest, 1982/83* (1982), pp. 13, 16, 22, 26, 33.
2. Jo Marney, "DM Plays Vital Role in the Total Media Mix," *Marketing* (12 July 1982), pp. 7-9.
3. "Coke Tops List of Brand Advertisers," *Marketing* (5 July 1982), p. 19.
4. "Auto Ad Spending to Stay on Par with '81," *Marketing* (22 February 1982), p. A8; see also Ted Wood, "Ah Yes, Those Were the Days," *Marketing* (22 February 1982), p. A4.
5. "The Feds Outspend Everyone," *Marketing* (19 April 1982), p. 22.
6. John R. Dickinson and Bent Stidsen, "Communication of Product and Service Concepts and Benefits: Is There a Fundamental Difference," *Developments in Canadian Marketing*, ed. Robert D. Tamilia (Administrative Sciences Association of Canada, 1979), pp. 166-75.
7. W.H. Mahatoo and D.E. Abraham, "The Marketing Concept—Its Relevance for Canadian Chartered Banks and the Public," *The Canadian Marketer* (Fall 1973), pp. 27-32.
8. John R.G. Jenkins, "The Canadian Advertising Industry in the 1980s," *Proceedings of the Third Annual Conference* (Administrative Sciences Association of Canada, 1975), Section 4, pp. 125-33.
9. Keith W.E. Warne, "Rent—Don't Hire—an Advertising Manager," *The Canadian Marketer* (Fall 1974), pp. 17-20.
10. Randy Scotland, "Are Agency Searches Turning Inside Out," *Marketing* (13 December 1982), pp. 48-50.
11. Nancy Church, "Source Credibility: Implications for Advocacy Advertising" (Working paper, Concordia University, 1983).
12. Philip Kotler, "A Generic Concept of Marketing," *Journal of Marketing* (April 1972), pp. 46-54; see also Philip Kotler and Gerald Zaltman, "Social Marketing: An Approach to Planned Social Changes," *Journal of Marketing* (July 1971), pp. 3-12.
13. G.H. Church and D.W. Gillingham, "The Description of Marketing Strategies and Their Influences

in the University Context," *Marketing*, ed. Vernon J. Jones (Administrative Sciences Association of Canada, 1980), pp. 107-16.

14. Gary A. Mauser, "Broadening Marketing: The Case of Political Marketing," *Marketing*, vol. 4, ed. James D. Forbes (Administrative Sciences Association of Canada, 1983), pp. 201-9; Gary A. Mauser, "Estimating Aggregate Share of Choice," *The Canadian Marketer*, 11, no. 1 (1980), 19-22.

15. G.H.G. McDougall, "Alternative Energy Conservation Appeals: Relative Effects," *Marketing in the 80s*, ed. Richard P. Bagozzi et al. (Chicago Marketing Association, 1980), pp. 432-35; C. Dennis Anderson and John D. Claxton, "Barriers to Consumer Choice of Energy Efficient Products," *Journal of Consumer Research* (September 1982), pp. 163-70; Sadrudin A. Ahmed and Douglas N. Jackson, "Psychographics for Social Policy Decisions: Welfare Assistance," *Journal of Consumer Research* (March 1979), pp. 220-39.

16. *Canadian Media Directors' Council Media Digest, 1982/83*, p. 10.

17. Bruce Mallen, *French Canadian Consumer Behaviour* (Montreal: Advertising and Sales Executives Club, 1977); M. Brisebois, "Industrial Advertising and Marketing in Quebec," *The Marketer*, 2, no. 1 (1966), 13; Robert M. MacGregor, "The Utilization of Originally Conceived French Language Advertisements in Parallel Canadian Magazines," *Marketing*, ed. Robert G. Wyckham (Administrative Sciences Association of Canada, 1981), pp. 186-95.

18. Harry Vredenburg and Peter Thirkell, "Canadian Regionalism: A Marketplace Reality," *Marketing*, ed. James D. Forbes (Administrative Sciences Association of Canada, 1983), pp. 360-70.

19. Erdener Kaynak and Lionel A. Mitchell, "A Study of Comparative Media Usage in Canada, the United Kingdom and Turkey," *Developments in Canadian Marketing*, ed. Robert D. Tamilia (Administrative Sciences Association of Canada, 1979), pp. 131-32.

20. P.C. Lefrançois and G. Chatel, "The French Canadian Consumer: Fact or Fancy?" *New Ideas for Successful Marketing*, ed. J.S. Wright and J.L. Goldstrucker (Chicago: American Marketing Association, 1966), pp. 706-15.

21. Arthur C. Fatt, "The Danger of 'Local' International Advertising," *Journal of Marketing* (January 1967), pp. 60-62.

22. Erik Elinder, "How International Can European Advertising Be," *Journal of Marketing* (April 1965), p. 7-11.

23. S.Watson Dunn, ed., *International Handbook of Advertising* (New York: McGraw-Hill, 1964), p. 71.

24. Robert D. Buzzell, "Can You Standardize Multinational Marketing," *Harvard Business Review* (November-December 1967), p. 102.

25. Ibid., pp. 102-13.

26. Joseph T. Plummer, "Consumer Focus in Cross-National Research," *Journal of Advertising* (Spring 1977), pp. 5-15.

27. Arthur C. Nielson, Jr., "Do's and Don'ts in Selling Abroad," *Journal of Marketing* (April 1959), pp. 405-11.

28. J.J. Boddewyn and K. Morton, *Comparison Advertising: A Worldwide Study* (New York: Hastings House, 1978).

29. J.P. Neelankavil and A.S. Stridsberg, *Advertising Self-Regulation: A Global Perspective* (New York: Hastings House, 1980).

30. E.T. Hall, "The Silent Language of Overseas Business," *Harvard Business Review* (May-June 1960), pp. 87-98.

31. Stephen J.F. Unwin, "How Culture Affects Advertising Expression and Communication Style," *Journal of Advertising* (Spring 1974), p. 24.

32. J. Lipton and R. Garza, "Responsibility Attribution Among Mexican-American, Black and Anglo Adolescents and Adults," *Journal of Cross-Cultural Psychology* (September 1977), pp. 259-72.

33. R. Green, W. Cunningham, and I. Cunningham, "The Effectiveness of Standardized Global Advertising," *Journal of Advertising* (Summer 1975), pp. 25-30.

34. Dunn, p. 71.

35. Ibid.

36. G.E. Miracle, "International Advertising Principles and Strategies," *MSU Business Topics*
(Autumn 1968), pp. 29-36.

37. D.M. Peebles, J.K. Ryans, and I.R. Vernon,
"Coordinating International Advertising," *Journal
of Marketing* (January 1978), pp. 28-34.

38. Warren J. Keegan, "Multinational Product Planning: Strategic Alternatives," *Journal of Marketing* (January 1969), pp. 58-62.

PLATE I
All the elements of this advertisement as well as their arrangement convey a luxurious atmosphere for the perfume.

Courtesy Jacqueline Cochran Inc.

Some of the best things
are measured by the ounce.

Seagram's V.O.

Canada's most respected 8 year old whisky. Only V.O. is V.O.

**PLATE II   The simplicity of this advertisement and the
illustration's small size in comparison to the total size
convey the idea of a precious, high-class product.**
Courtesy Joseph E. Seagram & Sons Limited

PLATE III The main idea of this advertisement is expressed graphically. The only written words needed are the brand's name, which is itself incorporated into the Gilbey's bottle representation.

Courtesy Gilbey's Canada

PLATE IV The mildness of Select is communicated in an atmosphere of elegance, romance, and luxury.

Courtesy R.J.R. MacDonald Inc.

THE PLEASURE IS ALL MILD.

Introducing Macdonald Select.
A unique new family of mild cigarettes
especially created for those who
select their pleasures with care.
Everything about them will please you.
In Special Mild, Ultra Mild and
Menthol Special Mild.

THE NAME SAYS IT ALL.

Wendy Henry on stubborn eaters, mealtime favourites and Maple Leaf.

There aren't many foods you can count on to please kids time after time. But Maple Leaf Hot Dogs can do the trick. They're always a treat because they're spiced just the way kids like. And they're made with only quality ingredients. So you get great taste at a sensible Maple Leaf price. And who can argue with that? **It's today's wise choice.**

PLATE V   Like any food product advertisement, appetite appeal is conveyed here by a photograph of the meals prepared with the advertised product and brand.

Courtesy Canada Packers

*In every woman there's a place
where life and vision interlace.
Where you look back to see
how far you've come,
and you know the best has just begun.
This is the place.
This is the Emeraude of your life.*

EMERAUDE

*Emeraude
Perfume by Coty.*

**PLATE VI   This painting conveys an atmosphere of elegance
and romance to the perfume.**
Courtesy Coty Division, Pfizer Inc.

PLATE VII   The selective use of colour for the brand illustration on a black and white background highlights the brand package and confers some distinction on the brand.

Courtesy Kimberley-Clark of Canada Limited

5

Canadian Print Media

Most media plans include advertising in print media. In 1982 Canadian advertising revenues for all print media accounted for more than 70 per cent of advertising revenues for all media.

A variety of print media are available for carrying advertising messages. The four general categories of print media in Canada are newspapers, periodicals, outdoor, and other print media.

Newspapers include dailies, weeklies, and semi-weeklies. Newspapers receive the largest share of advertising revenues of all media. In 1982, this share was 32 per cent, although it has been declining since 1977 (Table 5.1).

Periodicals include consumer magazines, business publications, and farm publications. They have grown rapidly in the past decade and in 1982 their share of revenues was about 14 per cent.

Outdoor media, including transit, has seen its share of advertising revenues decline slowly to 6.3 per cent in 1982.

Other print media are catalogues and direct mail. Those media increased their share of advertising revenues slightly to more than 20 per cent in 1982.[1]

Before looking at each type of media, it is important to understand three basic media terms. *Reach* (R) is the percentage of a target audience exposed at least once to one medium. *Frequency* (F) is the average number of times one member of the target audience is exposed to one medium. *Gross Rating Points* (GRPs) measure the number of times members of the target audience are exposed to one medium as

a percentage of the target audience. Unlike reach, GRP includes multiple exposure to the same person. The relationship among these concepts is reach multiplied by frequency equals gross rating points (R x F =GRP). A more complete treatment of these concepts, as well as their use in media planning, is presented in Chapter 14.

Newspapers

Evolution of Newspapers as an Advertising Medium

A Boston printer, Bartholomew Green, established the first Canadian newspaper, *The Halifax Gazette*, which appeared on March 23, 1752. His father printed the first American newspaper, *The Boston News Letter*, in 1704. This paper was one single sheet printed on both sides.

A Philadelphia printer, William Brown, founded *La Gazette de Québec*, in 1764. It was Canada's second newspaper and was printed in both French and English.

A Frenchman, Fleury de Mesplet, arrived in Quebec on May 6, 1776 to set up a printshop and publish a newspaper in order to assist Benjamin Franklin in wooing Quebec to become the fourteenth colony. When this plan failed, de Mesplet was arrested. Because of an acute need for a printer, however, he was released three weeks later to set up a print shop. On June 3, 1778, he published the first issue of *La Gazette*

101

TABLE 5.1   Components of Net Advertising Revenues by Print Media (in thousands of dollars)

Type of print medium	1977		1982		Average annual rate of growth (%)
	amount	%	amount	%	
NEWSPAPERS					
Dailies—*Total*	*703,605*	*28.6*	*1,155,000*	*26.0*	*10.4*
national	134,101	5.5	232,000	5.2	11.6
local	368,799	15.0	653,000	14.7	12.1
classified	200,705	8.2	270,000	6.2	6.1
Weekend Supplements—*Total*	*21,457*	*0.9*	*36,500*	*0.8*	*11.2*
national	17,945	0.7	30,000	0.7	10.8
local	3,512	0.1	6,500	0.1	13.1
Weeklies, semi, tri, etc. (including controlled distribution)—*Total*	*123,477*	*5.0*	*230,000*	*5.2*	*13.2*
national[1]	28,072	1.1	20,000	0.4	−6.6
local	95,405	3.9	210,000	4.7	17.1
PERIODICALS—*Total*	*330,649*	*13.5*	*615,200*	*13.8*	*13.2*
magazines, general	71,338	2.9	203,000	4.6	23.3
business papers[1]	78,120	3.2	139,000	3.1	12.2
farm papers	10,440	0.4	18,700	0.4	12.4
directories—phone, city	158,586	6.5	235,000	5.3	8.2
religious, school, and other	12,165	0.5	19,500	0.4	9.9
OTHER PRINT—*Total*	*471,574*	*19.2*	*892,000*	*20.1*	*13.6*
catalogues	92,891	3.8	160,000	3.6	11.5
other printed advertising	225,803	9.2	420,000	9.4	13.2
imported advtg. matter	32,880	1.3	52,000	1.2	9.6
postage cost**	120,000	4.9	260,000	5.8	16.7
OUTDOOR[2]—*Total*	*162,600*	*6.6*	*280,000*	*6.3*	*11.5*
TOTAL PRINT MEDIA	*1,813,362*	*73.8*	*3,208,700*	*72.2*	*12.1*
TOTAL ALL MEDIA	*2,458,006*	*100.0*	*4,445,700*	*100.0*	*12.6*

** Postage: 75 per cent of third class mail.
[1] Effective 1980, includes national financial publications previously included in weekly newspapers.
[2] Includes factory shipments of advertising signs and displays (Statistics Canada Catalogue 47-209) as well as firms in other outdoor advertising business (renting space, putting up billboards or other displays, placing advertising matter on streetcars, buses, and other transit systems, advertising revenue of other sign producers, show card writers, sign painters).
SOURCE: *Canadian Advertising Rates and Data* (February 1983), p. 156.
Courtesy Special Interest Network

du Commerce et Littéraire. This paper later became an English-language newspaper, *The Gazette* of Montreal.[2]

As the Canadian population and the volume of trade grew, so did the number of newspapers. By 1857, there were 243 publications. By 1981, this number had *quadrupled* to 1033 publications.[3] The real growth occurred in the circulation figures with the growth in population and trading activity. Between 1890 and 1980 Canada's population increased five times, while the average circulation per paper increased eleven times.

There are now 118 daily newspapers in Canada with a combined average circulation of 5.3 million copies a day.[4] Daily newspapers represent by far the largest medium in terms of net advertising revenues, which passed the $1.1 billion mark in 1982 for the first time (Table 5.1). They represent more than a quarter of net advertising revenues for all media. If one adds net advertising revenues for other types of newspapers (weekend supplements, weeklies, and others), the proportion is 32 per cent. Although the number of daily newspapers in Canada has not changed very much in the past thirty years, the industry has undergone major changes in distribution and structure. The number of cities with two or more daily newspapers is declining, while most of the new daily newspapers were originally weekly newspapers. Almost half of all Canadian daily newspapers and of the average daily circulation of newspapers is controlled by two chains: Southam Inc. and Thomson Ltd.

Competition from broadcast media and the declining household penetration of daily newspapers, from 1.06 copies daily per household in 1948 to 0.63 in 1981, has changed the nature of newspapers. They have evolved from a medium for informing people about major news events to a medium with in-depth analysis of news events, investigative reporting, local news, special sections, and so on. However, the number of people who read at least one newspaper per week has increased during the same period.[5] *Irregular* readers account for this increase. Newspapers are trying to make them regular readers so that present levels of penetration can be maintained or increased.

Differences among Newspapers

Newspapers have several formats and publication frequencies and provide different types of advertising services.

Formats

In Canada, two basic newspaper formats are used: the *broadsheet* and the *tabloid* (Figure 5.1). The broadsheet is a full-size newspaper approximately 380 mm wide and 560 mm deep (15″ x 22″). A *line* (or *agate line*) is a unit of space measurement one column wide and 1.8 mm (1/14″) deep. The number of columns is usually eight or nine, and each column has approximately 310 lines. The total number of lines per page varies from 2400 to 2900. Examples of broadsheets are *The Globe and Mail*, the Montreal *Gazette*, the *Vancouver Sun Province*, and the *Winnipeg Free Press*.

The tabloid is approximately 254 mm wide and 356 mm deep (10″ x 14″). The number of columns varies between five and seven, each column having approximately 200 lines. The total lines per page varies from 1000 to 1400. Examples of tabloids are the *Calgary Sun*, the *Toronto Sun*, *L'Evangeline*, and *The Chronicle-Herald*. Canada has 12 English and four French tabloid daily newspapers.

Publication Frequency

Newspapers are also classified by frequency of publication: daily and community newspapers.

DAILY NEWSPAPERS. In 1982 Canada had 118 daily newspapers with an average daily circulation of 5.3 million copies and net advertising revenues of $1.16 million.[6] Daily newspapers are published as morning or afternoon newspapers, but the trend has been toward morning newspapers. This is due to a shrinking "window of time" in the evening and the strong competition from television. Thus, the afternoon newspaper is slowly disappearing.

Most daily newspapers reach a high percentage of households within a particular *geographic* area. On the average, gross circulation as a percentage of households is about 70 per cent. This geographic characteristic of daily newspapers influences the type of news and other features carried, although more and more daily newspapers are including special sections like lifestyle or regional editions in large metropolitan areas in order to increase reader interest and daily circulation.

Some daily newspapers have developed into *national* daily newspapers. For example, *The*

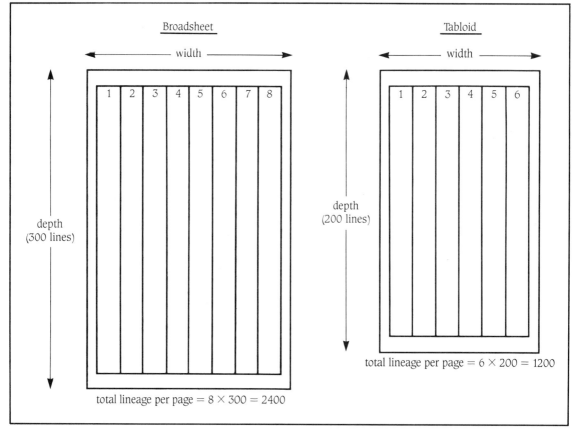

FIGURE 5.1   Characteristics of Broadsheets and Tabloids

Globe and Mail is sold in all provinces and territories and about 39 per cent of its circulation is outside its primary market area in Toronto.

Most newspapers are published Monday through Saturday and with special features that attempt to keep readership high. Some days have a high proportion of advertisements for food, banking services, and so on. This policy is a shopping convenience for readers and for advertisers it ensures high reader interest.

Some daily newspapers publish a Sunday edition similar in style to the Saturday edition of other daily newspapers, with a blend of news, news summaries and analysis, radio and television listings, comics, and special sections on sports, travel, and entertainment. In Canada the trend is to more Sunday editions of daily newspapers.[7]

COMMUNITY NEWSPAPERS.   This is the second major group of newspapers. Community newspapers are published three times a week or once a month, with circulation between 400 and 140 000 copies. Canada has approximately 1159 community newspapers, distributed as follows:[8]

Yukon and NWT	10
B.C., Alberta, Saskatchewan, and Manitoba	465
Ontario	378
Quebec	227
Atlantic provinces	79
Total	*1159*

The Canadian Community Newspaper Association (CCNA) has about 600 members and centralizes buying from all member papers.

Some community newspapers are distributed freely while others have a paid circulation. The increased number of free community weekly newspapers has led to a phenomenal growth in household penetration, from 0.66 copy per household per week in 1948 to 1.38 in 1978.[9] This trend contrasts with the decline of household penetration by daily newspapers and indicates a shift in the reporting of purely local news from the daily newspapers to the weekly newspapers. In the United States many large daily newspapers have separate community sections in the regular issues, particularly in the Sunday edition, to cover local news. These are distributed in large suburbs of major metropolitan areas. Canadian daily newspapers in large metropolitan areas may use this strategy to increase household penetration.

Additional Services Offered by Newspapers
In order to improve flexibility and compete with other media, newspapers provide a number of special advertising and printing services.

Colour has long been one of the main problems of newspapers because the quality of the standard newsprint is low. To correct this situation, advertisements are preprinted on higher quality paper and then fed in roll form into the newspaper during a normal run. Two types of pre-printed colour inserts are available: hi-fi and spectacolour. Hi-fi appears in a continuous pattern that bleeds off the top and bottom of the page. It is offered by most newspapers. Spectacolour has the width and depth of a newspaper page. More than seventeen Canadian dailies offer spectacolour to advertisers. In contrast to the preprinted advertisement, ROP (run of press) colour is printed on standard newsprint paper along with editorial material and other advertisements. Although the quality of ROP colour printing is still far from that of magazines, it is adequate for many creative requirements. Most daily newspapers offer ROP colour with minimum line requirements (600-1000 lines), and cost premiums depend on the number of colours.

Inserts are advertisements printed in advance by the advertiser and bound in or inserted into a newspaper by hand or by machine. Most newspapers offer this service.

Flexform is any advertising shape that does not conform to the standard rectangular format. Most daily newspapers offer this service for a premium charge.

Newspapers as an Advertising Medium

The main *advantages* of newspapers may be grouped into five categories:

Market coverage. Daily newspapers reach an average of 60 per cent of all adults (18 years and over) during the week and 65 per cent of all adults during the weekend. In metropolitan areas of 100 000 to one million inhabitants, these figures are, respectively, 67 per cent and 75 per cent.[10] The average daily reach has been falling since 1962, when it stood at 71 per cent.[11] Newspapers also provide advertisers with broad coverage of several demographic subgroups, although here the reach drops to 51 per cent of adults aged 18-24 and to 48 per cent of adults with less than a high school education.[12]

Flexibility. Newspapers allow very *short lead times* both for closing and cancelling advertisements. Advertisers may be allowed 24-hour notice in order to take advantage of fast-changing market conditions, fads, or to respond to actions by competitors.

In planning the campaign, since most newspapers are a *local* medium, they can be selected according to the brand's regional market conditions. In addition, newspapers provide merchandising properties (e.g., dealer tie-ins, co-operative plans, colour inserts, and couponing).

Newspapers provide *creative flexibility* for a low production cost. A wide range of space, sizes, and shapes is available. Time flexibility allows for creative use of news items and special events.

Reader interest. Canadians spend about $350 million a year on newspapers. Seventy-five per cent of readers go through daily papers page by page.[13] Readers differ, however, in the way they read the various sections of a newspaper.[14] Differences are also found between men and women's readership patterns.[15] Newspapers are an excellent medium for long copy and factual information. In addition, advertisers may benefit from the editorial environment in which their advertisement will appear.[16]

Many consumers use newspapers as a shopping guide when looking for a specific item (e.g., car, stereo system, or sports equipment), or before a shopping trip to a food store, a hardware store, or a car dealer.

High frequency potential. Daily publication of newspapers provides the advertiser with high frequency potential against a large number of readers. On an average weekday, daily newspapers provide about 60 per cent reach with a frequency of 1.3. Thus, on the average, readers are exposed to an advertisement 1.3 times.

Accessibility to small advertisers. Newspapers' high reach, timing, and creative flexibility make the medium accessible to advertisers with a small budget, particularly retail advertisers who are charged local rates and given free creative assistance.

The main *disadvantages* of newspapers may be grouped into three categories:

Creative negatives. Although the quality of ROP colour is constantly improving, newspapers cannot compete effectively with magazines. This is a serious drawback for campaigns in which colour is an important ingredient in communicating some product benefit, for example, for food products or fashionable clothes. Another drawback is that newspapers lack audio capabilities and movement, thus it is impossible to demonstrate a product in use or to use special effects. There is also the problem of *clutter*: newspaper advertisements have to compete for attention with many other advertisements and with a large number of inserts. Newspapers have a short life per issue. As a result, the advertisement must attract the reader the first time it is seen. Finally, advertisers have little control over an advertisement's position on a particular page, although newspapers try to accomodate the advertiser's requested position. Many newspapers have some form of position charges, which vary from newspaper to newspaper.

Audience selectivity. Because their coverage is broad, newspapers are an expensive medium for reaching a specific target group. The advertiser may be paying for a large amount of wasted circulation. This is also aggravated by a low pass-along circulation and the lower reach in such demographic groups as adults aged 18-24 and those with less than a high school education.

Problems for national advertisers. Newspapers require national advertisers to provide separate insertion orders and material, because space sizes are not standardized. Thus newspapers are a difficult medium in which to buy space. To alleviate this problem, the Newspaper Marketing Bureau (NMB) was formed in 1979. The NMB represents fifty of Canada's daily newspapers and three-quarters of daily newspaper circulation. It provides both centralized representation and centralized research with the Newspaper Audience Databank (NADbank).[17]

On a national basis, an advertising campaign run in daily newspapers is expensive. For example, a 1000-line black and white newspaper advertisement in all markets of more than 100 000 costs about $60,000. If the advertiser's audience is general, this may compare favourably with television, but if the audience is more selective, newspapers may be more expensive than television.

The Gazette

P.O. Box 4300
Montreal, Quebec H2Y 3S1

Tel: (514) 282-2750   Telex: 055-61767

Published Daily (M) — Except Sunday

MONTREAL

General Rate Card
No. 45

Effective
January 1, 1983

Contracts subject to written notice
of increase.

---

1. GENERAL ADVERTISING

	Per Agate Line	
	Mon.-Fri.	Sat.
Open rate	$2.84	20% extra

2. VOLUME CONTRACTS

2,500 lines	$2.62	20% extra
5,000 lines	$2.59	20% extra
10,000 lines	$2.57	20% extra
25,000 lines	$2.53	20% extra
50,000 lines	$2.48	20% extra

(Financial pages position plus 10%)
- Non-contract advertising ordered for three or more insertions at the same time within a 30-day period without copy change.

	Mon-Fri	Sat.
	$2.73	20% extra

3. SPECIAL CLASSIFICATIONS
- Appointment Notices — Photocomp prints acceptable. Glossy photos preferred. Appointment Notices will carry the word ''Appointment'' or ''Announcement'' at the top. Mon-Fri $7.42 . . . Sat. 20% extra
- Career Advtg. 1 insertion   Mon-Fri $2.84   Sat. 20% extra
  2 insertions   Mon-Fri $2.64   Sat. 20% extra
  3 insertions   Mon-Fri $2.44   Sat. 20% extra
- Legal Notices — Mon-Fri $2.84, Sat. 20% extra
- Resort & Travel Area rates available upon request.
- Dividends — financial premium applies
- Marine advertising published each Monday in The Gazette and also in the special Marine News mailer to over 12,000 importers, exporters and traffic managers every week. Rates available upon request.
- TV Times — Full-color offset magazine every Saturday. Flat rates for regular advertising units. Separate rate card available on request.
- Flexform Advertising. Charged at maximum depth of advertisement by 9 columns. Page exclusivity not included. Minimum size 810 lines.
- Reader Advertisements — carried under a double cut-off rule and marked ''Advt.'' Double applicable rate.
- Stand-by advertising — rates and requirements available upon request.
- Gatefold advertising — rates and requirements available upon request.

4. POSITION CHARGES & REQUIREMENTS (when available)
- No advertising on Front Page or Editorial pages. Mon-Sat.

	Widths	Line Depths	Premium
Page 2	3 & 6 col ads	min 100/max 150	25%
Page 3	3& 6 col ads	min 40/max 80	50%
Page 4	2 col ads min	min 50	25%
Pages 5-7-9	3 col ads min	min 100	25%

- Break pages (Sports, Business, Living, Entertainment — Mon-Fri)
  3 & 6 col ads   100 lines only   50%
- Other breaks — (Mon-Fri)
  4 to 9 cols   min 100/max 175   50%
- Saturday Breaks (except Weekly Review and Classified)
  6 cols   125 lines   50%
- Weekly Review (selected pages)
  6 cols   125 lines   50%
  9 cols   30 lines   50%
- Adjacency advertising — subject to editorial approval — 25% premium

5. COLOR ADVERTISING
- Available daily — 600 lines minimum, subject to confirmation.

B/W 1c	Mon-Fri	$1232	Sat. 20% extra
B/W 2c	Mon-Fri	$1484	Sat. 20% extra
B/W 3c	Mon-Fri	$1728	Sat. 20% extra

- Double truck: Appropriate color charge for each page used

6. SATURDAY COLOR COMIC ADVERTISING

	1 Time	6 Times	13 Times	26 Times	52 Times
Full page	$1140	$1083	$1026	$969	$912
½ page	684	656	627	599	570

- Full color included
- Mechanical and material requirements on request.

7. MINIMUM & MAXIMUM PAGE REQUIREMENTS
- Minimum depth 10 agate lines per column crossed. Advertisments ordered 280 lines or more in depth must occupy full column (310 lines).
- Tabloid: 165 agate line or more in depth must occupy full column (193 lines).
- Banner Advertising — Full width advertisements accepted, minimum depth 30 lines.

8. COPY & RESERVATION DEADLINES

	RESERVATIONS. CAMERA READY MATERIAL & COPY — NO PROOFS	COPY FOR PROOFS (MINIMUM 200 LINES)
• (Black & White)		
Monday	Fri - Noon	Wed -5 P.M.
Tuesday	Fri - 3 P.M.	Thurs - 5 P.M.
Wednesday	Mon - Noon	Fri - 5 P.M.
Thursday	Tues - Noon	Mon - 5 P.M.
Friday	Wed - Noon	Tues - 5 P.M.
Saturday	Thurs - Noon	Wed - 5 P.M.
• Travel Pages (Sat)	Wed - Noon	Tues - Noon
• Color Ads (Mon)	Thurs - Noon	Wed - 5 P.M.
• Color Ads (Tues-Sat)	3 Weekdays prior - Noon	4 Weekdays prior - Noon
• Flexform	3 Weekdays prior - Noon	4 Weekdays prior - 5 P.M.
• Double Trucks	3 Weekdays prior - Noon	4 Weekdays prior - 5 P.M.
• Color Comics	6 Weeks prior	

	RESERVATIONS	CAMERA READY MATERIAL & COPY — NO PROOFS	COPY FOR PROOFS (MIN. 200 LINES)
• Book & Art pages (Sat)	Wed - 5 P.M.	Thurs - Noon	Wed - 5 P.M.
• Restaurant pages (Fri)	Tues - 5 P.M.	Wed - Noon	Tues - 5 P.M.
• Marine News	Wed - 4 P.M.	Wed - 5 P.M.	Wed - 2 P.M.
• TV/Times	2½ wks prior	1½wks prior	2 wks prior
• Wednesday preprint	Fri - 5 P.M.	Mon - Noon	Thurs - 5 P.M.

- Inserts — Reservations — 2 weeks prior
  — Delivery for Sat. Insertion 8 weekdays prior
  — Delivery for weekday insertion — 5 weekdays prior
- Special Sections & Features — Deadlines available on request

9. MECHANICAL REQUIREMENTS
- Mechanical requirements of The Gazette are subject to change without notice.
- 9 cols per page — column width 8.4 ems.
- All advertisements set in photocomposition.
- Half-tone screen — 55.
- Printing process: Letterpress.
- Material Requirements — Black/White, Black/1 Color
  Material acceptable in the form of:
  1. Photocomp Prints (Velox Prints)
     Min. Diam. of Hi Lite Dot .... .0055''
     Min. Diam. of Shadow Dot .... .0085''
     Min. Diam. of Line Copy .... .0045''
  2. Repro Proofs on mat finish stock using heat dry inks
     Min. Diam. of Hi Line Dot .... .007''
     Min. Diam. of Shadow Dot .... .010''
     Min. Diam. of Line Copy .... .005''
  3. Negative film acceptable as complete copy providing it conforms to the following:
     Wrong reading with mat finish on emulsion side
     Min. Diam. of Hi Line Dot .... .005''
     Min. Diam. of Shadow Dot .... .008''
     Min. Diam. of Line Copy .... .004''
- Material Requirements — Black/2 Colors, Black/3 colors
  Minimum dot and line dimensions as above.
  For color material — photocomp negative on 20'' x 24'' film. To be same size as printed — full page 13¾'' wide x 22⅛'' deep. Partial page prepositioned to lower right-hand corner of 20'' x 24'' film, register marks in bearer area. Preferred film Dupont CLN II with right reading from emulsion side.
- For unregistered black material, photocomp print (velox) to make-up column width and depth shown in Mechanical Make-Up Requirements. Treat black as color if registered to another color.
- Acceptable: Photocomp prints (velox) for all color material to make-up column width and depth shown in Mechanical Make-Up Requirements.

FIGURE 5.2   General Rate Card for a Newspaper

Courtesy The Montreal *Gazette*

- One set of progressive proofs (preferred) or color keys to accompany material for process color advertising.
- Full page direct cast mats not acceptable.
- CDNPA Group #5.
- MAXIMUM WIDTHS FOR ALL MATERIAL

	Regular	Tabloid
1 column	1⅜''	1⅜''
2 ''	2 15/16''	2 15/16''
3 ''	4 7/16''	4 7/16''
4 ''	6''	6''
5 ''	7½''	7½''
6 ''	9 1/16''	9 1/16''
7 ''	10⅝''	10⅝''
8 ''	12 3/16''	
9 ''	13¾''	
Double Truck —	28¼''	22⅛''

Minimum 1500 lines. Use above column widths. Measure gutter column at ¾''.

10. TERMS OF PAYMENT
- Invoices payable 20 days after billing date. Agency commission 15% and cash discount 2% allowed only to advertising agencies as defined by the CDNPA.
- The publisher reserves the right to apply interest on overdue accounts at the rate of 1½% per month (18% per annum).

11. MISCELLANEOUS
a. The publisher reserves the right to increase the rate stipulated herein at any time upon notice in writing to the advertiser or his agent. The advertiser reserves the right to cancel at any date upon which the higher rates are made effective by the publisher. Furthermore, should publication of this paper be restricted or curtailed in any way, the rate quoted herein and the amount of space contracted for, as well as the size, location and volume of the advertisements, shall all be subject to revision or regulation by the publisher at any time without notice.
b. All advertising subject to publisher's approval. The publisher reserves the right to reject, discontinue or omit any advertisement, or to cancel any advertising contract for reasons satisfactory to the publisher without notice and without penalty to either party. The publisher reserves the option to insert the word ''advertisement'' above or below any copy. All advertising subject to Federal and Provincial Government regulations.
c. No contract made for a period exceeding 12 months.
d. Advertising instructions and/or information not in accordance with the current rate card will be regarded as a clerical error and any advertising will be billed at the rate in force.
e. All contracts are subject to the approval and written acceptance of the publisher or his appointed representative. The publisher shall not be bound by any stipulations or conditions other than those set out in contracts and evidenced by the signatures of the parties.
f. All telephone orders and cancellations must be confirmed in writing. Advertisements cancelled after reservation deadlines will be charged at full rate.

g. Failure to receive copies of The Gazette containing advertisements will not be considered reason to delay payment. Tearsheets for advertisements under 200 lines placed within the Census Metropolitan Area will not be mailed. Advertisers requiring tearsheets may pick them up at The Gazette Advertising Department, 250 St. Antoine St. W., Montreal.
h. Advertisements set and not used will be charged at $35. per hour (min. $35.).
i. The advertiser agrees that the publisher shall not be liable for any damages whatsoever arising from errors in advertisements beyond the actual amount paid for the space used by the part of the advertisement containing the error. Notice of such error is required before second insertion. The publisher shall not be liable for non-insertion of any advertisement.
j. All property rights, including copyright in the advertisement, shall be vested in and shall be the property of the newspaper. No such advertisement or any part thereof may be reproduced without the prior written consent of the newspaper.
k. Contest advertising shall include the publication of results.
l. Contingent orders not accepted.
m. Setting of key numbers not guaranteed.
n. Material sent collect or on which customs or excise taxes are charged, will be charged back to the client at our cost.

12. PRE-PRINTED INSERTS
Separate rate card available on request. Selective zone coverage available.

13. HI-FI, SPECTACOLOR
Not available.

14. REGULAR FEATURES & SECTIONS
List of features available on request. Reservations and material 7 days before insertion.

15. TIME AND DELIVERY OF PAPER
Mornings, Monday to Saturday.

16. CREATIVE SERVICES
Layout and copy services available at no extra charge. Charges for special artwork.

17. MASTHEAD SPOTS (earlugs)

	Front Page		Finance		Other Sections	
	Mon-Fri	Sat	Mon-Fri	Sat	Mon-Fri	Sat
13 wks	$284	$342	$213	$257	$171	$206
26 wks	$248	$298	$191	$230	$157	$189
52 wks	$199	$239	$163	$197	$142	$170

(position availabilities on request — non-cancellable).
Masthead spots — maximum size 2¾'' wide by 19 lines deep.

18. CLASSIFIED ADVERTISING
- General Advertising in Classified section — General Advertising rates apply.
- Classified Advertising format — 10 columns.

FIGURE 5.2 (continued)

National advertisers pay a higher rate than local advertisers, who are the daily newspapers' best customers. National advertisers have often argued against the dual rate structure. Newspaper publishers point to the higher costs involved in servicing national advertisers, including the 15 per cent commission paid to the advertising agency and the commission paid to media representatives.

Newspaper Advertising Rate Structures

Advertising rates depend on the nature of the advertising and the additional services requested of newspapers. There are three basic types of advertising rates for newspapers: general (or national) rates, retail (or local) rates, and classi-

fied rates. Information on rates and data about each type of advertising is available from each newspaper in the form of a *rate card*. Rates and data of interest to national advertisers are available in *Canadian Advertising Rates and Data (CARD)*.

General or *national* advertising is placed by an advertising agency and is subject to the traditional 15 per cent commission as well as cash discounts. Newspapers may also use the services of media representatives, who sell advertising space to agencies for a commission. For these reasons, general advertising rates exceed retail rates by about 50 per cent. Around 20 per cent of newspapers' net advertising revenues come from national advertising. The general rate card for the *Gazette* is reproduced in Figure 5.2. The types of rates and

The figure contains the following CARD listing information:

N0960

The Gazette

Member
CDNPA

A Southam Newspaper

Data confirmed for May/83 CARD

Est. 1778. Morn. ex. Sun.
Publishers: The Gazette Montreal/Montréal Limitée, 250 St. Antoine W., Montreal H2Y 3R7. Phone: 514-282-2750. Tlx.: 055-617-67.

CLOSING DATES
Regular page: b&w noon 2 days pre.; noon Fri. pre. for Mon. & Tues. If proof required, material & reservations 3 working days pre.
Travel pages (Sat.) noon Thurs.; book & art pages (Sat.) 5 p.m. Wed.; restaurant pages (Fri.) 5 p.m. Tues.; double truck: 3 days pre.
Color: Tues.-Sat. b& 1c, b & 2c, b & 3c: 3 weekdays pre. Thurs. for Mon. ed.
Special sections: 7 days pre. for reservations & mat'l.

COMMISSION & CASH DISCOUNT
15%; 2% 20th fol. mo.

GENERAL ADVERTISING
Rate Card No. 45. Effective Jan. 1, 1983.

LINE RATE:	M-F	Sat.
Transient		2.84)
Volume contracts:		
2,500 lines	2.62)	20%
5,000 lines	2.59)	extra
10,000 lines	2.57)	
25,000 lines	2.53)	
50,000 lines	2.48)	

Financial pages 10% extra.
Noncontract advtg. ordered for 3 or more insertions at the same time within 30-day period without copy change, Mon. to Fri. 2.73; Sat. 20% extra.
Contract & copy regulations subject to publisher's individual rate card.

COLOR	B/1c	B/2c	B/3c
M-F	$1232	$1484	$1728

Sat. 20% extra. Min. 600 lines.
Dbl. truck: appropriate color charge for each page used. Min. 1,500 lines overall.
MASTHEAD SPOTS (earlugs): noncancellable;

max. size 2-3/4 x 19 lines.

No. wks. (consec.)	13	26	52
	M-F	M-F	M-F
Front page	$284	$248	$199
Finance	213	191	163
Other sections	171	157	142
	Sat.	Sat.	Sat.
Front page	$342	$298	$239
Finance	257	230	197
Other sections	206	189	170

Max. size: 2-3/4 x 19.
Preprints: free standing—rates on request. Spectacolor & hi-fi roll-fed not available.
TV/TIMES—See Consumer Magazine Section.

SAT. COLOR COMIC BOOK ADVTG.

	1 ti.	6 ti.	13 ti.	26 ti.	52 ti.
1 page	$1140	$1083	$1026	$969	$912
1/2 page	684	656	627	599	570

Closing 6 weeks pre. Mechanical & material requirements—on request.

CLASSIFICATIONS
Appt. notices: photocomp prints acceptable. Glossy photos preferred.
Appt. notices will carry word "Appointment" or "Announcement" at top.
Mon.-Fri. 7.42; Sat. 20% extra.
Career advtg.: 1 insertion 2.84, 2 insertions 2.64, 3 insertions 2.44 (Mon.-Fri.); Sat. 20% extra.
Legal notices: Mon.-Fri. 2.84; Sat. 20% extra.
Resort & travel area rates on request.
Dividends: fin'l premium applies.
TV/Times: full-color offset magazine every Sat.—rates on request.
Stand-by & gatefold advtg.: rates & requirements on request.
Reader ads (carried under dbl. cutoff rule & marked "advt."). Dbl. rates apply.

FLEXFORM ADVERTISING
Charged at min. depth of ad by 9 cols. Page exclusivity not included. Min. size 810 lines.
Color add'l. Reservations 3 weekdays pre. Noncancellable.

POSITION CHARGES
(When available). No advtg. on front page or edit'l pages. Mon.-Sat.
Page 2, 3 & 6 col. ads, min. 100/max. 150 lines, extra 25%.
Page 3, 3 & 6 col. ads, min. 40/max. 80 lines, extra 50%.
Page 4, 2 col. ads min., min. 50 lines, extra 25%.
Pages 5-7-9, 3 col. ads min., min. 100 lines, extra 25%.

Break pages (Sports, Business, Living, Entertainment), Mon.-Fri., 3 & 6 col. ads, 100 lines only, extra 50%.
Other breaks (Mon.-Fri.), 4 to 9 cols., min. 100/max. 175 lines, extra 50%.
Sat. breaks (except Weekly Review & Classified), 6 cols., 125 lines, extra 50%.
Weekly Review (selected pages): 6 cols., 125 lines, extra 50%; 9 cols., 30 lines, extra 50%.
Adjacency advtg.: subject to edit'l approval, extra 25%.

MINIMUM & MAXIMUM REQUIREMENTS
Min. 14 lines.
10 lines for each col. crossed banner advts. accepted—min. 30 x 9 cols.; advts. exceeding 280 lines deep charged as full col.

MECHANICAL REQUIREMENTS
Printed space: 13 x 22-1/8.
Col. width: 8 ems. Depth: 310 lines.
No. of cols. 9.
Halftone screen: 55.
Advts. set photocomposition.
B&w, blk. & 1 color material: photocomp prints (Velox); repro proofs, negative film.
Full page direct cast mats not acceptable.

PERSONNEL
Pubr.: Robert McConnell.
Adv. Dir.: Bruce Stevenson.
Class Adv. Mgr.: James Thivierge.
Nat. Adv. Mgr.: Grant Crosbie.
Ret. Adv. Mgr.: J. T. Arklay.

BRANCH OFFICES/REPRESENTATIVES
Southam Newspapers:
Toronto M5S 2Y9: Clarence C. Heringer, Ste. 905, 150 Bloor St. W. Phone: 416-927-1877.
Vancouver V6B 3E4: Vernon J. Rumford, Media Representatives Ltd., Suite 16, 1035 Richards St. Phone: 604-669-0014.
New York 10022: Harvey Grotsky, #1402, 509 Madison Ave. Phone: 212-751-8412.
Florida & Caribbean: Hollywood, Fla. 33022, Hal Herman Associates Inc., P.O. Box 2226. Phone: 305-929-1956.
Mexico D. F.: 11500: Towmar Representaciones, Presa de la Angostura 8. Phone: 533-1596.

CIRCULATION
A.B.C. 30-9-82 pub. state.

Total:	Morn.	Sat.
City zone	166,454	217,815
Retail trading zone	16,691	29,253
All other	20,340	29,976
Paid excl. bulk	203,485	277,044

FIGURE 5.3 *CARD* Listing for a Newspaper

SOURCE: *Canadian Advertising Rates and Data* (1983), pp. 21, 23. *Courtesy* Special Interest Network

data available in *CARD* for a newspaper are shown in Figure 5.3. In 1983 the rate for a 1000-line black and white advertisement in a weekday edition of the *Gazette* was $2,840. A full-page advertisement cost $7,310. In addition, Figure 5.3 shows the special rates for special classifications of advertising: tender and legal notices, notices of redemption, career advertising, marine advertising, and reader advertisement. The latter classification uses the same type as for editorial matter and is marked "advertisement" at the top in order to identify it as such to the reader.

Retail (or *local*) advertising is placed directly by a retail store and is not commissionable. As mentioned before, the retail rates may be much lower than the general advertising rate. The retail rate card for the *Gazette* shown in Figure 5.4 can be compared with Figures 5.2 and 5.3. In 1983 the same advertisement mentioned

in the previous example cost a retailer $1,770; a full page advertisement cost $4,543.

Retailers provide newspapers with about 54 per cent of net advertising revenues (excluding classified advertising). Newspapers may be the best medium for retailers in terms of costs, timing, product presentation, and market coverage. Newspapers offer retailers assistance in designing their advertising creative and in selecting the size of the advertisement, the layout, and the illustrations.

Classified advertising may be placed by individuals or firms and is grouped according to various categories. Classified advertising rates are non-commissionable, except for general advertising placed by advertising agencies that is in regular or display classified style. Newspapers derive about 26 per cent of their net advertising revenues from this source.

The Gazette

A Division of Southam Inc.
C.P./P.O. Box 4300, Place d'Armes, Montréal, Qué. H2Y 3S1
Tel: (514) 282-2750   Telex: 055-61767
MEMBER: CDNPA, NAB, NMB, ABC, ACTA
Published Daily (M) — Except Sunday

**RETAIL
RATE CARD
NO. 44**

Effective
January 1, 1983

1. RETAIL DISPLAY ADVERTISING

		Mon./ Fri.	Sat.
Transient	per line	2.84	+ 20%
1,000 lines	per line	1.77	+ 20%
3,000 lines	per line	1.72	+ 20%
5,000 lines	per line	1.67	+ 20%
10,000 lines	per line	1.65	+ 20%
20,000 lines	per line	1.62	+ 20%
35,000 lines	per line	1.58	+ 20%
60,000 lines	per line	1.55	+ 20%
100,000 lines	per line	1.53	+ 20%
145,000 lines	per line	1.52	+ 20%
250,000 lines	per line	1.49	+ 20%
400,000 lines	per line	1.44	+ 20%
550,000 lines	per line	1.43	+ 20%
750,000 lines	per line	1.42	+ 20%
1,000,000 lines	per line	1.41	+ 20%
1,500,000 lines	per line	1.35	+ 20%
1,750,000 lines	per line	1.34	+ 20%
2,000,000 lines	per line	1.32	+ 20%

DISCOUNTS: Full page 8%; 150 lines & over x 9 columns 5%
Minimum space, display — 10 agate lines for each column crossed.

2. SPECIAL CLASSIFICATIONS

Religious services in Metropolitan Montreal
churches and synagogues appearing on
religion page   80¢ per line

Fund raising activities by
Metropolitan Montreal charitable
organizations   Mon./Fri. $1.02 per line   Sat. + 20%

Community and cultural organizations
which primarily serve
Metropolitan Montreal   Mon./Fri. $1.19 per line   Sat. + 20%

Political (& Para Political) organizations   See General Rate Card

Hookers   Mon./Fri. $20.00   Sat. + 20%

Appointment Notices   See General Rate Card

Business/Finance pages at 25% premium

Reader Advertisements   Double Retail Rate
(Carried under double cut-off rule and marked "Advt.")

Flexform Advertising
Charged at maximum depth of advertisement by 9 columns.
Page exclusivity not included. Minimum size 810 lines.

MASTHEAD SPOTS (Earlugs)

	Front Page		Finance		Other Sections	
	Mon./Fri.	Sat.	Mon./Fri.	Sat.	Mon./Fri.	Sat.
13 wks	$243	$292	$187	$224	$151	$181
26 wks	$215	$257	$164	$197	$135	$162
52 wks	$172	$206	$143	$172	$122	$146

(Position availabilities on request — non-cancellable)
Maximum size — 2¾'' wide by 19 lines deep.

SATURDAY COLOR COMIC ADVERTISING

Regular Saturday rates apply
Technical & Material requirements — on request
Closing date — 6 weeks in advance of issue date

TV TIMES

Full Color offset magazine every Saturday. Flat rates for regular
advertising units. Separate rate card available on request.

INSERTS

Separate rate card available on request.

3. POSITION

No advertising on first or editorial page. Page 3, break pages and
weekly review pages — 50% extra (when available). All other guaranteed positions — 25% extra. Additional information relating to
minimum/maximum ad size requirements on request.

4. COLOUR ADVERTISING

Minimum space — 600 lines

B/W 1 colour	$1,047	Sat. + 20%
B/W 2 colours	$1,196	Sat. + 20%
B/W 3 colours	$1,495	Sat. + 20%

One set of progressive proofs (preferred) or colour keys required for
process colour advertising.

Double truck: appropriate colour charge for each page used.
Gutter charged as extra column. Minimum 1,500 lines overall.

5. RESERVATIONS AND CLOSING

Traval pages: (Sat. insertion) 12 noon Wednesday
Art & Book pages (Sat. insertion) 5 P.M. Wednesday
Restaurant pages (Fri. insertion) 12 noon wednesday
Special sections: Reservations & Copy: 7 days before insertion
Regular paper: B/W advertising: 12 noon 2 days before insertion for
all material & copy; 3 working days before insertion if proofs re-
quired. (No proofs on advts. 200 lines or less.
For Monday issue: 12 noon Friday preceeding
For Tuesday issue: 3 P.M. Friday preceeding
Excessive copy changes or advertising copy set and not scheduled
will be charged at $40 per hour (min. $40).
Flexform Advertising: 4 days preceeding, non cancellable
Colour Advertising: B/1c — 3 working days before insertion for
order and material, non cancellable. B/2c-B/3c — 5 working days
before insertion for order and material, non cancellable.
Double Truck advertising — reservations and complete material 3
working days/non cancellable.

6. MECHANICAL REQUIREMENTS

Column width 1⅜' — depth 310 lines. Full page type space. 13¾'
x 22⅛'' — 9 cols. to a page. Half tone screen required — 55.
Double Truck material — minimum 1,500 lines overall. Normal
column widths apply to either page of a double truck. The gutter
space charged as an extra column, measures ¾'' or 4.5 picas.
Appropriate colour charge for each page used.
Any advertisement in excess of 280 lines will be given full depth of
column (310 lines) and charged accordingly. The mechanical requirements of The Gazette are subject to change without notice.
Material not claimed or used during a period of 4 months will be
destroyed at the option of the publisher.

7. TERMS OF PAYMENT

Invoices payable 30 days after billing date. The publisher reserves
the right to apply interest on overdue accounts at the rate of 1½%
per month (18% per annum).

8. MISCELLANEOUS

(a) The publisher reserves the right to increase the rates stipulated
herein at any time. The Advertiser reserves the right to cancel at
any time upon which higher rates are made effective by the
publisher. Furthermore, should publication of this paper be
restricted or curtailed in any way, the rate quoted herein and the
amount of space contracted for, as well as the size, location and
volume of the advertisements, shall be subject to revision or
regulation by the publisher at any time without notice.

(b) All advertising subject to publisher's approval. The publisher reserves the right to reject, discontinue or omit any advertisement, or to cancel any advertising contract for reasons satisfactory to the publisher without notice and without penalty to either
party. The publisher reserves the option to insert the word
"Advertisement" above or below any copy.

(c) All property rights, including copyright in the advertisement,
shall be vested in and be the property of the newspaper. No such
advertisement or any part thereof may be reproduced without
the prior written consent of the newspaper.

(d) No contract made for a period exceeding 12 months.

(e) Contest advertising shall include the publication of results.

(f) Tearsheets for advertisements under 300 lines placed within the
Census Metropolitan Area will not be mailed. Advertisers
requiring tearsheets may pick them up at The Gazette Advertising Department, 250 St. Antoine St. W., Montreal

(g) The advertiser agrees that the publisher shall not be liable for
any damages whatsoever arising from errors in advertisements
beyond actual amount paid for space used by that part of the
advertisment containing the error. Notice of such error is
required before second insertion. The publisher shall not be
liable for non-insertion of any advertisement.

(h) Contingent orders not accepted.

(i) Advertising instructions and/or information not in accordance
with the current rate card will be regarded as a clerical error and
any advertising will be billed at the rate in force.

ROBERT McCONNELL
Publisher

T. BRUCE STEVENSON
Advertising Director

JAMES T. ARKLAY
Sales Manager Retail Advertising

FIGURE 5.4   Retail Rate Card for a Newspaper

Courtesy The Montreal *Gazette*

Future of Newspapers as an Advertising Medium

As we have seen, the nature of newspapers has changed considerably over the past century and will likely evolve further as market conditions change and new technologies are implemented.

Newspapers have benefited greatly from the development of such technologies as offset printing and its superior reproduction quality, particularly for colour reproduction. The communications industry is one of the biggest users of computers in Canada and is rapidly adopting word processors, satellite transmission, fibre optics, and lasers.[18] Thus, the quality of newspapers will continue to improve.

Newspapers are strengthening their *market orientation* by better tailoring their content to readers' local interests and specific needs. They are improving their research capabilities and establishing data-bases on their audiences. Up-to-date and comprehensive information is essential to media buyers and should encourage greater use of newspaper advertising in national campaigns.[19]

In their role as a *communication* medium, newspapers will provide more information retrieval services, such as Southam/Torstar's Infomart or the *Globe and Mail*'s InfoGlobe. Such home-delivery information systems as videotex are still a few years away from the high penetration rate necessary for affordable advertising, but several forms of electronic publishing, especially the "electronic newspaper", are on the horizon. The impact of these developments on advertising revenues is difficult to estimate and depends on two factors:

How people will allocate their time among the various media; in particular, how much time they will spend reading newspapers.

How advertisers will allocate their advertising dollars among the growing number of media, particularly if the total media demand is not very elastic.[20]

Consumer Magazines

Consumer magazines are issued periodically and are intended for the ultimate consumers of retail goods and services. As an advertising medium, consumer magazines have experienced growth and have been able to adapt to advertisers' changing needs and to competition from other media.

Growth of Consumer Magazines as an Advertising Medium

In Canada and in the United States consumer magazines started as literary publications aimed at highly educated readers. Because Canada's population is so small and scattered, publishers had enormous financial difficulties and came to rely on advertising as a major source of revenue. Between 1833 and 1893, more than eighteen magazines appeared in Ontario; many of them survived only one to three years. The *Canadian Monthly* (1872) and the *New Dominion Monthly* (1867) lasted ten and eleven years, respectively. A French magazine, *Le Samedi*, founded in 1889, lasted more than fifty years.[21]

To survive, many literary magazines were forced to broaden their appeal or become more specialized. Even so, such magazines as *Canadian Magazine* (1893) was forced to cease publication.[22] Despite these difficulties, the number and circulation of magazines kept growing, and at a much faster rate since the early seventies. In 1982, there were about 390 consumer magazines with an average combined circulation of 27 million. This compares with 190 magazines in 1971 with an average combined issue circulation of 10 million.[23]

In addition to the difficulties of dealing with a small and sparsely distributed population and bilingualism, Canadian consumer magazines have had to withstand competition from U.S. magazines, which have used the Canadian market to extend their circulation and thus their advertising revenues. Canadian magazines, however, could not hope to penetrate the U.S. market to add to their already small Canadian-based circulation. In 1981, there were about 375 U.S. consumer magazines distributed in Canada, with an average combined issue circulation of eight million. This competition forced Canadian magazines to focus on Canadian concerns in terms of editorial policy. This strategy proved to benefit the industry greatly, as evidenced by the growth in numbers, circulation, and net advertising revenues. For 1982, Table 5.1 shows that the advertising revenues of consumer magazines reached $233 million. Their share of total *national* net advertising revenues among four media (consumer magazines, daily newspapers, radio, and television) reached 19.7 per cent,[24] compared with $87.6 million in revenues and a 16.9 per cent market share in 1976.[25]

The evolution of consumer magazines also resulted from competition from the other information and entertainment media—film, radio, and television. Radio forced some magazines to adopt the weekly news format, with narrative and photographs. Television pushed magazines into more audience specialization, with specific interests appealing to both readers and advertisers. Thus, one finds magazines on soccer, photography, nature, stamp collectors, vintage vehicles collectors, the military, and secretaries.[26] In effect, magazines have reacted to the threat of television by targeting markets, thereby offering advertisers a means to reach very specific audiences and to complement the coverage provided by television.

Various associations have played an active role in promoting magazines as a medium: Magazines Canada (The Magazine Association of Canada), the Canadian Periodical Publishers' Association (CPPA), the Magazine Publishers Association (MPA), and the Periodical Publishers Exchange (PPE).

Differences among Consumer Magazines

Like newspapers, magazines have various formats, frequencies of publication, editorial policies, circulation bases, and offer different types of special services to advertisers.

Format
Canadian magazines are published in formats ranging from the pocket size (14 × 19 cm) of the *Readers' Digest*, to the standard size (21 × 28 cm) of *Time* or *Chatelaine*, to larger sizes such as for *Decormag* (23 × 30 cm). Advertisements that are to appear in several magazines should be adapted to these sizes.

Frequency of Publication
Magazines vary greatly in frequency of publication, ranging from weekly magazines to quarterly magazines. About 28 per cent of consumer magazines are published monthly, 15 per cent are published bi-monthly, 17 per cent quarterly, 13 per cent weekly, and 11 per cent are published 10-11 times a year.[27] Frequency is an important consideration for advertisers concerned about message repetition, or for advertisers who are planning a new product introduction or promoting products whose sales are influenced by seasonal factors.

Editorial Policy
As was seen, magazines have developed editorial appeal *vertically*, i.e., by targeting a more or less narrowly defined audience. The thirty-two categories of consumer magazines listed in *CARD* in 1983 are provided in Table 5.2 according to distribution of titles. The most important group of magazines is "general editorial", with fifty-one titles. In this category one finds such diverse publications as *Canadian Geographic*, *Presbyterian Record*, and *Readers' Digest*. Other important categories are sports and recreation (49 titles), television and radio (32 titles), entertainment and shopping guides (36 titles), and women's magazines (22 titles). Their range of

editorial content and specific target market combined with high reader interest makes magazines an attractive advertising medium.

Circulation Base

Magazines may be classified into three categories according to their type of circulation: traditional, controlled circulation, and special interest.

Traditional magazines are the broad circulation magazines bought by subscription or on a newsstand, for example, *Chatelaine* or *Canadian Geographic.* Most of these magazines' circulation is from subscription. They are generally well established, with high prestige for advertisers.

Traditional magazines have maintained their circulation and volume of advertising revenues. In 1979, they represented 32 per cent of all magazines and 46 per cent of total circulation. Most of them are audited by the Audit Bureau of Circulation (ABC) and the Canadian Circulation Audit Board (CCAB).

Controlled circulation magazines are distributed without charge to a specific group of readers selected according to socio-demographic and economic variables, e.g., young apartment dwellers in downtown Montreal or Calgary. The first such magazines were the weekend newspaper magazine supplements (also called roto publications or rotogravures), which were introduced in 1951. *Homemaker's* and *Madame au Foyer* were controlled circulation magazines introduced in 1966 to selected groups of women. These magazines used research to prove to advertisers that they could not only provide efficient target group reach but also high readership levels.

Controlled circulation magazines is the fastest-growing category; in 1979, they represented 30 per cent of all magazines and of total circulation. This growth is largely responsible for the increase of household consumption of magazines from 69 per year in 1952 to 96 in 1979.[28]

Special interest magazines form the third category, and they also represent a fast-

TABLE 5.2 Types and Number of Consumer Magazines in Canada

Classification	Number of consumer magazines
Almanacs & directories	7
Animals	13
Arts	20
Automobile, cycle, & traffic	17
Babies & mothers	7
Boating & yachting	10
Brides	3
Comics	1
City magazines	36
Entertainment & shopping guides	13
Fishing & hunting	16
Food & beverage	6
Fraternal service clubs, associations	10
General editorial	51
Health	3
Hobbies	22
Homes	17
Labour	1
Men's	3
Military	1
Music	6
Nature	3
News	5
Photography	4
Political	3
Science	1
Social welfare	4
Sports & recreation	49
TV & radio	32
Travel & touring	22
Veterans	1
Women's	22
Youth	7
Total	*416*

SOURCE: Developed from *Canadian Advertising Rates and Data* (1983), p. 73.
Courtesy Special Interest Network

growing segment. Their average circulation is between 20 000 and 25 000 copies. There are more than 100 special interest magazines, among them *Bon Vivant, Artscanada, Hockey News,* and *The Atlantic Salmon Journal.* Of the three groups of magazines, they have the most selective audience and the most specific editorial environment, along with high reader interest.

Additional Services Offered by Consumer Magazines

COLOUR. In addition to excellent colour reproduction, some magazines offer five or more colours, instead of the traditional four, and metallic inks, which create striking effects. As printing technology improves, magazines will likely be the first to use the new processes.

BLEED PAGES. Bleed pages are printed to the edge of the paper; there is no margin whatsoever. They give advertisements a contemporary look and allow for special effects.

FREE FORM. This service, also called *flex-form*, allows creative directors to use an abstract form to contain the advertisement, subject to the magazine's mechanical requirements. The magazine runs editorial matter around the free-form advertisement. *Checkerboards* are a simple example of free-form: advertisements are made up of squares set up in the form of a checkerboard with alternating advertising and editorial material.

GATEFOLDS. Gatefolds are pages that fold out from a two-page spread advertisement. They are especially useful when an advertiser has lengthy copy or wants to make an impact by being the dominant advertiser in a magazine. Because they are physically different from the others, gatefolds are usually noticed by readers. Gatefolds are often used as an extension of the front or back covers of magazines.

SPECIAL POSITIONS. Most magazines offer two types of special positions: covers and guaranteed positions. (Magazines usually try to accommodate, without additional charges, the wishes of advertisers who have special positions.) These are often called *preferred* positions.

Covers. Of the four covers of a magazine, three are available for advertisements. The most expensive one is usually the back cover.

The second and third covers may be charged the same rate but at a premium to the four-colour page rate. For example, in 1983 the rate for the second and third covers (four colours) of *Maclean's* was $18,320. For the fourth cover it was $20,080, while the rate for one page, four colours, was $16,060.[29]

Guaranteed positions. These may be offered at a premium and are useful whenever the effectiveness of the advertisement may be enhanced by the proper editorial environment; for example, an advertisement for an album by a rock group next to a story on that group.

INSERTS. These may be supplied either by the advertiser or by the magazine. Inserts command more attention, because they may be printed on thicker paper, or appeal to the senses (e.g., smell, touch), or offer samples, or have a tear-off or cut-off postal card.

SPLIT RUNS. Some consumer magazines reproduce different advertisements in alternate copies of the magazine. This service allows the advertiser to test two creative approaches for their effectiveness on two matched samples.

REGIONAL EDITIONS. Consumer magazines may also offer some regional editions, thus offering more flexibility to advertisers.[30] *Chatelaine* with 19 editions and *Readers' Digest* with 18 editions offer the best market flexibility. Others include *Homemaker's*, *Maclean's*, and *TV Guide*.

Magazines as an Advertising Medium

The main *advantages* of magazines can be grouped into four categories:

High selectivity. By carefully selecting the appropriate magazines, advertisers can reach a target with minimal waste circulation, especially if the target is narrowly defined. Examples of magazines with narrow targets are shown in Figure 5.5.

Since magazines are mostly a national medium, the coverage of the target group is

FIGURE 5.5 Sometimes advertisers can obtain the best results by advertising in special interest magazines like those shown here.

Courtesy Moorshead Publications; Reprinted with permission, from CA Magazine (November 1983), published by the Canadian Institute of Chartered Accountants; The Canadian Booksellers Association.

presented on a *national* basis. Regional editions of magazines allow advertisers the flexibility to adjust for regional differences in product distribution and market penetration.

The wealth of information on magazine readers, their consumption patterns, and lifestyles is extremely useful to advertisers. Magazines understood very early the value of research as a tool for competing with other media. Starch Readership Studies and Print Measurement Bureau (PMB) studies have been largely sponsored by magazines and have helped magazines grow by convincing advertisers of magazine advertising's effectiveness

(Figure 5.6). These studies are described in detail in Chapter 15.

A high-quality medium. Magazines are a high-quality medium. The quality of *colour reproduction* of magazines is unsurpassed by newspapers or television, thus allowing advertisers to create a certain mood, present food and beverages in an appealing manner, build a prestigious image, or attract attention and interest by a dramatic use of colour. When combined with appropriate editorial content, colour advertisements are well read, since magazines' believability, authority, and prestige are often extended to advertisements. In addition, the editorial content stimulates the reader's information gathering, and advertisements are one readily available source of information. Finally, advertising in prestigious magazines enhances the advertiser's image in the eyes of both customers and distributors.

A durable medium. Magazines have a long life and may be read several times by one reader. Thus one advertisement may have been noticed several times. A study based on 39 consumer magazines shows that on the average, adult readers pick up a magazine on 3.2 separate reading occasions and spend about an hour reading one issue.[31]

Magazines also have a high secondary or passalong readership. What is important to advertisers is not a magazine's circulation, but its total audience, i.e., the number of people who read a particular issue. The total audience is made up of a primary and a secondary audience. The primary audience or readership is composed of individuals belonging to the subscribing or purchasing household. The secondary or passalong audience is composed of individuals who do not belong to the subscribing household but who receive the publication second hand. Magazines in the same study attracted an average of 3.1 readers per copy.[32]

The relationship among total audience, circulation and readers per copy is: total audience

PMB's biggest surprise?
Canadian Geographic!

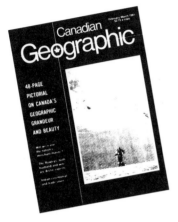

When the PMB III study was released, many people were surprised to see that *Canadian Geographic* had, by far, the largest readership per copy of all major national magazines. 7.9 readers enjoy each copy of our magazine as compared to 6.14 for *Time* and 3.72 for *Maclean's*

But we weren't in the least surprised because we've been increasing our press runs with every issue. *Canadian Geographic* brings the people and natural wonders of Canada to its readers in an interesting, colourful, high quality publication. And more and more people are reading it.

In fact, according to the December '80 ABC publisher's statement, our paid circulation was 97,302. Right now it is over 100,000 and we are guaranteeing a minimum of 110,000 for our next rate year.

Canadian Geographic. No surprise to over 800,000 readers!

Advertising Representatives

John McGown & Associates Inc.

785 Plymouth Avenue
Suite 310
Town of Mount Royal
Montreal, Quebec
H4P 1B3
(514) 735-5191

4800 Dundas Street West
Suite 105
Toronto, Ontario
M9A 1B1
(416) 232-1394

Doug Davison
Suite 414, Beatty Place
788 Beatty Street
Vancouver, B.C.
V6B 1A2
(604) 688-6819

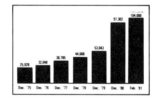

FIGURE 5.6
Advertisement for *Canadian Geographic* **Using Research Results to Promote the Magazine**
SOURCE: *Canadian Geographic*/The Royal Canadian Geographical Society.

= circulation × readers per copy. For example, in the *Canadian Geographic* advertisement reproduced in Figure 5.6, one finds that in 1980, there were 7.9 readers per copy and the paid circulation was 97 302. Thus in 1980 the total audience of *Canadian Geographic* was:

$$\text{total audience} = 97\ 302 \times 7.9 =$$
$$768\ 686 \text{ readers}$$

Additional Services. Additional services magazines provide are split-run and advertisement reprints, which are given to sales representatives who in turn distribute the advertisements to the trade.

There are four main *disadvantages* to using magazines as an advertising medium:

Lack of flexibility. Magazines lack flexibility for two main reasons. First, they require long lead times for including an advertisement in a specific issue. The closing date varies according to the type of magazine and is usually between four to twelve weeks before the issue (or cover) date. The *on-sale date* of a particular issue is often several days or weeks prior to the issue date. This long lead time does not allow advertisers to take account of rapid changes in market conditions. Second, magazines' circulation patterns do not always match a product's distribution pattern, and many magazines do not have regional editions. Even magazines with regional editions find it difficult to vary the intensity of advertising geographically. Finally, Canada does not have a *general interest* magazine, so it is impossible to reach men and women as a group with one publication or type of publication.

Low frequency and penetration. Magazines cannot offer high frequency of exposure and thus are inappropriate when high frequency is required. Because of its selectivity, the coverage offered by an individual magazine may be lower than for other media. Moreover, because a magazine is around for a long time, people do not read it right away. Although reach is not immediate as it is with TV or newspapers, people do look at a magazine several times, which increases the chances for an ad to be noticed. Thus the actual reach of a magazine may not be attained at the publication date. This is a corollary of the long life of a magazine.

Creative drawbacks. For the creative director, magazines present some problems. There is no limit on the number of advertising pages in a magazine, so the problem of clutter is very acute. This creates a difficult competitive environment for creative directors, who must find ways to improve an advertisement's chances of being noticed and read. A variety of techniques is used, often at a higher cost: special inks, preferred positions, covers, use of a celebrity endorsement, and large-size insertions. As with other print media, magazines do not have audio capabilities nor can they use movement to demonstrate a product.

High production costs. Magazine production costs are higher than for newspapers, particularly for four-colour advertising or special devices like metallic inks and microfragrances (e.g., for sampling a perfume).

Magazine Rate Structures

Magazine rates are determined according to circulation, audience, and editorial content. Circulation figures may be audited by the Audit Bureau of Circulation (ABC) or the Canadian Circulations Audit Board (CCAB). Magazines with audited circulation represent about 55 per cent of consumer magazines that report circulation. Other magazines provide either sworn statements or guarantees, and about 30 per cent of consumer magazines do not report circulation.[33]

This information, as well as all other relevant data, is provided by an individual magazine rate card, which is similar to the newspaper general rate card. A standardized version of the magazine rate card is available in *CARD*. Figure 5.7 shows the *CARD* listing for the *Financial Post Magazine.*

The rate structure for magazines may be based on regular rates, a variety of discounts, and additional services advertisers require.

Regular rate

The regular rate may vary according to an advertisement's size. Most magazines quote their rates according to a full page or a portion of a page. For example, for the *Financial Post Magazine* one finds the following symbols in Figure 5.7 with the corresponding four-colour rate:

1 p.	one page	$8743
2/3 p.	two-thirds of a page	$6819
1/3 p.	one-third of a page	$3935
1/6 p.	one-sixth of a page	Not Available

Advertising space covering two pages facing each other is called a *double-page spread* and may be sold at a discount. Part of a spread may also be bought, for example, a half-page spread. For the *Financial Post Magazine*, a four-colour double-page spread cost $15,737, while the one-half page spread cost $10,544, as shown in Figure 5.7. A gatefold allows an advertisement to run three pages or more and is subject to a special rate, usually at a discount from a multiple of the page rate.

Discounts

Some magazines offer discounts. Magazines that do not offer discounts have what is called a

001	C0850
03	**CANADIAN YACHTING** POWER & SAIL
04	(ABC) Member CPPA M. CDA LOGO
009	A Maclean Hunter Publication
010	*Data confirmed for Dec./83 CARD*
011	Est. 1976.
012	Published by Maclean Hunter Ltd., Maclean Hunter
013	Building, 777 Bay St., Toronto M5W 1A7. Phone:
014	416-596-5022. Tlx.: 06-219547.
015	Issued monthly.
016	───────── Closing dates ─────────
017	Issue:
018	1984	Ad.	Mat'l
021	Feb.	Dec. 10	Dec. 16
024	Mar.	Jan. 17	Jan. 23
027	Apr.	Feb. 13	Feb. 17
030	May	Mar. 12	Mar. 16
033	June	Apr. 11	Apr. 16
036	July	May 16	May 21
039	Aug.	June 6	June 14
042	Sept.	July 6	July 13
045	Oct.	Aug. 10	Aug. 17
048	Nov.	Sept. 7	Sept. 14
051	Dec.	Oct. 5	Oct. 12
054	1985:
055	Jan.	Nov. 7	Nov. 14
058	Per year, Canada $18, elsewhere $25.
059	NOTE: Ads scheduled in Canadian/Pacific
060	Yachting require duplicate film, progs etc. Ship to
061	Canadian Yachting.
062	SPECIAL ISSUES
063	Jan.: Annual Boat Show Issue; Sept.: Toronto, Van-
064	couver, Halifax Floating Boat Show Issue.
065	**COMMISSION & CASH DISCOUNT**
066	15%; 2% 10 days. Brokerage, Charter & Quarter-
067	deck/Aft Cabin rates shown are net. No agency
068	commission.
069	**GENERAL ADVERTISING**
070	Rate Card No. 8. Effective Nov. 1, 1983.
071	REGIONAL EAST
072	Sask., Man., Ont., Que. & Maritimes:

		1 ti.	6 ti.	12 ti.
073				
076	1 page	$1580	$1460	$1310
080	2/3 page	1265	1165	1045
084	1/2 page isl.	1105	1025	920
088	1/2 page	950	875	790
092	1/3 page	715	660	595
096	1/4 page	555	510	465
100	Dbl. 1/3 col.	510	475	425
104	1/3 col.	270	250	225
108	**COVERS**			
109	4-COLOR:			

		1 ti.	6 ti	12 ti.
113	2nd or 3rd	$2390	$2250	$2075
117	4th cover	2545	2395	2210
121	**COLOR**			
122	Process red, blue, or yellow, per page			$175
124	Special colors, per page			305
126	4-color process, per page			570
128	**CLASSIFICATIONS**			
129	Brokerage & Charter Advtg.:			

		1 ti.	6 ti.	12 ti.
133	1 page	$795	$735	$665
137	1/2 page	490	455	410
141	1/4 page	290	265	240
145	Quarter Deck Directory: consec. issues:			

		3 ti.	6 ti.	12 ti.
149	Per unit	$405	$750	$1320
153	Brokerage, Charter & Quarterdeck rates shown			
154	are net. No agency commission. Payment with or-			
155	der.			

156	REGIONAL WEST
157	See listing for Pacific Yachting.
158	CANADIAN/PACIFIC YACHTING
159	Pacific coast through to Maritimes:

		1 ti.	6 ti.	12 ti.
160				
163	1 page	$2790	$2590	$2360
167	2/3 page	2190	2030	1850
171	1/2 page isl.	1965	1830	1665
175	1/2 page	1700	1575	1440
179	1/3 page	1245	1155	1055
183	Dbl. 1/3 col.	880	820	745
187	1/3 col.	460	430	390
191	**COVERS**			
192	4-COLOR:			
193	2nd or 3rd cover	$4355	$4065	$3850
197	4th cover	4540	4380	4090
201	**COLOR**			
202	Process red, blue or yellow, per page			$325
204	Special colors, per page			570
206	4-color process, per page			1115
208	**CLASSIFICATIONS**			
209	Brokerage & Charter Advtg.:			

		1 ti.	6 ti.	12 ti.
213	1 page	$1520	$1410	$1295
217	1/2 page	940	875	800
221	1/4 page	535	490	465
225	Quarterdeck/Aft Cabin Dir. Consec. issues			

		3 ti.	6 ti.	12 ti.
226				
229	Per unit	$755	$1385	$2355
233	Brokerage, Charter & Quarterdeck/Aft Cabin rates			
234	shown are net. No agency commission.			
235	**CLASSIFIED**			
236	Rates on request.			
237	**POSITION CHARGES**			
238	Special or guaranteed positions, extra 15%			
239	**BLEED**			
240	No extra charge; full page only.			
241	**INSERTS**			
242	Rates on request.			
243	**MECHANICAL REQUIREMENTS**			
244	Printed offset.			
245	Type page: 7 x 10.			
246	Trim size: 8-3/16 x 11.			
247	Bleed size: 8-1/2 x 11-1/4.			
248	Quarter deck dir.: 3-3/8 x 1-3/4.			
249	Dbl. 1/3 col.: 4-5/8 x 3-1/8.			
250	Dbl. 1/3 col. stacked: 2-1/8 x 6-9/16.			
251	1/3 col.: 2-1/8 x 3-1/8.			

	Unit	Wide	Deep	Unit	Wide	Deep
252						
258	2/3 v.	4-5/8	10	1/3 v.	2-1/8	10
264	1/2 isl.	4-5/8	7-1/4	1/3 p.	4-5/8	4-7/8
270	1/2 h.	7	4-7/8	1/4 p.	3-3/8	4-7/8
276	PRINTING SPECIFICATIONS					
277	See Section A, inside back cover of CARD.					
278	**PERSONNEL**					
279	Editor: Penny Caldwell.					
280	Pubr.: Jas. A. Davidson.					
281	Classified & Prod.: Evelyn McCartney.					
282	**BRANCH OFFICES/REPRESENTATIVES**					
283	Vancouver V6B 2S2: Pacific Yachting Magazine,					
284	Ste. 202, 1132 Hamilton St. Phone: 604-687-1581.					
285	United Kingdom: Colin Turner (Trade) Press, Lon-					
286	don. Phone: 01-734-3052.					
287	**CIRCULATION**					
288	A.B.C. 30-6-83 pub. state.					
289	Average total subscriptions 17,688					
291	Average single copy sales 3,600					
293	Average total paid circulation 21,288					
295	Average total nonpaid distribution 1,016					
297	Total paid June 1983 issue 22,520					
299	Geographical Breakdown:					

300	Nfld.	392	Man.	530
302	N.S.	972	Sask.	372
304	P.E.I.	174	Alta.	826
306	N.B.	1,037	B.C.	1,835
308	Que.	4,116	U.S.	91
310	Ont.	12,136	Foreign	39
312	For national circulation include circulation for Pa-			
313	cific Yachting.			

FIGURE 5.7 *CARD* Listing for a Consumer Magazine

SOURCE: *Canadian Advertising Rates and Data* (1983), p. 104. *Courtesy* Special Interest Network

flat rate policy. There are several types of discounts, which may be combined according to the publication:

Frequency discounts are based on the number of issues in which the advertisement appears during a twelve-month period.

Volume discounts are based on the number of full (or equivalent) pages bought within a twelve-month period.

Continuity discounts are combined with volume discounts when an advertiser contracts for a space equivalent to one full page or more in each issue for 12, 24, or 36 consecutive months.

Consecutive-page discounts apply when several consecutive pages are bought in any one issue.

Run-of-book (ROB) discounts allow publishers flexibility in placing an advertisement.

Cash discounts of 2 per cent of net amount may be offered when the bill is paid within a specified period of time.

The *short rate* prevails if the advertiser does not use all the space contracted for. The adjustment is based on the discounts applicable to the amount of space used, and it results in amounts to be paid in excess of those already paid. If the amount of space used is higher than the one contracted for, the advertiser receives a *rebate* at the end of the year.

The Future of Magazines as an Advertising Medium

The evolution of magazines in response to competition from other media and U.S. magazines will likely take new directions with the introduction of new technologies.

New printing processes will improve the quality of magazines while new computerized colour graphic systems and other processes will allow a shortening of closing dates.

The *verticalization* of magazines is likely to continue, with the introduction of more special interest magazines that have smaller audiences but offer advertisers better advertising exposure. More national magazines will develop regional or city editions. City-oriented magazines (c.g., Toronto's *City Woman*) or even more restricted demographic areas like business districts or high-income, well-educated residential areas (e.g., Toronto's *Avenue Magazine*) will offer advertisers better quality audiences.[34]

The proliferation of media and the increased verticalization of magazines will increase the importance of the media director as well as the use of media research. To illustrate this point, the Print Measurement Bureau is increasing the frequency and scope of its research studies.[35]

The introduction of home-information delivery systems may eventually lead to the electronic magazine, allowing magazines to increase their coverage of a particular group and generate new revenues to cover increasing costs.[36]

Other Canadian Periodicals

In addition to consumer magazines, periodicals include business publications, farm publications, and directories as well as religious and school publications. Most of what has been said about consumer magazines applies to these periodicals, but there are some important differences.

Business Publications

Business publications developed in Canada with the growth of various trades or professions and were often started by a target group member as a business sideline. They preceded consumer magazines and some eventually became consumer magazines, such as the *Canadian Sportsman*, founded in 1870. Like consumer magazines, the mortality rate of these periodicals was high. The first business publications were aimed at trades or professions. The *Canadian Pharmaceutical Journal* was founded in 1868. The *Canadian Mining Journal* and the *Canada Lumberman* were founded in 1879 and 1880, respectively.[37]

In 1940, there were about 215 Canadian business papers under about 75 classifications, with a total circulation of about half a million.[38] By 1981, the number of Canadian business publications was 646 (triple the 1940 figures) under 118 classifications, with a total circulation of 97 million.[39] In 1982, net advertising revenues of business publications were $139 million (Table 5.1).

Differences from Consumer Magazines
Business publications are specialized and are used to advertise products or services to indus-

trial users, distributors, and other professional groups. Business publications differ from consumer magazines in several ways:

1. They are directed to professionals who are experts in their fields and for whom the advertising must be informative, and often precedes a sales call.

2. They are one of the few sources of new information for professionals.

3. They provide advertisers with less readership information than do consumer magazines or daily newspapers.

4. They are represented by several different organizations: the Canadian Business Press (CBP), which is the largest; the Periodical Publishers Exchange (PPE); the Canadian Periodical Publisher's Associations (CPPA); and the Canadian Management Press Association (CMPA).

5. Most business publications have low circulation figures (usually below 20 000 copies) compared to consumer magazines.

Rates and Rate Cards

The rate structure of business publications is similar to that of consumer magazines. Like consumer magazines, business publications are audited by the CCAB or ABC or give sworn statements. Since many business publications have controlled distribution, the accuracy of circulation figures is an important factor for advertisers to consider when buying space.

Business publications are expected to show growth in the future, with this growth coming from new publications and improvement in the "total product"—better information on circulation, audiences, and readership.

Farm Publications

Farm journals were one of the earliest types of periodicals in Canada, often associated with daily newspapers. The oldest survivor is the *Free Press Report on Farming*, founded in 1872.

Two of the oldest farm journals not associated with daily newspapers are *The Country Guide*, founded in 1882, and *The Grower*, an Ontario journal founded in 1879.[40]

As with other periodicals, farm journals evolved from a general publication to more specialized editorial content, often focusing on the managerial aspects of farming. This trend paralleled the transformation of farming from the small family farm to the large agribusiness. A high level of verticalization can be attributed to the heterogeneous farm audience in terms of climactic conditions and types of farm products and competition from other media. Thus, several farm magazines have regional editions. For example, the *Country Guide* offers national, regional, and provincial editions, plus demographic breakdowns by census division for producers with specific needs. This explains why most farm magazine advertising is placed in regional magazines or regional editions of national magazines.

Approximately ninety farm publications are listed in *CARD*. In 1982 net advertising revenues reached $18.7 million (Table 5.1).

Farm publications are expected to develop along the same lines as consumer magazines, with more specialization, particularly for the large publications.

Directories, Annuals, and Yellow Pages

These publications appear annually and usually contain an alphabetical or classified list of names, addresses, and other information. Advertisers may be charged to have their name listed or to have it appear in special type or to include an advertisement near their listing.

Approximately 127 directories and annuals are listed in *CARD*, 80 per cent of which are classified as business publications, 13 per cent as consumer magazines, and the rest as farm, university, and school publications. Examples are the *B.C. Fishing Guide*, the *Crops Guide*, the *Canadian Sporting Goods and Playthings*

Directory, and the *Canadian Directory of Pro-fessional Photography*.

Yellow page advertising is often the only form of advertising done by local merchants, since it is an effective and inexpensive medium. Canada has more than 330 yellow page directories with a total circulation of more than 23 million.[41] The large circulation explains why some national advertisers use the yellow pages for promoting a local branch or distributors or for providing information and other services to consumers.

Net advertising revenues for directories reached $275 million in 1982, or 5.3 per cent of all media advertising revenues, and these revenues are expected to grow. The medium will likely evolve along the same lines as other periodicals. For example, telephone directories may become available through such electronic systems as Telidon.

Religious, University, School, and Scholarly Publications

One early group of Canadian periodicals was the religious publication. Among the oldest surviving ones are the *Atlantic Baptist*, founded in 1827, and the *United Church Observer*, founded in 1829.[42] Twenty-six religious publications are listed in *CARD*, with circulation ranging from about 3000 to 300 000 and a total circulation of over one million.

About 102 university and school publications with a total circulation of over 320 000 are listed in *CARD*. Some of the oldest publications are *The Brunswickan*, established in 1865, and the *Queen's Journal*, established in 1873.[43] These publications may belong to one of two networks that centralize the selling of space: the Campus Network with sixteen members and a total circulation of over 100 000, and Campus Plus, with forty-eight members and a total circulation of over 270 000. In addition, there are about five scholarly publications with a total circulation of about 13 500.

Foreign-Language Publications

One manifestation of Canadian society's multicultural character is the growth in foreign-language publications (also called the *ethnic press*). This growth is consistent with the overall trend in magazines toward special interest groups. With foreign-language publications language and culture are the main segmenting characteristics. *CARD* lists approximately 167 publications belonging to 37 language or ethnic groups. The most important ones are shown in Table 5.3.

Most of these publications are recent, but some are quite old, such as the German semiweekly publication *Mennonitische Rundschau*, established in 1877, and the Icelandic weekly publication *Logberg-Heimskringla*, established in 1886.

Other Canadian Print Media

A variety of other print media is available to advertisers. *Out-of-home* advertising is growing rapidly and reached $280 million in net adver-

TABLE 5.3   Number of Foreign Language Publications in Canada

Language	Number		
Italian	23	Hungarian	5
Ukrainian	18	Korean	5
Arabic	10	Slovak/Czech	5
Greek	10	Spanish	5
Chinese	9	Polish	4
Portuguese	9	Punjabi	4
Urdu	7	Finnish	3
Croat, Serb,		Hindi	3
and Slovenian	6	Malayalam	3
Dutch	6	Romanian	3
German	6	Other*	24
Total 168			

* Armenian, Bulgarian, Byelorussian, Danish, Estonian, Gujarati, Icelandic, Japanese, Jewish, Latvian, Lithuanian, Norwegian, Pakistani, Philipino, Scandinavian, and Swedish.
SOURCE: Developed from *CARD* (March 1983), pp. 58-72.
Courtesy Special Interest Network

tising revenues in 1982 (Table 5.1). *Direct* advertising, particularly direct mail advertising, is becoming more sophisticated and will likely benefit from new technologies.

Outdoor Advertising

Outdoor advertising is a very old medium and may be traced back to Babylonian bas reliefs. Early in Canada, tradesmen and merchants used rocks, fences, barns, and chimneys to advertise their trade. Then came the printed poster, which was initially used by circuses, theatrical companies, and the patent medicine industry. In 1891, billposting companies formed the Associated Billposters and Distributors of the United States and Canada. This helped standardize poster sizes and rates. Painted-sign companies merged with the billposting companies in 1925 to form the forerunner of the Outdoor Advertising Association of Canada.[44] The most important factor in the growth of the medium was the growth of the automobile industry early in the twentieth century. Outdoor displays grew in size and in geographical coverage and the copy became simpler, thus effectively attracting attention. After standardization of sizes and rates, the most pressing need for advertisers was for research that would verify audience data. In 1933, the Traffic Audit Bureau was created for this purpose. Today, this task is performed by the Canadian Outdoor Measurement Bureau (COMB).

Types of Outdoor Formats

Space for outdoor advertising is usually offered as predetermined sets of packages in each city. For any market, the packages are designed according to daily circulation figures expressed as a set percentage of the total population: 25, 50, 75, and 100 GRPs. The number of panels needed for each level varies from market to market.

Poster panels are structures usually 746 cm × 366 cm (24′6″ × 12′) that can accommodate three different sizes of posters: the 24-sheet, the 30-sheet, and bleed posters (Figure 5.8). Posters are available in more than 400 Canadian markets and in 14 extended market areas, covering more than 70 per cent of the Canadian population.

Junior panels (also called eight-sheets) have a non-illuminated single pole structure of 366 cm × 183 cm (12′ × 6′) placed in six census metropolitan areas (CMAs). The actual copy area is 335 cm × 152 cm (11′ × 5′).

Superboards (also called painted bulletins) are hand painted or printed designs on structures larger than posters and are positioned at heavy traffic locations in major markets. The designs are rotated to different locations every two months to offer a more balanced coverage. Extensions made of wood or plastic and affixed to the unit may extend the face of the bulletin.

Backlights are units of 508 cm × 254 cm (20′ × 10′) located in high traffic areas, printed on reinforced translucent plastic, and illuminated from behind. They allow better colour reproduction, particularly at night.

Spectaculars are custom designed and come in varying shapes and sizes. They use electrical or mechanical devices or inflatable vinyl-coated nylon to create a three-dimensional display. Other devices can be used, such as steam in a cigarette advertisement, or reflective disks to create an impression of movement.

Other formats are mall posters, airport display panels, stoplights located in bus shelters, bench advertising, taxicab billboards, and golf course signs.

Strengths of Outdoor Advertising

Outdoor is a mass medium with *high reach*; it covers all demographic groups. In addition, outdoor provides *high frequency* very quickly because it has broad strategic location throughout a market.

Outdoor can be purchased market-by-market, thus providing advertisers with geographic *flexibility*. Also, advertisers may vary the time

The Poster

The standardized poster panel is usually 24 feet, 6 inches long and 12 feet high and can accommodate 3 different sizes of poster: the 24-sheet, the 30-sheet and the bleed. All 3 sizes involve a proportion of 2¼ to 1.

24-Sheet Poster
Many years ago when printing presses were smaller a poster panel required 24 sheets of paper. Today with larger presses, fewer sheets are needed, but the original term remains. Above right is a typical paper pattern for a 24-sheet poster, which measures 19 feet, 6 inches by 8 feet, 8 inches. The area between the design and the frame is covered with white blanking paper.

30-Sheet Poster
The 30-sheet poster, measuring 21 feet, 7 inches by 9 feet, 7 inches, provides about 25% more space for the design than does the 24-sheet poster. The additional space is taken from the blanking area. Middle right is a typical paper pattern for the 30-sheet poster. Through careful planning of the pattern, 4-color printing can be limited to a minimum number of sheets for lower production costs.

Bleed Poster
In the bleed poster—40% larger than the 24-sheet—the design is carried all the way to the frame. This is done by printing the minor variations in the overall size of poster panels, essential elements of the design— such as copy or logo—should be positioned at least 6 inches from the edges. This will ensure their appearance on the smallest panels.

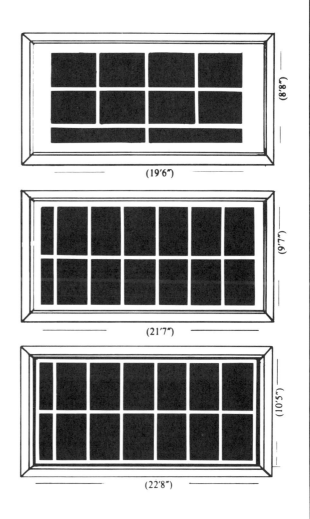

FIGURE 5.8   Characteristics of the Three Main Types of Standardized Poster
SOURCE: *The Instructor's Manual: An Inside Look at Outdoor Advertising* (New York: Gannett Foundation, 1981).

period for showing the advertisement.

Outdoor has a *long life*, and because of its size and artistic quality, it is an effective medium for many products that need reminder advertising or for new product introductions, which need quick brand awareness.

Outdoor is a relatively inexpensive medium on a relative cost-per-thousand-impressions basis.

Advertising messages can be placed close to the actual point-of-purchase, which is important during seasonal shopping rushes.

Weaknesses of Outdoor Advertising

Outdoor can only be used for *very short* product stories. The advertisement must use few words and illustrations in order for the message to be communicated effectively. In addition, the environment in which the advertisement is placed can be highly distracting, and there is no editorial or program content to enhance it.

The medium's broad reach means that it is difficult, if not impossible, to focus on a target group. Thus some circulation may be wasted. Outdoor is not consistently available in all major markets. It is banned in some cities (e.g., Victoria) or severely restricted (in Quebec only French copy is allowed).

The absolute costs for national coverage are high. Also, outdoor is not considered a prestigious medium and it may create some negative feelings among consumers who object to its environmental impact.

Statistics used to measure audiences reflect only the level of traffic flows by the boards and thus do not necessarily compare with those of other media.

Outdoor requires *long lead time* because of the long production time of outdoor messages. Often a two-month lead time is necessary. In addition, the production costs are fairly high compared to radio, magazines, and newspapers.

Outdoor Advertising Rate Structure

Rates for outdoor advertising are based on three main factors. The first is the level of daily GRPs, i.e., the average daily circulation as a percentage of the total population. The circulation figure is the number of persons walking or driving by the outdoor display each day. The most commonly used levels are 25, 50, 75, and 100 GRPs. Junior and mall posters use different levels. These rates are usually quoted for a four-week period, although short-term contracts are available at a premium.

Outdoor panels are *not* bought individually, and the number of panels that deliver 25 GRPs vary from market to market. For example, in 1982 the rate for all urban markets and 50 daily GRPs was about $250,000 for 718 panels.

Production charges must be added to the other costs, particularly for superboards, spectaculars, and backlights.

Continuity discounts based on the number of consecutives weeks purchased are available in some markets.

Future of Outdoor Advertising

Because its main strengths are high reach and frequency, outdoor is likely to grow as an advertising medium. The supply of outdoor space will have to increase *without* creating a negative public reaction, which would restrict its growth or even ban it from certain high traffic areas. Thus outdoor structures may become more adapted to their environment, making innovative use of available space, providing public services, such as time of day and news.

Transit Advertising

Streetcar advertising was first handled directly by the companies themselves. By 1902, street railways carried 135 million passengers in Canada, and by 1937 the number had grown to 827 million.[45] Advertising companies contracted with the various street railways for space to sell to advertisers. The industry grew with the number of passengers and number of public transportation systems. Today, most streetcars have been replaced by subways and buses.

Types of Transit Advertising
There are several types of transit advertising, the most important ones being interior transit cards and the exterior bus boards.

Interior transit cards (also called *car cards*) are displayed inside the vehicles. Because the travelling public is a captive audience, it is an effective communication medium. Car cards are available in more than 73 markets and are offered in standard sizes of 28 cm × 59, 71, 118, or 142 cm, depending on the market (11″ × 23¼″, 28″, 46½″, or 56″). Back-lit car cards are available in several markets.

Car cards are sold on the basis of level of service. Full service means that every vehicle has one or two cards. Service may also be offered in multiples or fractions. For example, half service means that half of the full service boards will be distributed among the vehicles, i.e., among every other vehicle or one card per vehicle instead of two. Car cards may also be sold on the same basis as for outdoor—by level of GRPs.

Exterior bus boards may be purchased for the front, sides, and back of vehicles. They are, in effect, travelling outdoor displays; their audience extends beyond the travelling public to pedestrians and motorists.

Exterior bus boards are available in more than 65 markets across Canada. The standard sizes are: king size, 76 cm × 353 cm (30″ × 139″); queen size, 53 cm × 223 cm (21″ × 88″); taillight, 53 cm × 178 cm (21″ × 70″).

They may be sold according to the number of boards (showings) per month, or according to set levels of weekly GRPs.

Other forms of transit advertising are subway posters, which may be platform posters on the walls of the platform, interior sidedoor cards located on each side of the car door, or back-lit displays placed in high traffic areas of subway stations; digital clock advertising within subway stations; and bus top spectaculars, custom-designed as for outdoor spectaculars.

Strengths of Transit Advertising
As for outdoor advertising, transit is a mass medium with a high degree of market flexibility. It also commands attention and has high visual impact. Other strengths are that advertising copy is often longer than for outdoor displays; it is a relatively inexpensive medium for reaching urban markets and operates close to the point-of-sale; it allows advertisers to provide riders with coupons or response cards.

Weaknesses of Transit Advertising
Weaknesses of transit are that it is inefficient for non-urban and narrow audiences; there is a lack of extensive audience research on transit that would provide information on audience characteristics and reach/frequency figures; the advertisements tend to be expensive and time-consuming to produce and thus have long lead times; it is not a prestigious medium among consumers and the trade.

Transit Advertising Rate Structure
The rate structure for transit is similar to that of outdoor advertising, although the actual rates may be different. For example, full service on a national basis for the smallest interior card size in 1982 cost about $37,000 per month, based on a three-month purchase.[46]

Future of Transit Advertising
The use of transit advertising will likely grow with the development of transit systems and with the increase in the proportion of the urban population using it instead of the automobile. Also, transit may benefit from the potential shortage of outdoor space. Better research may show that costs per thousand impressions are low, making transit a good buy for many small or medium-sized advertisers. Increased demand for transit space may bring about innovative ways of using the available space while maintaining reach and frequency levels.

Direct Mail Advertising

Direct mail advertising is the largest form of direct advertising. *Direct* advertising is defined as any form of advertising message that is sent directly to a pre-selected audience and includes direct mail and unmailed direct advertising. This term is not to be confused with *mail-order* selling. With the latter, orders for merchandise come through the mail, but the advertisement may have appeared first in a magazine, a newspaper, or even in the broadcast media, or the selling may be done through a direct mail piece.

Direct mail advertising was one of the first media used in Canada by merchants and has its roots in handbills and pamphlets as well as the advertising card. The growth of direct mail advertising was spurred by developments in printing technology, the growth in postal delivery methods and postal rate structures, as well as by efforts to organize the industry. In 1917, the Direct Mail Association of America was formed with the active participation of Canadian representatives.[47]

Direct mail has been growing rapidly in Canada—an average of 13.6 per cent per year between 1977 and 1982. Net advertising revenues of direct mail were $892 million in 1982, representing more than 20 per cent of all advertising revenues. Thus in terms of advertising revenues, direct mail is the *second largest medium* after daily newspapers. This growth is likely to continue. Americans receive three times the amount of direct mail material that Canadians do, but because Canadians are more collectively oriented than Americans, response rates in Canada are about 40 per cent higher than in the U.S.[48] Response rates are also higher in Quebec than in English Canada.[49]

Characteristics of Direct Mail Advertising
Direct mail is characterized by format and mailing lists, as well as production and distribution.

FORMATS. Direct mail comes in a variety of formats, with letters being the most commonly used format. Most people like to read interesting letters, so considerable work has been done to improve the effectiveness of the creative approaches in designing letters. New technologies are being incorporated in the production of direct mail material to make them more involving, interesting, and personalized. The wide use of computers in the last two decades brought about the computerized letter, which is becoming more and more sophisticated and attractive. For example, the use of laser processes for addressing allows the display of copy in half-inch type, adding strong visual impact to the message and increasing attention and response rates.

Other formats of direct mail materials may be used in conjunction with or instead of a letter. *Broadsides* (or bedsheets) are large sheets with full colour illustrations and folded for distribution. Layout and copy are very important in keeping the reader's interest. *Booklets* are used when the message is too long for a broadside or a folder, or when several offerings are described. *Folders* are commonly used to present short, simple printed messages and may be used with or without an accompanying letter. *Circulars* (or *leaflets, throwaways, fliers*) are one of the least expensive forms of direct mail advertising and are used for a quick impact, for example, to announce a special sale. *Brochures* are a more elaborate, higher quality type of booklet. *Postcards* are used for short and quick messages that need to be sent inexpensively. They may include a reply feature.

Finally, *catalogues* are books describing several or all of the products available from either a manufacturer or distributor. Because Canada's population has strong rural roots and is sparsely distributed, catalogues and particularly department store catalogues have always been popular[50] and will likely see rapid growth in the future.

MAILING LISTS. A good, up-to-date mailing list is an essential requirement in direct-mail advertising. A message is lost if the address is incorrect or if the recipient is not in the target market. Since direct mail is an expensive medium, it is particularly important to minimize wasted circulation. Mailing lists come from several sources:[51]

Internal lists are available to many advertisers from their own records of clients, distributors, stockholders, inquiries, complaints, and so on. Further breakdowns may be done based on the information available on these individuals or companies.

Solicitation lists of individuals who responded to various forms of direct mail solicitation or promotion incentives are available from specialized companies, some with demographic breakdowns.

Directories are another source of potentially useful mailing lists. Directories may be broad like the telephone directory, or very narrow like the list of members of the Administrative Sciences Association of Canada.

Compiled lists are developed by one organization and then made available to advertisers. These could include a list of new house buyers or graduating students.

PRODUCTION AND DISTRIBUTION. Production of direct mail pieces may be done by an advertiser or its agency or by a direct mail agency. These agencies handle all the details from the initial layout and the development of the mailing list to the final distribution program. Advertisers also use the services of freelance designers and/or writers for the creative side; a mailing list company or a broker for the rental, purchase, or creation of a mailing list; and *letter shops* (or fulfilment houses), which handle the actual printing of direct mail material and stuff, seal, and address the envelopes.

Strengths of Direct Mail Advertising
Direct mail is a highly *selective* medium; it allows advertisers to reach a narrowly defined target audience with a well-targeted message. Mailing lists often allow the advertiser to reach the best prospects for a product with a minimum amount of wasted circulation. In addition, direct mail allows flexibility in the degree of coverage to be reached by the campaign.

From the creative director's viewpoint, direct mail is a highly versatile medium. It is very flexible in the type of creative approaches, format, length of copy, and type of layouts it allows. In particular, the ability to use *long copy* is a strong point in favour of direct mail compared to other media. Communication with the market may be highly *personal*, *quick*, and has the possibility of *feedback* that can be measured. In addition, direct mail commands a high level of *attention*, free from the distraction of other media or competitive messages. Finally, a direct mail message may have a *long life*, with many prospects keeping it for future action, as a reminder, to show to a spouse, a friend, or to pass along.

From an overall communications viewpoint, direct mail provides a high degree of control. The advertiser has some certainty that the message has *reached* the intended audience. In addition, the advertiser may measure the performance of the campaign quite accurately, both for the total target or for some demographic or psychographic breakdowns.

Direct mail can also be used for a variety of sales promotion activities: to distribute coupons, refund offers, contest announcements, and small product samples.[52]

Weaknesses of Direct Mail Advertising
The major disadvantage of direct mail is its *high relative cost*. The costs per thousand impressions may run as much as 100 times the cost per thousand viewers for television. This high cost makes it imperative for the communication to be effective.

Direct mail has some creative negatives. The message must stand on its own, without editorial support, and the reader may have little interest in the material or have a negative reaction to this form of advertising. However, studies show that a very high percentage of people open their "junk mail". The response rate of direct mail is often extremely low. Although the response rate depends on several factors, such as the value of the item advertised or the type of market reached, it is not unusual for response rates to be less than 1 per cent.

The effectiveness of a direct mail advertising campaign depends heavily on the speed of postal delivery and on the accuracy of the information contained in the mailing list, including demographic and psychographic information.

Cost Structure of Direct Mail

The costs of a direct mail campaign are related to production, mailing lists, and distribution.

Production costs vary with the type, length, and quality of the message. A one-page black and white flyer costs much less than a four-colour broadsheet. The costs of the creative work for preparing the direct mail material must also be added.

Mailing lists may be rented, purchased, or compiled specifically for an advertiser. Costs vary with the type, length, and quality of the list.

A final cost factor is the *distribution* of the mailing, which involves folding, collating, stuffing, addressing, stamping, and bundling envelopes. The cost is based on the number of steps involved and the number of names in the list. One important item in the distribution is the cost of postal delivery, which varies according to the weight and the postal class used. For example, first class is the most expensive but also the fastest type of mail delivery, and it should be used when timing is important.

Future of Direct Mail Advertising

The future of direct mail will be influenced by innovations that will improve the attractiveness of a mailed advertisement and reduce its costs. The industry will continue to improve its use of computer technology, laser technology

and new printing processes. This will help make advertisements more personal, more relevant, and lower the cost per unit. Better research will help advertisers to target their audiences more selectively and increase the response rates.

Direct mail advertising may be affected by changes in public attitudes toward the medium and by deterioration (or improvement?) in postal delivery and costs. The industry will have to invest in home-delivery information systems (videotex and two-way cable), since these are expected to become very important in the 1980s and 1990s.

Minor Direct Media

One minor direct medium, *telemarketing*, has in recent years grown spectacularly and accounts for a large share of direct marketing revenues.[53] The main reasons for its popularity are first, that it is a fast method of reaching prospects, with a high degree of control; second, it can be used effectively with other promotional activities, such as direct mail and sales force efforts; third, the costs of a telephone call may vary between $3 and $10, compared to the cost of a sales call, which may reach $150.[54] Distribution of advertising messages through cable television will probably experience similar growth in the late 1980s with the diffusion of new communication technologies.[55]

Advertising specialties (or *remembrance advertising*) are a wide range of products that contain some form of advertising and that are given free or sold to a selected group. Because these products are practical and have a degree of permanence, they expose the recipient and users to the message every time the product is used.

Summary

There are various print media available in Canada for carrying advertising messages. Each medium has evolved to meet the needs of the advertiser and compete for a share of the advertising budget. They will continue to do so as needs change and new technologies transform the nature of the media.

Table 5.4 highlights the main strengths and weaknesses of each medium.

Newspapers provide high reach and coverage of most demographic subgroups. It is a flexible medium offering short lead times, regional flexibility, and good creative opportunities at low cost. Thus, it is a worthwhile medium for regional marketers or small local business. Colour reproduction is sometimes a problem, and national coverage may be relatively expensive and cumbersome to buy. Audience selectivity may be expensive for advertisers with specific audiences.

Periodicals, including consumer magazines, business, and farm publications, are aimed at a highly selected audience with a high passalong readership. High quality reproduction and long life of messages in a prestigious medium are the major advantages of periodicals. However, periodicals tend to have long lead times and a low penetration of some subgroups. High frequency is difficult to achieve, and the cost of production is often higher than for radio and newspapers.

Outdoor advertising is a mass medium with geographic flexibility. Its size and permanence provide impact and command attention. But messages must be short and universal (no selectivity). Production of outdoor messages leads to high costs and long closing dates.

Transit advertising is a mass medium in urban areas and it has some geographic flexibility. Size, permanence, and location provide for high readership, and relative costs per thousand impressions are low. As with outdoor advertising, production costs are high and closing dates can be long. Transit offers very little audience selectivity and only reaches consumers who use public transportation.

Direct advertising can be very selective and provides advertisers with a high degree of control and feedback. It is very flexible both in terms of creative content and market coverage. Without editorial support, however, the advertising message may lack credibility or be ignored. The relative costs are very high.

TABLE 5.4 Main Strengths and Weaknesses of Major Print Media

Medium	Strengths	Weaknesses
Newspaper	high reach & broad coverage flexible (time, geographic, creative) affordable to small business	colour reproduction audience selectivity national coverage is difficult/expensive
Periodicals	highly selective & pass along high-quality reproduction long life & prestige	little flexibility (lead time, low penetration) cost of production frequency
Outdoor	coverage & flexibility impact of message long life of message	short message no selectivity long closing dates
Transit	coverage & flexibility high readership low cost per thousand	no selectivity long closing dates high production costs
Direct	high selectivity & control flexible (creative, coverage)	high relative cost no editorial support

Questions for Study

1. Select the listing of one of your local newspapers in the latest *CARD* catalogue and try to describe its contents. What would a 1000-line black and white advertisement in the business section cost a national advertiser?

2. What are the pros and cons of the two-rate structure of national and local advertising? Present the two viewpoints and indicate the kind of policy you would follow as a newspaper publisher, a radio station owner, or a national advertiser.

3. Compare newspapers and consumer magazines as advertising media for (*a*) cigarettes; (*b*) power tools; and (*c*) cheese advertisements.

4. Find three different magazine or newspaper advertisements using flexform or freeform. Comment on the appropriateness of each. Under what conditions do you think a free-form advertisement would perform better than the traditional rectangular one?

5. Describe the similarities and dissimilarities of promotion through a sales force and through
   (*a*) newspapers
   (*b*) consumer magazines
   (*c*) business publications
   (*d*) outdoor and transit
   (*e*) direct mail

6. Find three different examples of the use of colour in newspaper advertising, and analyze for that product why newspaper was selected as the advertising medium as well as the role of colour in the advertisement. Answer the same question with consumer magazines.

7. What does verticalization of consumer magazines mean? Explain why this trend occurred. Do you believe it will continue? Justify your answer.

8. Explain how you would plan a direct mail advertising campaign. Develop a numerical example with a one-page black and white flyer addressed to homeowners in your community.

9. Provide some examples from your community of campaigns using outdoor or transit advertising. Evaluate this choice of medium for the particular products advertised.

10. Explain the rationale behind the use of specialty advertising. Give some good examples and others that you think are not appropriate.

Problems

1. Assume that you are a retailer of women's fashion shoes in the downtown area of a large metropolitan centre near your home. Your objective is to stimulate traffic in your showroom, and someone suggested that you advertise in one of the local print media. You have budgeted $5,000 for advertising, and you are deciding which print medium to use. In order to understand each medium, you have decided to look at each one separately and evaluate how much exposure your store would be getting by using that medium. Which medium seems to be the best one(s) for your store?

2. You have invented a revolutionary burglar-proof lock that works without a key. The lock operates with a small device attached to your wrist that emits a special coded sound. An electronics firm located in a nearby metropolitan area has agreed to produce the locks at $5.00 per unit provided that you order at least 5000 units. You have $20,000 of your own money, and a local bank has agreed to give you a loan of up to $50,000. You have decided that $15 is a good price for the new lock and that the best medium to

use is direct mail. You are thinking of naming your invention the Surelock, and your firm the Surelock Homes Company. Prepare a *complete* direct mail campaign in order to sell your lock to Canadian home-owners. Make sure that all assumptions are clearly stated, and that all the costs are accurate.

Notes

1. *Canadian Advertising Rates and Data* (March 1983), p. 154. Henceforth cited as *CARD*.
2. H.E. Stephenson and C. McNaught, *The Story of Advertising in Canada* (Toronto: The Ryerson Press, 1940), pp. 1-4.
3. Ibid., pp. 262-68.
4. *The Canadian Media Directors' Council Media Digest, 1982/83*, p. 28. Henceforth cited as *CMDC*.
5. T.R. Bird, "Analysis of the Impact of Electronic Systems on Advertising Revenues in Canada" (Working paper, Montreal: Institute for Research on Public Policy, 1982), p. 14.
6. *CARD*.
7. "An Interview with Roy Megarry," *Marketing* (2 November 1981), pp. 31-37.
8. *CMDC*, pp. 44-45.
9. Bird, p. 19.
10. *CMDC*, p. 28.
11. Bird, p. 14.
12. *CMDC*, pp. 30-31.
13. Newspaper Marketing Bureau, *Canadian Daily Newspapers: The Facts*, 15 March 1981, p. 30.
14. Fred H. Siller and Vernon J. Jones, "Newspaper Campaign Audience Segments," *Journal of Advertising Research* (June 1973), pp. 27-31.
15. Vernon J. Jones, "Dimensions of Audience Exposure to the Advertising Content of a Daily Newspaper," *Developments in Canadian Marketing*, ed. R.D. Tamilia, (Administrative Sciences Association of Canada, 1979), pp. 42-8.
16. James G. Barnes and G.A. Pynn, "A Hierarchical Model of Source Effect in Retail Newspaper Advertising," *Proceedings of the Fourth Annual Conference* (Administrative Sciences Association of Canada, 1976), Section 5, pp. 29-37.
17. "NMB Leads in Market Research," *Marketing* (2 November 1981), pp. 43-45.
18. John Foy, "Ad Revenues of $1 Billion Projected for Dailies in 1980," *Marketing* (21 January 1980), p. 25.
19. Leonard Kubas, "Recession Strengthening Marketing Muscle," *Marketing* (8 November 1982), pp. 11-12.
20. Joe Mullie, "The Videotex Threat? Fear and Loathing in the Newsroom," *Marketing* (2 November 1981), pp. 45-49.
21. Stephenson and McNaught, pp. 273-76.
22. Ibid., pp. 277-79.
23. Jo Marney, "Demographic Changes Favour Future Growth," *Marketing* (12 April 1982), pp. M6-7.
24. *CARD*, p. 154.
25. Marney, "Demographic Changes," p. M7.
26. *CARD*, p. 73.
27. Jo Marney, "In the Beginning was the Word . . . ," *Marketing* (22 June 1981), pp. 36-37.
28. Bird, p. 24.
29. *CARD*, p. 114.
30. Marney, "Demographic Changes," p. M6.
31. Karen Dean, "Magazines Canada Industry Round-Up," *Marketing* (12 April 1982), pp. M14-16.
32. Ibid p. M16.
33. Bird, p. 25.
34. "Magazine Sets Its Sights on City Core," *Marketing* (22 June 1981), p. 60.
35. Hugh Dow, "PMB Moves to Annual Reporting with the Release of 1983 Study," *Marketing* (12 April 1982), pp. M12-13.

36. Ibid.
37. Stephenson and McNaught, pp. 271-72.
38. Ibid., p. 272.
39. *CARD*, p. 154.
40. Stephenson and McNaught, p. 270.
41. *CMDC*, p. 46.
42. *CARD*, pp. 156-58.
43. Ibid., pp. 159-67.
44. Stephenson and McNaught, pp. 280-84.
45. Ibid., p. 284.
46. *CMDC*, p. 41.
47. Stephenson and McNaught, p. 284.
48. Stephen J. Arnold and James G. Barnes, "Canadians and Americans: Implications for Marketing," *Current Topics in Canadian Marketing*, ed. J.G. Barnes and M.S. Sommers (McGraw-Hill Ryerson, 1978), pp. 84-100. These figures were given by Frank C. Ferguson, president, Canadian Direct Marketing Association.
49. Ibid.
50. Jo Marney, "DM Plays Vital Role in the Total Media Mix," *Marketing* (12 July 1982), pp. 7-9.
51. R.S. Hodgson, *Direct Mail and Mail Order Handbook* (Chicago: Darnell Corp., 1965), p. 323.
52. Marney, "DM Plays Vital Role," p. 9.
53. Phil Brown, "A Direct Hit Is One in a Hundred," *Marketing* (12 July 1982), p. 12.
54. Nadine Lucki, "Ringing Phones Help Ring up Sales," *Marketing* (12 July 1982), p. 12.
55. Frank Ferguson, "CDMA Drops 'Mail' to Reflect Its New Status," *Marketing* (12 July 1982), p. 8; "Videotex Leads the Way in DM Revolution," *Marketing* (12 July 1982), p. 8.

Canadian
Broadcast Media

Canada has been among the foremost nations in introducing new technologies in the area of broadcast media. When they were first introduced, radio and television radically transformed the entertainment and advertising industries, and forced print media to change their strategies.

In net advertising revenues, radio has been growing at a slower rate than television, and its share of total advertising revenues has declined. Table 6.1 shows the components of net advertising revenues of radio and television. In 1982, net advertising revenues of radio reached $458 million, and its share of total revenues dropped to 10.3 per cent from 10.9 per cent in 1977. In contrast, television's net advertising revenues reached $779 million, which is more than double the 1977 figure, and its share of total revenues reached 17.5 per cent from 15.3 per cent in 1977. Television revenues gained market share from both national and local advertisers, while the reverse is true for radio.

Radio

The Changing Role of Radio as an Advertising Medium

In December 1920, the Canadian Marconi Company, located in Montreal, began regularly broadcasting on a wavelength of 1200 metres. From that first radio station *in the world*, the new medium grew rapidly. By 1923, 52 broadcasting licences had been granted.[1] The first

TABLE 6.1   Components of Net Advertising Revenues by Broadcasting Media (in thousands of dollars)

	1977		1982		Average annual rate of growth (%)
	amount	%	amount	%	
Radio—*Total*	269,080	10.9	458,000	10.3	11.2
national	73,034	3.0	129,000	2.9	12.1
local	196,046	8.0	329,000	7.4	10.9
Television—*Total*	375,564	15.3	779,000	17.5	15.7
national	278,651	11.3	591,000	13.3	16.2
local	96,913	3.9	188,000	4.2	14.2
Total broadcast media	644,644	26.2	1,237,000	27.8	13.9
Total all media	2,458,006	100.0	4,445,700	100.0	12.6

SOURCE: *Canadian Advertising Rates and Data* (1983), p. 154.
Courtesy Special Interest Network

receiving sets were battery-powered. The growth of radio penetration was based on improvements in technology and lower prices for receiving sets.

Because of the uneven distribution of the Canadian population, only large centres had operating radio stations and families with a set in other areas were listening to more powerful U.S. stations. The solution to the problem of providing radio programs to all Canadians was to set up a national broadcasting system, first as the Canadian Radio Broadcasting Commission, and in 1936 as the Canadian Radio Broadcasting Corporation (CBC), modelled after the British Broadcasting Corporation. Radio penetration grew rapidly, from 49 per cent in 1936 to 85 per cent in 1939, when 85 stations were in operation, nine of which were owned by the CBC. Initially, the CBC operated on licence fees levied on receiving sets as well as government loans and advertising revenues. In 1974, the CBC decided to stop selling advertising time for broadcast in all of its stations.

Battery-operated receiving sets received a strong impetus with the invention of the transistor in 1948. This allowed a reduction in size and an increase in mobility. The invention of the transistor allowed more cars to be equipped with radio. The growth and vitality of the medium was also spurred by other inventions and new technologies that led to FM (frequency modulation) and stereophonic broadcasting, more stable reception, and less interference.

In 1952 a new technology, that of television, pre-empted radio and soon became the favoured entertainment medium. In response to this competition, radio became more specialized and developed programming directed at specific target audiences. Radio changed from an involving entertainment medium to a background medium. Thus, radio came to be positioned as a complement of rather than a direct competitor to television.

In 1982, there were 531 independent stations, and 63 CBC owned and operated stations. About two-thirds are AM stations and one-third are FM stations. A breakdown by province is shown in Table 6.2. On the average, about 97 per cent of adults and teenagers listen to radio on a given week, and 98 per cent of all households own at least one set. Net advertising revenues of radio reached $458 million in

TABLE 6.2   Number of Originating Stations in Canada by Province (as of 31 March 1983)

Province	Private Independent*			CBC O&O			Total Stations		
	AM	FM	Total	AM	FM	Total	AM	FM	Total
Newfoundland	17	6	23	5	1	6	22	7	29
PEI	4	1	5	–	–	–	4	1	5
Nova Scotia	20	7	27	2	2	4	22	9	31
New Brunswick	14	5	19	5	1	6	19	6	25
Quebec	70	58	128	7	7	14	77	65	142
Ontario	94	67	161	6	5	11	100	72	172
Manitoba	17	6	23	3	1	4	20	7	27
Saskatchewan	19	9	28	1	2	3	20	11	31
Alberta	37	12	49	7	1	8	44	13	57
British Columbia	56	16	72	7	2	9	63	18	81
NWT	4	3	7	2	–	2	6	3	9
Yukon	1	3	4	1	–	1	2	3	5
TOTAL CANADA	353	193	546	46	22	68	399	215	614

*Including CBC affiliate stations
SOURCE: CRTC Annual Report 1982/83
Courtesy Canadian Radio–television and Telecommunications Commission

1982, or 10.3 per cent of the total for all media.[2] Between 1971 and 1981, radio advertising revenues grew by 274 per cent, which represents about 14 per cent per annum, with the biggest gain coming from local revenues.[3]

Characteristics of Radio

Radio stations are characterized by their mode of broadcasting, type of ownership, and programming.

Mode of Broadcasting

AM (amplitude modulation) stations transmit radio waves that may cover a very large area. AM stations are the most important in terms of numbers and amount of advertising carried. As seen in Table 6.3, there were 385 AM stations in Canada in 1980, or two-thirds of all radio stations. These AM stations received $328 in advertising revenues in 1980 or 85 per cent of total radio advertising revenues. About three-fourths of these revenues came from local advertisers, and this proportion has been on the increase for more than ten years.

FM (frequency modulation) stations cover a limited area, but their signal has the major advantage of clear reception. FM stations have seen rapid growth in their advertising revenues and audience share in recent years. Net advertising revenues of radio stations have increased by 197 per cent between 1976 and 1980 (Table 6.3) which is almost three and one-half times the growth rate for AM stations. This growth has been most pronounced in local revenues (202 per cent), but is still highly significant in national revenues (181 per cent). The FM share of total revenues has almost doubled between 1976 and 1980.[4] In addition, FM audience share has grown dramatically. In Montreal, the FM share of teenagers increased from 33 per cent in 1975 to 60 per cent in 1981, while the comparable figures for adults were 26 and 45 per cent. A similar growth was recorded in Toronto and other major cities.[5]

Types of Ownership

Radio stations may be classified into three groups according to the type of ownership: independent stations, network affiliates, and owned-and-operated stations.

Independent stations are individually responsible for programming and advertising. The majority of radio stations are in this category and the overwhelming majority of advertising

TABLE 6.3   Net Advertising Revenues of Radio Stations (1980)

Number	AM Stations 385	FM Stations 178	Total 563
Advertising revenues			
National			
amount ($ millions)	$ 83	$14	$ 97
change 1976-1980	41%	181%	52%
Local			
amount ($ millions)	$245	$43	$288
change 1976-1980	63%	202%	75%
Total			
amount ($ millions)	*$328*	*$57*	*$385*
change 1976-1980	*57%*	*197%*	*69%*

SOURCE: Leonard Kubas, "Radio to Chalk up Its First $½ Billion in Net Ad Revenues," *Marketing* (1 March 1982), pp. R12-13.
Courtesy Leonard Kubas/Kubas Retail

expenditures are placed with independent stations.

Network affiliates must carry *some* of the programs of the network, as well as the advertising sold by the network for some time periods. Otherwise, affiliates have complete responsibility for their programming. Examples of such networks are CKO All-News Radio Network, the Farm Market Network, and the Reseau des Appalaches Network.

Owned and operated (O + O) stations belong to one network, and individual stations have great flexibility for local programming. Examples of such networks are the CBC Network (no commercial advertising allowed), the Radio-mutuel Network, and the Reseau Laurentide Network.

Types of Programming

Radio stations define, attract, and hold their audience by the kind of programs they select. Programming decisions are based on demographic composition and tastes of the population covered by the station, changes in audience flow during the day, and competition from other stations.

MUSIC FORMATS. In Canada, there are basically six types of music formats used in radio programming:

Adult-contemporary stations play adult or easy listening music, show tunes, and popular music. These stations are sometimes called middle of the road (MOR) stations. Their audience is typically in their late 20s and up. Examples are CJOB in Winnipeg, CFRB in Toronto, and CJAD in Montreal.

Rock-oriented or top 40 stations play recent rock music and appeal mainly to teenagers and young adults. Most of them are AM stations.

Album-oriented rock (AOR) stations play rock albums on a continuing basis. They appeal mainly to teenagers and young adults. Most of them are FM stations. One example is CJAY-FM Calgary.

Country music stations play a variety of country music, which is most popular in the western provinces. One example is CKWX Vancouver. The audience tends to be downscale on the key demographic dimensions of occupation and income.

Classical music is played on many Canadian stations but only during certain times of the day. Except for the CBC network, there are no pure classical music stations in Canada. For most radio stations playing some classical music, the proportion of classical programming varies from 1 per cent to 25 per cent. The audience tends to be older, with higher education and income than for other music formats.

All-news stations do not play any music but provide local, regional, and national news and other related information on a 24-hour basis. These types of stations are relatively new in Canada and are growing in popularity. The CKO All-News Network started in 1977 in Toronto and Ottawa, and is now in seven cities.[6]

POPULATION COMPOSITION AND TASTES. Population characteristics of the area covered by a radio station can influence the type of programming. Age, sex, occupation, level of education, geographic location, and employment status affect the number of hours per day (or week) tuned to radio, AM or FM. Radio programming in a small town may be different from that in a large metropolitan or rural area. Examples of such differences are provided in Table 6.4 for age, education, occupational status, and occupation of full-time workers.

CHANGES IN AUDIENCE FLOW. The listening habits of various demographic groups are also quite important in deciding on programming formats, since there are major changes in audience composition during the average day. Between 8 A.M. and 4 P.M., there are more women listeners than men, while the reverse is true before 8 A.M. and after 4 P.M. Proportionally, more teenagers listen to radio than adults or children after 6 P.M.

TABLE 6.4   Characteristics of AM and FM Audiences

	Percentage distribution of reach	
	AM	FM
Age		
7-11	7	5
12-17	12	13
18-24	15	20
25-34	19	24
35-49	20	19
50-59	12	10
60+	15	10
Total	*100*	*100*
Education		
Grade school	19	12
Some high school	27	24
Completed high school	24	25
Completed technical college	13	17
Some university	8	11
Completed university	9	12
Total	*100*	*100*
Occupational status		
Work full time	45	50
Work part time	11	12
Not in labour force	44	28
Total	*100*	*100*
Occupation of full time workers		
Manager/Executive	14	15
Professional	20	22
Clerical	17	18
Sales	6	7
Farm/Fish	4	2
Skilled Tradesperson	18	17
Other	21	20
Total	*100*	*100*

	Percentage distribution of hours tuned	
	AM	FM
Age		
7-11	3	2
12-17	9	8
18-24	13	23
25-34	18	26
35-49	23	21
50-59	15	11
60+	19	10
Total	*100*	*100*

SOURCE: The Radio Bureau of Canada, *Radio 81/82*, p. 7.

Based on these characteristics, radio uses one of two programming strategies: a station selects a demographic group and caters to its tastes, developing a strong image as a rock station or an adult-contemporary station; or a station varies its programming in order to follow the audience flow pattern.

COMPETITIVE SITUATION.   In a given market, the amount of competition for the same audience may lead a station to change its music format or to expand its revenue base by targeting several groups at different times.

Radio as an Advertising Medium

The main advantages of radio can be grouped into five categories:

High frequency. Radio is the best medium for advertisers who require high message frequency at a relatively low cost. Specific audiences may be reached several times a day, for several days or weeks, to promote a local restaurant or a moving company. High frequency using one vehicle may allow the advertiser to qualify for a volume discount.

High potential reach. Because almost everybody listens to radio and most households own several sets, including car radios and portable radios, the medium has the potential for high reach by combining several stations. In addition, radio listenership is strong all year around. Radio's weekly reach by region is presented in Table 6.5. Reach figures are very high, especially for teenagers and adults.

Low cost. The costs of using radio are relatively low for four reasons. First, *production costs* of radio commercials are usually very low. Second, radio requires short deadlines and rapid copy changes can be made in order to take advantage of changes in market conditions. Third, *unit costs* of radio (the cost per thousand listeners) are among the lowest of all media, thus allowing advertisers to supplement the reach of other media or to generate high

TABLE 6.5   Weekly Radio Reach (in %) by Region

Region	Women 18+	Men 18+	Teens 12-17	Children 7-11
Maritimes	96.0	94.3	92.3	77.9
Quebec	97.0	95.3	93.1	74.1
Ontario	96.9	96.4	94.8	83.6
Prairies	97.3	96.1	93.3	76.8
B.C.	96.2	94.8	91.2	79.0
Canada	96.8	95.7	93.4	78.9

SOURCE: Bureau of Broadcast Measurment, Fall 1982

message frequency. Fourth, because of its relatively low production and time costs, advertising in radio is affordable to many retailers, with or without co-operative advertising dollars.

High selectivity. Radio stations have attracted very specific audiences through careful programming. Some stations appeal to narrowly defined demographic subgroups, thus allowing the advertiser to match the target market with the audience of one or several stations with a minimum of waste. Radio is considered the best medium to reach teenagers. Specific ethnic groups may be reached through ethnic radio stations or programs. Some stations, particularly in small communities, change programming during the day according to the changes in audience composition.

Great flexibility. Radio is a highly flexible medium. It allows *short lead times* in most markets for both production and scheduling, generally two to four weeks. In the top five or six markets, lead times of two to three months are often necessary, because of the nearly sold-out positions of the stations. Radio allows flexibility in *market coverage*, i.e., precise targeting both in terms of demographic characteristics and geographical coverage, which allows advertisers to vary the intensity of advertising according to market potential. Radio also allows a great deal of *creative flexibility* through a variety of sound effects, music, and voice

types, and by relying on listeners' imagination. Radio has often been termed "the theatre of the mind." Thus the message may be highly adaptable to a more heterogeneous audience. The low cost of producing radio commercials allows more experimenting with various approaches, until the right one is found.

The main *disadvantages* of radio may be grouped into three categories:

A low reach medium. Although it has the potential for high reach, radio can present many problems in terms of reach. First, the total audience for radio is often highly *fragmented*, depending on the number of stations available in a particular market and the changes in audience composition during the day. Second, the audience is segmented further due to differences in program quality, individual listening habits, and personal taste. Thus, radio is mostly a *high frequency/low reach* medium.

Creative negatives. For the creative director, radio presents several problems. Since radio is mostly a background medium, it has low listener attention levels. Message registration often requires repetition, attention-getting devices, and learning aids, such as catchy jingles and closure. A radio commercial has a very *short life* and has to accomplish its objectives in 30 or 60 seconds. In addition, particularly in AM radio, advertising messages have to compete for attention. Thus, *clutter* severely restricts the effectiveness of a particular message. Radio messages lack visual registration, particularly in providing package identification for products sold in self-service retail establishments. In writing radio commercials, it is inadvisable to use long copy because of low listener attention levels.

Media planning problems. Radio also presents several problems to the media planner. Most radio contracts contain a two-week cancellation clause, thus preventing the advertiser from responding within days to changes in the marketplace. It is often difficult to buy radio time in major markets because demand is high and availability limited. Stations are limited by law in the amount of commercial time they are allowed to sell. In a week, AM stations are allowed 1500 minutes; FM stations affiliated with AM stations are allowed 840 minutes; and independent FM stations are allowed 1050 minutes. Other constraints applying to FM stations limit the amount of commercial time per day or per hour. (See Appendix 1 for a listing of radio advertising regulations.) There is a need for more and better research data about radio in order to assist the media director in choosing vehicles and schedules. Although the use of market research is increasing, radio is still far from possessing the extent and quality of data that consumer magazines provide.[7] Finally, from the agency viewpoint, radio is an expensive medium for administrative costs because of the high number of independent stations.

Radio Advertising Rate Structure

The cost of advertising on Canadian radio depends on the nature of the advertiser, the scheduled time (daypart), the length of the commercial, package plans, and discounts or special features.

Nature of the Advertiser

There are two basic types of rates for radio: general and retail.

GENERAL (OR NATIONAL) RATES. General advertising is placed by agencies and is commissionable. General rates are published monthly in CARD. Unless noted in the general rate card, these rates are usually higher than local rates. On the average, national net advertising revenues represent 15 per cent of total revenues, as seen previously.

RETAIL (OR LOCAL) RATES. Retail rates are noncommissionable, and commercials are placed by a local businessperson, with or without production assistance from the station. Retail rates are generally lower than national rates, and these revenues provide an average of 85 per cent of total revenues (Table 6.3).

Time Classification (dayparts)

Radio time is usually divided into dayparts, and each such time segment has a different rate assigned to it. Unfortunately, dayparts are not standardized and the media buyer must look at each station's rate card. For example, two CARD listings are reproduced in Figure 6.1. The Vancouver station has three dayparts, like the Toronto station's three classes. For the Toronto station, the class AAA rates are from 5:30-10 A.M., Monday through Saturday, while for the Vancouver station the AAA rates are from 6 A.M. until noon, Monday through Friday.

The dayparts most often used as well as the audience composition by time period are shown in Figure 6.2. The pattern for adult men and children is rather flat, while that of adult women drops dramatically after 4 PM. The pattern for teenagers mirrors that for adult women.

Length of Commercial

All radio stations sell radio time by blocks of 30 or 60 seconds, the former being the most popular. Rates for 30 seconds are usually more than half the rate for 60 seconds.

Package Plans

Since one of the drawbacks of radio is low reach, stations have designed plans to maximize their reach. These plans are called reach plans or total audience plans (TAP). The rationale is that since audience composition varies with dayparts, the number of *different* people listening to the commercial may be increased if the commercial is *rotated* among various dayparts. In figure 6.1, CHUM-FM offers a choice of three reach plans, while CJOR offers one plan. The unit rate for these plans is offered at a discount from the regular rates.

R3090

Toronto—CHUM

Member CAB

Data confirmed for May/83 CARD

Est. 1945.
Owned & operated by CHUM Ltd.
Studio: 1331 Yonge St., Toronto, Ont. M4T 1Y1
Phone: 416-925-6666.
Transmitter: Clarkson, Ont.

WAVE—POWER—TIME
Power: 50,000 watts. Kilohertz: 1050.
Time: EST or EDT.

OPERATING SCHEDULE
24 hours daily.

TIME CLASSIFICATIONS
Class AAA: Breakfast rotation 5.30-10 a.m. Mon. to Sat. Available Mon. thru Sat. or Mon., Wed., Fri. alternating with Tues., Thurs., Fri.
Class AA: Supper rotation 3-8 p.m. Mon.-Fri.; 10 a.m.-6 p.m. Sat.
Class A: Daytime rotation 10 a.m.-3 p.m. Mon.-Fri. Evening rotation 8 p.m.-mid. Mon.-Fri.; Sat. 6 p.m.-mid.; All day Sun.

COMMISSION & CASH DISCOUNT
15% on station rates to all recognized advtg. agencies. No commission on talent. No cash discount. Invoices rendered monthly. Bills due & payable when rendered.

GENERAL ADVERTISING
Rate Card No. 30. Effective Dec. 15, 1981.

CLASS "AAA"

	1	260	500
*Feature insert	$225	$215	—
60 sec.	200	190	180
30 sec. or less	130	125	120

CLASS "AA"

*Feature insert	$150	$140	—
60 sec.	130	125	120
30 sec. or less	90	85	80

CLASS "A"

*Feature insert	$110	$100	—
60 sec.	95	85	80
30 sec. or less	70	60	55

*60 sec. anncts. in news & sports.

REACH PLAN
To be used within 1 b'cast. week.

	10*	15**	20***
60 sec.	$1000	$1500	$2000
30 sec.	700	1050	1400

Schedule: *3AAA, 3AA, 4A; **3AAA, 6AA. 6A, ***6AAA, 6AA, 8A.

RUN OF SCHEDULE
10 a.m.-mid. Mon. to Sun.

	10*	25**	50***	100****
60 sec.	$850	$2000	$3750	$7000
30 sec.	600	1375	2500	4500

R.O.S. packages, if available, station's choice of times & days & subject to change without notice & must be used within *1 b'cast week; **2 b'cast week; ***3 b'cast week; ****5 b'cast week.
Midnite to 5.30 a.m. rates on request.
Reach plan, run of schedule & regular anncts. cannot be combined for frequency discount.
Split 60 sec. anncts.—Dbl. 30 sec. rate.

PERSONNEL
Pres.: Allan Waters.
Vice-Pres. & Sales Dir.: Wes Armstrong.
Retail Sales Mgr.: Chuck Langdon.
Gen. Mgr.: J. Robert Wood.
Traffic Mgr.: Eileen Taylor.

REPRESENTATIVES
Can.: Major Market Broadcasters Ltd., Toronto, Montreal, Vancouver, Halifax, Winnipeg.
U.S.: Radio Station Representatives, Inc., New York.

R0740

Vancouver—CJOR

Member

Data confirmed for May/83 CARD

Est. 1926.
Owned & operated by CJOR, a Div. of Jim Pattison Industries Ltd.
Studio: 840 Howe Street, Vancouver, B.C. V6Z 1N6. Phone: (604) 669-6060.
Transmitter: R. R. 2 Eburne.

OPERATING SCHEDULE
24 hours daily.

WAVE—POWER—TIME
Power: 10,000 watts, Kilohertz: 600.
Time: PST or PDT.

TIME CLASSIFICATIONS
Class AAA: 6 a.m.-noon Mon. to Fri.
Class AA: 3-10 p.m. Mon. to Fri.; 6 a.m.-noon Sat./Sun.
Class A: Noon-3 p.m. Mon. to Fri.; Noon-10 p.m. Sat./Sun.

COMMISSION & CASH DISCOUNT
15% on station rates to all CAB enfranchised advtg. agencies. No commission on talent. No cash

discounts. Invoices rendered monthly. Bills due & payable when rendered.

GENERAL ADVERTISING
Rate card No. 3. Effective Jan. 1, 1983.
GRID:

CLASS AAA

	1	2	3	4	5
30 sec.	$33	$40	$45	$52	$60
60 sec.	50	60	70	80	90

CLASS AA

30 sec.	22	26	30	34	40
60 sec.	33	40	45	52	60

CLASS A

30 sec.	15	17	20	22	26
60 sec.	22	26	30	34	40

DRIVE BUY
AM/PM 50% AAA, 50% AA. Min. 10 anncts per week

30 sec.	25	30	35	40	45
60 sec.	39	45	53	60	69

BEST BUY (preemptible)
6 a.m.-mid. 6 days; min. 12 occas per week

30 sec.	12	15	18	21	24
60 sec.	18	23	27	33	36

REMOTE CONTROL
Full facilities for remote control pickups.

MECHANICAL PROGRAM EQUIPMENT
Equipped for continuous 33-1/3 & 45 r.p.m. recording. Tape recorders & cartridge tape facilities available.

PERSONNEL
Pres.: Jim Pattison.
Gen. Mgr.: Ron Vandenberg.
Prog. Dir.: Frank Callaghan.
Gen. Sales Mgr.: David Bremner.
Traffic Mgr.: Marilee Krogel.

REPRESENTATIVES
Can.: Radio-Television Representatives Ltd.: Toronto, Montreal, Calgary, Winnipeg.
U.S.: Hugh Wallace, Los Angeles & San Francisco; Canadian Standard Broadcast Sales, New York, Detroit;
Art Moore Inc., Seattle & Portland.

FIGURE 6.1 *CARD* **Listing for Two Radio Stations**
SOURCE: *Canadian Advertising Rates and Data* (May 1983), pp. 382, 409. *Courtesy* Special Interest Network

In addition, more specific rotations may be offered in order to increase reach. A *horizontal* rotation places a spot in the same daypart on different days, while a *vertical* rotation places a spot in different dayparts on the same day.

Other Discounts

Four types of discounts are available:

VOLUME DISCOUNTS. The unit rate is lower if a certain number of spots are purchased. For example, Toronto's CHUM-FM offers the first discount at 260 spots and the second at 500 spots (Figure 6.1).

FREQUENCY DISCOUNTS. The unit rate is lower if a certain number of spots are bought for a number of consecutive weeks.

RUN OF STATION (ROS) OR BEST TIME AVAILABLE (BTA). The radio station schedules the commercial at its discretion. ROS or BTA rates are often combined with a minimum volume (see Figure 6.1).

COMBINATION RATES. Discounts are offered when several stations (either AM, FM, or both) are owned by the same company and spots in two or more stations are bought.

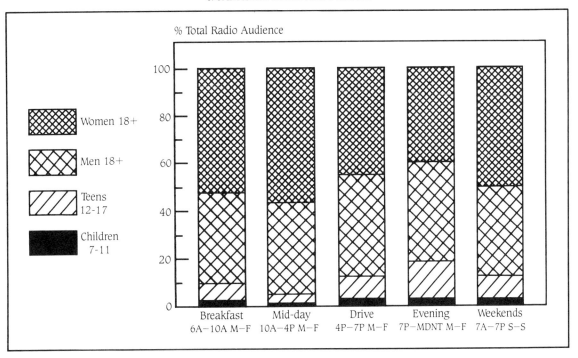

% Total Radio Audience

FIGURE 6.2 Audience Composition by Daypart
SOURCE: BBM Radio Fall 1982

Special Features

Special features offered to advertisers include sponsorship of a specific program, feature inserts, and tie-ins with retail outlets.

The Future of Radio as an Advertising Medium

The trend in favour of FM stations and an increasing use of radio by advertisers, particularly local advertisers, will likely continue because of cost considerations. The latter may be stimulated by industry efforts to improve their marketing orientation through standardization of rate cards, increased use of research beyond the mere demographic variables by using psychographic and other behavioural variables, and radio syndication in order to produce better programs and to spread the costs to larger audiences.[8]

Radio will be affected by *demographic* and *socio-economic trends* in the Canadian population: aging, working women, rising education levels, and changing leisure patterns.

Radio may be affected by new *technological developments*, but not as much as other media: increased penetration of cable, dish antennas, home information delivery systems, and other innovations related to the transmission of sound.

Television

Growth of Television as an Advertising Medium

Three years after it was introduced in the United States, television became the newest Canadian medium in 1952 with one station, CBFT, operating in Montreal and another, CBLT, in Toronto. Both stations were owned and operated by the Canadian Broadcasting Corporation.

As the CBC expanded its network and privately owned stations were licensed, by 1955 *seven* CBC and *nineteen* privately owned stations were reaching *ten* million Canadians. Based on the two main languages in Canada, the CBC expanded into a French and an English network.

In 1961 the third Canadian network, the CTV television network, was licensed to operate in eight major urban areas. The fourth Canadian network, the TVA television network, was established in 1971 to cover the province of Quebec. One year later the fifth Canadian network, the Global Television Network, was licensed to serve the province of Ontario.

In 1966, barely fourteen years after the introduction of television, another momentous development occurred: the introduction of *colour*. In 1970, about 12 per cent of Canadian households were equipped with a colour television set. By 1982, this figure had risen to 88 per cent.

The following technological developments are affecting the nature of the industry:

• Cable (or community antenna) television was first developed to reach areas with poor reception and came to be used to provide distant channels to the public in high density areas. Cable penetration of households rose from 25 per cent in 1970 to 57 per cent in 1982,[9] making Canada the *most "wired" nation in the world*.

• Converters allow the public to pick up more channels with a standard television set connected to a cable. About 26 per cent of all households owned a cable converter in 1982. The acquisition of a cable converter was found to increase total viewing and satisfaction with viewing.[10] However, the extent of switching among channels after acquisition of cable converters is not yet clear, although increases were found in the same studies.[11]

• Pay TV allows the public to receive selected commmercial-free programs for a fee through sets connected to a cable.

TABLE 6.6 Television—Cable, Cable Converters, Colour, and Multi-Set Penetration by Market (expressed by % of population 2+)

Central Markets	Cable %	Cable Converter %	Colour TV %	Multiple Sets %
Halifax	72	11	90	61
Saint John/Moncton	69	10	85	56
Quebec	54	36	90	63
Montreal	53	40	87	64
Ottawa	74	47	88	60
Toronto	77	61	90	58
Hamilton	71	57	92	58
Kitchener	82	67	89	49
London	81	55	89	54
Windsor	—	—	92	72
Thunder Bay	79	—	92	65
Winnipeg	86	7	93	60
Regina/Moose Jaw	78	20	95	61
Saskatoon	70	19	90	70
Calgary	79	28	94	61
Edmonton	79	9	90	57
Vancouver	90	59	93	52
Victoria	89	28	91	42
Canada	*57*	*26*	*88*	*56*

SOURCE: BBM Fall 1982 TV Sweep

- Satellites and dish antennas may improve the speed and efficiency of communication, particularly for business.

- Home video players/recorders allow the public to tape programs and delete commercials for viewing at a later date and to use their television sets to view commercial-free movies.

- Videotex systems/home computers allow the viewer to control the information received through the television set in the form of words or symbols. The Canadian videotex system, Telidon, is still being tested, and is expected to reach large numbers of consumers by the late 1980s.

- Two-way cable allows viewers and the cable company to control information other than text received through the television set. Two-way cable systems may be used to develop interactive programs such as electronic shopping or electronic market surveys.

This type of system is also in its infancy but it is expected to grow very rapidly in the late 1980s.

Thus, the medium of television, just over thirty years after its birth, is undergoing major changes that will shape its future. Today more than 97 per cent of Canadian households are equipped with at least one television set and more than 88 per cent own at least one colour set. More than 56 per cent own more than one set, and 57 per cent are equipped with cable.[12] Table 6.6 provides a breakdown by major markets. The highest penetration rate of cable is in Vancouver while 67 per cent of households in Kitchener own a cable converter. Regina/Moose Jaw has the highest percentage of households with a colour set (95 per cent).

There are currently 111 commercial television stations in Canada, reaching 35-45 per cent of all adults daily during prime time. On the average, more than 80 per cent of Canadians watch television at least once a day.[13] Figure 6.3

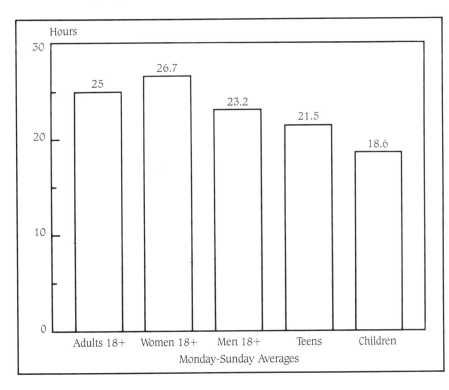

FIGURE 6.3
Average Weekly Hours Tuned Per Capita
SOURCE:
BBM Television Fall 1982

shows the average number of hours per week of television viewing for different groups. Women watch three and one-half hours more of television than men, and all adults watch more television than teenagers or children.

Net advertising revenues for television reached $779 million in 1982, more than twice the 1977 figure. Television increased its share of advertising revenues for all media from 15.3 per cent in 1977 to 17.5 per cent in 1982.

Television is mostly a *national* medium, with three-fourths of its revenues coming from national advertisers. It tends to be an expensive medium, well beyond the reach of small and medium-sized advertisers and thus is generally a medium for mass marketers, for example, packaged-goods companies. In addition, from 1978 to 1982, television rates increased 79 per cent and costs per thousand viewers went up by 62 per cent.[14]

Characteristics of Television

Television has various vehicles for carrying an advertising message: the type of station, the scheduled time period, and the type of program selected by the advertiser and its agency.

Type of station
Television stations are classified according to the frequency of transmission and the networks to which they are affiliated.

FREQUENCY. Since signals are transmitted by radio waves, television stations are assigned special frequencies by the CRTC. The first stations were assigned *very high frequencies* (VHF), which are channels 2 to 13. In 1982 there were 90 VHF stations in Canada. In 1972, when the VHF range could not accommodate more stations, *ultra high frequencies* (UHF) were assigned to new stations. These are channels 14 to 83. There were 22 UHF stations in Canada in 1982.

NETWORK OR INDIVIDUAL STATIONS. Television stations may be either independent or affiliated with one or several networks.

Independent stations, like CKND-TV (Winnipeg), are not affiliated with any network. They sell their time directly or through media representatives. There were 13 such stations in 1982.[15]

English CBC network stations are affiliated with the CBC English Network. There were 46 English stations in 1982, 20 owned and operated stations and 26 affiliates. The CBC Metronet network was comprised of the major stations affiliated with the CBC and included CBC stations in 14 markets. The coverage of the full network was about 98 per cent of households, while that of the Metronet was about 80 per cent.[16]

French CBC network stations are affiliated with the CBC French network. There were 17 French CBC station affiliates in 1982 (11 owned and operated stations and 6 affiliates), with a coverage of 32 per cent of Canadian households.

There were 26 stations affiliated with the CTV network in 1982. They have a 95 per cent household coverage. All CTV stations are independently owned and operated.

TVA television network is a French network with six affiliates in 1982 with a household coverage of about 30 per cent.

The Global network has six stations with a household coverage of 36 per cent.

The three non-commercial educational stations in Canada are located in Quebec and Ontario.

U.S. BORDER STATIONS. Another type of station that has a profound effect on Canadian television are U.S. border stations, which are powerful enough to broadcast to large populated areas in Canada. They further fragment the audience and put pressure on the operating costs of Canadian stations by pulling away advertising revenues from Canadian advertisers. Since 1976, however, these expenditures are *not* allowed as a deductible business expense (Bill c-58).[17] Nevertheless this competition makes it economically difficult for Canadian networks and

TABLE 6.7 U.S. Stations' Audience Share in Sixteen Major Canadian Markets

Central Market	ALL PERSONS 2+	
	Mon. – Sun. (6 a.m. – 2 a.m.) %	Mon. – Sun. (7 p.m. – 11 p.m.) %
Halifax	28	25
Saint-John/Moncton	29	25
Quebec	NA	NA
Montreal	16	15
Ottawa	12	14
Toronto	25	23
Hamilton	28	25
Kitchener	24	22
London	34	32
Windsor	77	79
Thunder Bay	39	33
Winnipeg	31	27
Calgary	24	23
Edmonton	23	23
Vancouver	38	36
Victoria	44	50

SOURCE: BBM Fall 1982

stations to develop the high quality programming needed to attract the large audiences advertisers seek. Since U.S. programs were developed for the large U.S. market, the high production costs are spread among many stations; the Canadian market is merely an opportunistic market for these programs. The same is true for the cable distribution of these U.S. stations and will continue as the penetration of cable television increases.

Table 6.7 gives the U.S. stations' share of the audience in 16 major markets. Windsor has the highest share, with 77-79 per cent of the audience viewing U.S. stations. Montreal has the lowest share of audience with 15 per cent on prime time.

To combat U.S. competition, Canadian stations have resorted to scheduling the same episode of a popular program at the same time as in the U.S. This practice is called *simulcasting*, and the station may demand that cable companies substitute their U.S.-originated signal, including commercials, with that of the Canadian station showing the same episode. With simul-

casting, the Canadian station can cater to the public taste for American programs and still receive additional revenues by offering Canadian advertisers a much larger Canadian audience.

Types of Advertising Time

For network affiliates, there are three types of advertising time: network, spot, and local. Independent stations have spot and local advertising.

NETWORK ADVERTISING. Network affiliates are linked by microwave relay stations or satellite transmission. Affiliates agree to carry a set of specific programs at a specific time, with the commercials sold by the network. These programs are mostly run during the evening prime time, with a few shown during the day. Commercials broadcast during these programs are called *network* advertising (or network time). For advertisers, the advantage of buying network time is in terms of the number of people reached during popular programs over a wide geographical area. This translates into high reach and low cost per thousand viewers. Another factor is the glamour or halo effect of advertising during popular programs, potentially giving additional status to the brand advertised and impressing the trade.

SPOT OR LOCAL ADVERTISING. Once a station agrees to carry the network programs and commercials, it is fully responsible for the balance of the schedule. The station may select its own programs and sell commercial time within the programs.

Commercial (non-network) time may be sold to a national advertiser, in which case it is called *spot* advertising. The advantage of spot advertising is that it allows advertisers to adjust the advertising pressure to local market conditions and to supplement basic network coverage.

Commercial (non-network) time may also be sold to local advertisers, such as retailers. This is *local* advertising and is non-commissionable.

TABLE 6.8   Audience Share by Program Category

Category of program	Group[1]		Males 18+ over		Females 18+ over		Teenagers 12-17		Children 2-11	
General drama and films	E	F	38	35	43	49	12	9	7	10
Suspense and adventure	E	F	36	36	37	36	12	13	15	15
Situation comedies	E	F	37	37	38	42	14	8	11	13
Variety shows	E	F	36	38	42	47	8	9	14	6
Documentaries	E	F	46	45	42	46	8	7	4	2
Talk shows and educational programs	E	F	48	42	45	52	5	2	2	4
Sports events	E	F	43	53	41	31	9	9	7	7
Early evening news	E	F	47	33	44	56	5	1	4	10
Late evening news	E	F	50	50	47	47	2	3	1	0
All television	E	F	36	36	38	38	11	11	15	15

[1] E = English
  F = French

SOURCE: A.C. Nielsen of Canada (1981)

About 25 per cent of net television advertising revenues come from local advertisers.[18]

Types of programming

The most important vehicle for carrying the advertising message is the program in which it is positioned. Since each type of program, and even each program, has its own individual audience composition, it is important to select the right one. Table 6.8 shows the nine categories of regularly scheduled programs and the audience share distribution of four demographic groups.

General drama and films attract a balanced distribution of both French and English viewers, with a bias toward more women than men and more French Canadian women than English Canadian women.

Suspense and adventure programs attract a balanced distribution of English and French Canadians.

Situation comedies are viewed more by French Canadian women than their English Canadian counterparts.

Variety shows are viewed more by women than men and least by teenagers in both French and English Canada.

Documentaries are viewed mostly by adults.

Talk shows and educational programs are also viewed mostly by adults, with a higher proportion of English Canadian men and French Canadian women.

Sports programs audiences are dominated by men.

News programs are mostly viewed by adults. The share of French Canadian males watching the early evening news is surprisingly low compared to the other groups, and conversely for females.

In addition to selecting the program, the advertiser has the option of *sponsoring* or *co-sponsoring* a particular program: one (or more) advertiser(s) agrees to buy all commercial time within that program. The advantage is for the advertiser to be associated with a popular program and to gain goodwill with a selected audience, for example, male adults watching a sports program. At the same time, the advertiser prevents other competitors from becoming associated with the program.

Television as an Advertising Medium

The main *advantages* of television can be grouped into four categories:

High message effectiveness. Television is *the* preferred medium of most creative personnel, and the best creative directors work more with television than with any other medium. Television allows an infinite variety of creative approaches by combining sight, sound, and motion to create a strong, effective impact. Television allows effective *demonstration* of the product in use, particularly for new product introductions; thus it is often the best medium for new product launches. Also, television is an intrusive medium; it encourages relatively high levels of attention thereby increasing the effectiveness of the communication. Finally, the advertiser selects the programs in which to broadcast a commercial, thus assuring compatible editorial content. Alternatively, the creative approach can be adapted to the type of program selected.

High reach and frequency. Because it is a mass medium with the potential to reach 97 per cent of Canadian households, television can deliver *high reach* for the advertiser. On the average, more than 80 per cent of Canadians turn on the television set at least once a day, of which 35-45 per cent do so during prime time. These figures mean that although television is expensive in absolute terms, it can be cost effective in terms of costs per thousand impressions (CPMs). Television can reach *all* demographic groups, thus providing unmatched high reach for mass marketers, such as Procter & Gamble and General Foods, which are among the heaviest users of television.[19] Again, this may lead to relatively low CPMs compared to other media.

For advertisers with large budgets, television provides a high level of message repetition, thus increasing reach and frequency. Messages may be repeated with any frequency within the hour, the day, or the week. Repetition is an important learning device and is critical to a product's success during the introduction, growth, and maturity stages. High frequency may also be attained by placing an advertisement within the same program over a period of time. There is viewer loyalty to certain programs or program types, and if the audience of the program matches the target market profile, frequency can be built.

A prestigious medium. There is a certain glamour associated with television advertising both from a consumer and trade perspective. Television allows advertisers to pre-sell products that are distributed in self-service retail establishments (i.e., a pull strategy). In particular, it promotes package identification, which is an important factor in that retail environment. Wholesalers and retailers are impressed with television advertising's ability to "pull" customers and increase their turnover rates.

Advertisers may sponsor (or co-sponsor) a popular program and provide worthwhile entertainment to the viewing public. This creates goodwill toward the advertiser and it is hoped the goodwill will carry over to the advertiser's products.

Some flexibility. Advertisers can complement the networks' broad coverage through spot buying to adjust the advertising emphasis to local market conditions. Advertisers may also adjust the schedule to seasonal variations in demand for their products.

The main *disadvantages* of television may be grouped into five categories:
High costs. Television is an expensive medium. Although the CPM may be relatively low, the *absolute* cost of advertising on television can be very high. A 30-second commercial on one

of the major national networks may cost more than $7,000 in air time alone during the regular season. Thus, television is often out of reach for the small or medium-sized advertiser.

Production costs for a commercial are also very high because of the technology involved, the cost of equipment, actors' fees, on-site filming, and special effects. More than one commercial is often produced and tested for effectiveness before it is aired, thus adding to the total cost. It is not unusual for the production of one 30-second spot to cost more than $75,000.

The *taxes* levied on advertising must also be added to the high budgets typical of television advertising. In Quebec, all broadcast advertising is subject to a two per cent tax on net dollars, while in Newfoundland all advertising (print and broadcast) is subject to a four per cent tax on net dollars (Bill 46).[20]

Lack of flexibility. Television is a rather inflexible medium for media buyers. It has *long lead times* both for booking and for production. Most networks are booked in the spring for the 52-week period that starts the following September. Usually these contracts are not cancellable. Other networks have minimum requirements for the length of a campaign. Selective spots may be purchased at any time but with two to four months' notice. Spots may be cancelled with a one month notice, but at least four weeks of the booking must be run and paid for.

Good time periods for advertising on television are limited and competition for them is stiff. Thus booking has to be done well in advance for the desired time slots.

Creative negatives. Television messages are very short; more than 85 per cent of all commercials sold are for 30 seconds. Thus, the commercial has to reach all of its objectives during this period. As a result, it is highly *perishable.*

Television is an entertainment medium and viewers often regard commercials as an annoyance,[21] often switching off, changing channels, or engaging in other activities while the commercials are being aired.

It is difficult to use long copy in television; the story must be short and simple.[22] One major selling point is usually the best strategy to follow.

There is the problem of *clutter,* which is the practice of clustering messages together during a station break.[23] Here the position of the message is important, with the first and the last receiving greater attention than the middle ones.

Commercials tend to *wear out*; they become stale and lose their effect over time. It is important to know when to pull a worn-out commercial and to replace it—at additional cost.

Reach problems. A problem of *audience fragmentation* results from the number of channels available to viewers. The audience is divided up and this leads to reduced reach and higher costs. The problem is aggravated in many markets by the powerful U.S. stations and by the penetration of cable, pay-TV, and cable converters. It may also be influenced by videotex systems, two-way cables, dish antennas, and video

TABLE 6.9 Television Summer Drop-Off: Adults 18+, Monday-Sunday 7-11 p.m.

Markets	Central Area Ratings (all stations) % difference
Halifax	−25
Quebec	−42
Montreal	−33
Ottawa	−31
Toronto	−29
Kitchener	−32
London	−36
Windsor	−33
Winnipeg	−32
Calgary	−33
Edmonton	−31
Vancouver	−26

SOURCE: BBM Fall 1981 vs. Summer 1982

recorders. Television viewing tends to drop dramatically during the summer, further reducing reach. Summer drop-off is not uniform across the country, as illustrated in Table 6.9 for adults in twelve major markets. The highest drop-off level in 1982 is found in Quebec City and the lowest in Halifax. Finally, network reach and frequency are uneven across Canada. This may create problems in using television networks in such highly fragmented markets as Toronto and Vancouver.

Heavy regulation. Because of its wide exposure and impact on the public, television is subject to a series of rules and regulations that can severely restrict advertising copy claims. The most important ones are:[24]

• The CRTC must approve all scripts for nationally aired commercials, in particular for food, drug, and cosmetic products.

• The Advertising Standards Council must approve all commercials directed to children 12 years old and under. "Directed" usually means either a commercial message designed for them, or run during children's programs.

• In Quebec, it is illegal to advertise to children 13 years old and under. The Committee for the Application of Articles 248 and 249 of the Quebec Consumer Protection Act gives written opinions on whether or not a commercial is directed to children under 13.

• The CBC Commercial Acceptance Committee must approve all commercials to be aired on CBC on the basis of good taste, factual (and documented) presentation, and competitive claims.

• The Telecaster Committee (CTV affiliates and one independent) must also approve all commercials to be aired on its stations.

• The federal Department of Consumer and Corporate Affairs must approve all national commercials for food products.

Television Advertising Rate Structures

Although television rates are often highly negotiable and based on demand and supply, rates also depend on the nature of the advertiser, the types of programs/dayparts, and the available discounts.

Nature of the Advertiser

There are three basic types of published rates for television advertising: network, spot, and local. Information and data for each type of advertising rate is available from the networks and/or stations in the form of a *rate card*. Rates and data of interest to national advertisers are available in *CARD*. An example of such a listing is provided in Figure 6.4.

Network advertising is placed by advertising agencies and is subject to the traditional 15 per cent commission. The rates are published in the network rate cards and in *CARD* under the name of the appropriate network. Most of the network time is booked well in advance, usually in late spring. Actual schedules must be negotiated with the networks, and the heavier advertisers tend to obtain the most desirable programs.

Selective spot advertising is also placed by advertising agencies and is subject to commission. The rates are published in the individual station rate cards and in *CARD* under the name of the station (Figure 6.4). Rates vary according to the daypart, and the time and the nature of the program.

Local advertising is sold directly to local businesses, mostly retailers, and is non-commissionable. Local rates are usually much lower than national rates. About one-fourth of net advertising revenues come from this source. Stations are trying to encourage local businesses to advertise on television, particularly by offering them creative counsel and technical assistance in producing commercials.

Types of Program/Daypart

Rates vary according to the type of program

FIGURE 6.4 *CARD* Listing for a Television Station

SOURCE: *Canadian Advertising Rates and Data* (May 1983), pp. 430-31.
Courtesy Special Interest Network

selected for the commercial and the time the program is aired. The rates take into account the audience available at a particular time segment as shown in Figure 6.5, as well as the individual ratings of a program. The three basic types of times and programs are prime time, fringe time, and daytime.

Prime time usually runs from 7-11 P.M. and is the most expensive time. Networks and independents schedule their most widely appealing programs during prime time and compete for a share of the viewing audience (Figure 6.5).

Fringe time precedes or follows prime time, from 5-7 P.M. and 11 P.M.-1 A.M. Early fringe

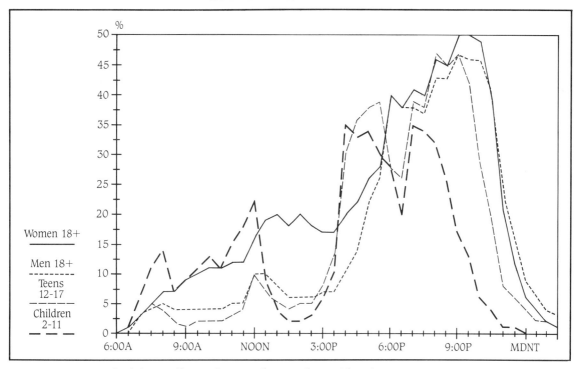

FIGURE 6.5   Television Daily Tuning Levels, Monday-Friday Average
SOURCE: BBM Fall 1982

time appeals primarily to individual adults or children returning from school.[25] Stations often schedule situation comedy reruns, talk shows, and local news during this period. Late fringe appeals primarily to young adults, and stations usually schedule talk shows or movies in this period.

Daytime runs from the morning to 5 P.M. and appeals primarily to women through local news programs, game shows, and soap operas. Some daytime programming is done by the networks.

Discounts

In addition to the published rates, various discounts are available.

Frequency discounts are earned when a minimum number of spots are purchased within a defined period, usually 13, 25, or 52 weeks.

Volume discounts are based on the amount of dollars spent within a period of time, usually 13, 25, or 52 weeks.

Continuity discounts are earned when a contract involves buying at least one spot *every* week over a given number of weeks.

Special package plans are offered by television stations to sell off fringe or daytime at a discount or in combination with prime time. Often the purchase of a package is mandatory for advertisers who want to buy prime time. Other packages include sports, movies, and entertainment specials.

Network discounts are available for buyers of full or partial network time slots or packages.

Special Rates

These include ROS or BTA, rotation, and pre-emption rates.

Run-of-schedule (ROS) or *best-time available* (BTA) is a discount the station offers advertisers if the station is allowed to schedule the commercial at its discretion.

Rotation is a discount the station offers for scheduling a commercial at will during specific programs or time periods. (See Figure 6.4 for an example of rotation.)

Pre-emption rates are lower rates given to the advertiser in exchange for the right to pre-empt a commercial with or without some notice by the commercial of another advertiser who is paying a higher rate or by an unexpected event, e.g., a major news story or a sports program. A pre-empted commercial is "made good"—the station will run it free later in an equally priced time segment.

The Future of Television as an Advertising Medium

Fragmentation of television audiences may continue as viewers are given more opportunities to use their sets with:

- increased penetration of cable television and of commercial-free pay television;
- home-delivery information systems, such as Telidon, with all its potential applications for entertainment, working at home, and electronic data transmission (e.g., directories and newspapers);
- television video games and home computers connected to television sets;
- dish antennas that pick up signals from satellites and bring programs from all over the world;
- video recorders that delete commercials, reschedule viewing, or allow for viewing of special tapes (movies and educational material) at home.

The important questions for advertisers concern audience viewing patterns and commercial exposure:

- Is total viewership going to increase with the penetration of new technologies?
- What is the composition of the new, smaller audiences, i.e., narrowcasting instead of broadcasting?
- What is the role of advertising in these new technologies?

The answers to these and other questions will determine the direction that advertising takes in the television medium. But it is very likely that the task of the media director will become much more complex in dealing with television.

Television may become an even more sophisticated *communication medium* by appealing to other senses like smell, using larger screens with three-dimensional capabilities, becoming more mobile. Thus, the creative director may have different ways to use its creative abilities.

The *costs* of advertising on television will likely continue to increase, not only as a result of inflation but also as the medium itself becomes more complex. Stations will have to find ways of incorporating the new technologies, of improving their programming to maintain audience share, and of strengthening their marketing orientation to compete with other stations and media for advertising revenues.

Research data on television viewing patterns will become more important to advertisers as audiences become more fragmented and stations try to attract more narrowly defined audiences. Research tools will become more sophisticated and may benefit from such new technologies as two-way cable and other interactive systems.

Summary

The two broadcast media available in Canada for carrying advertising messages are radio and television. Since the birth of broadcast media in 1920, with the *first* radio station in the world, Canada has been at the forefront of its technological and commercial development. Canada is the most "wired" nation in the world and is among the leading nations in developing videotext systems (Telidon), pay-TV, and two-way cable systems.

Table 6.10 highlights the strengths and weaknesses of each broadcast medium.

Radio is mainly a frequency medium, with high flexibility in terms of lead times and market coverage. The cost of radio time is relatively low. However, radio messages have a

TABLE 6.10   Main Strengths and Weaknesses of Major Broadcast Media

Medium	Strengths	Weaknesses
Radio	high frequency flexible (coverage, time) affordable to small business	fragmentation and clutter short life of message limited availability in major markets
Television	complete communication mass coverage flexible (geographic, creative)	high absolute costs (time, production) fragmentation short life of message

short life, the medium is not intrusive, and stations must compete for attention. Radio time in major markets is not always available when advertisers need it.

Television is the ultimate communication medium, providing mass coverage and geographic flexibility. It is the only medium that permits sound, colour, *and* motion, but television advertising is expensive both for time and for production. Television requires long lead times for both booking and for production. As is the case with radio, the television messages have a short life and must reach their objectives in spite of fragmentation, clutter, and negative viewer reactions.

Questions for Study

1. Compare television and radio as advertising media for *(a)* a moving company; *(b)* a restaurant; and *(c)* a political candidate.

2. Compare television and magazines as advertising media and give examples of products that should be mostly advertised in one of these media. Explain your choices.

3. Explain the problem of audience fragmentation and indicate how an advertiser may try to control it.

4. Explain the problem of commercial clutter and indicate how an advertiser may try to control it.

5. "Television is well suited to most advertising budgets." Do you agree? If not, explain under what conditions television should be used by a media planner.

6. It has been said that "radio is the theater of the mind." Explain what it means with three specific examples, and contrast the creative approaches and effectiveness of television and radio.

7. *(a)* Discuss the role of cable television in changing people's viewing patterns. What effect would increased penetration have on the advertising industry?
(b) Answer the same question for
   • converters and dish antennas
   • pay television
   • video recorders, home computers, and video games

8. Radio has been described as a frequency medium and a background medium. Do you agree? Explain your answer and develop the implications for you as an advertiser.

9. Under what conditions should spot radio commercials be used heavily? Spot television commercials?

10. Contrast AM and FM radio as an advertising medium for a retailer whose target market is composed of *(a)* teenagers, *(b)* young female adults, *(c)* young male adults.

Problems

1. You are the owner of Beefun, a small chain of fast food restaurants in your community that sells mostly hamburgers and french fries to teenagers and young adults. You have decided to advertise regularly on radio, using a humorous approach and emphasizing that eating in your restaurant is a fun experience with a relaxed atmosphere. You have determined that you should spend $50,000 a year for your advertising.

Develop the advertising strategy in detail and select the best radio station(s) and program(s) for carrying your radio commercial(s). Be sure to explain the reasons behind your choice *and* the rationale for rejecting the other stations.

2. You are the owner of the Surelock Homes Company (see Problem no. 2, Chapter 5). After looking at all the print media, you have decided to evaluate the use of broadcast media to advertise your lock.

(a) Construct a table summarizing the advantages and disadvantages of using *each* medium for your advertising.

(b) You think that you need to show your target market how the new lock works. Perhaps you may be forced to use television advertising. Since your advertising budget is limited, you are thinking of introducing your product in stages. The first market to enter is the largest metropolitan area in your province. Develop this strategy further, including your selection of television station(s) and program(s) as well as the rationale for rejecting the other stations.

Notes

1. H.E. Stephenson and C. McNaught, *The Story of Advertising in Canada* (Toronto: The Ryerson Press, 1940), p. 192; Sherri Craig, "Radio '80: Looking Forward to the Future with the Best in the Past," *Marketing* (3 March 1980), p. 9.
2. *Canadian Advertising Rates and Data* (March 1983), p. 154. Henceforth cited as *CARD*.
3. Leonard Kubas, "Radio to Chalk up Its First $½ Billion in Net Ad Revenues," *Marketing* (1 March 1982), pp. R12-13; see also Leonard Kubas, "Marketing Is Key to Success in '83," *Marketing* (14 February 1983), pp. 8-10.
4. Kubas, "Radio to chalk up . . .," p. R13.
5. "FM Stations Soar to the Top in Montreal," *Marketing* (1 March 1982), p. R11; see also Kubas, "Marketing is key . . .," p. 8.
6. "CKO Heads into the Black at Last," *Marketing* (1 March 1982), p. R2.
7. Kubas, "Radio to chalk up . . .," p. R13.
8. Jim Macdonald, "Syndication: For Some Clients It's a Great Way to Augment 'Spot' on Superior Programs," *Marketing* (23 February 1982), pp. 36-37.
9. T.R. Bird, "Analysis of the Impact of Electronic Systems on Advertising Revenues in Canada" (Working paper, Montreal: Institute for Research on Public Policy, 1982), p. 5.
10. Kenneth C. Hardy and Ian S. Spencer, "Television Viewers' Responses to Acquisition of a Cable Converter," *Marketing*, 1, ed. Vernon J. Jones (Administrative Sciences Association of Canada, 1980), pp. 172-78; see also Kenneth G. Hardy, John A. Quelch, Ian S. Spencer, and Hugh J. Munro, "The Effect of Increased Choice on Television Viewing Behaviour," *Developments in Canadian Marketing*, ed. Robert D. Tamilia, (Administrative Sciences Association of Canada, 1979), pp. 32-41.
11. Ibid., p. 40.
12. *The Canadian Media Directors' Council Media Digest*, 1982/83, p. 16. Henceforth cited as *CMDC*.

13. Ibid., p. 16; CRTC Annual Report 1981-1982, p. 55.
14. Ibid., p. 15.
15. Television Bureau of Canada, *TV Basics* (1981), pp. 4-5; CRTC Annual Report 1981-1982, p. 55; Bird, "Analysis of the Impact of Electronic Systems on Advertising Revenues in Canada" (Working paper, Institute for Research on Public Policy), p.5.
16. Ibid.
17. Vernon J. Jones and Sherry Monahan, "An Investigation into the Effects of Bill c-58 on Advertising Media Decisions," *Marketing 1977*, ed. Réjean Drolet and Gordon H.G. McDougall (Administrative Sciences Association of Canada, 1977), pp. 82-90.
18. *CARD*, p. 154.
19. *TV Basics*, p. 16.
20. *CMDC*, p. 21.
21. Peter M. Banting, A.K.P. Wensley, and Robert G. Wyckham, "Linguistic Usage in Television Advertising," in *Marketing*, 2, ed. Robert G. Wyckham (Administrative Sciences Association of Canada, 1981), pp. 21-7.
22. Gordon H.G. McDougall, "Alternative Energy Conservation Appeals: Relative Effects," *Marketing in the 80's*, ed. Richard P. Bagozzi et al. (Chicago: American Marketing Association, 1980), pp. 432-35.
23. Walter S. Good and Douglas C. Birdwise, "Clutter in Television Broadcasting," *The Canadian Marketer* (Spring 1977), pp. 9-14.
24. *CMDC*, pp. 20-21.
25. J. Barnes, K. Kelloway, and B.A. Russell, "Parental Influence on Children's Television Viewing Behaviour," *Marketing 1978*, ed. J.M. Boisvert and R. Savitt (Administrative Sciences Association of Canada, 1978), pp. 10-24.

CAMPAIGN HISTORIES FOR PART 2

1. Maher 1981-82 Campaign

2. Mazda 1981 Campaign

3. Roy & Gibson Co-op Advertising Campaign

CAMPAIGN HISTORY 1

MAHER 1981-82 CAMPAIGN
Developing a Good Relationship Between an Advertising Agency and a Retailer

ADVERTISER: Maher, Inc.
AGENCY: Promo Vision Communications Ltd.

Introduction

Maher, Inc. is a national chain of 120 Maher and specialty shoe stores. In 1977 Maher approached the people who now form Promo Vision Communications Ltd. (formerly McConnell/Cockfield Brown) and requested assistance with a small advertising project. Since that time, the relationship has grown and prospered as both companies have benefited from astute buying, good products displayed well, good marketing, and direct yet image-building advertising programs.

The majority of Maher's communications efforts have been project-oriented, and this description will concentrate on several of these projects. The overriding theme in all of Maher's communications is "Pleasure Your Feet At Maher". This slogan appears in-store on point-of-purchase material, on bags, in advertisements, and in commercials. It has been used without change for the past three years.

Marketing and Advertising Strategies

Our objective is to build store traffic and make the cash register ring. The advertising process on Maher's behalf begins with a review and in-depth analysis of the marketplace. Next, key marketing and advertising issues are analyzed. The third key element in this process is the continual updating and review of the "positioning process".

Positioning Process
The objective of this process is ultimately to end up with a positioning statement that will lead to the best advertising/ marketing strategy for Maher. Positioning is image. Image is two-fold.

1. Who is Maher? = Character
2. What is Maher? = Position

Maher cannot be all things to all people. The following exercise is an effective method for determining Maher's best image:

The key is to think of Maher as a person and to describe that person *(a)* as he/she currently is, in the mind of the consumer; or *(b)* as you would like him/her to be.

Target definition is an integral part of this exercise; however, until such time as research is conducted, we will be unable to define clearly and accurately who our primary, secondary, and tertiary targets will be. For this reason, we will not attach target definition at this time.

A psychographic research project that studies and describes the types of people by lifestyle who buy at different shoe stores, would answer the above information void. This could be conducted for approximately $15,000.

Creative Strategy
Once this process is completed and agreed upon by the client, the creative strategy is developed. The creative strategy has five key components:
Basic Benefit
Support
Imagery
Tone, Manner, Style
Target Audience

This form is prepared by client service and reviewed with the writer and artist prior to approval by client.

All creative is checked back to this form before layouts and copy are presented to client.

The newspaper advertisements included have been developed in the past year. They are:

1. Give Your Feet a Holiday
2. The Maher Cougar Family Sale
3. Maher's Kid's Shoe Sale

All the above advertisements reflect the following:

1. fashion (practical) yet good value
2. leadership
3. authority—knows quality

EXHIBIT 1
A Maher advertisement with the theme "Give Your Feet a Holiday"

EXHIBIT 2
A Maher advertisement announcing the "Maher Cougar Family Sale"

4. comfort

5. family store, yet still style (practical) conscious

6. are interesting, intrusive, and agreeably interrupting

Media Strategy

These promotions/sales are supported by radio advertising, utilizing a jingle that was developed three years ago. The length and weight of the campaign depends on the number of products purchased, competitive acitvity, and budget considerations. A typical sale lasts for 2-3 weeks and is promoted for ten days. The realm of retail advertising is so different from packaged goods that creative and media rationale do not play as important a role as they might in building an image for a soap product.

EXHIBIT 3

A Maher advertisement announcing the "Maher Kid's Shoe Sale"

CAMPAIGN HISTORY 2

MAZDA 1981 CAMPAIGN
Advertising a New Line of Cars

ADVERTISER: Mazda
AGENCY: Promo Vision Communications Ltd.

Revival of an Automobile Company

In the early 1970s, Mazda, the third largest Japanese automobile manufacturer, entered the Canadian market with a revolutionary new engine: the Wankel or rotary engine. The rotary engine was far less complicated than conventional power plants and contained far fewer moving parts while at the same time delivering a much higher power output than conventional engines of similar

EXHIBIT 1

size. The technological leadership implied by the rotary engine boosted Mazda's sales volumes to 9000 units in 1973. Then disaster sruck.

First, the energy crunch hit Canada, with a detrimental effect on the rather thirsty rotary-engined product.

Second, the engines themselves began to show a disconcerting tendency to wear prematurely, and total engine failure occurred in cars of relatively low mileage with alarming frequency. Mazda's reputation suffered immediately, and despite the offering of a five-year, 80 000 mile warranty, the rotary engine Mazda became a sales disaster. Volume fell by more than 50 per cent within a year and continued to slide even after the introduction of a conventional engined subcompact called the GLC.

Mazda's response to this falling sales volume situation was to engineer a complete new line of products, rushing them to market within two years, when the normal gestation period for the development of a new automobile is a minimum of five years and more often seven years in development.

These new vehicles utilized conventional engines packaged in extremely attractive vehicle designs. A new GLC with front-wheel drive and numerous product features and advantages, and the attractive 626 model were offered to consumers at extremely attractive prices, particularly considering their inherent quality and product benefits.

In addition, the rotary engine was re-engineered and made its appearance one more time in the sleek RX-7, Mazda's signal to the world that the rotary engine was far from dead. The interesting application of the rotary to the sports car range was also a clear signal to car buyers that the rotary engine was indeed a reliable, high-performance power plant with many advantages over conventional engines.

With this high-quality, highly reliable, and well-priced product range in place, Mazda's major marketing problem was to convince wary car buyers that the rotary engine fiasco of the early 1970s was an aberration, and that Mazda products were indeed worthy of consideration by discerning car purchasers anxious to spend their money wisely.

Advertising obviously had a key role to play in this strategy. It was essential that advertising communicate the quality and reliability story in a fresh way without referring to the past. In addition, the rotary engine RX-7 had to be presented in a way that would regain consumer confidence in the rotary concept and in Mazda as an engineering leader in the automobile business. A series of newspaper and magazine advertisements were developed for a campaign that was to span several years. These advertisements exuded a quiet confidence and quality while communicating product excellence at sensible prices. During this period, Mazda sales grew dramatically.

	1979	**1980**	**1981**
Number of units	8,095	17,071	32,042

The 1981 sales performance for Mazda was even more remarkable in that the company out-sold Datsun to become the third

EXHIBIT 2

best-selling import car line in Canada, behind Honda and Toyota. Obviously, superb product development and pricing were paramount in this market success, but consumer attitudes, especially negative attitudes, die hard, and advertising has been the primary catalyst in changing Canadian opinions of Mazda products, from extremely poor to extremely positive.

CAMPAIGN HISTORY 3

ROY & GIBSON CO-OP ADVERTISING CAMPAIGN
Developing a Co-op Program for Distributors

ADVERTISER: Roy & Gibson

Dealer Co-op advertising policy

GENERAL CONDITIONS

1. Allowed media are: dailies and weeklies · magazines · mailers · radio and television.

2. All advertising commitments must first be approved by your Roy & Gibson representative or the advertising manager of the company.

3. Only local rates will be accepted for any media selected by the dealer.

4. All advertising prepared by a dealer should be similar to the advertisements prepared by Roy & Gibson and include:

   a) The model number of each appliance being advertised.

   b) When a descriptive copy is used, it must correspond exactly to the unit being advertised.

   c) At least 50% of the space or time used must be devoted exclusively to Roy & Gibson. No competitive appliances can be shown in the same advertisement.

   d) The trade name Roy or Gibson must be at least as prominent as that of the dealer, in print as well as in radio or TV.

   e) To avoid any misunderstanding it is suggested that when in doubt, the advertisement be first submitted to Roy & Gibson for approval before printing or broadcasting.

5. The claim for credit must be filed within 30 days following publication of advertisement.

6. The amount of the credit will not exceed 50% of cost approved by Roy & Gibson.

7. Only the appliances listed on the current price list are eligible for co-op advertising credits.

8. Certain promotional material sold to dealers by Roy & Gibson may be claimed under the co-op advertising policy.

9. This policy is in force in all territories serviced directly by Roy & Gibson sales representatives.

PROCEDURE

A. Request for Advertising - (in cooperation with a Roy & Gibson sales representative).

   1. Dealer fills out co-operative advertising engagement form making sure all necessary information is given.

   2. Dealer returns blue, pink and yellow copy of form to the advertising manager for approval from company head office.

B. Claim for credit

   1. Dealer must send proof of advertising, plus paid invoice from media and blue copy of signed ad engagement form.

   2. This claim must be sent to the advertising manager, Roy & Gibson, L'Assomption, Qué.

   3. This claim must be filed within 30 days following ad publication.

EXHIBIT 1

COMPLETE LINE OF GIBSON BUILT-INS

"GRILL & GRIDDLE" GIBSON MODULAR RANGE

EXHIBIT 2

Every good refrigerator has a 5-year warranty.

Only Gibson gives you 10 years.

And more.

No other manufacturer offers you this kind of protection for your investment... 10 years warranted performance on the motor compressor, the heart of your refrigerator, of all Gibson Frost-Clear models. That's unbeatable quality and unbeatable value.

We build quality into every Gibson appliance.

Refrigerators, ranges, freezers, dishwashers, washers, dryers. Come in and see the Gibson line at our conveniently-located showroom.

Get a Gibson and you've got it for good.

EXHIBIT 3

Get a Gibson and you've got it for good.

There are more sales in store for you.

A great Gibson idea for the 1980's was to embark on a major National advertising campaign, from coast to coast, to create an even greater public awareness about Gibson appliances. As a result, Canadians will not only want to know more about Gibson appliances, they will also want to know where to see them and where to buy them. To help you cash-in on this new wave of buying power, we have produced this advertising kit which will enable you to prepare even more effective advertising for your store.

Our new advertising approach.

The overall objective of our National advertising campaign is brand awareness. We aim at nothing less than to place the brand name Gibson at the top of the list in the mind of Canadian consumers. Our radio commercials are different from anything you've ever heard. They were written to attract attention, to be highly memorable and to strongly relate the popularity of the name Gibson to that of major appliances. A clever emphasis was placed on quality, to appeal more directly to the segment of consumers who are right now in the market for major appliances.

EXHIBIT 4

The universality of our new Gibson slogan.

"Get a Gibson and you've got it for good". It's an action slogan. It's a slogan with a promise. It is as effective in print as it is on radio, in point-of-sale and other promotional material. Canadian consumers will be hearing and seeing it a lot in the months and years ahead.

Newspaper advertising.

The proven medium for effective retail advertising. It's where nearly everyone turns to for shopping ideas, to find out what's on sale and where it is being sold. Newspapers have proved their worth over and over in immediate, next-day results for retailers who have a consistent advertising program.

You'll find in this kit a choice of prepared advertisements as well as product line illustrations with a short text. The choice is yours. You can use the fully prepared advertisements by just adding your store's name, address and telephone number.

Change the product illustrated, to others more suitable to your audience and market. Or you can build an advertisement as you see fit using the line illustrations supplied. Whichever way you choose to follow, be sure to tie-in with the National Gibson theme. In all cases, your local newspaper will gladly assemble an advertisement to your liking. The fully prepared advertisements included in this kit are the first of a series. Others will follow, designed with seasonal appeal.

Radio advertising.

Radio is a powerful advertising medium. You'll find the text of our

commercials in this kit. Radio allows for numerous repetitions of a message and delivers high awareness and recall levels.

As in the case with newspapers, you can tailor your radio message to specific products and special events. At the end of each message, 6 seconds are left to allow for your store identification.

Here too, radio station representatives are experts in their field and can provide you with invaluable assistance in preparing your final messages and scheduling them.

Radio, in combination with newspaper advertising, is very effective.

Planning your advertising.

Our new slogan, the National radio campaign and this advertising kit are a winning combination which you should take full advantage of. Good planning of your advertising will ensure your success. Establish your sales objectives and your strategy to achieve them. Choose your media carefully and consult with media representatives for rates. Establish your advertising budget and schedule in relation to your sales objectives and the anticipated results will be forthcoming.

Judicious use of the advertising material, placed at your disposal in this kit, should reward you with increased sales and profits.

In-store point-of-sale and displays.

We will keep producing hard hitting in-store material as a further extension of the National radio campaign. Right now, we have two prominent displays readily available. One features the new "Grill and Griddle" modular range and the other our complete line of built-in models of appliances. They are illustrated on the back of this folder. Both are a proven sales aid for your floor salesmen and serve to remind your customers that you are selling Gibson appliances. Our sales representatives have all the details, but if you want to order your displays right away, a handy order card is enclosed.

EXHIBIT 4 (continued)

OPPORTUNITY
ANALYSIS
IN THE CANADIAN
ENVIRONMENT

In order to make sound decisions, advertisers should not only have a thorough knowledge of advertising institutions and the industry but should also be able to recognize and analyze the opportunities available in an ever-changing environment.

The third part of this text provides advertising students with a framework for recognizing and assessing advertising opportunities.

In order to design effective advertisements, an advertiser must first have a thorough knowledge of individual buyers' motives, attitudes, and purchasing habits, since advertising influences every buyer differently. Moreover, because advertising is a mass communication tool, advertisers must have an overall view of the market and an understanding of market mechanics and behaviour.

Chapter 7 analyzes advertising's potential effect on individual buyers' motivations and perceptions. Chapter 8 discusses the effect advertising can have on buyer attitudes. Chapter 9 describes the role advertising can play in the buyer's decision process. In Chapter 10 the effect of advertising is examined at a macro-level—how it affects the behaviour of an entire market.

Advertising and Buyers' Motivations and Perceptions

Why do advertisers need to understand human and market behaviour? Chapter 7 addresses this question and describes the basic market mechanisms that make advertising an efficient communication tool. A descriptive model is presented that shows how advertising, when properly used within the framework of a marketing program, can affect buyer behaviour.

Buyer and Market Behaviour

In Chapter 1, advertising was described as a communication process initiated by an organization and directed at the potential buyers of a firm's products, brands, or services or at potential subscribers to the advertised idea. To design an advertising campaign that has the effect intended, the advertising message must be compatible with the characteristics of the target audience, i.e., the consumers or potential buyers of the advertised brand. As is true of the design of the entire marketing program, an advertiser needs extensive knowledge of potential consumers in order to perform this task. For instance, how can a marketer advertise a certain brand of instant coffee if it is not known what benefits buyers are seeking when they purchase the product? Do they buy instant coffee because of the special aroma? Because of the speed and/or convenience of its preparation? Because it is cheaper? What are buyers' criteria for selecting a brand of instant coffee? These are only a few of the many questions an advertiser tries to answer before designing the message and the campaign. The answers to

these questions will influence strongly the type and content of the advertisements.

Because advertising is a mass communication tool, an understanding of individual buyers is necessary but not sufficient, as would be the case only if all buyers were motivated by the same forces and possessed identical attitudes toward the advertised ideas, products, brands, or companies. If this were true, a standardized advertising message could have approximately the same effect on all the individuals in a target market. Of course, people are extremely diverse. Some are economy oriented; others buy only luxury items. Some people like Mozart; others enjoy accordion music. Some consumers drive a Cadillac; others can afford only a bicycle.

The variety in individuals' tastes, preferences, lifestyles, and personalities is so wide that it can be reasonably asserted that no two consumers are perfectly identical. The market segmentation problem resulting from this diversity has always challenged marketers. It is linked to the concept of mass consumption, and to its consequence, mass communication. In short, segmenting a market consists in grouping together in some meaningful way buyers who exhibit sufficiently similar behaviour or, more exactly, responses to marketing instruments (advertising or any other marketing mix variable). The buyers in one specific market segment can then be efficiently subjected to the same marketing program.

The wide heterogeneity of audiences forces advertisers to develop a global understanding of the marketplace. Since advertising is a mass communication tool, it is intended to influence an entire market at a time. Thus, advertisers should know and be aware of the various flows of consumers in a target market. The problem is still more complex, however, because markets are not static; they evolve constantly. Some consumers enter and other leave the marketplace in more or less continuous flows. This explains the saying often heard in advertising circles that a firm does not advertise to an audience but to a parade.

An advertiser who is responsible for setting up a campaign for a brand of instant coffee generally tries to find answers to such questions as: Why is a significant proportion of consumers loyal to Maxwell House? Why are the consumers of some private brands the least loyal consumers, and have a propensity to switch to Nescafé, for instance. What is the proportion of potential customers who are aware of our brand? What is the percentage of these consumers who have a favourable attitude toward our brand? Why are the new buyers of instant coffee more likely to try a competing brand first? Here again, it is seen how different advertising message decisions are likely to result from the answers to these questions.

Advertisers need to have a micro view of the market, which is an understanding of individual potential buyers or of the different types of buyer for a product category, as well as a macro view of the market, which is market behaviour at an aggregate level (the whole mass market). (See Figure 7.1.) The objectives of an advertising campaign are based on both a micro *and* macro understanding of the market.[1] This is also true for budget decisions and for decisions on the measurement of campaign effectiveness, because these decisions are linked to objective setting. In contrast, decisions on the advertising message content and format, which must reach and influence each buyer individually, are based on a good understanding of buyer behaviour. Media buying decisions are based on the knowledge of where to reach consumers or what the media habits are in the market segments. These decisions imply that advertisers have a macro knowledge of the market.

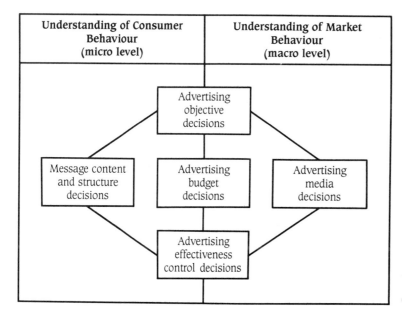

FIGURE 7.1 **Main Areas of Advertising Decisions and the Corresponding Level of Market Comprehension Required**

A Simplified Model of Advertising Effects

To apply the modern marketing concept, marketers and advertisers must be concerned with buyers' everyday lives. They must know buyers' needs, perceptions, and attitudes toward products and brands, purchasing habits, the kinds of change buyers want or are ready to accept. This is the reason why the field of buyer behaviour has considerably expanded over the last few years and is the subject of extensive research.

In order to explain purchasing behaviour, marketers have turned to the social sciences, especially psychology, sociology, social psychology, and cultural anthropology. Many authors have attempted to explain purchasing behaviour by borrowing from various schools of thought and from theories developed in other disciplines.[2] Unfortunately, these explanations may differ considerably depending on the theory and/or discipline on which they rely. Human behaviour results from a multitude of interrelated forces that evolve over time and depend on many environmental variables.

A general model of buyer behaviour is given in Figure 7.2. This view of market behaviour gives an opportunity to assess the effects of the main intervening forces on purchasing behaviour and reveals the complexity of such behaviour.[3]

In general, when buyers are subjected to certain marketing stimuli coming from the environment (such as a product or an advertising message) there is some probability they will respond. The behavioural response can be, for instance, the purchase of the product. The study of consumer behaviour is the determination of the elements that influence the consumer response.[4]

The model in Figure 7.2 is elaborated further in this chapter as well as in the following chapters. Figure 7.3 shows how the different parts of the model fit together.

Three basic conditions must be simultaneously met before potential buyers are willing to or even can buy a certain product or brand:

1. They must feel the need or have the desire to acquire a certain category of product or service. They should be motivated to fulfill a basic need or desire.

2. They must perceive the product and the brand as likely to fulfil this need. They should also have a sufficiently favourable attitude toward acquiring the product and the specific brand to consider purchasing it.

3. The product should be available for purchase (adequate distribution) and the consumer must be able to afford it (adequate pricing).

For instance, some individuals could have very favourable attitudes toward IBM and its products. However, they will not purchase an IBM electric typewriter unless they experience the need or desire to acquire one. Let us assume that one day one such potential buyer starts a business, hires an office assistant, and decides to buy a typewriter. The buyer may or may not decide to purchase an IBM typewriter, despite the buyer's decision to acquire such a piece of equipment and favourable attitude toward IBM. For instance, the typewriter may be too expensive or there may be no local IBM dealer. It may also be that the typewriter is too heavy to be carried along on business trips if necessary.

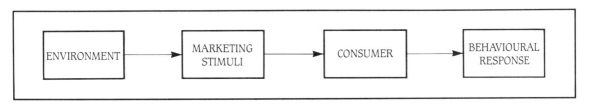

FIGURE 7.2   A Stimulus-Response View of Consumer Behaviour

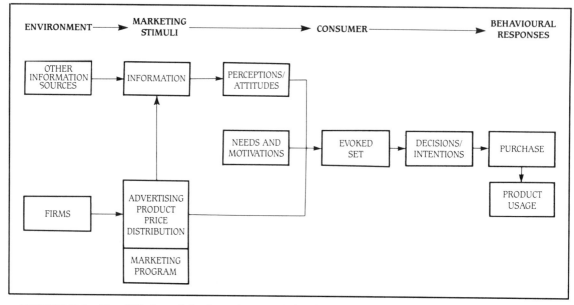

FIGURE 7.3 **Simplified Model of Marketing and Advertising Effects on Consumer Behaviour**

It may be, however, that this business person has a favourable attitude toward several brands and models of typewriters, and that several of these brands are approximately in the same price range and are available at a nearby dealer. In this case, which brand is the entrepreneur likely to select?

When a specific brand of a product category simultaneously meets the three essential prerequisites listed above, this brand is considered to be in the buyer's *evoked set*. A buyer's evoked set is composed of all the brands a potential buyer considers as possible purchase alternatives to satisfy the same general need or desire. Now, a buyer must decide which brand in the evoked set is likely to best satisfy. The outcome of this evaluation process is a purchase decision, generally followed by the purchase itself (behaviour) and by product usage. However, the outcome may also be a non-purchase decision.

In the preceding example, let us assume that the buyer has three brands in the evoked set for typewriters: IBM, Olivetti, and Olympia. The buyer must decide which among these three brands is most likely to best satisfy his specific need. After a careful evaluation of the features

of each typewriter in relation to his needs, he may select an Olivetti typewriter, purchase it, and use it. Under certain circumstances, however, he may decide that none of these three typewriters really fits his requirements and may decide to withhold his purchase decision until he finds a satisfactory solution or completely give up the idea of purchasing a typewriter.

To what extent does advertising play a role in the purchasing process? Advertising is an important marketing stimulus that provides *information* to consumers. However, as can be seen in Figure 7.3, it is *not* the unique source of marketing information used by consumers. The other elements of the marketing mix also convey a lot of information. Not only can they determine whether a brand is or is not part of a buyer's evoked set, but they can also carry information to potential buyers that can affect their attitudes toward the brand. Buyers also receive many pieces of marketing information from outside environmental groups (from family members, neighbours, or consumer associations).

Advertising and Buyers' Needs and Motivations

Motivations Defined

Motivations can be defined as the underlying force of any action. By inducing an individual to perform a certain act, this force tends to reduce the state of psychological tension generally aroused by an unsatisfied need or desire. Thus, motivations can be physiological (such as hunger, thirst, or sex) but, more often, they are psychological (for instance, security, esteem, or prestige).

Psychologists distinguish between positive and negative motivations. Positive motivations favour certain acts. They are often called needs or desires. Negative motivations, on the other hand, prevent the performance of certain acts. They are also called fears, aversions, or inhibitions.[5] Psychologists also recognize the complex interactions among various needs and give the generic term "motivations" to all the forces that trigger or favour the persistence of certain

behaviours. The implications of these two approaches for advertising will be examined later.

The Role of Motivations in Purchase Behaviour

Figure 7.4 lists propositions about motivations that have direct implications for advertisers.[6]

As shown in Figure 7.4, the products and services consumers buy reflect their needs. Consequently, a purchase cannot take place without a need being aroused, consciously or not. As will be discussed further in Chapter 16, advertising cannot induce consumers to buy products they do not need. In contrast, the same type of product may be bought by different consumers as the result of very different needs and motives. A car may fulfil a transportation need for some consumers and a social status need for others. The need for social status and recognition may have outlets other than buying a certain style of car, however.

These simple and somewhat intuitive facts have clear implications for advertisers. First, advertisers must make sure to identify properly the needs they want to satisfy through the advertised product. Second, they must identify actual competitors, i.e., the other consumption means typically used by consumers to fulfil the same need category. For instance, a car manufacturer may find that its main competitor is not General Motors but a a large travel agent or a well-known brand of stereophonic equipment. Finally, because advertising is part of a buyer's environment, it has the capacity to arouse certain needs in consumers (statement 5 of Figure 7.4).

Motivation Theories

Psychologists have proposed many different theories of motivation. In this analysis of the possible effects of advertising on motivations and needs, three theories are discussed: the theories of Maslow and Freud because of their

---

1. The motives of man form an organized and unified system.

2. The thought and action of the individual reflect his wants and goals.

3. On the one hand, *similar* actions may be related to *different* wants. On the other hand, *different* actions may reflect *similar* wants.

4. The wants and goals of the individual continuously develop and change . . . as a result of changes in the physiological states of the individual and his experiences as he interacts with objects and persons.

5. Most of the many wants of the individual are inactive or latent. . . . The arousal of a particular set of wants in the individual depends upon his physiological state, the environmental situation and his thoughts.

FIGURE 7.4   Propositions on Motivations from Social Psychology

SOURCE: David Krech, Richard S. Crutchfield, and Egerton A. Bellachey, *Individual in Society* (New York: McGraw-Hill, 1962).pp. Reproduced with permission of McGraw-Hill Book Company

impact on advertising and marketing thought, and a theory proposed by Kurt Lewin because of its usefulness in explaining advertising message effectiveness.

The Hierarchy of Needs Theory

Many psychologists have attempted—although with only limited success—to draw exhaustive lists of the needs underlying human behaviour.[7] These efforts to make accurate classifications have at least shown that human needs and motivations are numerous, complex, and diverse. The hierarchy of needs theory by Abraham Maslow relies on one such classification.[8] Although Maslow's hierarchy has a more intuitive than empirical foundation, it has often been cited for its potential in advertising.[9]

Maslow proposes five levels of human needs: physiological needs, safety needs, need for love and affection, needs for self-esteem and respect from others, and self-actualization needs. According to Maslow, these five levels of need constitute a hierarchy, and individuals go sequentially from one level of the hierarchy to the next. Thus, physiological needs must be completely (or almost completely) satisfied before the needs for safety can be felt. When the safety needs are completely (or almost completely) satisfied, then the needs for love and affection are aroused, and so on from the bottom to the top of the hierarchy (Figure 7.5).[10]

Maslow's theory may not prove very useful in explaining specific motives in a given purchase situation. But the concept of an ordered hierarchy of needs according to their relative strength is a useful tool for advertisers because of its implications for deciding on message content. As was already discussed, an advertised product or brand must satisfy some consumer need(s). Often, one single product or brand caters to different needs, which are sometimes at different levels in Maslow's hierarchy. Thus, to design an effective communication, an advertiser must appeal to the needs *actually felt* by consumers and that have not yet been satisfied.

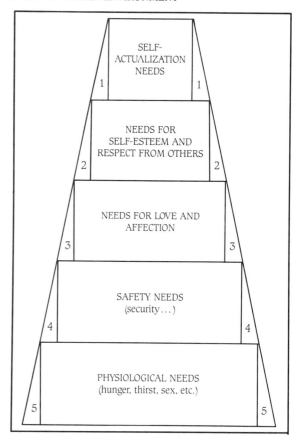

FIGURE 7.5 Maslow's Hierarchy of Needs

For instance, a cake mix might satisfy various needs: nutrition (level 1), the need for a mother to prove her love to her family and to receive their love (level 3), or a need for esteem, when a consumer wants to cultivate a reputation as a good cook (level 4). If a consumer has reached the third level in Maslow's hierarchy, there is no point in advertising the cake mix as having an outstanding nutritional value (level 1), or as the symbol of a *cordon bleu* (level 5). However, it would be relevant to build the advertisements around the satisfaction felt by family members when they eat a cake of the advertised brand.

Freudian Psychoanalytic Theory

The essence of Freudian psychoanalytic theory[11] is that as a child grows, he continuously experiences frustration for not being able to gratify his instincts by himself and for being dependent on the outside world.

> As he grows, his psyche becomes increasingly complex. A part of his psyche—the id—remains the reservoir of his strong drives and urges. Another part—the ego—becomes his conscious planning center for finding outlets for his drives. And a third part—his super-ego—channels his instinctive drives into socially approved outlets to avoid the pain of guilt or shame.[12]

Although it has been challenged and modified by Freud's disciples, Freudian theory has the merit of pointing at the existence of sub-conscious forces that shape an individual's behaviour. The application of these concepts to consumer behaviour has led to the advent of motivation studies. Motivation studies were popular in the United States during the 1950s. Their purpose was to try to find the "why" of consumers' behaviour and to discover the more or less conscious and recognized motivations that induced Mr. Smith to buy a sports car (as a substitute for a mistress) or prevented the Joneses from consuming prunes (symbol of patriarchal authority). Motivation studies as well as their merits and limitations are discussed in more detail in Chapter 15. Our purpose here is to underscore the contribution of Freudian theory in answering the "why" of consumer behaviour.

A second advantage of Freudian theory is to explain the conflict among the various motiva-tions felt by an individual. This conflict is sometimes quite violent. When a motivation is counterbalanced by "stronger" motives, it takes a negative value in the individual's eyes. For instance, for some people (and especially weight-conscious individuals), satisfying a sweet tooth is often a powerful motivation leading them to indulge in candies or pastries. When this motive conflicts with other motives that have high moral and social value (for instance, the "duty" to remain slim or to maintain one's self-control), it may become a negatively valued motivation. Consumers will consciously fight against such a negatively valued motivation,

depending on the strength of the conflict. Thus, when a motivation conflicts with other socially visible and accepted motivations, it may take on a negative connotation. Conversely, when it enhances these motivations, it may become a positively valued motive.

Two main factors affect the degree of the conflict. The first is how well entrenched are the social and cultural attitudes or taboos involved in the conflict. When a motivation conflicts with a social taboo, i.e., a cultural belief that cannot be transgressed without serious social sanctions (sexual freedom or easy and frivo-lous lifestyles have long been typical examples in the West), the chances are that it will become a very negatively valued motivation for the individual. Second, when the conflictual moti-vation is socially visible, it is likely to be more negatively valued. For instance, certain moti-vations can be satisfied without involving anyone else (such as hygiene needs). However, other needs can be satisfied only through actions that are highly visible to others or to social groups.

Advertisers must understand the nature and interaction of the motivations involved when consumers use a brand or product category. If the motivations are so negatively valued that they do not reach the consumers' conscious level, it would be extremely dangerous to talk about them: the message could be rejected, and the product could take on a negative connota-tion for the consumers. If the conflict takes place at the conscious level, a consumer is likely to rationalize the act that satisfied his or her needs. For instance, this consumer may say that eating candy increases his or her energy, because the health motive is socially more acceptable than the greed motive. An efficient advertiser must provide an outlet for the *true* motives and at the same time give consumers an opportunity to infer the real satisfaction being provided. Thus an advertisement might provide consumers with arguments to help them rationalize their purchasing the product. In that sense, the psychoanalytic approach is useful for understanding buyer motivations and helping advertisers design efficient communication strategies.

Lewin's Field Theory

According to Kurt Lewin[13] an individual's behaviour is the result of a number of motives and forces in this individual's *life space*, i.e., perceptions of the surrounding world (the environment). As a consequence, to understand buyer behaviour is to identify all the forces to which a potential buyer is subjected at the time he considers making a purchase and all the barriers that block efforts to reach these goals.

Certain forces induce buyers to purchase and are considered to have a *positive valence*. Forces that prevent them from buying have a *negative valence*. These forces can be represented by vectors, the direction of which would represent the valence of the motives. This set of vectors can be thought of as the configuration of the nature and the relative strength of the motivations involved in a certain purchase situation. The conflict between motivations with positive and negative valences generates a state of psychological tension, which is directly linked to the number and intensities of all the forces involved (Figure 7.6). Thus, the conflict-

ing nature of any human action, and of purchasing behaviour in particular, is highlighted here again. While certain motives induce a consumer to purchase a product, other motives (especially those urging the satisfaction of other needs) tend to prevent the purchase.[14]

This conceptualization of consumer behaviour as the result of acting and counteracting forces has a definite advantage: it applies to specific situations and specific decisions, such as a major purchase. It allows for an analysis of all the positive and negative forces pulling a potential buyer away or pushing him toward a specific purchase decision. From a psychological point of view, all the forces to which a buyer is subjected correspond to very precise, interrelated needs. As already discussed, one action or purchase can simultaneously satisfy several types of needs. For instance, buying a car may satisfy a transportation as well as a safety, an economy, and a social status need.

However, it would be unusual for a given action not to go against the satisfaction of other needs. This is always true of a purchase: when consumers buy a product, they give up a certain part of their purchasing power. In other words, they give up, at least temporarily, the possibility of using the same amount of money

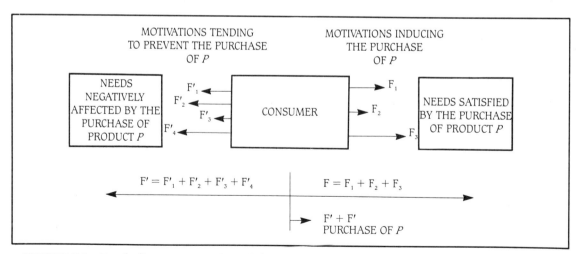

FIGURE 7.6   Symbolic Representation of the Positive and Negative Forces Influencing a Consumer on a Given Purchase Occasion *(P)*

to buy other products that could have satisfied other needs. For instance, when a consumer buys a car, he may subsequently give up the prospect of taking an expensive holiday or may postpone the long-contemplated purchase of a new home.

For example, let us assume that a student whose financial resources are somewhat limited is subjected to conflicting motives for buying a used car (Figure 7.7). Certain positive forces may induce the student to make such a purchase: the desire to drive to school more conveniently and pleasantly every morning; the need to impress friends (love needs); and the need to feel important (self-actualization need).

However, purchasing a car may be inhibited by other negative forces. For instance, the student may fear that the car could break down (security needs). Purchasing a car may also prevent the student from making some other expensive purchase.

If the sum of the forces pushing the student toward a purchase decision is larger than the sum of the forces pulling him or her away from this decision, the student will buy the used car; otherwise, the student will probably decide to postpone the purchase.

How Advertising Can Influence Consumer Needs

As previously discussed, the existence of a need or desire is an essential prerequisite for a purchasing decision. This is why it is important to know to what extent advertisers can "create" needs among consumers. If it were possible for advertisers to create consumer needs, it would be extremely advantageous for them to do so. If, on the contrary, they cannot do anything about them, how can they account for them as uncontrollable advertising variables?

The answers to these questions can be found in the fifth statement of Figure 7.4. It states that a latent desire can be stimulated by a subject's physiological change. For instance, hunger may result from the changes in an organism that are provoked by deprivation of food during a certain period of time. A latent desire can also be aroused by stimuli from the subject's environment. For instance, the subject may become thirsty at the mere sight of a bottle of Coca-Cola or the stimulus may be an advertising message that arouses a latent need or desire.

It must be stressed, however, that exciting a latent need is *not* "creating" a need. An

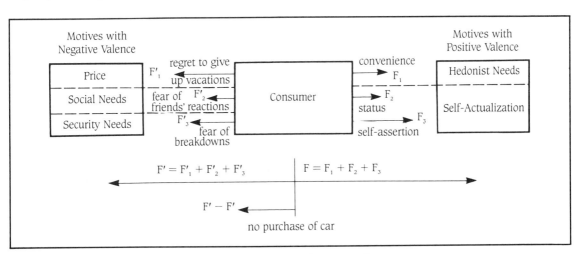

FIGURE 7.7 Example of Motive Conflict in a Used Car Purchase Decision for a Given Consumer

advertisement can awaken, reinforce, or even strongly stimulate a latent need. However, it cannot stimulate a desire that does not exist already. The sight of even the most delicate meal cannot arouse the appetite of anyone who has just finished a hearty meal. This is an important nuance, the implications of which are examined in Chapter 16, in which the limitations of advertising are discussed.

An advertiser can exert some action upon consumer needs only by remaining as present as possible in the consumer's environment in order to stimulate latent needs. This is especially true when the need is frequent and easily satisfied. Advertisements of drinks at points of purchase are an example of this.

Other Factors Influencing Needs and Motivations

In addition to being influenced by physiological changes, needs and motivations are also influ-

enced by a consumer's personality and past experience. Consumers' perception and awareness of their needs and the recognition that a product or a brand is likely to satisfy these needs are two essential prerequisites for a brand to be part of a consumer's evoked set (Figure 7.8).

Advertising and Buyer Perceptions

Buyers gain product and brand awareness and knowledge through the information flow they receive from various sources. They are exposed to at least four main sources of marketing information:

1. *Direct sensorial information.* Buyers receive such information through physical contact with the product. For instance, when they look at a product in a retail outlet or when they are exposed to the package, when they watch a commercial, when they see a

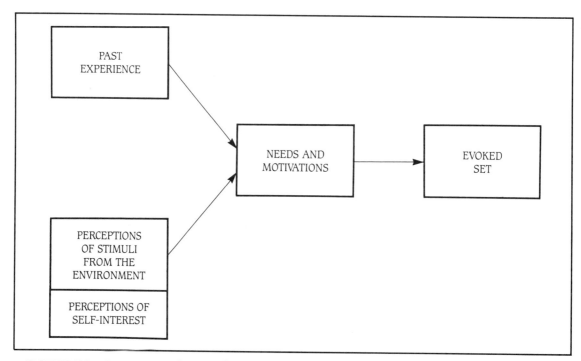

FIGURE 7.8   Some Determinants of Needs and Motivations

model in a showroom, or in any other circumstances, they receive or infer a certain amount of information about the product and/or the brand. Consumers may also infer information about the product characteristics after product usage.

2. *Retailer or seller's information.* A buyer may get product or brand information from retailers or from people in the distribution channels. Industrial buyers get valuable information from salespeople. This information may be factual, for instance, when it results from a demonstration of the product or from a description of the product's technical features and characteristics.

It may also be "subjective" information, as when the retailer tries to use persuasive arguments to induce the customer to buy a specific brand or when the customer asks the retailer's personal and subjective advice on which brand to select.

3. *Advertising information.* This is the bulk of information about companies, products, services, and brands that potential buyers receive through the advertising media.

4. *Inter-personal information.* Consumers receive a large amount of marketing information as they interact with various *reference groups*, which are the social groups to which they belong or to which they aspire to belong.

An important goal of any firm is to see its products, brands, and the firm itself perceived positively by potential customers. However, it is also important to keep in mind that buyers' perceptions are influenced strongly by the kind of communication message they receive and the media through which they receive the communication. Moreover, consumers often see a *risk* in the purchase decision, which may play an important part in the purchase decision process. Buyer perceptions are of paramount importance in advertising, since all stimuli must be perceived somehow—even if below the level of consumer consciousness—before they can trigger an affective and/or behavioural response.

Perceptual Defence Mechanisms

A perception is the mental configuration an individual has of a stimulus. People acquire some knowledge about the surrounding world through perceptions. No two individuals have identical perceptions of an object, however, because their perceptions of their environment are not likely to be exactly the same. Some generally accepted propositions about perceptions that are drawn from social psychology can be applied to an analysis of buyer behaviour and the role of advertising in influencing buyer behaviour (Figure 7.9).[15]

Selective Attention
Individuals filter and perceive only a small proportion of the stimuli to which they are exposed. This phenomenon is inherent in all

---

1. Each person has an individualized image of the world because his image is the product of...*his* physical and social environments, *his* physiological structure, *his* wants and goals, *his* past experience.

2. The cognitions of the individual are selectively organized....The selective organization of cognition is determined by two interacting sets of factors: stimulus factors and personal factors.

3. Cognitions develop into systems. The particular grouping of separate cognitions to form such systems is determined both by stimulus factors and personal factors, e.g., individual interests and experiences.

4. The properties of a cognition are influenced by the system of which it is a part.

5. Cognitive change is typically initiated by changes in the individual's information and wants.... Cognitive change is in part governed by the characteristics of pre-existing cognitive systems...and by personality factors.

FIGURE 7.9   Propositions on Perceptions and Cognitions from Social Psychology

SOURCE: Krech et al., *Individual in Society* (New York: McGraw-Hill, 1962), pp. 69-85. Reproduced with the permission of the McGraw-Hill Book Company.

communication processes and especially in those emanating from objects and products. Some buyers do not notice certain characteristics of a product, while they perceive other features at once. During interpersonal communications, such as a conversation with a neighbour, a friend, or a salesclerk, certain sentences and some details are not even "heard" by a subject, while other arguments have a very strong impact. But more than any others, mass communications and especially advertising are affected by the selective attention of audiences.

Three reasons may account for this phenomenon. First, because advertising is a nonpersonal form of communication, buyers do not have face-to-face contact with an individual to whom they must listen, even if out of sheer politeness. They are not forced to read an advertisement in a newspaper or in a magazine. They are not obliged to listen to a radio or watch a TV commercial. Consequently, there is very little to prevent selective attention. Second, advertising has become so ubiquitous in modern society that consumers cannot pay attention to every advertisement every day. Bauer and Greyser[16] have estimated that American consumers are potentially exposed to 1500 advertising messages every day. Out of these 1500 advertising stimuli, consumers perceive only 76 (12 of which induce some behavioural response). Finally, individuals and especially consumers develop a kind of reflex that permits them to filter and reject the largest proportion of the information that is irrelevant to their needs and/or wants. On the other hand, selective attention mechanisms permit them to select only the type of information in which they have some interest.

As shown in Figure 7.10, a subject's interests are shaped by the complex interactions among the subject's set of needs and wants. These interests are the gatekeepers that filter information relevant to the subject's need satisfaction. Some laboratory experiments can illustrate this point.[17]

It has been shown that deaf people are more likely to notice a very small advertisement in a newspaper bearing the simple headline "DEAF", followed by copy describing the merits of some hearing device. Deaf people have very specific needs related to their hearing problems and thus are likely to be alert to and interested in any information that may help them satisfy their needs. In this case, a deaf person's selective attention filters out larger attention-getting advertisements and retains a very small advertisement that contains relevant information.

This important observation gives a rationale for the advertising creation principles that are discussed in Part 4—that an advertising message built directly upon buyers' interests is more likely to go through the selective attention mechanisms than a message that merely tries to attract attention.

Besides considerations specific to individual buyers, message-related factors are likely to improve or prevent a message's passage through a potential buyer's attention filters. Consequently, a message is more likely to attract people's attention if its size increases and if it uses colour, is frequently repeated, has a high intensity (loudness, for instance), or uses motion.

Selective Distortion

Once a message has successfully found its way through selective attention mechanisms, it meets a second obstacle: selective distortion filters. Individuals have a somewhat distorted vision of the "objective" world. Perceptions are organized and have precise and often specific meanings for each individual. This is what is meant by the second statement in Figure 7.9. The selective distortion mechanisms affecting the information an individual receives are strongly influenced by need patterns. Bauer and Goodman[18] have shown in a now-classic study in psychology that unlike children from well-off families, children from poor families had a tendency to overestimate the size of

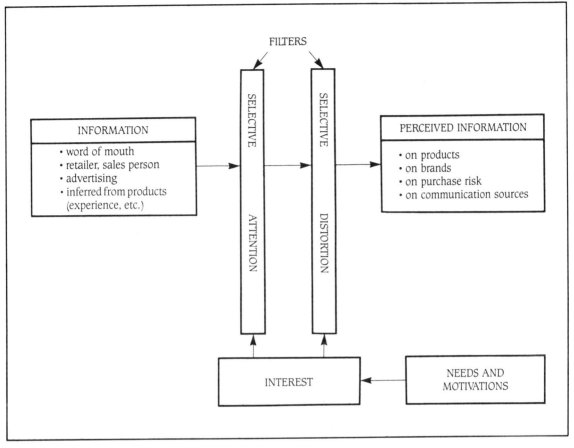

FILTERS

SELECTIVE ATTENTION

SELECTIVE DISTORTION

INFORMATION
- word of mouth
- retailer, sales person
- advertising
- inferred from products (experience, etc.)

PERCEIVED INFORMATION
- on products
- on brands
- on purchase risk
- on communication sources

INTEREST

NEEDS AND MOTIVATIONS

FIGURE 7.10 Information Perceived by Consumers

coins. This shows how the children's perceptions were influenced by their needs.

The marketing implications are obvious: in most cases, buyers see much more in a given product than a mere set of physical and objective characteristics. All products are perceived by consumers as having more or less important symbolic meanings, characteristics, and values. Consumers buy a product not only for what they expect the product to do but also for what it *means* to them.[19] This is why buyers are likely to have quite different perceptions of the products and their attributes, as of the information they receive about these products. These different perceptions depend on buyers' need patterns, their previous experiences, and/or personality.

The Nature of Buyer Perceptions

Buyer vs. Manufacturer Perceptions

Buyers develop specific perceptions of products and brands depending on their need and motivation patterns. It was seen in Chapter 1, however, that buyers and manufacturers have essentially different fields of experience as well as different needs and motives. Consequently, the two groups tend to develop different perceptions of products, brands, and communications. This has been highlighted by an experiment that was undertaken a few years ago by Blum and Appel.[20] In this experiment, the reactions of a firm's designers and marketing managers to 18 possible designs of a product were very different from the reactions of the consumers and the potential buyers of the product. It was shown that the evaluation criteria used by the two groups of respondents were quite different. The main conclusion suggested by this experiment is that marketing managers and advertisers should never try merely to guess how buyers are likely to perceive their product or their communication. In any circumstance, it is essential to obtain buyers' reactions by means of appropriate research methods and techniques, such as those which will be explained in Chapter 15.

Buyers' Perceptions of the Purchase Process Elements

Buyers see in products and brands more than a set of technical and physical attributes. The set of attributes that consumers perceive as being those of a brand is what is generally called the *brand image*. In other words, a brand image can be defined as the personality traits consumers ascribe to a brand.

Consumers are exposed to all kinds of marketing information about brands from various sources. Many information sources are involved, not only advertising but also communication with neighbours, retailers, salesclerks, and information included with a product's packaging. With the information received through these different communication channels, consumers develop a brand image that more or less matches the real and "objective" physical product. In other words, one could think of consumers as matching a brand with a typical consumer with a certain profile.

In a now-classic experiment, Mason Haire found that at the time instant coffee was introduced in the United States, the product was perceived as a product for "lazy and spendthrift housewives."[21] Thus, a brand image can also be viewed as the personality profile of the typical consumer of the brand as perceived by consumers themselves.

Another aspect of brand perception concerns one particular attribute of a product: its price. A product's price contributes to the brand image

consumers develop; thus buyers' perceptions of a product or a brand only imperfectly match the "objective" real world. In advertising, this image formation principle applies to the perceptions of a product category (product image), a certain brand (brand image), or a whole company (corporate image).

A brand image is favourable as long as a buyer perceives some congruence between needs (as perceived by the buyer) and the brand image. That is, the brand image is favourable if there is a small or no gap between buyers' perception of themselves (their self-concept) and the brand image. Conversely, the brand image may be unfavourable if there is too wide a gap between the two profiles. For instance, if a consumer perceives a certain brand of men's shoes as suitable for playboys, he will probably develop a positive attitude toward this brand *if* he perceives himself as a playboy. A conservative businessman, however, may develop a negative attitude toward the brand.

In this discussion of buyer brand preferences[22] it has been assumed that buyers had all the information they desired about products and brands. In practice, this is rarely the case. This is why buyers sometimes perceive an information gap between what they know about a product or brand and what they expect from a purchase. There is always some *risk* attached to any purchase situation. This risk is as high as consumers lack (or think they lack) the relevant information and is proportionate to the importance of the potential consequences of the purchase (a financial loss, for instance). Additional information will reduce the purchase risk. However, one other important aspect of information perceptions is that people perceive not all or part of the information conveyed by the communication but also infer some information from the elements of the communication (especially the source of the media used). These different elements of buyer perceptions of the purchasing process are represented in Figure 7.11.

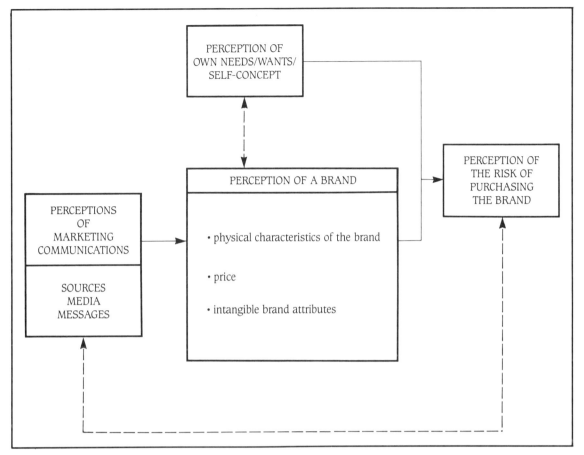

FIGURE 7.11   Consumers' Perceptions of the Purchase Process Elements

Buyer Perceptions of Brands

Buyer Perceptions of the Physical Attributes of a Brand

Buyers often have only a partial knowledge and understanding of the products they buy. Sometimes, the product is technically sophisticated (for example, a personal computer or video recorder). Therefore, unless consumers are electronics engineers or technicians they are unlikely to understand or evaluate all the technical and complex features of the product. Even when the product is not technically sophisticated, manufacturers are often surprised to learn through a market study that consumers have a high level of technical ignorance about facts that have become obvious and natural to them. Advertisers should thus be aware of the level of technical knowledge buyers have reached on a product if they want an advertising communication to be properly decoded by potential buyers.

Buyers tend to perceive only the attributes that are important to them. These are the *salient attributes*. Knowledge of which attributes are salient for which buyers in which circumstances is essential, since buyers are likely to compare the performance of the various brands available on these salient attributes before they purchase a brand. Moreover, consumers interpret and infer all kinds of information from certain physical attributes of the product.[23] This inferred information may seem absurd to a well-informed specialist. For instance, from the light weight of an electrical appliance, some consumers may (unconsciously) infer that the appliance is not sturdy, or that a piece of furniture is of inferior quality because some of its ornaments are made of plastic (for many consumers, a good piece of furniture can only be made of wood).

Buyer Perception of a Product's Price

The price charged for a product has different meanings for buyers. One is that part of the consumer's purchasing power must be sacrificed to acquire the product. Buying product A today often means giving up the prospects of buying products B, C, or D, which would satisfy other needs. This is why in *absolute terms* the price characteristic of a product can never be an inducement to purchase it. Classical economists have always recognized this aspect of price when they state that the demand schedule for a product decreases as its price increases.

Another meaning of price was not recognized, however, by classical economists, who assumed that consumers would have access to immediate, perfect, and free information. If this were the case, what would be the point of advertising? Price often gives consumers information about the quality of the product. In this case, the demand for a product increases as the price also increases, because as the price increases, consumers associate price with quality and the demand is higher for high quality products. Gabor and Granger[24] have hypothesized that buyers have in mind a range of possible prices for a certain product category, with an upper and a lower limit. Above the upper limit, the product is perceived as too expensive. Whatever its quality, it is perceived as not being worth its price by a large majority of potential buyers. Below the lower limit, the product is perceived as having too low a quality to be sold at such a reduced price. Between the two limits is a "fair" price that consumers may not be able to determine themselves because they cannot properly assess the "quality" of a product.

Therefore, within the admissible range, consumers tend to associate price and quality (the implicit assumption being that producers price their products on a cost-plus basis, which may not always be true).

Buyer Perceptions of a Brand's Intangible Attributes

It was shown how a product's physical characteristics and attributes, including its price, tend to generate in buyer's minds new attributes that may be real or sometimes irrelevant and false. As soon as a potential buyer gets into contact with a product, the brand image formation process starts. As shown in Figure 7.10, however, the product itself is not the only source of information for buyers. Advertisement for a brand, interpersonal communications about products, and in general everything that is related to a brand and falls into a buyer's visual field are also sources of infomation about a product. For instance, the general display at a bank head office, the thickness of the carpets at its branches, and the courtesy of its employees are but a few of the multitude of details that are visible to the public and that give a bank its personality (image).

Although advertising is not the only source of brand image formation, it is one of the few information sources that is often completely under a firm's control. Therefore, advertisers are generally interested in these kinds of questions: What is the present image of the brand as perceived by consumers? How is this image different from those of the competing brands? What is the "ideal" brand image toward which the brand should tend in a specific market segment? What should and could be done to bring the present brand image as close as possible to the ideal one? Consequently, brand image analysis is an important task of an advertiser.

According to Joannis,[25] brand image analysis can be conducted according to a brand's proximity, clarity, content, and value.

IMAGE PROXIMITY. Image proximity refers to how present a brand is in buyers' minds. Some brands are always present in practically every consumer's mind; others are not. To demonstrate this, one has only to ask people which brands of a product category they can mention without any aid. A brand with a high level of presence will always be among the first mentioned because it will probably come readily to consumers' minds as soon as they think of the relevant product category. For instance, when Canadian consumers are asked to give a few brand names of snowmobiles, Ski-doo is likely to be mentioned frequently, Eaton's for a department store, Kodak for a camera, Molson's for a beer, and so on.

In contrast, certain brand names are unknown to many consumers. Other brands are well known but not frequently mentioned because consumers do not readily think of such brands when they consider a product category. These brands have a low presence level in consumers' minds.

IMAGE CLARITY. A brand image is perceived more or less clearly. This is evidenced by the level of consensus among consumers as to what the personality of a brand is. Thus, a brand of detergent may be perceived by practically all customers as being young, modern, effective. This would be an example of a clear image. If, on the contrary, a brand is perceived as young, modern, and effective by certain customers, as old, traditional, and rather ineffective by others, and as a brand for poor or vulgar people by yet another group of consumers, this brand would not have a clear image in the market.

IMAGE CONTENT. The *content* of a brand includes all the personality traits that characterize the brand. As shown in Figure 7.12, two brands

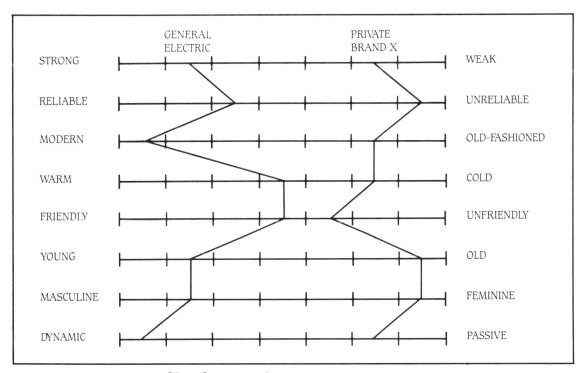

FIGURE 7.12 Image Profiles of Two Brands

(General Electric and private Brand X) could be perceived as having their profiles defined according to a set of bipolar adjectives[26] such as young-old, reliable-unreliable. Average profiles across consumers in a market segment are typically estimated on such scales for analyzing brand image content. Thus, in Figure 7.12, the General Electric brand would be perceived as more powerful, reliable, and modern than Brand X.

BRAND IMAGE VALUE. The profile of a certain brand image has little significance in itself. It gets its full meaning only when compared with the traits that buyers in a market segment would consider positive or negative for a brand in a particular product category. For instance, a brand can be perceived as feminine by consumers. This might be a positive characteristic for a beauty care product or for a brand of cigarettes directed at the women's market segment. However, it would certainly be an undesirable characteristic for an after-shave lotion or for a brand of cigarettes designed for heavy male smokers. These notions are discussed further in Chapter 8.

Brand Image and Brand Awareness

Brand awareness refers to the level of brand knowledge that consumers have acquired. It is one aspect of the proximity of a brand image (a well-known brand is often quite present in buyers' minds, although, as was pointed out, well-known brands may not be as present in all buyers' minds). That a brand is perceived as being well known or unknown is part of the content of its image. Consequently, brand awareness cannot be achieved without creating a brand image; to raise the awareness level, some information about the product and the brand must be communicated, which involves image formation.

Buyer Perceptual Maps

It was shown how buyers perceived a brand according to certain characteristics and attributes. These attributes can be objective (such as the package or product colours, or its shape), or abstract (such as masculine-feminine, or modern-old-fashioned). In practice, advertisers are interested not only in buyers' perceptions of their brand but also in how these perceptions compare with competing brands. The concept of a buyer perceptual map helps advertisers understand and "visualize" these perceptions of a buyer or of a whole market segment, if it can be assumed that buyers' perceptions of different brands are sufficiently similar to warrant their aggregation.

In the perceptual map, actual brands of a same product class are represented as points in a geometrical space. Interpoint distances between brands represent overall similarities as perceived by buyers of a market segment. The underlying dimensions of this space are considered to be the attributes used by buyers to discriminate among brands.

For instance, assume that a brand manager for Minute Maid, a fruit-juice company, wants to find out how consumers' perceptions of Minute Maid compare with two competing brands, Sun Pac and Tropicana. Also assume that only two main attributes are used by consumers to differentiate among the different brands,[27] for instance, sugar content and colour. (In practice, an advertiser does not know which or even how many attributes are used by consumers). Figure 7.13 shows how an average consumer in a market segment has rated Minute Maid, Sun Pac, and Tropicana on these two characteristics. It can be seen that Tropicana is perceived as being more similar to Minute Maid than is Sun Pac.

These data could be presented directly on the same diagram, where the two axes represent the two attributes and the scores of each brand on these two dimensions can be used as the co-ordinates to position each brand as a point in this two-dimensional space (Figure 7.14).[28]

If more brands and more attributes were involved, direct comparisons of the brands' relative positions would be very difficult. This

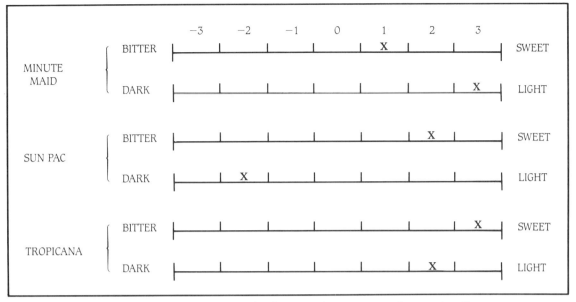

FIGURE 7.13   Perceptions of Three Brands of Fruit Juice on Two Relevant Attributes by a "Typical" Buyer

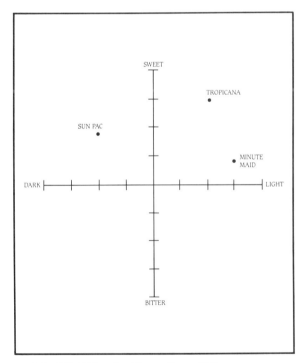

FIGURE 7.14   Configuration of Three Brands of Fruit Juice in a Consumer's Perceptual Space

is where the perceptual map concept can help an advertiser. Such techniques as multidimensional scaling and factor or discriminant analyses can provide the spatial representation of the perceptions of the various brands in buyers' minds; the number of relevant dimensions used by buyers to "perceive" brands; and the nature of these dimensions. The concept of perceptual maps can be extended to an analysis of buyers' perceptions and preferences.

Buyer Perceptions of a Purchase Risk

Like any decision, a purchase involves some risk for a consumer. Buyers generally perceive some risk in a purchase decision because they always see some uncertainty about the outcome of their decisions. The size of the risk involved in a purchase decision is influenced by at least two factors: First, it depends upon how important for a buyer are the consequences of the worst outcome of the purchase decision. This is an important aspect of industrial buying. Second, it depends on the level of uncertainty about the ability of the product or brand to satisfy needs and motives. As already mentioned, needs and motives may be personal, familial, or social in nature, and involve subjective and affective values for a buyer. Obviously, the lack of information about a product's ability to fulfil the needs involved in a purchase decision is the essence of buyers' uncertainty when they contemplate a certain purchase. As can be surmised, the more a product is complex and technically sophisticated, the larger is the information gap between what a buyer expects of the product on one hand, and what he knows about the product's future performance on the other. If consumers have had some experience with a product, they possess a substantial amount of information about the product's performance. At the other extreme, in the purchase of an innovation or an unknown product or brand, the uncertainty about actual product performance is generally substantial.

If the risk materializes, the consequences for buyers may involve the loss of all or part of the resources that have been devoted to acquiring the product. These may be financial resources. For instance, consumers risk losing an amount equal to the price paid for the product if the product does not meet their expectations. There may also be a physical risk if the product poses a health hazard. This would be the case if there was some risk in buying a deteriorated food product, an inefficient drug, or a cigarette brand that has more severe health effects than most other brands. These financial or physical risks are essentially associated with the non-satisfaction of personal or physiological needs and motives.

There is also a range of psychological and psycho-sociological risks. They essentially correspond to the non-satisfaction of familial or socially oriented motivations. The resources involved are the consumer's psychological and social equilibrium or balance. For instance, the purchase of a flashy suit may threaten a man's long-established reputation of good taste, simplicity, or elegance. Thus, as buyers put important and valued resources into a purchase,

they are likely to perceive a high risk in making a wrong decision.

It should be remembered that most products are likely to satisfy several buyer needs at a time. In such cases, a consumer may simultaneously perceive an economic risk (if, for example, the car does not perform as well as expected) and a psychological risk (if the reactions from the consumer's social groups are not those expected).

Bauer[29] has hypothesized that consumers act so as to minimize the risks they perceive in their purchase decisions. According to Figure 7.15, a buyer may succeed in minimizing the perceived risk through additional information, brand loyalty (past experience with the brand), and systematic information search from various sources (advertising, retailers, or friends).[30] The perceived risk can also be lowered by reducing the number and intensity of the motivations involved in the purchase; for instance, when buyers decide to lower their expectations of a product's performance. The same result can also be achieved by reducing the resources involved in the purchase (offering a smaller quantity of the product or offering goods on a trial basis). In short, the risks perceived by a consumer are likely to affect in many ways the information acquisition process in a purchase occasion, as well as the purchase behaviour.

Buyer Perceptions of the Communication Elements

All the elements of an advertising campaign contribute to brand image formation. When properly designed, a message conveys to consumers what the advertiser has to say about a product; in addition, the individual who actually delivers the message (source), the media vehicles carrying the ads, and the featured consumption scenario in which the product is advertised also communicate.

This is an important area for advertisers because an integrated brand image strategy

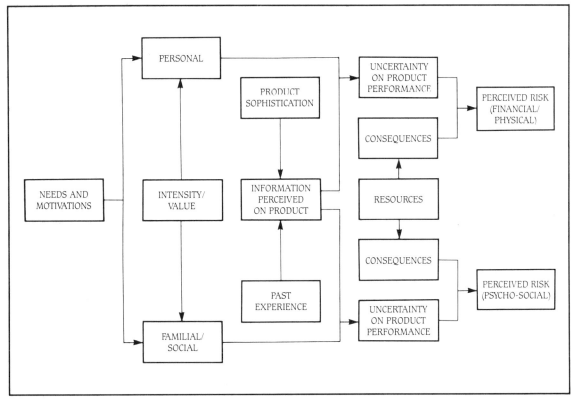

FIGURE 7.15 Relationships among Motivations and Needs, Product Perceptions, and Perceived Risks

should include only the elements that are compatible and are likely to convey the same information to the consumer or at least information that is not inconsistent with the target brand image.

The image potential of different communication elements in relation to the brand images has been shown in a pilot study that employed the concept of a perceptual map.[31] Using twenty attributes judged important a priori, each respondent in two samples of French and English Canadians was asked to evaluate:

1. different brands of beer presently on the market (Labatt 50, Laurentide, Molson, Carlsberg, O'Keefe, and Brador);
2. their ideal brand of beer (without specifying any consumption occasion);
3. what they would guess to be the ideal brand

of beer for various personalities generally known by the two communities (Frank Sinatra, Tex Lecor, Bobby Orr, and Guy Lafleur—two popular singers and two sportsmen, one French and one English speaking);
4. what they would consider the ideal brand of beer for a "typical" French Canadian and for a "typical" English Canadian;
5. what they would guess to be the ideal brand of beer for a "typical" reader of various English and French language media vehicles (*Playboy*, the *Gazette*, the *Financial Post*, *Le Devoir*);
6. the characteristics of the ideal beer to be consumed at various occasions (before dinner, with dinner, at a party).

The resulting two-dimensional configuration of the perceptual space is shown in Figure 7.16 for the French Canadian segment and in Figure 7.17 for the English Canadian segment. The location of each brand of beer is indicated relative to the two major dimensions. The original attributes that play a significant part in discriminating among the various brands are represented by vectors in the same space. These brand locations and the attributes' vector directions are derived simultaneously, so that the mean rating of each brand on each of the original attributes is shown by the relative position on each attribute vector (by merely dropping perpendicular lines from each brand onto each vector in turn). For instance, Carlsberg is perceived as being of higher quality, followed by Laurentide, O'Keefe, Brador, Molson, and Labatt 50.

The horizontal axis represents the price/quality dimension; the vertical axis is the light-ness dimension. The dimensions are easily identified by the original variables with which they are highly correlated.

Figures 7.16 and 7.17 show how the different possible communication sources, media, and scenarios are consistent with the different brand images, and how these perceptions are likely to vary from one market segment to another. For instance, if a beer manufacturer used the testimony of Bobby Orr or that of a French Canadian in an advertisement, the responses from the two original segments would most likely be different because of the opposite images cast on each market segment by these possible message sources. This is the reason an integrated brand image strategy can be built only for groups with the most homogeneous response possible to the selected advertising instruments.

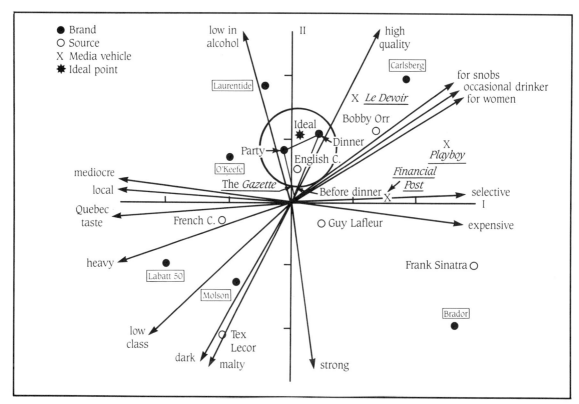

FIGURE 7.16   Multiple Joint Space of the French Canadian Market Segment

190

Buyer Perceptions of a Communication Source

SOURCE CREDIBILITY. Even before any communication takes place, a source is perceived by an audience as carrying a certain amount of information[32] and, hence, as more or less competent and credible. Source credibility is essential in advertising because communication effectiveness depends on it,[33] and as will be discussed in the next chapter, it is related to consumer attitude change. The source of a communication may be perceived as being either the firm advertising the brand or the individual(s) who deliver(s) the message, especially in the case of testimonial advertising. Source credibility depends on whether the source is perceived as being competent to make the statements contained in the message or whether the individual delivering the message

is considered truthful. Credibility has two major components: a cognitive and an affective component.[34] The cognitive component refers to the source's competence as perceived by the communication's recipient. A doctor is generally more credible when he makes a statement about some medical matter than would be a janitor. The affective component refers to whether the source is perceived as objective and trustworthy. A politician who makes a speech on the national economy may be perceived as competent but biased because of his political allegiance. Thus, credibility is not an intrinsic characteristic of a source; it is granted to the communicator by an individual. A source may well seem quite credible to one individual and absolutely untrustworthy to another. A consumer who is loyal to Coca-Cola can perceive an advertisement for this brand as credible,

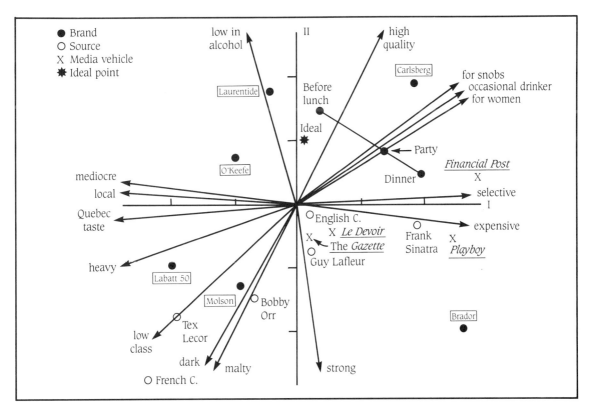

FIGURE 7.17   Multiple Joint Space of the English Canadian Market Segment

while another who is loyal to Pepsi-Cola may perceive the same advertisement as not credible because the ad is sponsored by a company toward which this consumer has a less favourable attitude.

Consequently, the first prerequisite for a source to be credible is that it be perceived as competent. Two factors enhance the perception of a source's competence. First, the source must be effectively recognized as an expert. Dentists (because of their officially recognized expertise) are more credible than a non-medical specialist when they make a statement concerning the effects of sugar consumption on cavity proneness. A second factor is the assurance with which the statement is made. The rationale is that experts are supposed to talk confidently about their field of expertise. This is why experts may lose some or all of their credibility[35] when they speak on topics outside their field.

The level of agreement between a communicator and an audience is a primary determinant of the affective component of source credibility. In other words, a source is more credible when it is perceived as holding opinions similar to those of the audience on other matters. One evidently tends to agree with people with whom one already shares a certain number of opinions. A second determinant is whether the source is perceived as having some interest in defending the stand taken in the message.

Various findings of social psychology have important advertising implications. One is that an advertiser should be perceived as a credible source, and this cannot be achieved unless the company is perceived as *competent* and *objective*. Although a company can build a reputation of expertise and competence, it will practically never be able to show it has no interest in convincing its audience, since advertisers have a vested interest in selling their products and services. Consequently, consumers will always attribute this intention to advertisers.[36] This reality may be somewhat overcome by a well-established reputation of competence.

FIGURE 7.18   The Use of a Recognized Expert for Testimonial Advertising
Courtesy Fisher-Price Canada

FIGURE 7.19   The Use of a "Typical" Consumer for Testimonial Advertising
Courtesy Regal Greetings & Gifts

A company that has not been able to establish such a reputation can use testimonial advertising. The objective of this approach is to dissociate the source of the message from the company. An advertiser can ask an outside person to "testify" for the product. Thus, the testimony of a recognized expert can be used to act upon the competence element[37] (Figure 7.18), while a "typical" consumer may be used to act upon the affective element by reporting on a positive experience with the product or service (Figure 7.19).

The assertive tone of most broadcast commercials can be also explained by advertisers' desire to ensure that the source is perceived as competent and credible. As will be discussed in Chapter 8, source credibility is important, since it is an essential element of buyer attitude change.

OTHER ASPECTS OF THE SOURCE IMAGE. Besides the credibility aspect, an audience perceives a communication source according to various qualitative considerations. In terms of the previous beer example, it is useful to measure the congruence or the gap between a brand image and the source image to predict the influence a potential source may have on brand image. For instance, if Frank Sinatra were hired to advertise beer, he would probably project the image of a strong, expensive beer. On the other hand, Bobby Orr would more likely convey to English Canadians the image of a malty, strong, and local beer. To French Canadians, the image would be of a high quality beer, low in alcohol, to be drunk by snobs and occasional beer drinkers.

The position given to a source by an audience on the perceptual map permits the advertiser to evaluate the plausibility of a message. To keep the same example, if Bobby Orr were asked to advertise a beer as light and low in alcohol, the message could be plausible to a French Canadian because these characteristics correspond to what French Canadians would assume to be Bobby Orr's favourite beer. This same message could seem implausible to an English Canadian. Message plausibility is important in advertising. Without plausibility, a message does not sound sincere and can be rejected by the audience. Source and brand credibility may also be affected.[38]

For the reasons mentioned above, advertisers should use a source whose image is as compatible as possible with the target image. Furthermore, an advertiser can compare various possible sources for ads on the basis of their respective distances to the objectives. Of course, this image element should be combined with other relevant source characteristics such as competence, credibility, and relevance to the product category.

Buyer Perceptions of a Communication Vehicle
In the same way as a communication source interacts with the message content, a particular medium can enhance or decrease the message credibility. For instance, information published in highly credible media is more likely to be believed, and this extends to the advertising published in such media. Thus, in Figure 7.17, *Playboy* or *The Financial Post* have an "expensive/selective" image that may be compatible with a brand like Brador or Carlsberg but less suited to Labatt's advertising. This is why the compatibility of brand and media images is a concern for media planners.

How Advertising Can Influence Buyer Perceptions

It was shown how advertising, like any buyer information source, must overcome buyers' perceptual defense mechanisms in order to increase their information level about an advertised product, brand, or service.[39] In order to break the barriers of selective attention, an advertiser can try to bypass the obstacle of selective attention and use what has been called *subliminal advertising*. Another method is the use of mechanical devices to attract the audience's attention.

Subliminal Advertising

One important question in advertising is to what extent communication can influence subjects without their being consciously aware that they have been exposed to the information. In other words, can a communication be effective when it is received by subjects at such a high speed that it falls below their perceptual threshold? Psychologists call this phenomenon *subliminal perceptions*. For advertisers, the problem is to assess whether subliminal advertising (advertising messages delivered so quickly that a subject has no time to consciously perceive them) can be effective in influencing consumers. (See also Chapter 16).

In an experiment carried out several years ago, two commercials for Coca-Cola and for popcorn were shown in a movie theater at a speed below consumers' perceptual threshold.[40] The reported results of this experiment showed a sales increase of 57.7 per cent for Coca-Cola and 18.1 per cent for popcorn at the theater. It should be underlined, however, that this experiment has often been criticized on methodological grounds and that the validity of these results is questionable. Furthermore, all the subsequent replications of this study have failed to produce similar results. The lack of effectiveness of subliminal advertising is supported by the conclusions of many experiments carried out by psychologists. These experiments have generally shown that subjects' perceptual defenses were still operative even at levels lower than their perceptual threshold.[41] At the extreme, when no perception is possible, the message has no effect whatsoever.[42] Therefore, the general conclusion is that there are at least serious doubts concerning the effectiveness of subliminal advertising, regardless of the ethical issues raised by this type of communication.[43]

Mechanical Devices

Factors such as the size of a print advertisement, the length of a telecast message, the use of colour, repetition, high message intensity, or motion can decrease the effectiveness of consumers' selective attention. Consequently, in order to be more effective communicators (regardless of the costs involved), advertisers are likely to prefer for magazine and newspaper advertisements:

- a full page to a half or quarter page
- four colours to black and white
- an advertisement that contrasts with the rest of the information conveyed by the medium.

For a broadcast commercial, advertisers generally prefer

- a one-minute commercial to a shorter one
- a commercial whose intensity contrasts with the rest of the program it is broadcast on.

For a flashlight billboard, advertisers should prefer

- the largest possible billboard
- the use of several colour lights
- the use of a moving rather than a still advertisement.

Another effective mechanical device that applies to all kinds of media is the use of message repetition. Several studies have shown a direct relationship between message repetition and message recall and comprehension. One study showed that the percentage of a television audience that could recall a telecast advertisement increased from 33 per cent to 65 per cent, depending on the total number of minutes the advertisements of the specific brand were seen.[44] Other studies have shown similar results.[45]

Keeping in mind that advertising is only one of several marketing information sources that can influence audiences, advertisers have at least three different ways of influencing buyer behaviour:

1. They can provide information in order to increase the buyer's information level about product characteristics and performance. Informative advertising can fulfil this objective. When an advertising campaign plays this role, it tends to reduce the risk that buyers perceive in the purchase decision

and, consequently, helps buyers make better purchase decisions.

2. They can help build a product or a brand image. Advertising can help give a brand favourable psychological attributes and, consequently, make it more desirable to buyers.

3. Advertising can be more effective if it uses communication sources that are perceived as credible. Competent and trustworthy experts can help bolster a company's credibility and reputation. Advertising is also more effective when attention-getting devices are used properly.

Summary

A simplified descriptive model of the effects of advertising on buyer behaviour gives some insight into how advertising works and can influence buyer behaviour. A purchase is a decision made by consumers on their evoked set of brands. In order to purchase a specific brand, a consumer should have a need or a desire to buy the product; perceive the brand as the most likely to fulfil his need or desire; and have the ability and the financial and physical resources to purchase the product.

There are two important dimensions of the purchase process: the effect of advertising on buyer needs and motives and its effects on buyer perceptions. A motivation is a force underlying a need or desire. There are various theories of motivations, among them Maslow's theory of a hierarchy of needs, the Freudian psychoanalytic theory, and the field theory of Kurt Lewin. An analysis of these theories leads to the conclusion that advertising cannot "create" consumer needs but can only stimulate needs that already exist, even if at the unconscious level.

Buyer perceptions may be described as a series of filters through which information and stimuli from the environment must pass to be integrated into the cognitive structures of the consumer's field of experience. There are two main kinds of filter: a buyer's selective perception sorts and rejects part of the information received, while through selective distortion other information is distorted. These concepts from social sciences can be applied to consumers to analyze their perceptions of brands (the set of objective and psychological attributes given to a brand by buyers), of price, of purchase risks, and the various elements of the communication process (especially the credibility of a source). This analysis of buyer perceptions leads to general principles that advertisers can and should follow in order to design effective advertising messages.

Questions for Study

1. Using Figure 7.3, explain why and how you made your most recent purchase of
   (a) a convenience product (food, cigarettes)
   (b) a durable good (furniture, car, stereophonic equipment)
   (c) a shopping good (clothing, camera)

   In each case, try to show the role advertising has had in your purchase decision.

2. Think of a major purchase you have made recently. Try to describe the role of advertising in this purchase decision. What was the role of all the other information sources that were involved? Which source had the most influence in your final decision? Be as specific as you can.

3. Answer as specifically as you can the two questions asked in the examples in the section "Consumer and Market Behaviour."

4. Find a print advertisement or a broadcast commercial that you think is effective in getting attention, and try to identify the perceptual mechanisms responsible for this effect.

5. Find a print advertisement or a broadcast commercial that appeals to the following motivations: (a) sex; (b) fear; (c) anxiety;

(d) security; and *(e)* social esteem. In each case, show how the appeal is being used and comment on the rationale of using such an appeal.

6. Can advertising "create" needs? Discuss. Give specific examples.

7. Discuss the concept of a brand image. Select a few advertisements or commercials for *(a)* cigarettes and *(b)* perfumes. For each, try to infer the kind of image you think the advertiser would like the brand to have among consumers. Explain why you think so.

8. Select a few brands of a product category. For each brand, investigate on a convenience sample of consumers the four dimensions of each brand image: its proximity, clarity, content, and value.

9. Explain the concept of a consumer perceptual map. How can this concept be useful to advertisers?

10. Find examples of print advertisements or broadcast commercials that use testimonial advertising and that are based:
    (a) on the competence of the source
    (b) on the affective "trustworthiness" of the source.

    Discuss the rationale for using these types of testimonials in each example.

Problems

1. You are the manager in charge of advertising for an important department store chain, Canadian Stores, operating in all Canadian cities. In the past, the stores have always tried to develop an image of offering a wide variety of merchandise. However, because of competing stores making similar claims, you are not sure that consumers in the Toronto market still perceive Canadian Stores as the department store where they can get almost every item they possibly would need. As a result, you have decided to analyze the Canadian Stores image in Toronto.
   (a) Outline the type of information you would like to obtain from the marketing research department, in order to have sufficient information about the store image strategy that you will follow for your next campaign.
   (b) Show how the results of this study are likely to affect the advertising strategy for the next campaigns.

2. As the advertiser for a medium-sized sports equipment firm, you are considering the following three alternatives for your next advertising campaign:
   - use the talents of a national hockey star as an "expert" source;
   - use a well-known television star as an "affective" trustworthy source;
   - use an "ordinary" actor to play a sportsman in the commercials.
   (a) How could the concept of the perceptual map be effectively used to select among these three alternatives?
   (b) How would you conduct a cost-benefit analysis to select the most profitable alternative?
   (c) On intuitive grounds, which alternative do you think is likely to be the most profitable for the company? Why?

Notes

1. Advertising objectives should include a definition of the target audience (macro) and a communication task to be performed on each individual consumer (micro). This is discussed in detail in Part 4.

2. See, for instance, Harold H. Kassarjian and Thomas S. Robertson, eds., *Perspectives in Consumer Behavior* (Glenview, Ill.: Scott, Fores-

man, 1968), pp. 439-526.

3. For more detailed models of consumer behaviour, see John Howard and Jagdish N. Sheth, *The Theory of Buyer Behavior* (New York: John Wiley and Sons, 1969); Francesco M. Nicosia, *Consumer Decision Process* (Englewood Cliffs, N.J.: Prentice-Hall, 1966); James F. Engel and Roger D. Blackwell, *Consumer Behavior* (New York: Holt, Rinehart and Winston, 1982).

4. Thomas S. Robertson, *Consumer Behavior* (Glenview, Ill.: Scott, Foresman, 1970), p. 2.

5. Kassarjian and Robertson, p. 69.

6. David Krech, Richard S. Crutchfield, and Eagerton A. Ballachey, *Individual in Society* (New York: McGraw-Hill, 1962), pp. 69-85.

7. Kassarjian and Robertson, p. 18.

8. Abraham H. Maslow, "A Theory of Human Motivation," *Psychological Review*, 50 (1943), 370-96.

9. Stephen D. Arnold, "Maslow's Humanistic Psychology and Consumer Behaviour Theory" (Presented at the 83rd annual conference of the American Psychological Association, Division 23-Consumer Psychology, Chicago, 1975).

10. Janice Hanna, A.N. Azim, and Barbara B. Skogen, "Maslow's Theory of Human Needs and Consumer Behaviour," ed. J.M. Boisvert and Ronald Savitt, *ASAC Proceedings* (1978), pp. 120-28.

11. For an excellent discussion of the Freudian and neo-Freudian theories, see Kassarjian and Robertson, pp. 195-99.

12. Philip Kotler, "Behavioural Models for Analyzing Buyers," *Journal of Marketing*, 29 (October 1965), 37-45.

13. Kurt Lewin, *A Dynamic Theory of Personality* (New York: McGraw-Hill, 1935). A more detailed exposition of this theory can be found in Joseph Clawson and W. Alderson, eds., *Theory in Marketing* (Homewood, Ill.: Irwin, 1950).

14. K.W. Kendall and D.J. Brown, "Effects of Threatening Advertising and Prior Information on Product Lastings," *Marketing*, ed. Robert G. Wyckham (Administrative Sciences Association of Canada, 1981), pp. 152-57.

15. Krech et al., pp. 17-46.

16. Raymond A. Bauer and Stephen A. Greyser, *Advertising in America: The Consumer View* (Boston: Division of Research, Graduate School of Business Administration, Harvard University, 1968).

17. See Jerome Bruner and Leo Postman, "An Approach to Social Perception," *Currrent Trends in Social Psychology*, ed. Wayne Dennis (Pittsburgh: University of Pittsburgh Press, 1955); R. Levine, I. Chein, and G. Murphy, "The Relation of Intensity of a Need to the Amount of Perceptual Distortion: A Preliminary Report," *Journal of Psychology*, 49 (1954), 129-34.

18. Jerome Bruner and Cecil C. Goodman, "Value and Need as Organizing Factors in Perception," *Journal of Abnormal and Social Psychology*, 42 (1947), 33-34.

19. Sidney J. Levy, "Symbols by Which We Buy," *Proceedings of the American Marketing Association* (1959), pp. 409-16.

20. Milton Blum and Valentine Appel, "Consumer Versus Management Reaction in New Package Development," *Journal of Applied Psychology*, 45 (August 1961), 222-24.

21. Mason Haire, "Projective Techniques in Marketing Research," *Journal of Marketing* (August 1950), pp. 649-56.

22. See, for instance, Franklin D. Evans, "Psychological and Objective Factors in the Prediction of Brand Choice: Ford Versus Chevrolet," *Journal of Business* (October 1959), pp. 345-69.

23. G.A. Mauser, D. McKinnon, and M. Nash, "The Effects of Taste and Brand Name on Perceptions and Preferences," *ASAC Proceedings* (1977), pp. 4-24.

24. André Gabor and C.W.J. Granger, "Price as an Indicator of Quality: Report on an Enquiry," *Economica*, 33 (February 1966), 43-47.

25. Henry Joannis, *De l'Etude de Motivation à la Création Publicitaire et à la Promotion des Ventes* (Paris: Dunod, 1966), p. 20.

26. The semantic differential scale is discussed in more detail in Chapter 15.

27. To keep this exposition as simple as possible, only two attributes are considered. However, the same principle applies to any number of attributes and to any number of brands.

$$S_{xa} = [\sum_{i=1}^{n} (S_{xi} - S_{ai})^2]^{1/2}$$

where:

S_{xa} = distance between two brands x and a
S_{xi} = score of brand x on attribute i
S_{ai} = score of brand a on attribute i
n = number of relevant attribute dimensions

In the reported example:

$$S_{xa} = [(1-2)^2 + (3+1)^2]^{1/2} = 4.123$$
$$S_{xb} = [(1-3)^2 + (3-2)^2]^{1/2} = 2.236$$

The distance from x to a (4.123) is larger than the distance from x to b (2.236)

28. Mathematically, the distance between two points can be represented by the Euclidian distance:

29. Raymond A. Bauer, "Consumer Behavior as Risk Taking," *Proceedings of the American Marketing Association*, ed. Martin Bell (Chicago: AMA, 1960), pp. 389-98.

30. Peter Thirhell and Harrie Vredenburg, "Individual and Situational Determinants of Purchase Information Search: A National Study of Canadian Automobile Buyers," *Marketing,* ed. Michel Laroche, Vol. 3 (Administrative Sciences Association of Canada, 1982), pp. 305-13.

31. René Y. Darmon, "Multiple Joint Space Analysis for Improved Advertising Strategy," *The Canadian Marketer*, 10, no. 1 (1979), 10-44.

32. J.G. Barnes and G.H. Pynn, "A Hierarchical Model of Source Effect in Retail Newspaper Advertising: Research Implications," *ASAC Proceedings* (1975), pp. 5-29.

33. Herbert C. Kelman and Carl I. Hovland, "Reinstatement of the Communicator in Delayed Measurement of Opinion Change," *Journal of Abnormal and Social Psychology*, 17 (1953), 327-35.

34. G.R. Rarick, "Effects of Two Components of Communication Prestige" (Paper presented at the Pacific chapter, American Association of Public Opinion Research, Asimolar, California, 1963).

35. See Ralph L. Rosnow and Edward J. Robinson, *Experiment in Persuasion* (New York: Academic Press, 1967), pp. 2-3.

36. See Bobby J. Calder and Robert D. Burnkrant, "Interpersonal Influence on Consumer Behaviour: An Attribution Theory Approach," *Journal of Consumer Research*, 4 (June 1977), 29-38; Linda L. Golden, "Attribution Theory Implications for Advertisement Claim Credibility," *Journal of Marketing Research*, 14 (February 1977), 115-17; Robert A. Hansen and Carol A. Scott, "Comments on Attributes Theory and Advertiser Credibility," *Journal of Marketing Research*, 13 (May 1976), 193-97.

37. This may also be the case when a message is approved by a recognized association of experts in the field.

38. Robert D. Tamilia, "A Cross-Cultural Study of Source Effects in a Canadian Advertising Situation," *ASAC Proceedings*, ed. J. Boisvert and Ronald Savitt (1978), pp. 250-56.

39. H.G. Gordon McDougall, "Cognitive Responses to Advertising Messages: A Diagnostic," *Marketing,* ed. Robert G. Wyckham (Administrative Sciences Association of Canada, 1981), pp. 205-15.

40. See W.N. Dember, *The Psychology of Perception* (New York: Holt, Rinehart and Winston, 1961), chapter 2.

41. E. McGuinnies, "Emotionality and Perceptual Defense," *Psychological Review*, 56 (1949), 244-51.

42. J.H. Voor, "Subliminal Perception and Subception," *Journal of Psychology*, 41 (1956), 437-58.

43. S.J. Arnold, J.G. Barnes, and K.B. Wong. "Subliminal Perception: Implications for Regulation," *ASAC Proceedings, 1975*, pp. 4-11.

44. "Frequency in Broadcast Advertising: 1," *Media/Scope* (February 1962).

45. See, for instance, "Frequency in Print Advertising: 1," *Media/Scope* (April 1962); *Recognition Increased with Advertising.... Dropped when Advertising Stopped* (New York: McGraw-Hill Advertising Laboratory, May 1961); E. Pomerance and H.A. Zielske, "How Frequently Should You Advertise," *Media/Scope* (September 1958), pp. 25-27.

8

Advertising and Buyers' Attitudes

In Chapter 7, it was emphasized that before buyers actually contemplate purchasing a product or a brand, they should have not only one (or several) need(s) that they think could be at least partially satisfied with the product or the brand, but also the physical and financial possibility to buy the product, as well as a sufficiently favourable attitude or preference toward the product or the brand.

Chapter 8 concentrates on this last condition of the purchase process. What roles do attitudes play in the consumer purchase process? How can consumer attitudes and preferences be studied? Can advertising change people's attitudes, and if yes, how?

Attitudes Defined

"Attitude" is a central concept in psychology and social psychology that can be used to explain buyer behaviour. It may be defined as a hypothetical construct that intervenes between buyers' perception formation process and their actual behaviour as they are exposed to stimuli and communications from the market environment. Broadly speaking, an individual's attitude toward an object is the inclination to act positively or negatively toward this object.

An individual's attitude or set of interrelated attitudes toward some object can be thought of as a reservoir of information, knowledge, and beliefs about some abstract or concrete object that is part of the individual's environment. It includes the individual's judgments about these objects and the affective reactions (e.g., liking or disliking) aroused by such information. When an individual has acquired a large amount of information and knowledge on the attitude's object or has had past experience related to it, or when these pieces of information are related to these strongly held affective values, the level of the reservoir is high (the subject holds strong attitudes toward the object). Conversely, when a consumer has only limited information about an object, and this information does not closely relate to important personal values, the level of the reservoir is low (the subject has no strongly held attitudes toward the object). This describes the quantity aspect of attitudes. As for their quality aspect, the fluid in the reservoir might be, for instance, pure water (if the attitude is positive), or pure vinegar (if the attitude is negative), or any mix of water and vinegar depending on how positive or negative the attitude toward the object is. Thus attitudes have a quantitative as well as qualitative aspect.

To keep the same comparison, the level of the reservoir as well as the composition of the mix is not constant, but varies over time. Attitudes are modified in strength and nature as new information from all kinds of sources is received, perceived, and processed by a consumer. As will be seen, the level of the attitude reservoir (in the absence of new information given to the consumer) has a tendency to decrease as time elapses as the result of forgetting.

Especially relevant to a study of buyer behaviour are buyers' attitudes toward products, product usage, firms, and the brands on the market. Other relevant attitudes are those toward various communication sources, different media vehicles, and buyers' attitudes toward risk.

To sum up, attitudes play a significant role in the buyer purchase process and in advertising effectiveness, because they are the links between information received (particularly through advertising) and selectively perceived by a buyer on the one hand, and the purchase decision on the other. Consequently, it is important to understand their structure formation process, and more importantly, why and how attitudes can be changed.

Attitude Structure

Figure 8.1 presents statements about attitudes that are generally accepted by social psychologists. The first statement defines an attitude structure as a system of positive or negative evaluations, emotional feelings, as well as pro or con action tendencies with respect to social objects. Three types of attitude components are identified: the cognitive, the affective, and conative elements.

Cognitive attitude components include the knowledge (or cognitions) individuals have acquired, as well as their evaluation of the importance of this information. During the evaluation process of the perceived information, a piece of information can be rejected if, for instance, it is not believed to be true. This information is likely to be rejected if it cannot be harmoniously integrated into the coherent system of cognitions that the individual has developed over the years. In other words, selective retention filters information that affects attitude formation. This process is shown in Figure 8.2.

For instance, a glue manufacturer advertised that a single drop of Krazy Glue is sufficient to keep a man hanging to a steel bar. One can easily imagine that this information—assuming that it can pass through the filters of selective attention and can be properly understood by consumers—runs a high risk of not being believed by potential customers. This is absolutely independent of the (possible) technical truth of this assertion. The fact that a message content is technically accurate is irrelevant. A message that is not perceived as truthful is rejected and cannot add to the consumer's knowledge about the product (glue) or the brand (Krazy Glue).

---

1. The social actions of the individual reflect his attitudes—enduring systems of positive or negative evaluations, emotional feelings, and pro or con action tendencies with respect to social objects.

2. Each of the three components of an attitude may vary in valence (i.e., their *degree* of favorability or unfavorability), and in degree of multiplexity (i.e., the number and variety of elements or parts making up a component.

3. Attitudes develop in the process of want satisfaction.

4. The attitudes of the individual are shaped by the information to which he is exposed.

5. The group affiliations of the individual help determine the formation of his attitudes.

6. The attitudes of the individual reflect his personality.

7. The modifiability of an attitude depends upon the characteristics of the attitude system, and the personality and group affiliations of the individual.

8. Attitude change is brought about through exposure to additional information, changes in the group affiliations of the individual, enforced modification of behaviour toward the object and through procedures which change personality.

9. The direction and degree of attitude change induced by additional information is a function of situational factors and of the source, medium, form, and content of the information.

FIGURE 8.1   Statements about Attitudes from Social Psychology
SOURCE: David Krech, Richard S. Crutchfield, and Egerton A. Bellachey, *Individual in Society* (New York: McGraw-Hill, 1962), pp. 139–42, 181–99, 216–26.

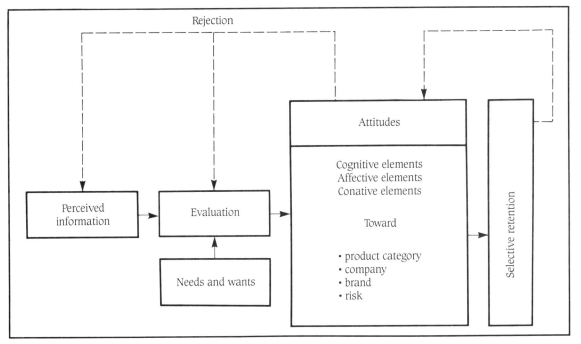

FIGURE 8.2   Representation of Consumers' Attitude Systems

Affective attitude components include the feelings and affective reactions provoked by the object toward which the attitude is being formed. These affective components are intimately linked to the evaluation of the information concerning the object. For instance, a piece of information is likely to be evaluated as important if it helps or hinders the satisfaction of some need(s). When it is perceived as hindering the satisfaction of some need or the aspirations of the individual, it is likely to generate negative affective reactions. Conversely, when it is perceived as helping to satisfy some needs and aspirations, it is likely to generate positive affective reactions.

Conative attitude components refer to an individual's tendency to act toward the attitude object. When positive affective elements dominate, these actions are likely to be in favour of the object. Otherwise, they are likely to be against the object. The conative elements of attitudes may be considered the logical consequence of the cognitive and affective attitude components.[1]

One important property of attitudes is that their elements tend to be consistent with one another. Thus, cognitive elements tend to be mutually compatible. In the same way, this is also true of the affective elements among themselves, as well as of the cognitive with the affective elements. Of course, attitude components are not organized into perfectly logical systems. People are often subjected to conflicting pieces of information or may simultaneously lean toward values that cannot be reconciled. Most individuals can cope with a certain amount of inconsistency among their attitudes or attitude components, but only to a certain extent. As an attitude includes elements that are inconsistent with one another, it becomes unstable, and as will be seen later, it can be easily changed. Conversely, as the attitude elements are homogeneous and consistent among themselves, the attitude is stable and difficult to change. At the extreme, when individuals are exposed to information that contradicts pre-existent attitudes, they are likely to reject the information, as was the case in the preceding example. But because the different elements that are part of an attitude are consistent among themselves, individuals' attitudes toward various aspects of their environment also tend to be consistent among themselves. Thus it is possible to speak of an individual's set of attitudes as a homogeneous and coherent system.

The various components of attitudes can also be characterized by their *valence* (intensity) and by their level of *multiplexity* (the number of elements that they include). (See statement 3 of Figure 8.1.) Thus, an attitude involving a large number of cognitive, affective, and conative elements can be characterized as a *central* attitude, because it involves important values to the individual. An attitude essentially involving one single affective dimension (product liking, for instance) would be simple, in contrast to an attitude that involves a large number of emotions such as fear, anxiety, and pleasure.

Attitude Models

The Communication Model of Attitude Formation

Some authors have postulated that potential customers who are exposed to persuasive communications are likely to go through a number of stages. These stages fall into the three main attitude components described previously.[2] Before buying or trying a product or a brand (behavioural stages), a buyer must be aware of the product, understand its characteristics and attributes (cognitive stages), and like or at least be favourable to the product and its features (affective stages). Four models have been proposed to describe the stages through which buyers supposedly progress when they receive persuasive communications. These models, which are also called *hierarchy of effects* models, are shown in Figure 8.3.

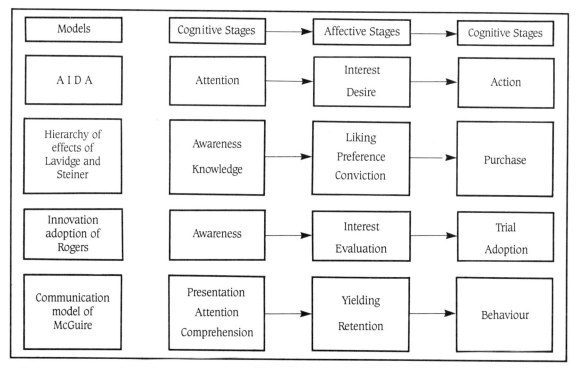

FIGURE 8.3   Models of Communication Effects on Consumers' Attitudes

1. *The AIDA Model.*[3] This model is one of the most popular in the advertising literature. According to this model, an effective advertisement should first attract a consumer's *A*ttention (cognitive stage), arouse *I*nterest and then *D*esire for the advertised product or brand (affective stage), and, finally, trigger an *A*ction, i.e., a trial or a purchase (conative stage).

2. *The Hierarchy of Effects Model.*[4] Lavidge and Steiner have proposed a six-step hierarchy through which buyers progress when they are exposed to advertising messages. These steps are: product-brand awareness, product knowledge, brand liking, brand preference, brand conviction, and purchase of the product or brand.

3. *The Innovation Diffusion Model.*[5] This model was proposed by Everett Rogers. It explains how innovators are likely to react to, try, and adopt a new idea. The model was originally proposed to explain farmers' acceptance of agricultural product innovations. Rogers postulated a five-stage process: product awareness, interest, evaluation, trial, and adoption.

4. *The Information Processing Model.*[6] This model proposed by McGuire describes how an individual is supposed to process information and how attitudes and behaviour are likely to be affected by such information. Six steps are hypothesized: message presentation, attention, comprehension, yielding, retention, and behaviour.

Verbal model	Probability for a consumer to be at each stage given that he is at the preceding stage	Probability for a consumer to be at a given stage
Message		
Presentation	$P(p)$	$P(p)$
Attention	$P(a\|p)$	$P(a) = P(a\|p) \cdot P(p)$
Comprehension	$P(c\|a)$	$P(c) = P(c\|a) \cdot P(a)$ $= P(c\|a) \cdot P(a\|p) \cdot P(p)$
Yielding	$P(y\|c)$	$P(y) = P(y\|c) \cdot P(c)$ $= P(y\|c) \cdot P(c\|a) \cdot P(a\|p) \cdot P(p)$
Retention	$P(r\|y)$	$P(r) = P(r\|y) \cdot P(y)$ $= P(r\|y) \cdot P(y\|c) \cdot P(c\|a) \cdot P(a\|p) \cdot P(p)$
Behaviour	$P(b\|r)$	$P(b) = P(b\|r) \cdot P(r)$ $= P(b\|r) \cdot P(r\|y) \cdot P(y\|c) \cdot P(c\|a) \cdot P(a\|p) \cdot P(p)$

FIGURE 8.4　**Mathematical Formulation of McGuire's Model**

All these models of the communication effects rely on certain assumptions that are more or less relevant depending on the purchase situation to which they are applied. Consequently, they have often been criticized. One of these assumptions is that consumers must go sequentially from one stage of the hierarchy to the next, that consumers cannot reach a certain stage without having gone through all the preceding stages of the hierarchy.

This assumption is clearer when the mathematical formulation of the McGuire model is considered (Figure 8.4). It is assumed that there is a certain probability that an individual will go from one stage to the next under the effect of an advertising message. Let us assume that the changes of going from one stage to the next are those indicated in Figure 8.4. Thus, the probability for one individual to reach each stage can be derived, using a multiplicative model. This multiplicative model implies that to reach a specific stage, an individual must necessarily go through all the preceding stages. For instance, the probability that buyers yield to an advertisement (P(y)) is the probability that they have attended a message presentation P(p) times the probability that they have also paid attention to the message, P(alp), times the probability that they have *also* understood the message P(cla), times the probability that they have *also* been convinced by the message, p(ylc). In mathematical notation:

$$P(y)=P(y|c) \cdot P(c|a) \cdot P(a|p) \cdot P(p)$$

Verbal Model	Probability for a consumer to be at each stage given that he is at preceding stage	Probability for a consumer to be at a given stage	Probability that a consumer at this stage will buy eventually
Message			P(b|m) .0112
Presentation	P(p) = .70	P(p) = .700	P(b|p) .016
Attention	P(a|p) = .50	P(a) = (.50)(.70) = .350	P(b|a) .0320
Comprehension	P(c|a) = .80	P(c) = (.80)(.35) = .280	P(b|c) .040
Yielding	P(y|c) = .40	P(y) = (.40)(.28) = .112	P(b|y) .10
Retention	P(r|y) = .20	P(r) = (.20)(.112) = .0224	P(b|r) .50
Behaviour	P(b|r) = .50	P(b) = (.50)(.0224) = .0112	P(b) 1.00

FIGURE 8.5   Numerical Examples of McGuire's Communication Model

Using a numerical example and assuming that the different probability values are those given in the second column of Figure 8.5, the same probability can be estimated as:

$$P(y)=(0.40)(0.80)(0.50)(0.70)=0.112$$

In the same way, the probability that an advertising message would result in a purchase, $P(b)$, is given by

$$P(b)=P(blr) \cdot P(ylc) \cdot P(cla) \cdot P(alp) \cdot P(p)$$

or in the numerical example in Figure 8.5:

$$P(b)=(0.50)(0.20)(0.40)(0.80)(0.50)(0.70)$$
$$=0.01112$$

As will be seen later, this assumption of sequential progression may not always hold.

A second assumption implied in all the communications effect models is that consumers' progression in the hierarchy is unidirectional (as shown by the direction of the arrows in Figure 8.3). Consequently, the purchase probability of consumers who are at each stage of the hierarchy increases as they get closer to the last stages, as shown in the last column of Figure 8.5.

Several weaknesses of these models can be pointed out.[7]

As was discussed previously, the cognitive and affective components of attitudes are not necessarily sequential and do not always follow a hierarchy. They are often simultaneous and interrelated. For instance, an advertiser may give some information about a product (cognitive elements) and, at the same time, try to push the buyer into liking the product (affective elements), and also induce the buyer to try the brand (conative elements). Consequently, an advertising message may have a simultaneous effect on the three attitude components by pushing a buyer into the cognitive, affective, and conative stages.

As was pointed by Palda[8] and Raymond,[9] the progression in the hierarchy is not necessarily unidirectional. For instance, brand preference often follows and seldom precedes the purchase or trial of a product. A consumer may well try a brand he or she was not even aware of, when the brand has been offered as a gift. In the same way consumers may "select" a brand they have not even heard of before because in an emergency situation, they had to buy the product and the brand may have been the only one available at the closest retail outlet.

Consequently, the communication models, although they certainly capture certain aspects of the effects of communication and of advertising on attitudes,[10] cannot explain everything. They should be considered oversimplifications of the real world.

The Fishbein Attitude Model

Let us assume that a consumer makes a series of perceptual and evaluative judgements about some product or brand (Figure 8.6). For instance, assume that he or she is considering the purchase of a new fruit juice brand. To do so, this consumer uses three attributes that are relevant for making such an evaluation. These attributes might be the fruit juice's sugar content, its thickness, and its refreshing aspect. Actually, one could expect that a much larger number of attributes would be judged by a consumer as relevant in deciding on the new brand. However, in this example, only three attributes will be used for the sake of simplicity.

In Chapter 7, it was seen how a consumer would *perceive* a certain Brand X on each of a set of dimensions relevant to his perceptions of the product category. As shown in Figure 8.6a, a consumer may perceive Minute Maid as being average in sugar content, rather thick, and with little refreshing value. At this stage, it is impossible to say if this consumer judges these (perceived) characteristics of Minute Maid as desirable or undesirable, positive or negative. To determine how this consumer feels about this brand, assume that this consumer is asked to make a series of evaluative judgments to assess how favourably he perceives Minute Maid with respect to each attribute. These evaluative judgments are shown in Figure 8.6b, as well as an overall evaluation of the taste of the Minute Maid fruit juice (pleasant-unpleasant scale).

In this example, the hypothetical consumer does not seem to be satisfied with the sugar content of Minute Maid's fruit juice, only mildly satisfied with its thickness, but very satisfied with its refreshing aspect, and rather satisfied with its overall good taste. The questions asked to elicit this consumer's evaluative judgements

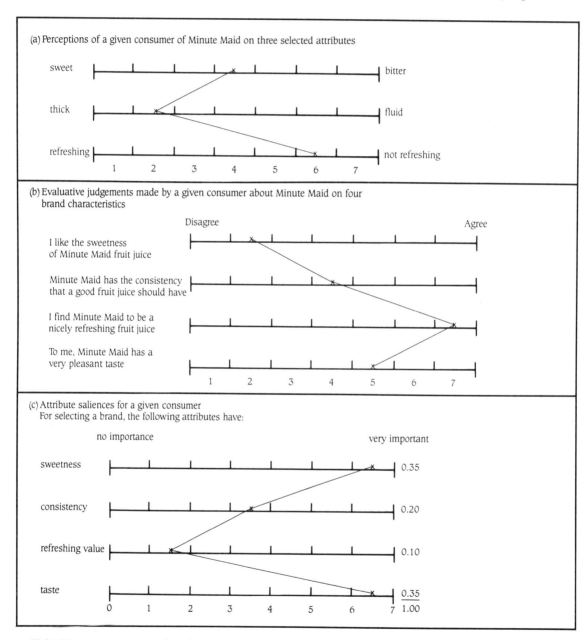

FIGURE 8.6 Perceptual and Evaluative Judgements about a Fruit Juice by a Given Consumer

more or less implicitly rely on a set of comparative judgements that a consumer makes between Minute Maid and a fictitious brand that could be called the ideal brand. This ideal brand would be the one that, if it were technically and economically feasible, would have all the main features and characteristics desired by the consumer. Thus, it is assumed that consumers always implicitly refer to a personal ideal brand when they assert that a certain brand of fruit juice does not have enough sugar, meaning that it actually has less sugar than the ideal brand would have (if it were on the market). As will be seen later, some models do explicitly take into account this concept of an ideal brand.

The importance of the concept of an ideal brand should be emphasized here, as it helps conceptualize the notion of *brand preference*. It is often assumed that the brand with a profile closest to that of the ideal point brand is the most preferred brand. More generally, a consumer prefers Minute Maid to Sun Squeeze if the profile of Minute Maid better matches the ideal brand profile than Sun Squeeze. (These concepts of an ideal brand and of an ideal point are elaborated in the discussion of the ideal point preference model.) It should be kept in mind that the concept of brand preference is closely related to the notion of attitude, in the same way as the concept of brand similarity is related to the notion of brand image or brand perceptions (Figure 8.7).

When individuals report their perceptions, they try as much as possible to report objective reality as they see it and to make abstractions from their feelings and evaluations. Consequently, they make some judgements about the stimuli, such as how similar the stimuli are among themselves, what properties they have,

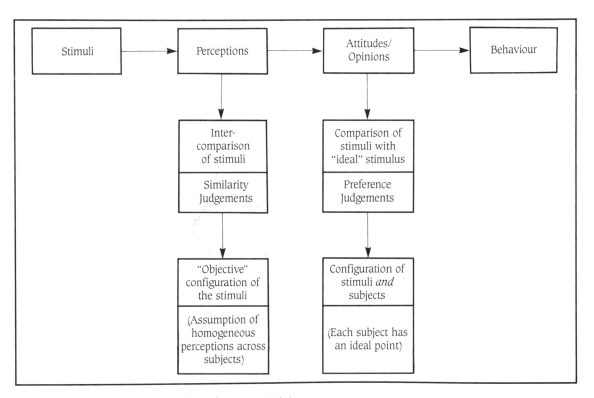

FIGURE 8.7 **Perception and Preference Models**

or how much of an attribute a particular stimulus possesses. When individuals report attitudes and preferences, they state their subjective preferences among the stimuli, or they pass affective judgements on the stimuli (whether they like them or not), on how much the stimuli depart from what they consider to be their *subjective* ideal. Therefore attitude scales, in addition to representing stimuli, should also include a representation of the relative position of an individual to show how he or she stands in comparison to the perceptions of the stimuli.

To what extent do all the judgements made on various brand attributes have the same importance in the attitude structure of a consumer? Do certain characteristics of a product have more weight than others for a given consumer? Or do they all have the same importance? Is the overall taste of a fruit juice more important than the sugar content for a given consumer in his global evaluation of a brand? In the example in Figure 8.6, taste and sugar content are judged by the hypothetical consumer as two very important attributes, much more so than the refreshing aspect of the juice.

In order to combine all these evaluative judgements on all these characteristics into a global attitude measure toward Brand X, Fishbein[11] has proposed the following combination rule:

$$A_{io} = \sum_{d=1}^{n} P_{id} \cdot a_{iod}$$

where:

A_{io} = attitude of individual i toward o

P_{id} = salience of the dimension d for individual i (with $\sum\limits_{d=1}^{n} P_{id} = 1$)

a_{iod} = attribute score given by individual i for the object o on dimension d

n = number of attributes of object o.

In the preceding example, the attitude score of the hypothetical consumer toward Minute Maid is:

$$A_{im} = (0.35)(2) + (0.20)(4) + (0.10)(7) + (0.35)(5) = 3.95$$

A simplified form of this model that has often been used in marketing consists in assuming that all the attributes have an equal salience for all customers. In mathematical form:

$$A_{io} = \frac{1}{n} \sum_{d=1}^{n} a_{iod}$$

i.e., in the given numerical example:
$$A_{ix} = (0.25)(2 + 4 + 7 + 5) = 4.5.$$

This simplified formulation has often given results comparable to those of the complete weighted Fishbein model or at least as satisfactory results.[12] A more complete form of the Fishbein model has also received a great deal of attention in the marketing literature.[13]

Four assumptions underlying the Fishbein model are:

1. The model assumes that all the relevant attributes accounting for an individual's attitude have been identified, i.e., that it is possible to make a priori an exhaustive list of all of them and that no important dimension has been omitted. For instance, in the first (weighted) version of the Fishbein model, an attribute that is not salient for an individual should be assigned a weight of zero and would be dropped from the model. If omitted, however, a salient dimension would change the overall attitude ratings.

2. The model assumes that attributes are uncorrelated, i.e., one attribute does not account for all or part of what is meant by another attribute. For instance, in Chapter 7, it was seen that the perceived quality of a product and its price were often highly correlated, especially for technologically sophisticated products. When this is the case,

the explicit or implicit weighting of the correlated attributes is overestimated in the Fishbein version of the attitude model.

3. The model also assumes it is possible to measure consumers' attitudes for every product dimension and especially that they can be measured with the kind of equal-appearing interval scales that have been used in the reported hypothetical example.

4. Finally, the model assumes that when a product or brand gets a high score on a specific attribute, the consumer's attitude toward this brand is more favourable. In many instances, this assumption is logical. For instance, if a product is perceived as having a pleasant aspect, a consumer's attitude toward the product should be more favourable. However, there are also cases where a consumer might prefer an optimal finite quantity of a certain attribute. Above and below this amount, a consumer's attitude may be somewhat less favourable. This could well be the case for such attributes as the sugar content of a fruit juice. If a consumer likes a certain level of sweetness in a fruit juice, below this amount he or she will find that the juice is too sour and above that amount, that it is too sweet.

If this attitude was represented by a vector, the direction of which would indicate the higher attribute levels, these two conceptualizations of an attitude could lead to two possible representations of an ideal brand (Figure 8.8).

In the first case, as is implicitly assumed in the Fishbein model, Minute Maid is represented by a certain level on a pleasant taste attribute. As far as this attribute is concerned, the ideal brand could be considered as being rejected toward infinity, in the positive direction of the vector. With increased levels of the attribute, the consumer's attitude toward the brand is more favourable.

In the second case, the ideal brand I could be represented by a specific point on the DA axis. The distance IM represents the gap between the ideal brand and Minute Maid on the sweetness attribute. Consequently, although the Fishbein model can give a good representation of the vector-type model of attitudes, it does not give an ideal point specification of the attribute model, which is not very appealing for certain types of attributes and brands.

The Preference Map Attitude Models

The Vector Model
The vector model in Figure 8.8 can be extended to deal with several attributes, but for the sake of simplicity, only two attributes will be discussed. Let us assume that the same brands of fruit juice—Minute Maid, Sun Pac, and Sun

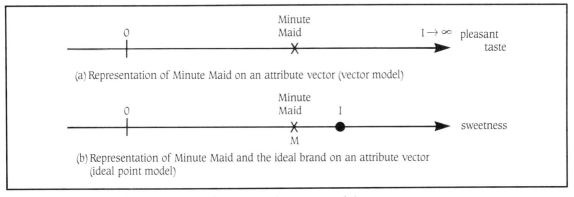

(a) Representation of Minute Maid on an attribute vector (vector model)

(b) Representation of Minute Maid and the ideal brand on an attribute vector (ideal point model)

FIGURE 8.8   Ideal Point and Unidimensional Vector Models

Squeeze—can be represented by points in the two-dimensional perceptual space, as was described in Chapter 7. Let us also assume that an individual, John, can be represented by a vector going through the origin of the two attribute axes. Assume that this vector is oriented in such a way that the perpendicular projections of each fruit juice brand onto the vector perfectly represent the relative preference positions of the three brands for John. Thus, as shown in Figure 8.9, John's preferences would go first toward Sun Squeeze, then to Minute Maid, and finally to Sun Pac. Note that the model assumes that John's ideal brand is rejected toward infinity, and that the more a brand can be projected far away in the positive

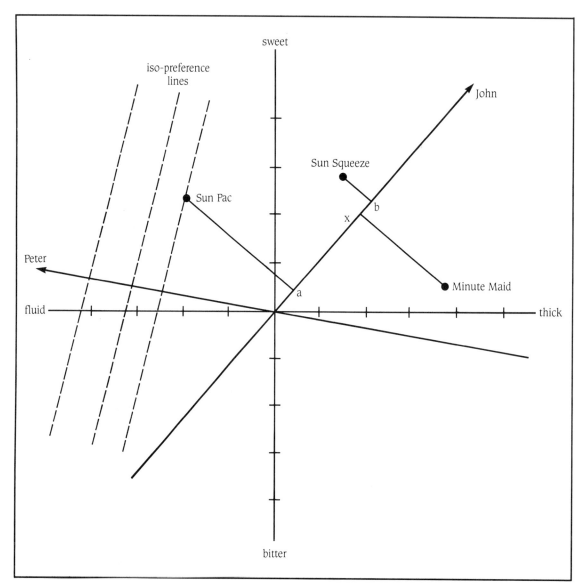

FIGURE 8.9   Vector Model of Consumer Preferences for Three Fruit Juice Brands

direction of the vector (i.e., the thicker and sweeter the juice is), the more it is likely to get a positive attitude response from John.

Let us assume now that a second consumer, Peter, shares the same perceptual map as John, i.e., that the perceptual configuration of the three brands is exactly the same.[14] Even if Peter shares with John the same perceptions of the three brands, Peter would probably have different preferences and attitudes toward the brands than would John. This is why Peter should also be represented by a separate vector that reflects his preferences among the three brands: Sun Pac, Sun Squeeze, and Minute Maid, in that order.

Here again, Peter's ideal brand is also rejected toward infinity, meaning that the more a juice is fluid and sweet, the more likely it is to be best liked by Peter. Thus, all the brand points on the same perpendicular to a vector are likely to be equally liked by the consumer represented by this vector, because all the orthogonal projections of these brands onto this vector fall exactly on the same preference point. In Figure 8.9 these perpendiculars to Peter's vector are his *isopreference curves*.

The Ideal Point Model

When a consumer has a definite preference for a specific and finite level of brand attribute, it is often better to use an attitude model where a consumer's ideal point falls at a specific place in the configuration (Figure 8.10). In the preceding example, there would be more consumers who prefer a level of sugar that is neither too sweet nor too bitter, and a level of juice thickness that is neither too thick nor too fluid, regardless of the level at which their ideal brand is located.

Let us assume that in the preceding example, two other consumers, Jack and Robert, who also share the same perceptual space as John and Peter, are asked to locate their ideal brand for a fruit juice, given the two relevant salient attributes. As shown in Figure 8.10a, Robert likes a fruit juice that is very sweet and thick. Jack has

a strong preference for a mildly sweet and very fluid juice. The configuration of Figure 8.10b or preference map is also called a joint space configuration because it gives a simultaneous representation on the same diagram of the (usually assumed common) perceptions of each brand for the group consumers as well as each subject's ideal brand in relation with the existing brands.

Thus, the notion of psychological distance mentioned in Chapter 7 applies here again. The closer a stimulus (brand) is to the ideal point (brand) specific to an individual (consumer), the more it is preferred to other stimuli that are further away. Consequently, a consumer's attitude toward a brand is inversely related to the distance between the stimulus and the ideal brand.[15]

Note that iso-preference curves are all the points located at the same distance from an ideal point, i.e., they are represented by a series of circles around each ideal brand, as is shown in Figure 8.10. The practical methods and techniques presently available to derive preference maps from consumer preference judgements are briefly outlined in Chapter 15.

Attitude Formation and Attitude Change

The Role of Communications in Attitude Formation and Change

A favourable attitude is generally a necessary condition for a consumer to buy a product, at least for repetitive or durable product purchases. Several studies have shown that purchase behaviour can be predicted from the attitude people hold toward the different brands of a product.[16] Therefore, advertisers have a vested interest in building favourable consumer attitudes toward their brands, especially in their target market segments.[17]

Advertisers may pursue several objectives concerning buyers' attitudes. They may try to:

1. create favourable buyer attitudes toward a brand, especially for new products introduced in the market.
2. change buyers' negative feelings into positive attitudes about the brand.
3. reinforce present customers' positive attitudes toward the brand.

In order to achieve these objectives, advertisers must understand how attitudes develop and know to what extent and how attitudes can be changed.

In the Fishbein model discussion, it was seen that an attitude could be considered as the summation of all relevant attributes of the

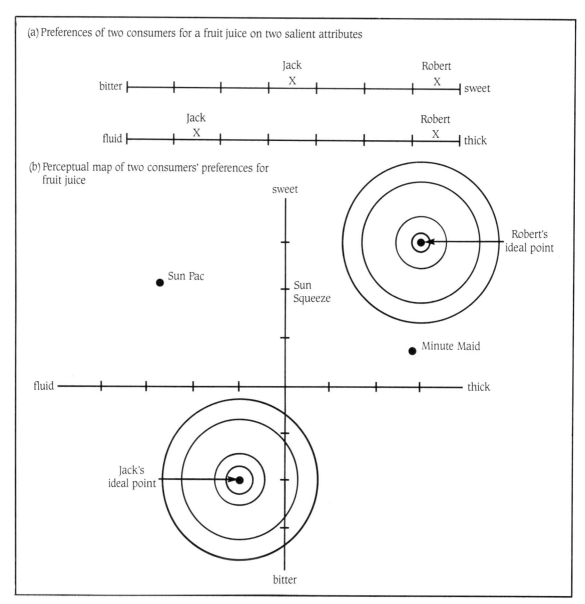

FIGURE 8.10 Ideal Point Model for Consumer Preferences

products of each brand attribute's intensity and salience. In order to build favourable attitudes toward a brand, advertisers can follow one of three strategies:

1. They can try to reinforce buyers' positive evaluation of certain brand attributes.
2. They can try to increase the salience of those brand attributes for which customers generally make positive judgements.
3. They can try to decrease the salience of those brand attributes for which buyers generally make negative judgements.

The advertiser of an important fruit juice brand may attempt to show consumers that a particular brand is high in vitamin content and that its consumption is very healthy. Thus, the advertiser would try to reinforce the health attribute of the brand (which appeals to the health motivation of consumers). This is an example of the first strategy. Alternatively, the advertiser may try to show that vitamins are not an important factor in fruit juice consumption because vitamins can be found in many other food products. This could be a desirable strategy if consumers perceive the advertised brand as low in vitamins. Then, by trying to decrease the salience of the vitamin content attribute on which the brand is negatively perceived, the advertiser would pursue the third strategy. Or the advertisements could suggest that a good fruit juice should be selected for its taste (an attribute on which a large number of consumers positively rate the brand). In so doing, the advertiser tries to increase the salience of the taste attribute in the fruit juice brand selection process, an example of the second strategy.

The third proposition in Figure 8.1 states that attitudes develop in the process of want satisfaction.[18] Thus, consumers develop favourable attitudes toward a brand to the extent that they perceive this brand can help them satisfy one or more needs or wants. If the product or brand is perceived as an obstacle to the achievement of some important goals or aspirations, con-

sumers will likely develop negative attitudes toward the brand.

Consider again the comparison between an attitude system and a reservoir. The information flow filtered and evaluated by individuals feeds the attitude reservoir and affects its whole content. Consequently, if for some reason the information flow is stopped, the reservoir content remains unaltered, at least for a time. Thus, an advertiser can stop or change the nature of the advertising information flowing into the consumer's attitude reservoir. However, it would be a formidable task to try to change the entire content of the attitude reservoir. Even if this were feasible, it would involve very large financial and time resources. This comparison highlights why changing unfavourable attitudes into favourable ones is generally a very long and very difficult communication task. Thus marketers often prefer to launch a new brand to replace a brand for which potential buyers have developed negative feelings. It takes generally less time and fewer resources to build favourable attitudes from neutral attitudes than to change negative attitudes into positive ones.

However, empirical evidence from psychology tends to support the proposition that individuals' attitudes are shaped by the information to which they are exposed, group affiliations, and personality (statements 4-6 in Figure 8.1). In the same way, changing an attitude implies a change in one or several attitude determinants (statements 7 and 8 in Figure 8.1). Among all these possibilities, an advertiser can only manipulate information through the mass media to influence or change buyers' attitudes. Obviously, consumers' social group affiliations cannot be manipulated, nor can consumers be forced to modify their behaviour. An advertiser can only achieve the goal of improving consumers' attitudes by making advertising as efficient a communication tool as possible.

As shown in statement 9 in Figure 8.1, the direction and attitude change induced by additional information is a function of situational factors and of the source, medium, form, and content of the information.

Situational Factors of the Audience

Substantial evidence from social psychology suggests that three situational factors favour an attitude change following a communication:

1. When the message is delivered to a homogeneous group of individuals. If the majority agrees with the message content, the communication will have been more effective and have provoked a more important attitude change than if each individual had been individually exposed to the message. If the group majority does *not* agree with the message content, the communication will have been less effective.[19]

2. When the recipient of the communication is publicly involved in the support of the communicator's position. The attitude change in the direction of the communication is likely to be more stable as the individual is supposed to acquire some ammunition against any counterpropaganda to which he might subsequently be exposed.[20]

3. When there is a group discussion. The communication may be more effective than when it is communicated without a discussion.[21]

Advertisers may draw distressing conclusions from these findings. Personal communications allow for a dialogue between communicator and audience, and in communications within a group, group pressure may be exerted on dissident minorities. Such communications are therefore more likely to be effective than impersonal communications delivered to passive groups (such as television advertisements), or to isolated individuals one at a time (such as magazine or newspaper advertisements).

Source-Related Factors

Research findings in psychology suggest that three source-related factors have important implications for the effectiveness of advertising messages: source credibility, attractiveness, and group affiliations.

Source Credibility

A number of studies in psychology have unequivocally shown that the source of a message is at least as important as the content of the message. Experiments by Hovland and Weiss,[22] and Kelman and Hovland[23] on communication source credibility have shown that a source perceived as credible by a certain audience is likely to generate a more important attitude change than would a source perceived as less credible. In one of these now classic experiments, the same communication was addressed to two groups of individuals. In the first group, the communication was attributed to a highly credible source, and in the second group, to a less credible source. Immediately following the experiment, the subjects who had received the high credibility source message showed significantly larger attitude changes (about 23 per cent of net attitude change)[24] than the subjects who had been exposed to the low credibility source (about six per cent of net attitude change only).

The results are supported on intuitive grounds and probably would not be surprising if the experiment had been stopped at this point. However, after a four-week period, new attitude change measurements were made for each individual in both groups. It was found that the group that had been exposed to the high credibility source recorded a drop in attitude change from 23 per cent to about 12 per cent. The second group, which had been exposed to the low credibility source, increased its attitude change in the direction advocated by the communicator to approximately 14 per cent. Psychologists have called this phenomenon the *sleeper effect*, meaning that as time elapses,

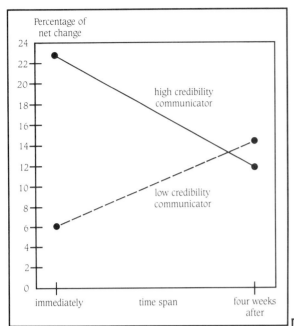

FIGURE 8.11 Attitude Change Provoked by High and Low Credibility Communicators ("sleeper effect")

SOURCE: Hovland and Weiss, "The Influences of Source Credibility on Communication Effectiveness," *Public Opinion Quarterly,* 15 (1951), pp. 635-50.

individuals submitted to persuasive communications tended to dissociate the communication content from the source (Figure 8.11).

When advertisers want to obtain an *immediate* effect from an advertising campaign, the use of a credible source is likely to generate more positive results. However, in the medium and long run, they suggest that the use and expenses of a credible expert may not be warranted, unless the message and its credible source are constantly associated through frequent repetition of the message.

Other experiments[25] have suggested that a message from a too high or a too low credibility source tended to be less remembered by the audience. A tentative explanation of this phenomenon is that it may be caused by the affective reactions provoked by the communication source.

Attractiveness of the Message Source

Another determinant of attitude change effectiveness is the perceived source attractiveness for the audience. Tannenbaum[26] has found that a positive attitude change was directly related to the degree of attractiveness of a source for its audience (see Figure 8.12a). When a communicator's message is in favour of a subject toward which the audience already has a positive attitude, the attitude toward the communication becomes more positive. Conversely, when an attractive communicator speaks against an object toward which the audience has a positive attitude (or for an object toward which the audience has a negative attitude), the audience's attitude toward the communicator evolves in the negative direction (see Figure 8.12 b).

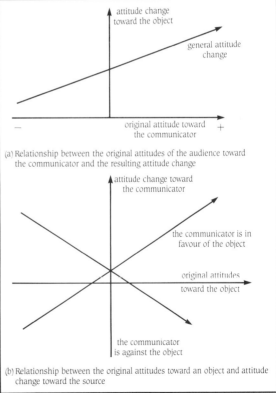

(a) Relationship between the original attitudes of the audience toward the communicator and the resulting attitude change

(b) Relationship between the original attitudes toward an object and attitude change toward the source

FIGURE 8.12 Attractiveness of Source and Attitude Changes

Translated into an advertising context, a firm or a communicator may wish to capitalize on a positive image to reduce or change the negative market reactions toward a particular brand.[27] The firm or the communicator may be successful, but they might at least partially lose their positive image in the corresponding target audience.

The Communicator's Affiliations

Attitude change is related to the way a communicator is perceived by the audience in terms of his or her affiliation to social groups.[28] A study by Katz and Lazarfeld[29] has shown that opinion leaders in a community generally were members of the social groups in which they exercised their leadership. Based on these conclusions,

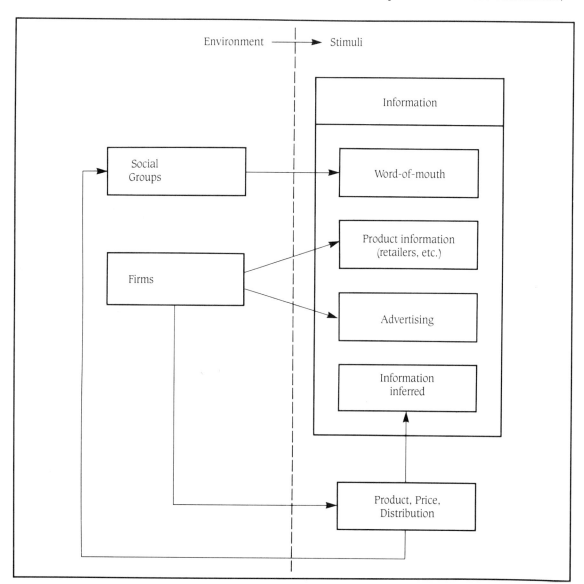

FIGURE 8.13   Consumer Information Sources

advertisers may, instead of using glamorous movie stars, use people with the same (obvious) social group characteristics as those of the target market. The rationale is that these people are more likely to be identified with an actual opinion leader from the same social group and the same social class than would be a movie star or another prestigious personality.

Media-Related Factors

As shown in Figure 8.13, individuals receive from various sources in their environment information that may influence or change their behaviour. Four main types of sources can be identified. Some information emanates from the product (i.e., the product's physical aspect, its price, the retail outlets in which it is sold). Some information on the products emanates directly from retailers or salesclerks. Product advertising is a third source of consumer information. Advertisers can have some control over these three information sources, since a firm has absolute control over its advertising content and can influence the kind of product information provided by retailers, retail sales-clerks, or by salespersons to buyers. To the extent that the marketing mix can be controlled, marketers can determine the information to emanate from the product package, its price, or from their choice of distribution outlets. In contrast, the fourth source of consumer information—the social groups to which consumers belong—is completely out of the advertiser's control.

Every morning, Mrs. Smith chats with her neighbour, Mr. Hughes. One of their favourite topics is the purchases they have made recently, the prices they have paid for various products, the bargains they have found in various stores, and the experiences they have had with good and bad products.

George Jones wants to buy a car. For some time, he has been visiting dealers' showrooms every Thursday night. He talks about his intended

purchase with friends and colleagues at work, especially with Robert Brown, who has just bought a new car. Robert Brown has a reputation of being an expert in mechanics and knows everything about the performance of any make of car on the market.

These are two examples of what everyone can observe every day. They point to the considerable amount of market data to which a consumer is exposed and which is channeled through word-of-mouth communications. Because social groups are influenced by their information sources and their past experience with the products and brands, there is only one means by which a firm can gain support of this type of information source. It is for the product's users not to have been deceived. Consumers who have used the product, the brand, or the service, must have been satisfied in order to transmit the results of their positive experience and positive product information to other potential buyers.

Then, the question of which communication channel is the most effective can be raised. Unfortunately for advertisers, the answer does not make their task easier. As was seen in Chapter 1, interpersonal communications, for example, word-of-mouth communications that take place among consumers or with salespeople, are likely to be more effective and persuasive than advertising through the mass media. Many studies in social psychology have clearly demonstrated this fact.[30] However, mass media play a more subtle role in transmitting information, if credit is given to the *two-step flow of communication* theory proposed by Katz and Lazarfeld.[31] According to this theory, ideas are transmitted through the mass media to the opinion leaders in a social group. Information then flows from these opinion leaders to less active segments of the population (Figure 8.14). To support their hypothesis, Katz and Lazarfeld were able to show that opinion leaders tend to have a wider exposure to the mass media than the rest of the population.

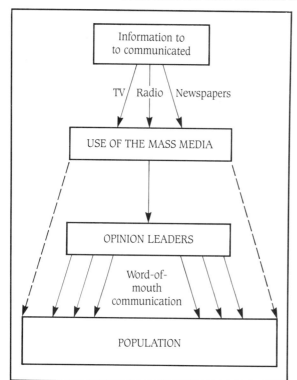

FIGURE 8.14   The Two-Step Flow of Communication Theory

Katz and Lazarfeld's theory is extremely appealing to advertisers. If there is a market segment constituted of opinion leaders who are more easily reached through mass media and more prone to be influenced than the rest of the market, an advertiser's task could be substantially simplified. Provided these leaders can be identified and located, advertisers could direct a campaign to this market segment at a relatively low cost. Then this restricted segment of opinion leaders could take charge of transmitting the information to the primary groups in which they exercise their opinion leadership.

Unfortunately, the reality of information diffusion is more complex than this oversimplified description of the two-step flow of communication theory implies.[32] There are no real "opinion leaders" who have definite and identifiable characteristics. An individual may be considered by peers as an opinion leader in cars, but

not be considered as a leader in food. Another individual may always be asked advice about electronics but will seek the advice of other well-informed people when it comes to subscribing to insurance.

Message-Content-Related Factors

To change an audience's attitudes, a communicator may try to change the cognitive and affective attitude components. Informative messages are designed to change the cognitive elements. Emotional appeal messages try to influence the affective elements.

Informative Advertising Messages

Two theories attempt to explain how an informative advertising message can influence buyers' attitudes: the *instrumental relation* hypothesis and the theory of *cognitive dissonance*.

INSTRUMENTAL RELATION HYPOTHESIS. This theory relies on the hypothesis that an attitude toward any object or situation is related to the ends to which the object serves, i.e., to its consequences. This is called the *instrumental relation*.[33] According to this assumption, to change an attitude, the instrumental value of the attitude must be altered through new beliefs. A study by Carlson[34] based on this hypothesis has shown a curvilinear relationship between an individual's initial attitude and the subsequent attitude change, as shown in Figure 8.15. Individuals holding extreme attitudes changed their attitudes less drastically than individuals holding moderate attitudes. At one extreme, the subjects are already in agreement with the communicator's arguments and there is probably little room for attitude changes. At the other extreme, the initial position of the subject is so far away from the position advocated by the communicator that the subject is "out of reach" of such drastically different opinions.

This theory has implications for determining the best possible message intensity for provok-

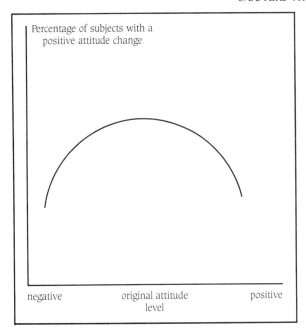

Percentage of subjects with a
positive attitude change

negative   original attitude   positive
                  level

**FIGURE 8.15   Relationship between Original
Attitude and Positive Attitude Change**

ing an attitude change in the direction desired by the communicator. It seems that the answer is highly related to how central the individual's attitude is. Results of experiments in social psychology suggest that if a subject is not very interested in the object of the attitude or the communication content, the message intensities and the corresponding attitude changes are positively related.[35] In contrast, if an individual is highly concerned about the object of the attitude, the relationship may be reversed. That is, the more the position advocated in the communication departs from the subject's position, the less important the attitude change is. Eventually, the message may have an effect opposite to that intended.[36]

What advertising principles can be drawn from these findings? First, it should be determined what a product represents for a consumer and what types of attitudes and attitude strength are involved. If the product does not relate to a consumer's important values or does not involve strong emotive values (salt or bread would be examples), it seems that the best results could be obtained through extreme advertising appeals, or what advertisers generally call "dramatizing" a product. The idea is to induce excitement for the product.

When the product is loaded with symbolic meanings that are highly valued by a consumer (most baby-related products that show some aspect of the highly emotional and valued relationship between a mother and her children would fall into this category), an advertiser should not take positions that depart too sharply from those generally held in the target market. A more effective strategy would be to induce consumers to change their attitudes little by little by making moderate statements rather than dramatic and extreme advertising appeals.

THEORY OF COGNITIVE DISSONANCE. Many persuasive communications rely on mechanisms that can be explained by the theory of cognitive dissonance.[37] This theory, developed by Leon Festinger, is based on two series of propositions. The theory states that when an individual is exposed to information that contradicts some already assimilated information and that constitutes his beliefs, the individual experiences a state of psychological tension or *cognitive dissonance*. The second series of propositions state that an individual who experiences cognitive dissonance tries to reduce the psychological tension. To do so, an individual can change attitudes and make his or her set of beliefs consonant with the new information just received; the new information can be rejected as being false or the credibility of the communicator can be challenged. The subject may also seek new information that could reinforce a new attitude change or, on the contrary, invalidate the dissonant information.

All advertising messages that rely heavily on superlatives are probably based on this theory. The rationale is to communicate to consumers the idea that they have not been using the "best" available product on the market. In this case, this information is inconsistent with the attitudes and behaviour of those consumers who do not use the advertised brand. The advertiser hopes that the resulting state of cognitive dissonance that some consumers will experience will result in an attitude change and possibly in the trial of the advertised product. Of course, consumers may also react by rejecting the communication or refusing to believe it.

Emotional Advertising Appeals

An advertiser can try to alter some affective elements of buyers' attitudes by following two essentially different approaches. Fear or negative appeals can be used or pleasant or positive appeals based on consumers' satisfaction can be used. Each approach is effective under different conditions.

FEAR APPEAL ADVERTISING. The use of fear appeals to change attitudes also relies on the theory of cognitive dissonance. The rationale is to show consumers the negative consequences that may result from not using a product or from using a brand different from the advertised one. Thus, buyers are given information on the consequences or the risks of the no-purchase decision that is inconsistent with the goals of well-being that most individuals pursue to some extent.

Insurance companies often use fear appeals in their advertisements to show potential customers the tragic consequences that may occur when they are not properly insured. For example, an advertisement may show children left without a means of support because the parents neglected to take out life insurance. The advertiser tries to plunge the consumer into a state of cognitive dissonance by creating a gap between present behaviour (no insurance) and what the consumer probably aspires to be (a good parent and father). The objective is to induce the non-insured customer to change behaviour and make him buy life insurance. However, the consumer may reduce dissonance by rejecting the information.

Are messages that use a fear appeal more effective? A study by Janis and Feshback[38] showed that the effects produced by a message based on fear and anxiety were inversely related to the intensity of the fear aroused in the subjects. According to these authors, the relative inefficiency of the fear appeal messages could be explained by the fact that the subjects tend to reduce their anxiety by developing hostile attitudes toward the communication. If this explanation holds, it suggests that a fear-arousing advertising campaign could produce adverse effects for advertisers, especially if the anxiety aroused among consumers passed a certain threshold. Other studies have shown, however, that the messages that aroused the highest levels of anxiety were the most effective, provided the communicator could suggest a convincing and plausible solution to reduce their anxiety.[39]

PLEASANT APPEAL ADVERTISING. The basic principle of pleasant appeal advertising is to try to associate a product/brand with pleasant events, objects, or feelings in the hope that buyers will continue to make the association in the future. Messages relying on humour often try to build on such associations. Unfortunately, there is a lack of research on whether messages relying on such positive appeals are more effective.

Message-Structure-Related Factors

Three message-structure-related factors likely to affect attitudes and attitude changes have been identified: the level of inference required of an audience to understand the message (conclusion drawing); the use of one-sided or two-sided arguments; and the order in which the arguments are presented to the audience.

The Level of Inference Built into the Message

Inference level is the extent to which the audience of a communication is free to draw its own conclusions from a message. For instance, an advertiser can give certain facts about a brand in an advertising message and let the buyer conclude that the product must be the best on the market. Or the message might state the conclusion that the advertiser wants potential buyers to draw.

Consider two themes that could be used by a hygiene product manufacturer for advertising Brand X toothpaste:

1. Keep your teeth white and shiny with Brand X.
2. New Brand X contains fluoride.

In the first case, the expected result from the product usage is directly described, i.e., the conclusion of the message is drawn: a consumer who uses Brand X toothpaste will have shiny white teeth.

In the second case, the message only states a fact: it describes an objective characteristic of the product and does not draw any conclusion. The consumer is expected to make the following inference: "New Brand X toothpaste contains fluoride; therefore it must make teeth white and shiny. Consequently, if I use Brand X, I will have white and shiny teeth."[40]

An experiment by Hovland and Mandell[41] has shown that when the conclusion of the message was explicitly drawn, the message was twice as effective as when subjects were left to draw their own conclusions. This may not be a surprising finding, because when an individual is free to draw conclusions from a message, nothing can prevent the individual from drawing conclusions that are completely different from those intended by the communicator. As was already seen, individuals have different perceptual mechanisms, different needs and motivations, and are likely to react differently to messages. In the preceding example, some people may draw conclusions that could have not even been suspected by the advertiser. For instance, they might make the following inferences: "Brand X contains fluoride; therefore it contains chemical products; therefore it may not be good for my health." In this case, the message

would have led consumers well away from the advertiser's communication objectives.

Despite these general results, other studies have pointed at three situations in which an implicit message would be more effective than a message with explicitly drawn conclusions. First, when the message is simple and the audience is intelligent, the audience may be irritated by what could be perceived as offensively repetitive statements by the communicator. Second, when the source of the message is not very credible, it is more effective to let the audience draw its own conclusions. Third, when the message deals with personal values or intimate feelings, a communicator who explicitly draws conclusions might be perceived as intruding on an audience's privacy.[42]

Drawing the conclusions of the message is often to make explicit statements about the benefits to the users of the advertised product or service (Figure 8.16). When an advertiser only describes the result of a product usage, the consumer has one inferential step to take: "If the product can do *this*, I should be able to get that *satisfaction* out of it." If the advertiser departs a little more from the consumer and gets closer to the advertised product, he may describe, for instance, a physical feature of the product. In this case, the consumer must draw two concluding statements: "If the product has that *feature*, then it should do *this*; if it does this, then I should be able to get such and such a satisfaction out of it."

A message that directly shows the benefits a consumer should get out of the advertised product has advantages and disadvantages. As has been mentioned, the message is less ambiguous for a consumer to decode. However, it is much less specific than a message about product characteristics. Many toothpaste advertisers can claim that their brand gives white and shiny teeth; only some of them can claim their product contains fluoride. A product-oriented message is also more credible and often more tolerable for consumers (especially in the case

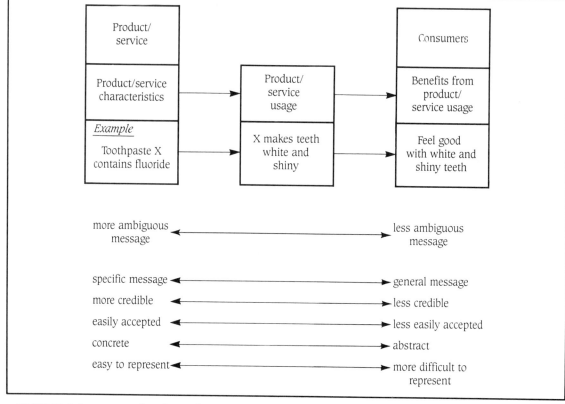

FIGURE 8.16   Example of Conclusion Drawing in Advertising Messages

of products loaded with emotional value), more concrete (a product characteristic is more easily understood than an abstract benefit), and in general it has a higher potential for visual representation in an advertisement.

However, an advertising message that stresses the benefits to consumers can also be based on product characteristics (for instance, "Keep your teeth white and shiny with fluoridated Brand X"). Thus the preceding analysis should not be considered an absolute dichotomy but rather a continuum on which an advertiser can select the best possible combination of elements in order to build a message.

One-sided or Two-sided Presentations

Is an attitude change more or less important when the audience is exposed only to arguments in support of the communicator's position or when a number of counterarguments are also acknowledged and refuted? In advertising, the large majority of advertisements are one-sided. There are some noteworthy exceptions: advertisements by Volkswagen (The Bug), or by Avis ("We are no. 2"), or by UNIVAC (the "other" computer company).

Experiments in social psychology have also shown that a one-sided presentation is generally more effective.[43] Exceptions occur when the communicator and the audience hold opposite stands at the beginning. Hence the use of counterarguments probably gives the appearance of objectivity and greater credibility to the communicator[44] when the audience is well-educated and when the subjects are likely to be subsequently exposed to counter propaganda. Counterarguments may have an immunizing effect, because the communicator has already presented counterarguments with the appropriate rebuttals. Since people are continuously subjected to conflicting advertising messages (identical to counter propaganda), it is surprising that advertisers have not made a more extensive use of two-sided advertising presentations.

Order of Presentation

Another problem for advertisers is to decide in which order different arguments should be presented to an audience. Should the strongest and most convincing arguments be presented first, in order to arouse the audience's interest and make the best impact while the audience is still attentive, or should they be presented last, in order to leave the audience with the stronger arguments?

Experiments dealing with two-sided presentations have not led to clear-cut conclusions. There are as many instances in which the greatest effectiveness was achieved when positive arguments were presented first as the other way around.[45] When only positive arguments are used, most studies have indicated that the order of the arguments was not a determinant of the message's effectiveness.[46] One study did find that it was more effective to present strong arguments first.[47]

What are the conclusions that advertisers can draw from these studies and their conflicting findings? Given that advertising is *not* the kind of communication that can benefit from sustained attention and interest from its audience, it may be more appropriate to use the best and more convincing arguments first. If they succeed, then the attention and interest of at least a part of the audience may be secured for a short period of time. If the weaker arguments are presented first, a large part of the audience may lose interest and will not pay attention to the more convincing selling points. More research in these areas is needed, not only in the social sciences but also in specific advertising contexts.

Selective Retention and Message Repetition

Forgetting and Repetition

Since Ebbinghaus,[48] a series of studies has shown that all information tends to be forgotten as time elapses. This forgetting takes place more or less rapidly depending on how important and valued the concerned attitude is within the individual's attitude system. In general, it occurs more rapidly if the information is inconsistent with the individual's attitude pattern. This phenomenon has been called *selective retention* by psychologists. Conversely, information is best remembered when it is well integrated and fits well into an individual's present attitude system.

The natural process of forgetting learned information can be overcome by message repetition. The quantity of recalled information varies in relation to the frequency with which a message is repeated[49] and in inverse relation to the time span between consecutive messages.[50] Experiments carried out by Zielske on the relationship between message repetition and forgetting are discussed more fully in Chapter 10.[51]

There seems to be a positive relationship between repetition and attitude change,[52] with the following exceptions:

1. when a message has been repeated a great number of times;[53]
2. when messages are repeated at too-short intervals;[54]
3. when message density (the frequency of all the messages, including competing advertisements) is too high.[55]

These results suggest that to be effective, advertising messages should be repeated, but that there is an upper limit to frequency and repetition. Advertisers have long recognized that one single message is of no use whatsoever for obtaining noticeable effects. In order to best understand these repetition and forgetting effects, the descriptive model of P. Langhoff can

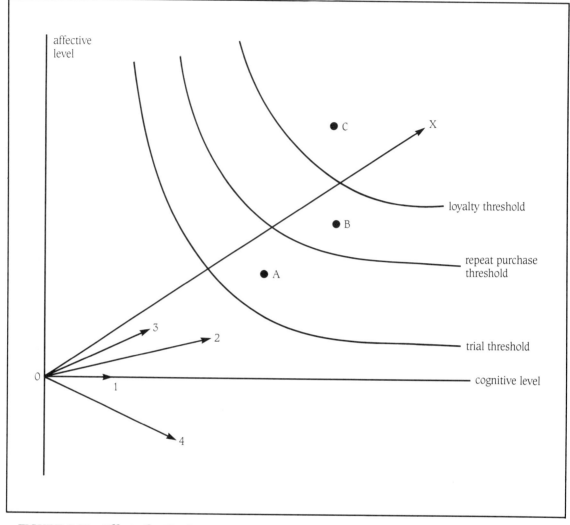

FIGURE 8.17   Effect of a Single Message on a Consumer's Attitudes

be used, first for a single message and then for a series of advertisements.[56]

Effects of One Message on an Individual's Attitudes

Let us assume that the attitudes of one specific individual toward a brand could be represented in a two-dimensional diagram. In Figure 8.17, the horizontal axis represents the level of product knowledge and brand awareness that this individual could reach (cognitive elements);

the vertical axis represents the various levels of affective feelings toward the brand that this individual could possibly reach (affective elements). The probability that an individual has a behavioural reaction toward the product—that he or she tries it, repeats the purchase, or develops a certain level of loyalty toward the brand—is likely to be higher as an individual has reached high levels on the cognitive and/or affective dimensions. These behavioural thresholds are represented in Figure 8.17 by the convex curves. When the consumer reaches points above each curve, for instance, A, B, or C, this consumer has a high probability of respectively trying the product, repeating the purchase, and developing a certain loyalty toward the brand. These curves show that the affective and cognitive elements of attitudes can be substituted for one another. The advertiser's problem, then, is to try to move this consumer up both the cognitive and affective scales, which in Figure 8.17 means as far as possible in the general direction of the Ox axis.

One advertisement is generally not sufficient to bring a consumer even above the first trial threshold. When a new product is involved, the consumer has not yet developed positive or negative attitudes toward the brand and is likely to start at point O, the origin of the two axes. Each ad may have quite different effects, however. These effects can be represented by vectors that show the path this consumer's attitude follows between the starting position (O) and the new attitude reached after the message has been heard or seen. It is to be hoped that this vector will fall in the first quadrant, which indicates a positive attitude change.

The direction and length of the vector depend on the new attitude position reached by an individual. The length of the vector is proportional to how well designed is the message's form and content for changing buyers' attitudes. The direction of the vector depends on the relative abilities of the message to make consumers progress on the cognitive and affective attitude scales.

Independently from the length of the vector that reflects higher or lower message effectiveness, the four messages in Figure 8.17 have different effects on this consumer's attitudes. Advertisement 1 conveys some information, but fails to create favourable feelings among customers. Advertisement 3 can do both things, but less so than advertisement 2. As for advertisement 4, it does convey positive information, but it triggers negative affective reactions from this consumer.

Effects of a Series of Messages on an Individual's Attitudes

Figure 8.18 shows the possible effects of two series of advertising messages on an individual's attitudes. The total effect depends on the effects of each individual message, with every message adding to the cumulative effects of the preceding ones. In series A, seven messages are needed to induce a consumer unaware of this brand to try it. More messages would be needed to bring this consumer to the higher threshold of repeat purchase or brand loyalty. The message series B does not succeed in inducing the consumer unaware of the brand to try it, and after the seventh message, negative effects are recorded. This negative response could be attributed to too-frequent repetition of the messages over a certain period, which irritated this consumer and provoked a negative reaction.[57]

Thus, too high a message frequency may adversely affect a communication's effectiveness. But as was previously emphasized, too low a frequency is also ineffective because during the time elapsed between two consecutive messages, a consumer may forget all or part of the information from previous messages. This is why each message-effectiveness vector always originates at the lower hand corner of the extremity of the preceding message vector in Figure 8.18.

Message Frequency and Campaign Effectiveness

The influence of message frequency on advertising effectiveness can be highlighted when the effectiveness of the series of messages is described over time. Figure 8.19 shows the various levels of the hierarchy of advertising effects. The curve represents the level or the degree of positiveness of an individual's attitudes as time elapses and as the individual is subjected to advertising messages about a given brand. Figure 8.19 also illustrates the

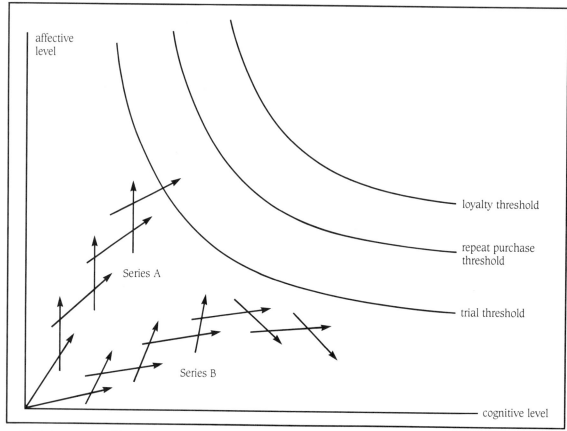

FIGURE 8.18   Effect of Two Series of Messages (A and B) on a Consumer's Attitudes

characteristics of advertising communications. These characteristics include the following:

1. The effectiveness of an advertising campaign depends upon the effectiveness of the various advertisements on which the campaign is based. As shown in Figure 8.19, the impact of each advertisement (A_1, A_2, A_3) on the attitudes of a given buyer may vary. This is represented by vectors of various lengths. The longer the vector, the more positive the effect of the message on attitudes, and the more it tends to bring the buyer to the top levels of the hierarchy.

2. Each advertisement has residual or carry-over effects that decrease as time elapses. In general, advertising effects can be felt not only during the period in which the campaign actually takes place but also in subsequent periods. However, without any reinforcement, these lagged effects decay very rapidly. This phenomenon is represented by the portions of curve C_1, C_2, C_3 in Figure 8.19. These lagged effects have been experimentally studied. In addition, advertising research studies that have taken these lagged effects into account have given better results than those in which they have been ignored. (See, for instance, the studies of Kristian Palda on the lagged effects of advertising.)[58]

3. The effectiveness of an advertising campaign depends upon the frequency of the messages. Figure 8.19 shows the extent to which the frequency at which advertising messages are

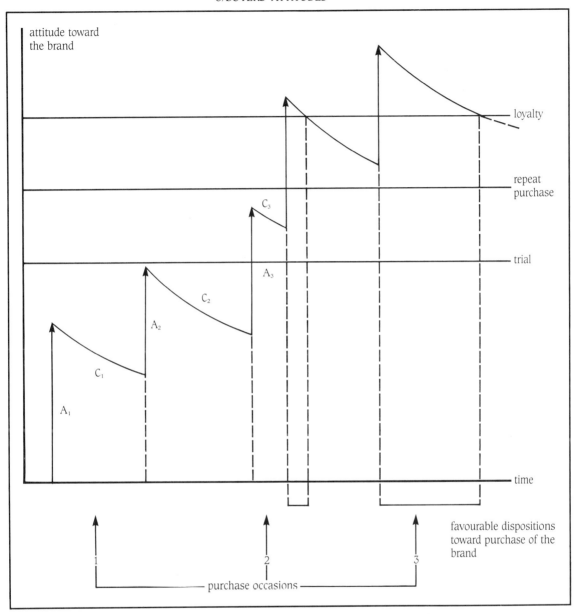

FIGURE 8.19 Effects of Advertising over Time on a Consumer's Attitudes

delivered can influence the general effect of an advertising campaign. If messages are delivered at very short intervals (i.e., with a high frequency), the effect of forgetting does not have sufficient time to take place and the cumulative effects of all the messages are important. In contrast, if too much time elapses between consecutive messages (i.e., messages are delivered with a low frequency), an important effect of forgetting is likely to be felt and an important part of the persuasion effect has to be built all over again with the following message. This results in a low advertising campaign efficiency.

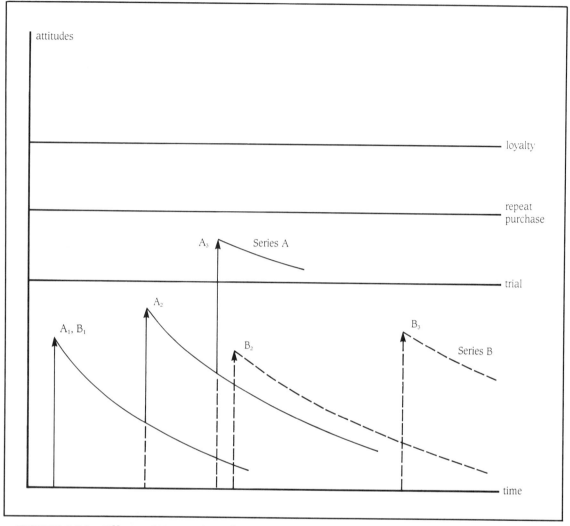

FIGURE 8.20   Effects of Two Series of Messages (A and B) with Different Frequencies on a Consumer's Attitudes

Figure 8.20 illustrates the effects of two series of messages A and B. The messages in both series are identical in every aspect (same copy, same media, same effectiveness of each single advertisement as represented by the same vector lengths $A_1 = B_1$, $A_2 = B_2$, and so on, and consequently, same total cost). The only difference between the two series is the different frequency level. It can be seen that with the concentrated frequency of the series A, the consumer can surpass the trial threshold, which cannot be achieved with the lower frequency of series B. This simple fact underlines the importance of the media scheduling problem that is discussed in detail in Chapter 14.

4. The effectiveness of an advertising campaign does not depend only upon consumer attitudes. As shown in Figure 8.19, favourable consumer attitudes toward a brand are not sufficient for consumers to buy it. First,

consumers should need the product. Second, a purchase can be made only if the product is available and if it is physically and economically feasible for the consumer to acquire the product. Instances of purchase occasions are represented by the arrows numbered 1, 2, 3 in Figure 8.19. In this example, it can be seen that the consumer will buy the brand only on the third purchase occasion because only by this time has he or she developed a sufficiently favourable attitude toward the brand to buy it and feels a need for the product.

How Advertising Can Influence Attitudes: An Overview

Information can influence or change an individual's attitudes. Thus advertising that supplies consumers with marketing information can also influence and change buyers' attitudes. Building as favourable attitudes as possible is an essential advertising objective. To do so, advertisers can apply several principles and guidelines, most of which are drawn from experimental evidence from the social sciences or from intuition and accepted advertising practice:

1. In order to positively influence a buyer's attitude toward a brand, an advertiser can:
   - reinforce consumers' positive evaluation of some of the brand attributes;
   - increase the salience of the brand attributes that are positively evaluated by the consumers;
   - decrease the salience of the brand attributes which are negatively evaluated by the consumers.

2. To achieve one of these objectives, an advertiser can build advertising messages with any of the following attitude change devices:
   - to use in their ads experts who are perceived as credible by consumers;
   - to build positively perceived brand and company images in order to gain a high level of credibility in the marketplace;
   - to use communicators who are perceived as being part of the same social groups as the target market segments;
   - to try to reach through the mass media opinion leaders who will in turn influence the rest of the population, according to the two-step flow of communication hypothesis of Katz and Lazarfeld;
   - to take into account the instrumental value of attitudes in satisfying consumer needs and wants;
   - to create a state of cognitive dissonance among consumers and, at the same time, to provide them with credible and plausible means to resolve their conflict;
   - to associate the product or the brand with positively perceived and pleasant elements that emphasize the benefits it can provide to consumers;
   - to design messages according to the principles outlined above with respect to the level of inference to be used and the nature, strength, and order of the arguments of the advertising message;
   - to use the principles of message repetition and frequency.

Summary

An understanding of the role of attitudes in purchase behaviour enables advertisers to influence or change such attitudes. Attitudes are the tendency for an individual to act pro or con certain objects, individuals, or events. According to social psychologists, attitudes include cognitive, affective, and conative elements. There are several attitude models, and two important communication models are Fishbein's attitude model and the multidimensional preference model.

Advertisers also need an understanding of the attitude formation and change processes. Attitudes can be compared to a reservoir, the level of which represents the intensity of the attitude, and the nature of its content the positiveness or negativeness of the attitude.

The reservoir is fed as new information is received from various sources, among them word-of-mouth, product, past experience, retailers, and advertising. Information is continuously pumped out of the reservoir through information forgetting as time elapses. Advertising communications can change consumer attitudes by applying such theories as the two-step flow of communication, the theory of attitude instrumentality, or the cognitive dissonance theory. Also, the principles relating to the design of more effective messages for changing people's attitudes may help guide the design of the advertising message content and format. The role of message repetition and frequency is of primary importance for advertisers.

Questions for Study

1. Find specific examples of print advertisements or broadcast commercials that use
   (a) reference groups
   (b) opinion leaders
   (c) word-of-mouth communication

2. Select a product category and a specific brand. Then, find a list of questions that you think could be helpful to an advertiser who wants to know what consumers' attitudes toward this brand are. Classify all the questions you think should be asked according to the type of attitude and elements they measure (cognitive, affective, or conative).

3. Find examples of print advertisements that you think might not be believed by important market segments. Which segments? Justify your answers.

4. Find examples of print advertisements or broadcast commercials that try to:
   (a) reinforce consumers' positive evaluation of certain product/brand attributes
   (b) increase the salience of attributes on which customers make positive judgements

(c) decrease the salience of attributes on which customers make negative judgements.
Justify in each case.

5. Find print advertisements or broadcast commercials in which the advertiser has tried to capitalize on the attractiveness of the source. Evaluate this approach in *this* specific context. Justify your answers.

6. Find print advertisements or broadcast commercials in which the message source is a "typical" member of the social groups of the (probably intended) target audience. Evaluate this approach in *this* specific context. Justify your answers.

7. Find examples of print advertisements using two-sided arguments. Study the order of the arguments. How would the principles outlined in the text have been applied? Discuss.

8. Find examples of print advertisements or broadcast commercials that
   (a) apply the theory of cognitive dissonance (superlative advertising)
   (b) are fear appeals
   Discuss the approach in the specific contexts of the advertisements.

9. Take several examples of broadcast commercials. Study the order in which the arguments are presented. Which do you think are the strongest arguments (given the probable target audience)? Discuss.

10. Take several examples of print advertisements. Study how the message is directly related to consumer benefits or infers these benefits. Find examples of different approaches to the benefit inference communication. Discuss.

11. When is it better for an advertiser to

concentrate his message over a short period of time within a year? When is it better to have a uniform spread of the message over an entire year? Try to answer the questions by using Figure 8.19.

Problems

1. The account executive in charge of advertising for an important manufacturer of pocket calculators (Brand X) has investigated the consumer choice process in a specific market segment. He has found that the "typical" buyer in this segment used the following criteria in his decision process: number of functions, energy source (battery and/or plug), warranty, and design. He also found that the importance attached to these criteria are respectively 7, 5, 5, and 2. Brand X, as well as the two leading competing brands (A and B) are evaluated by the typical consumer of the market segment as follows:

Brand	Number of Functions	Energy Source	Warranty	Design
X	7	4	2	2
A	5	6	3	3
B	4	4	4	4

(a) What conclusions can the account executive draw about consumers' preferences in this market segment?

(b) What do you think should be done? Why? How?

2. Select a convenience sample out of the market segment for hardware retailers in your city.

(a) Try to identify the choice criteria for such a retailer, the relative importance of these criteria, as well as the evaluation of the main competing hardware stores on these criteria.

(b) Do the same analysis as for problem 1 and answer the same questions.

(c) What problems do you see in the methodology you have used to evaluate consumers' preferences? Explain.

Notes

1. George David Hughes, *Attitude Measurement for Marketing Strategies* (Glenview, Ill.: Scott, Foresman, 1971), p. 9.

2. See, for instance, Philip Kotler, *Marketing Decision Making: A Model Building Approach* (New York: Holt, Rinehart and Winston, 1968), p. 536.

3. E.K. Strong, *The Psychology of Selling*, 1st ed. (New York: McGraw-Hill, 1925), p. 9.

4. Robert J. Lavidge and Gary A. Steiner, "A Model of Predictive Measurement of Advertising Effectiveness," *Journal of Marketing* (October 1961), p. 61.

5. Everett M. Rogers, *Diffusion of Innovations* (New York: The Free Press, 1962), pp. 79-86.

6. William J. McGuire, "Theory of the Structure of Human Thought," *Theories of Cognitive Consistency: A Source Book*, ed. Robert P. Abelson et al. (Chicago Ill.: Rand McNally, 1968), pp. 140-62.

7. John R.G. Jenkins, "The Hierarchy of Effects Theory of Consumer Decision Making: A Reevaluation," *ASAC Proceedings*, ed. J.M. Boisvert and R. Savitt (1978), pp. 139-48.

8. Kristian S. Palda, "The Hypothesis of a Hierarchy of Effects: A Partial Evaluation," *Journal of Marketing Research* (February 1966), pp. 13-24.

9. Charles K. Raymond, "Must Advertising Communicate to Sell," *Harvard Business Review* (September-October 1965), pp. 148-61.

10. John C. Maloney, "Attitude Measurement and Formation" (Paper presented at the Test Market Design and Measurement Workshop, American Marketing Association, Chicago, 1966).

11. Martin Fishbein, "Attitude and the Predictors of Behaviour," *Readings in Attitude Theory and Measurement*, ed. M. Fishbein (John Wiley and Sons, 1967).

12. See, for instance, Jagdish M. Sheth and W.W. Talarzik, "Relative Contribution of Perceived Instrumentality and Value Importance in Determining Attitude Toward Brand," *Abstracts*, ed. D.L. Sparks (Chicago: American Marketing Association, 1970), p. 35.

13. Martin Fishbein and I. Ajzen, *Belief, Attitude, Intention, and Behaviour: An Introduction to Theory and Research* (Reading, Mass.: Addison-Wesley, 1975). The extended Fishbein model can be expressed as:

$$B\text{-}BI = (A_B)W_1 + (SN)W_2$$

where B is overt behaviour; BI is intent (subjective probability) of performing behaviour; A_B is attitude toward (goodness or badness of) performing the behaviour; SN is subjective norm concerning the behaviour, and W_1 are empirically determined weights. The tilde between B and BI means that the degree of correspondence between behaviour and intent depends on a number of factors. See, for instance, Paul R. Warshaw, "A New Model for Predicting Behavioural Intentions: An Alternative to Fishbein," *Journal of Marketing Research*, 17 (May 1980), 154.

14. The assumption of homogeneity of perception has often been made in marketing research studies (despite the discussion about selective perception and selective distortion in Chapter 7).

15. Algebraically, the distance used to determine the brand preferences is given by:

$$A_{jo} = F[d_{jo}] = F\left[\sum_{k=1}^{n} (x_{ok} - y_{ik})^2 \right]^{1/2}$$

where:

A_{jo} = attitude of individual j towards object o

F = function relating the attitude of individual j toward object o to the psychological distance between the object and the individual's ideal point

d_{jo} = psychological distance between point o and the ideal point of subject j

x_{ok} = coordinates of object o on dimension k

y_{ik} = coordinates of the ideal point of subject i on dimension k

n = number of relevant perceptual dimensions

16. Alvin A. Adenbaum, "Knowledge is a Thing Called Measurement," *Attitude Research at Sea*, ed. Lee Adler and Irwin Crespi (Chicago: American Marketing Association, 1966), pp. 111-26; Henri Assael and Georges S. Day, "Attitudes and Awareness as Predictors of Market Share," *Journal of Advertising Research*, 8 (December 1968), 3-10.

17. S.A. Brown, "An Experimental Investigation of Attitude as a Determinant of Consumer Spatial Behavior," *ASAC Proceedings* (1975), pp. 5-75.

18. Michel Laroche, Michel Bergier, and Lee McGown, "Attitudes, Intentions, and the Effects of Competition," *Marketing*, ed. Vernon J. Jones, Vol. 1 (Administrative Sciences Association of Canada, 1980), pp. 222-29.

19. See, for instance, Kurt Lewin, "Group Decision and Social Change," *Readings in Social Psychology*, ed. G.E. Swanson, T.M. Newcomb, and L.E. Hartley, 2nd ed. (New York: Holt, 1952); Edith B. Bennett, "Discussion, Decision, Commitment, and Consensus in Group Decisions," *Human Relations*, 8 (1955), 251-73; D.F. Pennington, F. Hararey, and B.M. Bass, "Some Effects of Decision and Discussion on Coalescence, Change, and Effectiveness," *Journal of Applied Psychology*, 42 (1958), 404-8.

20. C.I. Hovland, Evid M. Campbell, and T. Brock, "The Effects of Commitment on Opinion Change Following Communication," *The Order of Presentation in Persuasion*, ed. C.I. Hovland et al. (New Haven: Yale University Press, 1957).

21. May Brodbeck, "The Role of Small Groups in Advertising the Effects of Propaganda," *Journal of Abnormal Psychology and Sociology*, 52 (1956), 166-70; L.L. Mitwich and E. McGuinnies, "Influencing Ethnocentrism in Small Discussion Groups Through a Film Communication," *Journal of Abnormal Sociology and Psychology*, 56 (1958), 82-90.

22. C.I. Hovland and W. Weiss, "The Influence of Source Credibility on Communication Effectiveness," *Public Opinion Quarterly*, 15 (1951), 635-50.

23. Herbert C. Kelman and Carl I. Hovland, "Reinstatement of the Communicator in Delayed

Measurement of Opinion Change," *Journal of Abnormal Sociology and Psychology*, 48 (1953), 327-35.

24. Net attitude change means the absolute difference between positive changes and negative changes.

25. G.R. Rarick, "Effects of Two Components of Communicator Prestige" (Paper presented at the American Association for Public Research, Pacific chapter, Asimolar, California, January 1963).

26. P.H. Tannenbaum, "Initial Attitude Toward Source and Concept as Factors in Attitude Change Through Communication," *Public Opinion Quarterly*, 20 (1956), 413-25.

27. Benny Rigaud-Bricmont, "Structure des attitudes du consommateur à l'égard des sources d'information qui l'entourent," *Marketing*, ed. Michel Laroche, Vol. 3 (Administrative Sciences Association of Canada, 1982), pp. 263-75.

28. Emmanuel Chéron and Michel Zins, "La théorie de l'attribution: Développements et applications pour le marketing," *Marketing*, ed. Vernon Jones, Vol. 1 (Administrative Sciences Association of Canada, 1980), pp. 97-106.

29. Elihu Katz and P.E. Lazarfeld, *Personal Influence: The Part Played by People in the Flow of Mass Communication* (Glencoe, Ill.: Free Press, 1955).

30. See, for instance, P.E. Lazarfeld, B. Berelson, and H. Gaudet, *The People's Choice* (New York: Duell, Sloan, and Pearce, 1944).

31. Katz and Lazarfeld.

32. Elihu Katz, "The Two-Step Flow of Communication: An Up-to-Date Report on an Hypothesis," *Public Opinion Quarterly*, 21 (Spring 1957), 61-78.

33. Helen Peak, "Attitude and Motivation," *Nebraska Symposium on Motivation 1955,* ed. M.R. Jones (Lincoln: University of Nebraska Press, 1955).

34. E.R. Carlson, "Attitude Change Through Modification of Attitude Structure," *Journal of Abnormal and Social Psychology*, 52 (1956), 256-61.

35. C.I. Hovland and H.A. Pritzker, "Extent of Opinion Change as a Function of the Amount of Change Advocated," *Journal of Abnormal and Social Psychology*, 54 (1957), 257-61; W. Weiss,

"The Relationship Between Judgments of a Communicator's Position and Extent of Opinion Change," *Journal of Abnormal and Social Psychology*, 56 (1958), 380-84.

36. Hovland and Pritzker p. 258.

37. Leon Festinger, *A Theory of Cognitive Dissonance* (New York: Harper and Row, 1957).

38. I.L. Janis and S. Fishback, "Effects of Fear-Arousing Communication," *Journal of Abnormal and Social Psychology*, 48 (1953), 78-92.

39. See Carl I. Hovland, Irving L. Janis, and Harold H. Kelly, *Communication and Persuasion* (New Haven: Yale University Press, 1953), pp. 87-88.

40. See, for instance, Henri Joannis, *De l'Etude de Motivation à la Rédaction Publicitaire et à la Promotion des Ventes* (Paris: Dunod, 1967).

41. Carl I. Hovland and Wallace Mandell, "An Experimental Comparison of Conclusion-Drawing by the Communication and by the Audience," *Journal of Abnormal and Social Psychology* (July 1952), pp. 581-88.

42. See Philip Kotler, *Marketing Management: Analysis, Planning, and Control*, 2nd ed. (Englewood Cliffs, N.J.: Prentice-Hall, 1972), p. 641.

43. See C.I. Hovland, A.A. Lumsdaine, and F.D. Sheffield, "Experiments in Mass Communication," *Studies in Social Psychology in World War II*, vol. 3 (Princeton, N.J.: Princeton University Press, 1948), chapter 8; A.A. Lumsdaine and I.L. Janis, "Resistance to Counter-Propaganda Produced by One-Sided and Two-Sided Propaganda Presentations," *Public Opinion Quarterly*, 17 (1953), 311-18.

44. E. Walster, E. Aronson, and D. Abrahams, "On Increasing the Persuasiveness of a Low Prestige Communicator," *Journal of Experimental Social Psychology*, 2 (1966), 325-42.

45. See, for instance, Brian Sternthal, "Persuasion and the Mass Communication Press" (Ph.D. diss., Ohio State University, 1972), chapter 8.

46. H. Gilkinson, S. Paulson, and D. Sinkink, "Effects of Order and Authority in an Argumentative Speech," *Quarterly Journal of Speech*, 40 (1954), 183-92; H. Galley and D. Berlo, "Effects of Intercellular and Intracellular

Speech Structure on Attitude Change and Learning," *Speech Monographs*, 23 (1956), 288-97.

47. H. Sponberg, "A Study of the Relative Effectiveness of Climax and Anti-Climax Order in an Argumentative Speech," *Speech Monographs*, 13 (1946), 35-44.

48. Ebbinghaus found in 1885 that one-third of the nonsense syllables he memorized were forgotten after twenty minutes and that nearly three-quarters were forgotten after six days. Quoted in James F. Engel, David T. Kollat, and Roger D. Blackwell, *Consumer Behavior*, 2nd ed. (New York: Holt, Rinehart and Winston, 1973), p. 340.

49. See H. Cromwell and R. Kunkel, "An Experimental Study of the Effect on Attitude of Listeners of Repeating the Same Oral Propaganda," *Journal of Social Psychology*, 35 (May 1952), 175-84.

50. E.K. Strong, "The Factors Affecting a Permanent Impression Developed Through Repetition," *Journal of Experimental Psychology*, 1 (1916), pp. 319-38.

51. Herbert Z. Zielske, "The Remembering and Forgetting of Advertising," *Journal of Marketing*, 23 (January 1959), 239-43.

52. See, for instance, "Frequency in Print Advertising: 1," *Media/Scope* (April 1962); "Frequency in Broadcast Advertising: 2," *Media/Scope* (March 1962).

53. "Frequency in Broadcast Advertising: 2," op. cit.

54. Michael Ray and Allan Sawyer, "Repetition in Media Models: A Laboratory Technique," *Journal Of Marketing Research*, 8 (1971), 20-29.

55. T. Cook and C. Insko, "Persistence of Attitude Change as a Function of Conclusion Re-exposure: A Laboratory Experiment," *Journal of Personality and Social Psychology*, 9 (1968), 243-64.

56. Adapted from Peter Langhoff, "Options in Campaign Evaluation," *Journal of Advertising Research* (December 1967), pp. 41-47, quoted by Philip Kotler, *Marketing Decision Making: A Model Building Approach* (New York: Holt, Rinehart and Winston, 1970), pp. 433-36.

57. "Frequency in Broadcast Advertising: 2," op. cit.

58. Kristian S. Palda, *The Measurement of Cumulative Advertising Effects* (Englewood Cliffs, N.J.: Prentice-Hall, 1964).

Advertising and the Buyer Decision Process

Needs and motivations are the starting points of purchase decisions. For a purchase to take place, buyers must experience sufficiently positive attitudes toward the product and the brand and more or less consciously felt needs. When all the elements of the marketing program are properly designed, a buyer will include the advertised brand in his or her evoked set of brands, which is all the brands that are considered for purchase. These elements of the marketing program include designing the product to have the attributes buyers seek, ensuring that the product is available at conveniently located retail stores, and setting a price that buyers perceive as reasonable. This chapter describes the process buyers follow to select a brand from within their evoked set. Emphasis is put on elements of the process that advertisers can influence through a well-designed communication program.

The Purchase Decision Process

Most purchases imply the decision to buy a product or service. This purchase decision process includes:

1. a goal to be reached (i.e., lessening the tension created by an unsatisfied need or desire);
2. a number of alternatives (i.e., competing products and brands). Products and brands are perceived, evaluated, and compared on the basis of their distinctive attributes and on their ability to satisfy a set of needs.

These alternatives also include the non-purchase decision;
3. some evaluation criteria for choosing the "best" alternative;
4. a state of doubt, arising from the impossibility of possessing all relevant information on the different products and brands. Buyers are always uncertain about how well a given product or brand will satisfy their needs or desires.

Because they must act on the basis of incomplete information, buyers automatically and consciously incur a risk in every purchase and non-purchase decision. The size of the risk buyers perceive depends on the importance of the particular purchase and on the quantity of relevant information about the product category and the competing brands. Potential buyers may act in two ways, depending upon their attitude toward risk and upon the time pressure exerted in the particular purchase situation. They may make an immediate decision based on their present information and buy the product they perceive as capable of procuring the most satisfaction. Or they may delay the purchase to seek additional information by comparison shopping, listening to commercials, making additional calls to sellers or retailers, or inquiring about the product among acquaintances, who may be the opinion leaders described previously in the theory of the two-step flow of communications.

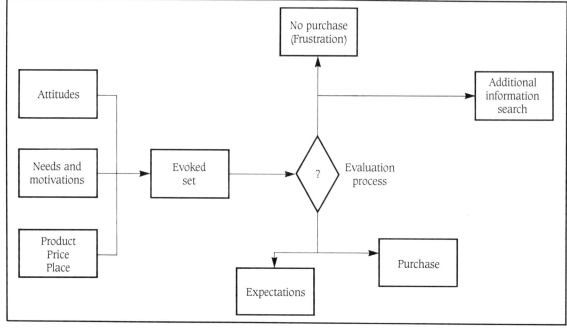

FIGURE 9.1   The Purchase Decision Process

When they buy a specific brand, buyers have expectations. This notion of expectation is intimately related to any purchase decision. A consumer who buys a product has developed definite expectations about the consumption of this product. Consumers buy a certain brand because it is preferable to competing brands; they have implicitly or explicitly anticipated that the selected brand will yield more satisfaction than the other brands and that it will respond more appropriately to the relevant set of felt needs. Hence, the amount of satisfaction consumers anticipate they will receive from a certain brand constitutes the *expectations* raised by the selected brand. A model of consumers' purchase decision process is shown in Figure 9.1.

The Purchase Decision: An Optimization Process

A purchase decision can be considered as an optimization process through which buyers

seek the product or the brand that will yield the greatest satisfaction. This process can be best understood when the brands in the evoked set are located in consumers' perceptual space, and when the ideal brand is located in the same space, as was discussed in Chapter 8.[1] Let us assume that an individual's utility function can be represented by a surface reaching its peak at the ideal point and, from there on, decreases regularly in all directions, as shown in Figure 9.2a. When this function is projected on the plane surface AB, the two-dimensional configuration shown in Figure 9.2b is obtained.

Thus, for this particular individual, who is characterized by a personal ideal brand, the iso-preference curves (i.e., the curves on which are located all the brands that are equally liked) consist in a series of concentric circles around this individual's ideal point (I). According to this model, two brands represented by the points M_1 and M_2 located on the same circle should be equally liked by individual I. On the other hand, the greater the distance between a brand and the ideal point, the less this brand is liked

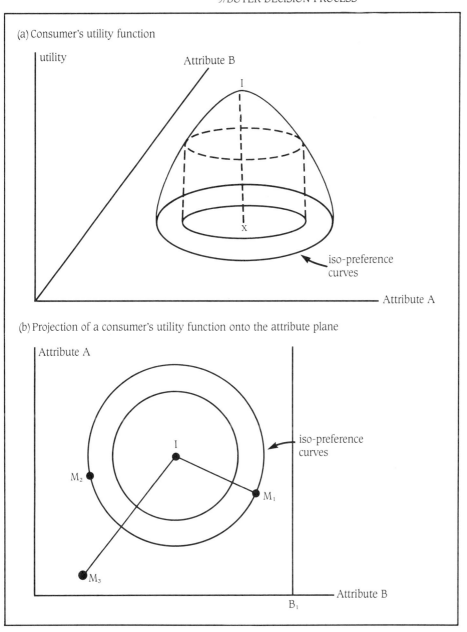

(a) Consumer's utility function

utility

Attribute B

I

X

iso-preference curves

Attribute A

(b) Projection of a consumer's utility function onto the attribute plane

Attribute A

I

M_2

M_1

iso-preference curves

M_3

Attribute B

B_1

FIGURE 9.2   Buyer's Utility for a Product Category

by the consumer. In this example, individual I would prefer brand M_1 to brand M_3. For a given buyer, the choice of one brand in the evoked set is an optimization process. Assuming this consumer knows exactly what he or she wants (i.e., the ideal point is well defined in the perceptual space) and possesses enough information to adequately position each brand in the perceptual space, the problem then consists of finding the brand located closest to the ideal point. This is the brand that should be preferred.

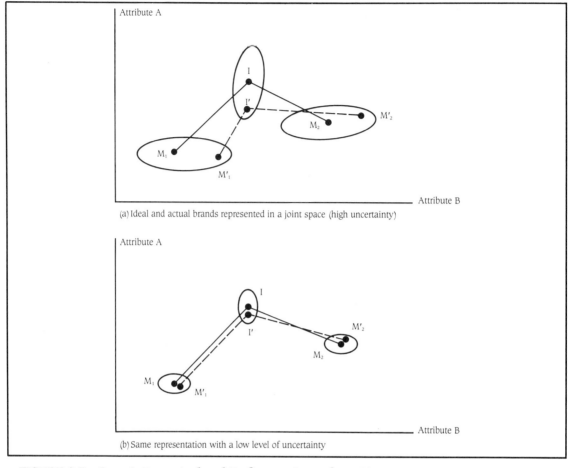

(a) Ideal and actual brands represented in a joint space (high uncertainty)

(b) Same representation with a low level of uncertainty

**FIGURE 9.3   Buyer's Perceptual and Preference Space for a Given
Product Category**

The uncertainty affecting a buyer's purchase decision is inversely related to the buyer's amount of information on the different products and brands. It affects the optimization process and the purchase decision in two ways. First, the buyer may have only a vague notion of the ideal brand's location in the perceptual space. This is the case of buyers who do not know exactly which attributes they should be looking for in a given product category, or which level of a given attribute would best respond to their set of needs. Second, since they are not perfectly informed about all products and brands, some buyers may have no precise idea of how to

evaluate the different brands according to those brand attributes that are most relevant to them.

In terms of the model described previously, this means that consumers often cannot represent brand perceptions and ideal brands by single points, but rather by zones. Thus, the centre of the zone constitutes only the "expected value" of the different (ideal or real) brand positions given by a buyer on different occasions. This "expected value" could be thought of as the mode of the *subjective* probability distribution that the buyer would associate to different levels and combinations of brand attributes. As we move closer to the periphery of the zone, the probability that this brand has the set of attributes at the corresponding levels decreases (Figure 9.3a).

Thus, if a buyer makes a purchase decision on the basis of present information, he will choose M_2, since it is closer to his (expected) ideal point I than M_1. On the other hand, the buyer very well realizes that he could be mistaken and be led to make a wrong decision. There is indeed a certain probability that M_1 will be closer to the ideal point as is shown in the example of $M'_1 I'$ which is shorter than the distance $M'_2 I'$. Obviously, the larger the ellipses representing the uncertainty zones, the greater the probability shall be for the consumer to make a wrong decision.[2]

If the buyer has sufficient information, however, thus considerably reducing the uncertainty, the probability of making a wrong decision decreases. This model, which has the merit of pointing at the potential role of information in a purchase decision, also has another advantage. It shows how different attributes influence the choice of one brand over another and indicates the attributes that enable consumers to evaluate and compare the different brands.

Assume that a buyer judges—wrongly or rightly—that all the brands of one product on the market have exactly the same level of a given attribute. This attribute does not enable the consumer to differentiate among different brands, since it is present in all of them. In terms of Figure 9.2b, this means that all the brands would be located on a vertical line B_1, with B representing the *inherent* attribute. Obviously, in this case, to choose a brand, one would have to compare the position of the different brands along attribute A and in relation to the position of the ideal point on attribute A. For example, a buyer may perhaps think that all the umbrellas on the market are waterproof, whether or not this opinion is technically well-founded. The consumer who perceives this as a fact cannot use the water-resistance attribute to compare umbrellas, since all the brands are perceived as being equal on this attribute.

A corollary of this observation is that brand comparison is possible only when a consumer considers those attributes on which some differences among brands can be perceived. These attributes are *distinctive* brand attributes. Consumers can compare different brands of umbrellas by their colour, style, or durability if they think these characteristics vary from one brand to another.[3]

To sum up, buyers dispose of incomplete information concerning the brand attributes they should seek and the attribute levels present in the different brands. Because of this uncertainty, a buyer must make a decision that is an optimization process under uncertainty. The search for more information reduces buyers' uncertainty about the attributes they should seek and about the levels of these desirable (and undesirable) attributes present in each brand. When buyers perceive all the brands as having the same level of a given attribute, this inherent attribute cannot be used as a criterion to evaluate and compare the different brands. Only the perceived distinctive attributes enable buyers to compare the different brands. The search for information causes the uncertainty to be reduced. One important question is to what extent buyers will try to reduce the uncertainty before making a decision, as they know that the degree of uncertainty is directly proportional to the probability of making a bad purchase decision.

The Purchase Decision: A Bayesian Process

The purchase decision problem as stated previously is essentially identical to the decision-making process according to the Bayesian approach.[4] This approach proposes a decision-making procedure that integrates different elements of decision making under risk. One principal element taken into account by this approach is the cost inherent in the decision problem. These costs are associated with delaying the final decision while more information is sought and the costs generated by this information search. The other principal element is the decision maker's subjective evaluation of the risks that result from the uncertainty caused by the decision maker's lack of information at a given time.

The decision-making process according to the Bayesian approach incorporates these elements into a formal model. This model enables a decision maker to estimate how accumulating additional information affects the subjective evaluation of the risks involved. These computations, relatively complex in practice if not in theory are based on Bayes' theorem, whence the name of the theory. Thus, the Bayesian process at any given point in time enables a decision-maker either to make an immediate decision and indicates which course of action should be followed; or to delay the decision to seek additional information, thus reducing the decision risks.

Theoretically, the Bayesian decision-making procedure and the purchase decision process are quite similar. A buyer who experiences the psychological tension caused by an unsatisfied need or desire faces a series of decision problems: What product should I buy? Which brand should I choose? These decisions may be described in terms of the Bayesian approach.

As was shown before, consumers run a certain risk in making a decision based on present information because this imperfect information does not enable them to predict exactly which product will procure the maximum satisfaction sought nor which brand really has the qualities desired (or that should be desired).

A certain number of costs are related to the risks taken by buyers. These costs are, for example, financial losses (if the product does not adequately satisfy all or part of a consumer's needs as it was hoped it would). The costs may also be physical (if, for instance, the realization of the risk endangers the consumer's life) or psycho-sociological (if a wrong purchase jeopardizes a consumer's reputation in one of his social groups, for example). As is shown by curve 1 in Figure 9.4, these costs are essentially associated with a fast decision (hence with a limited amount of information) and greatly decrease with time, because time has been used by the buyer to gather additional information, thus reducing the risk involved in the purchase.

However, when the buyer waits until more information is gathered before making a decision, costs associated with a delayed decision are incurred. This time, two types of cost are involved. First, there are "psychological opportunity" costs experienced by consumers who are deprived of the product they need and are consequently in a state of psychological tension. As time elapses, this psychological tension becomes more acute and eventually develops into a state of frustration. Second, buyers experience costs associated with the information-gathering effort. They must invest time and energy to visit several retailers, seek out and read advertisements, or inquire for other opinions about the best product to buy. These "delayed decision" costs are represented by curve 2 in Figure 9.4. These costs considerably increase as time elapses. Curve 3 in Figure 9.4 represents the total costs associated with a fast decision and those associated with a delayed decision, at each stage of the decision process. This curve first decreases, reaches a minimum t^*C^*, then starts to increase. Since buyers want to reduce the total costs associated with the decision as much as possible, they will seek the t^*C^* point that represents the best compromise between the costs associated with risky decisions and those associated with information-gathering activities.

Let us assume that a buyer located on the t_0 point experiences some need. Taking an immediate decision means running a risk equal to C_0. But this buyer may wait and call on several retailers to compare the product and brands which are offered on the market. This will require a certain amount of time equivalent to Δt_1. While reducing the risk, this visit to different retailers has caused the buyer the inconvenience of waiting and going to several

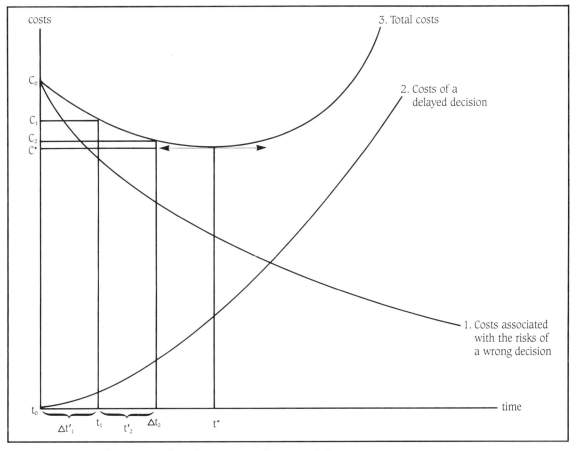

FIGURE 9.4   The Economics of Buyer Purchase Decisions

retailers. The risk that has been avoided is so important as to yield a total cost of C_1.

At the end of this round of retailers, however, the buyer is faced with the same problem. Must he make an immediate decision on the basis of present information (with an expected cost of C_1) or must he seek additional information, perhaps this time by consulting different consumer reports? This new search for information, which will require an amount of time equal to Δt_2, will deprive him of the product during this time, will cost purchase of various consumer reports, but will again enable him to reduce the purchase risk. The buyer will then reach a total cost of C_2, which is smaller than C_1. Consequently, this new step will have been well advised. The process will continue in this manner until the costs

involved in a new information search are superior to those of an immediate decision (past the t^*C^* point). As is shown in Figure 9.4, the buyer must seek information until it is felt (at least intuitively) that a search for additional information will bring about more costs than benefits.

Advertising Implications of the Purchase Decision Process

The Bayesian model showing the role of additional information in consumer purchase decisions has implications for advertisers. An advertisement reaching a potential buyer while the buyer is seeking information will have a greater impact, since the buyer is spared the time and effort needed to seek out this information himself and is less likely to turn to competing brand advertisements to obtain the additional information. In other words, buyers are generally more responsive to different brand advertisements while they are seeking information on these brands. This is why they become a choice target for the advertiser, provided the advertiser can identify and locate them. The strategy that consists of asking consumers to return a coupon at the bottom of a print advertisement is often devised along these principles. Thus, a consumer who is interested and is in an information-gathering stage is asked to return a coupon in order to obtain more information on the product or the brand. Then the advertiser takes advantage of the consumer's having identified him or herself to send a series of informative (and persuasive) messages or to send a salesperson who will try to conclude a sale. This strategy is currently used by life-insurance companies.

A second series of implications that this analysis of the buyer decision process has for advertising is that an advertiser must reduce the buyer's uncertainty about the *distinctive* attributes of the brand. Because a buyer takes only these attributes into consideration when comparing and evaluating brands, an advertiser normally tries to give positive information about the brand's performance on the distinctive attributes. An advertisement about the inherent attributes of a brand is bound to be ineffective. At best, it will be primary advertising for the whole product class, which will also promote the competing brands. This is why an advertiser must absolutely know which attributes in the relevant product category are perceived as inherent by the buyer, and what are the distinctive attributes on which the advertising effort should be concentrated.

Post-Purchase Reactions

Once a purchase is completed, a buyer has acquired a product or a service contract. Beyond the mere possession of the product, the buyer also has undergone some psychological change. The buyer has acquired *expectations* that go beyond the material possession of this product or this service contract; the buyer expects the products or services to provide the satisfaction he was seeking and that motivated the purchase. For goods with a short consumption cycle, consumers can judge if the product meets their expectations by using it immediately. But with durable products with long consumption cycles, consumers cannot tell immediately whether the product will meet their expectations.

A consumer buying a new cereal brand will know if his or her family likes it and if it is as good as expected by serving it for breakfast the next day. But a consumer who has just bought a new car may use it several weeks, even several months, and still wonder "is the motor strong enough to last 80 000 km? Will it really resist rust for several years, as promised by the dealer?" and not really be able to answer these questions.

Therefore a distinction must be drawn between the post-purchase feelings (Figure 9.5), which are essentially experienced during the period of relative uncertainty about the actual instrumental value of the purchased product, and which concern the occasional important and costly purchase; and between the post-usage feelings, when the consumer has evaluated the degree to which a product has met expectations.

Post-Purchase Feelings

Studies in social psychology and marketing have determined that an individual who has just made an important decision experienced post-decisional feelings.[5] In the consumer's case, these are post-purchase feelings. These post-purchase feelings can be explained by the theory of cognitive dissonance (Chapter 8).[6]

With a purchase decision, there are two possible causes of cognitive dissonance for a buyer. One is the risk inherent in all purchase decisions of not having made the best possible

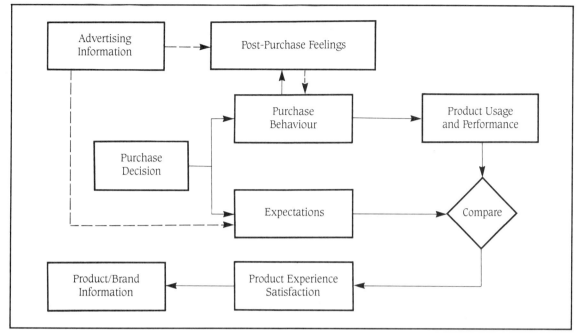

FIGURE 9.5   A Buyer's Post-Purchase Feelings

decision, since buyers can have only imperfect information on products and brands, as was seen previously. Thus, in terms of Figure 9.3b, the larger the ellipses (that is, the more important the probability of a wrong purchase decision), the greater the state of a buyer's cognitive dissonance. At this stage, the buyer's concern could be expressed as: "Have I bought the product that I should have to satisfy my needs?"

Second, buyers can experience cognitive dissonance because no product on the market exactly fits their ideal brand. Because of this inability to find an ideal product, buyers must compromise and select among the brands closest to the ideal. In making this compromise, they must give up certain desirable brand characteristics which are not present in the chosen brand for other desirable features which are present in the selected brand but not in the others. For example, the consumer in this type of situation can wonder: "Have I done well in choosing a four-door six-cylinder Pontiac Model A? Or should I have bought the Chevrolet Model X

that has an eight-cylinder motor, which I could have had with a Pontiac, but only with a coupé?" Thus, in terms of the diagram in Figure 9.3, this means that the more the brands on the market are clustered around the same iso-preference lines, the more the buyer should experience post-purchase feelings, because the compromise to be reached on the different brand characteristics is difficult to evaluate.

As was discussed previously, a subject in a state of cognitive dissonance tries to reduce his dissonance. An individual can become consonant by changing his or her behaviour to make it consistent with intimate convictions or may change some cognitive elements to make them more consistent with overt behaviour. Unfortunately, the theory does not enable us to predict which method a subject will choose to reduce his or her state of cognitive dissonance nor in which situation one way is more likely to be chosen than the other. Behavioural change corresponds to canceling a purchase if possible or brand switching, in the case of repetitive purchases. A change of opinion can be reached

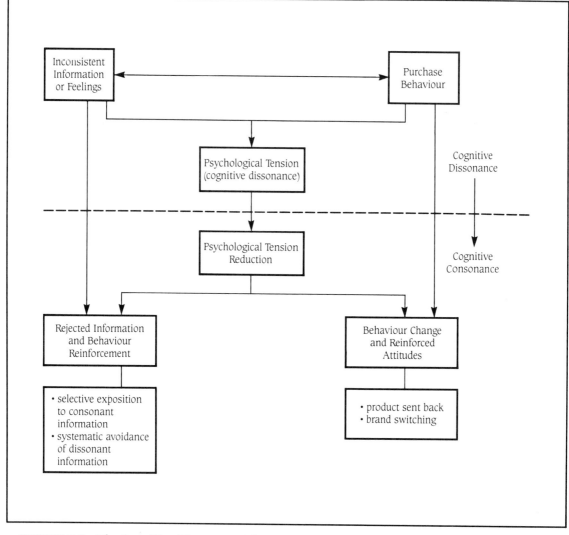

FIGURE 9.6   The Cognitive Dissonance Theory

if consumers are exposed to certain information. Thus, the subject may deliberately seek information that confirms the decision and try to avoid information questioning the merits of the choice (Figure 9.6). An experiment conducted by Ehrlich[7] is a classic illustration of this aspect of Festinger's theory. This experiment found that owners of a new car tended to notice and read advertising for the model they had just bought more so than advertising for the other brands.

The Role of Advertising in Post-Purchase Feeling Reduction

There is no empirical evidence yet to support the contention that advertisers can reduce buyers' post-purchase feelings. Some authors have said that an advertiser should undertake communication programs targeted at new buyers of a product.[8] This could be done, for instance, by sending leaflets on the newly bought products which would demonstrate the wisdom of the consumer's choice. It is not evident that manufacturers would benefit from such programs, however. If a consumer really seeks reasons to justify a choice, then the advertiser has nothing to do because the buyer will rationalize the purchase decision anyway. Except for an experiment conducted by Shelby Hunt, little research has been undertaken to test the effectiveness of post-purchase advertising.[9] Also, it must be questioned whether the manufacturer or the retailer is an adequate and sufficiently credible source to reduce dissonance. In the experiment by Hunt, disappointing conclusions were reached. In this experiment, consumers who just made a purchase received a message stating the merits of their choice. Some were made by mail, others by telephone. The clients who received a letter were less dissonant and developed more favourable attitudes toward the retailer than those who did not receive a letter. However, those who received the telephone communication were more subject to dissonance and developed less favourable attitudes toward the retailer than those who received no communication at all. Thus it is difficult to draw very firm conclusions on the usefulness of post-purchase advertising from this experiment, and no generalization should be attempted.

Post-Usage Feelings

As time elapses, post-purchase feelings give way to post-usage feelings, which are directly tied to a comparison of the product's performance with the consumer's expectations. It is to be hoped that the use of a product enables the consumer to attain a certain level of satisfaction. But the consumer does not judge the satisfaction obtained through product usage in absolute terms but rather in relation to what was expected of this product. A simple example can illustrate this idea.

A consumer tries a new detergent that has just been launched on the market. Suppose that for some reason, this consumer expects the new detergent to bleach more than the average brand. If after use this proves to be the case, this consumer will be "normally" satisfied with the product. If the product is superior to what was expected, the level of satisfaction will increase rapidly. However, if the product registers a performance inferior to what was expected, satisfaction would fall below the normal level. (See Figure 9.7a.)

Suppose now that another consumer expects the new detergent to be very much superior to the average, as is shown in Figure 9.7b. As for the previous consumer, the level of real satisfaction will be determined as a function of the difference between expectations and the product's actual performance. Thus, if a manufacturer tries to give a consumer a level of satisfaction S, the first consumer will have to reach the P_1 level of performance, which is substantially inferior to the P'_1 level that would be required to give the second consumer the same level of satisfaction S.

Of course, the consumer must have a sufficiently high level of expectation concerning the use of the product or the service for the purchase to materialize. Too high a level of expectation generally lowers the degree of satisfaction obtained by the consumer through consumption of the product. This degree of satisfaction as well as all the information on the product, the brand, and the use of the product, will increase the consumer's knowledge of the product class (i.e., improve the cognitive attitude components). In the same way, the consumer's evaluation of the product and brands during or after usage will improve or worsen attitudes toward the brand through a change in the affective attitude components.

The Role of Advertising in Post-Usage Feelings
An advertising message implicitly or explicitly promises a buyer a certain level of satisfaction through the purchase and consumption of the advertised product or service. In doing this, an advertiser raises a buyer's expectations. Consequently, the better the product performance

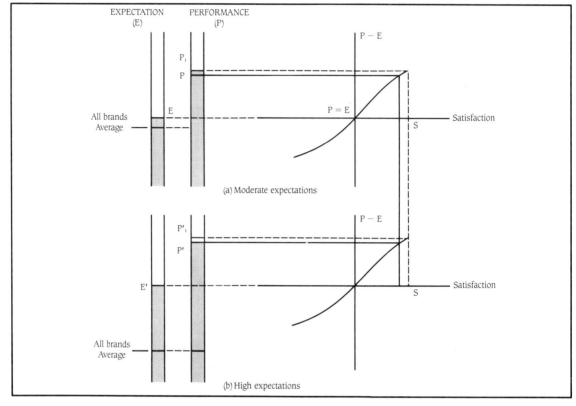

FIGURE 9.7   Relationship between a Consumer's Satisfaction and Expectations

will have to be for the consumer to feel the promised satisfaction. Advertisers who make exaggerated claims about the merits of a product or use deceptive advertisements have a short-term view of their place in the market. It may be easy to raise a buyer's expectations to sell a product, but if the product's performance does not meet these expectations, consumers will inevitably be dissatisfied and will not repeat their purchases.

Interpersonal Differences in Purchase Situations

The factors that lead to diverse behaviour within a single market segment are personal or psychographic characteristics, social factors, and cultural factors i.e., a consumer's cultural environment.

Personal or Psychographic Factors

Personal or psychographic factors characterize individuals at the psychological level and affect their lifestyles, behaviour, and purchase behaviour. An individual may be more or less impulsive, seek other people's company, act independently, or in a conservative and authoritative manner. These traits affect consumers' personality and influence their needs, motivations, perceptions, attitudes toward risk, and the decision and information processes. Certain consumers behave like energetic entrepreneurs and may be demanding of themselves and of others. An impulsive person wastes little time in seeking and processing information before making a purchase; an extrovert may make purchases that supposedly reflect personality.[10]

Advertisers and other communicators need to know whether consumers can be easily per-

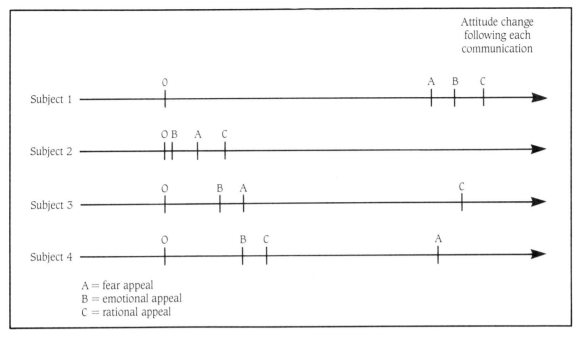

Attitude change
following each
communication

FIGURE 9.8   Reactions of Four Individuals with Various Persuasibility Levels to Three Communications (A, B, and C)

suaded. In Figure 9.8, four individuals are exposed to three messages concerning different subjects. Message A uses a fear appeal; B is an emotional appeal message; and C is a rational appeal message.[11] According to Janis and Hovland's nomenclature,[12] individual no. 1's reaction can be characterized as independent of the communication: he has been easily persuaded, whatever the nature of the appeal used. Individual no. 2 is the least persuasible of the four. Individual no. 3 is likely to be influenced more easily with messages using rational appeals, while the fourth individual is more likely to respond positively to messages based on fear. Persuasiveness is also tied to message characteristics and depends on the subject of the communication, the type of appeal used, the argument provided, or the style of the communication. In this example, persuasibility depends upon the communication.

The question which then arises for advertisers is to know whether they can identify the consumers who can be easily persuaded and who therefore are most influenced by advertising. If these consumers can be identified by easily observable characteristics, it would be easier to locate and reach them. Unfortunately, the numerous studies in social psychology conducted on this subject that sought the typical characteristics of persuasible individuals produced few sure conclusions. There is as much empirical evidence to suggest that a person's intelligence and propensity to be persuaded are positively,[13] negatively,[14] or not at all[15] related. The same statement applies to self-confidence.[16] In general, however, women seem easier to persuade than men.[17] Other factors that have been proposed as possible determinants of persuasibility are cognitive needs,[18] ego-defensiveness,[19] authoritarianism,[20] self-esteem,[21] aggressiveness,[22] the need for social approval,[23] and dogmatism.[24]

Thus, people differ as to the ease with which they are likely to accept a persuasive communication and tend to react differently after such a communication. Advertisers cannot, however, meaningfully use this criterion to segment an audience.

Socio-Economic Factors

Socio-economic factors characterize the social groups, formal or informal, structured or not, to which individuals belong, could belong, or would like to belong. These factors are an individual's age, sex, revenue, profession, education, religion, nationality, social class, size of the family, and the stage in the family's life cycle. These different characteristics lead to a better comprehension of consumers' behaviour. The needs of a young unmarried male are not those of a middle-aged married woman; the transportation needs of travelling salespeople are not similar to those of sedentary office employees. Education, profession, and social class affect consumers' perceptions and attitudes, just as an individual's income directly influences the brands that are included in the evoked set. Bank employees earning $18,000 a year will probably not include a Cadillac in their evoked set of brands when they consider buying a new car.

Because needs and attitudes differ from group to group, the pressures a group exerts on its members in order to induce them to comply to group norms must also be considered. Thus, if a bank clerk could afford the luxury of a Cadillac through some unexpected good fortune, he or she would probably incur the disapproval of colleagues, neighbours, and members of his or her social class.

Cultural Factors

Buyers must also be considered in the context of their cultural environment. Culture includes the knowledge, beliefs, art, ethics, law, customs, language, and all the other habits acquired by a society's members. Like socio-economic factors, these elements also influence behaviour and purchase behaviour. They are perhaps less visible since they are shared by all the consumers in a same market, as well as by the manufacturer and the advertiser. This is perhaps why cultural factors are less recognized by advertisers. However, if advertisers try to address market segments in which the cultural element is not the same for all consumers, an important dimension is without doubt added to the problem of buyer behaviour. This is the case when multinational firms must advertise in several countries to several different cultures, or of manufacturers who must, as in Canada, advertise in a bicultural environment.

The most subtle elements of a culture may create problems for a member of another culture. Concepts of time, space, friendship, the significance of material objects and of social conventions may be very different from one culture to another.[25] For example, in Arab countries, a mechanic feels pressured when asked to repair a car before a specific date and responds by slowing down or stopping work. A particular colour may have different meanings in different countries: a product with a green package might be accepted in Mexico and become a failure in Egypt. For each of these countries, green is a national colour, but differences in behaviour proceed from the attitudes toward its commercial use. A product with a green package might also be a failure in Malaysia because green is associated with the jungle and, therefore, with sickness. Thus it is essential for international marketing managers to know consumers well and to avoid using blanket approaches that may have succeeded in their native country. An advertising theme for a washing machine in Canada, where it is an essential good often put out of view of guests, could not be used in Mexico, where it is a luxury good, often displayed in the living-room as an indicator of high social class.[26]

Within one society, different cultural groups are identified by age, ethnic origin, geographical location, language, and religion. For example, Puerto Ricans in New York, the Pennsylvania Amish, and the Cubans in Miami might be

TABLE 9.1   Cultural Differences between English and French Canadians

Tendencies of Cultural Characteristics	English-Speaking	French-Speaking
Ethnic Origin	Anglo-Saxon	Latin
Religion	Protestant	Catholic
Language Spoken	English	French
Intellectual Attitude	Pragmatic	Theoretical
Family	Matriarchy	Patriarchy
Leisure Time	In function of the professional class	In function of the family circle
Individual vis-à-vis the Environment	More social	More individualistic
Business Management	Administrator	Innovator
Political Tendencies	Conservative	Liberal
Consumption Attitudes	Propensity to save; conformist; financier more than financed	Propensity to spend; innovator; financed more than a financier

SOURCE: Georges Hénault, "Les conséquences du biculturalisme sur la consommation," *Revue Commerce* (September 1971).

considered as distinct cultural groups within American society.

Canada is a multicultural society in which the two main cultures, the English and the French, can be identified by linguistic, geographical, and economic characteristics.[27] Lefrançois and Chatel define the French Canadian market as including, in addition to the province of Quebec, eight adjacent counties in Ontario and seven counties in New Brunswick.[28] These authors attribute the behavioural differences between the two groups to socio-economic differences, such as different income and educational levels, rates of urbanization, and employment profiles. According to this reasoning, an elimination of these differences could lead to a similarity in purchasing behaviour. This hypothesis was rejected by the findings of a study comparing consumption behaviour between families of the same size and the same income in Quebec and in Ontario.[29] Some of the cultural differences between Francophones and Anglophones are presented in Table 9.1.

Strong family ties may explain why home-made soups are served in 80 per cent of French Canadian families and in only 40 per cent of English Canadian families.[30] Also, because home cooking is an important aspect of family life, this might explain why French Canadians prefer to buy packaged soups and cake mixes rather than canned soups and ready-made cakes.[31] French Canadians have been found to be more introspective, more humanistic, more emotional, and less materialistic and pragmatic than English Canadians.[32] These qualities have led various authors to define specific consumption habits. For example, Quebec consumers have the largest per capita consumption of soft drinks, wines, maple syrup, and sweets, and they listen to the radio and watch television the most.[33] Expenditures for clothing are higher for French Canadians, and women in Quebec are more demanding about the quality of their clothes.[34]

How can it be explained that French Canadians consume more remedies against headaches and stomach aches, more decaffeinated coffee, and, in 90 per cent of the cases, more light beer or ale than their English counterparts? Why does perfume sell better in Quebec than in the rest of Canada?[35] These are questions that the marketing manager of a subsidiary of a foreign company, as much as a Canadian company, must answer in order to really know the market and avoid errors in judgement.

An examination of the liquor market further illustrates the impact of group cultures on consumption. The market has many segments, and liquor consumption varies widely in Canada, with the highest in the Yukon and the lowest in Quebec. Moreover, French Canadians drink almost all Geneva gin produced in Canada but only 9 per cent of sales of Canadian whisky, which is less than the Americans (12 per cent) and much less than the national average of 40 per cent. Similarly, Quebec consumers drink less vodka (8 per cent) than consumers in British Columbia (16 per cent). Rum is most popular in the Atlantic provinces because it was once an ocean trade commodity and has long been widely available in the coastal provinces.[36]

The reason for these different consumption patterns is that rum, vodka, and Geneva gin do not have the same meaning for a French Canadian and for an Albertan. Manufacturers who advertise such products in these provinces must be careful to refer to the proper values, meanings, and habits that are central to the consumption of these products in both cultures so that the advertising is understood and believed.

The Dynamics of Purchase Behaviour

The Determinants of Purchase Information-Seeking Activities

As we have seen, buyer behaviour is not static and changes over time; rather buyer behaviour and the information acquisition process can be viewed as a continuous system. To purchase a product or a brand, buyers need a certain level of information about the characteristics and the probable performance of various brands on the market. Pre-purchase information-seeking activities depend on four factors that have an important time dimension (Figure 9.9). Two factors are purchase-situation related: the urgency of the purchase situation and the level of information the buyer has acquired by the time of the purchase decision. The two other factors relate to the type of product and market: the length and regularity of the purchase cycle for a particular product type and the risk perceived by consumers in the purchase situation.

Urgency of the Purchase Situation
The urgency of the purchase situation affects the quantity and quality of information that a buyer has time to acquire before making a purchase decision. For instance, a consumer who suffers a severe migraine may go to the nearest drugstore to buy a pain reliever, and thus is acting under great time pressure. Because of this hasty decision, the consumer probably has not bought the same brand he might have if he was seeking a pain reliever for some future possible headache.[37]

Level of Information Already Acquired
Depending on the extent of market information, a buyer's decision process is more or less complex. A product's characteristics in relation to an individual's past experience determines the level of complexity of the decision process.

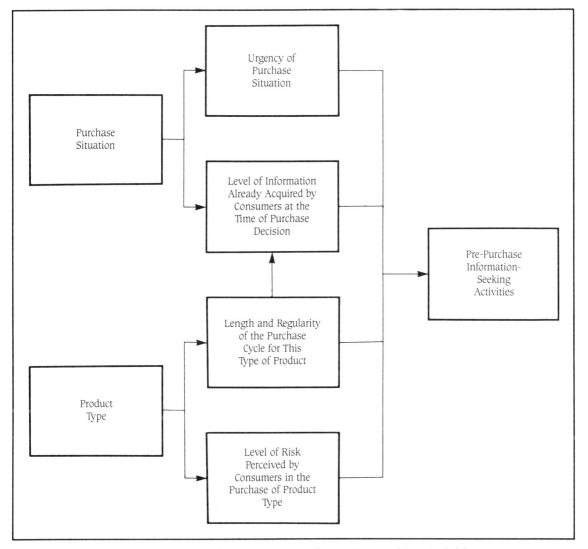

FIGURE 9.9   The Determinants of Pre-Purchase Information-Seeking Activities

Three possible cases can be identified:[38]

1. The consumer is very familiar with a product category and knows the characteristics of competing brands. This process is called *routinized response behaviour*.

2. The consumer knows the product category well but not the particular brand. For example, a new brand of pecan pie has been introduced on the market. The process through which the consumer becomes familiar with this brand is called *limited problem solving*.

3. The consumer does not know either the product category or the brand. For example, a newcomer to Canada must learn what a pecan pie is before deciding which brand to choose. Another example is UHT or long life milk which, at the time it was introduced, represented a totally new concept. This process is called *extensive problem solving*.

The level of information already acquired is directly affected by the length of the purchase cycle, because the rate of information forgetting depends on how frequently a product is purchased.

Length and Regularity of the Purchase Cycle

Purchase situations related to certain needs and wants occur at various frequencies and paces. Frequency is linked to the type of product and market. Based on the regularity and length of the purchase cycle, three main types of markets can be identified:

1. *Short purchase cycle markets* are characterized by routine purchase decision processes or by limited problem solving when a new brand is introduced on the market. Most food products, such as coffee, sugar, bread, soft drinks, canned vegetables, and household and beauty care products, fall into this category.

2. *Irregular purchase cycle markets* are characterized by products that are purchased more or less regularly. This category of products includes desserts, cookies, cake mixes, aperitif wines, and deluxe food products.

3. *Long or unpredictable purchase cycle markets* include all durable goods, such as cars, household appliances, and furniture. Also in this category are products for which occasions of purchase cannot be predicted, for example, drug products, which most consumers buy only occasionally.

Level of Perceived Risk

The role of the risk perceived by a consumer in a purchase situation was discussed in Chapter 7. In general, the nature of the risk—physical, financial, and/or psychological—as well as the level of the risk depend on the kind of purchase contemplated. Buying a candy bar typically does not involve the same level of risk as buying an expensive second-hand sports car. When buyers perceive a high risk in a purchase situation, they will generally require more infor-mation about the brand and the product class before making a decision. The relation between the size of the risk and the consumer's information research depends, in turn, on the consumer's attitude toward risk.

Brand Loyalty and Brand Switching

The information a buyer has already acquired, the urgency of the purchase, the type of product, and the risk involved interact with one another and determine a buyer's level of pre-purchase information-seeking activities. Once evaluated, this information is used to implicitly rank-order the different brands in the evoked set, and other conditions permitting, the most preferred brand will be purchased.

But for how long will this brand remain the most preferred? Is a buyer likely to switch to another brand at the next purchase? Learning theory may help answer these questions. According to psychologists, learning is the behavioural change resulting from previous behaviour in similar situations.[39] Learning theories postulate a state of tension as soon as a need is felt by an individual, in response to a stimulus in the environment (such as products or ads), which calls for the subject's response (a purchase decision). If the behaviour is rewarded by satisfaction and, consequently, by tension reduction, it is repeated when the need occurs again.

Learning is more likely to take place in short purchase cycle and routinized response behaviour situations. During the short time lag between two consecutive purchase occasions, only a fraction of information has been forgotten, and a substantial amount of additional information has been gained through using the selected brand. At the next purchase occasion, a buyer does not need and generally does not deliberately seek additional information. If the previously selected brand resulted in a positive experience, this buyer remains loyal to the brand with no further reassessment of purchase alternatives. Otherwise, if the preceding purchase has led to a negative evaluation of the brand, or if the buyer has been exposed to and has accepted new information that changed the order of the brands, then the conditions for *brand switching* are met. The buyer will try the new, most positively evaluated brand at the time of the next purchase.

Types of Market Situations and Advertising Implications

Because advertisers control only one of the buyer information sources, they can try to influence buyer behaviour by communicating information when it is needed. To be able to meet advertising objectives, advertisers must understand how buyers' information load varies over time in various types of markets.

Short Purchase Cycle Markets

A buyer's information load is likely to vary in short purchase cycle markets in the case of low risk products (for instance, candy bars) and of higher risk products (such as fashion items). In both cases, the first purchase is preceded by fairly extensive problem solving. However, for subsequent purchases the buyer has enough information and falls into routinized problem solving or limited problem solving. Depending on the nature of this information, the buyer may be loyal to one brand or to several brands, if each brand is bought for various consumption occasions, or switch to a new brand. However, in a low risk situation, buyers are unlikely to *actively* search for additional information, contrary to the higher risk situation.

In short purchase cycle markets advertisers may induce buyers who buy competitive brands to switch to the advertised brand, induce new buyers of the product class to try the advertised brand, or convince present users of the advertised brand that they should remain loyal to the brand.

ATTRACTING NEW BUYERS. To attract new buyers, advertisers should conduct a campaign that shows potential users of the product category that they have some unsatisfied needs of which they may not even be consciously aware and that the advertised brand can best fulfil these needs. The objective is not to "create" needs that consumers did not experience before. Advertising cannot sell skiing equipment in countries where it does not snow. The problem is, rather, to make consumers aware that they have a problem or need for which they have not found a satisfactory solution. For instance, a consumer may not have consciously recognized that he had to combat halitosis, because he did not know that products existed to solve this problem. The advertiser for a mouthwash product might show this consumer that his product can solve the problem of bad breath better than any other brand on the market.

ATTRACTING BUYERS FROM COMPETITIVE BRANDS. To attract buyers from competitive brands, advertisers can create a state of cognitive dissonance. The objective is to show consumers that they are not buying the best product, either because the advertised brand is superior to competitive brands or because the most positive attributes of the competitive brands are not the most important. The goal is to improve buyer attitudes toward the advertised product so as to make it preferable to the brand currently purchased. Advertisers try to encourage buyers who experience cognitive dissonance to reduce it by trying the new brand. In order to be effective, however, advertisements based on this principle should not be deceptive. Otherwise, unsatisfied customers will not repeat the purchase of the brand and will probably go back to their former brand.

RETAINING PRESENT BUYERS. To keep present buyers, advertisers attempt to combat the cognitive dissonance that competitors' advertising has created among their customers. They may emphasize arguments that buyers consider important or reinforce the importance of the brand attributes on which the advertisers have some competitive advantage.

Short and Irregular Purchase Cycle Markets

In short and irregular purchase cycle markets, an advertiser can attempt to increase the average consumption rate, i.e., shorten the length of the purchase cycle, or induce buyers to purchase more at each occasion.

INCREASING THE CONSUMPTION RATE. An advertiser may attempt to influence a buyer's memory by reminding him of the existence of the product and of the brand. This type of advertising is generally called *reminder advertising*. It is especially effective when it is made at the point of purchase. Suppose that a shopper in a supermarket is looking for a dessert and sees a large poster for Jello or a large Pepperidge Farm product display. If this person has already tried the brand and has been satisfied with it, he or she may decide to repeat the purchase. Without this advertisement, the shopper would probably not have thought of buying the product.

INCREASING THE PURCHASE VOLUME. In this case, an advertiser may suggest new uses for the product. For instance, Kraft often suggests new recipes to consumers, with Kraft cheeses as essential ingredients. A similar result can be obtained if new occasions to consume the product are suggested to potential buyers. For example, an advertisement for cheddar cheese states, "I feel like eating this cheese seven times a day." In both cases, an advertiser tries to increase buyers' information load concerning the possible uses of the products in question.

Long or Unpredictable Purchase Cycle Markets

Long or unpredictable purchase cycle products are the most difficult to advertise. It is practically impossible to identify potential buyers of these products in the market at a given time. This is why an advertiser should make sure that at any given time, potential buyers have a sufficiently positive attitude toward the brand so that they will probably select it when a purchase occasion arises. The advertiser's role is to give buyers all relevant information in order to build this favourable attitude. The advertiser may also give information that is likely to reduce the risk perceived by buyers when the product is purchased.

Summary of the Buyer Behaviour Model

The social groups, the culture to which buyers belong, and the firms that compete in the marketplace are part of buyers' environment (Figure 9.10). A great number of stimuli emanate from this environment. These stimuli can take the form of actual products and services that solicit the potential buyer (as well as all kinds of marketing information). The potential buyer overtly reacts to these stimuli either by the purchase and the consumption of the products or by a non-purchase, with or without a more or less active search for additional information on the products and brands. Because of their personality, past experience, personal characteristics, and the influence of the social and cultural groups to which they belong, buyers experience needs and motivations that make them more or less attentive at a given point in time to the purchase of a whole series of products and services. The presence of a product-stimulus in the buyer's environment, its physical and economic availability to the potential buyer, and the bulk of evaluative and affective information the buyer has on all the relevant elements of the purchase situation determine whether a product or a brand will or will not be part of a buyer's evoked set.

Of all the information that can affect a buyer's purchase situation, we will discuss only the sensorial information communicated by the product or the brand itself, or deduced from the buyer's past experience with the product. Much information that is directly controlled or controllable by a firm takes the form of communications through advertising, sales representatives, and advice given by a seller or a retailer. Finally,

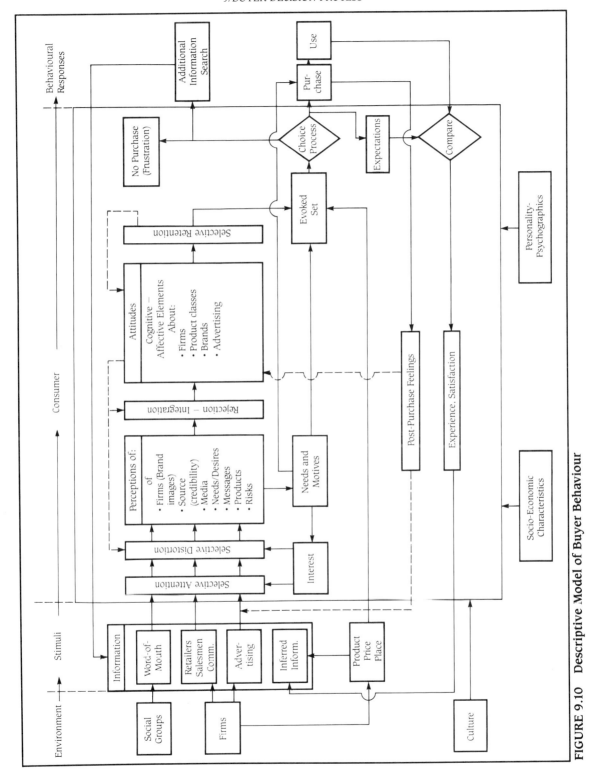

FIGURE 9.10 Descriptive Model of Buyer Behaviour

buyers receive a sizable amount of word-of-mouth information that is entirely controlled by the social groups to which they belong or wish to belong. Depending upon the source from which they emanate, these information flows pass through a buyer's selective attention and selective distortion filters. These filters depend on the buyer's interests and ego-involvement in the purchase situation, which in turn are determined by the importance and urgency of the needs involved. The information the buyer has thus received and perceived on the firms, the information sources, the media, the advertisement, the products and the risks of the situation are evaluated and constitute the large bank of objective and subjective data that make up the buyer's set of consistent and integrated attitudes. Of course, this data bank also loses information as time elapses, because of the consumer's information forgetting and as competing and contradictory information also tries to fit into the buyer's cognitive and affective attitude structures. Because the buyer tries to maintain coherent attitudes, he filters, distorts, and stores the received information in such a way as to remain psychologically coherent and consistent.

Depending upon the purchase situation, the buyer must choose a brand in the evoked set. This decision process can be blocked if one of the previous conditions is not fulfilled, that is, (1) if the product is not physically or economically available to the buyer; (2) if a buyer's attitudes are not sufficiently disposed toward at least one brand; or (3) if the buyer perceives so great a risk in the contemplated purchase that waiting and seeking additional information are warranted. The decision process continues in this way until the urgency and the costs associated with further delay of the purchase induce the potential buyer to give up the idea of purchasing the product or the brand, or to make the purchase and eventually use the product. In certain cases, the post-purchase feelings and the post-usage feelings alter the buyer's cognitive and affective elements con-

cerning the purchased product and/or brand.

This description of the purchase process refers more to an occasional purchase or to the first of a series of repetitive purchases (for example, the purchase of a first pack of cigarettes) where the search for information plays an important role. Fortunately, each individual purchase does not require the entire decision process; instead, a buyer uses past experience. This is what psychologists call learning. Learning is all the behavioural change that results from previous behaviour in a similar situation. Theories of learning postulate an impulsion, that is, a state of tension (or need) that calls for an action, and a stimulus in the environment, as, for example, an advertisement, which calls for a response from the subject (in this case, the purchase of the product). The behaviour is likely to be repeated if it is rewarded by satisfaction (by a reduction of the tension). This is how purchasing habits are formed in the case of repetitive purchases.

Learning is an important concept in marketing since it explains brand loyalty, an important goal sought by all manufacturers. Conversely, a responsibility of marketing managers is also to break buyers' loyalty to competing brands, which often requires, in addition to an adequate advertising campaign, the use of such promotional actions as free samples or discounts.

Summary of Advertising's Potential for Influencing Buyer Behaviour

The preceding analysis of buyer behaviour points out the possible impact of advertising (a persuasive communication) at three levels: on buyers' needs and motivations, on perceptions and attitudes, and on post-purchase feelings.

Effect on Buyers' Needs and Motivations

Advertising can influence buyer behaviour by

being present in the buyer's environment and by suggesting a solution to needs felt either consciously or in a less latent form. If advertising does not really "create" a need, it can act upon the buyer's emotional equilibrium by responding positively to motivations that would induce the buyer to make the purchase, or by decreasing the motivations with a negative valence that would prevent the potential buyer from purchasing. In this case, an advertisement will try to show the instrumental value of a product in responding to the buyer's needs (physical or psychological) and, consequently, in easing at least partially the tension caused by these needs.

Effects on Perceptions and Attitudes

An advertisement can try to act upon the buyer's perceptions to create a certain brand image in the market. More generally, advertising can try to cause changes in buyer attitudes and make them more favourable toward the consumption of the advertised brand.

To do this, advertising can provide information (cognitive elements) and/or act upon the affective elements of buyer attitudes. This should eventually result in a buyer's predisposition in favour of the purchase (conative elements). To make these changes, the advertiser can use the following research findings from social psychology:[40]

The Communicator

Manufacturers can identify themselves as the communicator and deliver the message. However, their credibility is weak because they have a visible interest in persuading buyers and inducing them to buy their brand. Manufacturers can also use an intermediary who will "testify" in favour of their product and deliver the advertising message. In this case:

1. The message will be as effective as the source is perceived to be credible. Credibility requires (a) expertise (extensive knowledge

about the subject of the communication) and (b) trustworthiness (motivation to communicate unbiased information).

2. The communicator's credibility has an impact on the immediate effectiveness of the advertisement and seems to be less important in the long run.

3. The message effectiveness is enhanced if the witness first expresses some ideas that are already shared by the audience.

4. The more an advertisement demands an important change on the part of its audience, the more the attitude change obtained by the advertiser is likely to be important. However, if the message is too far away from a buyer's initial position and if the "expert" is not credible enough, the attitude change will be less important.

5. Some of the communicator's characteristics that are not relevant to the message content can strongly influence the message's effectiveness (for example, an advertising message delivered by a black—an irrelevant characteristic—could be rejected by people with a racial prejudice).

6. In a more general way, what buyers think of an advertisement can affect their attitudes toward the communicator (the person who delivers the message or the brand).

The Message

1. Advertisers should present only those arguments that are in favour of the product: if the market already holds a favourable attitude toward the brand; if the market is not likely to be exposed to competing advertisements (a fairly unusual case); or when an immediate, albeit temporary, attitude change is sought.

2. Advertisers should present arguments in favour of and against their product if, for example, they want to convince users of another brand to switch to their brand, or if the buyers are likely to be exposed to competing advertisements. A relatively small

number of advertisers use this approach, yet it seems very effective.

3. If advertisers decide to use arguments and counter-arguments, those presented last are likely to be the most effective.

4. The message is more effective when the conclusions are explicitly drawn, rather than when buyers are left to infer conclusions. The exception to this rule would apply when the market segment targeted by the advertiser is highly intelligent.

5. The effectiveness of emotional versus factual messages depends upon the nature of the target market segment.

6. With advertisements using fear appeals, the effectiveness of the message will increase with the intensity of the provoked fear, provided clear solutions are proposed and provided these solutions are possible and seem plausible to the buyer. Otherwise, the message can have an effect opposite to the one intended.

7. There is no clear evidence indicating the order in which the arguments should be presented in terms of importance.

8. One can reasonably expect some resistance on the part of a buyer to persuasion by an advertisement. It could well be, however, that a distracting device simultaneously presented to the audience could decrease the audience's resistance to the persuasive communication.

The Buyer

1. Apparently, buyers seek selective exposure to messages that agree with their positions and avoid information that is inconsistent with their attitudes. Thus advertisers' ideal audience is generally composed of people who are the least likely to listen to their message.

2. The effectiveness of certain messages depends upon the audience's intelligence level.

3. An effective advertisement must take into account the reasons that motivate a buyer's attitudes; these reasons as well as the attitude must be changed.

4. Buyers' personality traits affect their propensity to be persuaded. Women or individuals with low self-esteem can generally be more easily influenced.

5. Buyers' ego-involvement with the advertised product (that is, as the product involves sensitive ideological values) decreases their acceptance of the message.

6. Buyers belonging to certain social groups are probably less influenced than others by an advertising message asking them to violate the norms of these groups.

7. It is easier to change a buyer's privately held opinions (such as opinions on products related to personal problems), than to change an opinion that has been publicly stated (such as opinions on products related to family or social environment).

Persistence of Advertising Effects

1. The effects of an advertising message tend to wear off over time. The effects of a message delivered by a positive source wear off more rapidly than those of an advertisement communicated by a negative source. A complex or subtle message, if it is understood, produces a slower decay of attitude change.

2. Repetition of an advertisement tends to extend its effect over time.

3. An attitude change can increase some time after the advertising message has been received by the audience (sleeper effect).

Effects on Post-Purchase Feelings

Advertising has a potential value in reducing a buyer's dissonant feelings after an important purchase. Although no sure evidence can give advertising a precise role in this area, there are at least theoretical arguments supporting such a role. Consequently, this possibility should be kept in mind in spite of the lack of empirical evidence.

The Limits of Advertising Communications

In the description of the potential of advertising communications, the (sometimes very particular) conditions under which an advertisement could be effective give an indication of advertising's limits. Advertising communications' main limitations can be grouped into three broad categories: message effectiveness, parallel communication channels, and other elements of the marketing mix.

Advertising Message Effectiveness

An advertising message's effectiveness depends on the communication format, the message content in relation to the buyer's initial attitude toward the advertised product, and the style of the message. These are the variables that have been considered by researchers in social psychology and that have led to precise conclusions. However, many content as well as format variables remain to be analyzed so that advertisers can draw useful conclusions for devising their messages. Thus, the length of the message, the message communicated through pictures, sounds, or words are other types of variables that are important to advertisers and on which few clear cut conclusions have been drawn.

Besides these structural variables that influence advertising effectiveness, one of the greatest limits of advertising was the ability of a message to pass successfully through the selective attention, selective distortion, and selective retention barriers. Of course, even if there are certain useful "gimmicks," for example, an appeal to the buyer's interests or the use of mechanical devices to attract the audience's attention, each message is one among hundreds vying for buyers' attention.

Buyer's Parallel Information Channels

Buyers generally do not rely on advertising for information. Indeed, buyers are faced with an information overload coming from different sources. Since they are unable to process all the information they are exposed to, buyers must consciously or unconsciously discard some information and select their information sources. This information overload is one of the principal limits to advertising effectiveness.

As was discussed, an advertising message must compete for the buyer's attention and against advertisements for the competing brands which, of course, generally give *contradictory* information. Furthermore, an advertisement also competes for the buyer's attention against all other advertisements. Indeed, if a consumer pays attention to a furniture advertisement, he or she cannot at the same time consider an advertisement describing the pleasures of a one-week vacation in Acapulco.

In addition, all advertising information received by a potential buyer is only a small part of this buyer's information about the products and brands on the market. Indeed, buyers' actions are very much influenced by the social groups to which they belong. First, a buyer's opinions and attitudes are influenced by these groups. Consumers are rewarded when their purchase behaviour complies with the norms of the group and are somehow sanctioned when it does not. Second, a great part of buyers' information originates from their social groups. Advertising through word-of-mouth plays a powerful role in buyer behaviour. According to the two-step flow of communication theory, advertising vehicled through the mass media influences only a small section of the market, which in turn can relay (or not relay) the advertiser's message.

Consequently, advertising is only one information source for the buyer. Unfortunately for the advertiser, this source is far from being the most effective, since personal communications considerably exceed mass communications in effectiveness. These important limits should be kept in mind when the effectiveness of advertising communications is assessed.

Other Elements of the Marketing Program

Another series of limits to advertising effectiveness can be found in the marketing program. As shown in Figure 9.10, buyer behaviour is far from being influenced only by advertising. The other marketing mix variables are also important: the product, the price, the distribution, and personal selling. As we have seen, advertising for a product is useless if this product is unlikely to respond effectively to some need of the consumer or if it cannot deliver the expected satisfaction. It is also useless to advertise a product if its price does not correspond to what the buyer is ready to pay or can pay to get it or if this product is not available at the buyer's local retailer.

Several conclusions can be drawn from these various constraints on the power of advertising. First, these constraints have the merit of showing that advertising is not independent from the other marketing tools. As was discussed in Chapter 2, the marketing program is a consistent and integrated plan with precise objectives. All the elements of the marketing program must be in harmony with these objectives. The role as well as the interdependence of the elements of the marketing program are highlighted in Figure 9.11.

Second, this interdependence shows that an advertising campaign must be devised in accordance with the other elements of the marketing program. *Otherwise, it cannot be effective.* Thus, the advertising message can be used only if the product does possess the advertised characteristics (otherwise the advertising would be deceptive, which, as we have already seen, would not be in the manufacturer's best long-run interest). Also, an advertiser cannot devise the campaign without considering the price of the product, which often influences the type and number of consumers who will be tempted by the product. In the same way, a campaign cannot ignore the product's distribution channels, because an advertising campaign must take into account the intermediaries in the distribution channels as well as the right mix of advertising and personal selling. This was discussed in Chapter 2, when the pull and push marketing strategies were outlined.

Finally, these constraints have an important impact on the advertiser's work method. Devising an advertising campaign is not the work of a single individual—the advertiser—nor the lonely creation of one artist. It is the task of an entire *marketing team*, for which the marketing program and the marketing objectives are of primary concern. Advertising must be integrated in this program and be given the role that only a mass communication tool can fulfil in a marketing program.

Industrial Buyer Behaviour

Although most of the principles of consumer behaviour apply to industrial advertising, industrial buyer behaviour does have unique characteristics.

Webster and Wind have developed a general model of organizational buying behaviour.[41] It identifies the important variables in the development of an industrial marketing strategy. The model does not describe any one specific buying situation; rather it brings together in a logical structure the variables known to influence industrial purchasing decisions.

According to this model, organizational buying behaviour is the result of four interrelated variables: the buying centre, buying tasks, organization structure, and buying technology. These variables are in turn influenced by such environmental factors as business fluctuations, governmental regulations, trade unions, and social and cultural values.

The Buying Centre

This concept encompasses all the members of

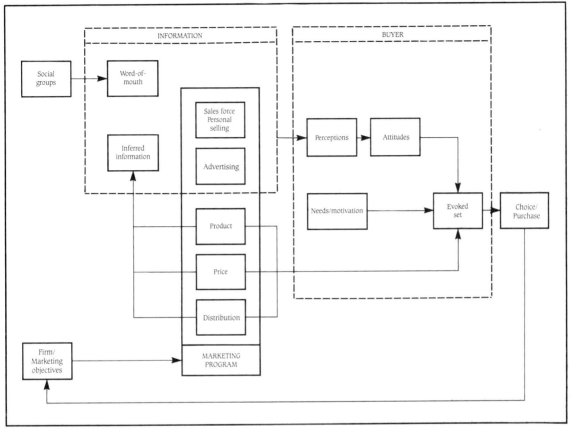

FIGURE 9.11   The Role of the Marketing Program in Influencing Buyer Behaviour

an organization that influence a buying decision. In discharging their duties, members of the buying centre have to perform the roles of users, buyers, influencers, deciders, and gate-keepers. An individual may occupy more than one role or several persons may share the same role. The purchasing agent is the person who usually places an order (buyer), and may also be the person who informs (gatekeeper) engineers and other production personnel (users and/or influencers) about available sources of supply.

Buying Tasks

The model defines five specific tasks outlined as five stages in a buying decision: identification of a need; establishment of specifications;

identification of alternatives; evaluation of alternatives; and selection of suppliers. At each of the five stages of the decision to buy, different members of the buying centre may be involved, different decision criteria are employed, and three different sources of information may be utilized.

Organizational Structure

The formal organizational structure consists of the sub-systems of communication, authority, status, rewards, and work flow. Some of these elements are evident from a company's formal organization chart, but industrial marketers must evaluate customers individually because the relationships among these sub-systems vary from one organization to another.

Buying Technology

The technology a company uses defines its plant and equipment. Its level of sophistication limits those products the company can buy and determines how it will buy them.

The model postulates that industrial buying is a problem-solving process. A problem is created when someone in the organization perceives a discrepancy between the present situation and a desired state of affairs. Although the model provides a useful framework for understanding how an organization behaves in order to solve its buying problems, it must be remembered that all organizational behaviour is human behaviour. Marketing efforts should always aim at the specific individuals who can influence the buying decision. Individual motives are both of a task and non-task nature. Task motives may predominate in most industrial buying situations. All other things being equal, non-task motives such as a pleasing personality, a free lunch, or a gift may influence a buyer to favour a particular source of supply.

Summary

The purchase process is a decision-making process under risk. The selection of one brand over all other brands is a process of optimizing the consumer's utility. This optimization is done under uncertainty, since the buyer does not have perfect information. Buyer decision-making can also be described as a Bayesian process. According to this process, buyers must always choose between making an immediate decision (to buy or not to buy) or delaying this decision to seek additional information, and thus reduce the decision risk. The buyer's post-purchase feelings may also be analyzed in the light of the theory of cognitive dissonance. Advertising has the potential to reduce a buyer's post-purchase feelings after an important purchase. A consumer's feelings after product usage can be described in terms of a simplified model of consumer behaviour that takes account of the psychographic, socio-economic, and cultural differences involved in the purchase process. To give a better understanding of the buyer decision process over time, buyers' information loads can be compared to a reservoir that is fed with new information and is drained through forgetting, as time elapses. In order to account for the time dimension of information processing by buyers and to assess the role of advertisers, different types of markets are identified.

Questions for Study

1. Consider an important purchase that you have made recently (for instance, stereo equipment, car, furniture, vacation tour). Show how the purchase process you followed was:

   (a) an optimization process.

   (b) a Bayesian decision-making process.

   Be specific.

2. Contrast the potential roles of advertising in pre-purchase and in post-purchase situations. Which role is likely to be more effective? Give specific examples.

3. Find examples of advertisements based on the theory of cognitive dissonance. Explain in what respects they apply this theory. Assess how adequately the theory applies to these specific situations.

4. Find examples of advertisements that you think make exaggerated advertising claims. Explain how these advertisements do or do not violate some of the principles discussed in this chapter. Can you suggest to the advertisers responsible for these ads plausible and more effective ways to advertise their products? Be specific.

5. Socio-economic and personality factors are likely to affect all the aspects of the consumer's decision process, which was described in chapters 7-9 and summarized in Figure 9.10. Suppose that a Canadian

travel agent wants to advertise a ten-day winter tour to Florida and is considering two possible market segments:

(a) higher income and higher-middle-class Canadians living in major Canadian cities;

(b) middle-income, lower-middle-class Canadians who are socially mobile and socially active.

6. Show how an important Canadian beer manufacturer should approach advertising a brand:
(a) in the Anglophone provinces
(b) in the Quebec market

7. Same question as 6, but the manufacturer considers exporting his beer to:
(a) Western European countries
(b) Eastern European countries
(c) Latin America

8. Explain the concept of a consumer's information reservoir. Why is this concept useful to an advertiser? Consider the cost-revenue aspects of the concept, from the consumer's point of view as well as from the advertiser's point of view.

9. How are the concepts of brand loyalty and brand switching related? Explain how these two concepts involve opportunities as well as liabilities to an advertiser.

10. Compare the behaviour of industrial buyers with that of ultimate consumers with respect to
(a) buyer motives and needs
(b) the number of people involved in the decision process
(c) the time it takes to sell the product
(d) the dollar value of the sales

Draw the corresponding implications for advertising targeted to these two types of market.

Using Figure 9.10, show how the purchase decision of the potential customers in the two market segments is likely to be different. How should or could an advertiser use these differences for designing an effective advertising campaign?

Problems

1. *(a)* A consumer is contemplating the purchase of a rather expensive watch. Using Figure 9.10, show how the purchase decision process is likely to differ when the purchase is intended
   • for the buyer
   • as a gift to a close relative.
(b) Does the model apply equally well to both situations? Explain.
(c) Outline plausible advertising strategies for both types of market segments, and contrast the major differences required for communicating with them.

2. *(a)* Find a family who has recently purchased a major durable good, such as an automobile. Through interviews with relevant members of the family, find out to what point the model of industrial buyer behaviour could apply to this purchase process.
(b) In the same way, after interviewing the purchasing agent of a medium or small sized firm about the typical decision process in the firm, find out to what point the purchase decision model in Figure 9.10 could be used to explain this process.

Notes

1. See, for instance, Paul E. Green and Frank J. Carmone, *Multidimensional Scaling and Related* *Techniques in Marketing Analysis* (Boston, Mass.: Allyn and Bacon, 1970).

2. For an operationalization of these concepts, see René Y. Darmon, "Extension du concept de carte perceptuelle aux perceptions floues," *Cahiers du 4e Séminaire de Méthodologie de la Recherche en Marketing* (Lille, France: Centre de Recherche d'Economie d'Entreprises, 1983), pp. 237-61.

3. Bent Stidsen, "Aspects of a Theory of Consumer Information Processing," *ASAC Proceedings* (1977), pp. 4-21.

4. For more details on this approach applied to marketing decision problems, see Paul E. Green, "Bayesian Statistics and Product Decisions," *Business Horizons* (Fall 1962), pp. 101-9.

5. See, for instance, M.T. O'Keefe, "The Anti-Smoking Commercials: A Study of Television's Impact on Behavior," *Public Opinion Quarterly*, 35 (1971), 242-48; J.H. Greenworld, "Dissonance and Relative vs. Absolute Attractiveness of Decision Alternatives," *Journal of Personality and Social Psychology*, 11 (1969), 328-33; J.W. Brehm and A.R. Cohen, "Re-evaluation of Choice Alternatives as a Function of Their Number and Qualitative Similarity," *Journal of Abnormal and Social Psychology*, 58 (1959), 373-78; J.W. Brehm and A.R. Cohen, *Exploration in Cognitive Dissonance* (New York: John Wiley and Sons, 1962).

6. Leon Festinger, *A Theory of Cognitive Dissonance* (Evanston, Ill.: Row, Peterson, 1957).

7. D. Ehrlick, I. Guttman, P. Schönback, and J. Mills, "Post Decision Exposure to Relevant Information," *Journal of Abnormal and Social Psychology*, 54 (1957), 98-102.

8. See, for instance, Leonard LoSciutto and Robert Perloff, "Influence of Product Preference on Dissonance Reduction," *Journal of Marketing Research*, 4 (August 1967), 286-90; Gerald D. Bell, "The Automobile Buyer After the Purchase," *Journal of Marketing*, 31 (July 1967), 12-16.

9. Shelby P. Hunt, "Post-Transaction Communication and Dissonance Reduction," *Journal of Marketing*, 34 (July 1970), 46-51.

10. S.A. Ahmed, "Personality Correlates of Product Purchase Behaviour: A Canadian Experience," *ASAC Proceedings* (1977), pp. 4-22.

11. See Ralph L. Rosnow and Edward J. Robinson, *Experiments in Persuasion* (New York: Academic Press, 1967), pp. 195-204.

12. I.L. Janis and C.I. Hovland, "An Overview of Persuasibility Research," *Personality and Persuasibility*, ed. I.L. Janis and C.I. Hovland (New Haven: Yale University Press, 1959), pp. 1-26.

13. H.H. Hyman and P.B. Sheatsley, "Some Reasons Why Information Campaigns Fail," *Public Opinion Quarterly*, 11 (1947), 412-23; C.E. Siranson, "Predicting Who Learns Factual Information from the Mass Media," *Groups, Leadership, and Men: Research in Human Relations*, ed. H. Guetzhow (Pittsburgh, Pa.: Carnegie Press, 1951).

14. H.J. Wegrocki, "The Effect of Prestige Suggestibility on Emotional Attitude," *Journal of Social Psychology*, 5 (1935), 382-94; D.W. Carment, C.G. Miles, and V.B. Cervin, "Persuasiveness and Persuasibility as Related to Intelligence and Extraversion," *British Journal of Social and Clinical Psychology*, 4 (1965), 1-7.

15. G. Murphy, L.B. Murphy, and T.M. Newcomb, *Experimental Social Psychology* (New York: Harper and Row, 1937), p. 930.

16. Donald F. Cox and Raymond A. Bauer, "Self-Confidence and Persuasibility in Women," *Public Opinion Quarterly* (Fall 1964), pp. 453-66; Abe Schuchman and Michael Perry, "Self-Confidence and Persuasibility in Marketing: A Reappraisal," *Journal of Marketing* (May 1969), pp. 146-54.

17. I.L. Janis and P.B. Field, "Sex Differences and Personality Factors Related to Persuasibility," *Personality and Persuasibility*, ed. I.L. Janis and C.I. Hovland (New Haven: Yale University Press, 1959), pp. 55-68.

18. A.R. Cohen, "Need for Cognition and Order of Communication as Determinants of Opinion Change," *The Order of Presentation in Persuasion*, ed. C.I. Hovland (New Haven: Yale University Press, 1957), pp. 79-97.

19. I. Sarnoff and D. Katz, "The Motivational Bases of Attitude Change," *Journal of Abnormal and Social Psychology*, 49 (1954), 115-24; D. Katz, C. McClintock, and I. Sarnoff, "The Measurement of Ego-Defense As Related to Attitude Change," *Journal of Personality*, 25 (1957), 465-74.

20. L. Berkowitz and R.M. Lundy, "Personality

Characteristics Related to Susceptibility to Influence by Peers or Authority Figures," *Journal of Personality*, 25 (1957), 306-16.

21. H. Leventhal and S.I. Perloe, "A Relationship Between Self-Esteem and Persuasiblity," *Journal of Abnormal and Social Psychology*, 64 (1962), 385-88.

22. A. Roland, "Persuasibility in Young Children as a Function of Aggressive Motivation and Aggression Conflict," *Journal of Abnormal and Social Psychology*, 66 (1963), 454-61.

23. D.P. Crowne and D. Marlowe, *The Approval Motive* (New York: John Wiley and Sons, 1964), chapter 8.

24. N. Miller, "Involvement and Dogmation as Inhibitors of Attitude Change," *Journal of Experimental Social Psychology*, 1 (1965), 121-32.

25. E.T. Hall, "The Silent Language in Overseas Business," *Harvard Business Review*, 38 (May-June 1960).

26. E. Dichter, "The World Customer," *Harvard Business Review*, 40 (July-August 1962), 113-22.

27. J.C. Chebat and G. Hénault, "The Cultural Behaviour of Canadian Consumers," *Cases and Readings in Marketing*, ed. V.H. Kirpalani and R.H. Rotenberg (Toronto: Holt, Rinehart and Winston, 1974), pp. 176-84; or in J.G. Barnes and M.S. Sommers, eds., *Current Topics in Canadian Marketing* (Toronto: McGraw-Hill Ryerson, 1978), pp. 74-84.

28. P.E. Lefrançois and G. Chatel, "The French Canadian Consumer: Fact and Fancy," *New Ideas for Successful Marketing Proceedings*, ed. J.S. Wright and J.L. Goldstucker (Chicago: American Marketing Association, 1966), pp. 706-15.

29. K.S. Palda, "A Comparison of Consumer Expenditures in Quebec and Ontario," *Canadian Journal of Economics and Political Science*, 35 (February 1967).

30. B. Mallen, "How Different is the French-Canadian Market," *Marketing: Canada*, ed. B. Mallen and I.A. Litvak (Toronto: McGraw-Hill, 1968), p. 26; also B. Mallen, *French Canadian Consumer Behavior* (Montreal: Advertising and Sales Executives Club, 1977).

31. M. Brisebois, "Industrial Advertising and Marketing in Quebec," *The Marketer*, 2, no. 1 (1960), 13.

32. Mallen, *French Canadian Consumer Behaviour*, p. 24.

33. Ibid., pp. 26-27.

34. N.K. Dhalla, *These Canadians* (Toronto: McGraw-Hill, 1966), p. 288.

35. Brisebois, pp. 13-14.

36. E. Clifford, "Tippers Reflect Diverse Tastes of National Mosaic," *The Globe and Mail*, 30 June 1979.

37. Roger M. Heeler and Rolf Seringhaus, "Buyer Behaviour in Emergency Situations," *Marketing*, vol. 2, ed. Robert G. Wyckham (Administrative Sciences Association of Canada, 1981), pp. 133-41

38. John A. Howard and Jagdish N. Sheth, *The Theory of Buyer Behavior* (New York: John Wiley and Sons, 1969), p. 150.

39. Bernard Berelson and Gary A. Steiner, *Human Behavior: An Inventory of Scientific Findings* (New York: Harcourt, Brace and World, 1964), p. 25.

40. Adapted from Philip Zimbardo and Ebbe B. Ebbesen, *Influencing Attitudes and Changing Behavior* (Reading, Mass.: Addison-Wesley, 1970), pp. 20-23.

41. Frederick E. Webster, Jr. and Yoram Wind, "A General Model for Understanding Organizational Buying Behaviour," *Journal of Marketing* (April 1972), pp. 12-19.

10

Advertising and Market Behaviour

The main challenge advertisers face is to design a single message for a large number of buyers who are essentially different. Although advertisers cannot hope to know all the consumers in the marketplace on an individual basis, they should still have an understanding of the aggregate market. That is, they should have as accurate a view as possible of the entire market *structure*—how buyers fall into various stages of the purchase behaviour process. This macro view of markets helps advertisers to make sound objective, budget, and media selection decisions. Chapter 10 describes markets at the macro level and assesses the effects of advertising on market behaviour.

A Static View of Market Behaviour

Market Structure at a Point in Time

Market Structure Analysis

As was seen in the preceding chapters, buyers in a market segment can be characterized by their status in the product/brand purchase decision process. At a certain time, not all buyers have reached the same stage because of different exposure to marketing information and past experience with the product class (Figure 10.1). Consequently, advertisers who want to understand the market structure need to know how many people have reached each stage of the process, and what are the main characteristics of the potential buyers in each stage of the purchase decision process.

Take, for example, a segment of the household coffee market. Among all the consumers who are potential coffee users, i.e., who could possibly experience a need or desire for coffee, only a certain percentage, say 95 per cent have perceived this need at a conscious level. The remaining 5 per cent may not be present in the coffee market because they are not aware of some desirable property of drinking coffee or for other reasons. The 95 per cent therefore constitute the market segment potential presently tapped by the coffee industry. Assume that 93 per cent of the hypothetical segment of the coffee market have sufficient knowledge as perceived by the consumers themselves about the product class to make an active transaction in the marketplace.

With respect to a specific brand, some buyers may or may not have achieved sufficient brand awareness. They may or may not know of the existence of the brand, or if they know of it, they may or may not feel that they have enough information about the attributes and characteristics of the brand. The percentage of brand aware consumers in a market segment is likely to vary widely depending on whether the brand is new or is well and long established in this market segment.

Assume that Brand X is well established and that 85 per cent of the consumers in this market segment have reached what can be considered a "sufficient" level of brand awareness. But people may be aware of a brand and still not consider buying it. Because of an outright negative evaluation of some brand characteristic, some consumers will not include this brand in

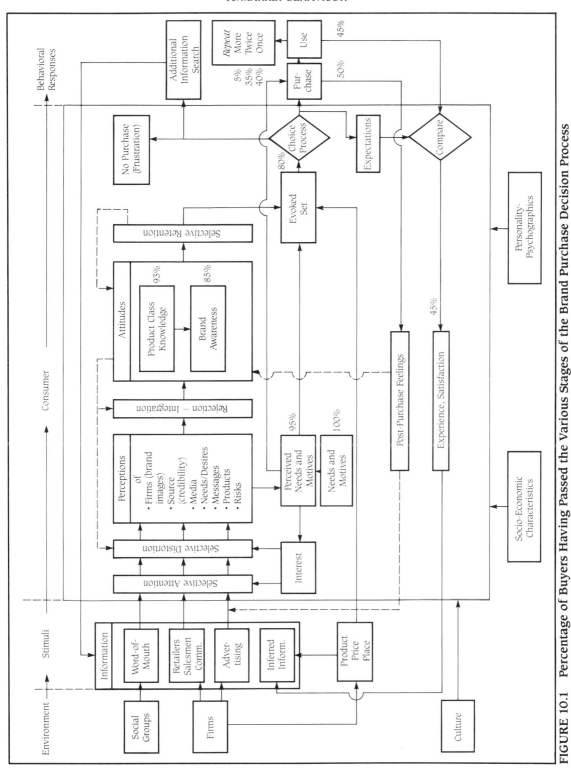

FIGURE 10.1   Percentage of Buyers Having Passed the Various Stages of the Brand Purchase Decision Process

their evoked set. If only a small fraction of brand aware consumers include the brand in their evoked set, this implies that the product is not considered a viable purchase. This can possibly happen if the communication program fails to properly communicate the advantages of using the brand, and/or if the purchase price falls beyond what the consumer is ready to pay, and/or if the brand is not conveniently available for purchase at retail outlets.

If a large proportion of brand aware consumers include the brand in their evoked set, this is an indication of a well accepted and potentially successful new product. Suppose 80 per cent of the potential consumers of coffee in the con-

TABLE 10.1 Buyers in the Different Stages of the Purchase Decision Process

Stages of the Purchase Decision Process	Percentage of Market Segment's Potential in Each Stage
1. Market segment's potential (needs)	100%
2. Market segment's perceived needs (tapped potential)	95%
3. Potential buyers perceiving they have enough knowledge about product class	93%
4. Buyers with sufficient brand awareness	85%
5. Buyers with brand in their evoked set (either tried or not)	80%
6. Buyers who have tried the brand at least once	50%
7. Buyers satisfied with first trial (i.e., keeping the brand in their evoked set as the brand preferred on certain purchase occasions)	45%
8. Buyers who have repeated the purchase at least once	40%
9. Buyers who have repeated the purchase more than once	35%
10. Buyers who insist on the brand in at least some purchase situations (perfect brand loyalty)	5%

sidered market segment include this rather well known and positively evaluated brand in their evoked set. Many of these consumers may not have tried the brand, for a number of reasons. For instance, a purchase occasion may not have arisen yet (this is more likely to be felt for long purchase cycle products such as ethical drugs); or the brand may compare less favourably on some key dimension with some competitive brand; or the consumer may lack information and has not yet decided which brand to select.

Assume that 50 per cent of the potential consumers have tried Brand X at least once. Among all those who have tried the product, a firm cannot expect all of them to still prefer its brand. Some of the triers will be completely dissatisfied with the brand. Others will rate the brand as inferior to others and will switch back to their usual brand. Others will prefer the brand in at least some purchase or consumption occasions and will keep the brand in their evoked set.

Assume that 45 per cent of the consumers in the market segment will have kept Brand X in their evoked set after trial. Some of them, say 40 per cent, will repeat the purchase at least once. Some people may not have had the chance to repeat the purchase because of the lack of consumption or purchase occasion, especially in the case of longer cycled consumption products. Some consumers may have repeated the purchase of Brand X more than once, let us say 35 per cent, and among them, a certain proportion might have reached "perfect" brand loyalty and may have bought only this brand over an extended period of time. Although this type of brand insistence is relatively rare for consumer products, it is not unusual for large-ticket items such as cars or electrical appliances.

Table 10.1 shows this hierarchy of buyer stages and the percentages of people who have completed one or more stages of the process at some point. This static view of a given market segment can be compared to an instant camera picture of the market at some point, where each buyer is "frozen" in whatever stage has been reached at the time of the picture.

The stages in the purchase decision process selected for this hypothetical case are not unique. Other intermediate stages could be included or deleted depending upon their relevance to the type of product under consideration. For instance, all the repeat purchase stages will be included for a well-established, frequently purchased brand. However, most of these stages will probably be deleted for some infrequently

purchased durable good. In the same way, the brand evaluation stages may be deleted in the case of well-established and well-known brands in a consumer product class, but they would give relevant information on a new brand trying to penetrate some market segment. The point here is that whatever the market, it can be broken down into a small and meaningful number of discrete stages. The number of potential buyers seen in this overall picture of a market at some point in time give a view of the present structure of a market segment.

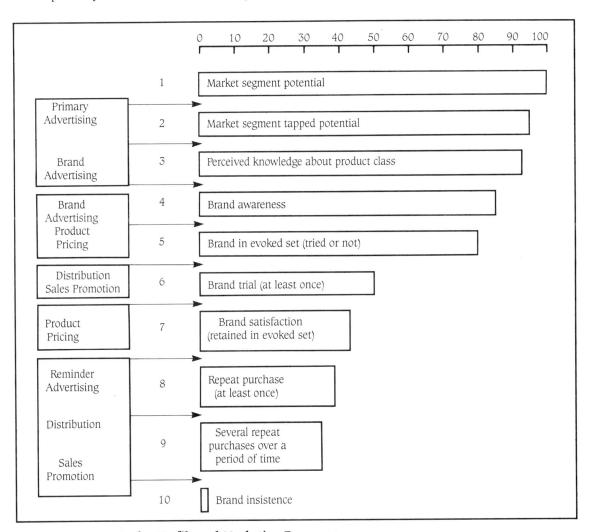

FIGURE 10.2 Market Profile and Marketing Programs

Market Structure and Marketing Program

A more detailed representation of a market structure is given in Figure 10.2, with the same example as that in Table 10.1.[1]

The number of individuals who are at a given stage of the decision process constitutes only a fraction of the number of those who are at the preceding stage, hence the diagram has a characteristic inverted pyramid shape. Obviously, as much as possible, a firm would like to obtain a diagram structure where all the bars would have the same length at 100 per cent. This would mean that 100 per cent brand insistence is achieved for the brand. This is practically impossible to achieve, of course, as this would imply complete saturation in a monopoly-type market. Thus, the sharper and thinner the inverted pyramid is at the bottom the less deeply the brand has penetrated a market.

The question then is, what can a marketer do to improve the shape of the pyramid for his brand? Or what can marketers and advertisers do to achieve a brand's market penetration? The main marketing tools and functions of the marketing program that are mostly involved between each two steps of the process are shown at the left of the diagram. Thus, primary advertising or industry advertising can bring product class awareness and information to potential consumers. Brand advertising promotes brand awareness. Product features, product quality, relative and absolute price levels, and attractiveness of a brand's characteristics help bring a specific brand into consumers' evoked sets. To induce consumers to try at least once a product which is in their evoked set, distribution and sales promotions are key elements of the marketing program. Whether consumers will be generally satisfied with their first experience with a brand depends essentially upon the product's actual performance and its performance in relation to price. Reminder advertising, distribution intensity, and sales promotion will induce consumers to repeat their purchases and will eventually bring consumers to the most desirable level of brand loyalty and brand insistence. Thus, it is essential that advertising be co-ordinated with the other elements of the marketing program in order to achieve market penetration.

Advertisers and marketers can address any group of consumers who are at any stage of the purchase process. They can attempt to bring any group to any state without necessarily having to bring all the consumers through all the consecutive stages. For instance, a brand manager can convert new consumers in the product class through free sample distribution, even though these consumers may not even be aware of the brand.

The Diagnostic Value of Market Structure Analysis

The value of a market structure analysis is its ability to diagnose potential weaknesses in a brand marketing program and/or in the advertising communication program.

The classification of products and brands in Figure 10.3 is based upon the efficiency of the product/price/distribution mixes and upon the efficiency of the advertising/promotion programs. Successful brands should have an efficient product/price/distribution mix as well as an effective communication program. These brands fall into the first quadrant of the classification.

A brand could be unsuccessful in terms of sales volume as a result of a poor communication/promotion program alone (these are products/brands in the fourth quadrant of the classification); as the result of ineffective product/price/distribution mixes alone (brands in the second quadrant); or the fault of both types of programs (brands in the third quadrant). The brands in the second and the third quadrants of the classification are generally impossible to salvage, especially if the product's quality and performance do not live up to consumers' expectations or if the marketing program has been directed toward the improper market segment. However, properly designed advertising/promotion campaigns can salvage potentially successful brands.

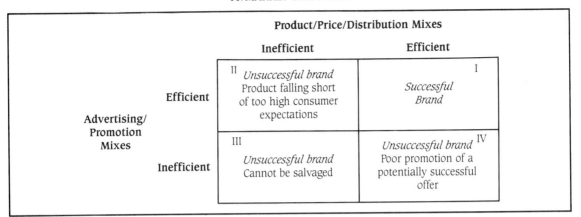

FIGURE 10.3   Classification of Successful and Unsuccessful Brands
According to Failing Marketing Mix Elements

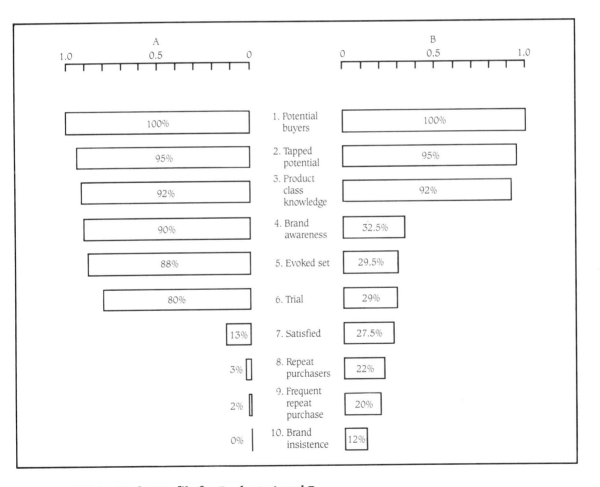

FIGURE 10.4   Market Profile for Products A and B

This idea is highlighted by the two brand profiles in Figure 10.4.

Brand profile A shows a product that falls into quadrant 2 of the preceding classification. A substantial proportion of the potential market, 80 per cent, has tried the brand at least once, which suggests an effective advertising/promotion program. However, only 20 per cent of those who have tried the product have been satisfied with the brand. This indicates that the product has failed to deliver the satisfaction and meet consumers' expectations raised by the advertising claims, because of unsatisfactory product performance, a relatively inferior product compared to competition, or an inadequately priced product.

Brand profile B is typical of a brand falling in quadrant 4 of the classification in Figure 10.3. A large proportion of people knowledgeable about the product class, 65 per cent, are not aware of the brand. This is the responsibility of the communication program. Among the consumers who are aware of the brand, a high proportion, 90 per cent, have tried the brand, which indicates effective distribution and sales promotion programs. A high proportion of the triers, 95 per cent, are satisfied with the product, and most of them (76 per cent) have repeated the purchase.

These examples of profiles A and B illustrate the diagnostic value of a market structure analysis. The information contained in a brand's profile sets the potential of an advertising campaign to deliver adequate and effective communications to the market and the limitations of advertising, since advertising alone cannot make up for poor programs in other areas of the marketing program. A clear understanding of the market profile is essential to advertisers for defining, as will be seen in Chapter 11, advertising objectives, when changing the orientation of an advertising campaign, or when pursuing a certain course of action.

Advertising Effects on Market Behaviour

Knowledge of the present state and structure of a market is not sufficient for designing an effective advertising campaign. It is also important to know how advertising can affect the various parts of a market and what advertising resources are needed to obtain a certain type and range of performance. This relationship between advertising resources or imputs and the market response or output is known as the *market response function to advertising.*

The Static Market Response Function to Advertising

Advertising effort is defined as all the resources involved in an advertising campaign—the amounts spent on advertising media, on research, and on production costs. This effort also includes such qualitative elements as the creative aspects, which is the effectiveness of individual advertisements in conveying the message to the market. The total amount of these resources will be designated by the letter E, assuming that all these resources could be estimated and accounted for.

As more resources are included in an advertising program, sales should increase. But according to the principle of decreasing marginal returns, as increasing amounts of advertising resources are invested in the same market, eventually marginal returns (additional sales) start declining. This is why sales are generally represented as an S-shaped curve (Figure 10.5a) or by a concave curve (Figure 10.5b).

The S-shaped curve in Figure 10.5a generally describes the sales curve for new products. If no advertising resources were invested in marketing the product, sales would certainly stay at zero level. If only a few resources were devoted to the advertising program, sales would still be extremely low, since few potential buyers would have the opportunity to learn about the product and retailers would not be interested in giving the product valuable shelf space. Only after a

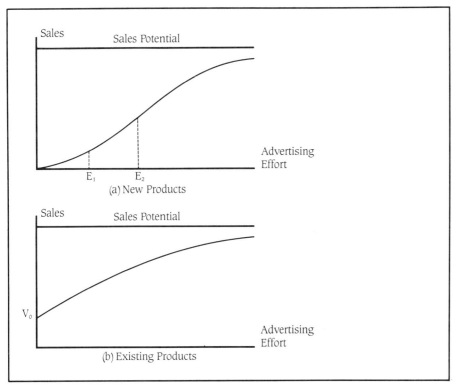

FIGURE 10.5   Sales Response Functions to Advertising Effort

certain marketing effort level (E_1 in Figure 10.5a) will the advertising program start producing valuable results and continue to a certain point (E_2). After this point, the principle of decreasing marginal returns applies. If the advertising effort were increased up to infinity, sales would approach a ceiling that could not be surpassed. Even on intuitive grounds, once a market is saturated, no additional advertising effort should be able to induce consumers to buy more of a certain product. This asymptotical upward limit of sales represented in Figure 10.5 by horizontal lines is what marketers usually call the company sales potential. For example, whatever the size of the marketing effort, a manufacturer of colour television sets would not be able to sell in one year more units than the number of households that do not yet own one colour television set. (One might also account for replacement needs and for households that want more than one set).

The second curve of Figure 10.5 more readily applies to the sales response function to advertising efforts for existing products. Here, the curve intercepts the sales axis at V_0. The rationale is that even with no marketing effort during the current year, the company would still sell some amount (V_0), as a result of advertising efforts initiated during preceding years and which continue to have some effect. These effects are called carry-over effects.

Some Empirical Evidence on the Advertising Sales Response Function

Several methods can be used to estimate the relationship between advertising and consumer information processing variables (such as brand awareness), or attitudinal variables (such as brand preference), and/or behavioural variables (such as sales). These methods include experimentation and statistical analysis and are discussed further in Chapter 15. This section is concerned with some important studies on the nature of the relationship between advertising and buyer response variables.

EXPERIMENTAL STUDIES.   Most empirical studies have shown a positive relationship between sales levels and advertising expenditures. In 1962, Du Pont conducted an experiment on the advertising for its Teflon finish for cookware.[2] Four cities received ten daytime commercial minutes per week during the autumn months, five cities received five minutes per week, and four cities in the control group did not receive any advertising. Sales of Teflon cookware were measured through personal interviews in all cities involved in the experiment. Total purchases of the cookware were found to be about 30 per cent higher in the cities with heavy advertising than in the cities with no advertising. In heavily advertised areas, the market share was nine per cent as compared to five per cent in the other cities.

A similar experiment was conducted by the Missouri Valley Petroleum Corporation.[3] The findings were that cutting advertising expenditures in half produced no significant sales decrease, which suggested that cutting the advertising appropriation could be done without loss in sales. Doubling the present level of advertising expenditures resulted in significant sales increases over a three-year period, while spending three times as much resulted in a smaller increase than did doubling the size of the present advertising budget. This experiment suggests that after a certain level, the sales response function may turn down, perhaps from over-saturation and fatigue on the part of consumers.

Another experiment by Eskin attempted to estimate the joint effects of advertising expenses and price variations (Figure 10.6).[4] This experiment involved 30 stores in each of four test cities. In two cities, a high level of advertising was used. In two other cities, a low level of advertising was implemented. In each city, three groups of ten stores were matched for

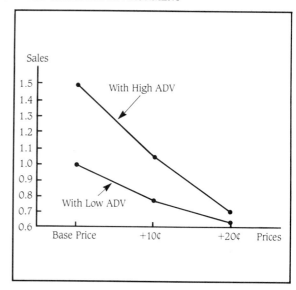

FIGURE 10.6   Results of the Eskin Experiment

SOURCE: Adapted from Gerald Eskin, "A Case for Test Market Experiments," *Journal of Advertising Research* (15 April 1975), pp. 29, 31.
Copyright © 1975 by the Sloan Management Review Association. All rights reserved.

identical sizes and other relevant factors. In each group of ten stores, prices were manipulated so as to be a base price—the base price of test items were below 50¢; a base price plus ten cents; and a base price plus 20¢, respectively. Each month the unit sales were recorded in each store.

This experiment led to several conclusions: the higher advertising level always led to higher sales; there was a strong interaction between the advertising levels and the price levels; higher advertising levels resulted in relatively higher sales at lower prices than lower advertising levels at lower prices; and both sales volumes were higher than high or low advertising levels at high prices.

An extensive series of experiments for the Budweiser Company started in 1962 and was conducted by two leading operations researchers, Ackoff and Emshoff.[5] These experiments found a double peaked sales response curve to advertising expenditures. As a possible

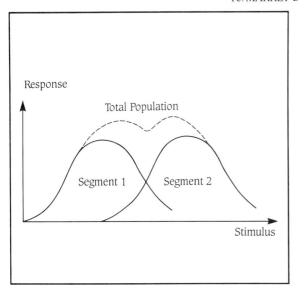

FIGURE 10.7   The Two Market Segment Hypothesis

SOURCE: Russell L. Ackoff and James R. Emshoff, "Advertising Research at Anheuser-Busch, Inc. (1963-68)," *Sloan Management Review* (Winter 1975), pp. 8-9.

explanation, the authors hypothesized two market segments with each segment displaying an increasing and then decreasing response function, but with each peak occurring at different advertising levels (Figure 10.7).

A more recent an experiment for AT&T by Kunitsky et al. on the effects of advertising also led to a positive relationship between sales and advertising level.[6]

THE DEMON MODEL.   Charnes et al. developed a well-documented model called DEMON (Decision Mapping Via Optimum Go-No Networks) for a leading advertising agency, Batton, Barton, Durstine, and Osborne (BBD&O).[7] (See Figure 10.8.) The portion of the model discussed here is limited to the sales response function to advertising dollars. The objective of this part of the DEMON model is to evaluate alternative introductory plans for new products. In order to achieve such an objective, an advertiser must specify the sales response function to advertis-

ing spending. Charnes's model formalizes and quantifies this relationship.

The link between advertising dollars and demand or sales dollars is specified as a succession of cause-effect relationships and is assessed in conjunction with other important marketing variables, particularly sales promotion, distribution, and price. These relationships were studied through statistical analysis of 200 packaged goods products in 16 product categories. The first relationship links gross rating points (GRP), a measure of audience size, to advertising expenditures. Because large media discounts are generally available to large scale volume purchasers, the function has the exponential shape shown in Figure 10.8.

In the same way, gross rating points have been related to the *unduplicated audience* (or *reach*) to whom the message has been communicated. As is discussed further in Chapter 14, the campaign reach is the number of individuals in the target audience exposed at least once to an advertisement during the campaign. *Frequency* refers to the average number of times that an individual in the target audience is exposed to an advertising message during the campaign. The relationship between gross rating points (GRP), reach (R), and frequency (F) is:

$$GRP = R \times F$$

Charnes et al. found the relationship between gross rating points and reach to be concave. Reach in turn is used to explain advertising awareness. Advertising awareness is defined as the number of people in the target audience who can recall having seen or heard the advertisement (i.e., people who not only can recall the brand but also are aware of the advertising claim). This relationship is found to be highly non-linear and can be expressed by several curves, depending on the rate of advertising spending relative to the industry and the creative value of the advertisements. Advertising awareness leads in turn to product trial. Trial is defined as the proportion of people in the target market who purchase the product

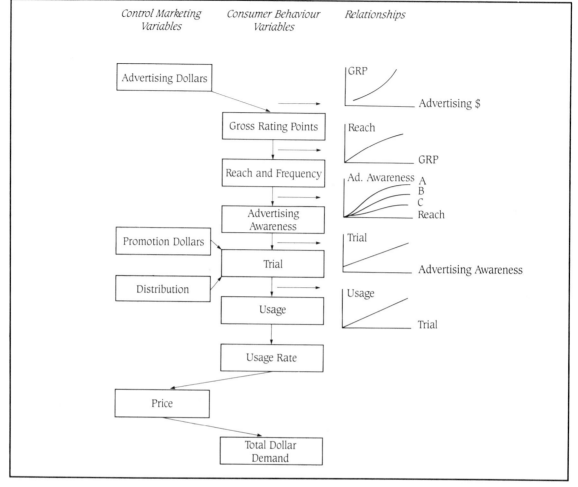

FIGURE 10.8   The DEMON Model

for the first time. The relationship between advertising awareness and trial is linear, as shown in Figure 10.8. In the same way, there is also a linear relationship between product trial and product usage. In this context, users are defined as consumers who purchase the product a second time.

Thus, given a certain advertising expenditure, it is possible to estimate the effect of product usage through this series of recursive relationships. With the estimate of the number of users and the distribution of the rate at which the product is used, multiplied by the unit price, an estimate of the sales volume in dollars can be derived. From here, an estimate of the corresponding profits can also be made by taking into account the marketing expenses involved in the marketing program.

The DEMON model is much more mathematically involved than the simple non-technical description given here. It has been extended to include a decision framework to balance the cost and benefits of additional research in order to decrease the risks (and the costs) of wrong estimates and bad advertising decisions. A complete description of this model is well beyond the scope of this chapter. Its purpose here is to serve as an example of how advertisers can fruitfully use the concepts of the communication process to better understand the relationship between advertising and sales, as well as to provide some empirical evidence for the nature of some of the relationships discussed previously.

The Dynamics of Market Behaviour

A good knowledge of the present state of a market is a necessary first step toward understanding the potential and the limits of advertising. However, marketers and advertisers as well should have a dynamic view of markets: how they evolve over time, how fast they change, what are the main flows of consumers within the market, and so on. This understanding is essential because advertising campaigns are not likely to be assigned the same role in a market that is relatively stable over time as in a very fast, evolving market. Because advertising campaigns must be planned well in advance, will be implemented in a more or less distant future, and will result in some future sales revenues, an advertiser must have as precise an idea as possible of what the market will look like at the time the advertising campaign will be actually run. The main time-related phenomena that affect consumers' responses to advertising actions are forgetting and remembering of brand attributes and advertising claims, as well as any relevant facts the consumers possess that bear upon a purchase decision.

Empirical Evidence on Remembering and Forgetting

A large amount of research supports the concepts of remembering, forgetting, and carry-over or lagged effects of communications. Some of this empirical evidence pertains to the assessment of the effects of advertising messages upon such communication variables as advertising recall or advertising awareness over time. Other research relates advertising expenditures to sales over time.

Communication Effect Studies

Remembering and forgetting were first studied at the individual level in laboratory experiments. Among the early works, the studies by Ebbinghaus[8] and, in an advertising context, by Strong[9] should be mentioned. However, the advertising forgetting and remembering phenomena at the aggregate or market level were first studied in a now-classic experiment by Hubert Zielske.[10] Zielske used thirteen different advertisements from the same national newspaper campaign for a widely used food product. The thirteen advertisements were mailed to two groups of women randomly drawn from the telephone directory, each group according to a different schedule.

The first group received the message at weekly intervals over a period of thirteen consecutive weeks, and the second group received the same thirteen advertisements mailed at the rate of one every four weeks, over a 52-week period.

Recall of advertising was measured through 3640 telephone interviews throughout the year, in such a way that respondents were interviewed only once. The rationale was to avoid the possible bias that could have been introduced, as previous interviewing might have artificially increased the recall level. The main results are shown in Figure 10.9.

The two curves of Figure 10.9 show the percentages of households who remembered the advertisements during the 52-week period of the study. For the first group which received the thirteen advertisements at a one-week interval, the rate of advertising recall grew faster relative to the number of advertisement than for the second group which was exposed to the messages at the four-week intervals. For the first group, the rate reached the peak after the thirteen weeks at the level of 63 per cent of the respondents remembering the advertise-

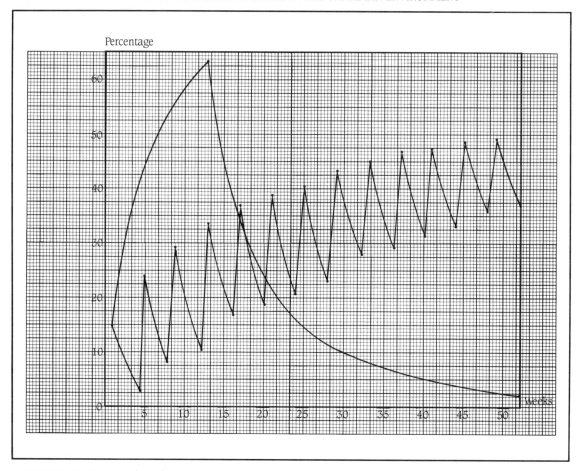

FIGURE 10.9   Results of Zielske's Experiment

ment, compared with 48 per cent after the thirteenth message for the second group.

The most striking finding of the study is the surprisingly high rate of forgetting. For the first group, four weeks after the last exposure the recall rate dropped from 63 to 32 per cent and eventually reached a low of four per cent at the end of the year. But, as can be seen on the recall rate curves of the second group, the rate of forgetting decreased as the number of exposures increased. Three weeks after the first exposure, the percentage of women who could remember the advertisement decreased from 14 per cent to three per cent, which is a decrease of 79 per cent [100 (14 − 3) ÷ 14].After the thirteenth exposure, the forgetting rate over

a similar four-week period was only 37 per cent, from 48 per cent.

These results have implications for scheduling advertising messages, as was suggested in Chapter 8. For instance, to sustain an overall level of awareness in the market, the spread-over-year exposure pattern gives better results (an average of 29 per cent of the households remembered the advertisement over the 52-week period of the experiment), than a burst of exposures within a short period of time (21 per cent for the second group). However, the second pattern gives better results to reach a peak during a certain period (as would be desirable for highly seasonal products), i.e., 63 per cent against 48 per cent of the spread-over pattern.

In 1978 Zielske and Henry extended this type of experiment to television advertising.[11] They expected to find some differences in the rates of response in comparison with the print experiment of 1959:

> ... The steepness of the curve is more characteristic of a television schedule. The reason is that the full audience of a television commercial is accumulated immediately, while the full audience of a magazine insertion takes weeks or even months to accumulate.[12]

They recorded and analyzed the unaided advertising recall measurements in 17 different tracking studies, which are studies that monitor the recall of advertisements by an audience over time. These studies involved a total of six products and services and were based on 25 000 interviews. The authors concluded that the mathematical model that best fitted the data was:

$$\triangle A_t = 0.030\, W_t - 0.92\, A_{t-1}$$

where:

$\triangle A_t$ = percentage change in unaided recall
W_t = target rating points in week t
A_{t-1} = unaided recall in t−1

In this equation, the first term, $0.030\, W_t$. is the average learning rate. Thus, if 100 target points were achieved in week t, this would result in three additional percentage points of unaided recall. The second term of the formula, $-0.92 A_{t-1}$ is the average forgetting rate. Thus, if in the previous week a level of 10 per cent of unaided recall had been achieved, it would drop to 9.08 per cent the following week as the sole result of forgetting. This study reached exactly the same conclusions as the 1959 study, except on one point: in 1978, no decrease in forgetting rates at higher exposure levels was found.

Several other studies have attempted to fit mathematical models to empirical advertising remembering and forgetting data. Strong proposed an equation that can simultaneously account for the forgetting and the reinforcement effects even during the period when an exposure takes place.[13] This equation was found to fit empirical data in a satisfactory way. Other recent attempts to model the dynamic communication response to advertising include those of Little,[14] Lodish,[15] Little and Lodish,[16] and Ray and Sawyer.[17] All these studies support the notions of forgetting, remembering, and diminishing marginal responses to additional advertising exposures.

Sales Response Studies

Sales response studies involve statistical analyses of time series sales and advertising expense data. For instance, one of the classical examples is Palda's study based on the Lydia Pinkham Company.[18] This study covered a 54-year period, from 1906 to 1960. The objective of the study was to explain sales as a function of advertising expenditures. The specific situation selected for this study was characterized by a large proportion of sales revenues spent on advertising (about 50 per cent), the only important marketing controllable variable for this product, and the product had no close substitute on the market, which gave Lydia Pinkham a monopoly position for this product category. Palda found that, among several models, the one which gave the best fit to the Lydia Pinkham data was the so-called Koyck's distributed lagged model, with three additional explanatory variables (time period, disposable personal income, and a shift in sales after 1925). The model is:

$$Q_t = -3649 + 1180 \log X_t + 0.665\, Q_{t-1} + 774\, D + 32\, t - 2.83\, Y_t$$

where:

Q_t = sales in thousands of dollars in year t
X_t = advertising expenditures in thousands of dollars in year t
D = a dummy variable taking the value 1 for years before 1926 and 0 after
Y_t = disposable personal income in billions of current dollars in year t.

Advertising expenditures best predict sales when they are expressed in logarithmic form. This suggests that sales increase at a diminishing marginal rate as advertising increases. On the other hand, the carry-over effect appears in the equation as the coefficient of $Q_{t-1}(0.665)$. From this equation, Palda derives the conclusion that one additional dollar spent on advertising would result in $1.44 in sales in the long run, although only $0.537 would be gained immediately.

In general, an accurate measurement of these carry-over effects is a difficult task because regression analysis, which is the underlying technique of analyzing the data, lacks sensitivity. Actually, the carry-over estimate is sensitive to the time periods into which the data have been broken down. As was shown by Clarke,[19] annual data tend to yield longer carry-over effect estimates than quarterly or monthly data.

Another difficulty with this type of analysis is that although a relationship between sales and advertising expenditures can often be detected, it is not too clear in what direction the causation runs. As will be seen in Chapter 11, a very popular (although theoretically unappealing) method of setting an advertising budget is to apply a certain fixed percentage to the sales volume achieved in the previous year. In such cases, it is not clear whether the advertising causes the sales volume or whether the sales volume is the cause of advertising expenditures. More sophisticated statistical techniques exist to address this problem, however. For instance, Bass[20] and Bass and Parsons[21] have used simultaneous equation systems to model these more complex two-way causal relationships.

To sum up, various experiments and analyses generally support the existence of important time-related aspects of the effects of advertising on communication variables and/or on sales. The presence of carry-over effects largely caused by advertising remembering, decay of past advertising effects mainly due to advertising forgetting, diminishing marginal responses to additional messages when they are concen-

trated in a relatively short period of time, are now widely demonstrated phenomena. As will be seen in Chapter 15, knowing and being able to properly estimate these effects have important implications for scheduling the advertising program and setting up the media plan. However, assessing the sales response functions to advertising is not an easy task in practice. As can be surmised, sales or even consumer stages in the communication process are only one result of advertising. Furthermore, these relationships are likely to display quite different outlooks depending on such external factors as the type of product and market under investigation, the economy, or the firm's competitive situation.

Dynamic Models of Market Behaviour

An Analytic View of Sales

In Chapter 9, different types of markets were described, as well as the types of action that an advertiser could undertake to increase sales. One essential question that must be addressed then is how an advertiser can select one type of action among the others. The answer depends on such questions as: How many consumers are loyal? How many consumers could be easily persuaded to switch to other brands? Are many consumers of other brands prone to switch to our brand? It also depends on the ability and the cost of advertising to perform one task rather than another. What is needed to answer these questions is not only a static view of the market but also an understanding of how consumers behave *over time* and how they choose one brand over another.

Advertisers often acquire insights into markets by considering the brand sales in units (S) as the product of three basic factors: the number of buyers in the market (n); the proportion of buyers who have purchased the brand during a considered period of time (p); and the average quantity of the brand purchased by each consumer in the market during the considered time period (q). In other words,

$$S = n \cdot p \cdot q$$

In short purchase cycle markets, such as the market for gasoline or cigarettes, a marketer can try to increase sales by increasing either n or p (n · p = N), which is the number of people buying the brand. In irregular purchase cycle markets (for products such as desserts), a marketer can often try to increase sales by acting on n or q. Finally, in long or unpredictable purchase cycle markets such as the market for most durables, an advertiser can influence sales by trying to increase p, the proportion of people who buy the brand or make in question. Although the following classifications of markets and corresponding advertising objectives do not cover all market situations, they are adaptable to a variety of situations.

Short Purchase Cycle Markets

MARKET SHARE ANALYSIS.   Short purchase cycle markets are characterized by routine purchase decision processes or limited problem solving (Chapter 9). Such markets are best thought of in terms of consumer flows observed between two consecutive periods of time. Let us consider as an example, some segment of the household coffee market. Assume that in this segment or area only four brands compete, brands A, B, C, and D. Let us also assume that households in this market segment buy roughly the same quantity at each purchase occasion, which occurs at roughly regular intervals of one month.

The first type of information that marketers would like to know when they want to understand market evolution, is how market shares have evolved over the relevant period of time. Let us assume that an advertiser has observed how the four competing brands, A, B, C, and D have shared the market in terms of number of purchases at the beginning and at the end of a one-month period, between two consecutive

TABLE 10.2   Market Shares in Two Consecutive Time Periods

	Market Shares at Time	
	t	t + 1
Brand A	20%	23%
Brand B	10%	11%
Brand C	30%	33%
Brand D	40%	33%
Total	*100%*	*100%*

consumer purchases. The brand shares at the beginning and at the end of the period are shown in Table 10.2.

It can be seen that Brand A has gained 3 percentage points of market share, that brands B and C have also gained 1 and 3 percentage points respectively, and that Brand D is the loser with a loss of 7 percentage points. However, a decreasing or an increasing market share does not say much about the cause of the decrease or increase. Furthermore, brand shares are often quite stable despite much brand switching.[22] A description of the consumer flows between the various brands purchased at the two consecutive purchase occasions gives some insight into market behaviour that market share analysis alone cannot provide.

CONSUMER FLOW ANALYSIS.   Let us assume then that an advertiser has also observed how *each* consumer in the coffee market segment has behaved over the one month period. As shown in Figure 10.10, potential customers may take one of 25 possible paths, represented by the arrows on the diagram. They could have taken one of the sixteen paths revealing that the two consecutive purchases they actually made were the brand at the start of the arrow for the first purchase to the end of the arrow for the second purchase. As can be seen in Figure 10.10, there are 12 possible paths that imply a brand switch (arrows from one brand to other brands), and four possible paths which imply "brand loyalty" (i.e., arrows from one brand to the same brand). In addition, the market observer could also notice that some people have entered the market by purchasing one of the four brands of coffee at the second period purchase occasion but not at the first. Conversely, some consumers have left the market by purchasing at the first occasion but not at the second. Finally, some potential consumers have stayed out of the market and have not purchased at all during the considered period of time.

Consumers enter and leave markets for many reasons. The flows of consumers in and out of the markets are represented by the arrows between brands and the outside of the market segment. What constitutes a market segment is not a steady set of customers, but rather a moving mass of individuals, some leaving and

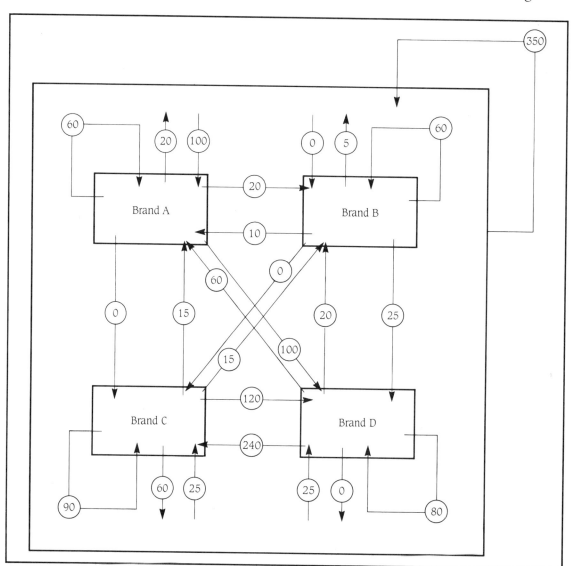

FIGURE 10.10   Consumer Flows within a Market Segment Between Two Points in Time

TABLE 10.3   Brand Switching Matrix

		PERIOD t + 1						
		Brand A	Brand B	Brand C	Brand D	0	Total	Market Shares
P	Brand A	60	20	0	100	20	*200*	20%
E	Brand B	10	60	0	25	5	*100*	10%
R	Brand C	15	15	90	120	60	*300*	30%
I	Brand D	60	20	240	80	0	*400*	40%
O	0	100	0	25	25	350	*500*	—
D								
t	Total	*245*	*115*	*355*	*350*	*435*	*1500*	100%
	Market Shares	23%	11%	33%	33%	—	100%	

some entering the market constantly. It is a well known saying in advertising circles that one does not advertise to an audience but to a parade.

Suppose that now there are 1500 potential consumers in this coffee market segment. Each potential consumer must have followed one of these 25 paths revealing his behaviour during the time period considered. The number that is circled in each arrow in Figure 10.10 represents the number of potential consumers who have followed each path. For instance, among the 1500 potential consumers of the market segment, 100 bought Brand B at the first purchase occasion. Among these 100 buyers of Brand B, 60 repeated their purchase at the following purchase occasion, while ten switched to A, none to C, 25 to D, and five left the market, and so on. Although Figure 10.10 conveys well the idea of consumer flows over time, it is not very convenient to analyze the flows. A better way is to summarize this information in the form of a *brand switching matrix* (Table 10.3).

The brand switching matrix shows how each of the 1500 consumers who were in a certain purchase status in period t have stayed in the same purchase category, or have switched to another brand, or have left the market at least for that period. The zero state, i.e., the no-purchase state, allows one to account for those consumers who have left, who have entered, or who have remained out of the market during the period under investigation. Thus, it can be seen by reading each row of the table that out of the 400 people who bought Brand D in period t, 60 switched to A, 20 to B, 240 to C; 80 repeated their purchase, and none left the market during this time period. A similar interpretation can be made for each row of the matrix.

It is now possible to understand why the market shares given in Table 10.2 have changed the way they did. It is apparent that there is a quite substantial switching activity among the different brands in this market segment. This switching activity would not have been detected if one had looked only at the market share variations of each brand over the considered period of time.

Another useful indication that could not be found by a simple market share analysis is an indication given by the brand switching matrix about market expansion or retraction during the time span covered by the analysis. The number of potential consumers who are not in the market at the beginning and at the end of the period gives a useful indication as to whether the market is expanding (i.e., if more new buyers have entered than left the market).

TABLE 10.4   Probability Transition Matrix

		PERIOD t + 1					
		Brand A	Brand B	Brand C	Brand D	0	Total
P E R I O D t	Brand A	0.30	0.10	0.00	0.50	0.10	*1.00*
	Brand B	0.10	0.60	0.00	0.25	0.05	*1.00*
	Brand C	0.05	0.05	0.30	0.40	0.20	*1.00*
	Brand D	0.15	0.05	0.60	0.20	0.00	*1.00*
	0	0.20	0.00	0.05	0.05	0.70	*1.00*

Conversely, if the number of potential customers who have not bought has increased, this is certainly an indication that the market has been shrinking. In the coffee market segment example, 500 potential consumers were not active buyers at the beginning of the period, against 435 at the end. Consequently, if this trend could be confirmed over a certain number of consecutive periods, this would be a clear indication of an expanding market segment.

PROBABILITY TRANSITION MATRIX ANALYSIS.   From the data of the brand switching matrix given in Table 10.3, another very useful matrix can be derived: the probability transition matrix (PTM). This matrix is obtained by dividing each cell of the brand switching matrix by the corresponding row total. Thus, the probability or, more exactly, the proportion of not switching or of switching to any other brand given that a consumer has purchased any given brand at the preceding purchase occasion can be obtained. For example, consumers who have purchased Brand C in period t have probabilities of 0.05, 0.05, and 0.40 to switch to brands A, B, and D, respectively. They have a probability of 0.30 to repeat their purchase of Brand C and a probability of 0.20 to leave the market, at least temporarily. A similar interpretation can be made of each row of the probability transition matrix. The PTM for the coffee market segment data is given in Table 10.4.

Operations researchers have used the probability transition matrix to forecast future market

shares.[23] By assuming that the probabilities remain constant in the probability transition matrix, it is possible to compute the market share for the following period. For instance, the number of consumers purchasing Brand A in period t + 2 would be:

$$(245 \times 0.30) + (115 \times 0.10) + (355 \times 0.05) + (350 \times 0.15) + (435 \times 0.20) \doteq 242$$

This simple type of computation applies to all the other brands as well, and therefore, one can derive the market shares for each brand in t + 2. If the process is kept going in the following periods (mathematicians call this process a stationary Markov chain), the market shares of each brand quickly tend to stabilize in an equilibrium. The assumption that the probability transition matrix is constant has been quite rightly challenged by marketers,[24] who have somewhat discredited the technique as a long-run forecasting device. What critics have often overlooked, though, is that the market probability transition matrix is a powerful analytical tool for understanding market dynamics and can be of valuable help, especially to advertising decision makers.

Analysis of the probability transition matrix of Table 10.4 gives insights into the dynamics of market behaviour. The following information can be systematically analyzed.

Market leaving rates.   The market leaving rates for each brand can be found in the rectangle in the right side of Table 10.5. As could be

TABLE 10.5   Market Leaving, Market Entering, and Brand Loyalty Rates

		PERIOD t + 1					
		Brand A	Brand B	Brand C	Brand D	0	Total
P E R I O D t	Brand A	0.30	0.10	0.00	0.50	0.10	*1.00*
	Brand B	0.10	0.60	0.00	0.25	0.05	*1.00*
	Brand C	0.05	0.05	0.30	0.40	0.20	*1.00*
	Brand D	0.15	0.05	0.60	0.20	0.00	*1.00*
	0	0.20	0.00	0.05	0.05	0.70	*1.00*

expected, the expansion or retraction rate of the market reflects the differences between new customers entering the market and those leaving the market. The same rate could result from both flows being large or small. In addition, it may be useful to know if all the brands in the market experience approximately the same leaving rates. For instance, in Table 10.5, the leaving rates might be judged to be overall on the high side (0, 5, 10, and 20 per cent). In addition, there are substantial differences among the brands. No consumer has left the market after an experience with brand D in period t. This may be an indication that consumers are satisfied with the product class after usage of Brand D. At the other extreme, 20 per cent of those having consumed Brand C have left the market at least temporarily, possibly for the opposite reason.

Market entering rates. The market entering rates appear in the rectangle in the last row of Table 10.5. As for the leaving rates, some brands may be able to attract new product class users better than others in the market. This can possibly happen as the result of deliberate marketing and advertising strategies designed to attract new product class users. As an example, consider the Commodore VIC-20 advertisement (Figure 10.11), which is directed at potential buyers of personal computers.

In the coffee market segment example, one can readily see that Brand A has been quite

successful in attracting new product users. At the other extreme, Brand B does not seem to

FIGURE 10.11   This advertisement directed at buyers entering the personal computer market uses the "reason-why" approach.
Courtesy Commodore Business Machines Limited

appeal to this category of customers, while brands C and D have been moderately successful in this respect.

Brand loyalty rates. In the same way, a market can be characterized by a general level of high or low brand loyalty. In relatively high loyalty markets, almost all the figures in the main diagonal of the probability transition matrix (Table 10.5) are high and can possibly approach one. Such markets consequently display relatively low brand switching rates. Conversely, low loyalty markets are characterized by relatively low rates in the main diagonal of the

FIGURE 10.12 By emphasizing "Now, more than ever...", Matinée is addressing its present customers and reinforcing the reasons for remaining loyal to the brand.
Courtesy Imperial Tobacco Limited, Montreal

matrix, and they must display high brand switching rates. In the example of the coffee market segment, loyalty is generally low, except for Brand B, which seems more able than its competitors to retain its own customers. This could be a strategy deliberately pursued by an advertiser. The Matinée advertisement (Figure 10.12) seems to have been designed to retain the brand's present customers and give them arguments for reinforcing their present attitude toward the brand.

A low or high loyalty rate has implications for scheduling the advertising messages, as confirmed by Kenneth Longman:

> .... If a brand has a good record of holding its new customers, it may be highly efficient to advertise in pulses rather than continuously. On the other hand, for a brand with a poor record of holding its new customers, the advertiser may need to keep up a steady effort in order to attract and hold customers.[25]

Brand switching—out rates. The values taken by these rates logically depend on the values taken by the loyalty rates, as was explained. Knowing which other brands were chosen by the customers who switch out of one brand generally provides advertisers with valuable information. If customers are more or less evenly lost to all the other brands in the market, this may indicate general dissatisfaction with the brand after it has been tried, especially if the switching out rates are higher than those experienced by most competitors. If, on the other hand, customers are lost to some competing brand more than to others, this may be the result of a competitor's deliberate advertising strategy. This competitor may be successfully using appeals to which the present users of the brand are more sensitive than others. The switching-out rates for Brand A arc given in the first-row rectangle in Table 10.6. In this case, it may be interesting to the advertiser of Brand A to notice that 50 per cent of customers switched to Brand D but none were lost to Brand C.

TABLE 10.6   Switching in and Switching out Rates for Four Different Brands

		PERIOD t + 1					
		Brand A	Brand B	Brand C	Brand D	0	Total
P E R I O D t	Brand A	0.30	0.10	0.00	0.50	0.10	*1.00*
	Brand B	0.10	0.60	0.00	0.25	0.05	*1.00*
	Brand C	0.05	0.05	0.30	0.40	0.20	*1.00*
	Brand D	0.15	0.05	0.60	0.20	0.00	*1.00*
	0	0.20	0.00	0.05	0.05	0.70	*1.00*

Brand switching—in rates. The switching-in rates for Brand A are indicated in the rectangle of the first column of Table 10.6. In this case, it can be seen that Brand A has been only moderately successful in attracting consumers from competing brands. It seems, though, that the consumers of Brand D are more susceptible than others to switch to Brand A. Actually, the relatively high mutual rates of switching in and out of brands A and D as well as brands C and D

FIGURE 10.13   Olivetti tries to attract buyers who may have been attracted to its leading competitor.

Courtesy Olivetti Canada Limited

(i.e., the customer exchange rates among two brands) suggest that the brand may be close enough in the consumer's mind and that competition is stronger among these pair of brands in this market segment. Advertisers can try to attract consumers from other brands, which is the goal of comparative advertising (Figure 10.13).

POSSIBLE ADVERTISING STRATEGIES. The analysis carried above for Brand A for the switching in and switching out rates can and should be done for all the competing brands in the market, in order to gain insight into market behaviour. It should be stressed, however, that the conclusions drawn from such market behaviour analyses are valuable only insofar as they are stable over time. Advertisers should observe behaviour over a sufficiently large number of periods until the flows observed reveal some consistent and meaningful pattern or trend. Only relatively stable trends should serve as a basis for advertising strategy decisions.

An advertiser who analyzes the consumer flows in the coffee market segment, assuming that what he can observe are typical of a trend, could make useful strategy decisions. For instance, the advertiser of Brand A could probably try to keep its appeal to new product category users, and at the same time try to keep them from switching to Brand D, by trying to build some brand loyalty. The advertiser of Brand B may decide to try to address new users in order to attract his fair share of this relatively large category of consumers. As for Brand C, it could capitalize on its ability to attract former customers of Brand D and retain them in larger proportions. Finally, Brand D is the more troublesome brand in the hypothetical market segment. Although it has an important capacity to attract customers from the other brands (especially brands A and C), it loses them in still larger numbers, especially to Brand C. Unless this is caused by poor product performance, an advertising campaign for Brand D could try to build up brand loyalty and prevent customers from leaving for Brand C, for instance.

The problem of advertising objective and strategy definition is even more complex, since consumers cannot be expected to buy the same quantity of the product. Moreover, the difficulty and cost of achieving the different tasks on various consumer groups should also be taken into account. For instance, are heavy users as responsive to advertising claims as light users? What about the small proportion of consumers who use a very large proportion of a product? As will be discussed in Chapter 11, such considerations affect the choice of specific advertising objectives.

From an operational point of view, market share analysis and brand switching or probability transition analyses are not difficult to carry out, not even when one must collect the relevant data. In consumer goods markets, most firms will have access to such data from syndicated consumer panels.[26] Such analyses provide a convenient framework in which advertising decisions can be made with a proper understanding of market behaviour. This framework can also be used to assess the effectiveness of specific advertising campaigns.[27]

Irregular Purchase Cycle Markets

MARKET ATTITUDE LEVEL DISTRIBUTIONS. In general, small ticket items are characterized by irregular purchase cycles. Desserts, for example, can be bought by consumers several weeks in a row. Then, many weeks or even months may elapse before the same consumer buys it again. In such cases, it is essential that potential consumers maintain a positive attitude toward the brand. But a more important consideration is that a firm create purchase occasions. The objective is to bring back as many consumers as possible and as often as possible into the active market, each period of time. This process can be understood by generalizing the individual attitude model described in Chapter 8 at the market level (Figure 10.14).

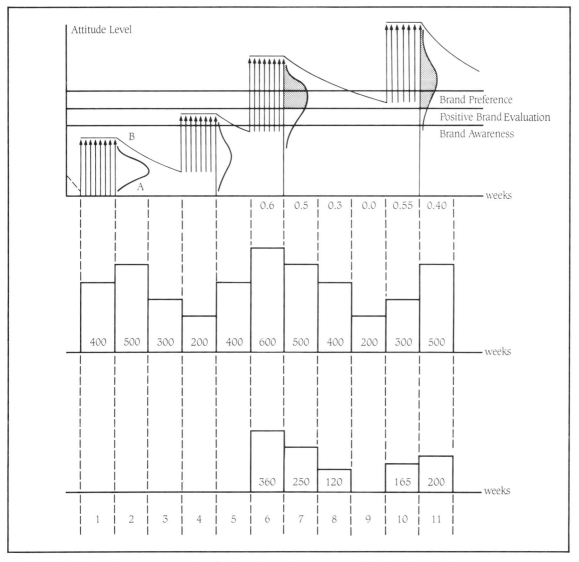

FIGURE 10.14 Consumer's Attitude, Purchase Occasion, and Sales Distributions

The upper diagram of Figure 10.14 describes the impact of a series of advertisements on consumer attitude levels. However, at the aggregate level, all the consumers in the market segment cannot be at the same stage of readiness to buy a certain brand, since not all buyers have been equally influenced by the advertisements, or buyers may experience different forgetting and remembering rates. Consequently, at the end of the first series of ads in week one of the example of Figure 10.14, each consumer may have reached an attitude level anywhere between, say A and B. The number of people who have reached the different levels between A and B can best be described as a distribution. This hypothetical distribution is represented besides the AB segment. Because no consumer has yet reached the necessary positive brand evaluation stage after week one, no sale of the brand can occur. Since no advertising takes place during weeks two and three, the general attitude level in the market decays as forgetting occurs. And the same process starts all over again with the new series of advertisements in week four, and so forth.

At the end of week six, the series of advertisements that have taken place during that week have brought a certain number of potential customers of the market segment above the level of positive brand evaluation required for brand purchase, if a purchase occasion does occur. According to the corresponding consumer distribution, about 60 per cent of the potential consumers in the market segment are above this level and consequently are potential candidates for a purchase that week. Because of the attitude decay when no advertising takes place, this proportion falls to 50 per cent, 30 per cent and zero per cent for weeks seven, eight, and nine, respectively. Because of the advertisements scheduled for week ten, this proportion is raised to 55 per cent in week ten and drops to 40 per cent in week 11 as no advertisement has been run, and so on.

PURCHASE OCCASION DISTRIBUTION. For a purchase to occur, not only should consumers be psychologically ready to buy a brand but a purchase occasion must also occur simultaneously. In irregular purchase cycle markets, purchase occasions are likely to occur over time with a certain distribution that reflects cyclical and seasonal variations. This distribution can be represented by the diagram in the middle of Figure 10.14. For instance, in week one, 400 consumers in the considered market segment have experienced a purchase occasion for this type of product. However, because none has yet reached a sufficient level of positive brand evaluation, no purchase can occur, as indicated on the diagram at the bottom of Figure 10.14. In week six, the first purchases of the brand can occur because 60 per cent of the consumers in the market segment have reached or surpassed this minimum attitude level. Since 600 purchase

occasions have occurred during this week, the brand can be expected to be bought 360 times (i.e., 600 x 0.6). The same reasoning applies to subsequent weeks, and consequently, the distribution of sales is shown at the bottom diagram of Figure 10.14. This sales distribution is the product of the number of consumers who are given the occasion and are willing to buy this type of product, and of the proportion of consumers in the market segment who have sufficiently positive attitudes toward the brand to buy it.

The great difficulty advertisers face in irregular purchase cycle markets is that they must simultaneously influence two aspects of the purchase process. First, they must try to improve consumers' attitudes and brand comprehension in order to bring as many consumers as possible above the minimum positive brand evaluation level. Second, they must also make sure that as many purchase occasions as possible are created in a given week. As was already seen, two types of strategies can be followed, depending on the type of product advertised. One strategy consists in increasing the average purchase volume of each consumer, for instance by suggesting new usages for the product, and at the same time showing that the brand is in a unique position to produce the desired results. This approach is used in Figure 10.15.

Advertisers may try to persuade consumers to buy more categories of the same brand by suggesting new purchase occasions and recipes for their products. Or they may attempt to encourage consumers to buy the brand at a faster pace through reminder advertising, promoting the features that distinguish the brand from other brands in the same general product category (see Figure 10.16).

As with short purchase cycle markets, the market model for irregular purchase cycle markets gives advertisers a useful framework for understanding the market, finding new advertising opportunities, and setting limitations on adver-

FIGURE 10.15 There are many occasions for consumers to use Campbell products. The company's special cookbook provides consumers with new ideas for using—and reasons for buying— Campbell products.
Courtesy Campbell Soup Company Ltd.

FIGURE 10.16 By proposing Hamburger Helper for occasions when consumers are in a hurry, the advertiser tries to sell the product for new usage occasions and accelerate the consumption rate.
Courtesy General Mills Canada Ltd.

tising. Consequently, it should also help decide on advertising objectives and strategies to be followed in any given market segment.

Long or Unpredictable Purchase Cycle Markets

For understanding and visualizing this type of market, the same framework as the one proposed for the irregular purchase cycle markets can be used. However, advertisers often have little or even no control over the purchase occasion distribution over time. In such markets, the role of the advertiser is to keep the largest possible proportion of potential buyers above the brand preference level. When the need arises, these consumers will select the advertised brand. This approach is illustrated by the Leo Chevalier advertisement (Figure 10.17).

Although product types and selling situations differ widely even within the three broad types of markets described above, the above framework for understanding and visualizing markets at the aggregate level encompasses sufficiently large number of situations to be of some value to advertisers and advertising students alike. In any case, advertisers should select the market model that can provide the best understanding of market behaviour and of possible advertising actions and market responses. The models proposed here should be viewed as convenient ways for advertisers to

FIGURE 10.17 With this advertisement Leo Chevalier is attempting to convey a positive image for its shirts—one that will pay off when a buyer enters the market occasionally.
Courtesy Leo Chevalier Men's Wear

who are at the various stages of the decision process. Such static market structure analyses have a diagnostic value, because they can be used to evaluate the potential and the limitations of advertising in the market behaviour influence process. The role of advertising in influencing market behaviour can also be analyzed in the context of market response functions to advertising.

The analysis can be extended to include the time dimension. Remembering and forgetting are important concepts at the global market level, and there is some empirical evidence to support the validity of these concepts. Different dynamic models of market behaviour that are useful for visualizing a market and for making sound objective and strategy decisions can be outlined for the three types of market: short, irregular, and long or unpredictable purchase cycle markets.

think about their markets and as an aid in designing sensible advertising campaigns with well-thought-out objectives.

Summary

Many of the concepts of individual buyer behaviour can be extended and studied at the aggregate market level, so that advertisers can gain a global view of a market and an understanding of an entire market's response to advertising actions. Such an understanding helps an advertiser to make sound objective, budgeting, and media decisions. A market can be described in terms of the number of buyers

Questions for Study

1. Using the framework described in Chapter 10 for static market structure analysis, provide a more specific model which, in your opinion, adequately describes the market for a brand of the following product categories:
   (a) a Jello-type product
   (b) kingsize filter cigarettes
   (c) compact cars
   (d) stereo equipment
   (e) shaving cream

2. Why is it important for an advertiser to have as explicit and as formal as possible an evaluation of:
   (a) the sales response function to advertising
   (b) the communication response functions to advertising

3. Using the probability transition matrix in Table 10.4, show how the market share of the different brands would stabilize.

(a) What would be the equilibrium market shares?

(b) After how many periods would this equilibrium be reached?

4. How should the probability transition analysis be modified to account for products that are bought in significantly different quantities by consumers? Give examples of such products.

5. How should the probability transition matrix analysis be modified to account for products for which the time span between consecutive purchases is very different from one consumer to another? Give examples of such products.

6. Why is it so important for advertisers to include the forgetting and remembering effects in the sales response function to advertising? Are such effects likely to be more important for certain products than for others?

7. Use whatever model of dynamic market behaviour you feel appropriately describes the following markets:
(a) Jello-type products
(b) kingsize filter cigarettes
(c) compact cars
(d) stereo equipment
(e) shaving cream

8. Look at a few recent issues of a magazine. Find some examples of what you think could illustrate the following advertising strategies:
(a) attracting new product users
(b) attracting buyers from competing brands
(c) preventing present customers from switching to other brands
(d) trying to accelerate the purchase rate

(e) increasing the average purchase volume of each consumer
(f) building positive attitudes while waiting for the purchase occasion to arise

Problems

1. Select a firm that conducts advertising campaigns and interview an advertising executive or manager. Find out which type of information this firm has about the sales response function to advertising from:
(a) formal data collection and analysis
(b) informal executive judgements

Critically evaluate these procedures. What recommendations (if any) would you make to this firm? Explain.

2. Select five major brands of gasoline sold in your area. Select two or three retail outlets for these brands and at each outlet interview at least five customers at the time they are purchasing gasoline at the station. Record the brand of their previous gasoline purchase. Assume that the data you have collected are representative of the local gasoline market.
(a) From these data, build a probability transition matrix for the gasoline market in your area.
(b) Analyze the consumer flows in this market and draw any relevant conclusions on market dynamics.
(c) What are the long-run market shares for the different brands?
(d) What marketing/advertising strategies would you recommend for each brand?
(e) What are the main limitations to the analysis you have just carried out?

Notes

1. The use of this type of analysis was first proposed by John C. Maloney, "Attitude Measurement and Formation" (Paper presented at the American Marketing Association Test Market Design and Measurement Workshop, Chicago, 11 April 1966).

2. James C. Becknell, Jr., and Robert W. McIsaac, "Test Marketing Cookware Coated with 'Teflon'," *Journal of Advertising Research*, 3 (September 1963), 4-5.

3. Charles M. Sevin, "What We Know About Measuring Ad Effectiveness," *Printer's Ink*, 9 July 1965, pp. 47-53; experiment discussed in David A. Aaker and John G. Myers, *Advertising Management,* 2nd ed. (Englewood Cliffs, N.J.: Prentice-Hall, 1982), p.70.

4. Gerald J. Eskin, "A Case for Test Market Experiments," *Journal of Advertising Research*, 15 (April 1975), 27-33.

5. Russell L. Ackoff and James R. Emshoff, "Advertising Research at Anheuser-Busch, Inc. (1963-1968)," *Sloan Management Review* (Winter 1975), pp. 1-15.

6. Alan Kunitski, Emily Bussam, Alvin Silk, and John D. Little, "Development, Testing, and Execution of a New Marketing Strategy at AT & T Long Lines," *Product Management: Quantitative Methods in Marketing*, Proceedings of the 9th International Research Seminar in Marketing (Aix-en-Provence, France: IAE, 1982), pp. 451-92. See also F.W.A. Bliemel, "Are Thresholds of Advertising Response Substantial?" *Linking Knowledge and Action*, ed. James D. Forbes, (Administrative Sciences Association of Canada, 1983) vol. 4, pp. 1-10.

7. A. Charnes, W.W. Cooper, J.K. De Voe, and D.B. Learner, "DEMON: Decision Mapping Via Optimum Go-No Networks—A Model for Marketing New Products," *Management Science*, 12, no. 11 (July 1966); A. Charnes, W.W. Cooper, J.K. De Voe, and D.B. Learner, "DEMON Mark II: An External Equation Approach to New Product Marketing," *Management Science*, 14, no. 9 (May 1968); D.B. Learner, "Profit Maximization through New Product Marketing, Planning, and Control," *Applications of the Sciences in Marketing Management,* ed. Frank M. Bass, Charles W. King, and Edgar A. Pessemier (New York: John Wiley and Sons, 1968), pp. 151-67.

8. Hermann Ebbinghaus, *Grundzuge der Psychologie* (Leipzig: Viet, 1902).

9. Edward K. Strong, "The Effect of Length of Series Upon Recognition," *Psychological Review*, 19 (January 1912), 44-7.

10. Hubert A. Zielske, "The Remembering and Forgetting of Advertising," *Journal of Marketing*, 23 (March 1959), pp. 239-43.

11. Hubert A. Zielske and Walter A. Henry, "Remembering and Forgetting Television Ads," *Journal of Advertising Research*, 20 (April 1980), 7-13.

12. Ibid., p. 7.

13. Edward C. Strong, "The Use of Field Experimental Observations in Estimating Advertising Recall," *Journal of Marketing Research*, 11 (November 1974), 369-78.

14. John D.C. Little, "Models and Managers: The Concept of a Decision Calculus," *Management Science* (April 1970), pp. 466-85.

15. Leonard M. Lodish, "Empirical Studies on Individual Responses to Exposure Patterns," *Journal of Marketing Research*, 8 (May 1971), 214-16.

16. John D.C. Little and Leonard M. Lodish, "A Media Planning Calculus," *Operations Research* (January-February 1969), pp. 1-35.

17. Michael L. Ray and Alan G. Sawyer, "Repetition in Media Models: A Laboratory Technique," *Journal of Marketing Research*, 8 (February 1971), 20-29.

18. Kristian S. Palda, *The Management of Cumulative Advertising Effects* (Englewood Cliffs, N.J.: Prentice-Hall, 1964).

19. Darral G. Clarke, "Econometric Measurement of the Duration of Advertising Effect on Sales," *Journal of Marketing Research*, 13 (November 1976), 345-57.

20. Frank M. Bass, "A Simultaneous Equation Regression Study of Advertising and Sales of Cigarettes," *Journal of Marketing Research*, 6 (August 1969), 291-300.

21. Frank M. Bass and Leonard L. Parsons, "Simultaneous Equation Regression Analysis of Sales and Advertising," *Applied Economics*, 1 (1969), 103-24.

22. Frank M. Bass, "The Theory of Stochastic Preference and Brand Switching," *Journal of Marketing Research* (February 1974), pp. 1-20.

23. See, for instance, Donald G. Morrison, "Testing Brand Switching Models," *Journal of Marketing Research*, 3 (November 1966), 401-9; David B. Montgomery, "A Stochastic Response Model with Application to Brand Choice," *Management Science*, 15 (March 1969), 323-37; David B. Montgomery, "Stochastic Consumer Models: Some Comparative Results," *Marketing and the New Science of Planning*, ed. R. King (Chicago: American Marketing Association, 1969).

24. A.S.C. Ehrenberg, "An Appraisal of Markov Brand Switching Models," *Journal of Marketing Research*, 7 (November 1965), 347-62.

25. Kenneth A. Longman, *Advertising* (New York: Harcourt Brace Jovanovich, 1976), p. 136.

26. These concepts are discussed more thoroughly in Chapter 15.

27. Irvin M. Grossack and Robert F. Kelly, "Measuring Advertising Effectiveness: Use of the PTM," *Business Horizons* (Fall 1963), pp. 83-88.

CAMPAIGN HISTORIES FOR PART 3

1. Air Canada Skifari 1981-82 Campaign

2. Knorr-Swiss Soups and Sauces

3. Atlas Copco Corporate Campaigns

CAMPAIGN HISTORY 1

AIR CANADA SKIFARI 1981-82 CAMPAIGN
Advertising a ski package to Western Canada

ADVERTISER: Air Canada
AGENCY: Publicité Foster Limitée

Situation Summary

Skifari is synonymous with the best ski packages to Western Canada. Since its inception in 1971, it has had an excellent response from consumers and the travel trade, which accounts for 85 per cent of total sales.

Skifari offers the Eastern skier the widest selection of ski packages to Western Canada at *very* competitive prices. The packages are to the following ski areas: Banff/Lake Louise, Jasper, Sunshine, and Whistler.

For the 1981-82 season the product has been expanded and improved. Skifari packages include five or six days of Western skiing, including accommodations, lift tickets, and transfers to and from the slopes. This year the Skifari skier has the option of a mid-week departure (for an additional $20.00 per booking) or a weekend departure. The product is available from December 1, 1981 to April 30, 1982.

Touram Inc. (an Air Canada company) is the exclusive wholesaler of the Skifari product. Hemisphere, Skican, and UTL are the three wholesalers for competing Western ski packages. Apart from Canada, the major competition consists of ski packages to Vail, Aspen, and Utah (offered by Toronto charter operators). Europe is not a significant factor.

Advertising Objectives

The objectives of the campaign are:

(a) to position the Skifari product as offering the best value in Western ski travel (i.e., the widest choice at competitive prices *plus* the Air Canada convenience and service) to the consumer and to the travel trade

(b) to communicate the product features and availability to target audiences

and, by doing so, to help sell 2000 Skifari packages together with attendant Air Canada travel.

Positioning Statement (Theme)

Skifari is the established brand—and the leader—in best-value ski travel to the best in Canadian skiing.

It is the leader because it offers
  • widest choice
  • competitive prices
  • flexible departure times
  • Air Canada service
  • Air Canada convenience
  • Air Canada dependability

Timing

Product availability: December 1, 1981—April 30, 1982
Selling period: October 1, 1981-April 30, 1982
Time horizon of the campaign: October 15, 1981—March 15, 1982

Target Audiences

1. Male and female skiers
  • both single/married
  • aged 18 + (with consideration in the 21-34 age group)
  • income of $15,000 +
  • living in or near
    —Quebec City
    —Montreal
    —Toronto
    —Ottawa

2. Travel agents operating in or near
- Quebec City
- Montreal
- Toronto
- Ottawa

Advertising Strategy

The Skifari product offers the consumer the top of the line in Canadian skiing—destinations that are famous for the best snow, the best runs, and the best conditions. Skifari offers the widest selections of packages to those destinations, at very competitive prices, together with the reliability of the Air Canada name. We intend to capitalize on the obvious appeal of that combination to both the confirmed and aspiring skier.

Our approach is calculated to generate the most excitement in the media most targeted to our specific audiences—in other words, reach them when and where it matters most. Consideration of Skifari travel patterns together with the advance booking requirement have led us to be highly selective as to the choice and emphasis of consumer media. This will be demonstrated in the media recommendations.

To reinforce our product awareness and strengthen our franchise among travel agents, we have planned that trade advertising be sustained throughout the selling period. As further support to our consumer and trade campaigns, we recommend the distribution of a Skifari poster to agencies and Air Canada locations within our specified geographic market. All elements should have a unified "Skifari 81-82" look in order to achieve maximum impact. We have also been organizing a promotional tie-in with Norvinca Inc. to support our primary campaign.

Creative Rationale

It is understood that the creative requirements for this year's Skifari campaign are:

1. consumer ads
2. trade ads
3. posters

Because of the important role that the brochure will play, we are recommending the retention of the photographic "theme" established by the brochure. The mountain visual immediately conveys to our audience what we believe to be the most important motivating factor: snow.

Price obviously plays an important part in the selection of a ski holiday. Our package prices will be featured in bold type, but will be secondary in emphasis to the main visual.

We feel our consumer ad headline, "SKI THE WEST FOR HIGH ADVENTURE," which relates to the slogan line on the brochure, positions the product more clearly as a Western Canada offering. This theme will be carried through trade advertising and other necessary collateral.

Media Objectives

1. Direct advertising to the following target audiences:
   (a) English- and French-speaking adults aged eighteen years and over, with emphasis on the 21-34 year age group with a personal income of $15,000 plus per year;
   (b) English- and French-speaking travel agents.
2. Advertise in Air Canada's following key markets:
   Montreal, Quebec, Ottawa/Hull, Toronto/Hamilton.
3. Schedule advertising from October 15, 1981 until March 15, 1982.
4. Re-create awareness of the Skifari product.
5. Select media in compliance with the creative strategy.

Media Strategy and Rationale

A combination of consumer ski magazines, daily newspapers, and travel trade publications is recommended to promote Skifari.

One-page black-and-red advertisements will be utilitized in *Ski-Québec* and the Eastern edition of *Ski Canada*. The November issue of *Evasion* has been recommended because of its special editorial on skiing, part of which will be on major ski areas in Western Canada. The publisher has guaranteed that the Skifari advertisement will run adjacent to editorial on Jasper. The agency is also recommending the Skifari advertisement be scheduled in "Ski-Mag," which will be a special pull-out section in the November issue of *Actualité*. "Ski-Mag" will have editorial matter on equipment, fashions, new ski trends, Canadian ski destinations, and ski holidays. The agency has negotiated with the publication to have the Skifari advertisement adjacent to editorial on Western Canadian ski resort destinations.

Six-hundred-line black-and-white newspaper advertisements will be utilized in special ski supplements or features where available. In all other instances, advertisements will be scheduled from mid-November 1981 through mid-March 1982. Should appropriate ski features become available, the agency recommends scheduling the advertisements into the features.

Six-hundred-line black-and-white advertisements have also been scheduled in the official language markets. English and French travel trade publications are recommended to promote Skifari to travel agents. Black-and-red 7″ × 10″ advertisements will be scheduled from mid-October 1981 until mid-March 1982. Editorial content on skiing has also been taken into consideration. The recommended travel trade publications were selected based on their ability to reach travel agents effectively.

Radio and television have been rejected because they are not affordable within the available budget.

Outdoor/transit were rejected because of non-compliance with creative strategy, and they are not affordable within the available budget.

Media Budget Summary

Magazines	23.5%
Newspapers	61.2%
Travel trade	14.7%
Media reserve	0.6%
Total	*100.0%*

EXHIBIT 1

CAMPAIGN HISTORY 2

KNORR-SWISS SOUPS AND SAUCES
Introducing a line of gourmet soups and sauces

ADVERTISER: Specialty products unit
Canada Starch Company Inc.
AGENCY: Publicité Foster Limitée

Background

While it is quite evident that both the Canadian soup and sauce markets are divided among major manufacturing entities such as Campbell's, Lipton's, Club House, French's, etc., the recent rise of the gourmet ethic has created new opportunities for smaller firms. It is the objective of Knorr-Swiss to make the most of these opportunities.

Target Group

Adults aged 20-54, living within a household of one or more, who may or may not be working and whose household income is $25 M plus (1981 dollars).

Target Markets

Major urban centres where the target group is concentrated:
Toronto, Hamilton, London, Kitchener, and Waterloo
Montreal and Quebec City
Vancouver, Victoria, Calgary, and Edmonton

Marketing Strategies

1. *Soups.* Positioning statement: Knorr-Swiss is a unique, high-quality soup with a rich, true flavour close to the standards of homemade, which can be enjoyed by the whole family.

2. *Sauces.* Positioning statement: Knorr-Swiss is a unique, high-quality flavourful sauce that adds to the enjoyment of home cooking.

Advertising Objectives

- Stimulate trial of Knorr-Swiss products by the defined target group
- Maintain and increase usage of Knorr-Swiss products by current users
- Maintain and increase awareness within the defined target group to an optimum of 100 per cent
- Communicate the aforementioned positioning statements

Advertising Strategies

Knorr-Swiss products are imported, are often quite different from what is offered by the competition, and have a highly rated performance. The product has, in fact, through its quality, variety, price, and origin, positioned itself in line with the growing consumer trend in favour of specialty products.

The advertising strategy is to underline this "uniqueness" to the brand's advantage. It shall be demonstrated through a well-targeted but unusual media mix, as well as through a highly original and therefore memorable creative approach.

Taste, satisfaction, and authenticity will be highlighted. It is assumed product performance will convert initial trial to retrial and eventually to regular use. Additionally, an important education job is to be done in regard to the usage of sauces outside of the very limited current practices.

In terms of seasonality, the advertising and promotion programs will follow the established sales pattern for the different product categories, i.e., fall and winter.

Creative Execution

As the primary objective is to persuade our audience to try our products, we will concentrate on the product performance element and present Knorr as the quality entry.

A combination of verbal and visual images is recommended in order to create a mood for the products as well as to maximize taste appeal opportunities.

As will be further explained in the following section on media, the combination will be of radio and of mall posters. The creative for radio will be geared to increase awareness by creating a positive and lasting brand name registration as well as by appealing to the listener's appetite. The mall posters provide visual support with the opportunity to maximize mouth-watering photography—one that shows the product and its ingredients to the best possible advantage. Strong package identification will ensure prompt recognition within the retail environment.

The creative platforms in both English and French will be:
Knorr-Swiss Knows . . . . soups, sauces, bouillon, etc.
Knorr-Suisse, le choix des gourmets.

Media Execution

The media objectives within the defined demographic, geographical, and seasonal parameters are:
• increase and maintain awareness;
• select media with good reach/frequency;
• select media compatible with creative.

The selection of mall posters is supported by research data indicating that the audience's recall factor of the posters ranges from 37 to 65 per cent and that 64 per cent of adults living in urban markets shop at mall locations an average of 7.3 times monthly. Mediacom studies also state that approximately 75 per cent of these shoppers visit two or more centres each month, thereby increasing both reach and frequency potential.

In the primary and secondary markets a posting level of 60 GRP is recommended. The first flight will be eight weeks in duration, from January 18 through March 14, 1982 (two consecutive posting blocks). The first four weeks will promote only soups and the latter four sauces. Against women 18 to 49 years of age, the average reach/frequency achieved will be 78%/7.7.

An eight-week hiatus will follow, and then a four-week posting for sauces will be scheduled from May 10 to May 31, 1982. This flight will provide an average reach of 70 per cent with an average frequency of 4.3.

In the tertiary markets a 40 GRP weekly level is recommended within the same schedule. This will take into consideration the relative objective of these markets within the marketing strategy and hence budgets.

Radio will be the medium used to generate high levels of awareness. PMB III research states that women aged 18-49 who are soup and sauce users and who reside in either Quebec, Ontario, Alberta, and British Columbia tend to range from medium to heavy radio listening. The "Women in the Market Place" study results indicate that working women and potential working women tend to be heavy radio listeners, while non-working women tend to be medium or above-average radio listeners.

The first radio flight will be of five weeks duration, from January 18 to February 21, 1982. The one week average reach/frequency achieved against our target group will be 42%/2.3. This will build to 52%/7.4 over the last four weeks. Soups will be featured.

A two-week hiatus will follow. The second flight will last six weeks, from March 9 through April 18, 1982. The initial weekly reach/flight frequency will be 40%/2.4 and will build to 52%/8.0. Aired material will be an even rotation of soup and sauce material.

Finally, a five-week campaign on sauces will get on the air between May 3 and June 6, 1982. A 30%/1.5 average reach/frequency will be achieved after one week, to crest at 48%/3.9 at the end of the flight.

To further explain the media combination, the following provides a quick review of the other media considered:

Television. Ideal mass medium combining the visual, sound, and motion elements in one effective package. However, production costs become a decisive factor, as well as the heavy investment required to provide an effective campaign.

Magazines. PMB III strongly proves women tend to read many magazines, and thus there exists very little loyalty to any one title. Thus, in order to provide an effective platform, a comprehensive package is required and this adds to the cost.

Newspapers. Advertising clutter and inconsistent quality of colour reproduction do not provide the high calibre required. It is not the correct environment for the developed positioning.

Outdoor/transit. The seasonality of the media buy indicates that poor weather conditions may affect adversely the visibility and thus the effectiveness of the campaign. PMB III states that the target group of women soup and sauce users are only light or medium outdoor viewers and extremely light transit riders.

Conclusion

The advertising strategy developed for Knorr-Swiss is consistent with the brand's marketing strategy, and the media and creative executions recommended will provide a good base for continued growth.

EXHIBIT 2

Foster Advertising	Radio script

Sponsor: KNORR-SWISS

Subject: SAUCES - "DON'T FORGET THE 'K' IN HOLLANDAISE"

Date: November 25, 1981 **Length:** 30"

Voice		Continuity
A	1	Knorr-Swiss knows sauces
B	2	Norr-Swiss?
A	3	Knorr-Swiss. Knorr-Swiss knows Hollandaise
B	4	Delicious on broccoli or asparagus
A	5	Superb for Eggs Benedict
B	6	I love it with salmon or almost any fish.
VO	7	A Knorr-Swiss sauce can add a gourmet touch to almost any meal.
	8	Ask for Knorr-Swiss sauces and gravies - in the red and green
	9	envelopes - in your supermarket or specialty store.
A	10	Don't forget the 'k'.
B	11	Knorr-Swiss knows sauces.
LYRIC	12	KNORR-SWISS
	13	KNORR-SWISS
	14	
	15	
	16	
	17	
	18	
	19	
	20	
	21	
	22	

EXHIBIT 1

EXHIBIT 3

CAMPAIGN HISTORY 3

ATLAS COPCO CORPORATE CAMPAIGNS
Corporate Advertising for an Industrial Firm by Using the Hierarchy of Effects

ADVERTISER: Atlas Copco Canada Inc.
AGENCIES: F.H. Hayhurst for the first campaign
Kitching Advertising for the second campaign

A subsidiary of an international organization headquartered in Stockholm, Atlas Copco Canada Inc. has had many years' experience in the Canadian market. Already a major supplier of compressed air equipment to Canada's mining industry, the company set out to increase that share of market and to become a key supplier to the country's construction and manufacturing industries. Advertising was to play a key role first by developing an awareness campaign during the early 1970s and next by designing a campaign to increase knowledge and liking of the company during the early 1980s.

1. Awareness Campaign for Atlas Copco (early 1970s)

The new goals were intended to lift the company to a broader sales plateau—to give it a new competitive footing. An early step in the marketing plan was a candid self-analysis. Through working closely with the company's agency, F.H. Hayhurst in Montreal, several important conclusions were reached:
- Although Atlas Copco was running a fairly substantial campaign in a number of trade journals, this kind of advertising alone could never achieve the exposure and growth that Atlas Copco management had in mind.
- Their trade campaign had been successful in selling specific kinds of equipment, but it wasn't designed to present the company's corporate breadth. The result was that many different groups of people had different, limited views of the company.
- While Atlas Copco had been established for some years as a supplier to the mining and heavy construction industries, they had not made significant inroads in lighter construction and in manufacturing.

The company was not as well known as the competition and was not being invited to quote on new jobs. As a result, it was losing out on new business. Taking into account the job to be done and the nature of the industries involved, it was felt that an influential segment of the Canadian population needed to be made aware of the Atlas Copco name, its areas of competence, and its superiorities.

This meant, in addition to product-oriented trade advertising, an image-building corporate campaign. But how? And where?

First, a "task budget" was established that was totally unrelated to the traditional advertising-to-sales ratio evaluation. Then a number of media combinations were analyzed.

Finally, the decision was made to launch a drive-to-work radio campaign on selected stations and to create a broad-based print campaign for *Time* magazine. Both were designed to develop a familiarity with the Atlas Copco name; the campaign in *Time* would have the added attraction of reaching a significant portion of the Canadian business community.

Why *Time*? Because it offered what Atlas Copco was looking for: stature, national coverage, international flavour, excellent colour reproduction, and the chance to be associated, through the magazine's other advertisers, with some of the country's best-known corporate names. Above all, *Time* offered exactly the right audience.

Bill Kitching, Hayhurst's Montreal manager, and the management group at Atlas Copco were convinced that the striking and informative campaign in *Time* would reap immeasurable benefits. Advertising and public relations manager Charles E. Laws put it this way: "Some of *Time*'s prestige rubbed off on us; it gave us wide recognition. It helped, too, that many industry officials, who saw the Atlas Copco name in connection with a specific product in a trade ad, came across the name in a broad corporate context in *Time*.

"Then, too, the network of people who influence a major purchase is formidable. How can you ever know that you're reaching all of them? Probably you can't. But *Time* gave us as much assurance as possible that we're not leaving out someone important."

In tackling the creative approach to the new print campaign, a purely industrial tone was scrapped in favour of one that would appeal to the average reader of *Time*, as well as to all those who would be interested professionally. And so a campaign was designed expressly for *Time*. (Happily, it turned out to be suitable for trade publications, too.)

The copy avoided the impulse to sell a specific product and, instead, strove to create a favourable corporate impression. The campaign consisted of seven two-page spreads—and the fact that they were four-colour bleed ads helped promote the image of a lively, contemporary corporation.

The "corporate" approach of the campaign reflected a philosophy long espoused by the company's Canadian management. According to Laws, "You don't really sell a five-ton piece of equipment through an advertisement in a magazine. What your ad in a magazine does—assuming it's done well and your original idea was a good one—is contribute an intangible impression of your company, of the quality of your products, and of the reliability of your service. Gradually—and this is a long-term project—the marketplace begins to feel the same way about your company as you do. In effect, your campaign is doing the ground work for your salesman. When he makes his next call to sell that five-ton machine, half the job is done because the potential customer has already been sold on the company."

The Atlas Copco campaign ran in the national edition of *Time* Canada for many years, and it received *Marketing Magazine*'s "Outstanding Ad Campaign" award. In announcing the prize, the judges noted that the campaign "established major-league style, stance, and image for the firm." This was testimony not only to the creativity of the advertising but also to the success of the campaign's purpose. Though the colour photos are strikingly different from each other, the ads carry a strong campaign look, a highly visible logo, and a short but succinct corporate product message.

An important adjunct to the external advertising campaign was an internal promotional campaign. The ads were mounted and displayed in branch offices across Canada; special reprints in *Time* cover format were prepared and circulated to their sales force, to prospects, and to clients. The impetus of the campaign was felt throughout the company, and the enthusiasm generated by telling "our story" paid off handsomely.

Perhaps one of the most significant testaments to the success of the campaign came from a senior executive, who said: "The campaign in *Time* worked exactly as we envisioned it would. It's especially difficult to become broadly recognized when your corporate name isn't at least a little self-explanatory, as would be the case with Philips Electronics or International Business Machines, for instance. We knew that we were starting from way back when we set out to promote the Atlas Copco name. Just open the telephone book to 'Atlas' and you'll know what I mean. The list of Atlases is endless—and we seemed to be competing with all of them. Our salesmen were tired of being greeted with a quizzical 'Atlas *who*?' Today, that doesn't happen. The campaign has given us stature, recognition—and in several cases—entrée through some previously hard-to-open doors. We've been able to measure real gains in all areas, but particularly in secondary manufacturing and construction."

2. Knowledge and Liking Campaign for Atlas Copco (early 1980s)

Many things have changed over the past decade since Atlas Copco commenced its hard-hitting industrial advertising campaign in *Time* magazine: a minor change in the company name to conform with Quebec language legislation; changes in top management; and the advent of many new products to meet the needs of the company's many customer groups.

One thing that did not basically change, however, was the company's attitude toward the top priority position of the function of marketing communications: advertising, public relations, and sales promotion. Nor did the fundamental strategy of maintaining a "different" look, creatively, in the corporate and product advertising placed in magazines and on radio across Canada. Because of major changes to the Canadian edition of *Time*, new thinking had to be given to the media mix, and considerable time was spent on analyzing the company's markets and the respective media reaching them.

Canadian Business magazine was selected as the "umbrella" vehicle for carrying the entire print campaign; a world-class business magazine, with a relatively large Canadian circulation, it suited the series perfectly. The program ran consistently during the early 1980s, until the economic downturn took its toll on Atlas Copco's communications budget. The same series of corporate/product advertisements were also used in selected business and technical journals in order to place greater emphasis on reaching specific job functions and/or target markets.

The series of seven advertisements was developed by Kitching Advertising, formerly the Montreal operations of Hayhurst Advertising. Kitching's creative director, Paul Henry, conceived the campaign, which used yet another unique and unusual (for an industrial advertiser) approach to obtain and focus reader attention on various key product features and benefits. A series of drawings executed by well-known Toronto artist Dino Kotopoulis depicted animals in a number of humorous situations relating to the clever headlines. Photographs of the product were conventional so as not to conflict with but rather present a pleasing contrast to the creative paintings.

A play on definitions, visually and verbally, as a way of promoting the company's reservoir of talent.

EXHIBIT 1

The campaign was produced in a variety of sizes ranging from one-half pages to two-thirds and full pages. Full colour was primarily used, although a selected number of advertisements were also produced in black and white.

In the mid-1970s Atlas Copco put in place a network of distributors across Canada, and this campaign was used as part of an integrated support program for them. All relevant dealers were listed in each advertisement, with the list being updated periodically.

Business-to-business communications need not be dull and mundane, and once again Atlas Copco proved the fact with this highly creative and extremely effective campaign.

EXHIBIT 2

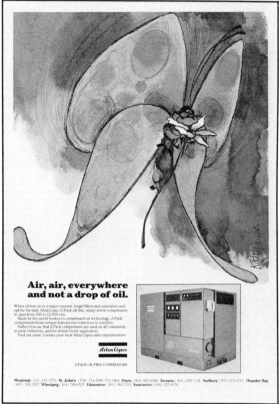

EXHIBIT 3

Advertisements that use humour to emphasize the reliability of Atlas Copco's air compressors and tools

EXHIBIT 4

PART

4

THE
MANAGEMENT
OF ADVERTISING
PROGRAMS
IN CANADA

The stage has been set for planning an advertising campaign. Part 1 described the nature and functions of advertising within the overall marketing mix and marketing plan. In Part 2 the respective roles of the advertiser, the advertising agency, and print and broadcast media were discussed as well as the Canadian environment in which the campaign is designed. The motivations, perceptions, attitudes, and other decision process variables of Canadian consumers that are useful to advertisers in all phases of campaign planning were outlined in Part 3.

Part 4 shows how to plan the overall advertising program. Setting the advertising objectives and budgets is explained in Chapter 11. Next, the process of developing effective print and broadcast messages that are consistent with advertising objectives is detailed in Chapters 12 and 13. The task of media planning, which is explained in Chapter 14, enables a message to effectively reach the target market specified in the objectives. Finally, the advertiser needs information at all levels of campaign planning, as well as for control of the advertising program. The various forms of advertising research are explained in Chapter 15.

CHAPTER 11

Planning the Campaign and Setting Advertising Objectives and Budgets

An effective advertising campaign takes a step-by-step approach to planning and management. Within the planning process, one of the major decisions is determining the direction and intensity of the advertising effort to achieve overall marketing objectives. This process involves two types of decision that are interdependent: setting precise and operational advertising objectives, and establishing the size and allocation of the advertising budget.

Planning, Executing, and Controlling an Advertising Campaign

The process of developing and managing an advertising campaign comprises the same steps, although the duration of each step may vary according to the market, company, and product. A new product may require a longer planning process and involve more participants than a mature product. Also, a firm with little marketing expertise may require a longer planning process than a firm with an advertising department. An advertising agency may play an important role in all phases of the planning process. If a firm is not using the services of an advertising agency, these functions must be performed internally or with the assistance of outside suppliers.

The complete process of planning, executing, and controlling an advertising campaign comprises six major steps (Figure 11.1).

Developing the Fact Book

A fact book is a summary of all relevant facts about a market and a brand or product (Figure 11.2). The fact book should be developed by both the advertising manager and the account executive. It represents the best available information about the industry, the trade, and the advertiser's brand. It is used at all levels in the advertiser's organization to appraise market opportunities and analyze the market in which the brand is to be advertised. The advertising agency often plays a critical role for many firms that lack marketing expertise and rely on the agency for marketing advice.

COMPANY FACTS. Information about the history of the company and the history of the product must be included in the fact book to assist the agency personnel who work on the marketing and advertising programs. For example, Kraft and Electrolux have used flashbacks about the company's history in their advertising to emphasize that their product and service is the same as in the "good old days." Company brochures and other promotional material contain some of these facts to convey that the company has been innovative and successful. Package designs or redesigns may use this information or incorporate some old symbols to convey the same message. It is essential that all agency personnel working on an account understand the company's objectives.

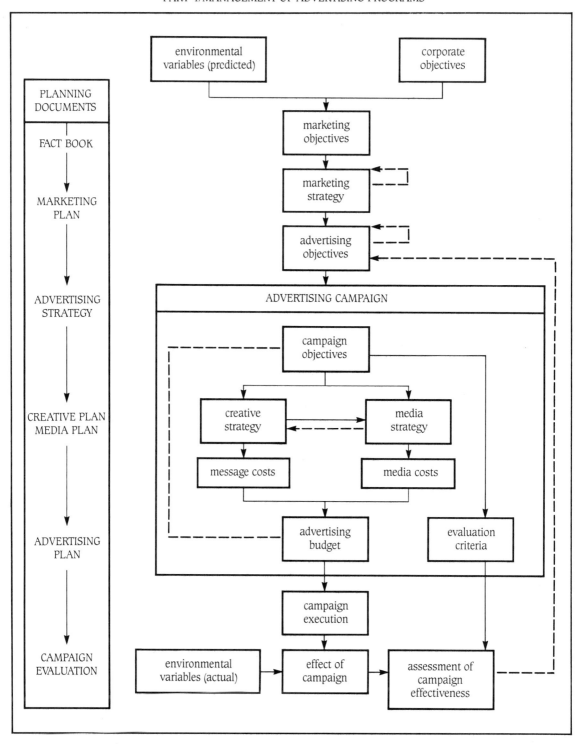

FIGURE 11.1   Planning, Executing, and Controlling the Advertising Campaign

```
┌─────────────────────────────────────────┐
│ FACT BOOK                                 │
│                                           │
│ A. COMPANY FACTS                          │
│    1. History of the company              │
│    2. History of the product             │
│    3. Corporate objectives               │
│                                           │
│ B. MARKET FACTS                           │
│    1. Environmental variables (predicted)│
│    2. Market size and trends             │
│    3. Segmentation and positioning       │
│    4. Channels of distribution           │
│    5. Competition                        │
│                                           │
│ C. BRAND FACTS                            │
│    1. Basic characteristics              │
│    2. Current marketing objectives       │
│    3. Current marketing strategy         │
│       • target definition                │
│       • marketing mix                    │
└─────────────────────────────────────────┘
```

FIGURE 11.2   Suggested Outline for the Fact Book

MARKET FACTS.   This section of the fact book develops an opportunity analysis for the firm. Major environmental variables—the economic, cultural, legal, or other uncontrollable variables affecting the market—are described first (Chapter 2). The size of the intended market, its predicted evolution, and a *thorough* analysis of market segmentation must also be included in this section. In particular, the nature and sizes of various market segments, as well as the positioning of competitive brands with respect to these segments should be well documented. For example, in the beer market it is important to know that the most important characteristics are strength and social image, the sizes and nature of the various market segments, and how well each competitive brand appeals to these segments. Information about distribution channels and how they relate to market segmentation and competition should also be included.

BRAND FACTS.   The last section of the fact book should include all relevant information about the brand to be advertised. It describes the brands' basic characteristics: history, evolution,

and benefits. Interesting information about the production process, quality control procedures, or a new innovative packaging process should be included here. Current marketing objectives and strategy for the brand are described in detail for the benefit of all individuals working on the marketing and advertising of the brand, particularly an agency's account service group.

Developing the Marketing Plan

Based on a thorough understanding of the market situation and the marketing objectives for a particular brand, a *marketing plan* must be developed, preferably with the assistance of agency personnel involved in advertising and sales promotion.[1] A study of planning procedures for packaged goods companies showed extensive use of the advertising agency, even by large firms, in developing the marketing plan.[2]

The marketing plan describes the overall marketing strategy that a company intends to follow for a product, i.e., the strategic decisions concerning the target market and the marketing-mix variables (the 4 Ps) as explained in Chapter 2. It also includes some critical implementation issues, such as timing, organizational changes, and information needs, as well as the marketing budget, sales and profit forecasts, and a timetable of activities. Figure 11.3 shows a suggested outline for a marketing plan.

The *summary of facts* highlights major points from the fact book as a result of the opportunity analysis done in the first planning document.

The *problems and opportunities* describe the options open to a company that result from the opportunity analysis in the fact book.

The *marketing objectives and strategy* make up the most important part of the marketing plan. It describes the firm's final decision on the marketing objectives and strategy for the next planning period. Depending on the marketing problem a company faces, these decisions may involve a slight modification to current market-

MARKETING PLAN

A. SUMMARY OF FACTS (from Fact Book)

B. PROBLEMS AND OPPORTUNITIES

C. MARKETING OBJECTIVES AND STRATEGY
   1. Long-range marketing objectives
   2. Target market
   3. Product policies
   4. Pricing policies
   5. Advertising plan
      (including sales promotion)
   6. Sales force policies
   7. Distribution policies
   8. Other considerations

D. PLAN FOR IMPLEMENTATION
   1. Short-run plan (if necessary)
   2. Timing
   3. Organizational changes (if necessary)
   4. Research activities
   5. Marketing budget
   6. Sales and profit forecasts

E. TIMETABLE OF ACTIVITIES

F. SUMMARY OF PLAN

FIGURE 11.3   Suggested Outline for the Marketing Plan

ing strategy or a radical departure. First, long-range marketing objectives must be stated clearly and in operational terms. Second, the target market must be defined precisely using information from the opportunity analysis. Finally, decisions on the marketing-mix variables (Chapter 2) are described. It is important to note that the advertising strategy is part of the overall marketing plan, but at this stage of planning, the marketing plan is used as input for developing a more detailed advertising plan.

The *plan for implementation* deals with critical implementation issues. Short-run plans (if any) are described. It may be essential for the plan to be implemented before a certain date because of competitive moves, or seasonal or cyclical factors. The plan may also require a reorganization of the marketing function. Research activities that must be undertaken during the next period must be properly planned and funded. The implementation plan also includes a description of the marketing budget and forecasts of sales and profits.

The *timetable of activities* co-ordinates all activities in order to maximize the impact of the marketing plan.

Developing a Preliminary Advertising Plan

The advertising plan is developed within the objectives defined by the marketing plan, in which the role and functions of advertising are defined as one of the marketing-mix variables. In the previous step, decisions are made about which overall marketing strategy is the best course for achieving marketing objectives. The next task for the advertiser and the agency is to develop the advertising component of the marketing mix.

Four major steps are involved in this task, which is often done by the agency or the advertising manager. First, precise and operational advertising objectives consistent with the marketing strategy are established. Second, the creative director develops a preliminary creative strategy for translating advertising objectives into an effective message. For example, the marketing strategy of appealing to teenagers to use a fruit-flavoured toothpaste may be translated into a social gathering where good breath is emphasized. Third, the media director develops a preliminary media strategy and a tentative advertising budget. Fourth, a tentative plan for evaluating the effects of the campaign is developed.

Developing the Final Advertising Plan

If the preliminary advertising plan is approved by the agency management or the plans board (Chapter 3), then the agency group working on the account presents the proposed campaign to the advertiser: campaign objectives, creative strategy, media plan, prototype advertisements, research, marketing services, and budget.

If the proposed campaign is approved by the advertiser, the account executive and the advertiser develop the final advertising plan. A suggested outline for the advertising plan is shown in Figure 11.4. The process of developing an advertising plan is an iterative process from the defining of the campaign objectives, the development of an advertising strategy consistent with these objectives, and the setting of a specific budget. If the client does not approve the plan, the process is repeated. Ultimately, the process stops when the agency and the advertiser agree with all of the decisions on objectives, strategy, budget, and control.

ADVERTISING PLAN

A. SUMMARY OF MARKETING PLAN
  1. Marketing objectives
  2. Target market characteristics
  3. Marketing-mix decisions
  4. Critical implementation issues

B. ADVERTISING OBJECTIVES

C. ADVERTISING STRATEGY
  1. Creative strategy and plan
    • rationale for creative strategy
    • copy platform
    • art
    • research on copy and layout
  2. Media plan
    • target audience
    • media strategy and rationale
    • media schedule and costs
    • media research

D. OTHER PROMOTIONAL ACTIVITIES:
   PLANNING AND/OR CO-ORDINATION

E. ADVERTISING BUDGET
  1. Appropriation
  2. Allocation

F. CAMPAIGN EVALUATION PLAN

G. SUMMARY OF PLAN

FIGURE 11.4 Suggested Outline for the Advertising Plan

The *summary of marketing strategy* highlights the key elements of the marketing plan. These are either developed by the agency for the client or derived from the marketing plan developed by the advertiser.

The *advertising objectives* are derived from the marketing objectives and strategy, and they should be stated in precise and operational terms. The agency helps the advertiser develop sound, realistic, and operational advertising objectives.

The *advertising strategy and plan* is presented in two parts. First, the creative strategy is described with a detailed rationale using facts from the opportunity analysis and research, if available. The creative strategy translates the marketing strategy into an effective message in order to achieve the advertising objectives. The rationale justifies the proposed message in terms of content and format. The two main ingredients of the creative strategy, copy and art, are developed in detail. Findings on pretesting of copy and layout are presented and used to evaluate the proposed creative execution. Planned copy post-testing activities may also be presented.

The *media plan* starts with a description of the target audience derived from the target market defined in the marketing plan. Then the media strategy is presented with a detailed rationale for the various media types and vehicles selected as well as for those rejected. Next, the media plan must contain a media schedule and an evaluation of the media budget. Finally, findings on media research from various sources are presented, as well as planned research activities on the selected media.

Other promotional activities involve such sales promotion techniques as product demonstrations, and publicity/public relations activities (Chapter 2). All these activities must be properly co-ordinated with advertising efforts and the rest of the marketing mix.

The *advertising budget* section provides the rationale for the advertising appropriation, as well as allocation to different markets, products, advertising functions, media, and time periods.

The *campaign evaluation plan* provides procedures for ascertaining the campaign's effects and whether the advertising objectives have been reached. This activity is critical for effective management of the advertising function (see Chapter 15).

Executing the Campaign

Once the advertising plan is approved by the advertiser, the account executive, in consultation with the client, co-ordinates the execution of the campaign. Production of advertisements or commercials must be completed in time for the start of the campaign and finished advertisements or commercials must be approved. The final media plan must be developed and approved by the advertiser before orders may be sent to the media for buying space and/or time.

Evaluating the Effects of the Campaign

After the campaign has run, the advertiser must determine if the advertising objectives have been reached. Research on the campaign's effects may be done by the firm's in-house advertising department, an outside research firm, or by the agency research group. Based on the information collected, a campaign evaluation report (Figure 11.5) is written, often by the account executive. The advertiser decides whether the marketing and advertising elements should be continued or modified or whether the campaign should be completely reworked for the next period.

The *summary of the advertising plan* states the main elements of the advertising campaign that are relevant to the evaluation. These elements are the advertising objectives (test criteria), the main copy points, and the selected media and vehicles.

The *research methodology* describes the methodology used to collect the data and analyze it.

CAMPAIGN EVALUATION REPORT

A. SUMMARY OF ADVERTISING PLAN
  1. Advertising objectives
  2. Advertising strategy
  3. Other promotional activities
  4. Campaign evaluation plan

B. RESEARCH METHODOLOGY
  1. Survey method
  2. Sample
  3. Questionnaire
  4. Data analysis

C. RESULTS
  1. Advertising objectives and campaign effectiveness
  2. Copy post-testing (optional)
  3. Media effectiveness (optional)

D. CONCLUSIONS AND RECOMMENDATIONS

FIGURE 11.5 Suggested Outline for the Campaign Evaluation Report

Procedures for these tasks are detailed in Chapter 15.

The *results* section evaluates the entire campaign by comparing the research results with the stated campaign objectives. If these activities were planned, results on copy post-testing and on different media and vehicle effectiveness are presented.

The *conclusions and recommendations* summarize the report's main findings and make recommendations on the advertising objectives, the advertising budget, the advertising strategy, the copy and layout of the messages, and the selected media or media vehicles for the next planning period.

Setting Advertising Objectives

From the statement of the marketing objectives and the marketing strategy, the objectives assigned to the advertising function are derived. Although marketing objectives may be stated in terms of sales, profit, or market shares, it is a *common fallacy* to state the advertising objectives in the same terms. Since advertising takes place toward the end of the implementation of the marketing plan, it seems natural to many marketers to relate this activity and that of the sales force to the ultimate sale. But sales are the results of the *total* marketing effort. Would advertising "sell" the product to the wrong target market? Would advertising "sell" if the product does not meet the needs and requirements of consumers? Would advertising "sell" if the price is too high in relation to competitive products? Would advertising "sell" if the product were not on the retail shelves? Questions like these may be asked for *every* aspect of the marketing plan. Only when one is reasonably assured of proper control of the other elements of the marketing mix and of similar uncontrollable factors can inferences be drawn about the effects of an advertising campaign on sales volume or market share.

The role of advertising within the marketing mix is to communicate with the market, i.e., to inform consumers about the contents of the marketing mix. Of course, communication takes place in other parts of the marketing mix, and these should be properly integrated with advertising. For example, price level often communicates something about the quality of the product;[3] the brand name may provide information about the product; the product packaging may provide information about the product. But the main task of communicating with the mass market is usually assigned to advertising.

Therefore, advertising objectives should be defined in terms of communication goals. This requires a sound understanding of how consumers process commercial and non-commercial information, and how this affects their decision process.

In addition, advertising objectives should be defined as precisely and completely as possible in order to help managers find the means to meet these objectives, as well as to assess whether the advertising campaign has been successful. Properly defined advertising objectives should help in efficiently managing this function. A clear understanding of what adver-

tising can or cannot do and how it contributes to the attainment of sales, profit, and market share objectives, should ensure and protect the means for carrying them out, which is the advertising budget.

Statement of Precise and Operational Advertising Objectives

The statement of precise and operational advertising objectives must include the "five Ts":
1. the *target audience*(s), which is the group(s) of individuals to whom the communication is directed;
2. the *theme*(s) of the campaign;
3. the *task*(s) of the communication, which is the campaign's intended effect(s) on the target audience;
4. the *time horizon* during which the communication task is to be accomplished;[4]
5. the *test criteria*, which will be used at the end of the time horizon to evaluate the campaign's effectiveness.[5]

A good example of a precise and operational objective is the following:

> To increase awareness of Brand X milk-based drink among teenagers and young adults aged 18-24 from the present ten per cent unaided recall of Brand X to a desired 50 per cent, within one year, by associating it with sports events, and presenting it as the drink of winners.

In this example, the five ingredients have been properly specified in operational terms:

Advertising Campaign Objectives

TARGET AUDIENCE: teenagers and young adults aged 18-24

THEME: the drink of winners in sports events

TASK: increase awareness of Brand X milk-based drink from the present 10 per cent to a desired 50 per cent.

TIME HORIZON: one year

TEST CRITERION: unaided recall of Brand X

Defining the Target Audience

The audience that is to receive the communication is derived from the target market identified in the marketing strategy. If this target market has been identified in precise and operational terms, and if it represents a unique segment of the market, then the target audience is quite similar to the target market.

If the market is comprised of different segments to which the same product is being offered, it may be more efficient to specify the advertising objectives in terms of a primary target audience and a secondary target audience. This is particularly important when the communication tasks and themes are different from one group to the other. When the differentiation is pronounced, different advertising campaigns may be used, as is often the case for products advertised to different cultural groups like the French and the English markets in Quebec, the French markets in Nova Scotia, or the English markets in Toronto, Calgary and Vancouver.[6]

The communication task may require a more precise definition of the target audience than the target market identified in the marketing plan. Again, one may introduce a primary target audience, a secondary target audience, and so on. For example, the target market for Milk Mate, a liquid milk modifier, may be defined as families with children aged 3-16.[7] In this case, the child is the user of the product and influences the parent's purchase decision. Or the primary target audience may be only children aged 3-16, and the advertising appeal may be "a tasty and fun drink". The secondary target audience may be parents with children aged 3-16, and the advertising appeal may stress convenience and nutrition.

Introducing the Theme of the Campaign

In developing the product's marketing strategy some differentiating measure(s) may have been selected, and one of the functions of advertising is to communicate this feature to the target audience. The basic theme(s) of the campaign must be based on the marketing strategy for the product.

For example, take the following statement: "to convince parents of children of ages 3-16 that Wonder Juice is the ideal drink to serve their children, because it is very nutritious and has a taste children always love". Here the strategy is to appeal to parents on the basis of good nutrition for their children, as well as ease of getting them to drink the juice.

Defining the Communication Task and the Appropriate Test Criteria

The statement of advertising objectives must clearly identify one or several communication tasks to be accomplished by the campaign within the time horizon specified. It is critical to define the main communication task, in order to select the type of campaign to be used, as well as the appropriate test criteria. Table 11.1 elaborates on advertising campaigns that are appropriate for selected communication tasks and target audiences.

If *brand awareness* is the selected communication task, the target audience may be all users of the product category; the type of campaign used may be an attention-getting campaign with teasers, a good slogan, or a catchy jingle, with the objective of increasing the number of users who remember the brand name from five per cent to 30 per cent. A brand awareness survey, using either aided or unaided recall, can determine the campaign's success. The advertisement for British Columbia (Figure 11.6) falls into this category.

If the selected communication task is *knowledge of brand attributes*, the target audience may be all the users who are aware of the brand name. The type of campaign used may rely on product demonstration, repetition of the brand's main attributes, or a catchy jingle or slogan, for example, "LSMFT: Lucky Strike Means Fine

TABLE 11.1   Some Examples of Relationships among Task, Target Audience, Test Criteria, and Type of Campaign

Related behavioural dimensions	Task of the communication	Primary target audience	Type of advertising campaign	Test criteria
Cognitive— the realm of thoughts	Awareness ↓	All users of product category	Attention-getting (teasers, slogan, jingles, humour)	Brand awareness (aided or unaided recall)
Ads provide information and facts	Knowledge ↓	Users aware of brand	Learning (repetition, description, demonstration)	Recall of copy
Affective— the realm of emotions	Liking ↓	Users aware of brand attributes	Competitive (argumentative, reason why, endorsements)	Attitudes or images; evoked set
Ads change attitudes and feelings	Preference ↓	Buyers of competitive brands	Aggressive (comparative, argumentative, status, testimonials)	Preference ranking
Conative— the realm of motives	Conviction ↓ Purchase	Present buyers of the brand Buyers of major brands	Reminder (reinforcements, image, new uses) Value-oriented (special, price deals, rebates, co-operative, direct-mail)	Intention to purchase Sales figures (with proper control)
Ads stimulate or direct desires				

SOURCE: Adapted from Robert J. Lavidge and Gary A. Steiner, "A Model for Predictive Measurement of Advertising Effectiveness", *Journal of Marketing* (October 1961), p. 61.
Courtesy American Marketing Association

Tobacco". An appropriate test criterion for the campaign's success may be aided or unaided recall of copy. The Air Canada advertisement shown in Figure 11.7 emphasizes knowledge of brand attributes.

If *brand liking* is the selected communication task, the target audience may be consumers who are aware of brand and its main attributes. The type of campaign used may be competitive, with both argumentative copy and image building techniques like endorsements or group identification, in order to induce consumers to include the brand in their evoked set. Appropriate test criteria may be attitude or image changes from 15 per cent to 25 per cent, as well as evoked set identification. Brand liking is the main objective of the Heineken advertisement (Figure 11.8).

If the selected communication task is *brand preference*, the target audience may be buyers of a competitor's brand. The type of campaign used may be aggressive, with comparative ads, argumentative copy, or the use of testimonials to confer status or glamour on the product. An appropriate test criterion is a measure of preference ranking to determine if improvements of preferences are taking place as a result of the campaign. The Dairy Bureau advertisement (Figure 11.9) attempts to develop consumers' preference for butter.

If *brand conviction* is the selected communication task, the primary target audience may be present buyers of the brand. The advertising campaign may be a reminder type of campaign, with a soft-sell approach to reinforce the brand image or to suggest new uses of the brand or new occasions to consume it. The appropriate test criterion may be changes in intention to purchase the brand. The Royal Bank advertise-

FIGURE 11.6 The object of this advertisement is to create *awareness* of British Columbia as a spring vacation spot, particularly among U.S. tourists.

Courtesy Tourism British Columbia.

FIGURE 11.7 This advertisement uses a combination of unusual headlines to lead into the copy, which emphasizes the attributes of Air Canada services for business travelers.

Courtesy Air Canada

FIGURE 11.8 This advertisement for Heinken uses very little copy because the product is already well-known to beer drinkers. The illustration and the copy suggest to the reader that Heineken should be part of their evoked set of brands.

Courtesy Sainsbury Limited

FIGURE 11.9 This advertisement attemps to develop a preference for butter instead or margarine by emphasizing butter natural process and taste.

Courtesy Dairy Bureau of Canada

FIGURE 11.10 This advertisement for the Royal Bank is attempting to convince the reader that it offers the best services, even overnight! The Royal Bank is well-known to the public, so the emphasis is on its improvements in services, every day.
Courtesy The Royal Bank of Canada

FIGURE 11.11 This newspaper advertisement for Intellevision uses an unusual layout to attract readers' attention. The offer of two cartridges is good only for two months, so quick action is required to take advantage of it.
Courtesy Mattel Canada Inc.

ment (Figure 11.10) attempts to create brand conviction.

In a situation where there is proper control of other marketing elements, the selected behavioural task may be brand purchase. The type of advertising campaign used may be value-oriented and stress reduced prices, price deals, rebates, or use co-operative or direct mail advertising. Assuming proper control of other marketing elements, the appropriate test criterion may be the changes in sales volume. The advertisement for Intellevision (Figure 11.11) calls for consumers to act immediately.

Specifying Test Criteria in Operational Terms

As was seen, the selection of test criteria is based on the communication task or on the campaign's intended effects on the target audience. To properly assess the effectiveness of the advertising campaign, both the present or pre-campaign levels of the test criteria *and* the desired or post-campaign levels of the test criteria must be stated.

In the example of Brand X milk-based drink, the test criterion was "unaided recall of Brand X." Before the campaign, unaided recall of Brand X was ten per cent of the target audience, and the campaign aimed at unaided recall of Brand X to be 50 per cent of the target audience at the end of the time horizon. Such benchmarks, which are related to the budget decision, provide advertisers with direction in designing the campaign and control over the campaign's effectiveness. If advertising is viewed as an investment—as part of the marketing effort—a realistic, quantified, and written goal may be considered an estimate of the return on that investment.

Effects of the Campaign on Other Behavioural Dimensions

Once a communication task has been selected and the campaign designed accordingly, the effects are felt at all levels of the hierarchy of effects model. An examination of these effects can help pinpoint weaknesses in the campaign. For example, an advertisement may be noticed but consumers may have difficulty remembering the brand name or cannot associate a brand name with the brand's main attributes.

A simplified example of how this type of analysis can help pinpoint problem areas and be used to design future campaigns is provided in Figure 11.12. The two campaigns both advertise the same product and have awareness as the major task of the campaign. Suppose both campaigns are equally effective in increasing brand awareness to 50 per cent of all users of the product category. One possible weakness of A is in translating brand knowledge into brand

liking, while for B, it is in the link between brand awareness and brand knowledge.

Avoiding Common Pitfalls of Campaign Planning

If developed properly, operational advertising objectives include the five Ts: the *T*arget audience(s), the *T*ask(s) of the communication, the *T*heme(s) of the campaign, the *T*ime horizon, and the *T*est criteria to be used at the end of the time horizon to determine the effectiveness of the campaign.

Critical as they are, these ingredients are often ignored in practice. One study of 135 campaigns created by 40 agencies showed that almost none of these agencies really knew or could know if their campaigns were really

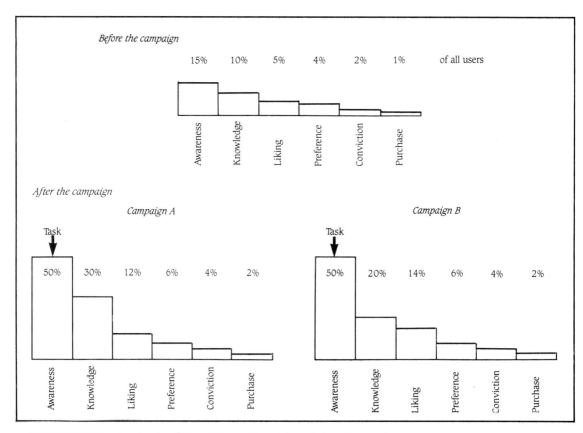

FIGURE 11.12   Analysis of Two Alternative Advertising Campaigns

successful. The most common pitfalls in stating the objectives and in relating the proof of success to the stated campaign objectives were:[8]

1. In the statement of objectives:
   (a) failure to state them in quantifiable terms (99 per cent);
   (b) failure to recognize that, in most cases, a sales increase is not a proper advertising objective (24 per cent);
   (c) failure to identify the advertising audience (16 per cent);
   (d) use of superlatives, which are unmeasurable (2 per cent).
2. In relating the "proof of success" to the stated objectives:
   (a) with awareness as objective, success was stated in terms of sales (68 per cent);
   (b) with a new image as objective, success was stated in terms of readership or inquiries (35 per cent);
   (c) with several objectives stated, success was mentioned only in relation to one of them (45 per cent).

The failure to state the advertising objectives properly is related to a lack of understanding of the role of advertising in general and advertising objectives in particular. For example, the client's misconception that advertising alone will increase sales or market share may cause an agency to present a campaign and its result in these terms. This attitude is unfortunate, because if advertising does not "deliver" right away, the temptation is great to change agencies, switch campaigns, or cut the advertising budget. In all cases, the effects of that decision may spell more problems for the brand.

Developing the Advertising Budget

The advertising budget is a detailed plan specifying how the total amount of money allocated to advertising is to be spent within a planning period. The *total sum* to be spent on advertising within the same period is called the advertising

appropriation. Thus, the budget decision includes the appropriation plus a scheme detailing how much is to be allocated to various media and other advertising functions, to sales territories, to different products, to different time periods, and so on.

It must be re-emphasized that all the major decisions are interrelated, and that the advertising budget is directly affected by decisions made on objectives, creative, media, and others. The planning process is an *iterative* process within the planning period and among successive periods. The involvement of senior managers, product managers, and advertising agency personnel is critical in order to maximize the effectiveness of these planning procedures.[9]

Factors to Consider in Developing the Advertising Appropriation

Before the methods for determining the appropriation are described, it is important to have an understanding of the conditions or constraints under which the appropriation is set. There are two general types of constraints: external and internal.

External Constraints

Four factors related to a market situation affect the size of the advertising appropriation:

THE STAGE IN THE PRODUCT LIFE-CYCLE. The amount of advertising spent on a product varies with the stage in the product's life-cycle. A brand at the introductory or the growth stage requires more spending in relation to sales than a product at the maturity or decline stages (Chapter 2).

THE TARGET MARKET. The size and composition of the target market affects the size of the appropriation and allocation to sales territories and market segments. Canadian markets tend to be widely dispersed and heterogeneous, thus the pattern of population density and the multicultural nature of Canadian consumers present a great challenge to advertisers. Advertisers' solutions to this problem have included:

- regional or cultural campaigns, as in Quebec and Ontario, or in both French and English;
- phased product introduction, by market, region, or segment;
- use of such lower cost media as newspaper or radio;
- segmenting the market to obtain smaller homogeneous targets who can be reached by low cost media.

COMPETITORS' STRATEGIES. Competitors' strategies should be taken into account when the advertising appropriation is determined. The same level of spending would not have the same effect if no one is advertising or if all major competitors are spending heavily on advertising. A small hamburger chain, for example, Harvey's, would be hard-pressed to match the $9 million in media space and time that McDonald's spent in 1982.[10] Such large, marketing-oriented companies as General Foods and Procter & Gamble often choose fragmented markets to introduce new products with heavy advertising spending, and often prefer television as the advertising medium. Small and medium-sized companies emphasize other variables in the mix, like pricing, display, and service, or use other media like radio, billboards, or transit advertising.

ENVIRONMENTAL VARIABLES. Environmental constraints may affect a company's ability to advertise. Poor economic conditions may force advertisers to cut their appropriations, as during the 1982 recession. Laws or voluntary self-regulation may force advertisers to avoid certain media, like television for cigarettes, or to limit the extent of their advertising.[11] Cultural norms may prohibit or discourage the use of certain media for advertising such products as contraceptive devices or guns.

Internal Factors

The most important internal factors affecting the budget decision are the nature of the marketing mix and of the organization.

THE NATURE OF THE MARKETING MIX. All decisions concerning the marketing-mix variables affect the size of the appropriation. If the product concept is clearly *differentiated* from the competition, the size of the appropriation would be lower than if differentiation is to be created by the advertising campaign. The role of advertising within the *promotional mix* affects the size of the appropriation. It will be higher for a pull strategy than for a push strategy. With a pull strategy, the role of advertising is to build interest in the brand, so that consumers will recognize it in retail stores, especially in self-service stores. The relationship between price and the advertising appropriation must also be considered. Higher prices lead to higher *unit profit margins*, thus allowing higher advertising appropriation per unit. This is not true for the total profit, which depends on the level of price elasticity. A high level of *brand loyalty* decreases price elasticity, and a heavily advertised brand may command a higher price. Otherwise, a lower price may lead to higher profits and a higher total appropriation. For example, in 1982 Rothmans of Canada spent $24.7 million, but the advertising cost per carton was low. Therefore, the relationship between advertising appropriation and unit profit margins depends on the level of price elasticity of the target market.

THE NATURE OF THE ORGANIZATION. Several organizational factors may affect the size of the appropriation. First, the size of the company and its financial strength will limit the amount to be spent in advertising. The objectives and organizational structure of the company and its *style of management* affect the decision on the degree of advertising support to be given to a new or an unsuccessful brand.[12] Some managers are willing to take some risks to ensure the success of a new brand, while others are more cautious and would tend to take conservative action. The degree of *influence* of the advertising agency, as well as the *confidence* of senior managers in the ability of the agency's account service group, may also affect the size of the appropriation. The account executive can ascertain the relationship among advertising objectives, strategy, and budget and thus advise the advertiser on the amount to spend on the forthcoming campaign. The final determination of the appropriation may or may not be influenced by this recommendation, depending on the relationship between advertising and agency personnel.

Methods for Determining the Advertising Appropriation

Setting the advertising appropriation implies formal or intuitive knowledge of the relationship between the amount spent on advertising and its contribution to the advertising objectives. Traditionally, three types of methods are used to determine the advertising appropriation: naive methods, economic models, and objective and task methods.

Naive Methods

Several naive (simplistic) methods are used to set the advertising budget.

AFFORDABLE BUDGET. The method of the *affordable budget* is a rudimentary procedure and consists of spending any amount on advertising in excess of an acceptable profit margin. In a study conducted among large companies, it was found that 28 per cent used the affordable method, both in nonconsumer and in consumer markets.[13] A related method is the *arbitrary method,* and the amount spent is arbitrarily based on what is spent on a similar product or some other rationale. By these methods, a company would only by pure chance be spending the optimal amount. More likely, the company would be spending too little or too much. With an affordable budget, an increase in the appropriation may, in conjunction with the rest of the marketing mix, lead to higher profits to absorb the increased spending. With the arbitrary method, a company spends wastefully, "just in case advertising works".[14,15] In one study, it was found that the arbitrary approach was used by 24 per cent of executives of firms dealing in non-consumer markets and by 16 per cent of executives in consumer markets.[16]

PERCENTAGE OF SALES METHODS. Some advertisers spend a certain percentage of past sales or of future sales on advertising, ignoring that, in theory, advertising should contribute to generating sales. This is a reverse approach, since sales determine the advertising expenditures. The main advantage of this method is its simplicity and its intuitive attractiveness to managers who think in terms of contribution to profits and not in terms of market demand. This method is similar to the cost-plus approach often used for pricing, instead of the more logical demand-based approach. Thus the method suffers from the same weaknesses, since the appropriation would be an optimal amount only by chance.

In highly turbulent markets, such a method can do considerable damage to a brand if past sales were at a peak or in a trough, or if sales forecasts were too optimistic or too pessimistic. In one study, San Augustine and Foley report that the method of percentage of future sales was used by 32 per cent and 52 per cent of executives in non-consumer and consumer markets, respectively. The corresponding figures for the method of percentage of past years' sales were 28 per cent and 16 per cent.[17]

Instead of using sales figures, another related method consists of setting the advertising appropriation as a *percentage of past or future profits*. This method magnifies the same drawbacks, since profits fluctuate more than sales.

Still another related method is setting a *fixed sum per unit* for advertising. For example, an appliance manufacturer would set eight dollars per refrigerator to be used for advertising and a brewery would set two dollars per case. The total appropriation would be obtained by multiplying the fixed-sum-per-unit by the anticipated sales in units or cases. The problems with this method are the same as with the others, but it is often used for its intuitive appeal, particularly in dealing with distributors, for example, in co-operative advertising programs. In the same study, San Augustine and Foley found that the method of unit anticipated sales was used by 12 per cent of executives in both consumer and nonconsumer markets. The corresponding figures for the method of unit past years' sales were 12 and four per cent.[18]

COMPETITIVE RELATIONSHIP METHODS. Some advertisers determine the advertising appropriation by looking at the amount their competitors spend; they rely on the "wisdom" of the industry. What they are really doing is following the industry's collective ignorance, and they fail to take advantage of a weapon that could help them gain an advantage over competitors. In addition, competitors may vary widely in size, follow different promotional strategies, or even marketing strategies. Can and/or should a small or medium-sized firm match the amount spent by the largest competitor?

A variant of this method is to spend more than a firm's share of the market to maintain or improve market share. For new products, a company's share of advertising expenditure should be twice the projected market share.[19] The method does recognize that advertising expenditures precede sales and may be considered an investment in market share, if the rest of the marketing program is also effective. Nevertheless, companies should not use this rule of thumb unless all the other competitive factors are considered.

Economic Models

An economic model for determining the advertising appropriation should take five elements into account (Figure 11.13).[20]

The first two elements characterizing the advertising expenditure-sales relationship are: the *marginal rate of advertising effectiveness* at various levels of advertising expenditure, which specifies the slope and curvature of the function; and the *market potential*, because whatever the amount spent on advertising, sales cannot exceed this upper asymptotical limit. The relationship between advertising expenditures and sales is represented in the first diagram in Figure 11.13.

The importance of advertising carry-over effects should also be taken into account in the advertising expenditure level determination process.[21] To account for carry-over effects in the advertising budget determination process, a third element, the *carry-over effect rate* of an advertising dollar over subsequent periods, should be included as well as the *discount rate*, a fourth element that is used to discount the future income stream of the advertising investment at its present value. These two new elements are essential in establishing the relationship represented in the second diagram of Figure 11.13, which relates advertising to the resulting long-run sales flow estimated at its present value.

The fifth element that should be taken into account in a theoretical model for setting the advertising appropriation is the *gross margin rate* prevailing at various sales levels for the company considered. This leads to an estimate of the third relationship in Figure 11.13 between advertising and gross contribution to profits. By subtracting the amounts invested in advertising (represented by the 45° line in the third diagram), from the gross contribution to profits, the fourth relationship can be derived, i.e., the relationship between advertising expenditures and net profits. This relationship has the highest significance for an advertiser, because it shows the optimal advertising expenditure level B*

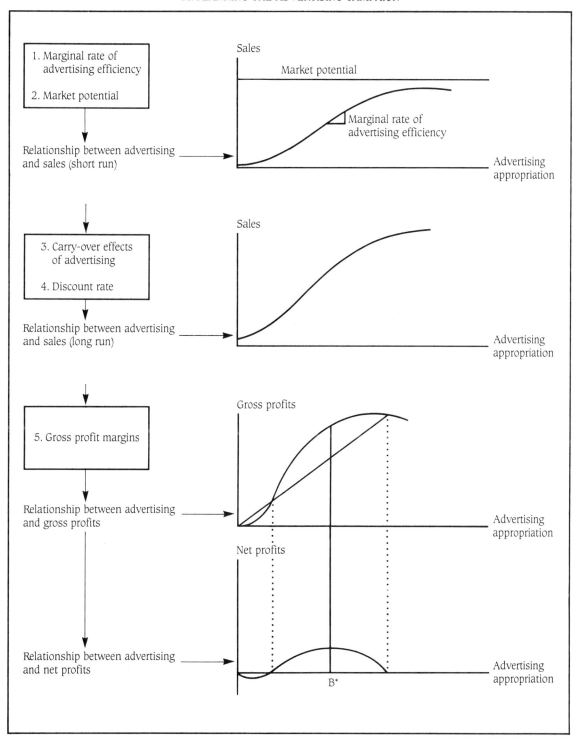

FIGURE 11.13   A Theoretical Model for Determining the Advertising Appropriation

that should be selected to maximize the company's long-run net profits.

LIMITATIONS OF THE ECONOMIC MODEL. Several assumptions are embedded in the economic model. One is that the shape of the advertising/ sales relationship is not greatly affected by media-mix decisions and creative decisions. Another is that this model does not explicitly take account of the interdependence between advertising and other marketing mix variables. For example, a change in price may affect the market potential and have a carry-over effect that interacts with the carry-over effect of advertising. Also, the model does not explicitly incorporate the effect of competition on the overall advertising effort. Finally, when several products of the same company are advertised, the model does not explicitly take into account the joint effect of advertising across all products. Nevertheless, despite these drawbacks, there are numerous practical approaches for determining the appropriation using the economic model.

SOME PRACTICAL APPROACHES USING THE ECONOMIC MODEL. Several attempts have been made to include many or all of various elements in a practical method for determining the optimal advertising appropriation. Examples are the method proposed by Vidale and Wolfe,[22] the DEMON model[23] used by the BBD&O advertising agency to estimate the advertising budgets at the introduction stage of new consumer products, and the adaptive control model of John Little.[24] All these methods share a common characteristic: they attempt to measure all or part of the relationship between advertising expenditures and sales in order to derive the optimal advertising appropriation. These procedures and models require a sophisticated level of mathematical training in order to be fully understood. In the San Augustine and Foley study, these types of quantitative models were found to be used only in the consumer markets,

and by only four per cent of the executives surveyed.[25]

Objective and Task Methods
As was emphasized earlier, an advertising campaign should contribute to the realization of precise marketing objectives, which in turn help realize a company's general objectives, given the marketing manager's predictions about environmental variables. From these objectives, an advertising manager derives the means necessary to meet them. These means include the advertising message content and format and the media selected to convey the message to the relevant market segments. Decisions about the structure and format of the message depend on the media selected and are guided by a *communication model*, for example, the hierarchy of effects model, and by the selected *communication task* indicated in the advertising objectives. This process is represented in Figure 11.14. These advertising tools involve costs that indicate the size of the budget needed to meet the advertising objectives.

This method of determining an advertising budget is known as the *objective and task method*. For an advertising campaign to be effective and profitable, advertisers should select objectives so that the costs warrant their pursuit. This is why it is always necessary to reassess the objectives in the light of costs whenever a harmonious equilibrium has not been reached between expected returns and costs. This is represented in Figure 11.14 by the feedback loop from approval of budget to the campaign objectives.

Procedures to measure an advertising campaign's effectiveness are typically designed to control the whole advertising process. From such an evaluation, the advertising strategy can be reassessed for the following period (year), because market penetration, the level of consumer awareness, or consumer attitudes achieved at the end of the current campaign can then be measured. This is represented in

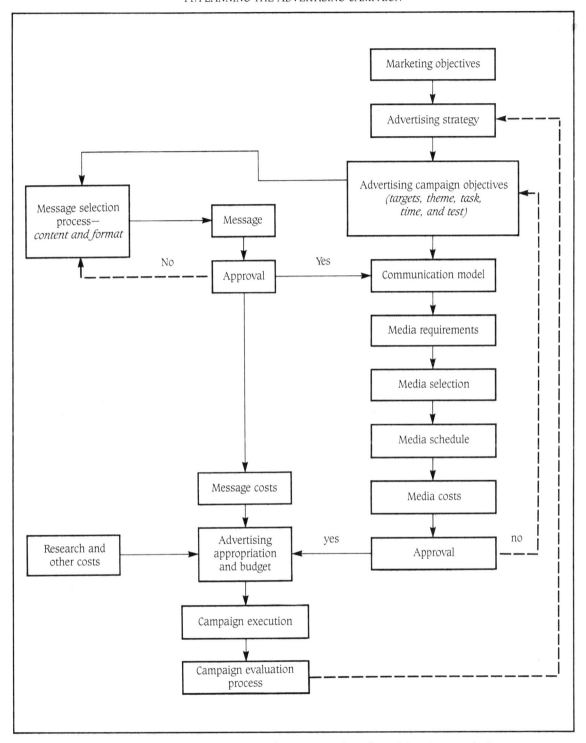

FIGURE 11.14   Objective and Task Method for Setting the Advertising Appropriation

Figure 11.14 by the feedback loop from campaign evaluation to advertising strategy.

The objective and task method is a logical method that allows advertisers to start from desired objectives and to follow a logical procedure. Its greatest strength is that efforts are made to determine the level of advertising appropriation that can best attain advertising objectives. It also forces advertisers to think through the whole process and acquire experience and competence in carrying out this difficult but rewarding process. An advertiser would be less likely to concur with John Wanamaker's statement that about 50 per cent of his advertising budget is wasted, but he doesn't know which half! San Augustine and Foley found that 20 per cent of non-consumer executives and 12 per cent of consumer executives used the objective and task method.[26]

When asked how he advises clients on budgeting effectively, Peter Swain, president of Media Buying Services in Toronto, reported:

Our methods vary with advertisers. The ideal circumstance is to work on a task method: define the objectives for a given point in the campaign, then determine the necessary budget.

Our primary concern should be to determine the needs. The more exactly we can pinpoint... needs and objectives, the more effectively we can use the budget to fulfil those objectives. When inflation takes a bigger chunk of our budget dollars, we may have to downscale objectives or decrease spending.

Hopefully in the 1980s, we will see a lot more advertising research on the advertiser's part. That's necessary because if we can predict effectively the value of the shift produced by advertising, we can judge whether increasing media costs are worthwhile. I suspect if we took this approach, we'd see that some of the increase in costs is quite reasonable.[27]

OBJECTIVE AND TASK METHOD AND PAYOUT PLANNING. With promising products, it may be advisable to plan the marketing and advertising effort over three years. The advertising effort would be higher in the earlier years, when awareness for the product has to be built, than in later years when preference would be the task. Since media costs are often higher in the earlier years, it may be better to invest in advertising early in a product's life cycle in order to improve the new product's chances of success.

The objective and task method may be used to estimate the advertising appropriation for each year of the three-year plan. The campaign objectives are set in terms of a communication model, and the criteria for approving the media costs are based on the long-term marketing objectives. If the estimated costs are still too high, a reassessment may have to be made of the campaign objectives.

A hypothetical example of a three-year payout based on the objective and task method is provided in Table 11.2. In the first year, the task of the campaign is to increase awareness of the brand name from ten per cent to 50 per cent. Based on the target market and the type of approach to be used, several media are selected. The total appropriation is then estimated to be $2,100,000. The total appropriation for the three-year period is thus estimated at about $5 million for projected sales of $28 million. Of that amount, 42 per cent is spent the first year; 32 per cent and 25 per cent the second and third year, respectively. The effect of such a spending pattern is to strongly support the brand when it needs it most, and to improve its chances of becoming a leading brand in its product category. It represents an investment in market share and in long-term profits.

Allocation of the Appropriation: The Advertising Budget

In the process of developing the appropriation, some consideration may or may not have been given to how the appropriation is to be spent. The advertising budget must, however, provide this information, including allocations by ad-

TABLE 11.2   A Hypothetical Example of a Three-Year Payout Plan

Year	Projected sales ($)	Market share	Price ($)	Distribution coverage	Communication task	Advertising appropriation ($)	Share of three-year advertising budget	A/S
1	5,000,000	10%	50	10%	50% awareness from 10%	2,100,000	42%	42
2	9,000,000	15%	45	30%	60% knowledge from 20%	1,600,000	32%	18
3	14,000,000	25%	35	60%	40% preference from 20%	1,300,000	26%	9
Total	*28,000,000*					*5,000,000*	*100%*	

vertising function, by medium and time period (schedule), by sales territory, and by product.

BY ADVERTISING FUNCTION.   The appropriation must cover all advertising activities, and allocations must be made for four categories of expenses:

1. total media allocation used to buy time or space in various media. These costs are roughly 70 to 90 per cent of the appropriation;
2. message production costs, which may be up to 15 per cent or 20 per cent of the appropriation;
3. research costs when research is used at any point in the development of the campaign (consumer, media, copy, and effectiveness research). These costs vary from zero to 15 per cent of the appropriation;
4. administrative overhead costs, including contingencies.

BY MEDIUM AND TIME PERIOD (SCHEDULE).   Decisions must be made on the allocation of total media expenditures to the various *media types*—newspaper, magazine, radio, television, direct mail, and other media. For instance, an advertiser may allocate 30 per cent of the media budget to magazines, 20 per cent to radio, and 50 per cent to television. With each type of medium, allocation of expenditures is made according to media vehicles, which are the individual magazines or newspapers, tele-

vision networks or radio stations, and the television shows during which the commercials will be broadcast. A media budget for magazines can be split equally among three vehicles, i.e., *Chatelaine, Homemaker's* magazine, and *Reader's Digest.* (See Chapter 14.)

The *media schedule* is worked out for each media vehicle. This schedule provides all the details about the issues of the magazines or newspapers, the days, and the time of the day at which each advertisement will appear or will be broadcast. The schedule also gives indications about the *media options* (the number of colours for print advertisements, the size of the advertisement or length of the commercial, the position of the advertisement in the vehicle).

BY SALES TERRITORY.   This task complements the previous one, since this allocation represents another breakdown of the total media budget. It concerns the disparities among sales territories in terms of penetration, sales potential, message appropriateness, and media availability. For example, how do you allocate the media budget according to the French and English markets in Montreal; the English, Italian, and French markets in Toronto; the English markets in Vancouver, Toronto, and Halifax? This allocation must answer such questions as sales potential, how well a brand is doing, how effective the message is to each group, and availability of media and differences in viewing patterns.

BY PRODUCT. When an advertising appropriation has been developed for a whole line of products, the budget must specify the amount allocated to each product in the line. Three types of allocation are possible:

1. a *proportional* allocation is made according to the share of each item in the total dollar volume of the line. New additions to the line may receive little advertising support other than the promotional value of the family name. An often used method is a small display of two or three low-selling items (receiving a small allocation) within the advertisement for the best-selling item.

2. a *concentrated* allocation is made to the best sellers in the line, in the hopes that increased spending on these items will create more goodwill toward the family name that will carry over to the other items.

3. an *unbalanced* allocation is made in favour of low-selling items with good potential. Some advertising support is withdrawn from the best sellers and for new items with fast growth potential. This is equivalent to the investment spending method used with the objective and task method.

Summary

Planning, executing, and controlling an advertising campaign involves a six-step approach: develop the fact book; develop the marketing plan; develop a preliminary advertising plan; complete and approve the advertising plan; execute the campaign; evaluate the campaign's effects.

Within this process, two critical and interrelated tasks are undertaken: setting the objectives of the advertising campaign and developing the advertising appropriation and budget. Although these are difficult tasks, they are essential steps in planning, executing, and controlling

the advertising function. If its existence is not properly justified, advertising is bound to suffer in times of economic slowdown.

Precise and operational advertising objectives must specify five ingredients: the Target audience, the Theme of the campaign, the Task of the communication over the Time Horizon, and the Test criteria for determining the effectiveness of the campaign.

The advertising budget includes the total appropriation as well as the exact allocation of the appropriation. Methods for determining the appropriation include naive methods, economic models, and objective and task methods. Allocation of the appropriation may be made according to advertising functions, media, time periods, sales territories, and products.

Decisions on the advertising objectives and budget are difficult ones for most situations. Since they are closely related to each other, and to the creative and media decisions, it is important that these two tasks be done properly. It may take several iterations between objectives and budget to arrive at a satisfactory set of decisions, but the overall campaign will be more consistent and effective. The client and the agency service group will gain useful insights that will make future campaign planning more efficient.

Questions for Study

1. "My only concern is whether or not I will sell more if I advertise". Comment.

2. Find some examples of print advertisements for each of the communication tasks in Table 11.1. Justify your choice.

3. Is it reasonable to expect advertisers or agencies to be able to state precise and operational objectives? If this is not done, who is most likely to be affected? Explain your answer.

4. Relate the following fictitious slogans to the hierarchy of effects model of Table 11.1. Justify your choice.

(a) "The best ice cream in all creation"
(b) "The newest show on earth" (an amusement park)
(c) "Help that counts" (personal computers)
(d) "Mr. Salad's best friend" (dressing)
(e) "Be at your best" (designer clothes)

5. Discuss under what conditions the percentage of sales methods may be a reasonable method for determining the size of the appropriation. What are the major risks in relying on it?

6. "Your share of advertising dollars should be equal or greater than your share of the market". Comment.

7. "The objective and task method is much too difficult for most advertisers or agencies to use". Do you agree with this statement?

8. Does it make sense to spend a much larger proportion of the appropriation on one or two items in a product line, rather than on the rest of the line? Explain.

9. "You cannot properly plan advertising expenditures because you never know how the market will respond to the creative approach of the campaign". Do you agree with this statement? Explain your answer.

10. "Advertising objectives must be stated in operational terms in order to plan the campaign effectively." Do you agree with this statement? Explain what form the statement of advertising objectives should take, and how they affect the other campaign decisions, i.e., creative, media, budget, and research.

Problems

1. Select a product with a low awareness level, and develop some advertising objectives and an advertising appropriation. Assume that your market is situated in an urban area, and that radio would be the best medium for that product. Indicate *all* the steps you would go through using the objec-tive and task method for the appropriation. Indicate also *all* the information you would need to complete this job.

2. You are the owner of AdVisor, a small advertising agency, and you have been hired by Mr. Watson, the owner of the Surelock Homes Company (see Chapter 5, problem no. 2). Mr. Watson, the inventor of the Surelock, has been able to interest some investors and a provincial agency in manufacturing the new product in your province. Mr. Watson has been able to ascertain the following facts through secondary sources (mainly Statistics Canada), and a small survey conducted in the Toronto metropolitan area using personal interviews:

(a) Only owners of private dwellings may be interested in the new lock. About 40 per cent of these owners say they are interested.

(b) The vast majority of those interested in the new lock are male heads of households.

(c) When *shown* the new lock, 30 per cent of those who claim to be interested in the new lock say they intend to purchase on the average two units if the price is between $10 and $15. This proportion drops to 25 per cent willing to purchase one unit if the lock is priced between $16 and $20. Above $20, only 10 per cent have a positive intention of purchasing the lock.

(d) These figures drop dramatically to 10, 5, and 1 per cent when the lock is only *described* (i.e., without demonstration).

(e) From the 1981 census, the number of owned dwellings in Canada is distributed as follows:

	Number (in '000 units)	%
Newfoundland	120	2.3
P.E.I.	28	0.5
Nova Scotia	195	3.8

New Brunswick	158	3.1
Quebec	1157	22.5
Ontario	1879	36.5
Manitoba	236	4.6
Saskatchewan	243	4.7
Alberta	478	9.3
British Columbia	641	12.5
Yukon and N.W.T.	7	0.1
Canada	*5142*	*100.0*

(f) Preliminary costing of the new product is as follows:

Volume		Average Cost Per Unit
0 – 200 000		$10.00
200 000 – 400 000		7.00
400 000 – 800 000		5.00
800 000 – 1 600 000		3.00

You are asked to develop a complete advertising plan for the Surelock Homes Company, paying particular attention to the advertising strategy, the campaign objectives, and the advertising budget.

You know from experience that you need at least five repetitions for a television commercial to make the audience learn the message, and twelve repetitions for a print advertisement. Finally, you know that a television commercial would cost about $50,000 to produce, while a print advertisement would cost $8,000 in colour and $3,000 in black and white.

Notes

1. Kenneth E. Bowes, "Develop Marketing Plan, with or without Agency, before Trying to Devise Ad Budget," *Marketing News*, 18 March 1983, Section 2, p. 17.
2. Stanley F. Stasch and Patricia Lanktree, "Can Your Marketing Planning Procedures Be Improved," *Journal of Marketing* (Summer 1980), pp. 79-90.
3. Deborah J. Nicholls and John P. Liefeld, "The Price (Brand) - Perceived Quality Relationship: Further Evidence," *The Canadian Marketer* (Fall 1973), pp. 21-24; see also Thomas E. Muller, "Price Awareness in the Supermarket," *Marketing*, ed. James D. Forbes, vol. 4 (Administrative Sciences Association of Canada, 1983), pp. 238-46.
4. Russell H. Colley, *Defining Advertising Goals for Measured Advertising Results* (New York: Association of National Advertisers, 1961).
5. Ibid.; see also Stuart H. Britt, "Are So-Called Successful Advertising Campaigns Really Successful," *Marketing Management and Administrative Action*, ed. S.H. Britt and H.W. Boyd, Jr.,
   3rd ed. (New York: McGraw-Hill, 1973), pp. 553-64.
6. G.H.G. McDougall, "Canadian Theme Appeals in Advertising," *Marketing 1978*, ed. J.M. Boisvert and R. Savitt (Administrative Sciences Association of Canada, 1978), pp. 178-88.
7. "Grenadier Chocolate Company Limited," *Canadian Problems in Marketing*, ed. Blair Little, John R. Kennedy, Donald H. Thain, and Robert E.M. Nourse, 4th ed. (Toronto: McGraw-Hill Ryerson), pp. 501-7.
8. Britt p. 562.
9. Stasch and Lanktree pp. 79 – 90.
10. Randy Scotland, "Feds Again Top the List on Ad Spending," *Marketing*, 11 April 1983, pp. 1, 35.
11. James G. Barnes, "Advertising and the Courts," *Canadian Business Review* (Autumn 1975), pp. 51-54.
12. Lionel A. Mitchell and Peter M. Banting, "Organization Structure and Factors Influencing Advertising Activities," *Marketing*, ed. James D. Forbes, vol. 4 (Administrative Sciences Association of Canada, 1983), pp. 220-29.

13. Lionel A. Mitchell, "Common Approaches to Budgeting Advertising: The Wheel of Advertising," *Developments in Canadian Marketing*, ed. Robert D. Tamilia (Administrative Sciences Association of Canada, 1978), pp. 30-31.

14. André J. San Augustine and William F. Foley, "How Large Advertisers Set Budgets," *Journal of Advertising Research* (October 1975), pp. 11-16.

15. "The Mackenzie Salt Company," *Canadian Problems in Marketing*, ibid., pp. 320-26.

16. "The Langton Company," *Canadian Problems in Marketing*, ibid., pp. 318-20.

17. San Augustine and Foley, pp. 11 – 16.

18. Ibid.

19. Ibid.

20. James O. Peckhan, "Can We Relate Advertising Dollars to Market Share Objectives?," *How Much to Spend For Advertising*?, ed. Malcolm A. McNiven (New York: Association of National Advertisers, 1969), p. 30.

21. Kenneth A. Longman, *Advertising* (New York: Harcourt Brace Jovanovich, 1971), p. 18; for threshold effects, see F.W.A. Bliemel, "Are Thresholds of Advertising Response Substantial," *Linking Knowledge and Action*, vol. 4, ed. James D. Forbes (Administrative Sciences Association of Canada, 1983), pp. 1-10.

22. M.L. Vidale and H.B. Wolfe, "An Operations-Research Study of Sales Response to Advertising," *Operations Research* (June 1957), pp. 370-80.

23. David B. Learner, "Profit Maximization through New Product Marketing Planning and Control," *Applications of the Sciences to Marketing Management*, ed. Frank M. Bass, Charles W. King, and Edgar A. Pessemier (New York: John Wiley and Sons, 1968), pp. 151-67.

24. John D.C. Little, "A Model of Adaptive Control of Promotional Spending," *Operations Research* (November 1966), pp. 1075-97.

25. San Augustine and Foley, pp. 11 – 16.

26. Ibid.

27. Michael Hallé, "Computers Can Help Agencies Save Costs, Increase Efficiency," *Marketing*, 25 February 1980.

Developing Effective Advertising Messages

After the advertising appropriation decision, the next important aspect of planning an advertising campaign is the development of the creative strategy and plan. The creative plan addresses the problem of translating the communication task specified in the campaign objectives into effective advertisements using specific themes and slogans for the campaign. The planning process of an advertising campaign, the creative and media plans should be developed at about the same time. It is nearly impossible for an agency's account executive or an art director to determine the advertising message content and format unless they know what type of media will be used. The design of a thirty second TV commercial has quite different considerations and constraints than a four-colour full-page advertisement in a national magazine. Consequently, the creative people should be informed of media decisions as soon as possible.

In the same way, the content of the message has obvious media implications. For instance, if product demonstration is an important ingredient in the advertising creative plan, television would almost certainly be used. High-quality image advertising is best conveyed by four-colour advertisements in prestige national magazines.

This chapter describes how advertisers can develop effective advertising messages.

The Advertising Creative Process

Advertising Message Creation

Developing the creative plan implies the steps listed in Figure 12.1. The whole creative process must start with an understanding of potential consumer behaviour and consumers' motives, knowledge, perceptions, attitudes, and buying habits with respect to the advertised product category. Then advertisers should select the advertising message content. This set of decisions is aimed at determining *what* should be said to potential buyers to induce them to purchase the advertised brand. The next set of decisions attempts to answer *how* the message should be put to woo potential buyers in the most effective way. Once these decisions on structure and format of the advertising message are resolved, the television or radio commercials or print advertisements are produced.

The task of deciding what to say is essentially the responsibility of the account executive, who is assisted by the agency's creative department, marketing executives, and research people working for the agency or the client. The decisions about the message structure and format—the words, images, and sounds used to convey the message—are the responsibility of the agency's creative department.

Creativity in Advertising

One of the simplest definitions of creativity is "the ability to formulate new combinations

Gentlemen Prefer Hanes.
Sensuously smooth, luxuriously sheer, undeniably silky, unmistakably Hanes.

PLATE VIII   In this advertisement, the layout is intended to make the reader's eye follow the stairway from top to bottom. The focal point has been placed in the middle of the bottom part.

Courtesy Hanes Hosiery, Inc.

The beginning of a beautiful past.

PLATE IX **The dramatic use of colour is well combined with the other elements of this advertisement, as well as with the symmetry of the composition.**
Courtesy Houbigant Inc.

PLATE X This type of layout evokes abundance. This feeling and message atmosphere might have been achieved at the expense of some clarity.

Courtesy General Mills Canada, Inc.

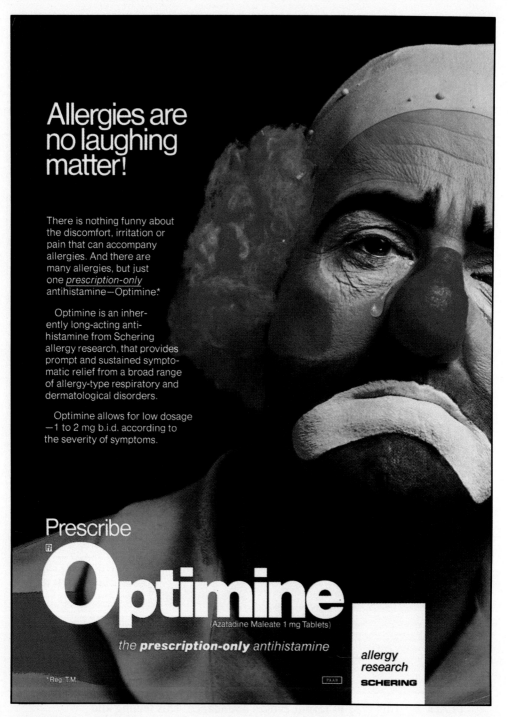

PLATE XI   The impression of numerous shades in this advertisement has been created by the superimposition of four plates: red, blue, yellow, and black.

Courtesy Schering Canada Inc.

Left is yellow only; right is red only.

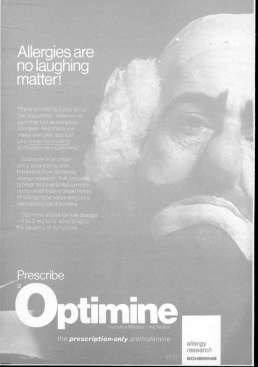

Top left is red and yellow; bottom left is blue only; on the right is blue and yellow.

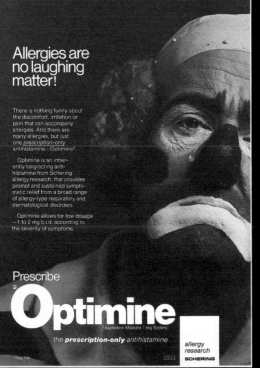

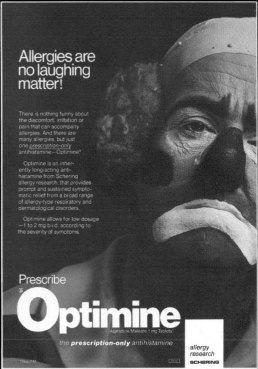

Left is blue and red; top right is red, blue and yellow; bottom right is black only.

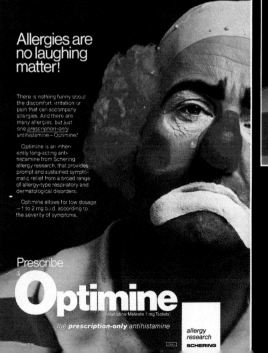

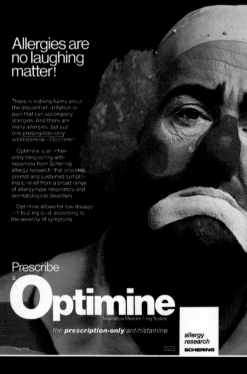

Top left is black, yellow and blue; bottom left is black, yellow and red; the right is in full colour (as in Plate X1)—red, blue, yellow and black.

1. Understanding of potential buyer behaviour with respect to product category and brands:
   • motives, needs, benefits
   • attitudes
   • perception, knowledge
   • buying habits

   ↓

2. Message content decisions: *What* should be said to potential buyers to motivate them to buy the brand?

   ↓

3. Message structure and format decisions: *How* should be said to be as effective as possible?

   ↓

4. Advertising message production:
   • print advertisements
   • radio commercials
   • TV commercials

FIGURE 12.1   Developing the Creative Plan

from two or more concepts already in the mind."[1] Although this definition may seem simple, the act of creating never is. Advertising creation is generally the result of hard work, sweat, and persistence. Advertising creative people who get "inspired" ideas that turn out to be great ideas is part of Madison Avenue folklore and bears little resemblance to reality.

What is needed to create a good and effective advertisement? Two ingredients are essential: people who are truly creative and a creative process that involves a method and discipline. Various studies have tried to identify the common characteristics of highly creative people.[2] Such characteristics are that creative people share a boundless curiosity. They are interested in practically every aspect of life, read a lot, and want to understand everything. They also are imaginative, capable of conceptual fluency;

they can generate many original ideas within a short period of time. They are empathetic—able to feel what others are feeling. Their sense of humour is more than average, and they tend to be more enthusiastic and less authoritarian than others, and they generally show a high degree of independence of judgment. People with this mix of qualities are a necessary but not sufficient ingredient for designing successful advertisements.

The Creative Process

The other prerequisite to successful advertising design is method and discipline in the creative process. Authors do not agree on the role and/or mechanisms of the creative process. Some describe the process of generating original ideas as one in which "talent plays a leading part in that which is known as association of ideas";[3] "the most [that] can honestly be said is that it usually includes some or all of these phases: orientation, preparation, analysis, hypothesis, incubation, synthesis, and verification."[4] Others see the creation process "as definite as the production of Fords."[5] The truth lies between these two extreme point of views. There are certain steps that promote the creative process. Frank Alexander Armstrong describes five basic steps: assessing the situation, defining the problem, using the subconscious, holding an idea-producing session, and using judgement in selecting ideas.[6]

Assessing the situation. The creative process should start with a clear understanding of the problem, the goals to be attained, and all the relevant facts. In an advertising context, a clear understanding of the marketing objectives, the market situation, the marketing strategy, and the brand's marketing mix are the starting point for designing an advertisement. Susan Kastner, vice-president and creative director at the Benton and Bowles advertising agency in Toronto, thinks that in order to create more effectively, the part of the marketing process that should be worked at hardest is: "Definitely the preparation for the creative, the planning, getting the marketing scene cold and clear."[7] To illustrate the point, Susan Kastner gives the example of Procter & Gamble, her agency's largest client: "When you have your marketing data and your strategy, then you can feed them into your creative."[8]

Defining the problem. In this phase of the creative process the problem is clearly understood and defined. It is practically impossible to solve a vaguely defined problem. In an advertising context, identification of the marketing and advertising objectives that specific advertisements should contribute to achieve, as well as the main constraints, are the second step to perform.

Using the subconscious. Creative people involved in the design of an advertisement should give the subconscious time to work on the problem. Working in a rush and under severe time pressure may prevent this step from taking place.

The idea-producing session. Once the subconscious has had time to work, the conscious mind can be put back to work to produce ideas. This can be done in a systematic way, either by an individual or in group sessions, known as brainstorming sessions.[9] The procedure is usually to gather a group of five to ten people. The problem is stated to the group, and each participant generates as many ideas as possible in a freewheeling discussion. At this stage, no criticisms are made, and all ideas, even the wildest, are encouraged, recorded, and considered.

Selecting the best idea. Once a large number of ideas have been generated, the best one is identified. The probability of finding a good idea out of a pool of ideas is greater when one starts with a large pool. All kinds of input are considered in order to find and refine ideas to arrive at the best possible selling advertisement or commercial.

Although the creative process depends on the individual talents of the creative staff, research plays an important role. This is also recognized by Susan Kastner, who asserts that to create more effective advertisements, research should be used "every step of the way. Research, to know your market, to discover how consumers view your product. Research during the making of the commercial to ensure the message is being produced more effectively, and research the ad after production to make sure you continue to say the right thing. . . . Research is absolutely indispensable."[10]

The Advertising Creation Budget

The ideas generated during the creative process are tried out and pre-tested on consumers. When many ideas are generated and many advertisements created and tested, the odds increase that the idea chosen is a very good one. But as an agency spends more time and resources to create and test alternate advertisements, costs also increase. Thus a compromise must be reached on the number of advertisements an advertising agency should create for its clients. The problem with advertising creation is that advertising agencies may lack the motivation to create as many advertisements as this optimal number. Indeed, it has often been said that expenditures on advertising creation are probably too small in comparison with media expenditures. Two reasons may account for this. One is that many advertising managers do not see advertising creation expenditures as yielding concrete results. The "quality" of advertisements may be improved, but how can message "quality" be measured? In contrast, money spent on the media can buy more advertisements or more time for the advertiser. Right or wrong, the latter often seem to be more concrete and profitable expenses to an advertising manager. The second reason can be found in the compensation structure of advertising agencies. When an agency is compensated with a 15 per cent commission on media billings, the creation costs are supported by the agency. At present, the costs of creating and pretesting advertisements typically run around five per cent of the advertising budget.

This problem has been analyzed in a study by Irwin Gross,[11] who showed that agencies generally create too few advertisements for pretesting. Advertisers thus do not necessarily get a good advertisement, but only the best out of the small number of advertisements created. Gross concluded that agencies should devote more of the advertising appropriation to creating more advertisements, at the expense of the media budget. He has suggested that as much as three to five times more than what is presently spent (i.e., at least 15 per cent of the advertising budget) should be allocated to advertising creation. These conclusions suggest that advertising creation—although it is often recognized as a critical part of the advertising process—may not get its fair share of the advertising dollar.

Advertising Message Content

Decisions about the advertising message content are influenced the most by the marketing and advertising objectives. For instance, when an advertiser decides to convince new buyers of a product category that the advertised brand is superior in a certain respect, this sets the stage for the type of message content that should be used. The type of product being advertised also gives more or less flexibility as to what can be said. For instance, a music lover's choice of a specific brand of stereo equipment may be influenced by the quality of sound, the power, the physical appearance, and the controls available. Each points at a possible advertising appeal. The list of possible advertising claims, however, becomes more limited when it comes to advertising a specific brand of gin, for instance. Advertising agencies develop specific creative styles and approaches that dictate the kind of advertising message content to be created and produced.

Advertising approaches can be classified according to the situation and considerations involved.[12] One convenient classification is based on the nature of the appeal, whether the advertising is argumentative or suggestive. Although the border between these two types of advertising may be difficult to draw with precision, it is nevertheless convenient. *Argumentative* advertisements give specific and explicit reasons for buying a product and a particular brand. The selling argument can be based on rational grounds, but this definition does not preclude the selling argument from arousing such emotions as pleasure or fear. The distinctive feature of this type of advertising is whether it explicitly uses arguments to sell the product or service. *Suggestive* advertising does not explicitly state any rationale for buying the product or brand. It appeals directly to consumers emotions and feelings and conveys a certain product or brand image.

Argumentative Advertising

Argumentative advertising may be approached in one of three ways: according to the target group to be reached, consumers' underlying motivations, or the differential advantages of a product.

The Target Group Approach
This approach uses as a basic advertising appeal the specification of the consumer group to which the product or service is intended. A well-known example of this type of advertisement is Pepsi-Cola's claim: "For Those Who Think Young." Cigarette manufacturers also use this approach. For instance, the du Maurier advertisement (Figure 12.2) states, "For People with a Taste for Something Better." Here the advertiser is attempting to have consumers associate the brand with a specific target audience profile—people who are striving for excellence. Some advertisers have criticized this approach as dogmatic.[13] This type of advertising gives little or no justification of

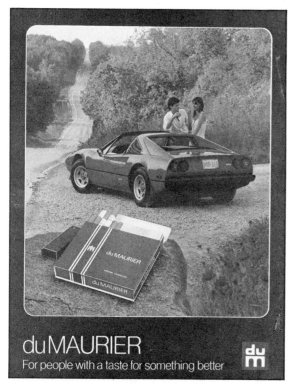

duMAURIER
For people with a taste for something better

FIGURE 12.2 **(du Maurier) The theme high-lights product or lifestyle excellence—real or aspirational. According to the advertising manager, the double entendre is intentional in the word "taste". This theme was selected after extensive consumer research had positioned du Maurier as an above-averge product and package, and the advertising campaign was designed to complement consumers' perceptions.**
Courtesy Imperial Tobacco Ltd.

the brand's appropriateness for this category of consumers. In the du Maurier advertisement, no justification is given for the statement that people with a taste for something better should use the brand or in what way du Maurier is the best brand to be smoked by this kind of people.

The target audience approach has often been effective, especially when it associates a product or brand with a certain reference group. For instance, the association between beer and sports fans has been a favourite theme of the Canadian beer industry; it attempts to associ-

ate beer drinking with a certain lifestyle. All those who are—or like thinking of themselves as—sports fans may develop a favourable attitude toward the brand, which becomes an additional symbol of what they are or would like to be associated with.

This approach, however, has major limitations. Some advertisers argue that associating a brand with its target group may be a desirable marketing objective but a poor advertising theme.[14] The argument is that there is no motivating element in the statement of the company's marketing objectives that may induce consumers to actually buy the brand. This approach also does not differentiate the advertised brand from its competitors, who can make the same claim. This is why many advertisers would favour the motivation or the differential product advantage approaches.

The Motivation Approach

The motivation approach is more commonly used, since it provides a framework that is useful for many situations and product categories. This approach has two major steps.[15] The first is the selection of some basic psychological element of buyer behaviour involved in the purchase of the specific product and brand. This element may be a specific benefit, a motivation, or even an inhibition that prevents some consumers from buying the brand or the product category. This psychological element will then be the prime target of the advertisement. Starting from this *abstract* definition and specification of the psychological element, an advertiser will then try to find the *concrete* elements that can best arouse or evoke in consumers' minds the selected satisfaction or motivation. The second stage of the selection process leads to the choice of a specific theme for the advertisement and/or the whole advertising campaign. It specifies the content of the advertising message.

SELECTION OF THE BASIC MOTIVE. To illustrate the process of selecting the best possible psychological element of the consumer purchase decision that advertising can influence, Kurt Lewin's theory briefly outlined in Chapter 7 can be used. It will be recalled that consumers are subjected to various forces or motives related to the purchase of a certain product and/or certain brand. The forces that induce the consumer to buy the brand are motives with a positive valence. Others tend to prevent a consumer from purchasing the product, and these are motives with a negative valence. Hence, any purchase decision can be viewed as a situation of conflict that involves motives with both positive and negative valences. No purchase decision can occur as long as the negative forces override the positive ones. Moreover, the number and strength of the positive and negative forces implied in a purchase decision create psychological tension for the consumer.

Examples of non-purchase situations. Consider two examples of a purchase decision. One involves great financial risk and psychological tension and consequently, high consumer ego-involvement, for instance the purchase of a microwave oven. The other situation involves the purchase of a product characterized by lesser tension and consumer ego-involvement, such as the selection of a brand of automatic dishwashing detergent.

With the microwave oven purchase, consumers may be submitted to forces or motives that induce them to buy the product, for instance, the time saved by fast cooking, especially for households in which both spouses work outside the home, and the convenience of quick defrosting of frozen food. Other positive motives might include a consumer's pride in possessing up-to-date appliances (social motives) or the pleasure of having a well-equipped and modern kitchen. Other factors prevent many households from indulging in the purchase of a microwave oven, for instance, the relatively high price of this equipment, the health hazards that may result from exposure to microwaves, or the fact that these ovens sometimes cook

food unevenly. In some households, limited kitchen space or a relatively limited range of usage occasions may also be constraining factors. Figure 12.3a represents this conflictual situation, which often results in a non-purchase situation.

Alternatively, let us consider the psychological elements involved in purchasing an automatic dishwashing detergent. Because fewer financial and psychological risks are involved and the product is purchased more frequently, fewer negative forces with less strength are involved. Thus, the relative price for this brand may be the main negative valence force. However, among the positive motivations, which may induce the consumers to buy the brand, one may find for instance the cleaning power of the detergent, its capacity to dissolve greasy elements, and perhaps its ability to give clear and neat cookware. This situation is depicted in Figure 12.3b. In this example, the decision is a non-purchase situation because the negative motives result in stronger forces than the positive ones.

Possible advertising actions. What can advertisers do to change a non-purchase situation? The advertiser can pursue three different types of action (as well as any combination of these three actions simultaneously) that start from a given non-purchase situation (Figure 12.4).

An advertiser may try to increase satisfaction, to a point at which the resulting force would change direction, i.e., where the consumer would lean toward a purchase decision (Figure 12.4b). This is what has been attempted in the advertisement for Cascade (Figure 12.5). By demonstrating how Cascade results in clear and spotless glasses, the advertiser has tried to increase the consumer's satisfaction of the good result obtained through brand usage and to induce this consumer to switch to Cascade.

The advertiser may bring a new satisfaction into the picture, i.e., a motive that was not felt before by the consumer with regard to this type of product (Figure 12.4c). For instance, advertising featuring a toy added in a package of cereals tries to add extra satisfaction that could induce a child to insist on buying a certain brand. As an example, this approach is followed in the advertisement for *Maclean's* (Figure 12.6), which promises the satisfaction of owning a free calculator (a satisfaction not typically experienced when subscribing to a magazine).

Finally, in order to achieve the same results, an advertiser could choose to suppress (or reduce) a negative valence motive which prevents

the purchase decision from taking place (Figure 12.4d). For instance, in the case of the microwave oven, the advertiser could select to suppress or reduce one of the major constraining forces, such as the uneven cooking argument. This is the approach followed by the General Electric advertisement (Figure 12.7), which demonstrates how the new models of General Electric and Hotpoint microwave ovens achieve evenness of cooking.

The basic motive selection procedure. Given that all the forces affecting a purchase decision

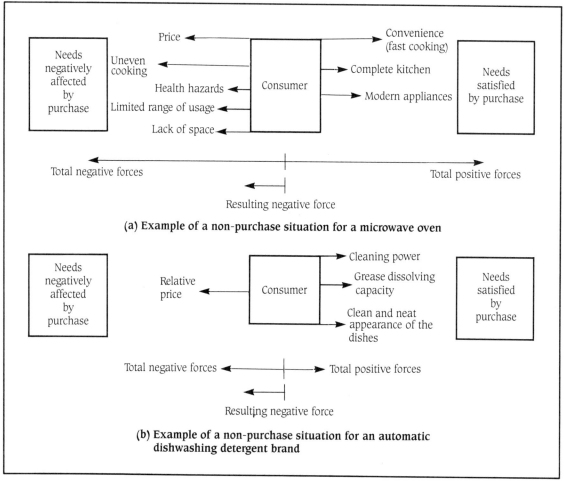

(a) **Example of a non-purchase situation for a microwave oven**

(b) **Example of a non-purchase situation for an automatic dishwashing detergent brand**

FIGURE 12.3 Examples of Two Non-Purchase Situations

are potential candidates for advertising actions, the problem arises of selecting the best one. There are several steps an advertiser can follow to select a good psychological element for building an advertising campaign.

An exhaustive list can be drawn of all the positive and negative valence motives involved in the purchase of the product category. This list should not be based on the advertisers' common sense alone. Motivation research,

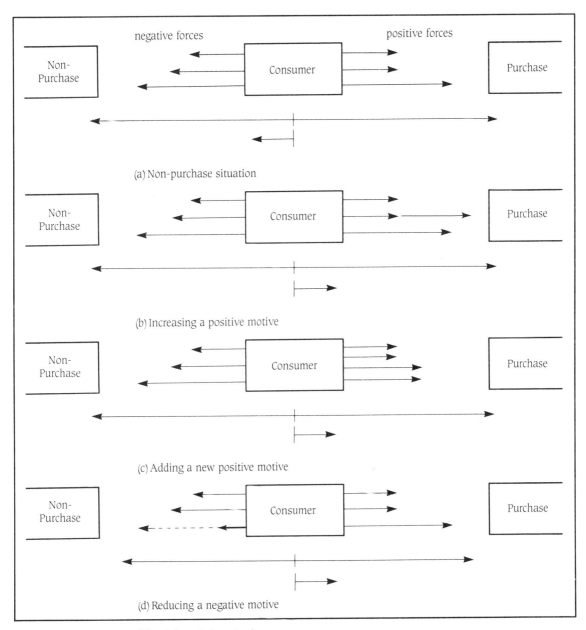

FIGURE 12.4   Possible Advertising Actions

FIGURE 12.5 To suggest the satisfaction obtained through product usages, the advertiser plays on the word "clear" with the headline, "The choice is clear." Every element in this advertisement has been designed to convey the promised benefit: clear and spotless glassware.
Courtesy Procter & Gamble Inc.

FIGURE 12.6 The main thrust of this advertisement is the offer of a free calculator. The main purchase, a subscription to *Maclean's*, almost seems incidental.
Courtesy Maclean-Hunter Ltd.

focus group interviews, and in-depth interviews are research methods and techniques that can help advertising researchers to develop the list. Research should supplement whatever knowledge marketing and advertising managers have of consumer behaviour concerning the purchase of their product category and brands.

In order to select the psychological element on which an advertising action could have the greatest effect, advertisers can apply a number of criteria and considerations to every possible motive involved in the purchase decision.

When a purchase decision simultaneously involves a product category purchase decision and a brand selection decision, then an advertiser should select a psychological element that can simultaneously influence the two interrelated decisions. This is the case with innovations or with most infrequently purchased durables, for example, a microwave oven. In such cases, advertisers can use the following criteria:

1. The selected motive, either positive or negative, should be strongly felt by individual consumers. If the selected psychological element is a strongly felt motivation that can be enhanced or a very serious constraint that can be removed or substantially decreased, then chances that the advertisements will affect individual consumer behaviour are greater. If a motive that is

FIGURE 12.7   This General Electric advertisement uses a technical demonstration to try to change consumers' perception of a drawback to using microwave ovens: unevenness of cooking.

Courtesy Canadian General Electric Company Limited/Camco Inc.

FIGURE 12.7   (continued)

not strongly felt is selected, even assuming that the advertisement is effective, it may not be sufficient to change the direction of the resulting forces toward a purchase decision.

2. The selected motive should be felt by a large proportion of consumers in the target market segment; the appeal should be relevant and effective not just for a small proportion of consumers but for the entire target audience. Obviously, it would not be very effective to select an appeal that can have an effect on only a fraction of the audience. This is especially true when the advertiser tries to remove or reduce a force inhibiting a purchase decision. If the negative force is not presently felt by a significant proportion of the market segment, then advertising may obtain results opposite to

the intended goal, by revealing to the majority of the market segment the existence of a negative argument. For instance, assume that a large proportion of potential microwave oven buyers were not aware that microwave ovens can produce uneven cooking. If an advertiser builds an advertising campaign on this argument, it may be not only ineffective with a large proportion of the market segment that did not feel this was a problem before, but it may also inform this part of the market that uneven cooking may be a drawback with this kind of product.

In addition to the above criteria, other considerations should be added so that not only the general product category is bought but also the *advertised brand*. Obviously, it is not effi-

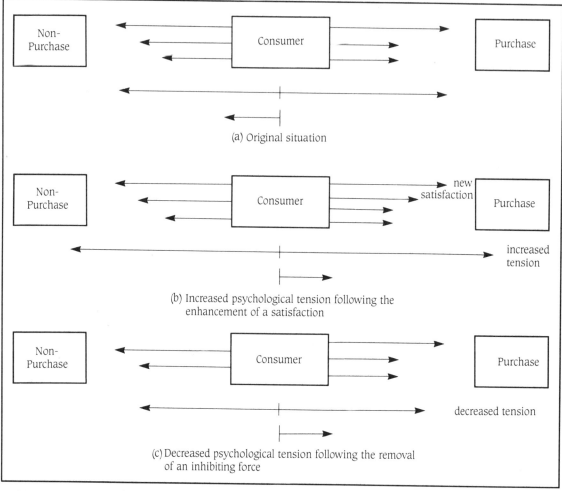

FIGURE 12.8   Psychological Tension as the Result of Different Advertising Actions

cient to induce consumers to buy a microwave oven if they end up selecting a competing brand. The motive selected should meet two other criteria:

1. The advertising claim used to enhance a motivation or reduce an inhibition should be specific to the brand and should not be applicable to the competing brands. In the microwave oven example, the product feature that promises evenness of cooking is a distinctive feature of General Electric and Hotpoint ovens and cannot be claimed by competing brands.

2. The claim must be true. This may seem obvious, but to keep the same example, it would have not been possible for General Electric to use this appeal if a technical breakthrough had not been made in the technology of microwave ovens.

Another determinant of the basic psychological element choice process is the kind of psychological tension that is aroused by the purchase decision. When the purchase of the product involves several powerful positive and negative forces, it is generally preferable to reduce or eliminate an element constraining the purchase of the brand, rather than trying to add a new motivation to buy. While the latter action would still increase the overall psychological

Nothing that comes out of a bag beats Betty Crocker cookies fresh from your oven.

Betty Crocker Cookie Mixes give you dozens of hot, fresh cookies in minutes.
Fresh homemade aroma, fresh homemade taste, because all of the good things in scratch cookies are right in the box.

Try all the delicious varieties of Betty Crocker Cookie Mixes. When it comes to taste, nothing that comes out of a bag beats Betty Crocker cookies fresh from your oven.

FIGURE 12.9   The satisfaction in eating fresh cookies is suggested by the child's smile.
Courtesy General Mills Canada, Inc.

tension of the purchase decision, the former action has a tendency to reduce the tension and to make it easier for the consumer to purchase the brand. (See Figure 12.8.)

SELECTION OF A SPECIFIC ADVERTISING THEME.   Once a basic motivating force of the consumer purchase decision has been selected, the next step is to select the advertisement theme. The advertisement theme is defined as the concept that concretely and effectively evokes in a consumer's mind the positive or negative psychological element that the advertiser has chosen. At this stage, it must be decided what should be said to consumers in order to act upon the selected motive. This step is essential, because consumers are not likely to understand abstract psychological language but only concrete facts

and words. There are several ways advertisers can translate general abstract psychological elements into concrete information and statements:

Direct description of the satisfaction.   The first possibility is to give a concrete description of the satisfaction that can be derived from using the brand. For instance, an advertiser for a toothpaste may have selected as the motivating force, parents' fear that their children may not have healthy teeth. The solution is to describe this satisfaction by demonstrating that with Toothpaste X, children will be kept away from the dentist. In the Betty Crocker advertisement reproduced in Figure 12.9, the satisfaction of having delicious fresh cookies with the cookie mix is directly described.

Inferring the satisfaction.   Joannis describes two methods of inferring the selected satisfaction.[16] First, an advertiser may try to infer the selected satisfaction by describing the product and/or brand action, and let consumers deduce the satisfaction that can be derived from using a brand. In the toothpaste example, an advertiser could state, "Toothpaste X fights cavities in youngsters' teeth." This approach is illustrated in the Canada telephone system advertisement (Figure 12.10). In this advertisement, the satisfaction is the time saving received from the telephone conference system. Instead of directly stating the underlying satisfaction: "Save time with the conference calling system," the ad says: "the fastest way to travel to business meetings." From this message business people will infer, "therefore I could save travelling time."

An advertiser can also try to further imply the selected satisfaction by describing a product feature that will result in a certain consequence, which in turn will yield the selected consumer satisfaction. Thus, an advertiser for toothpaste may state: "Toothpaste X contains sodium fluoride, an effective decay preventive agent." From this consumers might conclude "therefore it should protect against cavities" and,

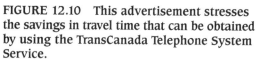

FIGURE 12.10   This advertisement stresses the savings in travel time that can be obtained by using the TransCanada Telephone System Service.

Courtesy Telecom Canada

FIGURE 12.11   Consumers who read only the headline in this advertisement have to make a two-step deduction in order to infer the underlying satisfaction to be gained through the product usage: healthy children's teeth.

Courtesy Procter & Gamble Inc.

consequently, "my kids would keep their healthy teeth." This approach is illustrated in the Crest advertisement (Figure 12.11).

Another example is the advertisement for Oh Henry bars (Figure 12.12), which features the product's physical characteristics—the bar is longer than any other brand. Hence, most consumers will or should conclude there is more to eat (the resulting consequence), and it would be a more enjoyable experience (the underlying consumer satisfaction).

Any approach that evokes the benefits a brand can bring to consumers has its merits and drawbacks. Directly describing the satisfaction is typically more abstract and generally

less credible than the two other approaches. However, it is less difficult to communicate to the market, because it is likely to be correctly understood by consumers who cannot be led astray in the stream of deductive statements they need to make to understand the satisfaction they can derive from this brand.

However, the second and especially the third inductive approach are more concrete because they directly relate to the product. Thus they are more likely to be believed, because the message is more fact- and product-feature oriented. Unfortunately, many consumers may not correctly deduce the proper satisfaction, or even worse, could derive quite different conclu-

FIGURE 12.12 **This is an example of an advertisement that few consumers would have difficulty understanding.**
Courtesy Lowney Inc.

sions from those intended. It is conceivable, for instance, that with the Oh Henry advertisement, some consumers may conclude that "there is more to eat, therefore it is higher in calorie content."

Selecting the proper theme or advertising claim for an advertisement and for the advertising campaign should be done according to how well each possible theme meets the following criteria: its likelihood of being properly understood by consumers, how brand specific it is, and how believable and how acceptable to consumers it is. Because the theme will be translated into specific advertisements and commercials, other criteria should include how well each advertisement concept lends itself to being easily and powerfully expressed by the agency's creative department.

The before–after demonstration. The advertising concept can often be best conveyed by showing or demonstrating the result of the product. One particular instance of product demonstration is to show the situation before and after product usage, and consequently, the substantial improvement in the consumer's

situation and satisfaction which has resulted from product consumption. The approach has often been used by advertisers of drugs, pharmaceutical products, and cosmetics. In this case, advertisers dramatically emphasize the difference between the situations before and after the advertised product has had its effects. This approach is illustrated in the advertisement reproduced in Figure 12.13.

Comparative advertising. Another approach for evoking product satisfaction is to make direct comparisons with competing brands. This style of advertising is relatively recent, at least on the scale at which it is presently used. A substantial proportion of advertising can now be classified under the heading of comparative advertising. Figures 12.14 and 12.15 show two examples following two different approaches. Olivetti undertakes a systematic comparison of its personal computer features with those of its identified competition—IBM, Apple, and Xerox. Note that only the characteristics for which Olivetti is better or equal to competitors have been retained. The Tide advertisement shows

A BEFORE AND AFTER STORY BY NIVEA CLEANSING MILK.

Whether you wear a little make-up or a lot, come clean with pure and simple Nivea Milk.
It works deep down to gently wash away all types of regular make-up.

It also replenishes your natural moisture to leave you looking and feeling terrific.
So cleanse your face with Nivea Milk every day.
You'll uncover beautiful, beautiful skin.
Nivea Milk.
For beautiful clean skin.

FIGURE 12.13   Before and after advertisements are often used for drugs and pharmaceutical products.
Courtesy Smith & Nephew, Inc.

how much better the product performs in comparison with other unnamed brands.

Sometimes, though, when using comparative advertising, an advertiser concedes some superiority to a competitor, capitalizing on the two-sided presentation discussed in Chapter 8. For example, recall Avis's advertisement: "We are number 2, so we try harder." Research on the effectiveness of comparative advertisements has led to mixed results. As will be discussed in Chapter 16, some authors have found comparative advertisements to be· more effective under certain circumstances, particularly for shopping goods[17] or for relatively unknown or small market share brands.[18] However, comparative advertising has also been found to be sometimes offensive[19] and less credible than non-comparative advertising.[20]

Testimonial advertising.   In order to translate concretely the basic motivation, advertisers can also use some credible source to testify for the product claim. This approach capitalizes on the concept of source credibility discussed in Chapter 9. The testimony may be provided by a celebrity who will be most likely viewed as a competent expert by consumers. When a famous hockey player makes a statement about ice skates, he is more likely to be believed. Chanel has used Catherine Deneuve to advertise its No. 5 perfume, and she is certainly a credible expert for beauty care products.

The testimony can also be that of "ordinary people," meaning people very similar to the target market segment. Here the rationale is to build the advertisement on the concepts of the two-step flow of communication and interpersonal influence. This type of advertising is shown in Figure 12.16 for Sanka coffee, in which ordinary people testify in a blindfold test that Sanka has a "terrific taste."

Should an advertiser use a celebrity, an expert, or a typical consumer? It has been suggested that the perceived risk involved should be the main criterion. Thus, when the risks associated with the purchase of a product are psychological and/or social, advertisers should use celebrities to endorse the product (this would be the case of Catherine Deneuve endorsing a perfume). When the risk is financial or physical, the expert endorser may be more effective. For products involving low risks, advertisers should use a typical consumer, as in the Sanka advertisement (Figure 12.16).[21]

The Differential Product Advantage Approach
The differential product advantage approach is similar to the motivation approach. The difference is that emphasis is put on finding advertising appeals that can provide consumers with benefits specific to the advertised brand. This approach has been advocated by

Building a better personal computer than IBM, Apple and Xerox wasn't easy. Thanks for waiting.

We know what you're thinking. How could Olivetti have developed a better computer than the rest?

The answer—in a word—is experience.

Since we introduced the world's first desktop model, in 1965, we've continued to market a variety of mini and microcomputers to a wide range of users.

Incorporating our experience and the latest technological advances—like our true 16-bit microprocessor.

And today the M20 proves that dollar for dollar, we've built the most powerful personal computer on the market.

Just look at the comparison chart.

The M20 has 100% more mass storage than a Xerox 820. Its 512K memory is twice as memorable as the Apple III's.

And it outperforms IBM right across the board.

It's easy to use, too, because the M20 teaches you about itself. One step at a time.

So you can handle most any application. Electronic spread sheets. Accounting. Data entry. Technical. Word processing. Communications. Scientific.

	OLIVETTI M20 PERSONAL COMPUTER	IBM PERSONAL COMPUTER	APPLE III PERSONAL COMPUTER	XEROX 820 PERSONAL COMPUTER
True 16-bit microprocessor*	YES	NO	NO	NO
Standard memory	128K	64K	128K	64K
Maximum memory	512K	256K	256K	64K
Expandability	5 extra expansion slots in sample configuration**	No extra expansion slots in sample configuration**	4 extra expansion slots in sample configuration**	No expansion slots
Diskette storage (per drive)	320K	160K	140K	92K
Mass storage (per drive)	11MB hard disk	None	5MB hard disk	None
Display capability	High-resolution B/W or high-resolution colour	High-resolution B/W or colour	High-resolution B/W or colour	High-resolution B/W
Built-in screen graphics	YES	NO	NO	NO

*Defined as 16-bit microprocessor with 16-bit bus.
**Sample configuration means system includes display, dual-disk drives, printer and RS 232C communicator. NOTE: Chart based on manufacturers' information and configuration available as of December, 1981.

Our exclusive disk-based operating system will make things easier and more productive still.

By managing the entire system, while providing a constant HELP function and more.

There's also a high-contrast colour screen, plus built-in software and growth capabilities.

And for a compatible letter printer, look no further than your Olivetti typewriter.

Finally, the M20 is backed by service that has satisfied Canadians for over 25 years.

Just call your nearby Olivetti branch or authorized dealer, to see how the M20's performance can help you outperform the competition.

Or return our coupon today.

olivetti
Olivetti outperforms you know who. Again.

I'd like to find out all about the M20 personal computer
☐ Please call me and arrange a demonstration.
☐ Please send me additional literature.

Name _____
Company _____ Title _____
Address _____
Postal Code _____ Telephone _____
To:
Mr. Paul Manina
Olivetti Canada Ltd.
1390 Don Mills Road
Don Mills, Ontario. M3B 2X3
Telephone: (416) 447-3351

FIGURE 12.14 This is a typical example of comparative advertising in which product features are compared with those of the main competing brands (see the table in the upper right corner).

Courtesy Olivetti Canada Limited

the Ted Bates advertising agency and is also known by the term USP (unique selling proposition). A USP may be defined as follows:[22]

A USP is a memorable set of words promising a unique benefit no one else can promise or does promise. This set of words must answer the consumer's basic question: "What benefit will I get from buying your brand that I won't get from buying other competitors' brand?" In other words, "Why is your brand superior?" The USP is a memorable set of words that sum up the unique reward or benefit. They must be *explicit*.

Figure 12.17 gives examples of successful USPs developed by the Ted Bates agency. USPs are product-oriented when they emphasize a benefit provided by a product feature; some are consumer end-benefit USPs when they directly describe the benefit.

Another characteristic of this approach is that once an effective USP has been developed, it should be kept indefinitely, or at least as long as the claim remains a USP. This may be difficult to apply in practice because many people directly associated with a campaign get

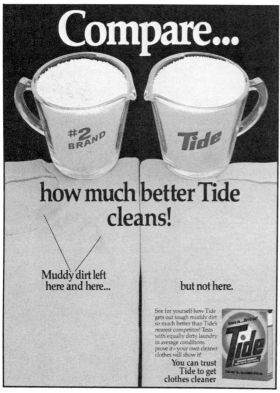

FIGURE 12.15 In this advertisement comparison is made with "Brand no. 2," which may be any competing brand. This type of comparison may be less credible than comparisons that name competing brands.
Courtesy Procter & Gamble Inc.

FIGURE 12.16 Typical consumers testify to the "rich taste" of Sanka coffee, which is a lower risk product category.
Courtesy General Foods Ltd.

---

1. **Product-oriented USPs:**

   M & Ms:
   "The Milk chocolate melts in your mouth—not in your hands."

   Shredded Wheat:
   "100% whole wheat—0% sugar."

   Kal Kan Cat Food:
   "So rich in nutrition, it's like getting a multi-vitamin in every can."

   Wonder Bread:
   "Helps build strong bodies 12 ways."

   Hefty Trash Bags:
   "Tough enough to overstuff."

   Halls Mentho-Lyptus Cough Tablets
   "Vapour Action"

2. **Consumer End-Benefit USPs:**

   Sanka:
   "Drink Sanka and be at your best—always."

   Panasonic:
   "Just slightly ahead of our time."

FIGURE 12.17 Examples of USPs
Courtesy Ted Bates Advertising Agency

bored with the theme, and get a false impression that any consumer in the market must be as bored as they are with the brand advertising.

The Ted Bates agency has a five-step procedure for developing effective USPs:

1. *Total immersion in the client's business.* All the agency personnel who work on the account—account executives, creative people, media and reseach groups—must be thoroughly familiar with the marketing mix, policies, and history of the product or brand to be advertised.

2. *Conduct additional research.* When all the information needed to develop an effective USP is not available, then the agency's research department conducts its own research, especially by using such qualitative techniques as focus groups.

3. *Strategic development and evaluation.* All product positioning strategies are enumerated and evaluated carefully. This includes a translation of all the possible strategies into ad concepts or statements and into rough ads or storyboards. Research can provide additional insight into the value of the different ad concepts.

4. *Develop an approved strategy.* The formal written strategy is prepared for client approval and then serves as the basis for providing the creative group with guidelines on writing and producing the advertisement.

5. *Create and test the USP.* The actual phrasing of the USP is developed and formally evaluated with qualitative and quantitative research techniques.

Suggestive Advertising

All the advertisements that have been discussed so far attempt to give consumers a rationale, an argument, or a reason why they should buy a certain product or brand. In contrast, suggestive advertising is not concerned with emphasizing some product features or consumer benefits but with building a positively valued brand image

in the target market segment. The objective is to ensure that consumers will have developed sufficiently positive attitudes toward the advertised brand and that they will consider purchasing it whenever the need or the occasion arises. Such an approach is best when the brands in a certain product category are fairly similar, since there is no strong physical product differentiation on which to build effective USPs or to use as a basic selling argument. Such product categories include cigarettes, perfumes, most beauty care products, and alcoholic beverages. In such cases, the idea is to attribute a specific personality to the brand in order to cater to specific market segments. This type of advertising is also called "emotional" or "mood" advertising, as it appeals to emotions, often aesthetic emotions, and creates a special mood or atmosphere. David Ogilvy, a leading advertiser, is a well-known advocate of this approach:[23]

> There isn't any significant difference between the various brands of whiskey, or cigarettes, or beer. They are all about the same. And so are the cake mixes and the detergents, and the margarines. The manufacturer who dedicates his advertising to building the most sharply defined personality for his brand will get the largest share of the market at the highest profit. By the same token, the manufacturers who will find themselves up the creek are those shortsighted opportunists who siphon off their advertising funds for promotions.

Examples of suggestive advertising are illustrated by the Nina Ricci advertisement reproduced in Plate I and the Seagram's V.O. advertisement in Plate II.

In order to build a suitable image, prestigious individuals are often used. The eye-patched character in the Hathaway shirt advertisement (Figure 12.18) is a case in point. But very often, celebrities are used in order to somehow "transfer" their personalities to a brand.

In *Confessions of an Advertising Man*, David Ogilvy gives his approach to advertising creation:[24]

10 good reasons why Hathaway puts a special signature on every shirt it makes.

FIGURE 12.18 The famous eye-patched Hathaway character is a distinctive feature of the brand.
Courtesy Warnaco of Canada

1. What you say is more important than how you say it. Two hundred years ago Dr. Johnson said, "Promise, large promise is the soul of an advertisement." When he auctioned off the contents of the Anchor Brewery he made the following promise: "We are not here to sell boilers and vats, but the potentiality of growing rich beyond the dreams of avarice."

2. Unless your campaign is built around a great idea, it will flop.

3. Give the facts. The consumer isn't a moron; she is your wife. You insult her intelligence if you assume that a mere slogan and a few vapid adjectives will persuade her to buy anything. She wants all the information you can give her.

4. You cannot bore people into buying. We make advertisements that people want to read. You can't save souls in an empty church.

5. Be well-mannered, but don't clown.

6. Make your advertising contemporary.

7. Committees can criticize advertisements, but they cannot write them.

8. If you are lucky enough to write a good advertisement, repeat it until it stops pulling. Sterling Getchel's famous advertisement for Plymouth ("Look at All Three") appeared only once, and was succeeded by a series of inferior variations which were quickly forgotten. But the Sherwin Cody School of English ran the same advertisement ("Do You Make Mistakes in English?") for forty-two years, changing only the type face and the color of Mr. Cody's beard.

9. Never write an advertisement which you wouldn't want your own family to read.

10. The image and the brand. It is the total personality of a brand rather than any trivial product difference which decides its ultimate position in the market.

11. Don't be a copy cat. Nobody has ever built a brand by imitating somebody else's advertising. Imitation may be the "sincerest form of plagiarism," but it is also the mark of an inferior person.

The Message Format Decision

Although in the process of translating advertising objectives into a specific advertising message the creative group of the advertising agency is involved, it is essentially the responsibility of the agency's marketing and account executives to find out *what* should be said to consumers. This section concerns the question of *how* to say it, i.e., what is the best combination of words, images, and sounds that will effectively convey the idea to the target market segment. This task is the main responsibility of the creative group at the advertising agency. It is now that the purely creative part of the adver-

Or buy a Volkswagen.

FIGURE 12.19 This award-winning full-page advertisement expresses consumers' frustration with the energy crisis.
Courtesy Volkswagen Canada Inc.

tising process begins. The rest of this chapter focuses on some basic principles that creative people follow in translating a message content into effective advertisements and commercials.

Principles for Creating Advertising Messages

In order to design effective advertising messages, advertisers may follow four simple and widely accepted principles:

Principle 1. An advertiser should try to communicate the message content as quickly as possible. The rationale is that the contact time between the consumers and a specific advertisement or commercial is often extremely short. For example, posters are seen in a glance as are magazine and newspaper advertisements. The time constraint is somewhat less stringent for broadcast commercials. If the message can be delivered during the first few seconds or even fraction of a second during which the consumer is exposed to it, this could make the difference between an effective advertisement and what could have been an ineffective message. At the other extreme are advertising messages that try to attract consumers' attention through means not directly related to the message or the advertised product. The rationale is to try to arouse consumers' interest (the fourth advertising creation principle) and then try to sell the product. Such advertisements strictly follow a hierarchy of effects sequence. They are likely to be much less if at all effective than messages that attempt to deliver the complete story at once and within the shortest possible period of time. Look at the Volkswagen advertisement in Figure 12.19. A mere glance is sufficient to grasp a somewhat complex idea. Because of its size (full page) and its simplicity it can effectively deliver the message in the shortest possible time.

Principle 2. All the communication elements of the advertising message should help express the idea selected as the campaign theme.

Whatever the medium, an advertising message is made up of a number of communication elements, and all of these communication elements convey information to consumers.

The *verbal message* is constituted of the written words in a print advertisement or the spoken and/or written words in a telecast commercial. *Visual elements* are the illustrations, the photograph, the graphical representation on a print advertisement, or the part of an advertising scenario that can be seen on a television screen. The *audio elements* are the sound effects and the music that are used in most broadcast commercials. Finally, the *general ambiance or atmosphere* of an advertisement or commercial also says something about the brand and/or the company to consumers. Because all these elements of the advertising message convey information, effective messages are those in which all the elements communicate all or part of the *same* idea or message.

For instance, a consumer watching a television commercial receives a visual message conveyed by the pictures. Simultaneously, the verbal message is spoken by an announcer, and the background music conveys another message. The advertisement would be much less effective if each element tried to convey unrelated meanings or contradictory meanings. If each communication element conveys different messages, none of the messages reaches its objectives and confusion may result.[25] In the Volkswagen advertisement in Figure 12.19, the visual and verbal elements complement each other to convey the same idea: "If you do not want to kill yourself paying outrageous gas bills" (expressed by the drawing), "buy a Volkswagen" (which constitutes the written headline).

Principle 3. If the medium permits, advertisers should try to convey as much of the message as possible with visual elements.

The rationale is that non-verbal communications are always more effective than verbal communications. What people do attracts more attention than what people say. Comedians know that the effect of a humorous reply can be "killed" if at the same time another actor starts moving on the stage. Teachers generally find it difficult to keep their students' attention when someone leaves the classroom during a lecture. These are examples of attention to verbal elements being distracted by visual elements. If, in spite of principle 2, the visual and the verbal elements do not contribute to the communication of the same idea, the visual elements can be expected to be the strongest. In the Volkswagen advertisement, the largest portion of the message is communicated by the drawing. The illustration is roughly equivalent to a statement that says: "If you think of killing

yourself because you cannot afford outrageous gasoline bills . . . ." The reader notices how much more effectively and rapidly the drawing delivers this idea. Only four words are needed to complete the sentence.

Sometimes an entire message can be expressed through visual elements. These are likely to be the most effective messages from a communication point of view. The Gilbey's gin advertisement reproduced in Plate III delivers the entire message in one picture: "Gilbey's gin has won its place in Manhattan, New York." In this case, the only word needed is the brand name, Gilbey's.

In a multicultural country like Canada, completely non-verbal advertising has the incomparable advantage of requiring the creation of one advertising message that can simultaneously be understood by both French and English speaking consumers.[26]

Principle 4: Advertisers should try to arouse consumers' interest as quickly as possible.

This principle is a corollary of principle 1. The classic hierarchy of effects model that suggests buyers' attention should be attracted first, before their interest can be aroused, may not be the most efficient advertising procedure. The rationale is that interested consumers will naturally pay more attention to the advertising message. In the Volkswagen advertisement, readers who are concerned (and therefore interested) about the soaring costs of energy and who are actively looking for new ways to save on gas are most likely to pay attention to the advertisement. Moreover, *because* they are interested, their attention will more likely be attracted by a message linked to energy savings. There is a strong tendency for people's attention to be attracted to what interests them.

The Atmosphere of Advertising Messages

Another dimension important to the visual and non-verbal elements of the advertising message is the ability to create an ambiance or an atmosphere that is loaded with meaning for consumers. The atmosphere created by an advertising message strongly influences the personality or image that consumers will assign to the advertised brand.

Influence of the Non-Verbal Elements

The setting in which products are used, the type of people who are shown on the illustration, the way they are dressed, how they look, what they do, give quite different personalities to an advertised brand. For instance, compare Plate IV and Figure 12.20. The Select advertisement evokes an atmosphere of luxury, romance, and a very special occasion, which well matches the brand name—Select. The du Maurier advertisement evokes an atmosphere of casual albeit above-average people, who are sports fans and like outdoor activities.

Objects, situations, or product usage scenarios also project a certain image as does the typeface used for the headline and the copy. But more important, beyond each specific detail, the general atmosphere evoked determines what personality consumers will attribute to the brand.

As was discussed in Chapter 1, consumers decode and interpret communication symbols through their fields of previous experience, knowledge, and their present situation and their aspirations for the future. As pointed out by Maurice Borts:

> This means that the content of an ad is often evaluated by potential consumers in terms of how well the messages fit in with the receiver's needs—current lifestyle and values. As a consequence, it is possible that the identical message would be interpreted differently by various individuals.[27]

For example, a well-dressed and elegant man in an advertisement could evoke to some people high class, expensive, and quality products. However, other people could infer from the same advertisement an image of a brand for snobbish, idle people. Thus marketers should

FIGURE 12.20   The mildness of du Maurier is suggested through an ambiance of outdoor activities of upper-middle-class people (suggested by the kind of boat pictured).
Courtesy Imperial Tobacco Limited

ensure that the proper interpretation of the advertisement's symbols is made by the target market segment.

The meaning of the symbols used in advertising messages is likely to evolve over time. For instance, failing to dress models according to the current fashion may have a positive or negative interpretation by consumers and an effect on the brand image.

Borts gives the following objectives for properly administering non-verbal messages:

- they reinforce the planned communication and not unintentionally create conflicting messages;
- they replace or support word messages that lack credibility or which cannot be adequately presented in words;

• communication barriers such as legal constraints, bilingual considerations, or the resistance that consumers build up against commercial communication can be circumvented.[28]

The Use of Humour

Humour is an important element that advertisers have often used to increase the effectiveness of their messages and that gives a unique atmosphere to an advertisement. However, the effectiveness of humour in advertising is still a subject of controversy in the advertising industry. There are as many examples of successful humorous advertising campaigns as examples of outright failures.

Humour is difficult to define, and there are many kinds of humour, some of them eliciting at best a smile, others triggering outbursts of laughter. Moreover, humour is not universal. An advertisement may be considered humorous by some and offensive or silly by others. One study using analytical techniques found eight types of humour in advertising.[29]

Some advertisers use empirical research to support their belief that humorous advertising may be more effective. Such studies suggest that humour tends to build a positive mood, enhance source credibility, and increase readership level. A recently published study[30] reached the conclusion that humour was most effective when used to promote brands that had already achieved a certain level of recognition among consumers in a market. According to the author, "humour out-performed the use of celebrities and 'real people' in commercials for established brands, but it can impede communication and hinder conviction for a product that has not had the opportunity to build a reputation and image."[31] The authors propose two reasons to explain these results. First, new product advertising generally has a lot of information to convey and the facts can be lost because the audience's attention is distracted by the humorous aspect of the story. Second, humorous advertising may project the image of a not

FIGURE 12.21   This advertisement uses humour to communicate and reinforce a selling idea that otherwise might seem exaggerated.
Courtesy Kraft Limited

too serious company. This effect is neutralized if the company is well established and taken seriously. However, it can have a quite negative impact for new product advertising, which may be rejected by consumers as "not serious." As Figure 12.21 illustrates, humour emphasizing a selling point can be effectively used by Miracle Whip, which is a well-known brand in the Canadian market.

Other arguments suggest that humour should be used with caution, since it may distract the audience from the main point of the advertisement. Furthermore, as already mentioned, humour is sometimes very personal and a humorous advertising message may often not be understood by some people in the audience. Thus, advertisers should try to avoid subtle wit, which may be lost on many consumers. For example, if some readers were not aware of the famous smile of the Mona Lisa, they would not understand the humour of the Participaction advertisement (Figure 12.22).

FITNESS NOW·AND HOW

How does this famous lady keep smiling?

Mona Lisa has been smiling for centuries. And for centuries, her beguiling smile has been a mystery.

Now, for the first time, Participaction can reveal the secret beneath the smile:

Mona Lisa is physically fit. Contrary to popular opinion, she has not just been sitting idly all these years, watching the world go by.

But until now, her active lifestyle has been concealed. Why?

Because until recently, the world has had some pretty misguided ideas about women and fitness. Fitness wasn't considered "ladylike". People thought that it meant big muscles and rough sports. What's worse, people thought that fitness was more important for men than for women — as if, somehow, there was something about men's lives and men's bodies which meant that they should be in better shape.

Of course, times have changed. And so have our ideas about women and fitness.

Today we realize that fitness is just as important for women as it is for men. And for the same reasons: because the shape you're in affects your energy, your vitality, your strength, your general health, your appearance, your ability to cope with stress and even the way you age.

In other words, fitness is important if you want to get the most out of life. Mona — a true Renaissance woman — understood this obvious point a long time ago.

Is regular physical activity the secret of Mona's smile? AND HOW!

PARTICIPACTION

FIGURE 12.22   In this advertisement the humour is the result of the contrast between Leonardo da Vinci's masterpiece and the jogger's outfit worn by the Mona Lisa.
Courtesy Participaction

From their review of the literature on the effectiveness of humour in advertising, Sternthal and Craig proposed the following generalizations:

1. Humorous messages attract attention.
2. Humorous messages may detrimentally affect comprehension.
3. Humor may distract the audience, yielding a reduction in counterargumentation and an increase in persuasion.
4. Humorous appeals appear to be persuasive, but the persuasive effect is at best no greater than that of serious appeals.
5. Humor tends to enhance source credibility.
6. Audience characteristics may confound the effect of humor.
7. A humorous context may increase liking for the source and create a positive mood. This may increase the persuasive effect of the message.
8. To the extent that a humorous context functions as a positive reinforcer, a persuasive communication placed in such a context may be more effective.[32]

Thus, advertisers should exercise judgement when using humour as an advertising tool.

Summary

The advertising creative process starts with a definition of the advertising message content. There are several possible approaches, such as the target group, the motivation, and the product advantage. These approaches lead to argumentative types of advertising and differ from suggestive (emotional or mood) advertising.

Creativity has been defined as the "ability to formulate new combinations from two or more concepts already in the mind," and the creative process was described. There are several principles for creating advertising messages and various elements that contribute to the atmosphere of the message. Non-verbal elements and humour play an important role in creating ambiance and influencing the brand image.

Questions for Study

1. Find a few examples of print ads that use
   (a) the target group approach
   (b) the motivation approach
   (c) the product differential advantage approach
   (d) the suggestive approach
   Compare them in terms of communicative effectiveness.

2. For which type(s) of product and/or service are the following techniques best suited? Why?
   (a) comparative advertising
   (b) use of humour
   (c) testimonial by celebrities
   (d) testimonial by "ordinary" people

3. Find examples of print ads that do not follow the creative principles given in the text. What test(s) could you do to confirm (or contradict) your opinion?

4. With a few examples of print advertisements, show how the different visual, verbal, and atmosphere elements all tend to convey a basic advertising message.

5. Find several advertisements using humour. Compare them in terms of the type of humour, the extent of their reliance on humour, and their effectiveness in communicating the advertising message. Evaluate each advertisement.

6. Find print advertisements in which the underlying consumer benefits are
   (a) directly described
   (b) inferred
   Discuss their relative communication effectiveness. Give reasons.

7. Find examples of advertising claims aimed at
   (a) increasing some motivation
   (b) reducing some fear
   Try to find the rationale for using these types of appeals.

8. Differential product advantage advertising tends to stress a product feature, while the motivation approach tends to stress a consumer benefit and may be more in line with the marketing concept. Discuss.

9. In order to be effective, an advertising message should bring the consumers along a hierarchy of effects model like AIDA. First, the message should attract attention. Then, it should arouse consumers' interest. Next, it should create desire, and finally, it should sell (action). Discuss.

10. Find examples of print advertisements in which all the elements do *not* tend to convey the same message. Give the reasons for your assessment.

Problems

1. Secure an interview with the advertising executive/and or manager of an important advertiser. During this interview, determine
   (a) what underlying *creative* approach is generally followed and the reasons why
   (b) how the creative aspects fit into the overall advertising strategy and in the marketing strategy of the product/brand
   (c) what are the manager's opinions about the use of humour, comparative advertising, testimonials, for advertising the firm's products and/or brands.

2. Find two print advertisements (if possible, for the same product category): one in which you think that all the elements tend to convey the same idea; one in which you think that inconsistent or conflicting meanings may be conveyed by the different channels.
   Show each advertisement to different people, varying the length of exposition (5, 10, 15, 30 seconds), and then measure what people recall and have understood.
   Do the results confirm your hypothesis? Discuss.

Notes

1. John W. Macfale, *Creativity and Innovation* (New York: Reinhold Publishing, 1962), p. 5.
2. See, for instance, W. Gordon, *Synectics: The Development of Creative Capacity* (New York: Harper and Row, 1961); G. Steiner, *The Creative Organization* (Chicago: University of Chicago Press, 1965).
3. Alex F. Osborn, *Applied Imagination*, rev. ed. (New York: Scribner's, 1957), pp. 110-14.
4. Ibid., p. 115.
5. Jane Webb Young, *A Technique for Producing Ideas,* 4th ed. (Chicago: Advertising Publications, 1960), p. 15.
6. Frank Alexander Armstrong, *Idea Teaching* (New York: Criterion Books, 1960), pp. 139-44.
7. Michael Hallé, "Creative Is Not Really Creative Unless It Sells," *Marketing* (July 1980), pp. 9-12.
8. Ibid., p. 10.
9. Osborn, p. 84.
10. Hallé, p. 12.
11. Irwin Gross, "The Creative Aspects of Advertising," *Sloan Management Review* (Fall 1972), pp. 83-109.
12. Kenneth A. Longman, *Advertising* (New York: Harcourt Brace Jovanovich, 1971).
13. Ibid., pp. 187-88.
14. Henri Joannis, *De l'Etude de Motivation à la Création Publicitaire et à la Promotion des Ventes* (Paris: Dunod, 1965).
15. Ibid., p. 113.
16. Ibid., p. 176.
17. Gordon M.C. McDougall, "Comparative Advertising: Consumer Issues and Attitudes," *Contemporary Marketing Thought*, ed. B.A. Greenberg and D.N. Bellanger (Chicago: American Marketing Association, 1977), pp. 286-91.
18. Edwin C. Kackleman and Subhash C. Jain, "An Experimental Analysis Toward Comparison and Non-Comparison Advertising," *Advances in Consumer Research*, 6 (Ann Arbor, Michigan: Association for Consumer Research, 1979).
19. Terence A. Shimp and David C. Dyer, "The Effects of Comparative Advertising Mediated by Market Position of Sponsoring Brand," *Journal of Advertising*, 8 (Summer 1978), 13-19.
20. Philip Levine, "Commercials That Name Competing Brands," *Journal of Advertising Research*, 16 (December 1976), 7-14; R. Dale Wilson, "An Empirical Evaluation of Comparative Advertising Messages: Subjects' Responses on Perceptual Dimensions," *Advances in Consumer Research,* ed. B.B. Anderson, 3 (Ann Arbor, Michigan: Association for Consumer Research, 1976), pp. 53-57.
21. See Jo Marney, "Testimonial Ads: Real People vs. Celebrities," *Marketing*, 13 September 1982, pp. 10-12.
22. Bob Jacoby, "Ted Bates: The USP Agency" (Speech delivered to Ted Bates Management Representatives, New York Management Reps, unpublished document 1981).
23. David Ogilvy, *Confessions of an Advertising Man* (New York: Atheneum, 1964).
24. Ibid., p. 93.
25. Maurice Borts, "Power of the Unspoken Word," *Marketing*, 3 December 1979, p. 20.
26. Ibid., pp. 22-23.
27. Ibid., p. 20.
28. Ibid., pp. 23-24.
29. Mervin D. Lynch and Richard C. Hartman, "Dimensions of Humor in Advertising," *Journal of Advertising Research*, 8 (December 1968), 39-45.
30. David Ogilvy and Joel Raphaelson, "Research on Ad Techniques That Work—and Don't Work," *Marketing News*, 17 September 1982, p. 2.
31. Ibid., p. 2.
32. Brian Sternthal and C. Samuel Craig, "Humor in Advertising," *Journal of Marketing*, 37 (October 1973), 12-18.

Developing Effective Print Advertisements and Broadcast Commercials

The principles and concepts described in Chapter 12 apply to the creation of all types of advertising messages, regardless of the media through which they are carried. This chapter deals with specific creative aspects of print advertisements and broadcast commercials. The first section shows how the visual, verbal, and atmosphere elements of a print advertisement are blended to communicate the selected advertising message effectively. The second section is devoted to the creation and production of broadcast commercials, with a special emphasis on television commercials.

Creating Print Advertisements

The principles of print advertisement creation are depicted in Figure 13.1, which shows how the visual, verbal, and ambiance elements can be combined into a unique piece of artwork.

The Visual Elements in Print Advertisements

The visual elements of a print advertisement must fulfil two basic functions. First, they must ensure that the advertised product, service, or brand can be recognized quickly by the public, if possible at a glance. For some products, this is a relatively easy task. It may be sufficient that the product, the brand name, or the package be easily visible in an advertisement. Other products are more difficult to identify quickly. How can a brand of carpets be advertised by depicting a luxuriously furnished living room with the advertised carpets, and make sure that readers do not assume that furniture or decoration services are being sold? This problem is shared by advertisers of household cleaning products and services in general. To convey the idea of the product and/or service being advertised, the art and expertise of talented photographers and artists are needed.

Second, the visual elements should express as much as possible of the message content. The expression of this task depends on the kind of message to be communicated. Figure 12.19 showed how the visual elements could express a substantial portion of the message and Plate III showed how they could express it all.

The illustration in a print advertisement often represents the product itself or part of the product if a special feature must be emphasized. Often, picturing the product in use or ready for use adds a suggestive dimension and interest and life to the advertisement. Consumers' satisfaction with product usage or ease of use may be effectively demonstrated in an illustration. To do so, the art director and the creative team use the combination of people, symbols, and objects that best communicate the basic message content.

Visual elements may be classified into photographs, drawings, and other types of artwork. Advertising experts disagree over the relative merits of these various types of visual elements for effectively conveying the advertising message. Each has its merits and drawbacks, depending on the advertising situation.

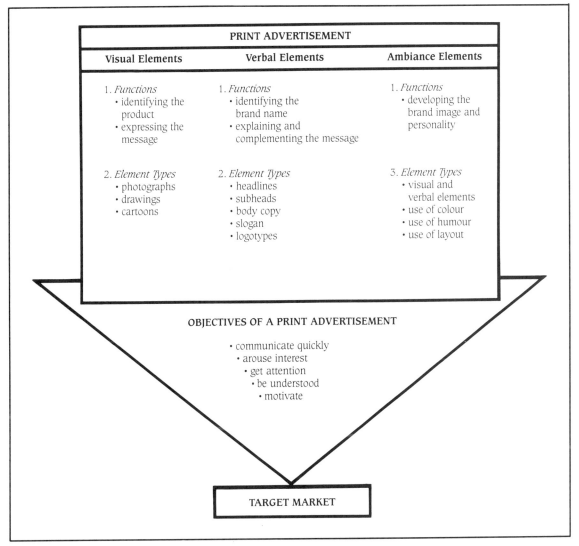

FIGURE 13.1   The Basic Elements of Print Advertisements

Photographs. Photographs lend realism, appeal, and credibility to an advertisement. Whenever advertisers want to depict real-life situations, the use of photographs is almost mandatory. Photographs are used to advertise product categories for which the visual element is important, such as food. In Plate V and Figure 13.2, photographs are the best means of appealing to consumers' appetites.

Since photographs are so vivid, they are an excellent way of capturing readers' attention.

Such advertisers as David Ogilvy unconditionally favour using photographs in print advertisements:

> Over and over again research has shown that photographs sell more than drawings. They attract more readers. They deliver more appetite appeal. They are better remembered. They pull more coupons. And they sell more merchandise. Photographs represent reality, whereas drawings represent fantasy, which is less believable.[1]

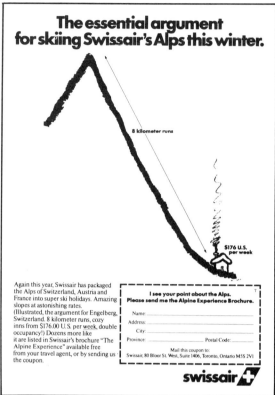

FIGURE 13.2 This photograph of the product is intended to be so suggestive and appetite arousing that consumers will buy it at the next purchase occasion.
Courtesy Kellogg Salada Canada Inc.

FIGURE 13.3 The simple line drawing communicates the advertisement's main selling arguments: (1) 8-km runs, and (2) $176 U.S. per week in a cosy inn.
Courtesy Swissair

Drawings. Because dramatic photographs have become ubiquitous in print advertisements, many advertisers are resorting to other techniques to make their advertisements more original and striking. Drawings have the advantage of standing out by contrasting with the more common photograph advertisements. When properly used, they create a special mood that will enhance a product image. In the Swissair advertisement reproduced in Figure 13.3, a drawing is used because its simplicity powerfully communicates two important selling arguments for taking Swissair winter vacations.

Other Types of Artwork. Paintings, cartoons, abstract drawings, and any other forms of

illustration also convey a special atmosphere or meaning to a print advertisement. A painting used to advertise a cologne or beauty product can project an image of exclusivity, elegance, and fantasy, as in the Emeraude advertisement in Plate VI. Because they are not often used in advertising, cartoons attract readers' attention and create a light, humorous and casual atmosphere, as in the Big Brothers' advertisement reproduced in Figure 13.4.

In the final analysis, the choice of a specific type of visual element should depend on the product advertised, the communication objectives, and the message content. Therefore, these different types of illustration should be evaluated on a case-by-case basis and be chosen to best fit the mood and the message to be conveyed by the advertisement.

The Verbal Element in Print Advertisements

The verbal elements of a print advertisement serve to identify the brand, to sign the advertisement, and to supplement the visual message. Readers cannot properly identify the brand being advertised unless it is written in the advertisement or on an illustration of the package. As with the Gilbey's gin advertisement (Plate III), even where the visual elements can express the whole message, it is still necessary to identify the brand name in writing. The only verbal element needed is the brand name on the package.

But in most instances, the message cannot be fully expressed by visual elements alone, and verbal elements are needed to "complete the message." The verbal part of the message should complement the illustration, so as to convey the entire message content to the reader.

The verbal elements that can be used in a print advertisement are the headline, a subhead, the body copy, a slogan, and a logotype. Each verbal element fulfills a specific role and function.

THE HEADLINE. Headlines are the most conspicuous verbal elements of a print advertisement. They are often the only elements of an advertisement that are read, since many readers just glance at advertisements and go on to the next page. Therefore, it is essential that the headline work with the visual element to convey the message in a striking, interesting manner.

A prerequisite for a headline is that it attract readers' attention. At the same time, the headline must also arouse interest, so readers will want to read the body of the advertisement. Furthermore, a headline must "discriminate" among potential readers and retain only those who would be likely to be interested in the

FIGURE 13.4 This cartoon-like illustration conveys the casual atmosphere of a kid's world and lends a light humorous tone to this advertisement.
Courtesy Big Brothers of Canada

product advertised. It can do this by directly identifying the consumers in the targeted audience or by addressing a concern common to the target market segment. For instance, the Hershey's cocoa advertisement reproduced in Figure 13.5 identifies a perceived target audience—recently married young women. The headline plays on the notion that women can impress their in-laws with good cooking.

The headline should complement the illustration of the print advertisement, not repeat it. A test advertisers often carry out is to hide the illustration and show only the headline to people who have not seen the ad before. If the reader can understand the whole message, the copy is inefficient. The reader may test this

FIGURE 13.5 This advertisement directly addresses just-married young women, and implies that there is no more severe a judge than a mother-in-law. From a marketing point of view, the advertisement addresses a target market that has not yet developed strong brand loyalty and that is ready to try many products and brands.
Courtesy Hershey Foods Corporation, Hershey, Pennsylvania, U.S.A.

FIGURE 13.6 This advertisement's headline directly promises a consumer benefit—good skin—with product usage.
Courtesy Noxell Corporation

principle on the Volkswagen advertisement in Figure 12.19. Without knowing what the illustration is, the written part—"or buy a Volkswagen"—does not convey the whole message. The whole message can only be fully understood when the visual *and* the verbal elements are put together.

The Headline's Information Content. Headlines can be used in several ways. One way is to make the headline an implicit or explicit statement of a promised reward to the consumer. Extensive research has shown that this approach is quite effective. The reward should represent the satisfaction of a conscious consumer need or desire, resulting from use of the product. Headlines can also stress the informational value of the body copy and therefore present the consumer with a reward that is not directly related to product consumption. The advertisements reproduced in Figures 13.6 and 13.7 give an example of each type of reward appeal. The Noxzema advertisement promises better skin for consumers who use Noxzema skin cream. In Figure 13.7, the headline promises a reward that bears no direct relation with the use of the advertised product; the reward is a "tip" on how to become beautiful by increasing one's self-confidence.

Headlines can be direct or indirect. Direct headlines present the product or product feature

FIGURE 13.7   This headline promises a reward—beauty—as a result of the self-confidence to be gained from using the product.This indirect approach is less product specific and could be used by other advertisers as well.

Courtesy Mary Kay Cosmetics, Inc.

FIGURE 13.8   Two product features—taste and preparation speed—are emphasized in the headline.

Courtesy American Home Products Corporation

in an informative, straightforward manner. For instance, the headline in the Chef Boyardee advertisement (Figure 13.8) directly states the product brand name along with two highly desirable product features. Headlines that present a product in a vivid, interesting manner are more likely to attract consumers' attention, as with the Buick Skylark advertisement reproduced in Figure 13.9.

Indirect headlines convey interesting information but do not pertain directly to the advertised product. As an example, the advertisement for Aim reproduced in Figure 13.10 is designed to stimulate parental interest by pre-senting the reader with a problem: that of preventing one's children from having cavities. The brand name is only identified in the sixth paragraph of the body copy. To be effective, this advertisement must be read in its entirety, and the headline is created to achieve just that purpose.

The Headline's Syntax. To communicate effectively in the shortest possible time span, attract consumers' attention, and arouse interest, the headline should be as short as possible. Every word in the headline should convey the right meaning to consumers. Some authors argue that it is always desirable to include the key words that are most likely to attract readers' attention. Among these key words, John Caples[2]

FIGURE 13.9 Two contradictory features of the Buick Skylark are emphasized in this headline: it is an economy car, but expensive-looking.
Courtesy General Motors of Canada Limited

FIGURE 13.10 As with any other indirect approach, the problem described may be solved by other means than the advertised brand—which is not emphasized in this advertisement.
Courtesy Lever Brothers Limited

mentions "announcing", "new", "now", "at last", "reduced", "free", "how to", "how", "why", "which", and "wanted". Such words can make a headline more striking and attention-grabbing.

Advertisements' headlines tend to follow one of several patterns. They can resemble a news headline, by announcing a new product discovery or by providing readers with some interesting and novel product information. The information conveyed in the headline should really be "newsworthy", i.e., it should not announce a fact already known to everyone or present untrue information. It should also remain as specific as possible, since a vague headline is not interesting. An example of a news headline is given in the L'Oréal advertisement reproduced in Figure 13.11.

Another interesting way of presenting a headline is by using the "how-to" approach. Such headlines suggest that the rest of the advertisement will provide the reader with a means of achieving a desirable objective. Advertisements employing the "How you can" approach are more personal, since they are addressed directly to the reader.

Attention can also be attracted by asking a question, which raises a problem and excites the reader's curiosity. It is hoped that readers will feel compelled to look at the rest of the advertisement, in order to find an answer to the question. A question can also be purely theoretical when the answer is self-evident. The question allows for a more striking presen-

372

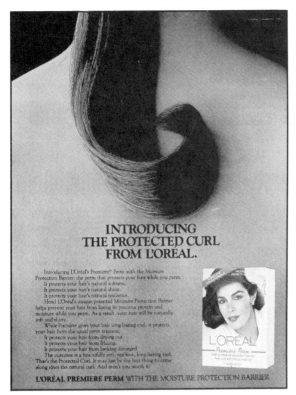

FIGURE 13.11 This headline presents new product information and reinforces the illustration.
Courtesy Cosmair Canada Inc.

FIGURE 13.12 Who would answer no to the question posed by this headline?
Courtesy Simon-Schuster Division, Gulf and Western Corporation

tation of the message. This is shown in the Silhouette Special Editions advertisement in Figure 13.12.

Headlines can also be expressed in the imperative form. This type of headline is generally used when immediate action is sought from the consumer. However, it tends to be less interesting than other approaches and in some instances may be less effective.

The different approaches to content and headlines can be combined, as is demonstrated in Table 13.1.

Selecting a Headline. How is an effective headline designed? There are no strict rules to abide to in order to achieve an effective headline; an advertiser must rely on common sense and intuition to select the most effective headline for a specific advertising situation.

Nonetheless, the probable effectiveness of a headline can be assessed by evaluating the concept according to the following criteria:

1. Does the headline attract a reader's attention?

2. Is it clearly understood? Does it convey the message in a straightforward, unambiguous way?

3. Does it identify the target audience either directly or by addressing a specific problem faced by this target audience?

4. Does it avoid banality and vagueness?

5. Does it properly supplement and is it consistent with the other elements of the advertisement, visual and verbal?

6. Does it effectively demonstrate how the

TABLE 13.1 Types of Content and Syntax in Headlines

TYPE OF HEADLINE	TYPE OF HEADLINE CONTENT	
	Direct	Indirect
News Headline	Introducing the Protected Curl from l'Oreal (FIGURE 13.11)	The six year molar may be the most important tooth in his mouth and the most vulnerable (FIGURE 13.10)
"How-to" Headline	How your hair can have beautiful body language (FIGURE 13.17)	How to prove to your mother-in-law that her son's in good hands (FIGURE 13.5)
Question Headline	Hotdog know how? Maple Leaf's got it! (PLATE V)	Are you ready for your next great romance? (FIGURE 13.12)
Command Headline	Watch good skin happen— Wash with Noxzema every day (FIGURE 13.6)	Learn how beautiful a little self-confidence can make you (FIGURE 13.7)

product can satisfy some consumer need, or does it lead toward such a demonstration?

THE SUBHEADS. The main headline may not be enough to make a point, but only attracts readers' attention. In these cases advertisers can explain the meaning of the headline in a subhead, which can develop a point raised by the headline or give additional information designed to reinforce the advertisement's main point. The Betty Crocker advertisement reproduced in Figure 13.13 gives a good example of effective use of subheads. Here the subhead identifies the brand and elaborates on the meaning of the headline.

THE BODY COPY. A headline and a visual element may be enough to drive home the point of the advertisement, and lengthy elaboration is unwarranted. The advertisements for Volkswagen (Figure 12.19), Gilbey's gin (Plate III), and Matinée (Figure 10.12) are cases in point. In some instances an advertiser may want to communicate additional product advantages or

factual information about the product, as in the Xerox advertisement shown in Figure 13.14. Or the advertisement can elaborate on the theme announced by the headline, as in Figure 13.15.

Advertisers usually resort to a written text or body copy to present more detailed selling arguments. The body copy may be quite lengthy, as for products that contain many technical features, for example, IBM microcomputers (Figure 13.16).

Few readers will likely read the body copy of this advertisement, and most of the technical points would not interest the layman. Therefore, this message is targeted at a limited market segment of people who want to buy a microcomputer and are seeking the type of information the copy provides. This example shows that the existence and length of copy depend on the nature of the product, as well as on the communication objectives of the advertisement.

Types of Body Copy. The type of body copy varies according to the nature of the appeal

Break the boring salad habit

tonight!

Why settle for the same old salad? Bac-Os® add a great bacony flavor and special crunch that can shake up your salad routine.

With the bacony Bac's crunch.

©General Mills, Inc. 1982   ®Bac*Os is a registered trademark of General Mills, Inc.

FIGURE 13.13
Without the subhead, the headline cannot be fully understood. The subhead is used to complete the message and emphasize the brand name.

Courtesy General Mills Canada, Inc.

Our new typewriter has more memory than what's their name's.

You know who we mean.
The one that sells the most typewriters.
The fact is, our new typewriters simply out-class theirs.

You see, not only can secretaries use the Xerox 610 Memorywriter just like the simple electric they're used to. But it also comes with a memory that saves them an incredible amount of time and trouble.

It handles margins, tabs, column alignment, indents, centering and underlining with unbelievable ease.

And can automatically erase what's been typed. Not just character by character, but entire lines at a single touch.

It lets you use three different type sizes and proportional spacing. All on one machine.

And the 610 Memorywriter remembers about 30% more characters than you-know-who's comparably priced model.

That's 30% more addresses, dates, names, phrases or entire paragraphs that your secretary doesn't have to keep retyping.

What's more, with any of the Xerox Memorywriters, you'll be able to add as much memory as you need. As you need it. Without changing machines.

So when you need a new typewriter, don't settle for an ordinary electric.
Especially when you can get your hands on a Xerox Memorywriter.
The typewriter that'll make you forget everyone else's.

For information, call 1-800-268-9074*, your local Xerox office, or mail in the coupon below.

☐ Please have a sales representative contact me. ☐ I'd like to see a demonstration. ☐ Please send me more information about your new Memorywriters.

Mail to: Xerox Canada Inc., P.O. Box 911, Station "U", Toronto, Ontario M8Z 5P9

Name_____ Title_____
Company_____
Address_____ City_____
Province_____ Postal Code_____ Phone_____
*In B.C. 112-800-268-9074.

S82TM7

Xerox Canada Inc.

XEROX

XEROX is a registered trademark of XEROX CORPORATION used by XEROX CANADA INC. as a registered user. 610 is a trademark of XEROX CORPORATION.

FIGURE 13.14 The body copy of this Xerox advertisement is used to develop selling arguments and give factual details about the product performance. This could also be an example of comparative advertising in which the leading competitor is not named but is supposedly known by readers.

Courtesy Xerox Canada Inc.

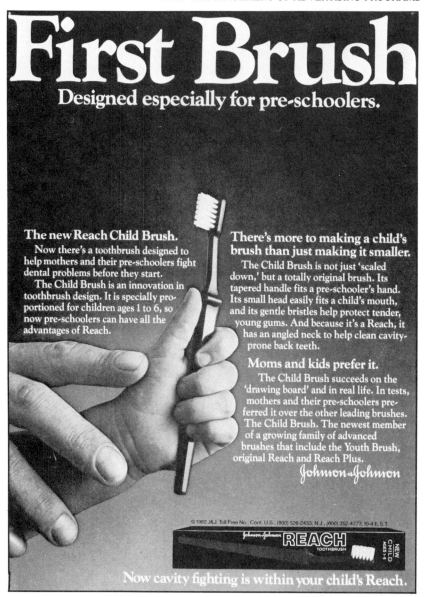

FIGURE 13.15 Here the body copy is used to reinforce and expand upon the message in the headline and subheads.

Courtesy Johnson & Johnson

used for the advertisement. Copy that gives consumers good reasons to buy a product is known as "reason-why" copy. The Enhance shampoo advertisement (Figure 13.17) is a good example, because it promises the reader a reward from using the shampoo.

Advertisers try to make a sales pitch more appealing by using humour in the body copy. For technically advanced products, descriptive copy provides a more elaborate description of the product than is possible in the headline or illustration. Testimonial advertising is another

FIGURE 13.16 The body copy constitutes the essential element of this advertisement and provides potential customers with a large amount of technical information.
Courtesy IBM Canada Ltd.

popular technique and was illustrated with the Fisher-Price and Regal advertisements in Chapter 7 (Figures 7.18 and 7.19).

Body copy can also take the form of a dialogue or a narrative text. The text should be interesting, precise, and well-written, because consumers will not otherwise be motivated to read lengthy copy.

Writing the Copy. As with headlines, there is no precise set of standards that determine good body copy. The copy should aim at brevity and clarity, but not at the expense of additional information or persuasive arguments. It should be interesting, specific, concise, easy to understand, and believable. It should never be vague or use unconvincing terms, as this would decrease the advertiser's credibility. Advertisers must strive to bolster a sales pitch with concrete examples and convincing arguments.

Just as in headline creation, the best tool to effective copy writing lies in advertisers' assessment of how to best meet the communication objectives for a particular situation. Therefore, much is left to the individual creator's common sense, intuition, and imagination.

SLOGANS. Slogans are somewhat like headlines, with a few differences. They may last for several years, throughout an entire advertising campaign, are intended to produce a lasting impression, and sum up the recurring theme of an advertising campaign. Examples are "Kentucky fried chicken is finger lickin' good" or "Drink Coca-Cola."

Good slogans are easy to remember. They are usually short, concise, and contain an inner

HOW YOUR HAIR CAN HAVE BEAUTIFUL BODY LANGUAGE.

HAIR THAT SAYS IT'S TOO DRY.   HAIR THAT SAYS IT'S GREASY.   HAIR THAT SAYS IT'S NATURALLY BALANCED.

Just as a person's body language can say something about the person, hair also has a body language all its own.

Sometimes hair can say uncomplimentary things.

Hair that's flyaway says it's too dry. Hair that's matted says it's greasy. Hair that's frizzy says it's unmanageable. Hair that says any of the above could be because it's lost its natural balance.

Natural balance?

Hair is mostly made up of protein and moisture. When hair is healthy these components are in "natural balance." In other words, healthy hair is neither greasy nor dry but somewhere in between.

However, this balance can be upset. By blow dryers, hot rollers, curling irons, or even your choice of shampoo or conditioner.

Now you can help restore your hair to its natural balance with new Enhance™ shampoo and Enhance® conditioner.

They contain special protein and moisturizers to help give your hair what it needs. Natural balance.

Try Enhance® conditioner and new Enhance™ shampoo. So your hair can have a beautiful body language all its own.

HELPS RESTORE HAIR TO ITS NATURAL BALANCE.

FIGURE 13.17   In this "reason-why" copy, the advertiser gives consumers arguments why they should use Enhance.
Courtesy S.C. Johnson & Son, Ltd.

rhyme, rhythm, or alliteration. A slogan such as "I like Ike," although not used in an advertising context, is striking and produces a lasting impression. There is no miracle recipe for creating effective slogans, however. Perhaps more than any element of print advertisement, they rely on the creator's stroke of genius. Slogans should, however, meet two standard requirements: they should be memorable; and they should effectively sum up the theme of the advertising campaign.

LOGOTYPES.   According to Hans Kleefeld, a logotype "derives from the Greek *logos*, meaning speech or word. Thus, logo strongly suggests a legible entity, e.g., a company's name. Visually,

such a company name may simply be represented in a particular type style—hence, logotype."[3] According to this definition, the name Swissair at the bottom of Figure 13.3 is a logotype. The concept of logotype may be extended to any non-verbal symbol used to identify a brand. Thus, the white cross in the same advertisement, which is used as a symbol for the company, can be considered part of its logotype.

Like a slogan, a logotype should be memorable and become associated in consumers' minds with the advertised brand. If a brand name is written in a distinctive manner, this style is considered a logotype, in that it identifies the company. Tourists who see a Coca-Cola sign written in Hebrew or Arabic will recognize the brand, even though they do not know either language. The purely non-verbal elements of the sign give added identity to the brand name and make them more readily identifiable by consumers. A logotype should not clash with the product image but serve to enhance it.

The Atmosphere Conveyed by Print Advertisements

The purpose of creating a certain ambiance or atmosphere with a print advertisement is to convey a specific personality or image to the brand that is consistent with the brand positioning strategy. As was seen in Chapter 12, all the visual and verbal elements in an advertisement generate an image. In Chapter 7, it was seen how specific characters, media vehicles, and consumption scenarios featured in the advertisement tend to convey definite images to a brand. Advertisers should try to control these elements and use them to confer the right image on the advertised product. To meet this objective, they can rely on intuition, experience, or on formal research techniques.[4]

It has been suggested that every detail of an advertisement contributes to brand image formation and that consequently, advertisers should try to control every detail of print

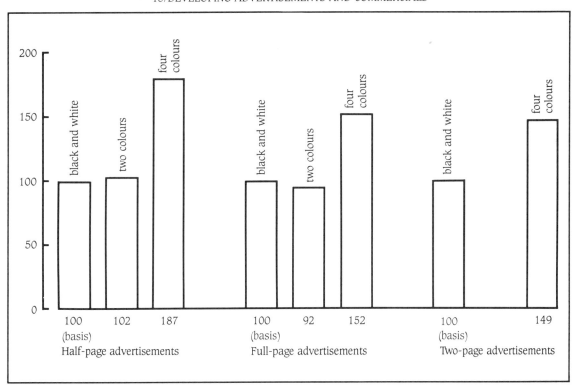

FIGURE 13.18   The Effectiveness of Colour Advertisements According to the Starch Study

advertisements so as to convey the desired brand image. Specific elements of an advertisement also convey a definite atmosphere. These include humour, as well as colour and the advertisement layout, which are exclusive characteristics of print advertisements.

THE USE OF COLOUR. In recent years, colour advertisements have gained wider usage; most magazine and an increasing number of newspaper advertisements are now run in colour. Colour can be used effectively to attract attention, make representations with complete fidelity, emphasize some part of the message, suggest abstract qualities, create pleasant first impressions or prestige for the product, service, or advertiser, and in readers' memory.[5]

Studies on the value of colour advertisements indicate that colour tends to increase the readership rate; enhance the prestige of the brand or the advertiser; and increase the retention rates for visual images among consumers. One study conducted by Daniel Starch on more than 25 000 advertisements in various product categories in national magazines, showed that four-colour advertisements were substantially more noticed in comparison with black and white or even two-colour advertisements, and this regardless of the advertisements' size. The results of this study are shown in Figure 13.18.[6]

Because colour advertising rates are substantially higher than rates for black and white advertisements, the question arises whether colour is really worth the extra cost. According to Starch, because four-colour rates are only 40 per cent above black and white rates for half-page advertisements, and about 35 per cent for one-page advertisements, four-colour advertisements seem to warrant the increased advertising costs.

Colour can be effectively used to attract readers' attention or to highlight certain parts

What Colors Should You Use?

Reaction to color, says Walter Margulies, is generally based on a man's national origin or race. For example, "warm" colors are red, yellow and orange; "these tend to stimulate, excite and create an active response." Those from a warmer clime, apparently, are most responsive to those colors.

Violet and "leaf green," fall right on the line between warm and cool. Each can be one or the other, depending on the shade used.

Here are some more Margulies observations:

Red Symbol of blood and fire. A runnerup to blue as man's "favorite color", but it is the most versatile, i.e., it's the hottest color with highest "action quotient." Appropriate for Campbell's Soups, Stouffer's frozen foods and meats. Conveys strong masculine appeal— shaving cream, Lucky Strike, Marlboro.

Brown Another masculine color, associated with earth, woods, mellowness, age, warmth, comfort, i.e., the essential male; used to sell men anything (even cosmetics), for example, Revlon's Braggi.

Yellow High impact to catch consumer's eye, particularly when used with black—psychologically right for corn, lemon or sun tan products.

Green Symbol of health, freshness—popular for tobacco products, especially mentholated, i.e., Salem, Pall Mall menthol.

Blue Coldest color, with most appeal, effective for frozen foods (ice impression); if used with lighter tints becomes "sweet"—Montclair cigarettes, Lowenbrau beer, Wondra flour.

Black Conveys sophistication, high-end merchandise or used to simulate expensive products; good as background and foil for other colors.

Orange Most "edible" color, especially in brown-tinged shades, evokes autumn and good things to eat.

FIGURE 13.19   The Symbolic Value of Colour

SOURCE: Walter Margulies, in *Media Decisions*, reproduced in Douglas Johnson, *Advertising Today*. (Chicago: Science Research Associates, 1978), p. 103.

KNOW YOUR STREET SIGNS

FIGURE 13.20   An advertisement with this type of layout tends to be dull.

of an advertisement. For example, the Kleenex advertisement in Plate VII, where only the product is in colour on a black and white background, was designed to focus on the product package.

Like any element of the advertisement, colour creates a certain mood. An advertiser should be well aware of the meaning of colour in order to make it enhance the atmosphere of the advertisement.

When food is being advertised, colour represents a definite advantage, since it appeals to consumers' senses. Using just the right colour is important; otherwise, the food in an illustration could look artificial and unappetizing. Colour also carries a great deal of symbolic information. For instance, cool colours are associated with relaxation and warm colours convey excitement. Also, colour preferences vary considerably according to cultural background, which is an important factor for a company that advertises on an international scale. Green is a symbol of life in our country but is associated with sickness and death in equatorial regions like Malaysia. Indications

FIGURE 13.21　**The use of white space in this advertisement evokes the cold and the snow and contrasts with the advertised product (wool).**
Courtesy The Wool Bureau of Canada

about the symbolic value of colours are reproduced in Figure 13.19.[7]

Unfortunately, the scant research conducted in this area provides little conclusive evidence on the symbolic meaning of the various colours. Therefore, the advertising creator must once again rely on artistic evaluation to choose colours that are consistent with the mood of the advertisement.

LAYOUT.　A layout is a working drawing showing how the various parts of an advertisement—the headline, subheads, illustration, copy, picture captions, trademarks, slogans, and logotype—fit together. Layouts generally fulfill two purposes. First, they are blueprints showing how the various elements of an advertisement must be placed in relation to one another; it is a guide for the artists and copywriters to show what is required to develop effective artwork.

Most importantly, the layout is often responsible for conveying the feeling or mood of the advertisement and thus has a psychological and symbolic function. Different positions, weights, and organization of the various elements of an advertisement may suggest

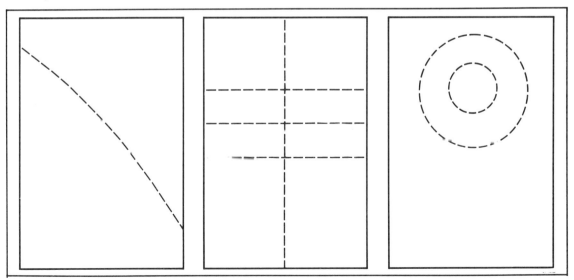

FIGURE 13.22　**Visual Path and Focal Point**

completely different atmospheres and convey very different brand images.

The most important features of a good layout are: interesting composition and balance, variety, simplicity, and intelligent positioning of the different units.

Composition and Balance. Arranging the various visual and verbal elements of a layout may seem like a simple task but in fact it is not. The visual elements should be positioned dramatically to avoid monotony and attract attention. Therefore, the visual elements should be of unequal sizes. This is a basic principle in art and photography. Figure 13.20 shows a layout that does not command attention because the four equally-divided squares seem monotonous. The advertisement in Plate VIII has a less conventional, more exciting layout.

Variety. Variety can be generated through such devices as dramatic use of colour (see the Houbigant advertisement in Plate IX), of blank space (such as in the Studio 55 ad in Figure 13.21), or different typefaces.

Simplicity. Cluttered layouts should be avoided. An illustration is best understood when it is kept simple. Only elements which add force to the communication should be kept. Plate X is an example of a layout that might be considered too crowded.

Positioning of the Units in the Layout. The first illustration of Figure 13.22 shows the visual path followed by the eye as it scans an advertisement. The eye does not always follow this path, however, but may be drawn to other interesting points. The point at which this happens most frequently is called the optical centre or focal point. It is located one-third of the way down from the top of the illustration, at the intersection of the vertical and horizontal lines, in illustration 2. The area surrounding this point, as shown in illustration 3, is the most frequently noticed by readers. Therefore, the most important element of an advertisement, which is usually the product, should be positioned in this very visible area.

Although advertising art directors or artists may find these guidelines useful in creating print advertisements, no principle can replace talent; creativity blended with communication abilities and common sense should yield effective advertising layouts.

Evaluating Print Advertisements

Once a print advertisement has been created, it must be formally evaluated before it can be accepted by the client. The objective is to ensure the advertisement meets some basic qualities, from a communication as well as from a marketing point of view. To make such an assessment, criteria and a formal procedure to test the advertisement should be set up.

Criteria for Evaluating Print Advertisements

A list of criteria for evaluating and selecting print advertisements has been proposed by Joannis.[8] This list gives a good idea of what an advertiser's concerns should be when an advertisement is created. Three criteria concern the advertisement's psychological effectiveness; two criteria concern its communicative effectiveness; and two criteria concern its marketing consistency.

PSYCHOLOGICAL EFFICIENCY CRITERIA.
Is the message powerful and distinctive? Is the motive or the satisfaction to which the advertisement appeals important to consumers? Does the message properly differentiate the brand from competitive products?

Is the message properly understood? Has the advertiser avoided making coding errors?

Does the message fit consumers' psychological background? Can the message be perceived by consumers as relating to their experience, culture, concerns, and psychological environment? Is it likely to be rejected? Does it go against consumers' moral, cultural, or aesthetic values?

COMMUNICATION EFFECTIVENESS CRITERIA.
Can the message be very quickly perceived and understood by the consumer? Can consumers

understand the meaning of the advertisement at a single glance (in this case, it has a high communicative value), or should the consumer be required to think in order to grasp the advertisement's meaning?

Is the message graphically powerful? Does the advertisement copy, the illustrations, and the advertisement layout powerfully communicate the idea that the advertiser wants to convey to consumers?

MARKETING CONSISTENCY CRITERIA.
Can the message be adapted to other types of media? Can the advertisement's appeal be easily adapted to other media if these other types of media must also be used for the advertising campaign?

Is the message consistent with other marketing constraints? Can the message be easily adapted to other promotional means (point-of-purchase advertising, posters, and displays)?

Research Evidence for Evaluating Print Advertisements

Formal research methodology for pretesting how well advertisements score in relation to each criterion is discussed in Chapter 15. Past research however, can also give clues as to what types of advertising format options have proved most effective.

Readership scores of 137 advertisements in the *American Builder* were found to be explained mainly by such factors as the size of the advertisement, the size of the illustration, and the number of colours. These were better explanatory variables than some message content variables.[9] A similar but more extensive study involved 1070 advertisements that appeared in *Life* magazine over a six-month period.[10] Here again, a substantial proportion of the variance in the reading scores provided by Starch was accounted for by such factors as the size of the advertisement (the scores were higher for a double page than for a single page, greater for a horizontal half page than for a vertical one) and the number of colours.

Advertisements with photographs scored higher than advertisements without visual elements. The scores had a tendency to drop sharply once the copy contained more than 50 words. It was also found that the brand or headline prominence in the advertisement had little or no effect.

Such results should not be considered as absolute truths, and they are highly situation dependent. It is somewhat artificial to consider each individual element of an advertisement separately. An advertisement is a whole that is greater than the sum of its parts, and it would be misleading to judge each element without considering the entire advertisement. These findings should be considered only as indications of general trends.

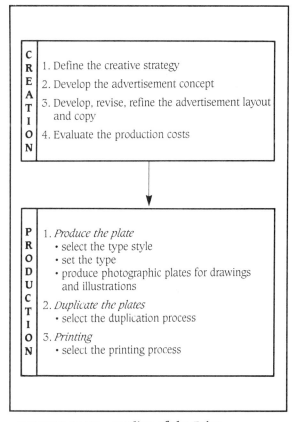

FIGURE 13.23 Outline of the Print Advertisement Production Process

Creating Other Types of Print Advertisements

Although most of the principles discussed above also apply to outdoor and transit advertising, some additional constraints must also be considered because of the special conditions in which the message must be conveyed to the audience.

Outdoor Advertising

Because consumers are likely to be exposed to an outdoor poster for only a short period of time, the principle of quick message delivery is more imperative than for magazine or newspaper advertising. Whether an advertiser designs new copy or adapts the copy already written for other media (as usually happens for national multi-media advertising campaigns), the problem is to simplify the copy as much as possible yet still make it powerful.

The copy should meet three basic requirements. First, the product and the brand should be attention-grabbing, which requires the use of bright colours. Also, the illustration should deliver as much of the message as possible. Third, headlines should be as short and unambiguous as possible. No other element should appear on the poster, because consumers might confuse the message.

Transit Advertising

Interior bus advertisements should follow about the same creation principles as magazine advertisements. But for outdoor car signs, the creation principles for outdoor advertising apply. The major difference between the two types of advertising lies in the horizontal format of bus signs, which requires a different layout.

Print Advertisement Production

After approval of the creative elements of the print advertisement, the production process begins. Print production has developed into a highly complex and technical process. There-fore, while it is neither possible nor even necessary that most advertising managers be versed in all the technical subtleties of this field, they must have at least a hands-on knowledge of its different phases in order to evaluate the costs, constraints, and opportunities in the production process. (See Appendix 2.)

As shown in Figure 13.23, the print advertisement production process can be divided into three stages. First the original plates for the advertisement are produced. Then this plate must be duplicated, especially if the advertisement is to be carried by several different publications. The third and final stage is the actual printing of the advertisement.

The original plate can be produced through a variety of techniques, depending on the type of print media that carries the advertisement, the quality and nature of the advertisement, the printing process, and other factors. One of the first decisions a producer must make are those concerning the different type styles for the advertisement's verbal elements. Next, the type must be set. Such mechanical typesetting methods as linotype or monotype are being replaced by newer, more efficient techniques that consist in exposing the text on photo-sensitive paper or film. If the advertisement contains an illustration, drawing, or photograph, this visual element will have to be etched on a separate plate. With colour advertisements, one plate must be designed for each colour. A full-colour advertisement needs four plates, one for each of the basic colours: red, blue, yellow, and black. These plates are then superimposed, creating the impression of numerous different shades, as is illustrated in Plate XI.

Several different publications may carry the same advertisement. This requires making a mould of the plate, either as a stereotype or as a more expensive, higher quality electrotype.

The printing process involves transferring the image of the advertisement from a press onto paper. The three most commonly used printing techniques are letterpress, gravure, and offset.

Creating Broadcast Commercials

Special Characteristics of Broadcast Commercials

The creation of broadcast commercials has some basic differences from print advertisements. These differences derive from the presence of another channel of communication: the audio element, a unique time dimension, and the particular medium/audience interface that broadcast media have developed.

The Audio Elements in Broadcast Commercials
A broadcast message contains an audio element not present in print advertisements. For television commercials, the audio elements are added to the three other communication channels of verbal, visual, and ambiance that characterize print advertisements. For radio commercials, they are a substitute for visual elements. Thus, the presence of audio elements changes the nature and effectiveness of the communication. When properly used, audio elements tend to increase a communication's effectiveness. There is typically a higher level of message retention among an audience exposed to a broadcast commercial, since a verbal message tends to be remembered better than the text in a print advertisement.

The Time Dimension of Broadcast Commercials
Whereas space is the limiting constraint for print advertisements, broadcast commercials are limited by time. The broadcast creator's problem is to deliver a message effectively in a brief period, usually 10, 30, or 60 seconds. Although these periods are often much longer than the amount of time that many readers of print advertisements devote to a single ad, the trend toward shorter, 30-second commercials (for obvious cost reasons) has caused the "commercial clutter" phenomenon. Television commercial time is filled with many 10-second and 30-second commercials, hence the increasing need for advertisers to vie aggressively for viewers' attention.

A second time-related difference lies in the relative control an advertiser has over the audience while the commercial is aired: Readers of a print advertisement are subjected to selected exposure to the selling arguments, since they may glance at some parts of an illustration, ignore others, and read only part of the text. With television or radio commercials, listeners are sequentially exposed to the various points, and advertisers have more control over the exact content of the message delivered.

The Consumer-Broadcast Media Interface
As most advertisers know, people frequently talk or engage in other activities while watching television. Audiences' low involvement in broadcast media is one manifestation of selective attention barriers that people use to screen out what they do not want to hear. Furthermore, Festinger found that people tend to argue mentally with commercials that are at variance with their own ideas, and that this counter-argumentation was listeners' attempt to resist commercial persuasion.[11] Consequently, this particular consumer-broadcast media interface tends to counterbalance the effectiveness of the audio elements.

Creating Television Commercials

Television's popularity and highly concentrated audiences make the medium an extremely powerful communications tool. This is why companies allocate an increasing amount of their advertising dollars to television. Because of its four parallel communication channels—visual, audio, verbal, and ambiance—television commercials are a more complete communication device. All the elements of every channel should be selected to communicate the desired message. This is represented in Figure 13.24.

The Functions of the Television Commercial Elements

VISUAL ELEMENTS. The functions of the visual and verbal elements of a television commercial

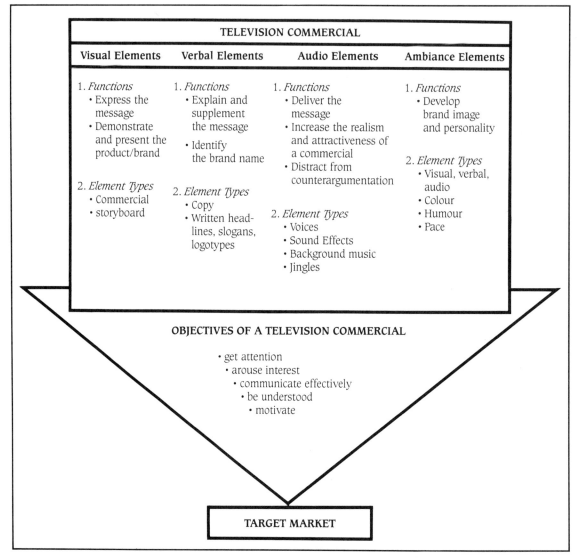

FIGURE 13.24   Elements of a Television Commercial

are closely related. As with print advertisements, the visual elements are assigned the function of expressing as much of the advertising message as possible. However, because of the relatively longer period of time to be filled by a commercial, advertisers are not limited to one major selling argument, as is the case for print advertisements. Depending on the duration of the commercial and the nature of the advertised product, advertisers can make several

selling points. Nonetheless, the visual elements should highlight the product and the brand, either in order to demonstrate its use or simply to make consumers aware of the package so that they would recognize the brand at a store. This is why a product or brand should be identified as early as possible during the television commercial. The visual elements, together with the verbal elements and the script, constitute the television commercial's scenario.

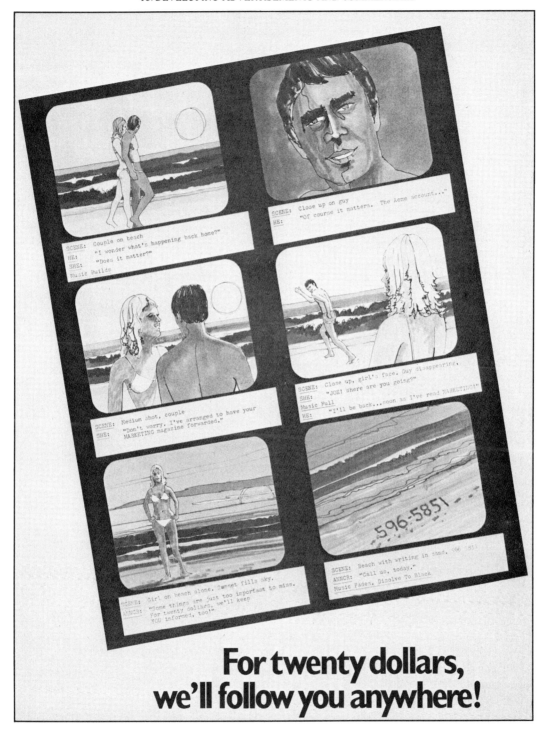

FIGURE 13.25   Storyboard for a Television Commercial
Courtesy Marketing Magazine

VERBAL ELEMENTS. The verbal elements—the script of the commercial scenario—are used to explain, reinforce, and complement the visual elements in order to communicate the advertising message effectively. Visual elements are needed to identify the brand name properly. As in print advertisements, this function can be performed in conjunction with written headlines, slogans, and logotypes.

AUDIO ELEMENTS. Audio elements in broadcast commercials fulfill three main functions: they deliver the verbal message; increase the message effectiveness through higher realism and attractiveness; and create a "distracting" element that is intended to reduce consumers' counter-argumentation during a commercial. Background music, sound effects, and jingles can be effectively used to achieve these three functions.

AMBIANCE ELEMENTS. Advertisers can build the proper atmosphere in a commercial that will generate the desired brand image and personality. All the visual, verbal, audio elements are likely to suggest symbolic interpretations, and the use of colours, the use of humour, as well as the pace of the commercial may create quite different moods.

Developing the Storyboard

A storyboard is the counterpart of a layout for print advertisements. It is a set of pictures or frames that describe each scene or movement during the commercial. At the bottom of every frame are indications about the copy, sound effects, and music that correspond to the scene. A storyboard is a detailed screenplay for a television commercial. A sample storyboard is shown in Figure 13.25.

Once an advertiser has described the main claim that will be emphasized in the commercial and for other related selling arguments, the approach to the commercial must be selected. There are a finite number of ways a commercial can be presented on television. The main categories for television commercials are:[12]

Story line. A commercial that tells a story; a clear, step-by-step unfolding of a message that has a definite beginning, middle, and end.

Problem-solving. Presents the viewer with a problem to be solved and the sponsor's product as the solution to that problem. Probably the most widely used and generally accepted example of a TV commercial.

Chronology. Delivers the message through a series of related scenes, each one growing out of the one before. Facts and events are presented sequentially as they occur.

Special effects. No strong structural pattern. Strives for and often achieves memorability through the use of some striking device, for example, an unusual musical sound or pictorial technique.

Testimonial. Also called "word-of-mouth" advertising, it uses well-known figures or an unknown "man in the street" to provide product testimonials.

Satire. A commercial that uses sophisticated wit to point out human foibles, generally produced in an exaggerated style. Parodies on James Bond movies, "Bonnie and Clyde," "Hair," and the like.

Spokesperson. The use of an on-camera announcer who basically "talks". Talk may be fast and hard sell or more personal, intimate sell.

Demonstration. Uses some physical apparatus to demonstrate a product's effectiveness. Analgesic, watch, and tire commercials employ this approach heavily.

Suspense. Somewhat similar to story-line or problem-solution structures, but the buildup of curiosity and suspense to final resolution is given a heightened sense of drama.

Slice-of-life. A variation of problem solution. Begins with a person at the point of, and just before the discovery of, an answer to a problem. Heavily used by detergent manufacturers.

Analogy. Offers an extraneous example, then attempts to relate it to the product message.

Straight Voice-of-Print. Very objective, non-emotional voice of a news announcer. Appeals particularly to men and is best suited to bank, financial institutions, car, truck, automobile accessories, sports event tickets, gasoline, insurance commercials.

Disk Jockey Announcer: Young, modern voice using casual and often confidential tone. Appeals to young people and is best suited for commercials on fashion clothes, musical happenings, music stores, hair care products.

Beery Announcer. Bass or baritone voice often used to announce beer or cigarettes, automobiles, or trucks. The leadership tone of the voice is effective in influencing men.

Pound-Pound, Hard-Hitter, Fast-Talker Announcer. Very assertive voice often used in discount store or second-hand car commercials.

Folksy Announcer. Use of regional pattern of speech and accent. Each best fits the area where it is typical or can be used as a symbol of the area.

Cosmetic Voice: Often used as voice-over in television (without the announcer being seen) to advertise perfume and cosmetics. Generally sexy, low, husky voice.

Impersonator Voice. Imitation of the voices of such well-known actors as Humphrey Bogart, Gary Cooper, or Mae West. If not carefully checked, this may involve legal complaints. Has high attention value.

Character Voice. Overacting of certain stereotypes (such as the henpecked husband or the rich dowager) depending on the screenplay of the commercial.

Personality, Star, Celebrity. These are actual celebrities used in testimonial commercials.

Real People. Untrained, natural voices of ordinary people used for certain types of testimonial commercials.

FIGURE 13.26   Types of Voices in Commercials
SOURCE: Adapted from Douglas Johnson, *Advertising Today* (Chicago: SRA, 1978), pp. 105-6.

Instead of delivering a message simply and directly, an analogy uses one example to explain another by comparison or implication. "Just as vitamins tone up your body, our product tones up your car's engine."

Fantasy. Uses caricatures or special effects to create fantasy surrounding product and product use: "Jolly Green Giant", "White Knight", "White Tornado", "the washing machine that becomes ten feet tall".

Personality. A technical variation of the spokes-person or announcer-on-camera, straight-sell structure. Relies on an actor or actress rather than an announcer to deliver the message. Uses a setting rather than the background of a studio. The actor plays a character who talks about the product, reacts to its use, or demonstrates its use or enjoyment directly to the camera.[13]

Selecting the Audio Elements

Because of their special importance for television commercials, audio elements should be selected carefully and should match the kind of story selected as a support to the sales pitch. Most important is the kind of voice selected to announce the product, the sound effects, the

background music, and the jingles. These bring life and realism to broadcast advertisements.

THE ANNOUNCER'S VOICE.   The selection of the proper voice can decide the success of a commercial, and a certain type of voice can give the right brand image or suggest the right product usage situation for the target market segment. J. Douglas Johnson recognizes ten voice styles for broadcast commercials, which are listed in Figure 13.26.[14]

A voice suitable for advertising a price cut at a discount store cannot be used to advertise expensive perfumes. Not only the voice itself, but also the tone of the voice, its nuance, the accent, and the emotion are loaded with information that is deciphered by the consumers and associated with the advertised brand.

SOUND EFFECTS.   There is a hierarchy of sound effects for use in a television commercial. Some sounds have an obvious raison d'être in a commercial because they are expected to be heard as the commercial unfolds. Their use is a question of realism. For instance, the roaring motor of cars passing on a highway, the noise of a lawn mower being demonstrated, the pop of a champagne cork, or the hiss sound of a spray can, are natural complements to the verbal part of the advertising message. At a higher level, an advertiser can make an effective use of sounds to say something about the product or the brand. For instance, a car door being slammed with a solid sound suggests a sturdy, well-built automobile; the fizz of sparkling natural water suggests the brand's thirst-quenching property; the crunch of a biscuit evokes freshness. At a more subtle level, sounds can build symbolic meanings around a brand and can be instrumental in brand image creation. The sound of a zipper being closed during a commercial for a diet drink evokes the ability of the product to help consumers stay thin (so that they can close the zippers without difficulty). Although nothing is said about the zipper, consumers clearly deduce the meaning.[15]

Thus, decisions about the choice and selection of sound effects are important because of the direct and symbolic information they convey to consumers.

THE USE OF MUSIC. Advertisers must decide what role music should play in the overall advertising message. Should the selling proposition be put into music (in this case, the music line is called a jingle), or should the music be assigned the role of setting a background to supplement the message? Should the music attract the listener's attention, or should it go unnoticed as an atmosphere-creating device? Should the music be already familiar to the consumers, or should it be created especially for the commercial? What instruments and orchestra should be used?

Music lends uniqueness and interest to a commercial. Depending on the effects being sought, music can be used either as background or as a jingle generally sang off screen. Whenever music is used as background, an advertiser can use *stock music*. Stock music is already orchestrated music corresponding to various moods advertisers want to create. This

music can be acquired at a reasonable cost from stock music companies. Or original music especially composed and recorded for a given commercial by an independent contractor may be used. This is certainly much more costly than stock music, but if a commercial is to be aired many times over an extended period, the higher cost of original music may be warranted.

Jingles fulfill a purpose quite different from that of background music. They help consumers identify a brand immediately, create almost constant presence, express the personality of the brand, product, and/or company, get a new brand across to a market quickly, and help keep a brand name or a slogan in people's memory.[16] An effective jingle can unforgettably associate in consumers' minds a brand name with a short advertising message. Thus, a jingle sets to music either the slogan for the advertised brand or lyrics written usually by the advertising agency.

Advertisers have several options for selecting music. Original music composed especially for the jingle can be used. Composing fees would have to be considered before this option was chosen. A popular song could also be used. The advantage of this option is that the public is already familiar with the tune and can memorize the jingle more quickly, with less message repetition. However, in this case advertisers must pay fees to the copyright owners. For songs in the public domain there is no fee to pay, but neither is there any guarantee that the song is not being or will not be used by other advertisers.

Evaluating Television Commercials
What makes a good and effective television commercial is somewhat hard to define. Creating a television commercial is as much an art as a science, and depends on such intangible and qualitative aspects as aesthetic values, emotional appeals, or credibility. But because of the high stakes involved in television advertising, advertisers have often tried to define the criteria that could help them to assess the quality of

television commercials. Some general criteria are:

Do the visual elements powerfully convey the message? Pictures are a powerful means of communication. Often, a single visual element can replace a lengthy description. Vivid pictures yield better results, attract more attention, increase reach, are most remembered by consumers, and generally make for a better advertisement. Striking pictures, if used judiciously, always reinforce the advertising message.

Has the commercial been kept simple? Typical television viewers are relaxing, and their concentration level is usually quite low. Thus they will reject subtle, complex, or muddled commercials. Therefore, the virtues of simplicity must once again be emphasized. The most powerful messages are always clear and straightforward.

Does the commercial make the best possible use of motion? A static picture will not hold viewers' attention. Fast-moving pictures generate interest in the commercial.

Does the commercial demonstrate the use of the product? Television is the best medium for product demonstration, especially for household and food products.

Is the commercial entertaining? Entertainment can make a commercial more lively and interesting. It should, however, be subordinated to the advertisement's communication objectives. It should not distract the audience from the main objective of the commercial, which is to convey certain product advantages and/or promote the product.

Is the commercial credible? Credibility is an essential prerequisite for *any* form of effective communication. Television advertising bears no exception to this rule. Commercials must avoid any kind of double talk, vague expressions, and inadequately backed claims that could ruin the sales presentation. In television advertising, this task becomes more complicated, because all the elements—setting, decor, acting, situation, language—must combine to create authenticity.

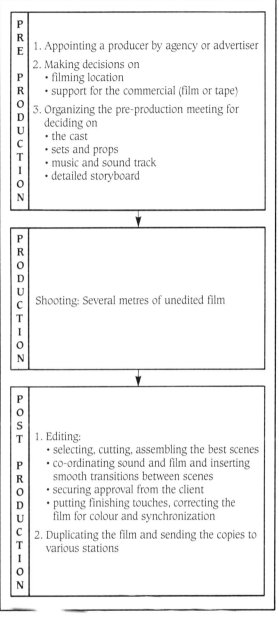

FIGURE 13.27   Outline of Television Commercial Production

Although a great deal of research has been conducted, scientific advances made in the field of television advertising are not being applied sufficiently in practice. David Ogilvy and Joel Raphaelson of Ogilvy and Mather, a

Chicago-based advertising agency, have deplored this lack of scientific attitude among advertising creators: "Advertising could achieve better results if more people who create it would take the time to learn which techniques are most likely to work."[17] Among the techniques that yielded above-average results in changing brand preferences, they found:

- problem solution;
- humour (when pertinent to the selling proposition);
- relevant characters (personalities, developed by the advertising, who become associated with the brand);
- slice-of-life (enactments in which a doubter is converted);
- news (new products, new uses, new ideas, new information);
- candid camera testimonials and demonstrations.

Commercials using celebrities were not found to be very effective. One explanation proposed was that "such messages focus attention on the celebrity rather than on the product."[18]

Other findings reported were:

- cartoons and animation are effective with children, but below average with adults;
- commercials with very short scenes and many changes of situations are below average;
- "supers" (words on the screen) add to a commercial's power to change brand preference, but the words must reinforce the main point;
- commercials that do not show the package, or that end without the brand name, are below average in changing brand preference;
- commercials that start with a key idea stand a better chance of holding attention and persuading the viewer. When you advertise fire extinguishers, open with the fire.

Television Commercial Production

A television commercial may start with a great concept and a clever storyboard, only to be spoiled by inadequate casting, poor lighting, amateurish filming, or any one of a hundred flaws in the production process. This is why production is a crucial stage in the development of a commercial and special care must be taken to ensure that nothing goes wrong. The production process for television commercials is divided into three stages, as is shown in Figure 13.27. The first stage involves the decisions that must be taken before the actual filming or recording is done, and is known as preproduction. Second, the storyboard is enacted and recorded on film or tape. Finally, the film is edited and submitted to the advertiser for approval. This last stage is postproduction.

PREPRODUCTION. Once a storyboard has been drafted and approved by the creative director of the advertising agency, the producer is summoned to oversee the actual production before the commercial is aired. The producer must decide on a studio or location in which the commercial will be shot. Then, a preproduction meeting is called, which is perhaps one of the most important stages of the entire production process. This meeting decides the schedule and the shooting: casting, music, sound effects, sets and props, lighting, camera angles, and other technical details. Nothing should be overlooked during this meeting, and the producer should "set everything straight" before the shooting. Even a minor snag noticed too late could result in time delays and costly overruns.

PRODUCTION. Since all of the important decisions have already been made at the preproduction level, shooting merely involves recording the commercial according to the detailed and precise instructions contained on the storyboard. Usually, the time alloted for filming each scene is kept to one day because of the high cost of labour, studio time, and actors. Since an agency can ill afford a mistake that would force it into costly retake, several versions are taken on each scene, and even superfluous scenes are

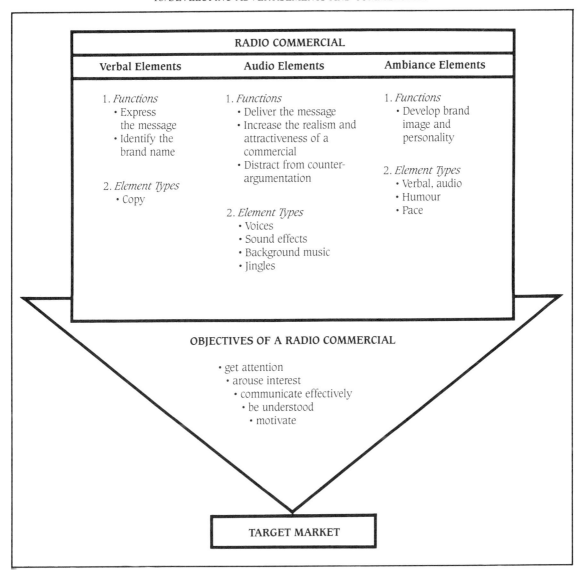

FIGURE 13.28 Elements of a Radio Commercial

sometimes added. For a typical 30-second spot, 600 to 900 metres of 35 mm film may be exposed, whereas only 15 metres will end up in the final commercial. If the commercial contains several different settings, the scenes are not filmed sequentially, for reasons of cost and efficiency.

POST-PRODUCTION. What finally comes out of the studio is an unfinished product: several

metres of film or tape, bearing a set of unrelated sequences. This rough copy is taken to the editor, who edits and cuts the film, selects the takes, recasts, improves, co-ordinates, and assembles the pictures into a coherent commercial. The film editor is in charge of the final stage of production. The creative department and the producer decide the content of an ad, but the editor makes their conception bear fruit and delivers the finished product, which can be aired once the client's approval is received. (See Appendix 2 for more information on the technical aspects of television commercial production.)

Creating Radio Commercials

Creating radio commercials bears some similarities to television commercial creation, but also a number of major differences. The first obvious difference is that radio commercials lack the visual elements of television. However, it would be wrong to conclude that radio commercials are nothing but the sound track of a corresponding television commercial. For television, the maximum amount of information must be conveyed through visual elements, and audio elements are used to supplement, reinforce, and make explicit the message to be communicated to the target audience. For a radio commercial, the audio elements are the only means available for conveying the message. The radio commercial communication process is represented in Figure 13.28. Consequently, the sound track of a radio commercial is likely to be substantially different from that of television.

In a given market, radio audiences are much more fragmented and segmented than television audiences. Depending on the types of programs and music aired, radio stations cater to audiences that vary according to age, social class, and education. Consequently, it may be desirable for advertisers to develop radio commercials built not only on the product to be advertised but also according to the different market segments reached by different kinds of stations.

Unlike television audiences, which are more homogeneous in their watching time and related activities while watching, radio audiences may be in different states of mind depending upon the time of the day and on the type of activity of the listener at the time the commercial is aired. For instance, radio listeners are not equally receptive when listening to a car radio while on the way to work, as when they listen to a transistor while relaxing on a beach. Copywriters must take these considerations into account when developing a radio commercial for a certain brand.

Copywriters have much more freedom in developing a radio than a television commercial. In creating a radio commercial, they are not constrained by the practical feasibility and/or the costs of developing the visual elements. With only words and sounds to manipulate, copywriters are limited only by their imagination. There are several types of radio commercials. Live or recorded commercials are the most common.

Types of Radio Commercial

Live commercials. The copy is prepared to be read "live" by a station personality or an announcer. Live commercial scripts are generally prepared in advance. They run about 100 to 120 words per minute so they can be read at a normal pace. Among other advantages, such messages tend to be more credible because they are read (and indirectly endorsed) by local personalities; they also are less costly than pre-recorded scripts. However, they cannot take full advantage of the audio elements, such as background music, jingles, or sound effects. They cannot rely on carefully selected voices and controlled diction of the message. This is why advertisers often prefer to use recorded commercials.

Announcer delivery. This type of commercial is much like a live commercial, but the script has been pre-recorded. Sound effects, background music, jingles, careful voice selection— all the audio elements—can be controlled, and the commercial can be revised until it fully satisfies the advertiser's requirements.

Musical commercials. Jingles and musical commercials can effectively associate a brand name with a slogan or a selling argument. All the characteristics of using music also apply to the development of good musical radio commercials.

Dialogue commercials. Dialogues make a radio commercial more lively and interesting. This approach also lends itself to the use of humour, which can enhance the positive image of a brand.

Testimonial commercials. The testimonial approach uses either real people or celebrities. Basically the same criteria for evaluating the effectiveness of commercials apply for radio and television commercials, but the entire communication is carried by the sound. A good radio commercial should entice consumers with interesting, informative content, provide lively soundtrack, and depict believable situations. The message should be kept simple, be repeated for added force, and the announcer should use short words and sentences so that the message is understood by consumers with the low level of concentration typical of radio listeners.

Radio Commercial Production

Radio production is much more simple and inexpensive than television. With a live recording, the production stage is almost inexistent, since the agency merely has to supply radio stations with a script. However, if the commercial is to be recorded, this implies the necessity of production.

The production of a radio commercial is straightforward. The advertiser appoints a director who selects a recording studio and a cast. Professional actors may be hired to read the script, musicians to play the music, or composers. Rehearsals may be held before the actual recording. Then the sound track and the music are prepared in a studio on separate tapes. The various elements are mixed at a later stage, yielding the master tape. After several such recordings have been made, the best is chosen and is duplicated, either on tape or on records. The commercials are then sent to various stations to be aired.

Summary

With print advertisements, the visual, verbal, and atmosphere-creating elements should be selected so as to be consistent and should help convey the basic advertising message to consumers. The visual elements are the most powerful in communicating to the market. They include photographs, drawings, or other kinds of artwork. Verbal elements should complete the message and supplement it. They include the advertisement headline, the subheads, the body copy, the slogan, and the logotype. In addition to the visual and verbal elements of an advertisement that tend to create a particular atmosphere and build a certain brand image, other elements are powerful in ambiance content. They include the use or non-use of colour and the layout for an advertisement. There are several criteria for evaluating print advertisements, as well as considerations that apply to outdoor and transit advertising.

Broadcast commercials have unique audio, time, and consumer medium interface characteristics. To develop effective commercials, advertisers must design a creative storyboard and make intelligent use of the announcer's voice, sound effects, and music. Although advertisers need not be versed in all the technical subtleties of producing commercials, they must have at least a hands-on knowledge of the different phases of production, in order to evaluate the costs, constraints, and also opportunities inherent in the production processes for the different media.

Questions for Study

1. Find two recent advertisements, one in a magazine, one in a newspaper. Using the criteria for print advertisement evaluation given in the text, evaluate these advertisements.

2. What is the most important part of a print advertisement? Advertisers' opinions vary;

some say it is the headline, others, the illustration; still others suggest that the whole concept is important, regardless of the type of advertisement. Discuss these viewpoints. What is your view? Elaborate with specific examples.

3. List all the elements in a print advertisement that, in your opinion, lead to image formation and/or atmosphere. Give specific examples.

4. List all the elements in a broadcast commercial (i.e., television *and* radio) that tend to convey some brand image.

5. Some advertisements have no illustration, only lengthy copy. Under what circumstances do you think such advertisements can be effective (if at all)?

6. In what way is it increasingly difficult or easy to create television commercials?

7. Take a few print advertisements in a magazine. Study and compare their layouts. If possible, find the rationale for each one.

8. For what kind of products might the use of a jingle be more appropriate? List some of the advantages and drawbacks of using jingles in *(a)* radio commercials and in *(b)* television commercials.

9. After reading Appendix 2, define the following terms: typography, roman, sans-serif, script, typesetting, handsetting, pica, em, monotype, phototypography, photo-text, monophoto.

10. After reading Appendix 2, define the following terms: letterpress, gravure, offset, photo-engraving, half-tone engraving, electrotype.

Problems

1. A group of accounting students at a university have set up a small non-profit organization to help individuals and small organizations figure their income tax. They have been given by a government agency a small budget to advertise in the local newspapers and on the local radio. Because of their limited resources, this group of students turns to you to ask you to write the advertisements (print and broadcast). You are free to select the creative approach you think is best, and you are responsible for the total creation and eventually the production of these advertisements.

2. Select a print advertisement in a magazine. Using the *same* concept as this advertisement *(a)* write a radio commercial and *(b)* create a television commercial storyboard for this same campaign, but using radio and television as the basic media.

Notes

1. David Ogilvy, *Confessions of an Advertising Man* (New York: Atheneum, 1964), p. 146.
2. John Caples, *Tested Advertising Methods*, rev. ed. (New York: Harper & Row, 1961), chapter 3.
3. Hans Kleefeld, "Symbol or Logo-What's the Difference," *Marketing*, 3 January 1983, p. 18.
4. See, for instance, René Y. Darmon, "Multiple Joint Space Analysis for Improved Advertising Strategy," *Canadian Marketer* (Fall 1979), pp. 10-14.
5. Thomas B. Stanley, *The Technique of Advertising Production*, 2nd ed. (New York: Prentice-Hall, 1954), p. 59.
6. Daniel Starch, *Measuring Advertising Readership and Results* (New York: McGraw-Hill, 1956), p. 59.

7. Walter Margulies, "Media Decisions," reproduced in J. Douglas Johnson, *Advertising Today* (Chicago: Science Research Associates, 1978), p. 103.

8. Henry Joannis, *De l'Etude de Motivation à la Création Publicitaire et à la Promotion des Ventes* (Paris: Dunod, 1965), pp. 285-87.

9. Dick Warren Twedt, "A Multiple Factor Analysis of Advertising Readership," *Journal of Applied Psychology* (June 1952), pp. 207-15.

10. Daniel Diamond, "A Quantitative Approach to Magazine Advertisement Format Selection," *Journal of Marketing Research* (November 1968), pp. 376-87.

11. Leon Festinger and Nathan Maccoby, "On Resistance to Persuasive Communication," *Journal of Abnormal and Social Psychology*, 4 (1968), 248-52.

12. Albert C. Book and Norman D. Cary, *The Television Commercial: Creativity and Craftsmanship* (New York: Decker Communications, 1970).

13. Ibid., p. 210.

14. Johnson, pp. 105-6.

15. Example given in Johnson, p. 108.

16. Ibid., p. 109.

17. David Ogilvy and Joel Raphaelson, "Research on Ad Techniques That Work—and Don't Work," *Marketing News*, 17 September 1982, p. 2.

18. Ibid., p. 2.

Developing a Media Plan

The role of the media director is to efficiently deliver an advertiser's message to a target audience. This is an enormous task, since a staggering amount of information on the markets, the media, and consumers' media habits must be processed. Also, the task of selecting media types, media vehicles and options, and developing a media schedule is extremely complex.

Computers can help media planners handle the information available and can suggest media selection and schedules by applying statistical and mathematical models. These decision tools are still being perfected, however, and media planners must use a great deal of individual judgement in working with them.

An understanding of the media planner's tasks is needed in order to arrive at the most efficient media schedule given the advertising objectives and the advertising budget.

Media planning is conducted in the general context of corporate, marketing, and advertising planning. Thus, it is important that media planners understand fully the objectives and strategies developed at higher levels. Advertising objectives and the advertising appropriation are the constraints within which the media director must work. Figure 14.1 outlines the media planning process.

The media director translates the advertising objectives into *media objectives* and strategies by using all information pertaining to the communication process, including the advertising message developed by the creative director. The media objectives in turn guide the selection of *media types* and *media vehicles*, i.e., a specific magazine, newspaper, radio station, or television program. Then is developed a detailed *media schedule* that indicates when, where, and how long each message is going to run. At any stage in this process the media planner may conduct research to get additional information for effective decision making. This planning process culminates in the *media plan* (Figure 14.2). Since media planning is part of overall campaign planning, the media plan is ultimately incorporated into the advertising plan. Nevertheless, a separate media plan is useful early in the planning process because it helps determine the overall appropriation. It is also necessary to know very early which vehicles are selected, since lead times, particularly for prime-time television, may be quite long.

Developing Media Objectives

The purpose of media objectives is to select the *best possible media* for reaching the advertising objectives for the selected target audience(s); the list of key market(s); the task of the communication; the creative execution of the message; and the advertising appropriation.

The media planner must make sure that the message reaches the right people at the right time, but in such a way as to ensure that effective communication takes place. The first task is most commonly associated with media directors, but the second is often as important in identifying the best conditions under which actual communication of the message (the work of the creative group) is to take place.

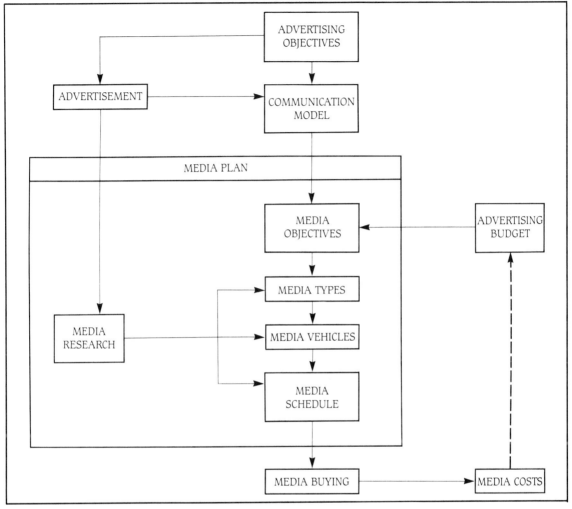

FIGURE 14.1   The Process of Developing the Media Plan

Media objectives must thus reflect these two tasks.

Making Decisions about the Target Audiences

As explained in Chapter 11, the advertising objectives define the main target audiences of the campaign.

The media director must take into account the target audiences in the statement of advertising objectives and select the advertising media according to the different values of the audience. To do so, a *weighting system*[1] is used that gives secondary and tertiary audiences lower weights than primary audiences. An example of the application of audience weights for a magazine is given in Table 14.1. The weight levels are determined by the media director based on judgement and past experience with the audience's level of interest in the advertised product.

Target audiences should be defined as precisely as possible in terms of demographic, economic, and psychographic variables. When a target audience is defined in the advertising

MEDIA PLAN

A. MEDIA OBJECTIVES: Select the best media for:
1. Target audience(s)
2. Key markets
3. Communication task
4. Creative execution
5. Advertising budget constraint

B. MEDIA SELECTION: Translate objectives into:
1. Reach/Frequency/Continuity/Intensity/Impact levels
2. The best media types
3. The best media vehicles

C. MEDIA SCHEDULE AND BUDGET
1. Media schedule
2. Media budget

D. MEDIA RESEARCH

FIGURE 14.2   Suggested Outline for the Media Plan

objectives, the task of the media director is a little easier, but it still may be necessary to apply weights according to the values of the various subgroups. For example, a subgroup of individuals or families who are heavy users of frozen pizzas should have a higher weight for an advertisement for that product than light users of the product class, particularly if marketing objectives call for market share gains rather than market development. This second

group of weights may be called demographic, economic, or psychographic weights depending on the variable(s) used to form the subgroups. Weights may also be derived from research data, either primary research or such syndicated sources as the PMB product profile studies and A.C. Nielsen.[2]

Target audiences have media usage habits that determine the use of certain media types or vehicles, if they are to be reached effectively. This section deals not with audience profiles of various media, which are used in the media selection process, but with factors called *media imperatives*. Although this term has been used mainly for magazines, it may be applied to any medium. A medium imperative calls for the media director to seriously consider using a particular medium because a substantial proportion of the target audience are heavy users of the medium *and* light users of the other media. For example, a large proportion of well-educated, high-income consumers watch very little television but read several magazines regularly. Thus these consumers may not be reached if magazines are not selected.

Making Decisions about the Key Markets in Which to Advertise

When a campaign is to run in several sales territories, it is necessary to develop the means for allocating the advertising effort among

TABLE 14.1   Numerical Application of the Audience Weighting System

Consumer magazine A (readership: 200 000) Advertisement for a women's perfume			
	Audience	Weight	Weighted audience
Primary target audience Women 18-45	100 000	1.0	100 000
Secondary target audience Men 18-45	50 000	0.5	25 000
Tertiary target audience Teenagers 14-18	40 000	0.3	12 000
		Total adjusted audience	*137 000*

various territories. This is often a marketing strategy decision, and the allocation among territories may be spelled out in the marketing plan. Such decisions may be in the form of marketing objectives, such as increasing penetration of the brand in territories with low or medium penetration or increasing market share in territories with high penetration.

Whatever options an advertiser selects, it is necessary to establish priorities for allocating the media budget. Media directors often use market weights and/or brand development indices in order to translate marketing objectives into an operational allocation to territories.

Market weights may be used to account for behavioural differences among various markets. For example, consumers in some territories may have historically been quite well disposed toward a brand, while in others they have been neutral or unaccepting. An advertisement for a brand may not be noticed and accepted to the same extent by consumers in these markets. Market weights take these differences into account, consistent with the selected marketing strategy. Applying the weights may well lead to a decision *not* to advertise in some markets.

Brand development indices (BDI) identify markets with low penetration and markets with high penetration. The BDI is an index of per capita sales of a brand in a given market compared to the national figure. An example of calculation of BDIs is provided in Table 14.2. In this example, the brand is doing very well in Nova Scotia, Quebec, and Manitoba, and poorly in Alberta and British Columbia. Based on the advertiser's marketing objectives, weights may be derived to account for these differences. In the case of BDI, the behavioural variable used is past purchase. Thus, weights derived from BDI are a special type of market weights.

Taking the Creative Execution into Account

Media planners must take into account the type of message created by the creative group and assess the requirements of the creative execution in terms of media types, media vehicles and media options, as well as the interactions among the message, the audiences, and the media types or vehicles.

Some creative approaches may require a specific medium. For example, an advertisement demonstrating a product in use may require television, or an advertisement with a jingle may require radio or television. Certain creative approaches may require a special editorial environment to be most effective, for example, an advertisement for sports equipment is aired during a sports program, or a testimonial advertisement using a specific actor or cartoon character may be shown during a film featuring the actor or character.

Creative execution may require certain media options that would eliminate some media types

TABLE 14.2   A Hypothetical Example of Calculating Brand Development Indices

Territories	(A) Distribution of brand volume	(B) Distribution of households	BDI = 100 A/B
Nova Scotia	5.0	3.7	135
Quebec	35.0	28.5	123
Ontario	35.0	39.0	90
Manitoba	6.0	4.7	128
Saskatchewan	4.0	4.2	95
Alberta	6.0	8.3	72
British Columbia	9.0	11.6	78
	100.0	100.0	

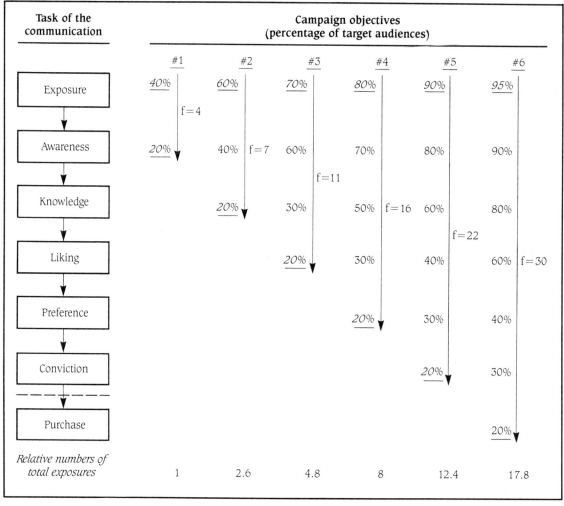

FIGURE 14.3 Hypothetical Example of the Relationship between Communication Task and Total Number of Exposures Required

or vehicles. For example, an advertisement requiring perfect colour reproduction would be best suited to magazines.

There may be interdependencies among the message, the audiences, and the media types or vehicles, since the same message may have very different effects if seen on television or in a magazine, or even on two different television programs when the audience predispositions are different. It is extremely difficult to account for those differences, but an experienced and knowledgeable media director can identify the most important interdependencies and weight them accordingly.

Taking the Communication Task into Account

The communication task set out in operational terms in the statement of advertising objectives is the critical element of the campaign. One task of the media director is to translate the advertising objectives into operational media objectives. This is a difficult step to undertake, but with experience the media director can develop reliable estimates. While some previous media objectives were concerned with maximizing the probability of *exposure to the medium*, here the concern is with the various steps involved in communicating the message, from exposure to the message to conviction about the brand. The media director does not supersede the work of the creative group but complements it by ensuring that the target audience is exposed to that message at the right time, in the right place, and with enough repetition to ensure that the communication task is completed.

To illustrate the relationship between the communication task and media objectives, a hypothetical example has been constructed in Figure 14.3, using the framework introduced in Chapter 11 and Figure 11.4. Assume that the brand is new. If increased awareness of the brand name is the campaign objective, it may be estimated that 40 per cent of the target audience should be exposed to the advertising message at least four times. Thus, the number of total exposures to the message may be calculated as follows: if the number of individual in the target audience is 100 000, the number of exposures should be:

10 000 $\times$ 40 per cent $\times$ 4 exposures/individual
= 160 000 exposures

This information, in turn, is used in the media selection process.

Similarly, if increased knowledge about the brand is the selected communication task, it may be estimated that at least 60 per cent of the target audience should be exposed to the message at least six times. This level of repetition may be necessary to ensure that copy claims about the brand are learned by the targeted number of individuals, which is 20 per cent of the target audience. The required number of gross exposures may be calculated as 420 000, i.e., 2.6 times the required number for increased awareness.

The same reasoning may be made for increased liking, preference, conviction, and

purchase. As shown in Figure 14.3, the relative number of total exposures required are, respectively, 4.8, 8, 12.4, and 17.8 times the required number for increased awareness of the new brand.

Although in practice it is often difficult to estimate the various numbers used in this example, the media director may derive these estimates from a variety of sources. First, there is a body of knowledge about learning, motivation, and attitude change that can help a media director evaluate the effect of a message on the various communication steps. The media director's past experience, particularly with similar campaigns, represents a more or less accurate estimate of the "response function" of the target audience. Research data on the target audience, and/or the product category, and/or the advertised brand, and information on the effectiveness of past campaigns for the brand, may be very useful if all the communication steps have been included in the test.

It must be emphasized that this exercise, however scarce the data available, is a necessary step in ensuring that the advertising objectives are guiding the media objectives.

Taking the Advertising Appropriation into Account

In general, the media director develops the media plan within the overall media appropriation. As explained in Chapter 11, the total advertising budget is based on the marketing and advertising objectives for the brand. Thus the role of the media director is to find the most effective media plan for this budget, i.e., one that meets these objectives.

The budget may affect the work of the media director in two ways. First, the size of the advertising appropriation may preclude the use of some media types or media vehicles. The most obvious example is television, which requires a very large budget, because of the costs involved. For example, during the 1982-83 season, the cost of one 30-second prime time commercial on the CBC network was $8,500. Second, if the budget allows for volume buying or for frequency or continuity buying of certain vehicles, the media planner may obtain significant discounts, thus allowing for more time and/or space to be bought. Similar reasoning may be used when lower rates can be negotiated, for example, when buying network television.

Writing Precise and Operational Media Objectives

The development of media strategies should start with well-defined and operational media objectives that take account of target audiences, key markets, creative execution, communication tasks, and the advertising appropriation.

For example, the media objectives derived from the advertising objectives in Chapter 11 may be as follows:

Advertising objectives: To increase the awareness of Brand X milk-based drink among teenagers and young adults aged 18-24 from the present 10 per cent unaided recall of Brand X to a desired 50 per cent within one year, by associating it with sports events, and presenting it as the drink of winners.

Media objectives: To maximize message frequency among teenagers and young adults aged 18-24 in metropolitan Toronto, Montreal, Vancouver, Ottawa-Hull, and Winnipeg by selecting media types and vehicles compatible with creative execution and media appropriation and reaching at least 50 per cent of the audience.

With such objectives, the media director still has leeway in developing an efficient media plan. In so doing, the media director works closely with the creative director and the account executive. But before developing a complete media strategy, the media director must collect a staggering amount of information, a great deal of which is available through direct computer access.

Planning the Media Strategy

In the process of developing a media plan, the media director must deal with several types of media and media vehicles. In order to make the appropriate selection of media types and vehicles, some general concepts are used. These include reach, frequency, gross rating points, impact, intensity and continuity.

Reach/Frequency Levels and Gross Rating Points

The concepts of reach and frequency apply to one or a combination of media vehicles, or to a media type.

Reach (R) is usually expressed as a percentage of the target audience exposed *once* to one or several vehicles. It is a measure of *unduplicated* audience, and thus represents the percentage of different units of the target audience exposed to the vehicle(s). For example, in Figure 14.4, the target audience is composed of 500 000 units (e.g., individuals, families, or firms). Medium or Vehicle A has a total audience of 300 000 units but only 200 000 belong to the target audience. Thus the reach of A is 40 per cent (200 000 ÷ 500 000). Similarly, B has a total audience of 200 000 units, but only half are members of the target audience. Thus, the reach of B is 20 per cent.

If there is no duplication of the target audience members by A and B, i.e., the 200 000 units of A are different from the 100 000 of B, then the reach of A and B is 60 per cent (300 000 ÷ 500 000).

On the other hand, if 75 000 units of the target audience are exposed to *both* A and B, then the number of units reached by A and B is 225 000 (300 000 less 75 000). Thus, the reach of A *and* B is 45 per cent.

From this example, it is evident that information on duplications between pairs of vehicles is important for estimating the reach of any pair of individual vehicles. If the information is not available, it may be assumed

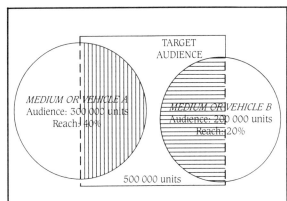

(a) The reach of two media or vehicles without duplication is 60 per cent— the sum of the reaches of A and B. The frequency of A and B is 1.

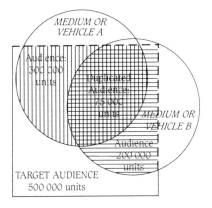

(b) The reach of two media or vehicles with duplication is based on the unduplicated audience of A and /or B—45 per cent. The frequency of A and B is 1.3.

FIGURE 14.4   Illustration of the Reach and Frequency Concepts

that duplication is random. For example, if A reaches 40 per cent of the target audience, 60 per cent are not reached by A. Since B reaches 20 per cent of the target audience, the possibility that those who are not reached by A are reached by B is 12 per cent (20 per cent of 60 per cent). In this case the reach of A and B is 52 per cent (40 per cent plus 12 per cent).

This method may be generalized to more than two vehicles. For example, if we have three vehicles with the following individual reaches:

A   50%
B   40%
C   30%

the net reach of A, B, *and* C is calculated as follows:

$$\text{net reach} = 50 + .50\,(40 + .60\,(30)) = 79\%$$

When information is available on duplication between pairs of vehicles, there are several methods available to calculate the net reach: the Agostini method[3] (see question no. 3 at the end of this chapter), the Metheringham method,[4] and the beta-binomial method.[5] Although it is beyond the scope of this book to explain these methods, readers should be aware that the issue is important, and that some of these methods may be incorporated into computer programs available to media planners.

Frequency is the number of times a member of the audience is reached by one or several vehicles. This concept is closely associated with the reach concept (Figure 14.4). If there is no duplication between A and B, and all 200 000 units of A and all 100 000 units of B are reached once, then the frequency of A and B is one.

If there is duplication between A and B, with 75 000 units exposed to both, then we have the frequency distribution indicated in Figure 14.5. Because of the duplication, 300 000 impressions were received by 225 000 units. Thus, each unit was reached an average of 1.3 times.

Although the average frequency is useful to know as an overall measure for the media or vehicles selected, it is equally important to use the *frequency distribution*. This is because one may expect an individual who has been exposed eight times to an advertisement to be at a higher level in the communication hierarchy than one who has been exposed only once. Thus the frequency distribution may be used in two ways. The numerical example in Table 14.3 will be used for illustrative purposes.

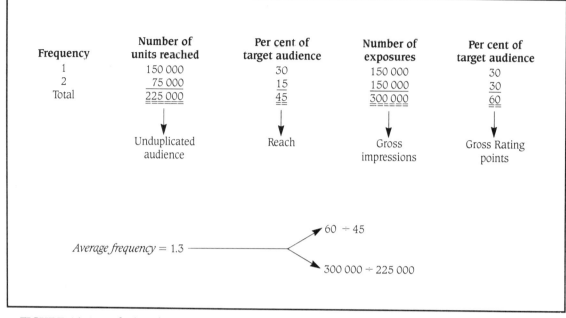

FIGURE 14.5   Relationship among Reach Frequency, GRP, Net and Gross Impressions

First, one may establish a *minimum* level of frequency necessary to move the average member of the target audience to accomplish the communication task stated in the advertising objectives. The minimum number of exposures within a four-week period may be set at four to move the prospects from awareness to knowledge. Thus a weight of zero may be assigned to prospects with less than four exposures and a weight of one to those with a frequency of

TABLE 14.3   Frequency Distribution and Effective Reach

Frequency	Per cent of audience	Cumulative reach(%)	Frequency weighting schemes		
			equal weights	minimum frequency	response function
1	20	85	100	0	50
2	15	65	100	0	65
3	12	50	100	0	85
4	8	38	100	100	100
5	7	30	100	100	105
6	5	23	100	100	110
7	4	18	100	100	115
8	4	14	100	100	120
9	3	10	100	100	125
10+	7	7	100	100	135
	85				
Effective reach			85%	38%	73%
Average frequency			4.0	6.7	4.9
Effective GRPs			340	255	358

four or more. This gives an effective reach of 38 per cent and an average frequency of 6.7, to be compared with a reach of 85 per cent and a frequency of four for the whole distribution.

If the previous method is considered too severe, one may weight the frequency levels according to their utility to the media director. Prospects with a frequency of one, two, or three may have moved toward the advertising goal and may be won over in the next campaign. Prospects with a frequency level of five and higher may have moved beyond the advertising goal, and thus may contribute to the marketing goal. Thus, the level of four exposures is indexed at 100, and frequency levels of less than four at less than 100, and those of five and more at more than 100. Using the example in Table 14.3, one finds an effective reach of 73 per cent and an average frequency of 4.9, again to be compared with 85 per cent and four for an equal weighting scheme. This general weighting is called *response function weighting*.[6]

The *gross rating points* concept has been developed to take into account the fact that some people may be exposed to the same vehicle more than once or exposed to more than one vehicle. Developed initially for television, the concept has found acceptance in other media. Gross rating points may be derived in three different ways:

From gross impressions. Gross impressions are the sum of all audiences of the selected media vehicles, including duplications. For example, in Figure 14.4, the gross impressions for A and B are 300 000 (200 000 plus 100 000). Viewed differently in Figure 14.5, the gross impressions of A and B are 300 000, i.e., 150 000 for the people exposed once to A or B, plus 150 000 for the people exposed to both A and B. Gross rating points may be defined as gross impressions as a percentage of the target audience—here 60 per cent (300 000 ÷ 500 000).

From ratings and coverages. The *rating* is expressed as the per cent of TV or radio households that are tuned, on the average, to

one time period (e.g., one quarter-hour) of a particular program. A similar concept in print media is called *coverage*, i.e., the per cent of members of a target audience who read an average issue of the publication. *Gross rating points* may be defined as the sum of individual ratings and coverages of the selected media vehicles. For example, in Figure 14.4, the gross rating points are 60 per cent (40 per cent plus 20 per cent).

From reach and frequency. Since the concepts of rating and coverage are special cases of the reach concept in broadcast and print media, it may be said that gross rating points are the sum of the individual reach of each vehicle. Since the reach of a set of vehicles is the percentage of unduplicated audience, gross rating points may be defined as the product of reach and average frequency (Figure 14.5).

Thus, one has the following relationship for a given set of vehicles:

$$GRP = reach \times frequency$$

The GRP Concept and Media Planning
The GRP concept is extremely useful in media planning, since it represents an operational measure of the campaign objectives. It can be used in many different markets, since it takes into account different competitive situations, rate structures, and fragmentation situations. Because of these properties, GRPs may be used for planning by allocating them to different markets according to a desired weight schedule and then calculating the desired number of announcements and insertions. This method is extremely useful for television and print media but difficult to use for radio, because of the complex interplay of reach and frequency, and the various rotation plans available. For radio, the accepted method is to first state the desired R/F levels, and then calculate the GRPs in each market and compare them in order to check for imbalances in market weighting.

Assume that an advertiser is faced with five markets of equal importance but with

TABLE 14.4 The Use of GRPs in Planning Television or Print Media

Market	GRPs/market	Coverage/issue or rating/spot (%)	Number of spots/ insertions required
A	100	10	10
B	100	20	5
C	100	25	4
D	100	33	3
E	100	50	2

varying situations. Each market is to receive 100 GRPs (Table 14.4). In market A, the average vehicle (spot or issue) has a reach (rating or coverage) of 10 per cent, because there is heavy competition among the various media in market A. By contrast, in market E, the corresponding reach is 50 per cent, because there is little competition among its media. In market A, the media planner will need ten spots or insertions in order to obtain 100 GRPs, while in market E, the media planner will need only two.

All spots or issues in each market may not have the same individual reach figures, but the principle of allocation is the same. The allocation of 100 GRPs may actually be made among four vehicles according to various patterns, as in Table 14.5, which illustrates how to calculate the reach of a set of vehicles. Table 14.4 does not provide the reach of the ten spots in market A or the two spots in market B, although they may be

estimated with the assumption of random duplication, or with actual measures of duplication in calculating reach and frequency levels in each market. Analysis of the examples in Table 14.5 leads to two observations:

1. Reach for a set of vehicles is higher than the highest reach of individual vehicles. Thus, if high reach is sought out by the media director, it is better to select vehicles with high individual reach.
2. Frequency increases as the number of vehicles increases, and the range of individual reaches decreases, assuming that there is a fair amount of duplication among vehicles. Thus, if high frequency is sought, it is better to select many vehicles with a low reach.

Allocation Strategies Table 14.6 illustrates the various allocation strategies which may be used

TABLE 14.5 Hypothetical Examples of R/F Levels for Various Vehicle Selections with 100 GRPs

Markets	Reach of each vehicle (%)				R/F levels for the selected vehicles	
	V1	V2	V3	V4	Reach (%)	Frequency
1	25	25	25	25	68.4	1.46
2	40	20	20	20	69.3	1.44
3	40	30	30		70.6	1.42
4	50	30	20		72.0	1.39
5	60	20	20		74.4	1.34
6	60	40			76.0	1.32
7	80	20			84.0	1.19
8	100				100.0	1.00

TABLE 14.6   Hypothetical Example of the Effects of Three Media Strategies

Target markets	Size	Heavy users	Proportional allocation strategy		Profile-matching strategy		High-assay strategy	
			GRPs %	Heavy users[1] (000s)	GRPs %	Heavy users[1] (000s)	GRPs %	Heavy users[1] (000s)
Halifax	300	100	30	3	17	1.7	0	0
Montreal	1000	900	100	90	156	140.4	130	117
Toronto	1500	1000	150	150	173	173.0	250	250
Calgary	500	100	50	5	17	1.7	0	0
Vancouver	500	100	50	5	17	1.7	0	0
Total	*3800*	*2200*	*380*	*253*	*380*	*311.5*	*380*	*367*

[1]Number of effective gross impressions (on heavy users).

by the media director, who is faced with five markets of different sizes and concentrations of heavy users of the product category. Three different strategies may be used to allocate the 380 GRPs to the five markets:

1. The *proportional allocation strategy* allocates the total GRPs according to the relative sizes of the markets. This is done in column 4 of Table 14.6. If the primary targets are the heavy users in each market, then the number of effective gross impressions may be calculated, as shown in column 5. This strategy leads to the delivery of 253 000 gross impressions to heavy users.

2. The *profile-matching strategy* allocates the total GRPs according to the relative sizes of the primary target audiences. This is done in column 6 of Table 14.6, and the resulting number of effective gross impressions is shown in column 7. This strategy leads to the delivery of 318 500 gross impressions to the heavy users. It is clearly superior to the relative allocation strategy, since it focuses directly on the primary target audience. The first strategy would use general media and waste a large amount of gross impressions on audiences outside of the primary target audiences, and this would not contribute to the advertising objectives. In contrast, the profile-matching strategy, which is the most commonly used, relics on information about demographic, eco-nomic, and psychographic profiles of both the users of the product category and the various media. Its name refers to the matching of these two profiles.

3. The *high-assay* strategy[7] allocates the total GRPs first to the market with the "richest" collection of heavy users, in the same way the gold miner starts mining a vein with the highest assay of ore. This is done in columns 8 and 9 of Table 14.6. Here it is assumed that all 380 GRPs cannot be allocated to Toronto, and that 250 GRPs is the maximum. This leaves 130 GRPs to be allocated to the next best market—Montreal. Thus, this strategy leads to the delivery of 367 000 gross impressions to heavy users. The high-assay strategy is clearly superior to the previous two strategies. It requires the availability of very specialized media vehicles allowing the media director to precisely target heavy users in order to minimize wasted circulation.

Continuity and Intensity of the Campaign

The concept of *continuity* is related to the overall *pattern* of advertising exposures over the time horizon of the campaign. As defined, it only affects the distribution of advertising weights over time. Changes in campaign continuity do not greatly affect the media budget, assuming that everything else stays constant. For example, Figure 14.6 has two different patterns of distributing 2400 GRPs. The first one is a steady campaign using 200 GRPs per month for 12 months. The advantage of a steady campaign is that the product is advertised regularly and the effects are accumulated over time, minimizing forgetting between exposures.[8] The second pattern shown in Figure 14.6 is a concentrated pattern, also called a *flight* when concentrated in one medium, in which the whole campaign runs from March to June. The rationale of a concentrated pattern of exposures is to try to bring a large number of consumers through several steps in the hierarchy of communication effects until the advertising objectives have been reached.

There are, of course, a variety of distribution patterns of the total effort, over the time horizon, and across media types or vehicles. These are described in detail in the scheduling section, but from the media strategy viewpoint a decision must be made on the type of continuity most likely to contribute to the advertising objectives.

Contrary to the continuity concept, which implies different options for allocating the same total effort, the level of intensity of the campaign can have a great impact on the advertising budget. *Intensity* may be defined as the average monthly GRPs over the time horizon. Figure 14.7 illustrates this point. Campaign A has an average intensity of 200 GRPs per month, while campaign B with the same pattern of continuity has an average intensity of 100 GRPs per month. Thus the media budget for A is likely to be much larger than that for B. If one starts with a given media budget, the implication is that increased intensity can only be accomplished by lowering the cost per GRP. For example, whole regions or provinces may be excluded, size may be reduced, some media options cancelled, spot may be substituted to network time, and fringe to prime time. Again, a strategic decision must be made on the

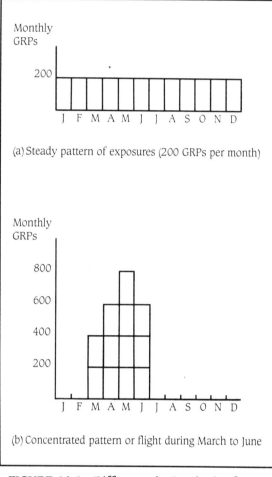

(a) Steady pattern of exposures (200 GRPs per month)

(b) Concentrated pattern or flight during March to June

FIGURE 14.6   Difference in Continuity for Two Campaigns with 1200 GRPs

desirability of increased intensity versus size, options, media types, and media vehicles.

Impact of the Campaign

Another important strategic decision relates to the desired impact of the campaign. *Impact* refers to all the physical characteristics of the advertisement that may increase its effectiveness given a basic creative execution. Examples of these characteristics, often referred to as *media options*, are:

• size of the messages in terms of the number of lines in a newspaper, the number

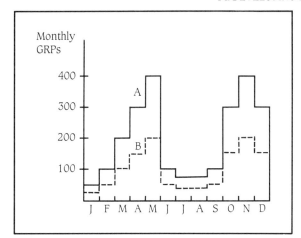

FIGURE 14.7 Difference in Intensity Levels for Two Campaigns with the Same Pattern of Continuity

or fractions of pages in a magazine, or the number of seconds in a radio or a television program;

- the shape of the advertisement, as in free-form;
- the number of colours in a print advertisement;
- a preferred position in the vehicle;
- some degree of exclusivity or dominance in the vehicle, as in multiple-page advertisements or sponsorship of a radio or television program.

All decisions relate to an advertiser's desire, as expressed in the campaign objectives, to establish the brand name in a leadership position in the market by impressing both consumers and distributors. The impact of the advertisement may then improve the image of the brand and give it a favourable market position.

Increasing the impact of the campaign leads to an increase in the cost per GRP and a decrease in the average intensity of the campaign in the context of a fixed media budget. A decrease in intensity will in turn lead to lower reach and/or frequency levels.

In the same way as there is a trade-off between reach and frequency for a given GRP level, there is a trade-off between average

intensity and impact of the campaign. For example, given a fixed media budget, doubling the size of a print advertisement leads to a large decrease in reach and/or frequency of the campaign, since more dollars are spent for each insertion.

Selection of Media Types

Based on the media objectives and the decisions on the previously developed dimensions, media types are selected. This selection process is based on media characteristics, competitive analysis, and campaign requirements.

Media Characteristics
Each medium has strengths and weaknesses (Table 14.7), which were outlined in chapters 5 and 6. Each medium has a given profile of its audience, in particular in terms of light use of the medium.[9] Thus, comparison of various media types according to these characteristics and their suitability for the product category and/or brand to be advertised may lead to a rejection or combination of some of these media types. For example, radio may be rejected for a new disposable razor, if demonstration and package identification are important, and newspaper may be rejected for a food product if good colour reproduction is important. Media may be combined to increase reach or according to the media imperative concept. Thus television and magazines, or television and radio are often used together. In particular, radio may be used as a low-cost extension of a television commercial by using the mind's ability to relive a commercial from hearing the audio component of that commercial, once it has been registered in long-term memory. This is called image transference.

Competitive Analysis
Since most advertisers are competing with other advertisers for consumers' attention, it is important to analyze what competitors' media decisions are. This analysis may affect an

TABLE 14.7   Main Strengths and Weaknesses of Major Media Types

Media Types	Strengths	Weaknesses
Newspaper	high reach & broad coverage flexible (time, geographic, creative) affordable to small business	colour reproduction audience selectivity national coverage difficult/expensive
Periodicals	highly selective & pass along high-quality reproduction long life & prestige	flexibility (lead time, low penetration) cost of production low frequency
Radio	high frequency flexible (coverage, time) affordable to small business	fragmentation & clutter short life of message limited availability in major markets
Television	complete communication mass coverage flexible (geographic, creative)	high absolute costs (time, production) fragmentation short life of message
Outdoor	coverage & flexibility impact of message long life of message	short message no selectivity long closing dates
Transit	coverage & flexibility high readership low cost per thousand	no selectivity long closing dates high production costs
Direct Mail	high selectivity & control flexible (creative, coverage)	high relative cost no editorial support

advertiser's media selection process at two levels.

MEDIA TYPES USED BY COMPETITORS. The types of media used by most competitors in the same product category *may* be an indication of their effectiveness. This point should be thoroughly investigated since, if true, it may require that an advertiser should use the same types of media. The rationale may be in terms of traditional media usage or in terms of information processing needs.

First, the medium may be heavily used by the selected target audience for the brand and thus may be the best one for carrying the advertisement. This does not, however, guarantee exposure to an advertisement, especially if it has to compete with similar ones.

Second, a medium may not be heavily used by the target audience but the probability of exposure to the advertisement by the target audience may be high because of consumers' *overt* information search at the time of purchase. For example, a couple looking for a new car may look at several consumer magazines because this medium has traditionally been used by car manufacturers. Similarly, since retailers often use newspapers for advertisements, these may be consulted by consumers looking for specials in food, hardware, and appliances. Thus, the advertiser may be able to capitalize on this learned overt behaviour in order to improve

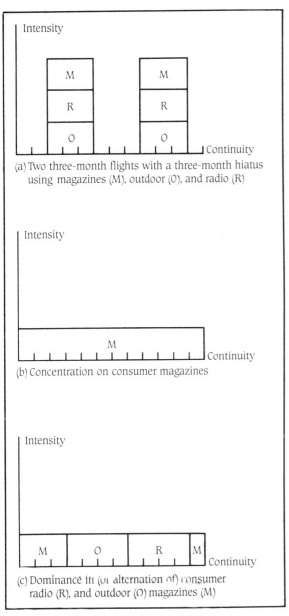

(a) Two three-month flights with a three-month hiatus using magazines (M), outdoor (O), and radio (R)

(b) Concentration on consumer magazines

(c) Dominance in (or alternation of) consumer radio (R), and outdoor (O) magazines (M)

FIGURE 14.8   Comparison of Flighting, Media Concentration, and Media-Mix Dominance Strategies

exposure to an advertisement. Of course, the message still must compete with similar messages, and many factors may determine its effectiveness, such as marketing-mix dimensions, creative execution, and clutter.

COMPETITIVE CAMPAIGN INTENSITIES.   The extent of advertising in a given medium by competitors may not be matched by small-budget advertisers, who cannot afford the level of intensity of large advertisers. Thus, many small-budget advertisers try to achieve high intensity within a *limited period* or in a *limited media mix*.

With the first strategy, media planners may advertise heavily during *flights* in order to achieve a high initial impact and break the barrier of heavy competitive advertising. This situation is illustrated in Figure 14.6, in which a steady pattern may not be able to break through the clutter, while a four-month flight may make a lasting impact with memorable creative. On the other hand, forgetting between flights may be a serious problem, and flighting may carry additional expense since some discounts (e.g., for continuity) may be lost. Thus the length and frequency of flights should be selected carefully (Figure 14.8).

With the second strategy, the media planner may select to advertise in one medium only during the time horizon or to use a few flights, one for each medium. *Media concentration strategy* is used when a large proportion of the target audience may be reached with one medium (Figure 14.8). In this case, it makes sense to use the entire media appropriation in that medium and to try for increased frequency and/or impact to move these prospects up the communication ladder. In addition, continuity of advertising may bring some media discounts and lower the unit cost of exposure. But if one medium is insufficient to reach a large proportion of the target audience, the media planner may decide to divide the media budget among two or three media and use the flighting technique for each one (Figure 14.8). If two or three flights cover the same period, the first strategy applies (Figure 14.8a). If these flights are used sequentially to cover a large portion of the campaign's time horizon, this is called *media-mix dominance strategy* (or media alternation strategy). This strategy shares some of the problems of the flighting strategy in terms of forgetting and media discounts.

Campaign Requirements

The objectives of the campaign as translated into media terms influence the selection of media types. Budget constraints may influence the choice of media types at several levels:

• the size of the budget may preclude the use of such media as television, even if one of the previous strategies is used.
• the allocation of the budget among media types must rely on some form of inter-media cost comparison. Because costs and audiences are not standardized across media types, this is a difficult task to accomplish. The most commonly used measure of media efficiency is the cost per thousand impressions introduced in Chapter 5, which is

$$CPM = \frac{\text{unit cost of a message}}{\text{audience size (in 000s)}}$$

The media objectives require different levels of reach and/or frequency. A *reach dominant strategy* requires the use of a variety of media types selected according to their individual reach of the target audience and the corresponding CPM. Consideration can also be given to frequency levels when several media mixes are equally attractive. A *frequency dominant strategy* requires that a few media be used in order to reach the same prospects many times. The selection may be based on minimum reach levels and the corresponding CPM.

The nature of the communication task as well as the creative execution may lead to a preference for some media types, based on an assessment of the communication environment and the principles developed in chapters 7-9.

To conclude, it is essential that a detailed rationale be given in the media plan both for the *selected* and the *rejected* media. It is important to state why certain types were selected, and how the media budget was allocated among these media. It is equally important to state why the other media were not selected.

Selection of the Media Vehicles

The next step after the selection of the media types to be used in the campaign is the selection of actual media vehicle(s) within each type. For example, if the consumer magazine medium was selected, which consumer magazine(s) should be used? Similarly, if television was selected, which television program(s) should carry the commercial?

The selection of media vehicles is based on the campaign requirements, the characteristics of each vehicle, and cost comparisons among vehicles.

Campaign Requirements and Vehicle Characteristics

The selection of media vehicles is influenced by seven factors:

1. The media director must look at the *creative execution* of the message and its requirements in terms of media options. Some vehicles may thus be eliminated because some options are not available or cannot be negotiated satisfactorily. Examples of such options are flexform, spectacolour, and split run. In addition to these special services, some vehicles may have restrictions that are listed in *CARD* under the heading "mechanical requirements." These restrictions may affect the decision to select a vehicle.

2. The media director must consider a vehicle's ability to reach the target audience(s) specified in the media objectives. *Demographic* and *psychographic* profiles of the vehicle must be compared with the target audience to determine the vehicle's ability to achieve the objectives. Also, the audience's *geographic* distribution must be compared with the key markets specified in the media objectives, in order to assess the vehicle's ability to deliver audiences in the key markets. Some vehicles are more selective than others in reaching specific groups defined by demographic, psychographic, or geographic variables, and thus may be more efficient on a relative cost basis (as will be seen later in this chapter).[10] Thus, this factor is related to the campaign's reach targets, as defined in the media objectives, with respect to the definition of the target audience(s) and the selection of key markets.

3. The media director must consider several factors related to the communication task. The vehicle's *editorial environment* is evaluated in terms of the message and the target audiences. The degree of interest of the target audience with respect to the editorial may promote proper communication of the advertiser's message through exposure and other steps in the communication hierarchy. The degree of interest in the editorial may be obtained by looking at the trend in circulation figures of the vehicle. Increased circulation indicates that interest in the vehicle is high, and vice-versa. Another factor that may hamper the communication process is the amount of *clutter*, the number of advertisements competing for attention. Thus, the media planner may prefer a particular vehicle because it offers a better opportunity for a message to be noticed. If a vehicle must be used for other reasons, it may be necessary to use preferred positions in the vehicle. The effect of clutter can be lessened if a campaign has been highly successful in the past, and the advertisement is recognized by the audience. Finally, the *time* of exposure to the message may be quite important for some products, because the target audience may be in the right frame of mind for buying the product category. Food advertisements usually appear before the weekly shopping trip, advertisements for movies and/or restaurants toward the end of the week, or commercials for snack foods during early to late evening television programs.

4. Media planners must compare the *discount structures* offered by different vehicles. This factor considerably complicates the selection task, since a vehicle that has a high relative cost without any discount may become very

attractive with one or several discounts (e.g., volume, continuity). The discount structure is thus heavily influenced by decisions on the levels of frequency, intensity, and continuity. When one or several of these factors are emphasized, it is relatively easy to take advantage of discounts. When reach is emphasized, this task is more difficult, since it is often better to use several vehicles.

5. The media director must verify the *availability* of certain vehicles. For example, a certain magazine may not be distributed in a key market, or a particular program may be completely booked by the time media planning is done. Since many popular vehicles, particularly in television, radio, and outdoor, are booked well in advance, it is important to begin the vehicle selection process as soon as possible. Sometimes a large agency may book blocks of time in advance to insure that these time periods are available to their clients. Of course, this is a risky strategy if all time periods are not used by these clients, and it is often not recommended. An agency may, however, use this strategy to attract good clients by guaranteeing popular programs.

6. Media planners must take into account the use of each vehicle by *competitors*, in order to determine which vehicle(s) to use and to what extent. The considerations here are similar to those used to select media types. If one vehicle must be used because of the audience's characteristics, then consideration must be given to improving the message's chances to be noticed, e.g., a cover position or near some particular editorial matter. In this case, decisions on the advertisement's impact in a particular medium may influence the selection of the vehicle(s), and vice-versa.

7. The vehicle selection process is constrained by the *budget* allocated to each media type. Thus, some vehicles may be eliminated if the budget is insufficient for certain vehicles because their absolute cost is too high.

TABLE 14.8   Calculation of the Page Cost for Newspapers

Newspaper	Number of columns (1)	Depth (2)	Line rate (3)	Page cost (1)×(2)×(3)
Globe and Mail	9	308 lines	6.52 (Ont. ed.)	$18,073
Toronto Star	9	308 lines	6.71 (M-F)	$18,600
Toronto Sun	6	200 lines	2.89 (M-F)	$ 3,468

SOURCE: Adapted from *CARD* (May 1983)

Vehicle Cost Comparisons

The absolute cost of using a particular vehicle with or without any discount is available through the various rate cards discussed in chapters 5 and 6. The absolute cost is often not a valid measure for comparing vehicles within a given type of media, because different vehicles have different audience sizes, space sizes, and so on. Thus, various relative cost measures have been developed in order to compare various vehicles within a given medium.

Although the CPM measure is used for all media types, it cannot be used to compare vehicles in *different* media types, since there is no widely accepted definition of a unit across media types. For example, is a one page, four-colour bleed advertisement in a magazine the same unit as a 1000 line, black-and-white advertisement in a newspaper, or a 30-second prime time commercial? A similar question arises with respect to the definition of the audience for the message.

Within a particular medium, it is possible to minimize these problems by using the same definition for both units and audiences. Nevertheless, these measures suffer from the lack of standardization across vehicles. For example, a major problem in comparing newspapers is the lack of standardization of space sizes and circulation figures. A numerical example is provided in tables 14.8 and 14.9 for three Toronto newspapers with different numbers of columns and lines (depth), and using the circulation figures for the primary market only.

For *newspapers*, what unit of space should be used to compare them? Two measures have been widely used, the milline rate and page costs.

MILLINE RATE.   If the unit of space is 1000 lines, black and white, and the audience is the circulation figure (in 000s), then the CPM definition is identical to the *milline rate* introduced in Chapter 5. Calculation of the milline rates for the three Toronto newspapers is done in Table 14.9. Thus, although the *Star* has the highest line rate, its milline rate is much lower than that of the *Globe and Mail*. On the other hand, the *Globe and Mail* has a much larger circulation outside the primary market, and on a national basis its milline rate would be much lower than for its primary market. Circulation figures do not indicate the actual audience of the newspaper in terms of how many different people

TABLE 14.9   Calculation of the Milline Rate and the CPM for Newspapers

Newspaper	Circulation in thousands (1) (primary market)	Line rate (2)	Milline rate 1000×(2)÷(1)	Page cost (3)	CPM for one page (3)÷(1)
Globe and Mail	201.707	6.52 (Ont. ed.)	$32.32	$18,073	$89.60
Toronto Star	385.822	6.71 (M-F)	$17.39	$18,600	$48.21
Toronto Sun	228.297	2.89 (M-F)	$12.66	$ 3,468	$15.19

SOURCE: Adapted from *CARD* (March 1983)

read each copy (i.e., readers per copy), and the members of the target audience who read that newspaper. If the information is available, more meaningful measures of milline rates may be used. But a serious problem remains with this definition: would a 1000-line advertisement in the *Sun* be equivalent to 1000 lines in the *Star*? The answer is obviously no, since the same advertisement in the *Sun* would occupy more than 83 per cent of the page, while in the *Star* it would occupy 36 per cent of the page.

PAGE COSTS AND CPM. Many media buyers prefer using one newspaper page as the unit of space. The calculations for the page costs are provided in Table 14.8 and for the CPM in Table 14.9. For newspapers with the same dimensions, the two definitions lead to the same relative measures: $32.32 \div 17.39 = 89.60 \div 48.21$. The significant difference is between broadsheets and tabloids. The milline rate for the *Sun* is about 80 per cent of the rate for the *Star*, while in terms of CPMs (per page), the ratio is now 34 per cent. For the milline rate, a more meaningful measure of the CPM is derived by using the number of people in the target audience who read the newspaper, whether or not they have bought it, to divide the page cost.

Magazines and other periodicals cost comparisons. For magazines and other periodicals, the unit of space commonly used is one page, four colours. The audience figure may be either the circulation figure or the total readers, including both primary readers (members of the subscribing or purchasing household) and secondary readers. Alternatively, the total readership is obtained by multiplying the circulation figure by the number of readers per copy. Table 14.10 provides examples of CPM calculations for selected consumer magazines and for both male and female adults. A better measure of audience is derived from the previous analysis of members of the target audience and their geographic distribution.

A similar analysis may be made by changing the unit of space to one page black and white or by adding the premium cost for bleed to the cost of the one page, four-colour unit. It must be emphasized here that this comparison of CPM is only one factor in the selection process of the vehicle, which includes the other considerations mentioned previously.

Radio cost comparisons. For *radio*, the unit of time often used to compare vehicles is the cost of one minute of commercial time. Care should be taken in using the same classification in calculating and comparing CPMs for radio. Ideally the audience factor should be the number of listeners who belong to the target audience(s).

Media planners use another measure of efficiency based on the GRP system. The *cost per rating point* (CPRP) is useful for comparing vehicles or combinations of vehicles, that is, alternative radio scheduling units. It is calculated by dividing the cost of the scheduling unit by the GRPs delivered by that unit. For one vehicle, the CPRP is defined as:

$$CPRP = \text{cost per time unit} \div \text{rating}$$

For more than one vehicle, the CPRP is defined as:

$$CPRP = \text{cost per schedule} \div \text{total GRPs of schedule}$$

Since it is difficult to use the GRP concept for selecting radio vehicles, the accepted practice is to base the radio schedule and vehicle selection on reach and frequency targets. These alternative selections may then be compared in terms of GRPs and CPRP, and the decision is based on this information and other cost comparisons.

Television cost comparisons. For television, the unit of time most often used to compare vehicles is the cost of one 30-second block of commercial time. One must ensure that the same time classification for calculating CPMs is used. The audience factor may be calculated in terms of viewers or households tuned to a program. Again, the closer the definition of the audience factor is to that of the target audience(s), the more useful is the CPM measure.

The cost per rating point (CPRP) is often used in television to compare the cost of various

TABLE 14.10   Consumer Magazines: Costs & CPM Comparisons (PMB '83 Cost Analysis)

ENGLISH CANADA	COST PG. 4/C $	CIRC.	CPM $	MEN 18+ PRIMARY (000)	CPM $	TOTAL (000)	CPM $	WOMEN 18+ PRIMARY (000)	CPM $	TOTAL (000)	CPM $
PUBLICATION											
Alberta Report	2820	51237	55.03	53	53.20	156	18.07	39	72.30	115	24.52
Atlantic Insight	3180	43996	72.27	40	79.50	89	35.73	54	58.88	125	25.44
Broadcast Week	4325	213082	20.29	179	24.16	196	22.06	180	24.02	197	21.95
Calgary Magazine	2225	59803	37.20	57	39.03	53	41.98	42	52.97	33	67.42
Canadian Geographic	4795	105123	45.61	122	39.30	301	15.93	80	59.93	211	22.72
Canadian Living	8165	369480	22.09	147	55.54	334	24.44	457	17.86	1212	6.73
Chatelaine	19660	1087378	18.08	429	45.82	653	30.10	1279	15.37	2142	9.17
City Women	9750	301482	32.34	122	79.91	117	83.33	369	26.42	340	28.67
Decormag	2930	49590	59.07	25	117.20	103	28.44	52	56.34	222	13.19
Edmonton Magazine	2225	59872	37.16	61	36.47	41	54.26	44	50.56	26	85.57
Financial Post Magazine	8743	218199	40.06	240	36.42	362	24.15	128	68.30	177	49.39
Flare	6790	203924	33.29	38	178.68	109	62.29	232	29.26	549	12.36
Hamilton Magazine	2190	47779	45.83	32	68.43	29	75.51	30	73.00	27	81.11
Harrowsmith	5000	146092	34.22	123	40.65	221	22.62	128	39.06	202	24.75
Homemakers Magazine	19705	1335726	14.75	650	30.31	558	35.31	1324	14.88	1298	15.18
Legion Magazine	5400	512721	10.53	456	11.84	445	12.13	273	19.78	254	21.25
Leisure Ways	4465	375915	11.87	293	15.23	188	23.75	255	17.50	152	29.37
Maclean's	16060	632187	25.40	540	29.74	1155	13.90	508	31.61	1045	15.36
Marquee	7415	509750	14.54	N/A	N/A	280	26.48	N/A	N/A	268	27.66
Montreal Calendar	3310	80393	41.17	43	76.97	35	94.57	49	67.55	35	94.57
Quest	17980	712658	25.22	594	30.26	505	35.60	525	34.24	423	42.50
Reader's Digest	16695	1334650	12.50	998	16.72	1561	10.69	1327	12.58	1966	8.49
Saturday Night	5800	133232	43.53	111	52.25	175	33.14	99	58.56	136	42.64
Star Week	10155	835868	12.14	764	13.29	809	12.55	764	13.29	792	12.82
Time	7420	331384	22.39	317	23.40	1007	7.36	248	29.91	749	9.90
Toronto Life	4650	83265	55.84	66	70.45	166	28.01	74	62.83	156	29.80
TV Guide Magazine	11285	876634	12.87	722	15.63	1019	11.07	842	13.40	1219	9.25
TV Times	16995	1643562	10.34	1339	12.69	1325	12.82	1369	12.41	1368	12.42
TV Week Mag Van/Vic	2400	72778	32.97	71	33.80	112	21.42	56	42.85	83	28.91
United Church Observer	3510	301558	11.63	165	21.27	190	18.47	297	11.81	330	10.63
Vancouver Magazine	3110	99759	31.17	88	35.34	104	29.90	79	39.36	94	33.08
Western Living—Alberta	3280	93150	35.21	77	42.59	66	49.69	81	40.49	75	43.73
Western Living—B.C.	3720	102725	36.21	68	54.70	106	35.09	90	41.33	124	30.00
Westworld Magazine	5450	279375	19.50	208	26.20	198	27.52	208	26.20	202	26.98

SOURCE: *The Canadian Media Directors' Media Digest, 1983/84*

vehicles or combinations of vehicles. Since the GRP concept is widely used in television planning, the CPRP concept is the logical measure of efficiency. When the information is available, ratings and GRPs may be broken down into demographic or psychographic subgroups and/or weighted according to primary, secondary, and tertiary target audiences.

Out-of-home cost comparisons. For *outdoor* and *transit*, the unit of space used may be the daily showing according to a given GRP level. Thus the cost per unit may be calculated by converting the monthly cost on a daily basis. For outdoor or transit the CPM definition may be stated as:

CPM = daily cost ÷ daily circulation (in 000s)

As for other media, circulation figures may be weighted according to various subgroups in the target audiences.

Conclusions

Based on the budget allocated to a specific media type, media planners must consider both qualitative and quantitative factors when selecting vehicles. The environment for communicating the message must be favourable, through decisions on media options, editorial, level of clutter, timing of exposure, and competitive use of vehicles. The right audience must be selected at the lowest possible cost, and the selection is affected by market coverage, unit rates and discounts, availability, and vehicle cost comparisons weighted by the target audiences. Once the selection process is completed, the media planner must justify the choice of vehicles. Each vehicle must have a rationale.

Developing the Media Schedule and Budget

After the media vehicles are determined, the final step in developing the media plan is the *media schedule*. The media schedule is a calendar indicating how and when the selected vehicles are to carry the advertisement over the campaign's time horizon.

The scheduling strategies are based on the selected communication task and the media planner's knowledge about the various steps in the communication process:

- consumer motivations (Chapter 7) and the proper timing of response to the advertisement when the prospect is in the right frame of mind, e.g., a beer spot during the early fringe on television;

- consumer perceptions (Chapter 7), consumer attitudes (Chapter 8), and the proper placement and spacing of a series of advertisements to improve attention and learning (and minimize forgetting), and its effects on the attitudes of consumers. (See especially the last section of Chapter 8.);

- the dynamics of purchase behaviour (chap-

ters 9 and 10) and the influence of purchase cycles on the media scheduling strategy.

Media Scheduling Strategies

Although several schedules may be compatible with the media objectives and strategy for frequency and continuity, there are six types of scheduling strategies (Figure 14.9):[11]

1. Steady. This strategy consists in using a vehicle regularly in order to produce an even flow of exposures and increase the effect of the message (Figure 14.9a). The critical problem here is inter-exposure time. If it is too large, some forgetting may take place.[12] Reducing this interval of time may, however, only be done by increasing the size of the budget or reducing the size or length of the message. This type of scheduling strategy is usually applied to products that are well known and that have a constant probability of purchase across the campaign's time horizon.

2. Seasonal pulse. This strategy consists in timing the advertising to precede or coincide with the sales pattern. Thus, the media schedule will have heavy advertising just before or during the high-sales periods. The advantage of this strategy is high impact. It reaches prospects when they are gathering information and making decisions to buy a product (Figure 14.9b). Examples of products with seasonal pulse strategies are lawn mowers, toys, and moving companies. The problem with such a strategy is that considerable forgetting may take place during the off-season period, depending on the length of each period.[13]

3. Periodic pulse. This strategy consists in placing short pulses or flights at regular intervals during the time horizon (Figure 14.9c). These flights may not necessarily be related to seasonal patterns. This strategy is used when the effects of each flight can be sustained without too much forgetting and consumers need to be reminded regularly of the product. For example, such strategies may be used for

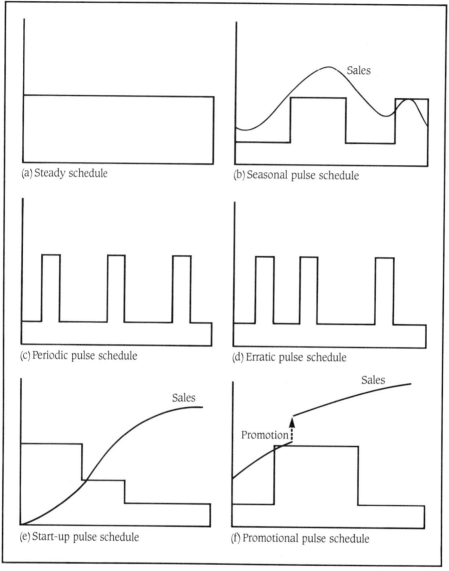

(a) Steady schedule

(b) Seasonal pulse schedule

Sales

(c) Periodic pulse schedule

(d) Erratic pulse schedule

(e) Start-up pulse schedule

Sales

(f) Promotional pulse schedule

Sales

Promotion

FIGURE 14.9   Six Basic Types of Scheduling Strategy

well-known brands like Coke or Pepsi, or for food products like cheeses and snack foods. When the creative execution uses approaches that tend to wear out rapidly, like humour, this strategy can restore the message impact by allowing some forgetting to take place.

4. Erratic pulse. This strategy is similar in principle to the periodic pulse strategy, except that the flights are not spaced regularly (Figure

14.9d). It may be used to take advantage of specific market conditions, or because the purchase cycles are irregular, or to modify purchase cycles. Products that may use such a strategy are desserts, aperitif wines, turkeys, and cranberry sauce. The difficulty with this strategy lies in determining the intervals between flights.

5. Start-up pulse. This strategy consists in advertising heavily when a new product is introduced in order to stimulate adoption and trial (Figure 14.9e). It is used for new consumer products and services as well as for new models of automobiles and other durable products.

6. Promotional pulse. This strategy calls for heavy advertising during a promotional campaign, such as sampling and couponing (Figure 14.9f). This type of pulsing is designed to increase the target market's response to the promotional tool by encouraging trial, repeat purchase, or multiple purchases.

Media Scheduling Models

Traditionally, the media selection problem has been solved with a sequential approach. The advertising budget is first split among the different types of media. For instance, an advertiser may decide to allocate 60 per cent of the advertising budget to print media and 40 per cent to broadcast media. Then, within each class of media, the budget is further split among media vehicles. Finally, the *media schedule* is worked out for each media vehicle. The media schedule also specifies the media options that have been selected. Nonetheless, even if it were possible to make optimal decisions at each different decision level (i.e., budget allocation among media types, media vehicles, media options), this procedure would not lead to an overall optimal media schedule. Optimizing each part of a system is not the same as optimizing the entire system. Thus a better approach is to derive an optimal media schedule immediately.[14]

Media Selection through Mathematical Programming

Because the media selection problem is an optimization problem (i.e., maximization of profits, sales or exposure value) under constraint (the advertising budget, the maximum and minimum number of insertions that should or could be made in each media vehicle), it is one of the first problems operations researchers tackled when they turned to marketing problems.

The application of linear programming was first proposed in 1961.[15] Unfortunately, when these techniques were first applied to media selection, the problem was grossly oversimplified. Most relationships are not linear. Moreover, the principle of diminishing marginal returns applies in many circumstances, and an optimal solution implies that the media vehicles and the media schedule should be determined simultaneously. Nowadays, several of these methods have been improved, and the problem is normally solved through mathematical programming rather than linear programming. Such methods determine the media schedule, which maximizes either the total number of media exposures of the schedules, or sales, or profits. Among such models, one of the most complete to date is MEDIAC.[16]

In principle, MEDIAC is an interactive computer system where a manager interacts with a model on the conversational mode. The purpose of this model is to determine the media schedule that maximizes a firm's profits for a given advertising budget. A marketing manager supplies basic data about the audience and the cost structures of each advertising media vehicle, and also judgemental estimates on the appropriateness of each advertising vehicle for the advertiser's purpose. The system yields output on the best media schedule. In addition, the model user can change basic estimates and assess the impact of the proposed schedule.[17]

High Assay Method

This method is used by the Young and Rubicam advertising agency.[18] It consists of making a purchase in the media vehicle that is the most profitable for a given period. The profitability of the media vehicle purchase is assessed in terms of a given criterion, for instance, the media insertions that yield the best results per dollar spent. Then, taking into account the effect of this first purchase on the duplicated audiences with all other available media vehicles, and on the costs of subsequent purchases in the media vehicle (because of quantity discounts), the second best purchase is made, and so on. This procedure is continued until a certain objective has been met for a given period of time.[19] Typically, this objective is a function of several variables, among them the number of potential customers and the product life-cycle stage of the brand.

Simulation Models

Other authors have solved the media selection problem through simulation. The effect of a

given media schedule is simulated on a fictitious population that is a small-scale representation of the actual target market segment. The most likely effect of a given advertising schedule on this simulated market segment is estimated and then inferred to the whole population of interest.[20] The basic structure of one media planning model is shown in Figure 14.10.[21]

After reviewing and evaluating most of the approaches used in the past 30 years in order to deal with the huge amount of data in media planning, Calantone and de Brentani concluded:

> . . . Media scheduling models still must undergo substantial refinements before they can be expected to reach the levels of accuracy and realism that is required by advertisers. Nevertheless, it is also clear from this chronological discussion, that in less than twenty years media models have moved from a state where they comprised a set of very simplistic arithmetic operations to one where they include highly sophisticated mathematical formulations. If future research continues to focus on "cleaning up" the details of the most feasible models, it is very possible that, to an increasing degree, the media scheduling function will be carried out by these models.

At the same time, it is important to remember that advertising involves people, competitors, products and a changing environment. Above all, it calls for creativity and innovativeness and it is highly unlikely that any mathematical model, no matter how elegant, can ever find effective solutions to the media selection problem, let alone the entire advertising. But if to an increasing degree, the analytical details can be handled by a computer that is endowed with a really good model, advertising executives can spend more time and energy on these creative aspects and hence altogether make much more effective advertising decisions.[22]

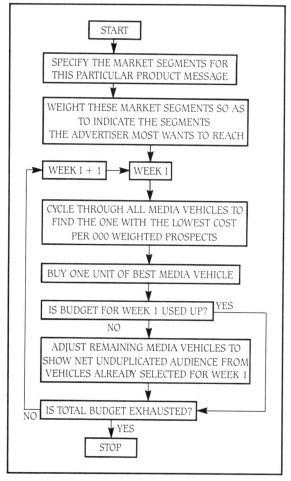

FIGURE 14.10   Gensch's Model of Media Planning

SOURCE: Dennis H. Gensch, *Advertising Planning: Mathematical Models in Advertising Media Planning* (Amsterdam: Elsevier Scientific, 1973), p. 48.

This view is consistent with the actual use of media models for the purpose of scheduling, which is quite low, according to a study by McDougall and Simpson, who surveyed media decision-makers in both companies and advertising agencies.[23]

Media Schedule and Budget

The media *schedule* must include a list of all the vehicles that were selected and regrouped according to the various media types; the amount of time or space to be bought in each vehicle, with the indication of the various media options selected; and the dates when the advertisements are to appear.

A useful document that accompanies the schedule and summarizes it is called a *blocking chart*. An example of a completed blocking chart is reproduced for the campaign in Part 5.

The final media *budget* indicates how much money is allocated to each vehicle and each key market. Often, a detailed expenditure statement by month or quarter is also provided.

Media Buying

Once the media schedule has been prepared, the actual execution of the media plan is the responsibility of media buyers. Since media buying is a complicated and time-consuming task, many agencies use different specialists for print, television, and radio. Thus, the media service group represented in Figure 3.5 has a television time buyer, a radio time buyer, and a print buyer. These specialists may be assisted by estimators in preparing, negotiating, and controlling the various buys.

Media buyers have an important role to play in three areas. They have to interpret the work of the media planner in making decisions on actual buys or in finding a suitable replacement if a particular vehicle is not available. Often, in the course of negotiation, it is too late for the buyer to consult the media planner when some problems arise.

They are skilled in negotiating with media representatives for better rates, favourable positions, and any other factors that will enhance the message's effectiveness within a given schedule. In doing so, they stretch the efficiency of the media budget.

They have to make tactical decisions during the campaign, when schedule changes are required by a competitor's move, a shift in the editorial environment of the vehicle, or anything else that can affect the media schedule.

The *process* of media buying follows five steps:

- gathering all the relevant information about the campaign and the media plan;
- requesting submissions from the media representatives of each vehicle;
- evaluating each submission and, if necessary, requesting more information or another submission;
- negotiating the media purchase and signing a contract;
- reporting the total schedule.

Once the media buying has been completed, the agency or advertiser must *control* or *verify* that the advertisement or commercial has been run. Most print media vehicles provide the agency with a tear sheet, which is a copy of the page in which the advertisement appeared. For broadcast media vehicles, the usual practice is an affidavit from the station or network that the commercial was aired. Otherwise, suitable replacements must be negotiated at no extra cost to the advertiser.

Summary

The development of a media plan is a difficult and complicated task. Since most advertising dollars go to purchasing media time or space, it must be done efficiently.

The development of the media plan starts with the advertising objectives, which are in turn reworked and stated as media objectives. These are developed in terms of target audiences, key markets, creative execution, and the selected task of the communication within various constraints.

The media strategy for achieving these objectives is designed around such basic planning dimensions as reach, frequency, continuity, intensity, and impact of the campaign, and some relative cost measures. The strategy involves selecting the media types and media vehicles consistent with the media objectives and the decisions on the previous dimensions.

The sequence an advertisement or commercial appears in the selected vehicle is called the media schedule. Six basic scheduling strategies may be used: steady, seasonal, periodic, erratic, start-up, and promotional pulses. Some mathematical models developed in the last thirty years can help media planners process the huge amount of information available and arrive at an optimal schedule. Nevertheless, they are still being refined, and are not in widespread use. Computers, however, are heavily used in media departments for many basic operations, and it is likely that in the future, some of these models will gain acceptance by media planners.

Once the media schedule has been prepared, the task of media buying and verification is undertaken.

Questions for Study

1. Find some examples of advertisements where the creative execution had a great influence on the choice of media types and/or vehicles. Explain your choice.

2. Explain the concepts of reach and frequency and their usefulness in the media planning process. When would high reach be more important than high frequency as a media strategy?
Give some examples of campaigns
(a) with high reach and low frequency
(b) with low reach and high frequency
(c) where both reach and frequency are important

3. The Agostini method for calculating net reach is based on the following formula:

$$NR = 100 \frac{A}{TA} \div (1 + \frac{KD}{A})$$

where NR = net reach of all vehicles
A = sum of the audiences of all vehicles
TA = target audience
D = sum of all pairwise duplications
K = Agostini's constant of 1.125

(a) Calculate the net reach for five magazines, with the following information:

Magazine	Net reach of each magazine	Duplication with			
		B	C	D	E
A	12%	13000	14000	15000	16000
B	16%	—	12000	13000	14000
C	20%		—	15000	16000
D	24%			—	14000
E	28%				—

The size of the target audience is 250 000.
(b) Calculate the net reach for the five magazines using the assumption of random duplications.

4. Discuss the advantages and disadvantages of the flighting strategy, the media concentration strategy, and the media-mix dominance strategy. Give a numerical example of each, assuming that you have a media budget of $300,000 for a chain of jewellery stores in your province.

5. How do the media decisions of competitors affect those of
(a) a chain of supermarkets
(b) a French restaurant owner
(c) a toy manufacturer?

6. Give some detailed examples of campaigns for each one of the six basic media scheduling strategies.

7. Select three consumer magazines and explain how you would use the main factors in vehicle selection described in Chapter 14.

8. Explain the CPM concept in the context of the main media types: television, radio, newspapers, magazines, out-of-home, direct mail. Compare all the major vehicles in your area using the CPM concept and using the most common unit of space in each medium: one page/four colours, 1000 lines/black and white, 30" prime time television, 60" prime time radio, 100 GRP.

9. What are the main advantages and disadvantages of using media models in planning the media plan? Why are so few of them used in practice?

10. Explain when and why weekly newspapers are considered for a media plan. In a market with more than one daily newspaper, how would you go about selecting the vehicle(s) to include in your media plan?

Problems

1. Considering the situation described in Problem 2 of Chapter 11, you are asked to develop a complete media plan for the Surelock Homes Company, paying particular attention to media objectives and strategy. If you have to make assumptions, please state them clearly.

2. Given the following information, put together the best possible TV buy and then explain your choice of programming.

	CFTO	CITY	CHCH	CBLT
Program	Academy	Laverne/MASH	Event TV	Early News
Cost	1025.00	945.00	1750.00	800.00
GRP	8	7	11	5
CPR	128.13	135.00	159.09	160.00
Audience	232,200	199,100	431,000	199,000
CPM	4.41	4.75	4.06	4.02
Program	Late News	Late Movies	Sat. Sports	Journal/Late News
Cost	525.00	405.00	100.00	700.00
GRP	3	3	2	4
CPR	175.00	135.00	50.00	175.00
Audience	140,000	71,800	74,000	145,600
CPM	3.74	5.64	1.35	4.81
Program	Burnet/News	Sun. Movies	Renovating Home	Disney
Cost	1025.00	405.00	100.00	800.00
GRP	8	3	1	7
CPR	128.13	135.00	100.00	114.29
Audience	449,800	94,700	7,800	268,600
CPM	2.28	4.28	12.82	2.98

Client: Paint company
Target: Homeowners 25 years and over
Market: Toronto
GRP Obj.: 30
Budget: $4,000.00

Present the result of your work in the form of a media plan.

Notes

1. Tony Jarvis, "Time to Play the Weighting Game," *Marketing*, 22 June 1981, pp. 52-53; see also L. Van Esch and R.A. Powell, "Preference for Choice and Its Applications to Marketing," *Marketing*, vol. 4, ed. James D. Forbes (Administrative Sciences Association of Canada, 1983), pp. 351-59.
2. *Canadian Media Directors' Council Media Digest, 1982/83*, pp. 48-59.
3. J.M. Agostini, "How to Estimate Unduplicated Audiences," *Journal of Advertising Research* (March 1961), pp. 11-14; see also H.J. Claycamp and C.W. McClelland, "Estimating Reach and the Value of K," *Journal of Advertising Research* (June 1968), pp. 44-51.
4. R.A. Metheringham, "Measuring the Net Cumulative Coverage of a Print Campaign," *Journal of Advertising Research* (December 1964), pp. 23-28.
5. Robert S. Headen, Jay E. Klompmaker, and Jesse E. Teel, Jr., "Predicting Audience Exposure to Spot TV Advertising Schedules," *Journal of Marketing Research* (February 1977), pp. 1-9.
6. Jarvis, p. 53.
7. William T. Moran, "Practical Media Decisions and the Computer," *Journal of Marketing* (July 1963), pp. 26-30.
8. Hubert A. Zielske, "The Remembering and Forgetting of Advertising," *Journal of Marketing* (January 1959), pp. 239-43.
9. Gary A. Mauser, "Segmenting Media Usage: A Case of Methodological Triangulation," *1976 Proceedings* (Administrative Sciences Association of Canada, 1976), Section 5, pp. 221-27.
10. For example, see S.A. Ahmed and J.R. Kennedy, "Factor Analytic Search for Television Programs," *1976 Proceedings* (Administrative Sciences Association of Canada, 1976), Section 5, pp. 1-9; also S.A. Ahmed, "Prime-time TV Viewing Correlates," *1975 Proceedings* (Administrative Sciences Association of Canada, 1975), Section 4, pp. 1-7.
11. Kenneth A. Longman, *Advertising* (New York: Harcourt Brace Jovanovich, 1971), pp. 371-72.
12. Zielske.
13. Ibid pp. 293-43.
14. E. Brian Bimm and Allan D. Millman, "A Model of Planning TV in Canada," *Journal of Advertising Research* (August 1978), pp. 43-48.
15. See, for instance, Frank M. Bass and Ronald T. Londsdale, "An Exploration of Linear Programming Method in Media Selection," *Journal of Marketing Research* (May 1966), pp. 179-88.
16. John D.C. Little and Leonard M. Lodish, "A Media Planning Calculus," *Operations Research* (January-February 1969), pp. 1-35.
17. Ibid.
18. William T. Moran, "Practical Media Decisions and the Computer," *Journal of Marketing* (July 1963), pp. 26-30.
19. Note that this method does not lead to media schedule optimization because the algorithm may find a local but not the global optimum.
20. *Simulatics Media-Mix: Technical Description* (New York: The Simulatics Corporation, October 1962).
21. Dennis Gensch, *Advertising Planning: Mathematical Models in Advertising Media Planning* (Amsterdam: Elsevier Publishing, 1973).
22. Roger J. Calantone and U. de Brentani-Todorovic, "The Maturation of the Science of Media Selection," *Journal of the Academy of Marketing Science* (Fall 1981), pp. 490-524.
23. Gordon McDougall and Gerald Simpson, "Media Planning in Advertising: the Practitioner's Viewpoint," *Marketing 77*, ed. G.H.G. McDougall and R. Drolet (Administrative Sciences Association of Canada, 1977), pp. 91-98.

Finding the Relevant Information for Analyzing, Planning, and Controlling the Advertising Program

Although judgement plays an important part in the analysis and solution of many advertising problems, advertisers also have at their disposal analytical tools that range from simple procedures to sophisticated decision systems. Even though advertisers must use their judgement to make decisions this does not prevent them from using scientific methods or from finding objective solutions. Advertisers should and must bring original and creative thinking to rigorous scientific analysis.

Thus, advertising communication, like any element of the marketing mix, is elaborated from precise knowledge of consumers' needs, motivations, attitudes, opinions, behaviour, and purchasing habits. Because of the high costs involved, advertising communications must not be inefficient and a burden to the company. It costs only a fraction of a cent to reach a potential customer with an advertising message, but a large number of potential customers must be reached several times in order to move them up the attitudinal hierarchy. In addition, since media audiences include thousands and sometimes millions of individuals, the cost of effectively delivering an advertising message is relatively high.

Because of the potential competitive advantage that an efficient advertising campaign can give a firm, no elements of the advertising communications program can be neglected. This is why they have been the object of formal research by advertisers and advertising agencies. Research projects can be either systematic and recurrent, such as those which are periodically undertaken on the audiences of media vehicles, or occasional, when they are carried out every time a new advertising campaign is planned. This chapter first describes the means available to advertisers and agency personnel to obtain and analyse advertising data. Then the various types of advertising research for different types of advertising decisions are detailed.

Methods for Finding Information Relevant to an Advertising Program

The nature of research in advertising includes obtaining information relevant to the decision-making process and presenting this information in a manner that relates directly to the problem. The information seeker may be the advertising manager, the account executive, the copywriter, the creative director, or the media director. Of course, advertising research is a special application of marketing research and uses many of the standard marketing research techniques and methods. Nevertheless, some types of advertising research, for example, copy testing and research on media habits, are carried out by organizations separate from the traditional market research organizations.

Sources of Advertising Data

Advertising data may be collected on a regular basis in order to control the effectiveness of various campaigns or flights, or data may be collected through *ad hoc* research in order to assist in a precise advertising decision.

Advertising data come from different sources. They come from *secondary sources* when they have already been collected for purposes other than those of the advertising manager. Secondary data sources may be internal or external to a firm. Advertising data come from *primary sources* when they have not been collected before and are collected for a particular need of a marketing unit.

Internal Secondary Sources

Companies collect information on their customers in the normal course of business transactions. The internal accounting system, the customer relations department, and the company sales force may all provide valuable information on customers' characteristics, their geographic and demographic distribution, and their reactions to packaging and advertising.

External Secondary Sources

Several media organizations collect data regularly on the viewing or reading habits of consumers, as well as demographic and psychographic information. Examples of external secondary sources are the Print Measurement Bureau (PMB) studies and the Newspaper Marketing Bureau studies.

Radio and television audience panels operate under the principle that audience members are required to record their television viewing and/or their radio listening behaviour in a diary. Through inference, the audience size of certain programs and stations can be estimated. In Canada, A.C. Nielsen and the Bureau of Broadcast Measurement provide such services.

Secondary sources of information are among the least costly for a company to obtain. Consequently, before trying to obtain information from primary sources, researchers should make sure that the information is not available elsewhere.

Primary Sources of Advertising Data

Primary source data are collected for a specific purpose. In other words, it is information that has not already been collected or is not readily available. Thus researchers must design a specific project for collecting the desired data. This type of advertising research is generally expensive. Some companies organize "home-panel" or ongoing tracking studies, and market research studies are also carried out at intervals. However, the trend is for primary data research to be carried out on an *ad hoc* basis, according to the specific requirements of the advertising problem to be solved at a given time.

Primary data may be collected through observation, experimentation, and surveys. The latter technique has reached such a high stage of development and has been so widely used that it has almost become synonymous with advertising research.

OBSERVATION. This is the most elementary data collection procedure. It consists solely of observing consumer behaviour. Obviously, what can be observed is only overt behaviour. No indication is given about the thoughts, opinions, and deeper attitudes of the observed subjects. However, even when behavioural responses are the only types of information an advertiser is looking for, two important sources of error can affect the results of observation studies. These are the biases of the observer and the biases of the subjects when they know they are being observed. This is why some researchers use recording devices, such as cameras and tape recorders and conceal the recording devices. Data collected through observational procedures are essentially descriptive and may need to be supplemented with other types of data.

EXPERIMENTATION. When a researcher attempts to infer a causal relationship between two sets of events, the most appropriate research method is experimentation.[1] For instance, if a researcher wants to find out which advertising budget level has the greatest effect on sales, a causal relationship is implied between advertising and sales. The experiment should show the nature of the relationship, its direction, shape, and amplitude. In practice, sales are likely to vary because of factors other than the variable under investigation. Therefore the principle of experimentation consists of studying how one phenomenon varies (the dependent variable) as another variable (the causal or independent variable) is submitted to some variation while all other factors are kept at a constant, or while the variations of other factors are at least controlled. This principle is simple enough but difficult to apply in practice. Various experimental designs or methods are used to partially solve these problems, but each experimental design has possibilities for error.[2]

Experimentation has had only limited application to advertising problems. There are serious problems in setting up experimental designs where environmental variables can be manipulated by the researcher,[3] since advertising decisions are made in a complex environment. Moreover, the costs of experimentation in advertising are substantial. Besides the direct research costs, the opportunity costs are often very high. For instance, to assess the effects of various advertising themes implies that less effective themes are purposely tried out in some markets. This results in opportunity losses, which are substantial and lasting. For all these reasons then, experimentation and observation may be useful techniques for obtaining certain types of information but are generally less than ideal methods for collecting primary data.

Surveys

Because each advertising campaign is different, surveys are the most widely used technique for collecting information. The principle of a survey is to interview individuals or other units by means of a questionnaire. The respondents are often consumers. In most cases, advertisers want to ask consumers about their past or present behaviour, their buying intentions or intended buying behaviour, as well as their perceptions, preferences, attitudes, and opinions. Because interviewing *all* the consumers in a market segment would not be practical and is too costly and time consuming, only a sample of the whole population is selected and interviewed. If the sample of respondents has been drawn according to statistical procedures, the probability that the sample has the same characteristics as the whole population can be calculated. Sampling errors can be computed and the confidence intervals of the computed statistics can also be estimated by simple formulas derived from statistical theory. Thus, by accepting calculated risks or errors, a researcher need not interview the whole population.

Each step in a market survey involves the risk of committing various errors. Some types of error can, to a certain extent, be controlled. Other types can be avoided only through the expertise of the researcher. In any survey, there is room for judgement, and generally a researcher's experience cannot be superseded by a set of "recipes." This is why two surveys with the same general objectives may yield different results.

The steps a researcher follows in conducting a market survey are shown in Figure 15.1.

Once a marketing or advertising problem has been identified and has been properly translated into a research problem, the objectives of the research study should be stated clearly. Then, to design the survey, decisions must be made in three fundamental areas: the questionnaire, the sample, and the survey method. In designing the questionnaire, the marketing researcher is concerned with the question: *Which* information should the respondents be asked? The sampling procedure involves the question: To *whom* should the information be asked? The survey method is directed to the question: *How* should this information be obtained? Of course, the decisions concerning the survey design cannot be made independently. All the questions must be answered with the other questions in mind, in order to arrive at a coherent survey design.

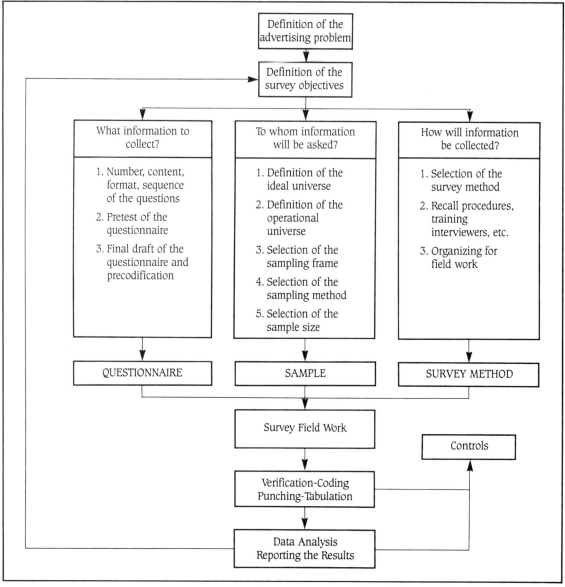

FIGURE 15.1   Steps to Be Completed in a Typical Advertising Survey

THE QUESTIONNAIRE.   A questionnaire is characterized by the number of questions, the content and wording of each question, as well as by the sequence of questions a respondent is asked. There are no widely accepted rules concerning the *number of questions* that should be asked in a survey. However, respondents cope with a larger number of questions when a personal, rather than telephone, interview is used. The length of an interview varies according to the questions asked and the subject matter of the survey. If the subject matter is interesting to the respondents, they will be motivated to give their opinions more readily. When designing a questionnaire, market researchers attempt to collect only the information needed to meet the objectives of the survey with the smallest possible number of questions.

Researchers should ask only those quesions that can be answered with an acceptable level of accuracy.[4] This principle may seem obvious, but it is difficult to apply it well. Sometimes a question can elicit inaccurate answers or even none at all when a respondent does not know the answer or does not want to furnish the information. An example of the first type of question is: "Where did you see the advertisement for product X?" Questions leading to voluntarily inaccurate answers or no answer at all are those relating to personal and sensitive issues, such as "How old are you?" "What is your annual income", or questions with high social status connotations, such as "How much do you spend each year for beauty care products?"

There are "tricks" for by-passing these problems. Questions may be worded in such a way as to elicit more truthful answers, and answers can be cross-checked with similar questions to detect inaccuracies.

The *wording* of the questions depends on the survey medium. Some questions involve sensitive issues and may require the use of various projective techniques to elicit accurate and truthful answers. The principle of projective techniques is to induce a respondent to reveal personal deep feelings by making a third person answer instead. This third person bears the responsibility for the opinion expressed, not the respondent. For instance, a respondent might say that most of his or her neighbours are afraid to fly, but would deny such a feeling because of fearing to appear cowardly or give a negative image to the interviewer.

Questions with no pre-coded answers are called *open* questions. A respondent is given complete freedom to answer. For instance, "What do you think of Brand X?" is an open question. When a researcher can predict all the possible answers to a question, a multiple choice or a dichotomous question is generally used. An example of a multiple choice question is: "Which brand of razor blades are you using presently? None? Brand A? Brand B? Brand C? Any other brand?" If only two choices are possible, the question is said to be dichotomous. Other questions may best be answered with rating scales when more subtle answers are needed. For instance, the following scales may be part of a survey asking, "How would you describe Brand X?":

Unpleasant	1 2 3 4 5 6 7	Pleasant
Weak	1 2 3 4 5 6 7	Strong
Cheap	1 2 3 4 5 6 7	Expensive

Rating scales (also called semantic differential scales) have been used to measure consumer attitudes and opinions.

The wording of a question is also affected by the survey medium. For example, most semantic differential scales would not be suitable for telephone interviews. A mail survey should not ask too many open questions, because respondents should be able to answer the questions without help and in a relatively short period of time.

The *sequence* of the questions is another concern in questionnaire design. Questions should follow a logical order so that each question is easily understood by respondents. The first few questions should be easy to answer, almost trivial, just to induce a respondent to start answering. Once the process is started, it is psychologically more difficult for a respondent to end the interview. The more personal and time-consuming items, such as open questions, should be placed near the end of the questionnaire, to avoid discouraging respondents.

No matter how experienced a researcher is, the first draft of a questionnaire will never be perfect. Some questions may not be properly understood by certain individuals. Some words may be ambiguous and sometimes are not given the same meaning by everyone; a question may be offensive to some respondents; sometimes respondents unexpectedly cannot answer certain questions. For these reasons, researchers should pre-test the questionnaire before using it on a large scale for the survey. During the pre-test phase, the questionnaire is completed by a few respondents who have the same general characteristics as the individuals who will be interviewed in the actual survey. After the pre-test results are analyzed, the questionnaire is modified and again pre-tested. The process continues until the questionnaire no longer requires substantial modification. In the final form, the questionnaire is usually pre-coded. This step makes the codification task much easier once the questionnaires are completed.

SAMPLING. To obtain an adequate sample, the ideal universe to be studied should be properly and carefully defined, as well as the operational universe that will be used. Then the sampling frame, the sampling method, and the sample sizes are determined.[5]

The *ideal universe* is composed of all the individuals or sampling units that possess the information the advertising researcher wants to collect. Theoretically, this universe is all the individuals—and only those individuals—who should be interviewed if it were decided to collect the information through a complete census of the population. These individuals are likely to be difficult to locate and sometimes cannot be properly identified. Even when they can be identified, the costs of reaching some of them may be prohibitive. Thus advertising researchers must settle for an *operational universe*, which is a more practical definition of the individuals who can be interviewed. For instance, a razor blade advertiser may define its ideal universe as all the male adults living in the Calgary metropolitan area (CMA). As it may be too difficult to identify all these individuals, the advertiser may define its operational universe as all the male adults living in the metropolitan area whose households are listed in the telephone book. By clearly defining ideal and operational universes, advertising

researchers can assess the compromises to be made and the kinds of error that can result from the operational definition of the universe. In the preceding case, one individual with several telephone numbers could be included several times in the operational universe. Similarly, individuals who are not listed in the directory will be systematically excluded from the survey. Excluded individuals might correspond to an under-representation of lower income families who may not have a telephone and higher income professionals who have unlisted numbers.

If the compromises on the definition of an operational universe are acceptable to the advertising researcher, the next step is to obtain a *sampling frame*, which is a list of the units to be interviewed. This could be a list of the households, individuals, or any other unit. In the preceding example, the sampling frame would be constituted by the names under which each household is listed in the telephone directory of the CMA, excluding all firms, organizations, and public administrations. By identifying all the male adults in each household, an advertising manager can sample an operational universe. Here again, the quality of the sampling frame must be assessed. Is it up to date? When was it most recently updated? In the example above, some telephone subscribers could have left the Calgary area and the names of recently arrived people would not yet be listed. As before, researchers should assess the risks of systematic errors before deciding on a specific sampling frame.

At the same time as the decision to use a given sampling frame is made, the researcher must also decide which *sampling method* to follow. A sampling method is generally selected according to three criteria: the objectives of the survey, the quality and costs of the available sampling frames, and the costs of interviewing the selected sample units. If the research is exploratory, there is no need to draw a simple random and representative sample of the population. However, if the survey objective is to estimate a population parameter, for example, the mean number of units of a certain brand consumed by households, the statistical sampling method that most readily gives estimates on sampling errors and confidence intervals for the estimated parameters is a simple *random sample*. The researcher draws the desired number of units in the sample, following certain random procedures. In practice, a sampling frame may not be readily available, or may not lend itself to such a procedure, and the costs of interviewing distant and scattered individuals may be prohibitive. In such cases, other more practical sampling methods can be used.

The sampling plan must also specify the sample *size*. A sample size is chosen on the basis of the results to be achieved, the sampling method to be selected, the expected rate of non-response, and the size of the research budget. When a researcher needs greater precision in the survey results, the confidence intervals in which the true parameter values should fall are small, and consequently the sample size should be large. As the selected sampling method departs from a purely random procedure, the sample size should increase for a given precision level. In selecting the sample size, researchers should predict the non-response rate. Then the sample size should be adjusted so that the number of completed questionnaires yields the desired level of precision in the results. Finally, the budget for the research project often acts as a more or less binding constraint, limiting the sample size used.

SURVEY METHODS. At an early stage of the survey design, an advertising researcher must decide which method will be used to collect data—a personal, telephone, or mail survey. The selection of the survey method depends on the type of information to be collected and the costs involved weighed against the expected benefits of the study.

From a technical point of view, the *personal interview* is always the best method of collecting information from respondents. When pro-

jective techniques must be used, it is the only practical method. The personal interview is also the most adequate data collection procedure when lengthy explanations must be given or when it is important to ascertain whether respondents correctly understood a question or what has been asked of them. Response rates are generally higher for personal interviews than for any other type of survey, but a major drawback is the cost. An interviewer must contact each respondent and spend time in completing the questionnaire. Besides the travelling time involved in this type of procedure, there is also waiting time and time spent calling back individuals who were not at home during the first call. When respondents are geographically scattered, personal interviews can seldom be combined with simple random samples.

Telephone interviews share many advantages with personal interviews because they allow for personal contact between interviewers and respondents. They are also less expensive than personal interviews. Respondents who were not at home during the first call can be called back several times at minimal additional costs. However, respondents are sometimes reluctant to give personal data or even talk over the telephone to a so-called interviewer that they do not know and see in person. It is also much easier for a respondent to end an interview by hanging up the telephone than by closing the door on an interviewer. Telephone interviews are best suited for short questionnaires that do not deal with personal or sensitive issues.[6]

Mail surveys are generally selected as a survey method when cost constraints are very important. Mail surveys typically have high non-response rates, especially when respondents are consumers chosen from the general public. A mail survey is used when it is essential that a simple random sample be used and when the research budget does not allow for personal or telephone interviews. Like telephone surveys, questionnaires used for mail surveys should be short enough to keep the non-response rate as low as possible and at the same time obtain data as accurate and complete as possible.[7] Various methods can be used to lower the non-response rate. But before these devices are used, the costs should be compared with the expected benefits of additional and better quality data. The response rate to a mail survey can be increased by giving some premium to the respondents, by sending reminders to the individuals who have not yet answered, by including addressed and pre-paid envelopes, or by sending a covering letter that carefully explains the survey's objectives and stresses the importance of the selected respondents' co-operation if the objectives are to be met.

The response rate in personal or telephone interviews can be substantially increased when interviewers are courteous, when they take the time to explain the main objectives of a survey, and when they can gain respondents' co-operation.

Recently, new research technologies have been developed using improvements of such methods as WATS telephone centres interviewing or cathode-ray tube (CRT) interviewing machines in shopping centres, or in the home through a two-way cable system. Since we are experiencing an information revolution, one may expect the introduction of other forms of survey methods.

TRAINING INTERVIEWERS. Interviewing is not an amateur's job. On the contrary, professional interviewers undergo extensive training and development. In addition to establishing contact and gaining respondents' confidence, interviewers must be absolutely neutral when they ask questions in order to get unbiased answers. If an interviewer is not professionally trained, a word, a gesture, a smile, or a nod may induce a respondent to give answers that the respondent thinks the interviewer expects. Thus before field work is begun, interviewers should receive training on the survey's general objectives and instructions on the way the interviews should be carried out. Interviewers must know who should be interviewed, when they should be

interviewed, how many calls to make before giving up on a respondent, how to behave when a respondent asks certain questions, and what to do with completed questionnaires.

Once the field work starts, interviewers must be given a precise work schedule and the researcher must have a replacement team ready, in case some interviewers do not show up on certain days. Also, controls must be set up to minimize the errors caused by interviewers who disregard the rules.[8]

STEPS OF THE SURVEY FIELD WORK. After the questionnaire is in its final form, the sample drawn, and all the practical details of the field work arranged, the actual field work can start. Once the questionnaires are filled out, they should be checked individually to detect recording errors or to identify questionnaires that were carelessly answered and that would seriously distort the results if they were not corrected or discarded in some cases. After this verification step is completed, each answer must be given a prespecified code that allows the survey data to be computerized. Then, data are punched on computer cards and the computerized data are checked to ensure they are free from punching or mechanographical errors. Then the survey data are ready for analysis.

Analyzing the Data

The raw data relevant to advertising decisions does not always help advertisers make better decisions, since survey results usually come in the form of computer printouts and statistical tables. Large numbers of figures do not reveal what they mean right away. Generally, meaningful results can be achieved only through careful data processing. When analyzing data, researchers may have several goals that are not necessarily incompatible. One goal may be to reduce large amounts of data to only a few numbers or into a graph that can reveal the meaning of the data at a glance. This most elementary objective can be achieved by *descriptive statistics*. At a higher level of sophistication, researchers may need statistical techniques to make inferences about the population as a whole from observations made on a sample. *Inferential statistics* allow researchers to achieve such objectives. When the data alone, even properly summarized and applicable to the whole population, cannot be readily translated into a specific decision, an additional tool is needed to bridge the gap between marketing data and marketing decisions. Such tools are *advertising decision models.*

Statistical Techniques

In the last few years, multivariate statistical techniques have been increasingly used to analyze marketing data.[9] These techniques are suitable for analyzing phenomena subjected to a multitude of variables. These techniques are multi-dimensional scaling,[10] multiple regression analysis, canonical correlation, factor analysis,[11] correspondence analysis,[12] and clustering techniques. Even a superficial description of these techniques requires a basic knowledge of statistics and is well beyond the scope of this book. However, a non-technical example of such a technique that can be illustrated easily is the data reduction technique. Data reduction is a recurrent task in analyzing marketing data. For instance, a researcher who wanted to know what the consumption of soft drinks in British Columbia is could list all the households in the province, and note in front of each name the yearly soft drink consumption of the household. The huge report that would result would not be very informative for an advertiser. It makes more sense to compute the mean consumption over all the households, and to say that the average household consumption of soft drinks in British Columbia is ten litres a month. By so doing, the researcher summarizes the information collected by computing the mean. Other statistics would yield summary measures of different aspects of the data.

For instance, assume that a researcher wants to know how various brands of beer are perceived by a market segment in Quebec.[13]

One may start by finding all the attributes that one thinks and/or knows consumers use to differentiate among brands of beer. Assume that the researcher has found 50 such attributes, and that you want to know how five popular brands (Labatt 50, O'Keefe, Brador, Molson Export, Carlsberg) are perceived. In this case, you select a sample of 1000 beer drinkers in the market segment with a relevant statistical sampling procedure. The researcher asks each respondent in the sample to rate each brand on the 50 attributes on a seven-point scale. Once this task is completed, the researcher has 250 000 numbers to deal with: 5 brands $\times$ 50 attributes $\times$ 1000 respondents. If the analysis were stopped at this stage, the advertiser would have learned very little about consumer perceptions of various brands of beer.

Several assumptions can be made. One, chances are great that several attributes among the 50 are very closely related. Second, certain attributes are likely very important for consumers and others are less so. Using multiple discriminant analysis, which is a multivariate statistical technique, the collected data can be represented by the graph in Figure 15.2.

Figure 15.2 shows clearly that consumers essentially use *two* sets of attributes to differentiate among brands. The horizontal axis is a high price-high quality, lower price-lower quality dimension. The vertical axis is a light-heavy dimension. The attributes consumers use to differentiate among the brands are shown on the diagram and are as close to an axis as they are correlated with this dimension. The mean perceptions for each brand by the consumers are also positioned on the graph. Thus, Carlsberg is perceived by this segment of Quebec consumers as a high-quality beer, low in alcohol, with a snobbish, feminine, occasional drinker connotation. In contrast, Molson Export is perceived as a rather heavy, strong, darker, and more popular beer. This example shows how this analysis has extracted meaning from 250 000 pieces of data, and has yielded simple and easily interpreted statistical inferences.

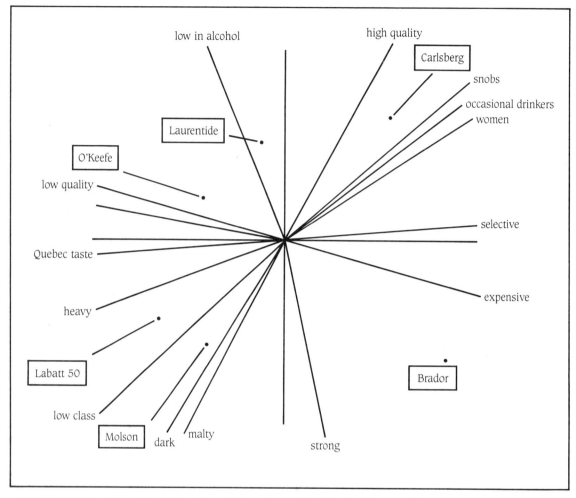

FIGURE 15.2 Perceptual Mapping of Beer Brands in the Quebec Market

Advertising Decision Models[14]

A model is a simplified replication of the real world. An advertising model presents an advertising phenomenon from which the less important or irrelevant variables have been deleted and which retains the most relevant aspects of the real world for the purpose of the model user.

Two types of marketing models have proved very helpful in solving advertising problems: optimization and simulation models. With an *optimization model*, an advertiser provides basic data, which are the model's parameters, and the system yields the values of the decision variables that maximize a certain criterion variable,

for instance, what advertising budget would maximize profits.[15] The ADBUDG system falls into this category. *Simulation models*, as their name implies, simulate the real world. Thus, a marketing manager can manipulate this simulated environment to test the effects various decisions would have on such other variables as sales, profits, or market share. For instance, how would sales be affected by a 10 per cent increase in the advertising budget? The PERCEPTOR system falls into the simulation category.

Whatever the type, the trend over the last few years has been to build simple advertising models that are easy to communicate with, can be accessed by a computer, and are easy to understand.

The ADBUDG decision model is designed to help advertisers select the proper level of advertising expenditure. An advertiser makes a series of judgements about expected sales territory responses to different levels of advertising expenditure. These judgemental estimates are processed through a computer-based model that assesses the underlying profit response functions to advertising and estimates the corresponding optimal advertising budget for which profits are maximized.[16]

The same problem can be solved with a simulation model. In this case, the population of Canada is simulated by means of a sample of fictitious individuals.

With PERCEPTOR, expected market performance for a new product can be predicted. Information collected during the pre-test stage of new product development becomes the input data. The system uses product perceptual maps similar to the one shown in Figure 15.2 and predicts the long-run market share that the new product idea could capture.[17]

These are only a few examples of a new generation of advertising models that have been designed for decision-makers. These models should be used only after a study of the costs of development, implementation, the data requirements, the managerial time needed, and the expectations of benefits. With the greater use of time-sharing and mini-computers, these management tools will likely become available to more medium and small size firms.

Information Relevant to Analyzing and Planning for an Advertising Program

Marketing and advertising research activities grew from the need of the full-service advertising agencies early in the twentieth century for information needed to solve marketing and advertising problems. In 1929, Warren Brown, president of National Publicity, created the first Canadian marketing research department. In 1932, Ethel Fulford and Associates was founded in Toronto as the first independent research firm. In 1943, it became known as Canadian Facts Ltd. Four other independent firms were created by 1945: Elliott-Hayes, which became Elliott Research, the Canadian Institute of Public Opinion, which became the Gallup Poll of Canada, A.C. Nielsen of Canada, and International Surveys.[18]

To help advance the discipline, practice, and professional standards of advertising research, several organizations were created. The Canadian Advertising Research Foundation is a non-profit organization supported by advertisers, advertising agencies, and media. Its objectives are to develop new research methods and techniques, to analyze and evaluate existing methods and techniques, and to establish research standards. One useful booklet it distributes is "Media Research Standards and Full Consultation Procedures and Requirements."[19] Several advertising agencies have adopted nine principles of copy testing called PACT (positioning advertising copy testing).[20] Two other professional organizations assist members in improving the quality of research: the Professional Market Research Society and the Canadian Association of Market Research Organizations.

Depending on the stage of the planning process, there are four main types of research on which advertising decisions rely. Following the order in which an advertiser plans a campaign (which is the reverse of the order in which the communication takes place), they are: market and consumer research, media research, advertising copy research, and advertising effectiveness research (Figure 15.3).

Information for the Marketing and Advertising Plans

Qualitative Methods
These methods are motivation research, focus groups, in-depth interviews, attitude scaling,

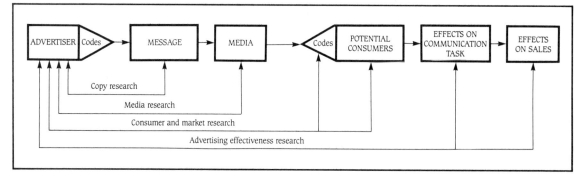

FIGURE 15.3   Types of Advertising Research Undertaken by or for Advertisers

and/or projective techniques. Studies are usually carried out on small samples of consumers drawn from the target market. The objective of *motivation research* is to unveil motives that are often hidden or buried in the consumer's subconscious mind and that may explain purchasing behaviour patterns.[21] However, the diagnosis phase that should follow analysis of the psychological material gathered from in-depth interviews with consumers required more expertise than that possessed by amateurs. The relatively small sample sizes, sometimes as few as 50 people, cast doubt on the reliability of such research studies' findings. Motivation research is not the end of the research process but only a first step toward a formulation of hypotheses about consumer behaviour. These hypotheses must be tested through large-scale studies that use more conventional techniques.

Focus groups are made up of about ten to 15 individuals who are similar to the product target group. The group leader elicits responses from the group members in a non-directive manner.[22] Focus groups may be used for new concept testing, brand name selection, brand image, and package testing.

In-depth interviews are conducted with one representative individual at a time by a trained interviewer who probes the individual's reactions to a new concept, a prototype new product, a brand name, or a new package. As with motivation research, this method is quite expensive and only provides directions for further analysis and research.

Attitude scaling and *projective techniques* can be administered much more quickly and cheaply. Both may be done through a self-administered questionnaire. With attitude scaling, an introduction describes the concept, mentions the brand name, or asks respondents to look at the prototype product or package accompanying the questionnaire. The respondent is then asked both closed and open-ended questions. With projective techniques, indirect questioning provides more accurate answers. Individuals are asked to assume the identity of another person, like a neighbour, a character in a drawing (as in the Thematic Apperception Test, or a balloon test), or in a verbal statement. Respondents are then asked to record their reactions to the material provided, or to make a statement in answer to a question based on, or included in, the material.[23]

Quantitative Methods
This type of study uses market surveys with structured questionnaires and multiple choice questions that can be easily pre-coded. The surveys are taken on larger samples drawn from the entire population of potential or actual customers in order to draw conclusions about the whole population. These types of research studies provide input into the development of the marketing plan and help define the target market more precisely.

Quantitative research may be conducted either by the advertiser's research department or by an outside supplier, which may be the research group of an advertising agency or a private research house. Another alternative is for an advertiser to participate in an *omnibus* study, in which advertisers share the cost of research. Several research companies regularly conduct omnibus studies.

Information on the nature and extent of *competitive advertising* is very useful in the planning stages. For example, an outside supplier may specialize in providing estimates of national advertising expenditures for companies or brands. This is done by monitoring advertising in daily newspapers, weekend supplements, consumer magazines, farm publications, radio and television stations, and by estimating the expenditures for space and time by brand and company. Results are published monthly and sent to subscribers. Additional information an advertiser requires may also be obtained on a custom basis. Advertisers can purchase scripts of radio commercials and photographic story boards from research houses that specialize in monitoring and recording competitive creative activity in the broadcast media.

Information for the Media Plan

The object of research is to analyze the media exposure habits of consumers in various market segments. Advertisers use the results to select the most appropriate media vehicles for reaching selected market segments. The management of many media vehicles often sponsor such studies in order to identify their audiences' socio-economic characteristics or purchasing habits. The objective is to furnish media representatives with arguments to help them sell advertising space or time to potential advertisers.

Print Media Research

The object of print media research is to measure audiences and readership, to determine the profile of print media readers, and to correlate the profiles with consumption patterns. Research may be done by media, co-operative associations, or individual vehicles.

DAILY NEWSPAPERS. Data on daily newspapers are collected on a regular basis by the Audit Bureau of Circulation (ABC), the Canadian Daily Newspaper Publishers Association (CDNPA), and the Newspaper Marketing Bureau.

The Audit Bureau of Circulations is an association of over 4000 advertisers, advertising agencies, and publishers in seven countries, including Canada. Its objectives are: (1) to issue standardized statements of circulation and other data reported by members; (2) to verify these figures; and (3) to disseminate them, without opinion. To be eligible for ABC membership, a publication must have at least 70 per cent *paid* circulation. ABC publishes a number of reports, including the *Canadian Newspaper Factbook*, which includes circulation figures by individual newspapers, countries, and major markets for dailies (and by province for weeklies).

The Canadian Daily Newspaper Publishers Association represents 83 daily newspapers and about 86 per cent of the total circulation of Canadian dailies. It provides extensive research support to the industry, including the *cost estimator*, which is a computer system for on-line costing of newspapers' advertising schedules.

The Newspaper Marketing Bureau represents 44 daily newspapers in order to promote newspapers as viable national advertising vehicles. The Newspaper Audience Databank (NADbank) is an integrated source of newspaper audience information available through on-line computer access. It contains readership data for 29 newspapers in 15 major Canadian markets, with a wide range of demographic information for both weekday and weekend newspapers.

Individual newspapers may, in co-operation with other dailies, conduct readership studies in order to develop demographic or psychographic profiles. For example, a study was conducted in 1980 in the Montreal census metropolitan area to determine a demographic profile of the readers of four newspapers. A total of 2562 interviews were completed, and

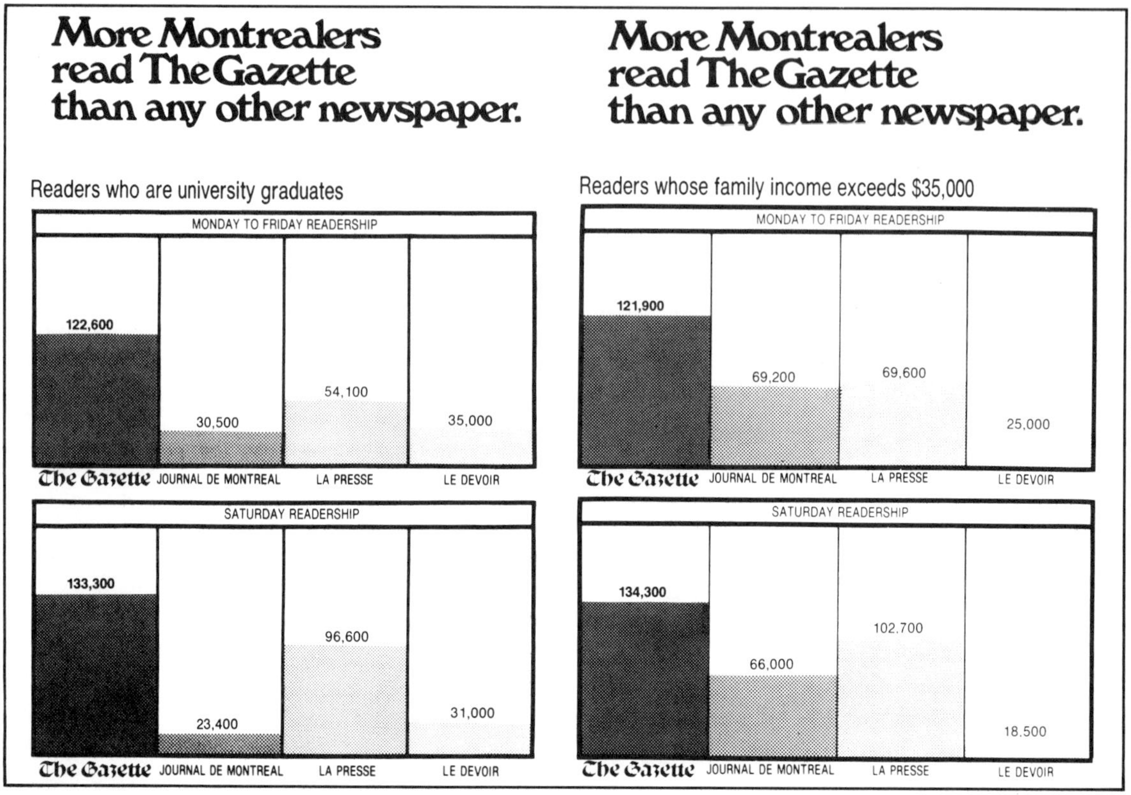
More Montrealers read The Gazette than any other newspaper.
Readers who are university graduates
MONDAY TO FRIDAY READERSHIP
122,600
30,500
54,100
35,000
The Gazette
JOURNAL DE MONTREAL
LA PRESSE
LE DEVOIR
SATURDAY READERSHIP
133,300
23,400
96,600
31,000
The Gazette
JOURNAL DE MONTREAL
LA PRESSE
LE DEVOIR
More Montrealers read The Gazette than any other newspaper.
Readers whose family income exceeds $35,000
MONDAY TO FRIDAY READERSHIP
121,900
69,200
69,600
25,000
The Gazette
JOURNAL DE MONTREAL
LA PRESSE
LE DEVOIR
SATURDAY READERSHIP
134,300
66,000
102.700
18.500
The Gazette
JOURNAL DE MONTREAL
LA PRESSE
LE DEVOIR

FIGURE 15.4 An example of media audience research undertaken by the vehicles themselves, here newspapers in Montreal. These two diagrams are part of a package used by the Montreal *Gazette* to promote the newspaper.
Courtesy The Montreal *Gazette*

some of the results are shown in Figure 15.4 for two subgroups.

MAGAZINES. Data on magazines are collected on a regular basis by the Audit Bureau of Circulation (ABC), the Canadian Circulations Audit Board (CCAB), Magazines Canada (MC), and the Print Measurement Bureau (PMB).

The role of ABC for magazines is similar to that of daily newspapers. The CCAB audits business publications as well as several large controlled-circulation consumer magazines. MC's objective is to promote the use of magazines as an advertising medium, and it collects and publishes research data on magazines.

The Print Measurement Bureau is a non-profit organization of advertisers, advertising agencies, and magazine publishers. It was established in 1971 to provide readership data on consumer magazines. The first PMB study was conducted in 1973 with 20 consumer magazines. The next two studies were conducted every three years and each added questions on product usage, general media habits (for cross media comparisons), and psychographics. The third study (PMB III), conducted in 1979, cost $1.7 million and the results were made available through subscription by advertisers and agencies. In addition, participating magazines contributed about 60 per cent of the total cost of the study. Starting in 1983, PMB is conducting annual studies with about 6000 interviews, and it will publish annual reports by combining the data for two years, i.e., a sample size of about 12 000.

About 47 consumer magazines participated in the 1982-83 study.

The PMB reports contain data on readership of consumer magazines, with demographic subgroups, duplications of readership, and accumulation of audience; exposure to major media for selected demographics; and qualitative readership data on reading occasions, editorial interest, and others.

In addition, the PMB product profile study measures purchasing and usage of 668 product categories covering some 26 product fields, as listed in Table 15.1. The data contain usage information on products or services (light, medium, or heavy user), demographics, psy-

chographics, and media habits covering the 47 magazines plus all other major media for cross-media comparisons. The subscriber to the study receives the standard published information (on microfiche) on the product categories requested. In addition, the subscriber may, through computer access, conduct additional analysis on the data by cross-classification of product usage with media habits or psychographic information. For example, one may want to find the media habits of heavy users of decaffeinated coffee and their type of lifestyle. The information is useful not only for developing the marketing and advertising plans, but also for the media planner and the creative

TABLE 15.1 Types of Products Included in the PMB III Product Profile Study

Product field	Number of product categories
1. Food Shopping, Cooking and Baking	24
2. Vegetables, Soups, Condiments and Spreads	20
3. Dairy and Breakfast Foods, Jams and Jellies	15
4. Snacks, Desserts, Confectionery	17
5. Meat, Fish, Prepared Meals	22
6. Hot Beverages, Juices and Soft Drinks	29
7. Children's Products, Cats and Dogs	13
8. Laundry and Cleaning Products	25
9. Household Products	16
10. Personal Care, Glasses and Dentures	30
11. Hair Care, Shaving	20
12. Medicinal Remedies	18
13. Women's Cosmetics and Feminine Hygiene	30
14. Women's Fragrances and Fashion	18
15. Driving, Cars and Trucks, Recreational Vehicles	33
16. Leisure Activities and Sports	32
17. Beer, Wines, Fortified Wines and Aperitifs	22
18. Liquor, Liqueurs	16
19. Smoking	10
20. Pleasure Travel	26
21. Business Travel, Business Entertainment and Car Travel	25
22. Home and Home Improvements, Household Appliances, Tools and Equipment	60
23. TV, Radio, Cameras, Personal Goods, Tableware	39
24. Financial, Insurance, Credit Cards	39
25. Shopping, Gift Giving, Clubs, Books, Magazines, Lotteries	46
26. Entertainment, Eating Out, Personal Long-Distance Telephone Calls	23
Pre-Publication Total:	*668*

SOURCE: Print Measurement Bureau

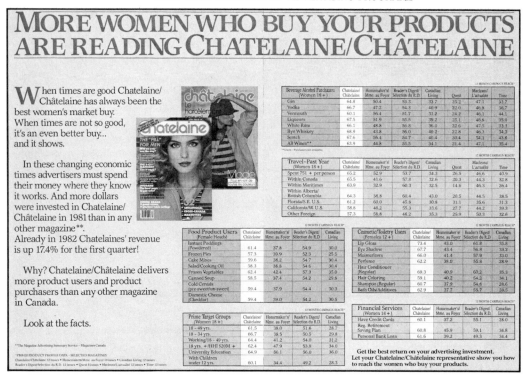

FIGURE 15.5   An advertisement for *Chatelaine* using results from Magazines Canada Summary Service and the PMB III Product Profile Study to demonstrate that the magazine is a superior vehicle for reaching users of selected product categories.
Courtesy Chatelaine/Châtelaine/Maclean-Hunter Ltd.

director. For instance, if such a heavy user plays tennis several times a week, this may suggest to the creative director to set the creative execution on a tennis court or to use a known tennis player in the television commercial.

Magazines may also use the results from these studies to sell advertising space to major advertisers. For example, the *Chatelaine* advertisement reproduced in Figure 15.5 uses results from the PMB III study and Magazines Canada to show that its magazine delivers the highest reach for selected usage of products and services among adult women.

OTHER PRINT MEDIA. Organizations representing other print media are attempting to develop similar types of data on individual vehicles. PMB studies include other *general* media such

as outdoor and transit, which may assist the media planner in comparing major media. Outdoor traffic circulation is measured every year for one-quarter of the boards in Canada by the Canadian Outdoor Measurement Bureau. Similar studies are conducted for transit audiences in major markets by means of a camera mounted in cars and buses and analyzed later for calculating traffic (pedestrians and cars) and exposure to a board. Nevertheless, for many advertisers and media planners, more and better data are necessary, and it is likely that additional research will be done by media organizations or individual media vehicles.

Broadcast Media Research
The object of broadcast media research is often to produce estimates of Canadian audiences

and program ratings, as well as to determine the audience composition of broadcast media and correlate it with consumption patterns. Research may be done by syndicated rating services, media associations, or individual vehicles or networks.

RADIO. Data on radio audiences are collected on a regular basis by the Bureau of Broadcast Measurement (BBM) and the Radio Bureau of Canada (RBC).

The BBM is a non-profit organization of advertisers, advertising agencies, and broadcasters. It was founded in 1942 to survey radio audiences and to provide estimates of the audiences to its members. The mandate of the BBM was enlarged about a decade later to include television audiences.

BBM radio reports are based on the results of a personal *diary* survey normally conducted during three consecutive weeks and averaged over the three-week period. Audience estimates are calculated by projecting diary information to the total population and according to age, sex, and language subgroups. The fall survey covers all subscribing stations, the spring one most medium and large markets, and the summer one covers 14 major markets in alternate years.

For the purpose of a BBM radio or television survey, the whole of Canada, except the Yukon and the Northwest Territories, is divided into 370 sampling cells. Within each sampling cell, a random sample is drawn from a list of telephone households in cities and towns. Each household is then called, using bilingual operators where necessary, in order to obtain a list of persons living at that address. The actual number of selected households is designed to provide a *sampling frame* containing a sufficient number of names for all the BBM surveys in one year. This number is currently over one million.

Each radio diary sample is then randomly selected from the sampling frame. The sampling

method is to select respondents from a random starting point within each of thirteen demographic subgroups in each sampling cell. Finally, each individual in the sample receives a diary by mail with a monetary incentive to gain co-operation. The diary contains a brief demographic questionnaire, and a daily log to record radio listening by quarter hour, every day for seven days. When completed, the diary is mailed back to BBM. A reminder card is sent in order to increase the response rate, which averages 50 per cent. A sample page of a radio diary is reproduced in Figure 15.6. A sample page of a BBM radio report is provided in Figure 15.7.

In addition to the standard reports, the BBM data may be accessed directly in order to interrogate it or to perform some specific operation of interest to the member. Finally, BBM may undertake proprietary studies requested by a member.

The RBC is a non-profit association of commercial radio broadcasters set up to promote radio as an advertising medium. Each year it publishes a fact book containing a summary of the latest available radio statistics. More detailed information is available without charge to advertisers and agencies from the RBC's Marketing Data Centre, which also contains the world's largest library of indexed commercials and related sonic material.

TELEVISION. Data on television audiences are collected on a regular basis by the BBM, A.C. Nielsen, and the Television Bureau of Canada (TVB).

The BBM television surveys follow the same basic methodology as for the radio surveys. Both network and individual television market surveys are conducted. Each network survey is issued as a series of 25 one-week reports. On the other hand, each television market survey is taken over two or three weeks, and the total number of weeks surveyed for each market is as follows:

	TUESDAY ②				**DAYTIME**		**TUESDAY** ②				**EVENING**

DAYTIME — TUESDAY ②

	TIME	STATION CALL-LETTERS	AM	FM	WHERE LISTENED At home	Away from home
01	5.00-5.15AM					
02	5.15-5.30					
03	5.30-5.45					
04	5.45-6.00					
05	6.00-6.15					
06	6.15-6.30					
07	6.30-6.45					
08	6.45-7.00					
09	7.00-7.15					
10	7.15-7.30					
11	7.30-7.45					
12	7.45-8.00					
13	8.00-8.15					
14	8.15-8.30					
15	8.30-8.45					
16	8.45-9.00					
17	9.00-9.15					
18	9.15-9.30					
19	9.30-9.45					
20	9.45-10.00					
21	10.00-10.15					
22	10.15-10.30					
23	10.30-10.45					
24	10.45-11.00					
25	11.00-11.15					
26	11.15-11.30					
27	11.30-11.45					
28	11.45-12.00					
29	12.00-12.15PM					
30	12.15-12.30					
31	12.30-12.45					
32	12.45-1.00					
33	1.00-1.15					
34	1.15-1.30					
35	1.30-1.45					
36	1.45-2.00					
37	2.00-2.15					
38	2.15-2.30					
39	2.30-2.45					
40	2.45-3.00					

EVENING — TUESDAY ②

	TIME	STATION CALL-LETTERS	AM	FM	WHERE LISTENED At home	Away from home
41	3.00-3.15PM					
42	3.15-3.30					
43	3.30-3.45					
44	3.45-4.00					
45	4.00-4.15					
46	4.15-4.30					
47	4.30-4.45					
48	4.45-5.00					
49	5.00-5.15					
50	5.15-5.30					
51	5.30-5.45					
52	5.45-6.00					
53	6.00-6.15					
54	6.15-6.30					
55	6.30-6.45					
56	6.45-7.00					
57	7.00-7.15					
58	7.15-7.30					
59	7.30-7.45					
60	7.45-8.00					
61	8.00-8.15					
62	8.15-8.30					
63	8.30-8.45					
64	8.45-9.00					
65	9.00-9.15					
66	9.15-9.30					
67	9.30-9.45					
68	9.45-10.00					
69	10.00-10.15					
70	10.15-10.30					
71	10.30-10.45					
72	10.45-11.00					
73	11.00-11.15					
74	11.15-11.30					
75	11.30-11.45					
76	11.45-12.00					
77	12.00-12.15AM					
78	12.15-12.30					
79	12.30-12.45					
80	12.45-1.00					

Please check (✔) box if you did *not* listen at all today ☐

10   11

FIGURE 15.6   Sample Page of a BBM Radio Diary
Courtesy Bureau of Broadcast Measurement

17 weeks: Toronto, Montreal, Vancouver
11 weeks: Halifax, Quebec City, Ottawa,
Kitchener, London, Winnipeg,
Calgary, Edmonton
9 weeks: Windsor, Hamilton, Victoria
6 weeks: all other markets

The BBM television diary is similar to the radio diary, and a sample page is reproduced in Figure 15.8. Information on cable television is also included in the brief questionnaire. A sample page of a BBM television report is provided in Figure 15.9.

CJRC
OTTAWA-HULL

SONDAGES BBM SURVEYS CANADA

SPRING 1982 PRINTEMPS

Average ¼ hour audience by hours–Saturday   Auditoires moyens (par ¼ d'heure) pour des heures–Samedi

FULL COVERAGE - IN HUNDREDS (00)   TERRITOIRE DE RAYONNEMENT EN CENTAINES (00)   CENTRAL AREA   REGION CENTRALE

Average ¼ hour audience by hours–Sunday   Auditoires moyens (par ¼ d'heure) pour des heures–Dimanche

Audience Profile – Full Coverage   Structure de l'Auditoire – Rayonnement

STATIONS

FIGURE 15.7   Sample Page of a BBM Radio Report
Courtesy Bureau of Broadcast Measurement

2 Mardi / Tuesday Jour / Daytime Soir / Evening

#	heure time	station	canal channel	émission program	#	heure time	station	canal channel	émission program
01	6.00-6.15 am				41	4.00-4.15			
02	6.15-6.30				42	4.15-4.30			
03	6.30-6.45				43	4.30-4.45			
04	6.45-7.00				44	4.45-5.00			
05	7.00-7.15				45	5.00-5.15			
06	7.15-7.30				46	5.15-5.30			
07	7.30-7.45				47	5.30-5.45			
08	7.45-8.00				48	5.45-6.00			
09	8.00-8.15				49	6.00-6.15			
10	8.15-8.30				50	6.15-6.30			
11	8.30-8.45				51	6.30-6.45			
12	8.45-9.00				52	6.45-7.00			
13	9.00-9.15				53	7.00-7.15			
14	9.15-9.30				54	7.15-7.30			
15	9.30-9.45				55	7.30-7.45			
16	9.45-10.00				56	7.45-8.00			
17	10.00-10.15				57	8.00-8.15			
18	10.15-10.30				58	8.15-8.30			
19	10.30-10.45				59	8.30-8.45			
20	10.45-11.00				60	8.45-9.00			
21	11.00-11.15				61	9.00-9.15			
22	11.15-11.30				62	9.15-9.30			
23	11.30-11.45				63	9.30-9.45			
24	11.45-12.00				64	9.45-10.00			
25	12.00-12.15 pm				65	10.00-10.15			
26	12.15-12.30				66	10.15-10.30			
27	12.30-12.45				67	10.30-10.45			
28	12.45-1.00				68	10.45-11.00			
29	1.00-1.15				69	11.00-11.15			
30	1.15-1.30				70	11.15-11.30			
31	1.30-1.45				71	11.30-11.45			
32	1.45-2.00				72	11.45-12.00			
33	2.00-2.15				73	12.00-12.15 am			
34	2.15-2.30				74	12.15-12.30			
35	2.30-2.45				75	12.30-12.45			
36	2.45-3.00				76	12.45-1.00			
37	3.00-3.15				77	1.00-1.15			
38	3.15-3.30				78	1.15-1.30			
39	3.30-3.45				79	1.30-1.45			
40	3.45-4.00				80	1.45-2.00			

6   Cochez s.v.p. (✔) si vous n'avez pas regardé la télé aujourd'hui ☐ Please check (✔) here if you watched NO TV today

FIGURE 15.8 Sample Page of a BBM Television Diary
Courtesy Bureau of Broadcast Measurement

As for radio, the BBM data may be accessed directly, and proprietary studies may be done for a member.

A.C. Nielsen of Canada is a privately owned company that provides television audience estimates, program ratings, and special analysis services. It issues two reports. The *Nielsen Television Index (NTI) Network Report* covers all Canadian networks for 37 weeks per year, including three weeks in the summer. The *Nielsen Broadcast Index (NBI) Local Market Report* measures station audiences per quarter hour in 41 designated market areas and covering from three to 18 weeks depending on the size of the market.

SONDAGES BBM SURVEYS CANADA

TORONTO Spring 1982 Printemps

MONDAY
4:00 P.M.–2:00 A.M.
LUNDI

PAGE 8

TIME — HEURE		W K S / S E M	CENTRAL MARKET % MARCHE CENTRAL									EXTENDED MARKET % MARCHE ETENDU									FULL COVERAGE AUDIENCES (00) AUDITOIRES DANS RAYONNEMENT (00)								¼ HOUR AVERAGES MOYENNES PAR ¼ D'HEURE	
			TOTAL 2+ TOUS		AD 18+ AD	WOMEN FEMMES		MEN HOMMES		12/17	2/11	TOTAL 2+ TOUS		AD 18+ AD	WOMEN FEMMES		MEN HOMMES		12/17	2/11	TOTAL 2+ TOUS	AD 18+ AD	WOMEN — FEMMES			MEN — HOMMES			12/17	2/11
STATION	PROGRAM/EMISSION		RTG COTE	SHR PART		18+	18/49	18+	18/49			RTG COTE	SHR PART		18+	18/49	18+	18/49					18+	18-49	18-34	18+	18-49	18-34		
						RATINGS			COTES						RATINGS			COTES												
400- 430 PM	ALL STNS	123	23	100	17	20	19	14	13	45	37	23	100	18	22	20	14	12	46	35										
CBLFT	BOBINO	123	-	1	-	-	-	-	-	-	1	-	-	-	-	-	-	-	-	1	77	11	6	6	3	5	-	-	11	55
CBLT	AFTER SCHOOL	123	-	1	-	-	-	-	-	-	-	-	1	-	-	-	-	-	-	-	165	135	89	29	17	46	37	17	6	24
CFMT	WORKING WORLD	123	-	-	-	-	-	-	-	-	-	-	-	-	-	-	-	-	-	-	1	1	1	-	-	-	-	-	-	-
CFTO	MOVIE	123	3	12	3	3	2	3	3	3	1	2	11	3	3	2	3	3	3	1	1531	1206	609	299	156	597	393	273	232	93
CHCH	YOUNG & RESTLESS	123	6	26	6	10	9	2	2	13	1	7	29	7	11	11	3	2	12	1	3431	2753	2240	1461	1106	512	321	223	561	117
CICO	PASSE-PARTOUT	123	-	-	-	-	-	-	-	-	-	-	-	-	-	-	-	-	-	-	60	25	12	12	12	12	7	-	4	32
CITY	ROCKFORD FILES	123	1	6	1	1	1	2	1	2	-	1	6	1	1	1	2	1	2	-	533	457	140	93	71	317	172	136	76	-
WGR	VARIOUS	123	2	7	1	1	1	1	1	9	2	2	7	1	1	1	1	1	9	2	818	277	122	101	42	155	129	83	389	152
	WHAT'S HAPPENING	23	2	8	1	1	1	1	1	9	1	2	8	1	1	1	1	1	9	2	921	355	150	130	41	204	166	102	415	152
	RICHARD SIMMONS	1	1	5	-	-	1	-	-			1	5	-	-	-	-	-	8	1	612	122	66	43	43	56	56	45	338	153
WIVB	STREETS/SAN/FRAN	123	2	7	2	2	1	2	1	1	1	2	7	2	2	1	2	1	2	1	895	761	417	108	64	343	138	70	92	42
WKBW	HAPPY DAYS AGAIN	123	3	13	1	1	2	1	1	10	8	3	14	1	1	2	1	2	12	7	1884	651	327	295	241	324	294	241	605	628
WUTV	LOST IN SPACE	123	2	8	1	-	1	1	1	2	7	2	8	1	1	1	1	2	3	7	982	297	99	93	50	198	182	182	120	565
CKGN	VARIOUS	123	2	8	1	1	1	-	-	2	8	2	7	1	1	1	-	-	2	7										
	GODZILLA	23	2	8	1	1	1	-	-	3	6	2	7	1	1	1	-	-	3	7										
	HERCULES	1	2	9	1	1	1	-	-			2	7	1	1	1	-	-	-	8										
OTHERS		123	2	10	1	1	1	1	1	3	9	2	9	1	1	1	1	1	3	8										
430- 500 PM	ALL STNS	123	25	100	19	23	21	15	14	47	42	26	100	20	24	22	16	14	48	42										
CBLFT	EDGAR ALLAN	123	-	-	-	-	-	-	-	-	-	-	-	-	-	-	-	-	-	-	25	9	4	4	4	5	-	-	8	8
CBLT	BEACHCOMBERS	123	1	3	1	1	1	-	-	3	1	1	4	1	1	1	-	-	3	1	410	207	137	64	37	71	39	24	117	85
CFMT	JUST LIKE MOM	123	-	1	-	-	-	-	-	1	1	-	1	-	-	-	-	-	-	-	62	24	24	24	10	-	-	-	16	22
CFTO	MOVIE	123	3	11	3	3	2	3	3	3	1	3	10	3	3	2	3	3	4	1	1622	1224	615	325	172	609	395	259	272	127
CHCH	YOUNG & RESTLESS	123	6	25	6	10	10	2	2	13	1	7	26	7	11	11	3	2	12	1	3495	2776	2262	1495	1089	514	335	227	583	136
CICO	VARIOUS	123	-	-	-	-	-	-	-	-	-	-	-	-	-	-	-	-	-	-	85	41	35	35	27	6	3	-	-	44
	TELL ME A STORY	123	-		-	-	-	-	-	-	-	-		-	-	-	-	-	-	-	82	41	35	35	27	6	3	-	-	41
	ROBIN AND ROSIE	123	-		-	-	-	-	-	-	-	-		-	-	-	-	-	-	-	87	41	35	35	27	6	3	-	-	47
CITY	ROCKFORD FILES	123	1	5	2	1	1	2	1	1	-	1	5	2	1	1	2	2	2	-	563	487	151	103	82	337	180	143	67	9
WGR	ROCKFORD FILES	123	1	5	1	1	1	1	1	3	1	1	5	1	1	1	1	1	3	1	589	382	188	78	71	194	149	142	127	80
WIVB	STREETS/SAN/FRAN	123	2	7	2	2	1	2	1	1	1	2	7	2	2	1	2	1	2	1	887	741	413	107	63	328	114	46	96	50
WKBW	LITTLE HOUSE/PR.	123	2	8	1	1	2	1	1	6	4	2	8	1	2	2	1	1	7	4	1321	596	378	249	185	218	186	132	330	395
WUTV	LOST IN SPACE	123	2	7	1	-	1	1	1	2	6	2	7	1	1	1	1	1	2	6	977	315	118	104	60	197	181	181	154	508
CKGN	BATTLE PLANETS	123	2	9	1	1	-	1	-	3	10	2	8	1	1	-	1	-	3	10										
OTHERS		123	5	20	2	2	3	2	3	10	17	5	19	2	2	3	2	3	10	15										
500- 530 PM	ALL STNS	123	28	100	22	22	19	23	22	51	45	28	100	22	22	19	22	22	54	45										
CBLFT	HOMME ET LA CITE	123	-	-	-	-	-	-	-	-	-	-	-	-	-	-	-	-	-	-	35	18	11	9	9	7	7	7	12	5
CBLT	HAPPY DAYS	123	5	18	2	2	2	2	2	14	15	5	16	2	2	2	2	2	14	13	2306	719	323	228	161	396	330	239	663	924
CFMT	PORTUGAL TODAY	123	-	1	-	1	1	-	-	-	-	-	1	-	-	1	-	-	-	-	104	97	60	60	31	37	32	32	7	-
CFTO	MOVIE	123	3	10	3	3	3	4	4	2	1	3	11	3	3	2	4	4	3	2	1763	1357	642	361	233	715	501	301	273	133
CHCH	RHODA	123	2	6	2	3	2	1	1	3	-	2	5	2	3	2	1	1	3	-	902	689	538	334	262	151	80	69	167	46
CICO	SESAME STREET	123	2	6	1	-	1	1	1	-	10	2	6	-	-	1	1	1	-	10	1314	288	162	150	133	127	118	74	-	1026
CITY	PRICE IS RIGHT	123	3	9	3	3	2	3	2	2	-	2	9	3	4	2	2	2	2	-	1052	954	575	264	145	379	184	94	69	29
WGR	ROCKFORD FILES	123	1	5	1	1	1	1	1	4	1	1	5	1	1	1	1	1	3	1	638	423	197	81	61	227	163	141	126	87
WIVB	M.A.S.H.	123	5	16	4	3	3	6	6	11	2	5	17	5	3	3	6	6	13	1	2506	1864	775	423	322	1089	802	648	533	109
WKBW	LITTLE HOUSE/PR.	123	2	7	1	1	2	1	1	6	3	2	7	1	1	1	1	1	6	4	1209	541	352	232	177	188	156	102	335	333
WUTV	WONDER WOMAN	123	1	4	1	1	1	1	1	1	3	1	4	1	1	1	1	1	1	4	681	236	123	89	63	113	111	94	50	395
CKGN	STARSKY & HUTCH	123	3	10	2	2	2	3	3	7	4	3	10	2	2	2	3	3	7	3										
OTHERS		123	2	8	2	2	1	2	1	1	6	2	9	2	2	2	2	2	2	6										
530- 600 PM	ALL STNS	123	26	100	23	21	18	25	24	38	36	26	100	23	22	18	24	23	44	34										
CBLFT	HOMME ET LA CITE	123	-	-	-	-	-	-	-	-	-	-	-	-	-	-	-	-	-	-	32	17	11	9	9	7	7	7	12	2
CBLT	MUPPET SHOW	123	3	11	2	3	3	1	1	3	8	3	10	2	2	3	1	1	4	7	1373	674	457	306	215	217	116	66	174	524
CFMT	VARIOUS	123	-	1	-	-	1	-	-	-	-	-	1	-	-	-	-	-	-	-	99	92	48	48	15	43	38	38	7	-
	PORTUGAL TODAY	123	-		-	1	1	-	-	-	-	-		-	-	1	-	-	-	-	114	107	64	64	31	43	38	38	7	-
	NEWS LINE	123	-		-	-	-	-	-	-	-	-		-	-	-	-	-	-	-	84	76	33	33	-	43	38	38	7	-
CFTO	MOVIE	123	3	13	4	3	3	4	4	4	1	3	12	3	3	3	4	4	5	2	1912	1440	658	394	250	782	554	337	325	148
CHCH	YAN CAN	123	1	2	1	1	-	-	-	-	-	1	2	1	1	-	-	-	-	-	311	285	205	41	35	81	46	39	12	13
CICO	SESAME STREET	123	2	7	-	-	-	1	1	-	10	2	7	-	-	-	1	1	-	10	1294	276	155	155	136	121	113	74	-	1018
CITY	PRICE IS RIGHT	123	3	11	3	4	3	3	2	3	1	3	11	3	4	3	2	2	2	1	1179	1027	630	302	167	398	212	100	88	64
WGR	NEWCENTR-2 AT530	123	-	1	-	-	-	-	-	1	-	-	1	-	-	-	-	-	-	-	194	163	62	11	1	101	56	42	18	13
WIVB	BARNEY MILLER	123	4	15	4	3	2	6	5	4	2	4	16	5	3	2	6	5	6	1	2291	1918	776	370	276	1141	745	638	263	111
WKBW	JEFFERSONS	123	3	13	2	2	3	2	3	10	5	4	14	3	3	3	2	2	12	5	1973	1066	600	448	297	466	330	227	551	355
WUTV	WONDER WOMAN	123	1	5	1	1	1	1	1	1	4	1	4	1	1	1	1	1	1	4	698	255	133	83	69	121	119	102	68	375
CKGN	STARSKY & HUTCH	123	3	11	3	2	2	3	3	7	3	3	11	2	2	2	3	3	8	2										
OTHERS		123	3	10	2	1	1	3	4	6	3	3	10	2	2	1	3	3	6	2										
600- 630 PM	ALL STNS	123	33	100	33	31	25	35	32	39	33	34	100	34	33	25	35	31	37	31										
CBLFT	DIVERS	123	-	-	-	-	-	-	-	-	-	-	-	-	-	-	-	-	-	-	77	74	31	14	11	44	11	11	2	-
	CE SOIR-NOUV NAT	123	-		-	-	-	-	-	-	-	-		-	-	-	-	-	-	-	87	82	35	17	11	47	14	14	5	-
	NOUV.REGIONALES	123	-		-	-	-	-	-	-	-	-		-	-	-	-	-	-	-	66	66	26	12	11	40	7	7	-	-
CBLT	CBC(1)EARLY NEWS	123	6	17	7	7	4	7	5	1	1	5	16	7	7	3	7	5	1	1	2707	2578	1339	409	167	1240	585	299	65	64
CFMT	MOVIE	123	1	2	1	1	1	1	1	1	-	1	2	1	1	1	1	1	1	-	303	265	140	61	32	125	85	57	27	11
CFTO	CAROL BURNETT	123	9	26	7	8	8	7	6	19	10	9	25	7	8	8	7	6	18	9	4348	2762	1505	981	721	1257	849	547	899	687
CHCH	NEWSROOM	123	-	1	-	-	-	-	-	-	-	2	6	2	3	1	2	1	1	-	929	864	519	159	46	345	117	43	34	31
CICO	POLKA DOT DOOR	123	2	5	-	-	-	1	1	1	9	2	5	-	-	1	-	1	-	10	1830	316	178	171	130	138	138	59	23	1491
CITY	CITYPULSE AT SIX	123	5	15	5	5	5	5	5	6	2	4	13	5	5	4	5	4	4	1	1786	1541	814	441	239	727	472	234	153	93
WGR	6 OCLOCK REPORT	123	-	1	-	-	-	1	-	-	-	-	1	-	-	-	-	-	-	-	183	171	48	36	21	123	41	37	9	3
WIVB	NEWS 4	123	-	1	1	1	-	-	-	1	-	-	1	1	1	-	-	-	-	-	296	280	146	43	33	134	81	62	16	-
WKBW	EYEWITNESS NEWS	123	-	1	-	-	-	-	-	1	-	-	1	-	-	-	-	-	1	-	428	293	149	68	31	144	76	63	82	54
WUTV	TWILIGHT ZONE	123	2	6	2	2	2	3	4	3	1	2	6	2	1	2	2	3	3	2	959	692	243	201	192	449	418	370	137	129
CKGN	NEWS HOUR	123	4	13	5	5	4	6	5	2	1	4	13	5	5	4	6	5	1	1										
OTHERS		123	4	12	3	1	1	5	4	6	8	4	11	3	2	1	4	4	6	7										
630- 700 PM	ALL STNS	123	34	100	36	31	28	38	33	26	28	34	100	36	36	28	37	31	24	27										
CBLFT	NOUV.REGIONALES	123	-	-	-	-	-	-	-	-	-	-	-		-	-	-	-	-	-	44	44	22	13	9	22	7	7	-	-
CBLT	CBC(1)EARLY NEWS	123	4	11	5	4	3	6	4	1	-	4	11	5	4	3	5	4	1	-	1912	1813	867	331	149	951	441	307	55	44
CFMT	MOVIE	123	1	2	1	1	-	1	1	1	1	1	2	1	1	-	1	1	1	-	308	254	131	34	7	123	83	66	33	22
CFTO	WORLD BEAT NEWS	123	10	29	12	12	8	11	8	8	3	10	29	12	12	8	11	8	7	3	4789	4310	2270	946	493	2040	989	462	295	105
CHCH	NEWSROOM	123	-	-	-	-	-	-	-	-	-	1	3	1	2	1	1	-	1	-	546	521	306	78	49	216	80	42	24	-
CICO	VARIOUS	123	2	5	1	-	1	1	1	1	10	2	6	1	-	1	1	1	1	10	1723	365	192	177	135	173	173	90	49	1309
	TALES OF MAGIC	123	2		1	-	1	1	1	1	10	2		1	-	1	1	1	1	10	1657	362	198	184	142	164	164	97	55	1239
	JEREMY	123	2		1	-	-	1	1	1	10	2		1	-	-	1	1	1	11	1789	367	186	170	128	181	181	84	42	1379
CITY	CITYPULSE AT SIX	123	4	12	4	4	4	4	4	5	3	4	11	4	4	4	4	4	4	3	1549	1231	665	400	235	566	407	203	152	167
WGR	NBC NIGHTLY NEWS	123	1	2	1	1	-	1	1	-	-	1	2	1	1	-	1	1	-	-	324	288	90	41	30	198	71	36	16	20
WIVB	CBS EVENING NEWS	123	1	4	2	1	1	2	2	-	-	1	4	2	1	1	2	2	-	-	666	631	193	81	48	437	267	127	12	23
WKBW	ABC WORLD NEWS	123	1	3	1	1	1	1	1	1	1	1	3	1	1	1	1	1	1	1	602	491	268	146	55	223	158	121	56	56
WUTV	MARY TYLER MOORE	123	2	7	3	3	3	3	3	4	1	2	7	3	3	3	2	3	4	1	1338	1057	544	447	391	513	460	368	170	111
CKGN	NEWS HOUR	123	4	10	4	4	3	5	4	-	1	3	10	4	4	3	4	4	-	1										
OTHERS		123	4	13	4	3	4	4	4	4	8	4	12	3	3	3	4	4	5	7										

FIGURE 15.9 Sample Page of a BBM Television Report (for all Toronto stations)

Courtesy Bureau of Broadcast Measurement

Here's how to keep your TV Diary:

In columns 1, 2, 3 . . . at the right, **please fill in the NAMES, AGE and SEX** of all household members. Except for those outside of Canada, **do not include persons away from home this week.** See Example below for typical entries. If no Man or Lady of House, write NONE in that column.

IF YOU HAVE SEVERAL TV's, you probably received several diaries. Please write names in same order in each diary, and keep one diary with each TV. (If you didn't receive a diary for each TV, **see instructions inside back cover.**)

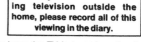

> If a family member was watching television outside the home, please record all of this viewing in the diary.

(A) **WHEN THE TV IS "OFF"**
Draw a line down the "OFF" column for all quarter-hours the TV is off.

(B) **WHEN THE TV IS "ON"**
Put an X in the "ON" column for each quarter-hour the TV is turned on for six minutes or longer. Please be especially sure to show all **late-evening** TV use.

Write in Station Call Letters, Channel Number, and Name of Program. For Movies, please write "Movie" and Name of Movie. Please record all viewing including **all** local cable programs. (See Example, below.)

Put an X in the column under the name of each person watching six minutes or longer during each quarter-hour the TV is "ON".

(C) If an entry in a column does not change from one quarter-hour to the next, DRAW A LINE down that column to show entry did not change. (See Example, below.)

(D) If the TV is "ON" but no one is watching, fill in the station and program information and put "0" in the first person column.

(E) If you have a visitor watching this TV, write "VISITOR" in one of the blank name columns along with visitor's age and sex. (If exact age is not known, put in approximate age.) If you do not have room to write in any more names, write in the **number** of other persons watching in the column marked "OTHERS."

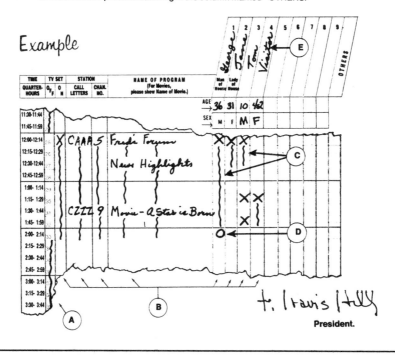

FIGURE 15.10 Nielsen TV Viewing Diary: Instructions and Sample Page

Courtesy A.C. Nielsen of Canada

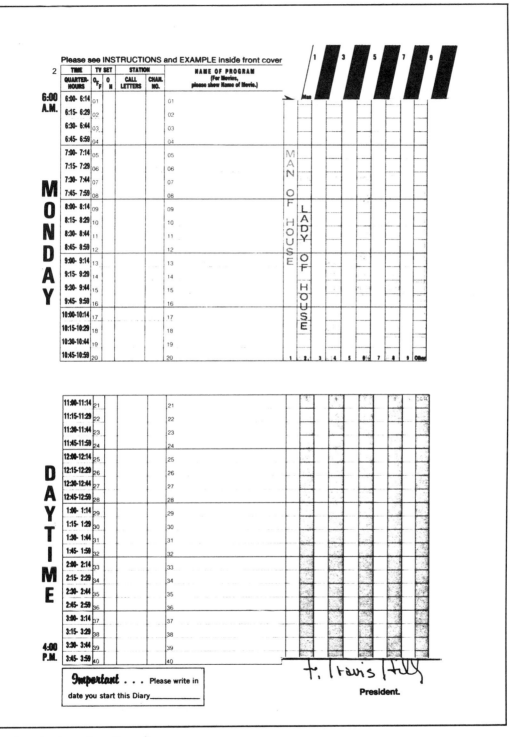

FIGURE 15.10 (continued)

The sampling procedure followed by A.C. Nielsen is also a two-step procedure. First, some areas are defined as measurement cells. The sampling frame is drawn from telephone directories, and a sample of *households* is selected, with the possibility of selecting a household which has participated in one or two past surveys and has agreed to participate again. The sample must contain less than half of such respondents. The others are selected randomly from the sampling frame.

As mentioned before, the sample contains households who are sent a diary with some monetary incentive. Here *all* individuals in the household participate in the study by recording the station call letters, channel number, and program name when the set is on. When completed, the diary is mailed back to A.C. Nielsen. A reminder card is also sent to increase the response rate, which is around 50 per cent. A sample page of a Nielsen diary is reproducucd in Figure 15.10. Sample pages of an NTI Network Report and of an NBI Local Market Report are reproduced in Figures 15.11 and 15.12.

In addition to its regular reports, Nielsen publishes a series of supplementary reports and may conduct some special analysis services, such as audience duplication studies, viewer preference studies, and audience fragmentation studies.

The TVB is a non-profit organization set up by the television industry to promote the use of television as an advertising medium. Each year it publishes *TV Basics*, a fact book that contains the latest available information on television. A data bank of statistics on television is also available to advertisers and agencies.

NIELSEN WEEK/SEMAINE
Apr 26 Avr, 1982

CBC-DAY AND TIME TV LISTINGS | **CBC-LISTE CHRONOLOGIQUE**

DAY(S) JOUR(S)	TIME START/DEBUT	DUR. 1/4 HRS.	PROGRAM/EMISSION	* STNS.	AVERAGE 1/4 HOUR AUDIENCE AUDITOIRE MOYEN PAR 1/4 D'HEURE (000) HOUSEHOLDS FOYERS TOTAL	HOUSEHOLDS FOYERS RTG COT	VIEWERS/TELESP. 2+	VIEWERS/TELESP. 12+	VIEWERS/TELESP. 18+	WOMEN/FEMMES 18+	WOMEN/FEMMES 18-34	WOMEN/FEMMES 18-49	MEN/HOMMES 18+	MEN/HOMMES 18-34	MEN/HOMMES 18-49	TEENS ADOLESCENTS 12-17	TEENS ADOLESCENTS GIRLS FILLES	CHILD ENFANT 2-11	LOH VM TOTAL
			---MONDAY/LUNDI---																
MON/LUN	9.45A	1	FRIENDLY GIANT	15	45	.5	64	IFR	IFR	IFR	IFR	IFR	IFR	IFR	IFR	IFR	IFR	64	IFR
MON/LUN	10.30A	2	MR. DRESSUP	38	346	4.2	403	39	35	31	23	31	4	IFR	4	4	IFR	364	29
MON/LUN	11.00A	4	SESAME STREET	15	283	3.5	293	26	26	22	1	14	4	IFR	IFR	IFR	IFR	267	21
MON/LUN	12.30P	4	MCLEAN AT LARGE	15	88	1.1	110	105	105	75	6	10	30	3	8	IFR	IFR	5	63
MON/LUN	1.30P	2	REGIONAL PROGRAMS	14	IFR														
MON/LUN	2.00P	2	WOK WITH YAN	15	60	.7	73	73	73	61	35	43	12	2	2	IFR	IFR	IFR	50
MON/LUN	2.30P	2	CORONATION STREET	38	80	1.0	72	72	72	55	IFR	8	17	IFR	IFR	IFR	IFR	IFR	55
MON/LUN	3.00P	2	EDGE OF NIGHT	37	150	1.8	210	194	183	151	31	73	32	9	17	11	11	16	130
MOM/LUN	3.30P	2	TAKE THIRTY	38	137	1.7	137	137	137	109	19	31	28	11	18	IFR	IFR	IFR	94
MON/LUN	4.00P	2	ARK ON THE MOVE	15	60	.7	64	55	48	37	5	9	11	11	11	7	IFR	9	30
MON/LUN	4.30P	2	BEACHCOMBERS	15	149	1.8	277	204	120	62	27	31	58	24	46	84	25	73	46
MON/LUN	5.00P	2	HAPPY DAYS	14	577	7.0	1149	863	502	236	157	172	266	184	224	361	135	286	178
MON/LUN	5.30P	2	MUPPET SHOW	14	344	4.2	623	367	270	132	66	92	138	62	109	97	33	256	101
MON/LUN	6.00P	4	CBC EARLY EVE NEWS	15	622	7.6	1095	1075	1041	541	112	220	500	111	221	34	16	20	460
MON/LUN	7.30P	2	JOHN ALLEN CAMERON	15	228	2.8	350	321	272	171	14	47	101	IFR	35	49	42	29	140
MON/LUN	8.00P	8	NWS SP:SAS PROV ELEC	6	132	1.6	239	236	216	103	15	44	113	29	53	20	20	3	90
MON/LUN	8.00P	2	PRIVATE BENJAMIN	31	820	10.0	1608	1365	1181	650	296	410	491	204	329	184	108	243	562
MON/LUN	8.30P	2	THREES COMPANY	31	1080	13.2	2154	1849	1530	833	308	475	697	281	438	319	175	305	723
MON/LUN	9.00P	2	M*A*S*H	31	1432	17.5	2548	2385	2058	1011	460	643	1047	577	809	327	133	163	899
MON/LUN	9.30P	2	WKRP IN CINCINNATI	31	1242	15.1	2175	2064	1780	854	388	540	926	515	719	284	142	111	730
MON/LUN	10.00P	1	CBC NATIONAL NEWS	38	1362	16.6	2265	2235	2130	972	157	447	1158	304	621	105	13	30	866
MON/LUN	10.15P	3	CBC JOURNAL	38	1177	14.4	1867	1859	1776	775	89	322	1001	256	518	83	4	8	702
MON/LUN	11.00P	1	CBC UPDATE/LOCAL	15	392	4.8	572	572	572	259	25	70	313	77	101	IFR	IFR	IFR	227
MON/LUN	11.15P	1	CBC NEWS/VARIOUS	15	318	3.9	466	466	466	206	16	57	260	61	73	IFR	IFR	IFR	191
MON/LUN	11.30P	2	BARNEY MILLER	14	175	2.1	267	267	253	120	38	53	133	59	80	14	IFR	IFR	113
			---TUESDAY/MARDI---																
TUE/MAR	9.45A	1	FRIENDLY GIANT	15	47	.6	77	64	64	41	IFR	9	23	IFR	IFR	IFR	IFR	13	41

FIGURE 15.11 Sample Data from a Nielsen NTI Report for the CBC Network
Courtesy A.C. Nielsen of Canada

9 NBI PROGRAM AVERAGES/SECTION MOYENNES DES EMISSIONS NBI   TORONTO/HAMILTON   MARCH/MARS 1982

PROGRAM/EMISSION STATION DAY/JOUR TIME/DEBUT	METRO AGGLO HOUSEHOLDS % FOYERS				DESIGNATED MARKET AREA/MARCHE DESIGNE														STATION TOTAL AUDIENCES (000) AUDITOIRES DE ZONE DE RAYONNEMENT (000)															STATION START TIME/ DEBUT DAY/JOUR	NUMBER OF QUARTER-HOURS AVERAGED DUREE MOYENNE EN QUARTS D' HEURE		
					HH % FOYERS MULTI-WEEK AVERAGES MOYENNE MULTI-HEBDO		DEMOGRAPHIC RATINGS % COTES DEMOGRAPHIQUES %								HH FOY-	VIEWERS TOTAL TELESP	WOMEN FEMMES			MEN HOMMES			TEENS ADOL	CHD ENF	LOH MM		WK 1 SEM	WK 2 SEM	WK 3 SEM
	TOR		HAML			SHARE/PART	VIEWERS TOTAL TELESP	WOMEN FEMMES		MEN HOMMES		TNS ADO	CHD ENF																
	RTG COT	SHR PAR	RTG COT	SHR PAR	RTG COT	HAR '82	HAR '81	CAB	2+	18+	TO-TAL	18-49	TO-TAL	18-49	12-17	2-11	ERS	2+	18+	TOTAL	18-34	18-49	WKG TRA	TOTAL	18-34	18-49	12-17 GIRLS FILLES	2-11	TOTAL				
	1	2	3	4	5	6	11	7	14	15	16	17	21	22	26	28	29	30	31	32	33	34	54	37	38	39	42	43	44	45		50	51	52
A BUNKER PLACE WIVB																															WIVB			
SUN 8.00PM	7	12	7	12	8	14		61	5	6	6	5	5	4	5	2	145	256	211	121	43	67	44	90	24	50	28	9	17	110	8.00 SUN	4	2	2
NOR 8.00PM	7	13	8	13	8	15	19	61	5	6	7	5	5	4	4	2	149	255	220	129	43	69	47	90	23	43	19	5	16	117	8.00 NOR	2	2	2
A HITCHCOCK WUTV															•																WUTV			
MON 10.00PM	<<		1	1	<<	2											8	12	12	5	2	3	1	6	5	5				6	10.00 MON	2	2	2
TUE 10.00PM	<<		<<			1											5	6	6	5	4	6	6	1	1	1				5	10.00 TUE	2	2	2
WED 10.00PM	1	1	1	1	1	1	1			1							10	12	12	9	5	5		3	1	1				4	10.00 WED	2	2	2
THU 10.00PM	<<		<<		<<	1											4	7	7	4	1	1		4	1	1				4	10.00 THU	2	2	2
FRI 10.00PM	1	1	<<		1	1	1			1			1				9	18	18	6	5	5	3	12	5	5				2	10.00 FRI	2	2	2
AV5 10.00PM	<<		<<		<<	1				1							8	11	11	6	3	4	2	6	3	3				4	AV5	10	8	10
A.M. WEATHER WNED																															WNED			
M-F 6.45AM	<<		1	36	<<												2	2	2					2		1					6.45 M-F	5	5	5
ABBTT&COSTELLO CITY																															CITY			
M-F 12.00NN	1	10	1	6	1	8	3		1						1	3	19	37	12	7	5	5	2	5	4	4	4	3	22	6	12.00 M-F	10	10	10
ABBTT&COSTELLO WUTV																															WUTV			
SAT 4.30PM	3	12	2	5	3	11	12	69	2	2	2	2	3	4	3	2	54	104	78	26	16	22	11	52	26	46	11	5	15	17	4.30 SAT	6	6	6
ABC MON-MOV WKBW																															WKBW			
MON 9.00PM	2	2	5	6	3	4	12	20	2	3	3	3	2	3			63	122	118	68	22	49	21	50	30	40	4	4		49	9.00 MON	8		
ABC MOV SPCL WKBW																															WKBW			
FRI 8.30PM	6	10	10	15	6	10	2	50	4	4	4	5	5	7	2		119	231	188	77	51	67	19	111	69	88	29	6	14	64	8.30 FRI			6
ABC MOV-WEEK WKBW																															WKBW			
MON 12.00MD	<<		1	13	1	8											10	11	11	5	2	2	1	6	2	3				5	12.00 MON	8	8	8
ABC NWS-SUN WKBW																															WKBW			
SUN 1.00AM	1		1	10	1	23	17				1	1					16	15	15	9		6	5	7	4	4				9	1.00 SUN	2	2	
ABC SUN-MOV WKBW																															WKBW			
SUN 9.00PM	5	9	9	15	7	12		64	5	5	6	7	5	6	7	1	133	281	226	113	57	93	39	113	54	91	43	17	11	91	9.00 SUN	11	8	9
NOR 9.00PM	6	10	10	16	8	13	12X	62	6	6	6	8	6	7	8	1	147	315	253	127	64	104	43	126	61	102	49	19	13	101	9.00 NOR	8	8	8
ABC THEATRE WKBW																															WKBW			
MON 9.00PM	4	7	2	2	5	7	12	55	3	3	3	5	2	3	4	1	88	139	112	65	45	60	18	47	18	44	19	15	8	45	9.00 MON	2		
ABC WKEND SPCL WKBW																															WKBW			
SAT 12.00NN	2	17	3	14	2	16	20X	76	1		1	1		1	2	2	38	45	14	8	5	6	4	6	6	10	4	21	5	12.00 SAT	2	2	2
ABC-NITELINE WKBW																															WKBW			
MON 11.30PM	1	8	2	7	2	8		93	1	1	1	1	1	1			24	36	36	14	5	7	7	22	6	12				11	11.30 MON	2	2	2
TUE 11.30PM	<<		3	10	1	4	4			1				1			16	23	22	9	1	3		13	2	6	1	1		8	11.30 TUE	2	2	2
WED 11.30PM	1	4	2	6	1	3											14	15	15	7	2	2	3	8		3				5	11.30 WED	2	2	2
THU 11.30PM	1	6	1	4	1	5	3				1						13	15	15	9	5	7		8		1				10	11.30 THU	2	2	2
FRI 11.30PM	1	3	2	7	1	4	5			1		1		1			18	21	21	10	3	3	5	12	2	5				8	11.30 FRI	2	2	2
AV5 11.30PM	1	5	2	7	1	5	3			1	1		1				17	22	22	10	3	5	4	12	2	6				8	AV5	10	10	10
ABC-WORLD NWS WKBW																															WKBW			
MON 6.30PM	1	2	5	8	3	5	5X	59	2	2	2	2	2	2			45	70	68	35	16	19	14	33	6	17			2	33	6.30 MON	2	2	2
TUE 6.30PM	1	6	6	10	2	4	6X	70	1	1	1	1	1				36	42	41	20	10	10	5	20	3	11	1	1		34	6.30 TUE	2	2	2
WED 6.30PM	2	3	3	6	3	5	6X	52	1	2	2	1	2	2			45	59	57	33	9	16	12	25	8	18	2	2		34	6.30 WED	2	2	2
THU 6.30PM	1	2	5	9	3	5	5X	64	1	2	2	1	2	1	1	1	42	57	49	26	9	11	7	23	3	12	2	2	6	28	6.30 THU	2	2	2
FRI 6.30PM	2	4	4	8	3	6	5X	56	2	2	2	1	2	1	2		40	65	54	30	9	13	8	24	5	10	9	9	2	28	6.30 FRI	2	2	2
AV5 6.30PM	1	2	5	8	3	5	6X	59	1	2	2	1	2	1	1		42	59	54	29	11	14	9	25	5	13	3	3	2	28	AV5	10	10	10
ACADEMY PRFRMC CFTO																															CFTO			
SAT 9.00PM	9	15	7	12	8	14	13	66	5	7	6	7	7	8	4		162	315	284	131	69	98	49	152	85	119	28	8	3	101	9.00 SAT	8	8	8
ACADEMY PRFRMC CKCO																															CKCO			
SAT 8.00PM	2	4	5	8	3	4	X	81	2	2	2	1	2	1	1	1															8.00 SAT	8	8	8
ADVNTR OUTDOOR CICA																															CICA			
SAT 10.00AM	<<		2	21	<<																										10.00 SAT			2
AFTER BENNY WGR																															WGR			
SUN 12.00MD	1	16	4	31	1	16	27		1	1	1	1	1	2			29	51	51	14	6	9	2	37	18	31				13	12.00 SUN	2	2	2

For explanation of symbols, see Table 9 of the Market Data Section/
Pour une explication des symboles, consulter le Tableau 9 de la Section des Données sur le Marché.

FIGURE 15.12   Sample data from a Nielsen NBI Report for the Toronto/Hamilton Designated Market Area

Courtesy A.C. Nielsen of Canada

Information for the Creative Plan

Advertising research that provides information on the creative part of the campaign is called *copy research*. In effect, it represents creative research since all creative aspects, including execution, may be tested. Depending on the information required from copy testing, one must differentiate between strategic and executional research. *Strategic copy testing* is used to differentiate between two or more creative strategies. In this case an advertiser wants to ensure that a message has the *intended* effect on consumers, i.e., the communication task of the campaign as developed in Chapter 11. *Executional copy testing* is used to differentiate

between two or more executions of the same creative strategy. These tests determine whether the message is correctly understood by consumers, whether it has good attention value, and whether the theme of the message is remembered correctly.

Copy testing may be conducted before a message is finally selected for an advertising campaign, either to select the best message from several possibilities or to make any minor changes before the campaign is actually run. These are called advertising copy *pre-tests*.

Copy testing carried out after the message has actually run is a *post-test*. The objective is to assess the effectiveness of each advertisement in the *actual environment* in which it will appear and as consumers will see it within the media vehicle and among competitive advertisements.

Copy Pre-testing

Pre-testing of a message is becoming more common as advertisers realize it is better to identify weaknesses in the message before it is produced.[24] Three types of pretesting methods may be used: indirect questioning, direct questioning, or laboratory tests.

PROJECTIVE TECHNIQUES OR IN-DEPTH INTERVIEWS. The projective techniques for copy testing are similar to those for market and consumer research.[25] Here the researcher is interested in the reactions of selected individual(s) to the proposed creative execution of an advertising message. Often, the message is in the initial stages of development, i.e., rough sketches, animatics, or storyboards. The respondent is asked third-person reactions to the whole message or to the headline or the slogan. Test methods include the (cartoon-type) balloon tests, the sentence completion tests, the Thematic Apperception Tests (TAT), and word association tests.

In-depth interviews may also be used to pre-test copy. A trained interviewer probes an individual's reactions to a message and its components (the headline, subheads, body copy, and slogan). The message may be a rough sketch, a radio commercial, or a storyboard. Because of the depth of probing, the pre-test provides a detailed qualitative evaluation of the message's effects. Weaknesses in the copy are identified and interpreted, thus pointing toward some improvements. This method is expensive, however, and the results are based on a small, often non-random, sample of consumers. The cost varies between $50-$300 per interview.

DIRECT QUESTIONING METHODS. Copy pre-testing may also be done by asking a selected group of individuals a series of questions. For focus group testing, the groups may be small or large for mall or theatre testing. The questioning may be unstructured or structured.

Focus groups usually involve ten to 15 individuals with the demographic characteristics of the brand's target group. These individuals are brought together in a room equipped with one-way mirrors and audio-visual equipment. A trained moderator defines the areas for informal exchange among the participants.[26] The stimulus for the group may have one of the following formats:

- showing one advertising message in rough or finished form. A finished advertisement is always superior for reliable results;
- showing a series of unrelated advertising messages with the test message "buried" in the series;
- showing several versions of the same advertising message;
- showing a whole package with some editorial matter and the test message(s) placed within it.

For print, this method is called the *portfolio test*, and each portfolio resembles a newspaper or a magazine.

Group members are then asked to comment on what they have seen, or heard, or read. They may also be asked to choose one or several brands among a display, and explain their choice.

Depending on the complexity of the procedure, a focus group interview takes between one and two hours. At least two focus groups should be run on the same procedure in order to minimize a chance occurrence that may distort the results.

Several focus groups may also be used to test different versions of the same message. Instead of showing all the versions to the same group, each group is exposed to a different version within the same procedure. If the groups are properly *matched*, each version may be pretested for major flaws. It is also advisable to have two groups per version, as mentioned before. The cost of this method varies from $800 to $1500 per group.

Mall tests or *ad hoc* commercial testing are conducted with respondents intercepted in shopping malls and plazas, and recruited according to certain demographic characteristics. They participate in an interview that may involve showing some advertising messages and commenting on them. This kind of test has also drawbacks. The population sampled may be biased because of the neighbourhood in which the mall is situated or the kind of people it attracts. In addition, the interview must be short since most respondents are intercepted while on a shopping trip. On the other hand, this method is relatively inexpensive, can accommodate large samples, and gives fast answers to copy problems. Safeguards may be taken to ensure proper coverage of the target group and to improve the accuracy of the data obtained.

One example of a mall test is the Dadson Compare Test, which uses two groups for testing a commercial: one test group and one control group. A series of questions on attitudes toward the product and on intention to buy the product are asked of individuals in the control groups. They are not shown the commercial. The test group is shown the commercial and then asked the same battery of questions. Differences between the two groups' responses are measured and analyzed. The cost of such a method is about $1800 per group.

Theatre tests are conducted with a large group of people selected according to demographic characteristics, who have agreed to go to a theatre at a certain time to preview a television program. The time period may be during lunch time on weekdays, or in the evening, or during the weekend. The television program shown contains commercials to be pre-tested. After the program is played, respondents are asked to answer a questionnaire designed to assess the effects of the test commercial, and how it achieves the advertiser's communication task. A theatre test is relatively expensive, however, takes place in an artificial setting, and

tends to measure only verbal communication elements. Nevertheless, it is a useful diagnostic tool for copy testing.

The best known theatre test in Canada is the *Clucas method,* which can be used for both rough and finished commercials. About 100 respondents are randomly selected and asked to go to an auditorium one evening to view a twenty-five minute program.

LABORATORY TECHNIQUES. This type of advertising copy pre-testing is not commonly used in Canada but may become more popular. In the *laboratory* type of experiments consumers are exposed to a message and their reactions observed, recorded, and measured with sophisticated equipment. What these instruments measure is still being debated, and the techniques of measurement are still being developed. Some of these techniques are:

The *eye-movement* camera[27] records the path of eye travel as a respondent looks at a message. It can test layout or determine if and how the copy is read.

Pupilometric devices measure a respondent's pupil dilation as a message is shown. These changes may be correlated to the attention level and emotional responses of the respondent, but more work is needed to validate the technique.[28]

The *psychogalvanometer* measures the level of perspiration on the hand of the respondent, which is correlated with interest in the message. Here, too, more development is needed to validate the technique.[29]

Electroencephalographs (EEGs) measure brain wave activity as a respondent views the message.[30] Its use is still limited.

Voice-pitch analysis is a computer analysis of changes in voice pitch of a respondent reacting verbally to viewing a message. It is assumed that voice pitch correlates with emotional reaction to the message.[31]

A *tachistoscope* is a device for varying the length of exposure to a message and then measures the rate of perception and comprehension of the advertising message. It allows advertisers to test a message for its effectiveness in gaining attention and registering the brand name in the context of quick exposure, as for outdoor, or with high clutter in magazines or television. Of all the laboratory techniques, this is probably the most commonly used.

The *Facial Action Coding System* (FACS) consists in recording respondents' facial expressions as they view a commercial. From the subtle muscle movements recorded by the camera are identified various emotions generated by different parts of the commercial.

Copy Post-Testing

There are three basic methods of testing copy after the message has appeared in print or broadcast media: the day-after-recall (DAR) method, the Starch recognition method, and the split-run method.

DAY-AFTER-RECALL. The day-after-recall (DAR) method is used to test television commercials and may be used to test radio commercials. The day after a commercial is first aired, a telephone survey is conducted with about 150 randomly selected target group members who saw the commercial. They are asked to recall and play back the commercial's main messages and to indicate what they liked or disliked. Results are then compared to norms developed for each product category. Reporting of results is usually fast. One drawback is that only recall of verbal communication elements is available. Because the test is done on one exposure only, it does not measure the effects of multiple exposures.

STARCH METHOD. The Starch recognition method was developed in 1921 by Daniel Starch. It measures the degree to which a print advertisement is seen and read.[32] The method uses a through-the-book or recognition technique for a particular issue of a publication, after a suitable waiting period to give readers the

opportunity to read the issue. This period varies from two days for a daily publication to three weeks for a monthly one. Starch uses a minimum of 100 readers per sex, who are sampled according to the target audience's geographic and demographic distribution.

Interviewers carry a copy of the test issue, coded according to the list of advertisements to be tested and the starting point of the interview. Each interviewer is assigned a different starting point in order to minimize the order effect. To minimize boredom, no more than 90 items are tested with one respondent. The interviewer follows the same procedure with each respondent who meets the quota requirements, who has read or looked through the particular issue of the publication, and who agrees to cooperate. With the issue at hand, and starting from the assigned page, the interviewer turns the pages and asks a series of questions about each advertisement to be studied, such as seeing and reading the headline, the illustration, the brand name, the signature, and the copy blocks.

For each advertisement, the respondent is classified as follows:

1. Ad-as-a-Whole: A "Noted" reader if the respondent has previously seen this advertisement; *an "Associated" reader* if the respondent also saw or read some part of the advertisement that clearly indicated the brand or the advertiser; *a "Read Most" reader* if the respondent read half or more of the written material in the advertisement.

2. Copy blocks. A "Read Some" reader if the respondent read some of the copy.

3. Headline, slogan, signature or illustration. The appropriate item is checked if the respondent saw the illustration or the signature or read the headline, or the slogan.

After all advertisements have been tested, the interviewer ends the interview by asking some basic demographic data for cross-tabulation purposes.

Data from all interviews are compiled and analyzed and a report is sent to all subscribers.

This *Starch Readership Report* contains the following items:

1. A labelled issue of the magazine that is a copy of the study issue with labels affixed on the tested advertisements and that contains the percentage of some group of readers (e.g., male adults) in each of the previous categories. A sample page of a labelled advertisement is provided in Figure 15.13.

2. A summary report listing the summary readership figures for all tested advertisements and arranged according to the product category and insertion size. Also included in the report are the advertisement rank in the issue according to the numbers of readers, and readership indexes based on the issue median.

FIGURE 15.13   A sample page from a labelled issue of a Starch Report. The results are given for male readers and the illustration, headline, slogan, and signature were tested.
Courtesy Starch INRA Hooper

3. Adnorm data reports contain figures for two years of the study publication. These are used to compare results with a norm for a similar advertisement (in size and colour).

Interpretation of these numbers may be done along the following lines: the "noted" score may relate to attention to the advertisement; the "associated" score may relate to recognition of the brand name, i.e., the source of the message; the "read-most" score may relate to interest or involvement in the message. The pattern among this set of numbers for this advertisement and for competitive ones may be useful for pinpointing copy or layout problems.

The Starch readership service is a reasonable and relatively inexpensive test of an advertisement, particularly the copy elements, in an actual environment.

By analyzing results across a number of advertisements and campaigns, the researcher may be able to determine actionable trends and principles, which are then communicated to the creative director. But the method does have methodological weaknesses in terms of sampling and measurement. In particular, the "recognized" advertisement may have been seen in previous issues or in other magazines. This potential overstatement should be kept in mind when using this method.

SPLIT-RUN METHOD. The split-run method is a controlled experiment in which one version of an advertisement is printed in half the issues of a publication, and the other version in the other half. Many parts of the advertisement's copy may be tested with this method. Each advertisement contains some form of offer calling for a response from the reader. Each advertisement is coded in order to trace the responses and to determine which one generated the largest number of responses.

This method is used with newspapers and magazines and will come into use in broadcast media when dual cable systems become more common. This method is ideally suited to direct mail where many variations are possible.

Information for Controlling the Advertising Program

The fourth type of research that advertisers undertake concerns the effects of advertising campaigns *after* the campaign has been executed. These effects may be tested by using various research designs. In addition, the advertising researcher needs to know *what* to measure and *when* to measure them.

Effectiveness Research Designs

Depending on the research budget and the complexity of the sampling procedure, the research designs are based on the number of measurement points and the use of a control group. There are four simple research designs.

The first design uses a single group after the campaign has run and is the least expensive. There is no benchmark, however, to which results can be compared, unless the information is available by other means. It is often used to check consumers' reaction to the campaign, but as mentioned in Chapter 11, this is often not sufficient.

The second design uses two groups after the campaign has run, with one group exposed to the campaign and one control group not exposed to it. The main assumption is that both populations had the same level of the measured variable(s) before the campaign started and that environmental conditions were the same during the campaign. This design has the merit of isolating the effect of the campaign from other effects, for example, from distribution or competitive advertising.

The third design also uses two groups, one before the campaign starts and the other after it has run. The main problem with this design is that the effects of the campaign often cannot be isolated from the effects of such other variables as distribution or competitive advertising, even when the same measures are made of the other brands. Nevertheless, this design is often preferable to the previous one.

The fourth design uses four groups and combines the advantages of the previous two designs. Two populations are identified, one of which is to be exposed to the advertising campaign. Then one group is selected in each population before the campaign starts. After the campaign has ended, another group is selected in each population. The differences between both groups represent the changes that would have taken place without the campaign. The effects of the campaign are measured by subtracting the changes recorded in the control groups to those recorded in the test groups. Because it involves four groups of respondents, this design is the most expensive of the four.

Testing the Effectiveness of the Campaign

Depending on how the advertising objectives have been stated, advertisers measure the effects of an advertising campaign on intermediate variables, such as consumer awareness, brand recall, brand preference, attitude toward the brand, or *when possible*, on the end variable, which is sales. It may be useful here to review Table 11.1 for the relationship between objectives and advertising effectiveness research.

Research into the communication effects of advertising attempts to measure how effectively a campaign has moved consumers up the first two levels of the hierarchy of effects—the cognitive and affective levels. The cognitive level involves effects on brand awareness and knowledge of brand attributes. The affective level involves effects on variables such as liking and preference and is generally much more difficult to test.

The hierarchy of effect models has been criticized because of its failure to explain several types of consumer behaviour. For example, a

consumer may prefer a brand only after it has been tried or a may try a product only because it was received as a gift. Therefore some advertisers try to measure the effects of advertising on sales. In terms of the above-mentioned hierarchy, these advertisers are only interested in the *conative* stage of consumer behaviour. Methods that directly measure the advertising-sales relationship include experiments, econometric methods, and mathematical models. But, as was mentioned, sales are the result of many factors besides advertising (including each of three other P's of the marketing mix), and the effect of advertising on sales has not yet been satisfactorily established.

Objectives with Cognitive Variables

When advertising campaign objectives are expressed in terms of such cognitive variables as awareness or recall of copy, advertisers may use a syndicated service, participate in an omnibus study, or conduct a special research project often by using telephone interviewing.

If the communication task is to *change brand awareness*, the test criteria may be top-of-mind recall, unaided recall, share-of-mind recall, or aided recall. *Top-of-mind recall* of a brand is the percentage of individuals mentioning this brand as the first one that comes to mind. *Unaided recall* of a brand is the percentage of individuals mentioning this brand when asked to name all brands of which they can think. *Share-of-mind recall* of a brand is the percentage of all brands mentioned unaided. It may also be obtained by normalizing unaided recall scores. Finally, *aided recall* of a brand is the percentage of individuals indicating that they have heard of a brand when presented with a list of brand names. For any of these measures, the result is generally compared with the target defined in the statement of advertising objectives.

If an advertiser wants to measure whether a campaign has had a strong impact and in what media, research questions are intended to determine *advertising awareness*, either unaided or aided. An unaided measure would be to ask if the respondent has heard, seen and/or read any advertising message for a product category, and if yes, for which brand(s). An aided measure would be to ask if the respondent has heard, seen, and/or read any advertising for Brand X. In both cases, follow-up questions ask which of a list of media the advertising messages appeared in.

If the communication task is to increase *knowledge* about the brand's attributes, test criteria may ask for recall of copy points, brand identification, importance, believability and exclusiveness of copy claims. *Recall of copy points* measures the amount and type of information about the brand that the respondent remembered. It measures only what the respondent can remember from the advertising campaign, and thus does not measure the full extent of the communication, e.g., changes in the amount of information about the brand due to the campaign. The latter may be done by measuring *brand identification* before and after the campaign, i.e., how much a respondent knows about a particular brand.[33] As seen in Chapter 8, for a communication to be effective, the source must be credible and the respondent must *believe* the claims made in the copy. Otherwise, even if the claims are learned by the respondent, they may not be used in the latter stages leading to purchase.

Two other measures testing copy claims may shed some light on the communication's effectiveness during the campaign. The *saliency or importance* of the copy claims can be measured when the advertiser aims at positioning the brand along dimensions that are important to the respondent. Also, among the important claims a respondent remembers are some that are common to competitive brands, and some are particular to the advertiser's brand. It is the *exclusiveness* of the advertiser's copy claims that should be measured.

Objectives with Affective and/or Conative Variables

When the advertising campaign objectives are stated in terms of affective and/or conative variables, such as attitudes or preference ranking or trial, advertisers tend to use a custom designed research project, often with personal interviews. Three types of information may be collected.

If the communication task is stated in terms of brand *liking*, the test criteria measure attitude and attitude change as well as inclusion in the evoked set or brand satisfaction. By recording *attitudes* toward the brand, advertisers determine if the brand is viewed positively by the target market. *Attitude change* measures the campaign's effect on the target market's attitude toward the brand and is a better measure of the communication's persuasiveness. Measuring inclusion of the brand in consumers' *evoked set*[34] is an important indication that the brand has been properly positioned, for brands in the evoked set have a much higher chance of being purchased.[35] Measuring *brand satisfaction* helps advertisers determine problems with the brand or if the product is unsatisfactory in view of the copy claims.

If the task of the communication is *brand preference*, the test criteria measure attitude or preference ranking. Here an advertiser wants to know if the brand is the most liked or preferred brand among all major competing brands. *Preference ranking* may be measured by asking a straight ranking of the brand, or by making pairwise comparisons. Changes in the brand position before and after the campaign is often a good measure of the effectiveness of the advertising strategy.

If the task of communication is in terms of *conviction* or *trial*, the test criteria measure intention to buy or to try the brand. *Intention to buy* may be measured by asking the degree of intention to purchase the brand within a specific period. Another measure may be in terms of probability to purchase that brand. A third measure may be to ask to indicate the brand(s) to be bought in the next 10, 20, or 100 purchases of the product category. *Trial* may be asked directly and the length of time should be consistent with the length of the campaign. More important are the reasons for trial or non-trial of the brand, which may indicate how the campaign affected the trial rate. This is particularly important for a new product, a new service, or an idea such as energy conservation.[36]

Measuring the Wearout Factor

Studies have shown that television commercials have an initial impact on the audience, but with subsequent exposure to the same commercial, attention, recall, and liking level off and ultimately decline.[37] This phenomenon is called *wearout*.

To reduce wearout, advertisers have used three strategies to enhance attention to the message and, thus, its effectiveness. First, the inter-exposure time is increased to allow some forgetting to occur, particularly with humorous commercials. Since frequency declines, the exposure value of the campaign is reduced. Second, multiple executions of the message are used to maintain frequency and allow some forgetting of each execution to take place. This strategy is quite expensive, however, since the cost of production is increased by multiples of the number of executions. Third, attention to the message can be increased by dominating the media environment and lowering the level of clutter. This strategy is also expensive, since the impact of the campaign must be increased.

Television commercial wearout can occur even if these strategies are used.[38] Thus, careful consideration is necessary to weigh the benefits of various strategies against the additional costs, since more research on the wearout factor is needed.

Tracing the Effects on Sales

As was mentioned in Chapter 11, a natural inclination is to judge the results of an advertising campaign in terms of sales. Several kinds of research may be conducted to determine the relationship between sales and other variables. Some of these studies were described in Chapter 10 and will not be reviewed here. Instead, this section provides an overview of various approaches to the problem of tracing the effects of advertising on sales.

Researchers can study the *evolution* of a previous variable and compare it to sales figures of the product. The problem with this method is that sales may be affected by other factors during the same time period, and it is risky to attribute the changes in sales figures to advertising. A better procedure is to gather information on such other factors as price, competitive advertising, and distribution coverage, and to relate sales to all the relevant factors, including advertising.[39] Techniques such as multiple regression analysis may be used.

Another variable in relating advertising to sales is the *time*: when does an advertising campaign take effect and for how long (the carry-over effect). These effects were discussed in Chapter 11, in the context of economic models of budget setting. Techniques that may be used here are spectral analysis of time series[40] and econometric techniques.[41]

Still another category of research includes all *controlled experiments* in which the advertising component is manipulated while other factors are left reasonably constant. This method is useful mainly when an advertiser is interested in the *short-term effect* of advertising on sales. One example of such a study involved placing advertisements in daily newspapers in six cities. In each city, two matched samples of home delivery routes were selected, one test group and one control group. About 30 hours after delivery of the morning newspaper, about 200 housewives in each of the two matched groups and the six cities were personally interviewed. On the average, researchers found that the group exposed to the advertisement purchased 14 per cent more of the test brand than the control group. It was also found that although most advertisements did produce some positive results, three out of 31 advertisements actually produced *negative* results.[42]

This method can be used by broadcast media with a dual cable system covering the same market, thus controlling for many variables. Other forms of controlled experiments are split-run tests, direct-mail experiments, and tests of retail advertising based on short-term deals, specials, and rebates, as well as for market tests in which the advertising effort or strategy is manipulated across various test markets.

Summary

Advertising research is an integral part of the advertising plan. Advertisers can use general sources of information for advertising decision making, as well as the methods used to obtain and analyze information.

Various kinds of research are done at each stage in the planning, execution, and control of the campaign. Market or consumer research may be either qualitative or quantitative. Media research is used to measure audiences, as well as exposure patterns to media types and media vehicles. Media information is available from syndicated services, media or industry associations, or through custom studies.

Copy research is useful in determining whether the message is properly designed by the creative group and properly understood by the target audience. Methods for copy research involve projective techniques, in-depth interviews, direct questioning, laboratory techniques, and post-testing techniques.

The effectiveness of the campaign as set out in the campaign objectives may be assessed in order to control the budget. Various research designs may be used. Depending on the communication task, emphasis may be put on cognitive measures (awareness), affective measures (attitude), or conative measures (trial). There are several methods available for determining the effect of advertising on sales.

Questions for Study

1. "Research is the last thing I want to include in my advertising budget." Do you agree? Comment.

2. Compare the Nielsen and BBM services for television media research. Evaluate the research methodology of these two companies, particularly their sampling procedures.

3. What are the problems associated with the use of sophisticated laboratory equipment for copy testing?

4. What are the strengths and weaknesses of the day-after-recall method for copy testing?

5. Why is it so difficult to measure the extent of the effects of an advertising campaign in the field?

6. Explain what each of the Ad-As-A-Whole Starch scores measures and compare them. How would you use them, and which one would you use most often? Answer the same question for the other types of score, i.e., copy blocks, headlines, slogan, signature, and illustration.

7. What are the advantages and disadvantages of pre-testing advertisements? Answer the same question for post-testing. Compare the two methods.

8. What should be the relationship between the advertising research group and the creative group? Between the research group and the account service group? What do you see as potential conflicts, and how can these be avoided?

9. Should research on campaign effectiveness be part of every advertising plan? Comment.

10. Is copy testing a necessary research activity for each advertising campaign? Explain.

Problems

1. Assume that you are the advertising manager of Camelback, a moving company in your town, and that you are advertising on radio during May-June in order to increase awareness of your name during the heavy moving season. You have to develop a complete research program in order to evaluate the effects of your campaign. Write a complete campaign evaluation plan along the lines described in Chapter 11, including the choice of the survey method, the sampling methodology, and the questionnaire that you will be using.

2. An insurance company wants to estimate the market potential for a new kind of life insurance it contemplates selling in the Maritimes. The ideal universe is defined as all the households in the Maritimes that have not yet subscribed to a life insurance policy. Because he wants to obtain a certain precision level in the results, the company statistician tells the marketing manager that for a probability sample he should get about 1000 answers. Which survey methods would you recommend (i.e., telephone, mail, or personal survey)? Why? What are the problems likely to be encountered with each method?

Notes

1. For a discussion of experimental designs, see, for instance, Donald T. Campbell and Julian C. Stanley, *Experimental and Quasi-Experimental Designs for Research* (Chicago: Rand McNally and Co., 1963).
2. See, for instance, Seymour Banks, *Experimentation in Marketing* (New York: McGraw-Hill, 1965).
3. Thomas E. Muller, "Information Load at the Point of Purchase: Extending the Research," *Marketing*, ed. Michel Laroche (Administrative Sciences Association of Canada, 1982), pp. 193-202.
4. Stanley L. Payne, *The Art of Asking Questions* (Princeton, N.J.: Princeton University Press, 1951).
5. Sampling is discussed in great detail in Morris H. Hansen, William N. Hurwitz, and William G. Neadow, *Sample Survey Methods and Theory*, vol. 2 (New York: John Wiley and Sons, 1953).
6. Douglas J. Tigert, James G. Barnes, and Jacques C. Bourgeois, "Research on Research: Mail Panel Versus Telephone Survey in Retail Image Analysis," *The Canadian Marketer* (Winter 1975), pp. 22-27.
7. Ibid.
8. Ethical problems in marketing research have been discussed, for instance, by George S. Day,

"The Threat to Marketing Research," *Journal of Marketing Research* (November 1975); George S. Day and Adrian B. Ryans, "The Changing Environment in Marketing Research in Canada," *Problems in Canadian Marketing*, ed. Donald N. Thompson (Chicago: American Marketing Association, 1977), pp. 203-22.
9. A good treatment of statistical multivariate techniques applied to marketing is given in Paul E. Green and Donald S. Tull, *Research for Marketing Decisions,* 3rd ed. (Englewood Cliffs, N.J.: Prentice-Hall, 1975).
10. Paul E. Green and Frank J. Carmone, *Multidimensional Scaling and Related Techniques in Marketing Analysis* (Boston: Allyn and Bacon, 1970).
11. Examples of application of techniques to marketing problems can be found in David A. Aaker, *Multivariate Analysis in Marketing: Theory and Application* (Belmont, Cal.: Wadsworth Publishing, 1971); Jagdish N. Sheth, ed., *Multivariate Methods for Market and Survey Research* (Chicago: American Marketing Association, 1977).
12. See, for instance, Ludovic Lebart and Jean-Pierre Fenelon, *Statistique et Informatique Appliquées*, 3rd ed. (Paris: Dunod, 1975).

13. René Y. Darmon, "Multiple Joint Space Analysis for Improved Advertising Strategy," *The Canadian Marketer*, 10 (1979), 10-14.

14. A more complete treatment is given in David B. Montgomery and Glen L. Urban, *Management Science in Marketing* (Englewood Cliffs, N.J.: Prentice-Hall, 1969); and in Philip Kotler, *Marketing Decision Making: A Model Building Approach* (New York: Holt, Rinehart and Winston, 1971).

15. Roger G. Calantone and Donald H. Drury, "Advertising Agency Compensation: A Model for Incentive and Control," *Management Science* (July 1979), pp. 632-42.

16. John D.C. Little, "Models and Manager: The Concept of a Decision Calculus," *Management Science* (April 1970) pp. 466-485.

17. Glenn L. Urban, "Perceptor: A Model for Product Positioning," *Management Science*, 21 (April 1975), 858-71.

18. Jo Marney, "Beyond the Six Ps of Market Research," *Marketing*, 25 April 1983, p. 8.

19. Canadian Advertising Research Foundation (Toronto).

20. "Twenty-one Ad Agencies Endorse Copy Testing Principles," *Marketing News*, 19 February 1982, pp. 1, 9.

21. George H. Smith, *Motivation Research in Advertising and Marketing* (New York: McGraw-Hill, 1954); Rena Bartos and Arthur S. Pearson, "The Founding Fathers of Advertising Research: Ernest Dichter: Motive Interpreter," *Journal of Advertising Research* (June 1977), p. 4.

22. Keith J. Cox, James B. Higginbotham, and John Burton, "Applications of Focus Group Interviews in Marketing," *Journal of Marketing* (January 1976), p. 79; Bobby J. Calder, "Focus Groups and the Nature of Qualitative Marketing Research," *Journal of Marketing Research* (August 1977), pp. 353-64.

23. Mason Haire, "Projective Techniques in Marketing Research," *Journal of Marketing* (April 1950), pp. 649-56.

24. Mark Lowell, "Pretests Taking the Lead," *Creativity* (Spring 1980), pp. 27-28.

25. Haire pp. 649-56.

26. Cox et al.; Calder pp. 353-64.

27. Norman H. Mackworth, "A Stand Camera for Line-of-Sight Recording," *Perception and Psychophysics* (March 1967), pp. 119-27.

28. Roger D. Blackwell, James S. Hensel, and Brian Sternthal, "Pupil Dilation: What Does it Measure," *Journal of Advertising Research*, 10, no. 4 (1970), 15-18.

29. "Psychogalvanometer Testing Most Productive," *Marketing News*, 16 June 1978, p. 11.

30. Herbert E. Krugman, "Brain Wave Measures of Media Involvement," *Journal of Advertising Research*, 11, no. 1 (1971), 3-9.

31. "Voice Analysis May Give Insights into Consumer Advertising Attitudes," *Product Marketing* (April 1977), pp. 14-17.

32. For outdoor posters, Starch uses a port-a-scope, which shows a poster with varying threshold levels, from one to five seconds. The respondent is questioned after each of the three exposures.

33. John A. Howard, *Consumer Behavior: Application of Theory* (New York: McGraw-Hill, 1977), pp. 46-49.

34. Ibid., p. 32.

35. Jacques E. Brisoux and Michel Laroche, "Evoked Set Formation and Composition: An Empirical Investigation in a Routinized Response Behavior Situation," *Advances in Consumer Research*, ed. Kent B. Monroe, Vol. 8 (Chicago: Association for Consumer Research, 1980), pp. 357-61; see also Michel Laroche and Jacques E. Brisoux, "A Test of Competitive Effects in the Relationship Among Attitudes and Intentions," *The Changing Marketing Environment: New Theories and Applications*, ed. Ken Bernhardt et al. (Chicago: American Marketing Association, 1981), pp. 213-16.

36. Gordon H.G. McDougall, "Cognitive Responses to Advertising Messages: A Diagnostic," *Marketing*, ed. Robert G. Wyckham (Administrative Sciences Association of Canada, 1981), pp. 205-15.

37. Bobby J. Calder and Brian Sternthal, "Television Commercial Wearout: An Information Proces-

sing View," *Journal of Marketing Research* (May 1980), pp. 173-86.

38. Ibid., p. 186.

39. N.K. Dhalla and S. Yuspeh, "Forget the Product Life-Cycle Concept," *Harvard Business Review* (January-February 1976), pp. 102-12; see also the discussion in Kenneth G. Hardy, "Procedures and Problems in Evaluating Sales Promotions," in *Marketing*, vol. 4, ed. James D. Forbes, (Administrative Sciences Association of Canada, 1983), pp. 142-50.

40. C.W.J. Granger and M. Hatanaka, *Spectral Analysis of Economic Times Series* (Princeton, N.J.: Princeton University Press, 1964).

41. Richard F. Quandt, "Estimating Advertising Effectiveness and Some Pitfalls in Econometric Methods," *Journal of Marketing Research* (May 1964), p. 60; Kristian S. Palda, *The Measurement of Cumulative Advertising Effects* (Englewood Cliffs, N.J.: Prentice-Hall, 1964).

42. Leo Bogart, B. Stuart Tolley, and Frank Orenstein, "What One Little Ad Can Do," *Journal of Advertising Research*, 10 (August 1970), 3-13.

CAMPAIGN HISTORIES FOR PART 4

1. Royale Bathroom Tissue

2. The Montreal Expos

3. Wonder Cola 1985 Campaign

CAMPAIGN HISTORY 1

ROYALE BATHROOM TISSUE
Developing a Campaign with High Borrowed Interest from White Persian Kittens

ADVERTISER: Facelle Company Ltd.
AGENCY: F. H. Hayhurst

Situation

The bathroom tissue market is a highly developed and competitive one. Volume growth has paralleled population growth and there are no seasonal skews to purchases.

In the Canadian market there are five major brands, six generic, and a host of private label brands.

At launch of advertising, Royale was the only two-ply bathroom tissue on the market. This product differentiation offered Facelle a competitive advantage to its advertising. Since Royale's two plies were stronger than one-ply tissues, Facelle could legitimately claim that their bathroom tissue was both *strong and absorbent*. The two-ply construction provided a rationale for the consumer benefit as well as substantiating Royale's premium price.

This situation did not prevail for long, however, as competition soon saw that the marketplace was strongly attracted to two-ply tissue. Soon there were a number of competitors vying for this segment of the market. Facelle's follow-up consumer research and brand audits began to indicate that consumers rated softness as a more important attribute for bathroom tissue than strength and absorbency. This dictated a change in strategy.

Predicated on this consumer research, it was decided to focus advertising on *softness*.

Creative Strategy/Execution

The creative strategy required that Facelle Royale be presented as a premium-quality bathroom tissue that is extremely soft yet strong. Based on this strategy, the "Kittens" commercial was created.

The commercial setting, a white-on-white bathroom with soft white shag carpet everywhere, contributes to the impression of softness that the spot makes. The sound track with its simple message and haunting quality amplifies the singleminded softness message as does the announcer voice-over and the signature, "The Soft Touch".

Central to the effectiveness of the execution, however, are the white Persian kittens—an ingenious and compelling metaphor. Without clumsy and often hollow words this visual metaphor symbolizes the softness, the purity, and the gentleness inherent in Facelle Royale bathroom tissue. The kittens clawing at the tissue expresses a certain quality of strength. At the same time the kittens have created a unique and enviable personality for Royale—there is an innocence, a guilelessness, a believability, and a charm about Royale that, given competitors' efforts to epitomize softness in their advertising, is the envy of the market category. Plus, the eminent "watchability" of the kittens supplies enormous borrowed interest in a very low-interest category.

Media Strategy

In addition to delivering large numbers of prospects (women 25-49) efficiently, television with its dimensions of sight, sound, and motion, provided the best medium to present the brand image of softness.

Periodically, for a change of pace, the brand employed print in the form of outdoor posters, newspapers, and magazines, but always with the visual of a kitten uppermost. Despite these forays into alternate media, television was consistently the primary medium.

Since the launch of the "Kittens" commercial, most major brands have built their advertising themes and brand images on the claim of outstanding softness. Cottonelle uses testimonials/consumer comments in the advertising to convey that their product is "soft as cotton". Delsey claims to be "soft as a cloud"—softer, fluffier, and more absorbent. Similar emphasis on softness as the primary benefit is seen in Purex advertising—"pillowy soft"; White Swan—"soft as a swan"; Charmin advertising—"squeezably soft"; and so on.

Results

As a result of advertising, Facelle enjoyed increased market share on an equivalent case index basis as follows:

	1977	1978	1979	1980	1981
Royale B.T.	100	104	113	121	121

Furthermore the "Kittens" commercial was an outstanding creative success.

The visual metaphor that is the kittens has built an emotional bridge between Royale and the viewer's life. Thus the kittens have become one of the most recognized and most loved mnemonic devices in Canadian advertising.

In its first year, 1974, the commercial won the *Marketing Magazine* award as the best TV commercial in its category.

The print ad received almost perfect Starch scores and was even acclaimed in the U.S., where it received the American Newspaper Publishers' award as the outstanding four-colour ad of the year.

In 1977 the Kitten billboard won runner-up in the quarterly *Outdoor Advertising* competition, and in that same year both *Homemaker's* magazine and *Reader's Digest* used the print ad in their new business presentation. The accolades did not stop there. Simpson's re-designed the front cover of their health and beauty aid catalogue to feature the Royale kitten and Royale product line.

The Future

Unlike many commercials, which would have experienced "wear-out" with such extensive exposure, the Royale "Kittens" commercial still elicits desired consumer responses.

Creative research conducted in 1981 demonstrated that the perception of Royale softness is still conveyed by the commercial, and no major signs of viewer boredom or wear-out were evidenced.

The kittens visual is so closely tied to Royale that it has become an extremely valuable franchise that will be retained and enhanced whenever possible.

In 1982 the Royale package graphics will be changed to include a visual of the kittens, thereby creating further synergism with advertising. The kittens are now synonymous with Royale bathroom tissue. The raison d'être of the package is based on image transference and the equity established through advertising. The new package dictates new creative. Assuredly, the kittens will not be abandoned as the visual device used to connote softness.

EXHIBIT 1 Print advertisement for Royale with a mail-in, product-related, self-liquidating premium—a Royale kitten.

EXHIBIT 2

CAMPAIGN HISTORY 2

THE MONTREAL EXPOS
Advertising a Baseball Club to the Home Audience in 1983

ADVERTISER: Montreal Baseball Club Ltd.
AGENCY: Jean Lévcillé & Associés Inc.

Marketing Objectives

For the 1983 campaign, the marketing objectives are:
1. to bring the baseball enthusiasts along to buy several tickets for several games of the Montreal Expos;
2. to broaden the base of baseball lovers who buy tickets;
3. to maintain some continuity in the new communication program;
4. to maintain the good image of the Expos among the public, the media, and sports organizations.

Advertising Objectives and Strategies

Target audiences

The primary target audience for 1983 is selected as non-buyers, men and women, aged 30 years and more (66 per cent), and earning $25,000 or more (39 per cent). These have the highest potential among ticket buyers.

The secondary target audience is selected as buyers, men (77 per cent), between the ages of 15 and 40 (68 per cent), franco-phones (84 per cent), and earning $25,000 or more (64 per cent).

Geographic Location

The primary market area is the Montreal metropolitan area, where 76 per cent of ticket buyers are located. A secondary area comprises Three Rivers, Sherbrooke, Ottawa-Hull, and Plattsburg-Burlington, where 9 per cent of ticket buyers are located.

Advertising Promise (Theme)

Going to see the Expos at the Olympic Stadium is an event totally satisfying when shared with family or friends.

Creative Plan and Rationale

First, as a pre-campaign (December to February), we produce three pamphlets aimed at buyers of season tickets, mini-season tickets, and group tickets. Second, the objective of the 1983 campaign is to bring non-buying baseball fans to Olympic Stadium. We propose to use two radio commercials and transit panels (subways and buses). In addition, the second group (buyers) is given information on the various season tickets through two print advertisements. One is directed to the entire public and the other to businesspersons.

Supports to Promise

The strategy is to convey the idea that to be in Olympic Stadium watching the Montreal Expos is to:

• please family members and friends
• relax
• participate in the excitement of the game
• enjoy oneself in the outdoors.

Copy Platforms

The primary target audience should be very receptive to a slogan that confers on baseball and the Expos a high social acceptability, respect, and admiration. The slogan must also contain the reasons for coming to the stadium. For one person, it may be an outing; for another, a picnic, and so on. We need a short slogan that conveys all these benefits. We need to find the idea of total pleasure in being at the stadium and living a social, sensorial, fun experience.

Thus, the selected slogan is:
"See the Expos at the stadium . . . *the summertime treat.*"

The art treatment amplifies the slogan. It uses a baseball-apple—the fruit of temptation, the temptation of trying it yourself.

In the radio commercials, we used common people: kids in the first one; in the second one, a husband and a wife in conversation. The tone is light and humourous, emphasizing the temptation of going to see the Expos at the stadium.

Media Objectives

The media objectives of the 1983 campaign are:

1. to reach as efficiently as possible the following two groups:
primary (weight 80 per cent): non-buyers, between the ages of 30 and 59, residing in the Montreal metropolitan area, with a family income of $25,000 or more, with high school completed;
secondary (weight 20 per cent): male francophone buyers, between the ages of 15 and 40, residing in the Montreal metropolitan area, with a family income of more than $25,000;

2. to maximize the impact in (order of priority):
  • the Montreal metropolitan area;
  • towns located within 100 miles;
  • Burlington and Plattsburg;

3. to maximize reach and frequency within the appropriation;

4. to schedule advertising to coincide with selling periods;
  • advertisement "businessperson": week of 28 February;
  • advertisement "selling of tickets": week of 28 February;
  • beginning of the season: mid-April to mid-June.

Media Strategies and Recommendations

1. Use the following media:
  (a) radio (French and English) as the primary medium
  (b) transit posters (French) as a supportive medium
  (c) super panels (French) as a supportive medium
  (d) *TV Hebdo* (French) as a tactical medium
  (e) daily newspapers (French and English) and *Les Affaires* (French) as tactical media.

2. Advertise monthly during May and June in order to maximize the impact on the primary target audience:
  (a) radio (30-second commercial): 41 days during April, May, and June
  (b) backlight posters: 3 months (June to August)
  (c) *TV Hebdo:* 2 months (May and June)
  (d) newspapers (800 lines): week of 28 February.

Calendar of Activities

PHASE 1 (December-February):
the emphasis is on buyers and on providing information
PHASE 2 (March):
the target audience is the businessperson, and the emphasis
is on providing information
PHASE 3 (May-June):
the emphasis is on non-buyers, developing the image of the
Expos, and urging participation
PHASE 4 (April-September):
the emphasis is on promotion and image maintenance

Promotional Activity	Target Audience	
	Buyers	Non-Buyers
Radio-christmas (December)	X	X
Folders (January)	X	
Business persons (March)	X	
Mastercard holder (March)	X	X
Selling tickets (March)	X	
Season's opening (April)	X	
Transit posters (April-September)	X	X
Radio (May-June)		X
TV English (May-September)		X
Outdoor backlight panels (June-August)		X

EXHIBIT 1 Specifically Planned Activities

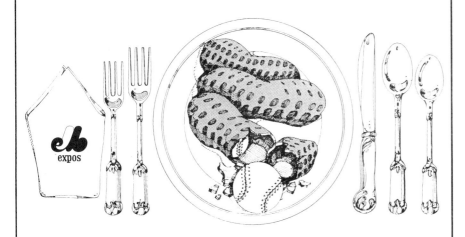

CLINCH A DEAL OVER THE EXPOS' HOME PLATE!

A business lunch is one way of pleasing your clients and friends. But if you really want to score big, treat them to Expos tickets. This year, the Expos are offering three great ticket packages.

Mix business with pleasure: offer your clients and friends tickets to Expos baseball.

For more information, call **Expos-Tel†** at **253-3434** or dial toll-free **1-800-361-6807**. Or simply fill out the coupon below and mail it to the following address:

Ticket Office
Montreal Baseball Club Ltd.
P.O. Box 500
Station M
Montreal   H1V 3P2

expos

① EXPOS-SEASON

See all **81 Expos games** in the seat of your choice. For post-season action, season tickets also give you first option on the same seats plus the chance to buy an additional ticket for each seat you hold.

Level	Total price	Regular price/ ticket	Your price/ ticket
200	$795	$10.50	$9.93
300	$660	$ 8.75	$8.25
400	$545	$ 7.50	$6.81

② EXPOS 600

Catch the **50 best games** of the season. Same advantages as season-ticket holders.

Games	Total price	Regular price/ ticket	Your price/ ticket
50	$195*	$4.75	$3.90

*At regular price, these tickets sell for $237.50

③ EXPOS 400   EXPOS-NIGHTS, EXPOS-WEEKENDS, EXPOS-SELECT   16 games

EXPOS-NIGHTS and **EXPOS-WEEKENDS:** See the Expos play **each** National League team at least once during the season.

EXPOS-SELECT: The choice is yours. Just select 16 games from the home game schedule.

Games	Total price	Regular price/ ticket	Your price/ ticket
16	$110*	$7.50	$6.87

*At regular price, these tickets sell for $120

The Expos guarantee you the best seats available at the time of purchase.

Please send me information on:
Expos-Season ☐   Expos-600 ☐   Expos 400 ☐   Please print

Name _____

Address _____   Tel _____

City _____   Postal Code _____

EXHIBIT 2   Newspaper Advertisement Directed to the Expo's Business Audience

EXHIBIT 3   Transit Poster

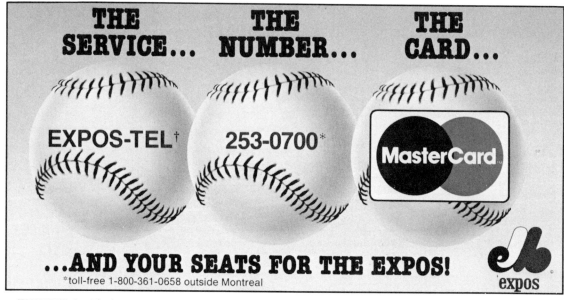

EXHIBIT 4   Tie-in Promotion with MasterCard

CAMPAIGN HISTORY 3

WONDER COLA 1985 CAMPAIGN
*Developing a Media Plan Checklist for Preparation of the Media
Strategy*

ADVERTISER: Universal Foods
PREPARED BY: Harold J. Simpkins

Media Plan Checklist

This checklist has been designed to provide a formal collection of
the data judged necessary for the development of a media plan.
The checklist ensures that no information requirement is overlooked and that a documented data source is available for
reference purposes. It is important therefore that information be
both accurate and up to date.

The completed checklist will enable the preparation of a media
strategy. Upon approval and agreement a full media plan will
then be developed. The checklist will be included as an appendix
in the final plan.

Client

ACCOUNT: Universal Foods
DIVISION: Soft Drinks
PRODUCT/SERVICE: Wonder Cola

Due Dates

CHECKLIST PREPARED: 27 April 1984
ORIGINAL/REVISED: Original
STRATEGY: 10 May 1984
PLAN—INTERNAL: 24 May 1984
PLAN—CLIENT: 1 June 1984

Timing

FISCAL YEAR: 1 Sept. 84—31 Aug. 85
CAMPAIGN PERIOD: same

Personnel

ACCOUNT STAFF: L. Martin
MEDIA SUPERVISOR: J. Roy

Budget

WORKING MEDIA: $2,000,000   NET:
PRODUCTION: $ 125,000   GROSS: X
TOTAL: $2,125,000

SPECIAL DIRECTIVES: Wonder Cola has been a sponsor of major amateur and professional sports events and programs for the past five years (i.e., baseball, hockey, football, and soccer). Historically, 40 per cent of the media budget has been to television time on selected high profile sports programs. Research and sales results have shown the allocation to be highly effective.

Regional/Language Requirements

PLAN TO PROVIDE COVERAGE: ETHNIC MEDIA COVERAGE.
                            LIST LANGUAGE REQUIREMENTS:

NATIONALLY: X   None
ENGLISH ONLY:
FRENCH ONLY:

SPECIFIC MARKET LIST:
Halifax, Sydney, St. John's, St. John, Charlottetown, Quebec City, Trois Rivières, Chicoutimi/Jonquières, Montreal, Ottawa/Hull, Kingston, Oshawa, Toronto, Hamilton, Sudbury, Timmins, North Bay, London, Kitchener, Windsor, Winnipeg, Regina, Saskatoon, Calgary, Edmonton, Vancouver, Victoria.

Objectives/Strategy

Marketing Objectives

1. To increase market share as follows:
   English Canada—from 3 per cent to 4 per cent
   French Canada—from 2 per cent to 2.5 per cent.

2. To successfully introduce new aluminum can packages to replace current tinplate cans, starting January 1, 1985. (Cans account for 35 per cent of Wonder Cola's sales; bottles represent 65 per cent of sales.)
3. To expand usage of Wonder Cola's 1-litre bottle, from 1 per cent of households to 2 per cent in English Canada, and from 0.8 per cent to 1.5 per cent in French Canada.

Marketing Strategy

1. Continue positioning as the lively, better tasting cola that is a real break from ordinary colas. Support positioning with aggressive advertising and sales promotion throughout the year, with emphasis on summer.
2. Advertising spending in Quebec will be increased by 30 per cent, and new commercials and advertisements will be produced to increase awareness and trial. A Quebec sports personality will be featured in the new advertising campaign.
3. The new aluminum can will be introduced to the distributive trade in November 1984, with advertising and sales promotion support ("Buy five get one free").
4. Distribution of the 1-litre bottle will be expanded from 40 per cent to 50 per cent nationally in supermarkets and convenience stores. Trial-inducing price-off deals supported by advertising will be offered in June and December 1984.
5. National distribution will be expanded in sports arenas and sporting events from 75 per cent to 90 per cent, and the brand will continue to be a sponsor of major sporting events and programs.

Advertising Objectives

1. Increase unaided brand awareness from 75 per cent to 85 per cent in English Canada and from 50 per cent to 70 per cent in French Canada.
2. Increase the past 12-month trial levels as follows: English Canada, from 6 per cent to 8 per cent; French Canada, from 4 per cent to 5.5 per cent.
3. Maintain a brand preference rating of 70 per cent among triers on a national basis.

4. Encourage adults who are current brand users of the 10-oz. size to purchase the 1-litre size instead of the comparable sizes of competitive brands.
5. Develop positive attitudes among Wonder Cola's user group toward the new aluminum can prior to and during its introductory stage.

Media History

Brief Details of Previous Media Plans and Budgets:
See media plan.

Target Audience

	Per cent Population	Per cent Prospects	Development Index
Sex			
Male	49.7	55.5	112
Female	50.3	44.5	88
Age			
12 - 17	10.4	20.1	193
18 - 24	13.4	28.2	210
25 - 34	17.3	20.3	117
35 - 49	17.3	14.4	83
50 - 64	14.0	5.5	39
65+	9.7	2.6	27
H/Hold Income			
Under $10M	14.6	18.5	127
$10-15M	11.7	23.0	197
$15-20M	12.7	25.7	202
$20-25M	14.1	11.2	79
$25-35M	23.0	12.5	54
$35M+	29.3	9.1	31

	Per cent Population	Per cent Prospects	Development Index
Education			
Public or Grade	21.9	27.5	126
Some High School	23.0	30.7	133
Completed High	19.4	22.7	117
Community College	19.7	10.3	52
Some University	8.0	4.6	58
Completed University	8.0	4.2	53
Occupation			
Owner/Manager			
Professional	22.9	10.5	46
Clerical	17.6	20.2	115
Sales	10.4	15.5	149
Farmer	6.2	4.2	68
Skilled	25.6	30.1	118
Other Workers	17.3	19.5	113

Other Criteria:
Wonder Cola users tend to be more physically active than the general population. They are above-average participants in and spectators of sporting activities.

Source of Population and Prospect Data: 1981 Census, Statistics Canada, and Universal Foods records.

Sales Data

By Province

	Per cent Population	Per cent Category	Sales Brand	Development Indices Market	Brand
Newfoundland	2.3	2.2	2.1	96	91
Prince Edward Island	0.5	0.5	0.4	100	80
Nova Scotia	3.5	3.4	3.3	97	94
New Brunswick	2.9	2.8	2.5	97	86
Quebec	26.4	27.5	20.1	104	76

	Per cent Population	Per cent Category	Sales Brand	Development Indices Market	Brand
Ontario	35.4	35.1	39.6	99	112
Manitoba	4.2	4.3	5.4	102	129
Saskatchewan	4.0	4.1	4.1	102	103
Alberta	9.2	8.9	10.5	97	114
British Columbia	11.3	11.0	12.0	97	106
Yukon	0.1	0.1	0.0	100	0
N.W.T.	0.2	0.1	0.0	50	0

By City Size

	Per cent Population	Per cent Category	Sales Brand	Development Indices Market	Brand
1 000 000+	29.4	31.0	33.0	107	112
100 000– 1 000 000	27.1	27.0	27.0	100	100
Under 100 000	43.5	42.0	40.0	97	92

By Month

	Per cent Sales		Monthly Indices	
	Category	Brand	Market	Brand
January	5.5	5.4	66	98
February	5.4	5.2	65	96
March	6.5	6.0	78	92
April	7.1	7.0	85	99
May	9.3	9.2	112	99
June	10.2	11.1	122	109
July	11.4	12.3	137	108
August	11.8	12.0	142	102
September	9.1	8.7	109	96
October	6.9	6.5	83	94
November	6.8	6.5	82	96
December	10.0	10.1	120	101

Other seasonal aspects, e.g., special events:

Wonder Cola is under contract to sponsor the World Series baseball games, the Stanley Cup playoffs, and the Grey Cup game.

Source of Population and Sales Data: 1981 Census, Statistics Canada; Sales: Universal Foods records

Market Shares—Competitors

Market and Brand Growth
Per cent change past year—market   2.1%
Per cent change past year—brand   5.6%

Historical comments:
Wonder Cola has outpaced market growth for the past three years.

Market Share and Position

	Share %	Position #	Significant Regional Variations:			
			Region	Share	Postion	% Change Past Year
Brand	3	5	Maritimes	2.5	6	5.0
Competition	97	—	Quebec	2.0	7	5.2
Coke	24	1	Ontario	3.8	5	6.1
Pepsi	19	2	Prairies	3.0	5	4.8
Seven-Up	8	3	B.C.	3.1	5	4.8

Production Distribution
Describe channels:
Supermarkets and convenience stores —75%
Restaurants and snack bars   —15%
Sports arenas and events   —10%

Purchase Cycle
1. Single serving sizes—daily, high impulse component
2. One litre size and larger sizes—weekly

Price
Brand: At parity prices except during special price promotions.
Competitors: Same

Competitive Activity
Highly Competitive   X
Moderate Competition
Minimal Competition
No Competition

Competitive Brands	Media Used	Estimated Budgets
Coca Cola	Television, radio, outdoor, print	$9,000,000
Pepsi Cola	Television, print	$4,500,000
Seven-Up	Television	$3,000,000

Creative Requirements/Government Regulations

Creative Requirements:
This section provides the Media planner with guidance as to the creative parameters that will be required in the selection of media. It does not necessarily represent any creative executional directives.

	Primary Requirement	Secondary Requirement	Comments/Rationale
Visual	X		
Demonstration		X	
Package identification	X		
Sound		X	
Colour		X	
Long Copy		X	
Short Copy	X		
Announcement, News Approach		X	
High Quality Reproduction		X	
Dominance		X	
Mood	X		
Other: sports/Active environment	X		

Creative Strategy
Wonder Cola will be presented as the better-tasting alternative to competitive soft drink brands, with particular appeal to teenagers and young adults who are physically active (or who perceive themselves to be so).

Government Regulations
Specify any regulations that could affect media selection/scheduling:
Do *not* schedule advertising in time periods whose audience

is composed of a majority of children under 13 years of age in Quebec.

Provincial Advertising Taxes

Indicate whether budget includes or excludes allowances for provincial taxes:
Budget *excludes* provincial taxes.

Non-Tax-Deductible Advertising

Indicate if U.S. media can be used and how non-deductibility should be accommodated:
Double estimated cost of U.S. media for budget purposes.

Spill/Promotional Plans

U.S. Spill-in Advertising

Indicate medium, commercial unit: Television—30 seconds
Print—Full page, 4 colours

Indicate compatibility in:
Packaging: Same as in Canada
Creative Strategy: Same as in English Canada only

Provide indication of weight levels, markets and seasonality:
June to August: 125 GRPs weekly television in all border markets.
April to October: Full page insertion every month in U.S. national issues of *Sports Illustrated, People, Cosmopolitan, Road & Track.*

Special Promotional Plans

Provide dates and content of plans:
January 1985—Introduction of new aluminum cans with the "Buy five, get one free" deal.
March/April 1985—Stanley Cup contest
June 1985—Trial price offer on 1-litre size
September/October 1985—World Series contest
December 1985—Trial price offer on 1 litre size

Special Client Directives

Provide details of special client requests that could affect media selection or scheduling:
1. All savings that accrue because of buying effectiveness to be returned to client.

2. Do *not* schedule advertising in vehicles with a high level of sex and/or violence.
3. When efficient, purchase time on blockbuster movies and dramatic specials.
4. If using newspapers, ensure placement in sports, food, or entertainment sections.

Attachments

List of attachments supplied for background:
1. U.S. media plan with tearsheets of U.S. print advertisements
2. Media plan for previous year
3. Analysis of major competitive promotional activities
4. Samples of competitive print and broadcast media
5. Creative strategy documentation

THE EFFECTS
OF ADVERTISING
ON CANADIAN
SOCIETY

Throughout this text, the role played by advertising in the marketing programs of Canadian consumer, industrial, and non-profit organizations has been discussed from the viewpoint of advertisers. An overview was provided of the workings of advertising in the Canadian environment, of advertising's role in a marketing program, and of the tools and techniques available to advertisers to fulfil their communication tasks. The point of view taken was a micro view of an organization communicating with its markets.

To complete the analysis, Part 5 gives a macro view of advertising's effects on Canada's economy and society.

The Economic and
Social Effects
of Advertising

Critics and advocates of advertising all too often rely on impressions rather than facts. Of course, assessing the economic and social effects of advertising (Figure 16.1) is difficult, and the complex issues involved are far from being resolved. This chapter discusses the effects of advertising on the economy and society, and examines the protections against abuses from unethical advertising practices that are available to Canadian consumers. Figure 16.1 outlines some negative and positive effects of advertising.

The Economic Effects of Advertising

The main economic consequences attributed to advertising concern consumers' information load; the process of new product development and/or product proliferation; consumer prices, through its impact on distribution costs and market competition; business cycles; and the media and media economics. These issues can be grouped into three categories (Figure 16.2). The first two—that advertising provides consumers with product and service information and enhances the new product development process—are often advanced by advocates of advertising as proof of its positive economic function. If properly fulfilled, these roles of advertising would tend to benefit the consumer. Critics of advertising argue that advertising results in increased consumer prices, through the two abovementioned effects on distribution

costs and on the market competitive structure. Thus, if this latter argument is true, advertising would also involve some disutilities to consumers. The third category is based on the fact that advertising has two important "side effects" that indirectly impinge upon consumers' welfare. They are called side effects because they do not directly affect the marketing process but have consequences for business cycles and the economics of the various media.

Advertising and Consumer Utility

Advertising and Consumers' Informational Utility
Even the most vocal critics admit that advertising's objective is to provide consumers with information about products and services. The dream of classical economists, who conceived of perfect and free information available to all consumers, bears little resemblance with the reality of the market. As was shown in Part 3, consumers look for information to make better choices and to reduce the risks of their purchase decisions. Advertising is such an information source and should fulfil the essential role of providing information on the products and services available in the marketplace.

One important way in which advertising can meet this informational objective is to build brand awareness and favourable brand images. Brand names constitute an investment for a manufacturer, because consumers can expect a certain quality level associated with a specific brand name. The role of a brand name is more important for products that involve high risks

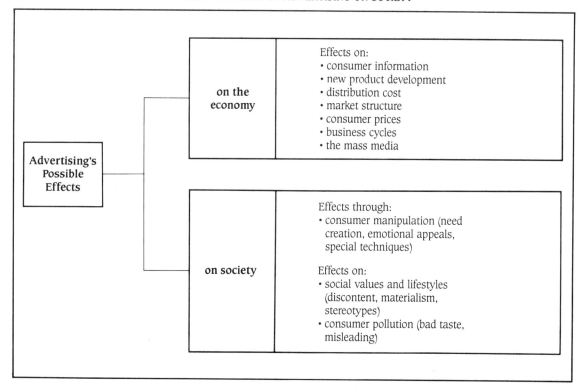

FIGURE 16.1 Possible Effects of Advertising on the Economy and on Society

for consumers and also for products whose quality consumers are not technically competent to assess directly, especially before they use the product. Thus, a well-known brand name has high informational value and an economic raison d'être. Consequently, when advertisers build a brand name or a brand image, they also build a name that has some informational value for consumers. They are then committed to delivering a product quality that is consistent with advertising claims and consumers' expectations.

Therefore deceptive advertising or advertising claims that induce consumers to make suboptimal choices constitute a disutility for these consumers, and is not in a company's best long-term interests. If advertising fails to provide consumers with *relevant* information, it is ineffective. Although critics and advocates of advertising might agree with these statements, they may disagree over what constitutes

"relevant" information. Some economists define such information as "objective" information about the technical features and/or the physical characteristics of the brand.

According to critics, only informational advertising should be permissible while so-called "persuasive" advertising should be banned. For instance, Richard Caves writes: "At the point where advertising departs from its function of informing and seeks to persuade, it tends to become a waste of resources."[1] Similar claims can be found in Roger Leroy Miller's work[2] and have been reported by Ivan Preston.[3] However, in a convincing article, Shelby Hunt has shown that the informative-persuasive advertising dilemma is a false dichotomy.[4] Using the basic concepts of information theory, Hunt shows that "if advertising critics really believe that persuasive advertising should not be permitted, they are actually proposing that no advertising be allowed, since the purpose of advertising is

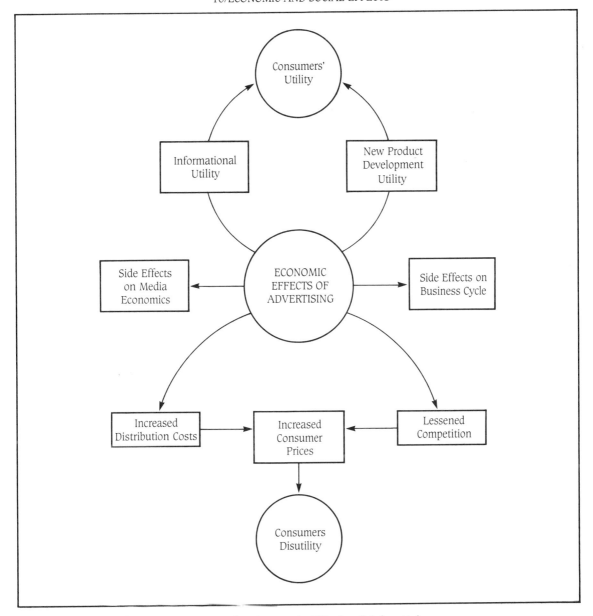

FIGURE 16.2   The Controversy on the Economic Effects of Advertising

to persuade."[5] On another possible distinction between low vs. high information content advertising, Hunt also convincingly demonstrates that the quantity of information in a message cannot be meaningfully measured independently from the quality or usefulness of the information, which in turn, is essentially "individual specific". Advertisements with a high information content for one consumer may have a low information value for another, and vice-versa. Thus, marketers who recognize that consumers use several dimensions, some objective, others subjective, to evaluate brands, would broaden the definition of what constitutes "relevant information" to include any information that consumers process to help them make a purchase decision.

In the same vein, economists who perceive the consumer as close to the "ideal" rational economic man argue that advertising designed to create certain moods or to associate products with certain lifestyles or activities is completely void of information content. In contrast, marketers have long recognized that consumer behaviour is essentially rational but is also affected by psychological, social, or cultural values, and that such motives are at least as powerful as economic motives in the consumer's logic. These marketers would argue that mood or lifestyle advertising adds to consumers' utility, since consumers buy not only physical products but also the set of meanings attached to the products.[6] The quarrel between advocates and critics of advertising can be traced to both groups' disagreement over this extended concept of a product. However, if consumers find additional value and utility in these meanings, the role of advertising should be to establish such meanings through mood or lifestyle advertising and to communicate them to the market.

Advertising and New Product Development
Advertising—and sometimes only advertising—can efficiently inform consumers about new products and innovations. If such a convenient and relatively inexpensive device were not available for communicating the existence of new products or new ideas to potential buyers, the new product development process would be seriously impaired. Without advertising, the large number of product improvements and innovations that characterize our economy might not have been possible.

Critics of advertising challenge the role of advertising in providing consumers with real new product utilities. They argue that by focusing on inconsequential product features, advertisers attempt to differentiate products in ways that are not beneficial to the consumer. Mar-

keters would answer such criticisms by saying that as long as a market segment responds positively to a certain product with specific advertised features, *knowingly and in the absence of any deceptive advertising claim*, then these consumers find some real value and satisfaction in the brand they purchase. Since what constitutes value to one customer may be worthless to another, one should guard against imposing one's value judgments on a market or on society. This endless quest for meaningful product differentiation is a powerful economic catalyst. Because firms always try to find and promote products with differential advantages, meaningful innovations often—if not always—reach the marketplace.

When properly used by companies that refrain from deceptive or exaggerated claims, advertising fulfils an essential economic role. It provides consumers with informational utility, keeping in mind that consumers need not only "objective" information but also meanings, moods, and "subjective" information. This information is often built into brand names. Consumers are also provided with utility derived from innovations that try to cater to consumer needs and desires in order to secure competitive advantages.

Obviously, there are costs attached to all these benefits. It is often difficult to find the limits between "informative" and "noninformative" advertising. In addition, non-informative advertising (as perceived by consumers) is likely to be ineffective and constitutes an economic waste. Moreover, product differentiation may be pushed to a point at which the differences do not warrant introducing a new product on the market. Much of the controversy between critics and advocates of advertising lies in their view of what constitutes "informative advertising" and "value to the consumer." Much of the difference lies in the implicit assumption made by advertising critics that consumers are "rational economic individuals," while marketers and advertisers view consumers as rational beings motivated not only by economic forces but also by psychological, social, and cultural values.

Advertising and Consumer Disutility

Among the most vocal critics of advertising are economists who advance the argument that advertising increases the prices paid by consumers for goods and services. They suggest two broad types of mechanism through which consumer prices could increase as the result of advertising: consumer prices could be inflated as the result of increased distribution costs and/or lessened competition and concentrated market structures.

Advertising and Distribution Costs
Critics of advertising claim that advertising expenditures are a waste of economic resources and that advertising expenses are often a substantial part of the good sold. Consequently, consumers in the end pay for these additional selling expenses, since the selling price must recover these costs if a company is to make a profit. This argument has been extended to all the promotional devices marketers use to enhance consumer sales.

Although this argument may seem to carry some weight, it must be seriously qualified. First, two underlying assumptions in this criticism of advertising do not always hold. The first assumption is that marketers always use a cost-oriented pricing strategy (such as cost-plus pricing). This is not always the case. If a demand-oriented pricing approach is followed—and assuming that advertising expenses can be spread without decreasing the demand for a product—then any cost reduction would not be passed on to consumers but would increase the company's profits.

The second assumption is that advertising has no definite impact on sales and that marketers could do without it at no extra cost. Obviously, this assertion is at variance with what has been discussed previously. Advertising fulfills an important information function in a marketing program. If advertising were not used for this essential marketing information function, marketers would have to use something else, for instance, personal selling, and the information cost would be transferred to other marketing expense accounts. Moreover, these costs would probably increase dramatically, because only advertising can efficiently perform certain tasks of mass communication.

Although the argument that advertising increases the retail price of goods rests on two questionable assumptions, there are strong arguments that suggest the contrary—that advertising can decrease the unit distribution cost of products. This idea is conveyed by the upper part of Figure 16.3, which shows how the unit cost of a certain product varies at different levels of output and sales. The unit cost has been split between production and advertising cost. The (M) curve presents the typical U-shaped manufacturing cost curve. As economies of scale are felt, the unit manufacturing cost drops and then increases as diseconomies of scale are involved. The lower part of the diagram represents the sales response function to advertising expenditures, which has been described in Chapter 10. Thus, if no advertising expenditures were made, the firm could probably sell a certain quantity S_0 (although a small one) because of the effects of the other elements of the marketing mix. It can be seen on the upper part of the diagram that at the S_0 sales level, the unit cost of the product could be C_0.

Now consider what happens when this firm decides to spend some money on advertising (for instance, A). These additional advertising costs should be added to the manufacturing costs. The unit advertising costs at various sales levels are respresented by the curve (C_A). This curve starts at S_0 and increases at an increasing rate ($C_A = A/S$), because the sales response gets smaller for successive equal additional increments of advertising expenditures, which is the result of the law of diminish-

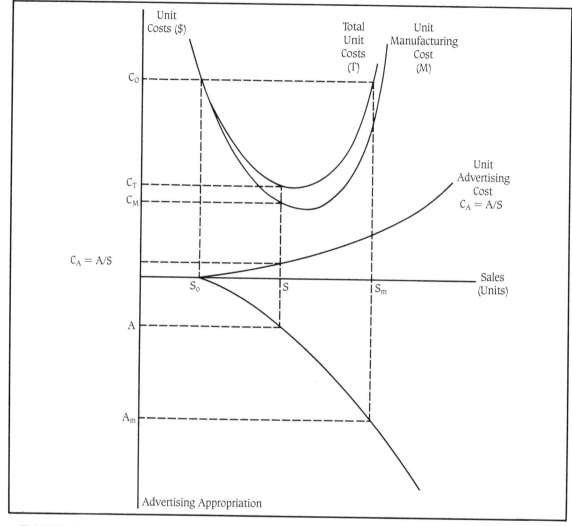

FIGURE 16.3   Unit Cost of a Product and Different Output/Sales Levels

ing marginal returns. The (T) curve is the vertical summation of the manufacturing and advertising costs that are needed at the different contemplated sales levels. When the firm spends A on advertising, the *total unit cost* of the product drops from C_O to C_T. The reason becomes evident when Figure 16.3 is considered: advertising can increase demand so that the economies of scale that are now possible result in a decreased average manufacturing cost (from C_O to C_M) that is still larger than the additional advertising cost per unit (C_A).

It may also turn out that advertising does result in an increased total unit cost. This may happen if the resulting sales level falls at the right of S_M (i.e., if the advertising expenses are larger than A_M) for one of three reasons:

1. The firm continues to stimulate demand for the product when production is close to capacity (with very high marginal manufacturing costs). This happens when the firm overspends on advertising.

2. The demand for the product cannot be stimulated any more, because the market is saturated or close to the saturation level (i.e., the sales curve is in its flat part). Here again the firm has overspent on advertising.

3. For some reason, advertising is ineffective.

All three cases may occur as the result of marketers making inefficient use of advertising dollars. They constitute marketing mistakes that marketers try to avoid. Nevertheless, the inefficient use of tools and techniques is not restricted solely to advertising, or even marketing. It can also be present in the other elements of the marketing mix (such as personal selling or pricing policies) or in other aspects of the firm's management (financial or personnel management).

To sum up, advertising can result in a consumer price increase when (1) marketers follow a cost-oriented pricing strategy and (2) marketers use advertising dollars inefficiently by overspending and/or conducting ineffective advertising campaigns.

Advertising and Market Structure

That advertising leads to higher consumer prices and higher profits through market concentration is a more subtle argument. Economists have studied this problem theoretically and empirically, and although there is no clear evidence in either direction, this argument can be substantiated more than the preceding one. Figure 16.4 illustrates these hypothetical market mechanisms.

OVERVIEW OF THE MODEL. According to economists, advertising can lead to market concentration and to higher consumer prices. At first glance this process resembles an endless loop. In other words, advertising leads to market concentration, which leads to more advertising, and so on. The upper part of the loop, which represents how advertising could lead to market concentration, is believed to be a barrier to market entry. Such barriers are said to exist when a new

company finds it difficult to enter a market and compete with well-entrenched firms.

There are three ways in which advertising can give a company differential advantages that may constitute a barrier to entry. One is that advertisers can build brand loyalty. Economists argue that new competitors may find it very difficult to break the loyalty that consumers have developed to well-established brands. Loyal customers are essentially satisfied consumers and breaking loyalty patterns is a difficult endeavour. A second way is that advertisers can gain preferential treatment from the media that could not be obtained by a smaller newcomer. A third way is that, as was discussed in Chapter 10, there is a threshold effect for advertising before it can be effective. Thus the large resources required to overcome this handicap may discourage a new competitor from entering the market.

As shown in Figure 16.4, barrier to entry eventually leads to market concentration, which means that a small number of competitors share a substantial part of a market. Market concentration leads to lower competition and decreased price competition. The rationale of this assertion is that when only a small number of large competitors share a market, that is, when a market has an oligopolistic structure, a price decrease initiated by any manufacturer is likely to be immediately matched by competitors. Consequently, there is no incentive to compete on prices. Lack of price competition usually means higher prices for consumers and larger profits for the manufacturer.

As can be seen in Figure 16.4, three feedback loops tend to perpetuate and even accelerate this process. First, market concentration can lead to product differentiation. Because firms in a concentrated industry do not compete on prices, they differentiate products that are essentially similar in their primary function, by artificially altering some secondary attributes. From an economic point of view, product differentiation is not a bad strategy when it better serves the differentiated needs of consumers. However, if this process is pursued to an extreme, it can result in an artificial proliferation of brands. As was pointed out by Neil Borden in his classic study of advertising's economic effects, an expanding set of product options can be disadvantageous for consumers when they involve only minor differences over existing brands that add little to consumers' real utility.[7] In this case, it can be argued that a large number of brands increases distribution costs and makes consumer buying more difficult and less efficient. But the objective of product differentiation is to build brand loyalty by increasing consumers' preferences for a specific set of product attributes, and brand loyalty is a major cause of barrier to entry.

Second, lack of price competition in a concentrated industry leads not only to product differentiation but also to advertising competition to promote the artificial differences of a product. If the additional advertising costs are passed on to consumers, then this competition may lead to higher consumer prices and certainly to more advertising.

Third, higher prices and profits are believed to lead to increased advertising expenses because manufacturers have an incentive to promote highly profitable items more aggressively.

ANALYSIS OF SOME KEY RELATIONSHIPS. The preceding argument rests on hypothesized relationships, some of them real and well documented and others not as well established. Some of the relationships of the model are quite controversial.

Advertising and preferential treatment from the media. Although theoretically correct, this advantage does not seem to materialize in practice and at best seems a rather weak relationship. (This relationship is analyzed fully later in this chapter, in the discussion of the effect of advertising on media economics.)

Advertising and brand loyalty. Advertising plays an important role and function in estab-lishing brand names and in establishing a close relationship between the brand name and consumers' expectations of a certain level of quality. When advertisers spend large amounts of money on advertising, they want to build some brand loyalty for products or brands by promising something unique, usually the assurance of a certain quality level. If advertising is aimed at building brand loyalty, industries with the largest advertising expenditures would show the most stable market shares. Although market share stability does not necessarily imply brand loyalty, since a large amount of brand switching can take place with relatively stable market shares,[8] brand loyalty should definitely result in stable market shares. A study carried out a few years ago showed an *inverse* relationship between these two variables.[9] Also, in such heavily advertised industries as beer or cigarettes, brand shares tend to show high variability. From a marketing point of view, these findings are not surprising when one considers that in a heavily advertised market, consumers of a certain brand who are exposed to advertising that induces them to remain loyal to the brand are also exposed to advertisements that induce them to switch brands. Consequently, the hypothesized direct relationship between advertising and brand loyalty does not have conclusive support from empirical data.

Advertising and market concentration. If advertising leads to market concentration, one could observe an association between advertising levels and market concentration. In other words, those spending the most on advertising should be the most concentrated industries. Most empirical studies that have attempted to test the existence of this relationship have reached contradictory conclusions. Some studies, including the most famous attempt by Lester Telser,[10] have concluded that no significant relationship existed.[11] Other studies have reached the opposite conclusion.[12] These conflicting results may find at least some partial explanation in the substantial difficulties that researchers

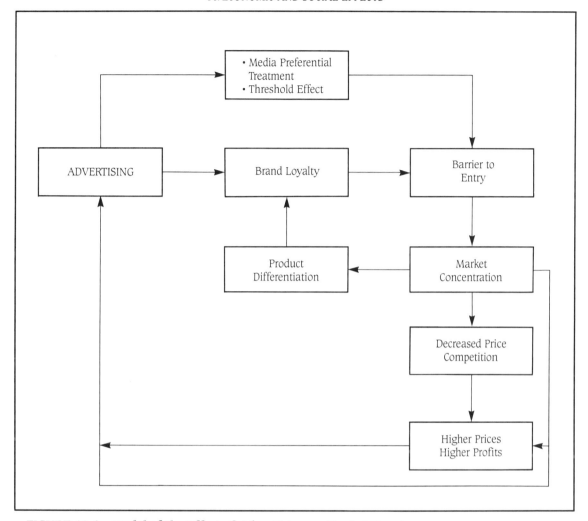

FIGURE 16.4 Model of the Effect of Advertising on Market Structure

face when they have to operationally define and measure such concepts as industry, industry advertising, and market concentration. Industries are generally defined according to the Standard Industry Classification (SIC) provided by the U.S. Census Bureau. Unfortunately, this classification for which industry data are available has somewhat arbitrary boundaries that do not always suit the purposes of researchers. Industry advertising is typically measured by the advertising to sales ratio (A/S), which reflects the percentage of an industry expenditures devoted to advertising. Here again, this ratio may be a poor indicator of the level of advertising, because it is highly dependent on the type of product characterizing each industry. Finally, market concentration is often measured by the concentration ratio. This ratio measures the market share held by the four largest competitors in an industry.[13] This widely accepted measure of industry concentration is also highly dependent not only on industry definition but also on its variability when firms or brands are considered as the competitors in an industry.

The inconclusive evidence for a relationship between the amounts spent on advertising and the level of industry concentration suggests that if the relationship exists, it is not as strong as some economists have believed.

Market concentration and increased prices.
Although economic theory shows that market concentration leads to higher consumer prices, in at least two situations this may not be necessarily true. For instance, when a firm enters a market on a local or a regional basis and competes with national firms by catering to local needs better than a national firm can, it becomes quite feasible for a newcomer to enter a highly concentrated market and to compete on price with well-entrenched companies. In addition, buyers in a concentrated industry can form an association in order to negotiate better prices from the concentrated industry. This tendency has been noted, especially in the distribution channels of consumer products.[14] Consequently, here again, even if there exists a relationship between market concentration and increased prices, it may not be as strong as is shown in Figure 16.4.

Advertising and profits. There is stronger empirical evidence to support a positive relationship between advertising expenditures and profitability across industries.[15] An empirical study by Comanor and Wilson concluded that industries with the largest advertising expenditures had profits approximately 50 per cent in excess of other industries.[16] Although the authors explained their results by the barriers to entry created by large advertising outlays, the association does not necessarily imply causation. If there is a causal relationship, no conclusion can be safely drawn as to which direction the causation runs, that is, whether advertising leads to higher profitability or if profitability leads to more advertising, as is suggested by Figure 16.4. It may also be the case that advertising expenditures and profitability are both positively or negatively related to a third extraneous variable.

Product differentiation and brand loyalty. One basic objective of the strategy of product differentiation is to build customer loyalty by better meeting consumers' needs and desires than any other brands. Although few empirical studies have been done in this area, it seems reasonable to conclude that when product differentiation is substantial enough and corresponds to actual differences in customers' needs, product or brand loyalty can be and is created. As was noted, few economists argue against this type of product differentiation. They instead challenge the concept of product differentiation when it is based on immaterial product characteristics, which leads to a proliferation of nearly identical brands. It is also reasonable to assume that the brand loyalty created by such secondary features is not as strong and thus can be broken more easily, especially as similar new brands appear on the market.

In conclusion it can be said that Figure 16.4, which summarizes the argument that advertising increases consumer prices through increased market concentration, should not be considered as a definite causal model but as suggestive of some plausible market mechanisms. Although this model embodies some real and theoretically true relationships, these relationships may not be as strong and prevalent as they seem. More empirical research is needed before conclusions can be drawn on all the issues involved.

Advertising and Retail Price Competition
Farris and Albion[17] have noticed that with a single exception, empirical studies reporting that advertising increases price sensitivity looked at *consumer* prices,[18] and studies reporting that advertising decreases price sensitivity examined *factory* prices.[19] Advertising has also been positively associated to *factory* price levels[20] and negatively to *consumer* price levels.[21]

Lee Benham conducted a study to compare the prices of eye examinations and eyeglasses in states that permit advertising versus those that do not. After allowing for possible differences in income and socio-demographic characteristics of the various state populations, Benham concluded that the prices paid by consumers for these products and services were an average of $4.43 cheaper in those states where advertising was allowed.[22] These results can be explained by Steiner's theories[23] about the role of retailers as links between manufacturers and consumers. According to Steiner, retailers may price highly advertised products in such a way that they earn a lower gross profit margin than on unadvertised products (such as private label brands).

Two reasons may account for this retailer's pricing behaviour. First, advertised brands have a higher turnover rate than less advertised products, and this tends to keep down the retailer's inventory cost per unit. Because retailers often use a cost-plus approach to set their prices, one can expect lower retail selling prices and retail gross margins for advertised brands. As reported by Farris, retailers may "prefer a quick nickel to a slow dime."[24] Second, highly advertised brands are often used by retailers as loss leaders. The rationale for using advertised brands rather than less known brands as loss leaders is that consumers are more likely to know the prices of such brands and should be able to use those prices as benchmarks to compare the prices charged by competing retailers. According to Farris and Albion:

> Both of these factors increase the probability that a price cut on advertised brands will bring more customers into the store (where they may also buy other items . . . perhaps at higher gross profit margins) than a price cut on unknown unadvertised brands.[25]

If only the differences in unit sales and in retail prices between advertised and unadvertised brands are considered, the value of advertising would be underestimated. Actually, the differences between manufacturers' prices are very pronounced and relevant to an evaluation of advertising's contribution to profitability. Because retailers are willing to cut their profit margins to provide consumers with low prices, part or all of these differences are not felt at the consumers' level.

Economic Side Effects of Advertising

Advertising also has important side effects. They are called side effects in the sense that they only indirectly affect consumers' utility. Advertising may also affect business cycles and the economics of the mass media.

Advertising and Business Cycles

Advertising is believed to have a negative impact on business cycles. An economic analysis reached the conclusion that advertising expenditures had a tendency to follow the same pattern as business cycles,[26] because advertisers tend to increase advertising when the economy is booming and to curtail advertising expenditures when sales are weak. As discussed previously, many advertisers determine their advertising expenditures by applying a fixed percentage to their sales. Even those advertisers who do not follow such rigid rules may take into account the current sales level to decide how much to spend on advertising. From a theoretical point of view, the opposite practice should prevail: advertisers should reduce advertising expenditures when they foresee a booming economy and increase advertising budgets in periods of economic recession, to try to alleviate the extremes of business cycles. Although the practice seems to contradict theory, Simon notes that even if advertising has a negative impact on economic cycles, this effect is probably relatively small in comparison with major determinants of business cycles.

Advertising and the Mass Media

A large part of the amount spent on advertising (about 75 per cent) is used to buy advertising space and time. These amounts collected by selling advertising space and time are a major—and sometimes the sole—source of income for the mass media. The remaining 25 per cent is devoted to production and administrative costs. It has been estimated that in the United States about 60 per cent of the cost of periodicals, about 70 per cent of the cost of newspapers, and practically 100 per cent of the cost of radio and television are covered by advertising revenues.[27] Similar figures have been reported for Canada.[28] When consumers buy a product (which includes some advertising cost), they also buy, in addition to the satisfaction directly derived from the consumption of the product, the possibility of watching a TV or radio program or a substantial reduction in the price of a favourite magazine or newspaper. If we could imagine a world without advertising, other means of financing the mass media would have to be found. In the final analysis, consumers would have to pay the bill, either through direct radio or TV taxes and duties, as is presently done in some European countries, and higher prices for each issue of newspapers and magazines, or through additional taxes. Thus, consumers recover a great amount of the money spent on advertising through media attendance (watching TV, listening to the radio, reading newspapers and magazines) at a substantially reduced cost.

It has been argued that the financial support advertisers give to the mass media is not without a social cost, since advertisers try to exercise control over the media contents. This control can reduce a medium's freedom to report some anti-business news or articles and programs that may have a negative impact on large advertisers. There certainly is a danger of pressure being exerted by important advertisers. It may also be argued, however, that it is better to have pressure exerted on the media by several advertisers whose interests often conflict than to have the mass media under the sole control of government. Governments are run by political parties whose objectives, motives, and interests are more obvious and definitely more homogeneous than those of various businesses.

It has also been argued that through rate schedules, the media could favour large advertisers at the expense of small advertisers. The media generally do offer large discounts to volume purchasers, but the allegation of discriminatory pricing practices does not hold. For instance, many time slots on TV that are not sold in advance are offered to all advertisers at substantial discounts, regardless of the advertiser's total commitment. This is why smaller advertisers can also purchase time slots at substantially reduced prices.[29] Thus the present pricing structure does not really give a substantial differential advantage to large advertisers.

Conclusions on the Economic Effects of Advertising

The model in Figure 16.3 indicates that advocates of advertising stress two broad types of economic benefits to consumers, i.e., that advertising fulfills the useful role of providing information to consumers and of enhancing new product development.

Critics point to the upward pressure advertising may exert on prices as the result of increased distribution costs or because of lessened competition. Here again, critics and advocates of advertising are likely to disagree on where the limits stand between what is truth and what is speculation.

Advertising does have desirable and undesirable economic effects. The real problem is to assess whether the benefits of using advertising are worth the economic cost. One answer is that advertising plays a role no other communication tool can fulfill as efficiently. From an economic point of view, if it were possible to get rid of advertising, the costs would certainly be much higher than the cost of keeping—and at the same time trying to refine and improve—this economic institution.

The Social Effects of Advertising

Critics of advertising who are concerned with the impact this economic institution has upon our social life, stress two main arguments for questioning the relevance of advertising for our social well-being (Figure 16.5). One is that advertising manipulates consumers. The second is that advertising has undesirable social effects on lifestyles, values, and culture.

Does Advertising Manipulate Consumers?

This argument can be examined by emphasizing various aspects of the advertising communication process. Advertising has been accused of having the immediate *effect* of manipulating consumers by "creating" needs. At the level of the *message*, advertising could possibly manipulate its audience by intensively appealing to emotions. Critics view the use of appeals based on sex, fear, or love as attempts to manipulate consumers by making extreme appeals to their emotions. Other social critics view advertising as manipulating through its use of *tools and techniques* that seek to influence consumers at a subconscious level. Motivation research and subliminal advertising are cases in point. Finally, advertising has also been considered as manipulating such persuasible audiences as children.

Can Advertising Create Needs?

Critics of advertising have argued that advertising can create needs among consumers and induce them to buy products that they do not otherwise want. They picture advertisers as unscrupulous individuals who persuade consumers to buy against their will products and services that do not or cannot bring any satisfaction. The view that advertising can create some kind of irresistible desire and can change otherwise intelligent consumers into robots that advertisers can manipulate is far removed from the real world of advertising communications.

At this point it should be asked whether advertising experts can cause consumers to purchase products they do not need. "Need" is a relative concept, since psychological needs can be as important as and sometimes are more important than physical needs. What is con-

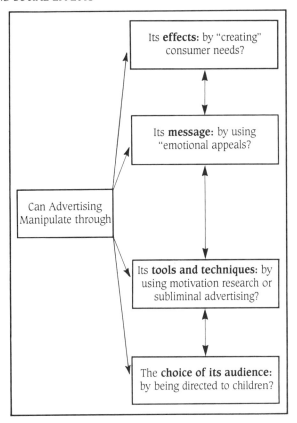

FIGURE 16.5 Questions Raised by Social Critics of Advertising

sidered a necessity by one individual may be trivia to another individual; a necessity in one society may be a luxury in another. For instance, vacuum cleaners and refrigerators are considered by Canadians as necessities. However, such items are unaffordable luxuries for many African villagers.

Statistics show that 80 per cent of new products introduced into the market are rejected by consumers.[30] A well-known example is the Edsel automobile, which was introduced by the Ford Motor Company in 1957. This pioneer of the automobile industry lacked neither promotional funds, expertise in engineering, or sophistication, but the Edsel proved to be a monumental failure.

This particular case has been analyzed from many different angles. The results of all available analyses point to one fundamental fact: the company tried to sell a product for which there was absolutely no need or desire at the time. This point cannot be over-emphasized. Vast amounts of money spent on advertising and publicity to promote a given brand of cigarettes will not persuade a non-smoker to smoke. The opposite is also true: thus far, advertising efforts to reduce the intake of cigarette smokers have failed.[31]

What then is the value of advertising? Why promote a product if consumers cannot be induced to purchase it? Is advertising a useless endeavour? Much to the contrary. As was shown throughout this text, advertising exerts a powerful influence on consumer behaviour. However, rather than creating needs, advertising stimulates existing needs. That is, it arouses latent needs that consumers do not feel strongly or consciously.

From a marketing standpoint, viewing advertisers as creating needs negates the marketing concept. While these critics see manufacturers as making up products, and then creating the need for the product, marketers know the process goes in a reverse order. The marketer first recognizes, identifies, and discovers unsatisfied consumer needs in order to design products and services that are wanted and are acceptable to the consumers.

Should Advertising Use Emotional Appeals?
Those who contend that advertising manipulates often point at the extensive use advertisers make of emotional appeals, especially for household or beauty care products. They imply that advertising should use only "rational" appeals, such as economy, or provide consumers with "objective" information about the physical characteristics of the product. Consider an advertiser faced with the problem of advertising a beauty care or grooming product. Obviously, this advertiser could advertise the product's price, its chemical ingredients, or any other "objective" characteristic of the product. But how would that relate to the profound motives of most people

when they make such purchase decisions? Most buyers of beauty care or grooming products use such products in order to look attractive, to feel better, or for other emotional reasons.

When advertisers promise people that they will look more attractive if they use the brand, the advertiser attempts to use the same language that consumers probably use when they contemplate making such purchases. As was emphasized, consumers make choices and purchase choices (and the more so for products and services that have strong psychological and social meanings), by using a large number of criteria and dimensions, emotional as well as economic and "objective." In other words, what economists or social critics label emotional appeal is what marketers call making a sales presentation that uses the consumers' logic and language. For marketers, even highly emotional motives are considered rational, because buyer behaviour is rational behaviour. The problem of many critics can often be traced to their denial of rationality to anyone who does not use their own value judgements and behaviour standards!

Another dimension to this problem is whether it is legitimate for advertisers to promise greater attractiveness or to hint at irresistible success with the opposite sex if their products are purchased. Advertisers are often guilty of exaggeration. Some critics would view these as outright deceptive claims, and in some ways, they are right. It is true that advertisers do not and cannot believe that their brand of detergent can fulfill a consumer's life. The question is whether people can really be deceived by such statements.

Language is full of exaggeration, even if one ignores advertisements. Who has not been "terribly sorry" for some cigarette ashes falling on a carpet? Or who has never expressed "profound sympathy" to a neighbour who is experiencing some painful event? To highlight this point further, think of the cards that people send to their families and friends to celebrate the main events of their lives. From these cards one can draw a good sample of dramatized overstatements and could conclude that this type of language has become part of our culture. In the same way, people have become accustomed to advertising's inflated language and have learned to discount the exaggerated claims that are part of advertising. Thus, in many cases, what at first glance seems to be outright lies, is simply one among the many overstatements that are part of our culture. Such advertisements are effective not because they exaggerate, but because they appeal to the right motivation.

Does Advertising Use Powerful Tools And Techniques?

The tools and techniques at the disposal of advertisers are far from perfect; they have only a *limited* effect even when they are properly used. Two common charges are that advertisers manipulate consumers into buying unwanted products and services through motivation research and subliminal advertising.

MOTIVATION RESEARCH. The objective of motivation research is to unveil motives hidden or buried in consumers' subconscious mind. Such unconscious motives may explain purchasing patterns. As seen in Chapter 7, prune consumption has been reported to be associated in consumers' minds with old age and parental authority, or the purchase of a convertible car was subconsciously thought of as a substitute for a mistress.[32] When motivation research techniques were introduced, one author, Vance Packard, objected strongly to the manipulation of consumers. In the *Hidden Persuaders* he wrote:

People's surface desires, needs, and drives were probed in order to find their points of vulnerability. Among the surface motivating factors found in the emotional profile of most of us, for example, were the drive to conformity, need for oral stimulation, yearning for security. Once these points of vulnerability were isolated, the psychological hooks were fashioned and

baited and placed deep in the merchandising sea for unwary prospective customers.[33]

However, motivation research soon revealed its limitations. The interpretation of the extensive psychological material gathered from consumers' in-depth interviews required more expertise than that of the personnel commonly working with the data. The relatively small sample sizes, with sometimes as few as 50 people, cast serious doubts on the findings of such research studies. Motivation researchers reached very different conclusions from an analysis of the same data. Even assuming that the interpretation of the data was correct, a substantial gap had to be filled before research results could be translated into "manipulative" and "effective" advertising campaigns.

For these reasons, motivation research has not lived up to its promise of being the advertiser's panacea. At present, it is viewed as a first step in the research process that generally leads to the formulation of hypotheses about consumer behaviour that must be tested through large-scale surveys.

SUBLIMINAL ADVERTISING. Chapter 7 showed that the effect of subliminal advertising was extremely limited. However, some critics have raised strong objections to its use on ethical grounds and have also attributed to advertisers the power of manipulating consumers through subliminal messages. Given the lack of positive evidence about its effectiveness and uncertainty about the ethical issues involved, subliminal advertising is not likely to become an actual advertising technique. After an extensive review of the relevant literature, Timothy E. Moore concluded, "In general, the literature on subliminal perceptions shows that the most clearly documented effects are obtained only in highly contrived and artificial situations. These effects when present are brief and of small magnitude . . . . These processes have no apparent relevance to the goals of advertising."[34]

From the evidence at hand, accusing advertisers of having at their disposal tools and techniques for manipulating consumers at a subconscious level overestimates grossly the power of these techniques. As has been seen, advertisers have only limited tools and techniques to deal with what is extremely complex and heterogeneous human behaviour. Accusing advertisers of being able to manipulate consumers reveals a fundamental misunderstanding of the advertising process and of consumer behaviour as well.

Are Children More Persuasible?

More serious is the argument that advertising induces children to desire objects that parents cannot afford or may not wish to give to their children. This has been a relatively recent concern with the increased presence of television and cable TV in North American homes. A recent study conducted in Canada concluded that children in homes with cable television watch more television and do more of that watching alone than children whose homes receive only conventional television.[35] This has led the province of Quebec to pass laws forbidding advertising directed at children and has also motivated formal research in the United States and Canada.

Are children especially persuasible through advertising? If so, until what age? Until they are 13 years old, as specified by Quebec law? A study conducted by Robertson and Rossiter[36] showed that toy advertising influenced children's choices, especially during the Christmas season. Thus the effectiveness of advertising cannot be doubted. However, Robertson and Rossiter's study also shows that the effects of advertising on children are relatively limited. Advertising increased by only five per cent the quantity of toys and games chosen by children as Christmas presents (only for those items that were heavily advertised during the Christmas season). One other interesting fact is this: the increase was not related to the children's age, which was 7, 9, and 11 years. Another study conducted by Scott Ward, Daniel Wackman, and Ellen Wartella[37] arrives at identical conclusions and suggests that the effects of advertising on children have been grossly overestimated. According to their results, children develop skeptical attitudes and defense mechanisms against advertising messages at an early age.

That children develop defense mechanisms against advertising was also demonstrated in a previous study by Robertson and Rossiter,[38] which showed that children can detect the persuasive intent of an advertising message. Furthermore, once a child can detect this intention, he reacts against the persuasion. According to the authors, a child capable of detecting a persuasive intent is less influenced by advertising because he places less confidence in it, likes the advertisement less, and tends to make less purchase demands.

Furthermore, the ability to recognize persuasive intent is directly related to a child's age. In the study just cited, this ability was found in 53 per cent of all first-graders, 87 per cent of all third-graders, and 99 per cent of fifth-graders. This study has two implications for advertising: Since fifth-graders can be no more influenced than adults, the legal limit of 13 years of age is perhaps too high. Moreover, the ability to detect persuasive intent is directly related to age. However, for Jean Piaget, a leading child psychologist,[39] age represents two things: maturity and acquired experience. Thus, isolating a child from advertising may delay the formation of the mechanisms through which he resists advertising persuasion. Some children, however, may be badly in need of these mechanisms in the first stages of adolescence. A study conducted by Goldberg and Gorn[40] showed that a child's behaviour and attitudes are affected by advertising. Furthermore, children who have the best chance of obtaining whatever they desire are the most affected. This suggests that advertising is more effective with children who know their parents are likely to give in to their demands. Another study conducted by these two authors points out that, just like adults, children are subject to advertising saturation effects. Thus, after a certain number of message repetitions, the advertising effects would become negative.[41]

Thus research conducted in this field seems to conclude that the efficiency of advertising aimed at children, while real, has often been exaggerated. Children perceive at quite an early stage the persuasive intent of an advertisement, develop mechanisms against it, are submitted to the same saturation effects as adults, and are more influenced if they know parents are likely to give in to their demands. To illustrate these limits placed on the efficiency of advertising aimed at children, one would only have to point out that 75 per cent of all toys advertised on television in the United States every year are market failures!

Another interesting question is whether children exert pressure on parents and whether they give in. Ward and Wackman[42] found only a slight correlation between five to ten year olds' attempts at exerting influence and the actual instances in which parents have given in to such pressure, when the age factor was not considered. However, when age is considered, it was found that children's attempts to pressure parents decrease with age, and the instances in which parents give in to their children's demands increase with age. This phenomenon seems quite normal, since parents lend more judgement to their children as they grow older. Wells[43] concludes his research by suggesting that parents often give in to their child's preferences when they lack other criteria on which to base their decision.

A study conducted by Berey and Pollay[44] examined the influence of children on the choice of a particular brand of cereals. Their findings suggest that mothers who cared a lot about their children were less likely to buy the cereals their children wanted than mothers who were less centred on their children. This conclusion suggests that mothers who care about their children's well-being buy what they deem best for their child rather than buying what the child wants.

These studies, although incomplete, point out that in general, parents do not give in to pressure exerted by their children and that this pressure decreases as the child gets older. The role of parents as educators, particularly their role in forming their child's buying habits, must be underlined. However, a child is not always "a gullible agent working unknowingly for the manufacturer," who is used by the advertiser to influence parents. A child usually has more judgement than some legislators think, as is pointed out in a study by Mark Lovell.[45] According to this study, children may show interest in advertisements directed at adults when they are concerned about the advertised product. Moreover, they can remember the product brands much better than their parents can.

A child is not only an "agent" but also a consumer, who often disposes of limited purchasing power. In order to use this purchasing power in an intelligent way, a child needs and is entitled to information provided by advertising.

Thus, the stereotype of the naive child who is manipulated by advertising into demanding all that he sees may be more a cliché than a reality.

Does Advertising Have Negative Social Effects?

There is a high level of subjectivity in this area of assessment of advertising effects, because it is related to social values, lifestyles and tastes, and to our social and economic system. Contradictory points of view can be quite legitimately held about the role and effects of advertising depending on one's values and views of what society is or should be. There is no one truth in this controversy over advertising because it is not a controversy over facts but over value systems.

There are two aspects of the argument over the possible negative social effects of advertising. First, some critics see advertising as a force that negatively affects our values and life styles. Other critics, without necessarily granting such power to advertising, deplore its "polluting" effects and argue that it undermines aesthetic and intellectual values.

Does Advertising Affect Values and Lifestyles Negatively?

Advertising has been accused of unduly raising the expectations of economically deprived segments of our society and of enhancing materialistic values. Others point out that it promotes undesirable social stereotypes, for example, the stereotyping of women.

ADVERTISING, SOCIAL DISCONTENT, AND MATERIALISM. The process through which advertising is seen to lead to consumers discontent and/or materialism is outlined in Figure 16.6. By making consumers aware of products and services and by inducing them to buy, advertising encourages consumers to desire products that they would not even dream of if they were not advertised. If a consumer cannot financially afford the advertised and desired product, advertising can lead to frustration and discontent. This problem is more acute for consumers who are not affluent and who must cope with many advertising stimuli.

If consumers can afford to buy the advertised products, critics argue that advertising fosters materialism. Materialism refers to excessive importance given to material welfare as compared to such nonmaterial values as love, freedom, and intellectual development.

Following this line of thought, advertising involves negative social effects by the mere fact of generating consumer wants. This proposition is related to the charge that advertising can create unwarranted needs and wants. As has been pointed out, "Much of the criticism that advertising sells people things they do not need is directed more at the fact that people buy things the critic does not think they should want."[46] Thus, if consumers are considered to be adults who should enjoy freedom of choice, this argu-

ment does not hold unless one believes that wants are legitimate, when they originate from the individual and are not induced by such external forces as advertising. This view emanates from the economic theory that resource allocation should serve consumers and should maximize consumers' satisfaction; it should not be in the hands of persuaders or advertisers. This view of our society is somewhat naive. Advertising is only one stimulus that consumers receive about products and services. Even if consumers—financially deprived or not—could be completely isolated from advertising, they would see expensive cars in the streets, they could see displays of fine foods in supermarkets or luxury clothes in stores, see well-off people consuming all kinds of goods that they sometimes could afford, and sometimes not. Consequently, although the argument of consumer discontent and materialism may be valid, it cannot be attributed to advertising alone. The criticism should be more adequately addressed to our society and our economic system, which favour and are built on mass consumption. Advertising is part of the system because it is an institution designed to serve this society and this economic system. However, if the value system on which society is built or its economic system are responsible for people's discontent or materialism, it is useless and misleading to attack an institution that is only one of its logical consequences; the debate should focus instead on the roots of the problem rather than on its symptoms.

Those who blame advertising for being the result of our economic system should remember that whatever the social and political system, advertising must play a part because it fulfills essential economic functions. For example, the U.S.S.R. is presently using advertising:

Thanks to well-organized advertising, the consumer can more rapidly find the goods needed by him, purchase them with a smaller expenditure of time, and select the goods according to his taste . . . . This function of advertising not only reflects the new relation to the consumer,

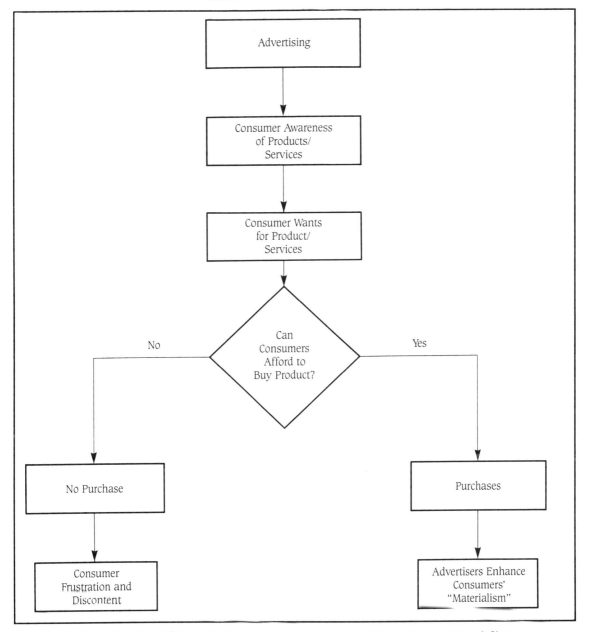

FIGURE 16.6   Possible Effect of Advertising on Consumers' Discontent or Materialism

care about the population, and its needs, but it also has important economic significance. It creates the precondition for a more economic and rational use of material goods which are created by society, and permits a more satisfied consumer.[47]

The report of the Prairie Provinces Royal Commission on Consumer Problems and Inflation commented:

Though advertising has long been regarded by the Russians as the result of sinful capitalist aggression for markets, the overwhelming requirement for information for the consumer simply forces the acceptance of this solution.[48]

Those who are satisfied with our economic system do not always view consumer discontent as an evil. Of course, if discontent is the chronic state of a consumer with low economic status, it is certainly regrettable. But instead of hiding goods from the sight of the poor, a more logical approach to the problem is to improve their economic welfare until they can afford these products. Here again, this is a social problem that goes well beyond the effects of advertising. Moreover, the proponents of our economic system argue that consumer discontent in not so extreme cases may be an economic catalyst, since major innovations and inventions have evolved from consumer discontent.

As for the third relationship in Figure 16.6, which specifies that consumers who want and purchase goods pursue materialistic goals, it can be argued that people often buy products to pursue non-materialistic goals. For instance, one may purchase products as gifts to express love or esteem, or books and records for intellectual development. In our society, consumption has become one of the most natural ways by which one achieves even nonmaterial goals. Here again, the argument implies a condemnation of the Western way of life, which relies heavily on mass consumption.

The argument that advertising leads to consumer discontent and materialism can be differently appreciated by the proponents and critics of advertising. However, as advertising is an institution of the free enterprise economic system, it tends to foster the values and principles on which this society is built. But it is only one and probably not the strongest of the forces that shape values and culture. The divergent views about the social effects of advertising often point to different beliefs about what society should be.

ADVERTISING AND STEREOTYPES. Advertising messages sometimes feature "slices of life"; they picture consumers in various roles and situations, as they are—or supposedly are—in their daily lives. Inasmuch as advertisers assign definite roles to various types of individuals, such as minority groups or women, it can promote or perpetuate certain stereotypes. This is also true of any mass communication. This argument against advertising originated in the United States when minority groups, particularly blacks, accused advertisers of picturing them in low status roles. Since the 1970s advertisers have used "integrated" advertising, which portrays blacks in higher status roles.[49]

More recently, women's associations have charged that advertisers portray women in limited and traditional roles, such as housewives, clerks, or secretaries, and seldom in higher occupational levels. As put by Robert Oliver, then president of the Canadian Advertising Advisory Board:

> If advertising does help perpetuate such stereotypes, does it, in the process, erect one more psychological barrier to human freedom? To the degree that it does, is this aspect of advertising not a negative social force? Do some advertising portrayals by their very nature constitute an affront to women?[50]

These questions have led to a number of studies in the United States[51] and in Canada. A 1971 study of 729 advertisements in eight general interest magazines concluded that feminists were at least partially justified in saying that women were not portrayed in the variety of roles they actually play in American society. Most frequently, women's roles were stereotyped as follows:

• women do not make important decisions
• women need men's protection
• a woman's place is in the home
• men regard women essentially as sex objects.[52]

Subsequent studies by Wagner and Banos[53] and by Venkatesan and Losco[54] showed that between

1959 and 1971 the stereotypes of women were unchanged, except for a substantial decrease in the number of women portrayed as sex objects.[55]

In a cross-cultural study involving 2977 general interest magazine advertisements carried out in 1975 and involving the U.S., Canada (French and English), the U.K., and France, it was found that women are *not* caricatured in magazine advertisements as useless, decorative sex objects *any more than men*. Female decorative models outnumber male models in such advertisements, because women's clothing and beauty products are more heavily advertised in magazines. It was found that in Canada, discrimination in advertising role portrayal is more a function of social class than sex; for example, blue collar workers are severely underrepresented.[56] Finally, a study reported in Canada by Kindra and involving 861 advertisements in eight magazines published in 1981 suggested that "although the portrayal of women in traditional roles had declined, their projected image continues to be narrow and limited."[57]

Thus there is empirical evidence to suggest that advertisers have lagged behind in portraying women in new roles. One explanation could be that advertisers fear to arouse negative reactions from audiences if they used a so-called liberated type of advertising. However, one study conducted in 1976 by the Task Force on Women of the Canadian Advertising Advisory Board concluded that the fear that such advertising would lack impact and arouse negative reactions is unwarranted. On the contrary, such messages tend to overcome the traditional type of message.[58] These results were confirmed to a large extent by a Quebec study carried out by Petrof et al.[59] Similar conclusions were reached by a study on integrated advertising in the United States, which found that such advertising tended to have positive effects on black audiences, and a neutral impact on white audiences.[60]

One might question whether advertising should promote new ideas and/or fight undesirable social stereotypes or should communicate effectively with markets. As the role of women

in society changes, it is normal and probably more efficient for advertisers to picture women in new roles. Advertisers should not be geared to the past but should reflect the present values and lifestyles of the market rather than picture what society could or should be. As the task force on women reported:

> . . . . But at the same time, today's woman becomes irritated by advertising that shows women and men in an exaggerated and unrealistic way. For maximum effectiveness, the advertisers must understand the reality of today's women and ensure that the portrayals of both women and men are genuine (or reflect that reality).[61]

Does Advertising Have "Polluting" Effects?

Advertising is omnipresent. If all or part of what consumers see or hear in commercials and advertisements offend their feelings or aesthetic values, then advertising can be considered a polluting agent. Commercials are often criticized for being too loud, too repetitive, boring, overusing sex or fear appeals, emphasizing "sensitive" product classes, i.e., products that some consumers would not like to see openly advertised or even talked about, for example, personal hygiene products, drugs, or alcoholic beverages, commercials that insult consumers' intelligence, use unpleasant or stupid jingles, or messages that are dishonest or misleading.[62]

ADVERTISING AND BAD TASTE. Taste is not universally shared. What is considered good taste by some individuals may be viewed as stupid or offensive by others. This is true of advertising as of anything else. Rock music may be considered sheer noise by classical music lovers. All gourmets do not favour the same dishes, and the list could go on. Consequently, it is inevitable that advertising messages are diversely evaluated and judged by various segments of the market.

Not all advertising to which the public is exposed is conceived and created by responsible professionals. Some advertising is also the work of individuals with the unfortunate marketing philosophy of selling at any cost. These people have typically little concern about the aesthetic value of their advertisements. It is true that a certain percentage (it is hoped a small one) of advertisements fall into the latter category, but this is sufficient to give the entire advertising industry a poor image. Just as a single misdeed can spoil an individual's reputation for exemplary behaviour, a few poorly conceived advertisements can give advertising a reputation of bad taste, in spite of a substantial proportion of well conceived and responsible advertisements.

Consumers may see bad taste in some advertisements as the result of what has been called "imperfect segmentation".[63] Because the media cannot perfectly match advertisers' desired target audience, some consumers may see or hear what is not intended for them. They may consider silly or offensive messages that are directed at market segments that would not find such messages as offensive because the messages have been designed for them specifically. As Gist points out:

> . . . . To the extent that pinpoint accuracy cannot be accomplished, we must logically expect some messages to fall on the "wrong" ears. Or, what is the same thing, we will encounter messages so compromised by the "general" nature of the audience that they are very likely to offend with their blandness. It is particularly true of our general media—television and general appeal printed media—that a pinpoint matching of messages and tastes is very nearly impossible.[64]

The same question concerning stereotypes applies to the taste and aesthetics of advertisements: Should advertisers be concerned with and try to promote "good taste", or should they be interested only in the long-run efficiency of their communications with the market? Evidence suggests that very pleasant and also very unpleasant advertisements are more effective than those in between.[65] Obviously, the two objectives can be somewhat reconciled. Shouldn't a lawyer take into account the laws or the facts of a case when delivering an effective address to the court? Can't an architect design a masterpiece and still meet the functional constraints of the building? In the same way, advertisers should reconcile art and marketing communications. Their responsibility is to translate selling arguments into words and images that are likely to induce consumers to buy what the economy has produced for them.

TRUTH IN ADVERTISING.   The charge that advertising is dishonest and tells lies or only part truths is often raised. Although the public may tend to put all advertisements "in the same bag", several situations should be recognized. Some advertisements may constitute outright lies, for instance, claiming that a product does things that it cannot do, or is made of substances it does not contain, or has characteristics it does not possess. In such cases, there is an obvious and deliberate intent to deceive and mislead consumers into buying the advertised product, whether or not the product can provide promised satisfaction. All professional advertisers vigorously condemn such practices. Besides the fact that such practices are illegal, advertisers who subscribe to the Canadian Code of Advertising Standards are not likely to indulge in unethical practices.

The argument of half-truths is more subtle. Advertisers of two competitive products might both claim that their respective products are the "best" or the "first." Some advertisers might also claim that their product is, for example, "unbreakable." Besides exaggeration, which dramatizes the product and would not deceive most consumers, advertisers could claim the superiority of their product by referring to specific functions or characteristics, or to a specific usage occasion, or they could use a different product category than that used by a competitor making a similar claim. Sometimes there are subtle and very technical arguments involved in these claims that are impossible to explain in a short commercial. Obviously, in such cases consumers receive imperfect information, but it is not possible for an advertiser in a thirty second commercial or in a half page ad to give all the facts. Consequently, advertisers must exercise judgement as to what should be said to consumers. It is only logical that the facts or aspects of the product that give a differential advantage over competitive products would be emphasized.

In the same way, claiming that a product is "unbreakable" seems to be an outright exaggeration. There is no such thing as an unbreakable product, provided the proper destructive means are employed. An "unbreakable" watch would not resist a steamroller. What the advertiser's claim generally means is that a product is unbreakable under normal and typical usage conditions. Here again, because of time and space constraints and because of the need to sustain consumers' attention and interest for extended periods, advertisers are obliged to use short-cuts that may seem to be, if not pure lies, at least overstatements or part-truths. Do consumers really need to know that an unbreakable watch could not actually resist a steamroller?

Conclusions on the Social Effects of Advertising

In general, it can be said that advertising's effects on consumer behaviour have been overestimated. Advertising cannot "create" consumer needs. It can stimulate latent needs, perhaps unconsciously felt by the consumers, but does not manipulate consumers.

Whether advertising has undesirable social effects on value systems, lifestyles, on social discontent, whether it is deceptive, or in bad taste, or perpetuates undesirable stereotypes, are more complex issues to assess. There are a number of situations ranging from a minority of outright deceptive and unprofessional advertisements, which are vigorously condemned by the advertising industry, to well done, professional, and sometimes artistic advertising. Thus the quality of advertising should not be the subject of unwarranted generalizations. Another im-

portant conclusion is that the quarrel between critics and advocates of advertising often rests on a criticism or a defense of the social and economic system and values that are based on free enterprise and stress mass consumption.

Advertising is a tool, and a tool is never good or bad in itself. Rather, those who handle the tool can make good or bad use of it. In the same way, critics should address many of their questions to our social system, which uses advertising as one of its efficient and logical institutions.

Consumer Protection

We have seen that it is extremely difficult to assess the true impact of advertising on the economy and on our social and personal lives. The mechanisms through which advertising exerts its influence are complex, and every argument that can be advanced for or against advertising can be matched by counter-arguments. This leads to the question how consumers are and should be protected against the potential abuses of advertisers and against advertising that they judge offensive or in bad taste. Consumers can find some protection through the law, by the self-regulation of the advertising industry, and they can also protect themselves.

Legal Protection

In Canada consumers have some legal protection. Parts of the Criminal Code forbid, at a penalty, the publishing of outright falsehoods. However, because the advertising process is so complex, it is often difficult to ascertain what exactly constitutes a falsehood. Since consumers have failed so far to bring pressure to bear on attorneys-general to have charges laid under the provisions of the Criminal Code, there is no body of case law on which to rely. The lack of misleading advertising cases tried under the Criminal Code may be due to the extent of federal and provincial legislation restricting advertising content in Canada.

Nevertheless, under the various sales of goods acts, consumers have recourse against manufacturers when products do not perform as specified. As stated in the report of the Prairie Provinces Royal Commission on Consumer Problems and Inflation, this is of limited value:

> First, just what it was said the good in question would do, and under what conditions, is not usually easy to establish in sufficiently precise terms to secure a judgement in the consumer's favour. Second, and much more important, it is usually too costly to obtain recourse in view of the expected recovery. The law, then, contains only limited attempts to grapple with potential abuses in advertising, and such legal enactions as there are have experienced only very limited application and enforcement.[66]

Most provinces find it more efficient to enforce consumer legislation that is more specific about the acceptability of product and service representation. Canada does not have a body similar to the U.S. Federal Trade Commission, which can order advertising campaigns to be stopped without going through full criminal proceedings against the advertiser. However, there are a number of Canadian federal and provincial regulations that deal with advertising. Although much of the legislation deals with broadcast advertising, some laws, such as the Combines Investigation Act and the provincial consumer protection acts, deal with any form of advertising.

What characterizes the Canadian legislation about advertising is the great number of laws and bills both at the federal and the provincial levels that attempt to constrain the work of advertisers. As pointed out by Rafe Engle, "... there are possibly more active curbs and constraints on advertising and marketing in Canada than in any other business-oriented society."[67] This legislation is changing and growing rapidly, which made the same author write: "If Canada's past is any forecast of its future, then governments, crown corporations, trade associations, and consumerists will soon make yesterday's controls look archaic and mild."[68]

Federal Government Regulations[69]

The main pieces of federal legislation dealing with advertising are listed in Figure 16.7.

One of the most important pieces of federal legislation concerning advertising is Article 36 of the Combines Investigation Act (see Figure 16.8). This part of the act forbids and defines misleading advertising. Prosecution for violating the law can result from the general impression conveyed by a representation as well as the literal meaning of the representation. In addition, articles 36.1 and 36.2 of the Combines Investigation Act deal with testimonials and tests represented in advertisements, and forbid the practices and advertising of double ticketing.

The Combines Investigation Act does not *require* advertisers to clear advertisements prior to publication. Moreover, advertisers have the option to use the so-called "program of compliance." According to this program advertisers may submit advertising material to the Marketing Practices Branch of the Bureau of Competition Policy of the Department of Consumer and Corporate Affairs. Advertisers are then notified whether action will be taken on the material submitted.

Television advertising of foods, drugs, cosmetics, devices, beer, and wine comes directly under the control of the Canadian Radio-Television and Telecommunications Commission (CRTC). Radio and television broadcast regulations require that the Food and Drug Directorate, Health Protection Branch, Health and Welfare Canada, pre-clear all drug, cosmetic, device, and broadcast advertising. They also require that all food broadcast advertising be pre-cleared by the Department of Consumer and Corporate Affairs. The CRTC sets technical standards, such as 12 minutes of advertising per hour, prohibits subliminal advertising, and sets standards for good taste. It is also involved in licensing stations and setting regulations for programming.[70]

The CRTC together with the provinces review liquor, wine, and beer advertising; each province has a liquor control board with a different set of

Federal Acts

Broadcasting Act (Sections 5, 8, 8a, 8c, 16)

Regulations: 9) Advertising Generally
10) Liquor, Beer, Wine, and Cider
Beer, Wine, and Cider Advertising
Criteria
11) Food and Drugs, Proprietary or
Patent Medicines
Circulars
Clearance of Food and Drug Commercials
Food Advertising
Registration Procedures for TV Commercials
Canadian Human Rights Act
Combines Investigation Act
Consumer Packaging & Labelling Act
Copyright Act
Criminal Code
Department of National Revenue—Customs and
Excise Tariff item 99221-1, Schedule C,
June 30, 1972
Food & Drug Act
Hazardous Products Act
Income Tax Act (Section 19)
National Trade Mark & True Labelling Act
Official Languages Act
Textile Labelling Act
Trade Marks Act

FIGURE 16.7   Federal Legislation Affecting Advertising

standards for the amount and kind of liquor, beer, and wine advertising that can appear in all media. Some provinces do not allow any liquor advertising. In addition, *all* commercials to be aired on the CBC require preclearance.

Provincial Government Regulations

The main provincial laws that deal with advertising are listed in Figure 16.9.

Various provincial consumer protection and trade practices acts affect advertising in all media in that they deal with "representations made . . . ," "paid messages . . . ," when outlining laws on misleading advertising and trade practices.[71]

Some Possible Effects of Canadian Legislation

These laws and bills constraining advertising in Canada are the result of a long history during which pieces of legislation have been added over the last few decades. Presently, the control of Canadian advertising is characterized by "fragmental law and piecemeal regulation."[72] What have been the effects of this legislation on advertising in Canada?

Some authors have questioned the benefits of Canadian advertising legislation. For instance, Sweitzer, Temple, and Barnett write: "Whenever regulations fail to specify adequate models of audience behaviour [and the authors demonstrate they do], the quality of regulation will suffer. Such questionable quality in the face of increasing government costs suggests that the answer to the question: 'Is it worth it?' is a simple: 'No'."[73]

However, despite the need for simplification and unification of Canadian advertising laws, the regulations have decreased the amount of advertising that is in poor taste or misleading. In addition, the complexity of Canadian law might have been a factor in inducing Canadian advertisers to develop stricter codes of ethics. By adhering to such codes, advertisers can stay within the limits of the law. Enforcement of advertising legislation has given way to new advertising practices, i.e., comparative advertising and corrective advertising.

Comparative advertising[74] has been encouraged by the Federal Trade Commission since 1972. The underlying assumption of the legislator was that naming competing brands would oblige advertisers to be more truthful about their claims. This was followed in 1976 by guidelines issued by the Federal Department of Consumer and Corporate Affairs concerning comparative advertising.

Ever since, advertisers have had mixed reactions about this form of advertising. Some argue that comparative advertising gives better information to the consumers. Critics charge that it confuses consumers and increases skepticism about advertising or that such advertising benefits the competitors named in the advertisements. Research in the United States[75] and in Canada[76] has failed so far to show clear consumer benefits from competitive advertising.

Misleading advertising

36. (1) No person shall, for the purpose of promoting, directly or indirectly, the supply or use of a product or for the purpose of promoting, directly or indirectly, any business interest, by any means whatever,

(a) make a representation to the public that is false or misleading in a material respect;

(b) make a representation to the public in the form of a statement, warranty or guarantee of the performance, efficacy or length of life of a product that is not based on an adequate and proper test thereof, the proof of which lies upon the person making the representation;

(c) make a representation to the public in a form that purports to be

(i) a warranty or guarantee of a product, or

(ii) a promise to replace, maintain or repair an article or any part thereof or to repeat or continue a service until it has achieved a specified result

if such form of purported warranty or guarantee or promise is materially misleading or if there is no reasonable prospect that it will be carried out; or

(d) make a materially misleading representation to the public concerning the price at which a product or like products have been, are or will be ordinarily sold; and for the purposes of this paragraph a representation as to price is deemed to refer to the price at which the product has been sold by sellers generally in the relevant market unless it is clearly specified to be the price at which the product has been sold by the person by whom or on whose behalf the representation is made.

Deemed representation to public

(2) For the purposes of this section and section 36.1, a representation that is

(a) expressed on an article offered or displayed for sale, its wrapper or container,

(b) expressed on anything attached to, inserted in or accompanying an article offered or displayed for sale, its wrapper or container, or anything on which the article is mounted for display or sale,

(c) expressed on an in-store or other point-of-purchase display,

(d) made in the course of in-store, door-to-door or telephone selling to a person as ultimate user, or

(e) contained in or on anything that is sold, sent, delivered, transmitted or in any other manner whatever made available to a member of the public,

FIGURE 16.8   Abstract from the Combines Investigation Act

SOURCE: Government of Canada, *Combines Investigation Act* (Ottawa: 1978). Reproduced with the permission of the Minister of Supply and Services Canada.

Amendments to the Combines Investigation Act have resulted in more *corrective advertising* in Canada.[77] According to Section 37, 3(2) of the Act, advertisers may use corrective advertising as a defence for misleading representations. Misleading advertisements must be the result of an error, reasonable precautions must have been taken to prevent the error, and the corrective advertisement must be placed immediately and so as to reach the same audience as effectively.[78]

In the United States, corrective advertising is used by the courts as a sanction against advertisers convicted for misleading advertising. Because an advertisement can be established as misleading only after its publication, corrective advertising is needed to deprive advertisers of these "immoral" gains, as well as to rectify consumers' false information. Reviewing this American experience[79] in view of its possible future application to the Canadian scene, Wyckham identifies five unresolved issues about corrective advertising:

1. What objectives can corrective advertising effectively pursue?

2. Has misleading advertising long-run effects on consumers, in order to justify the need for corrective advertisements?

3. Can consumers be "inoculated" against corrective advertising by actions of the firm, as was suggested by an experimental study by Hunt?[80]

4. What is the optimal time lag between the false and the corrective advertisements?

5. What should be the best duration, budget, copy and media to run corrective advertisements?[81]

shall be deemed to be made to the public by and only by the person who caused the representation to be so expressed, made or contained and, where that person is outside Canada, by

(f) the person who imported the article into Canada, in a case described in paragraph (a), (b) or (e), and

(g) the person who imported the display into Canada, in a case described in paragraph (c).

Idem (3) Subject to subsection (2), every one who, for the purpose of promoting, directly or indirectly, the supply or use of a product or any business interest, supplies to a wholesaler, retailer or other distributor of a product any material or thing that contains a representation of a nature referred to in subsection (1) shall be deemed to have made that representation to the public.

General impression to be considered (4) In any prosecution for a violation of this section, the general impression conveyed by a representation as well as the literal meaning thereof shall be taken into account in determining whether or not the representation is false or misleading in a material respect.

Punishment (5) Any person who violates subsection (1) is guilty of an offence and is liable

(a) on conviction on indictment, to a fine in the discretion of the court or to imprisonment for five years or to both; or

(b) on summary conviction, to a fine of twenty-five thousand dollars or to imprisonment for one year or to both. R.S., c. C-23, s. 36; 1974-75-76, c. 76, s. 18.

Representation as to reasonable test and publication of testimonials **36.1** (1) No person shall, for the purpose of promoting, directly or indirectly, the supply or use of any product, or for the purpose of promoting, directly or indirectly, any business interest

(a) make a representation to the public that a test as to the performance, efficacy

or length of life of the product has been made by any person, or

(b) publish a testimonial with respect to the product,

except where he can establish that

(c) the representation or testimonial was previously made or published by the person by whom the test was made or the testimonial was given, as the case may be, or

(d) the representation or testimonial was, before being made or published, approved and permission to make or publish it was given in writing by the person by whom the test was made or the testimonial was given, as the case may be,

and the representation or testimonial accords with the representation or testimonial previously made, published or approved.

Punishment (2) Any person who violates subsection (1) is guilty of an offence and is liable

(a) on conviction on indictment, to a fine in the discretion of the court or to imprisonment for five years, or to both; or

(b) on summary conviction, to a fine of twenty-five thousand dollars or to imprisonment for one year or to both. 1974-75-76, c. 76, s. 18.

Double ticketing **36.2** (1) No person shall supply a product at a price that exceeds the lowest of two or more prices clearly expressed by him or on his behalf, in respect of the product in the quantity in which it is so supplied and at the time at which it is so supplied,

(a) on the product, its wrapper or container;

(b) on anything attached to, inserted in or accompanying the product, its wrapper or container or anything on which the product is mounted for display or sale; or

(c) on an in-store or other point-of-purchase display or advertisement.

Punishment (2) Any person who violates subsection (1) is guilty of an offence and is liable on summary conviction to a fine not exceeding ten thousand dollars or to imprisonment for one year or to both. 1974-75-76, c. 76, s. 18.

FIGURE 16.8 Continued

Provincial Acts

Alberta
The Unfair Trade Practices Act
Credit and Loan Agreements Act
Liquor, Beer, and Wine Advertising Regulations

British Columbia
Trade Practices Act
Consumer Protection Act and Regulations
Closing Out Sales Act
Motor Dealer Guidelines
Liquor, Beer, and Wine Advertising Regulations

Ontario
Business Practices Act
Consumer Protection Act
Human Rights Code
Regulation 128 (Credit Advertising)
Liquor Control Act

Quebec
Charter of the French Language
Regulations—Language of Business and Commerce
Consumer Protection Act
Regulation—Children's Advertising
Lotteries Act
Broadcast Advertising Tax Act
Agricultural Products and Food Act
Liquor, Beer, and Wine Advertising Regulations
Pharmacy, Professional Advertising Regulations
Roadside Advertising Act
Quebec Class Actions Act

Saskatchewan
Consumer Products Warranties Act
Cost of Credit Disclosure Act
Liquor, Beer, and Wine Advertising Regulations

Manitoba
Consumer Protection Act
Trade Practices Inquiry Act
Liquor, Beer, and Wine Advertising Regulations

New Brunswick
Consumer Product Warranty and Liability Act
Cost of Credit Disclosure Act

Nova Scotia
Consumer Protection Act
Liquor, Beer, and Wine Advertising Regulations

Prince Edward Island
Business Practices Act
Consumer Protection Act
Highway Advertisements Act
Liquor, Beer, and Wine Advertising Regulations

Newfoundland
Trade Practices Act
Consumer Protection Act
Exhibition of Advertisements Act
Liquor, Beer, and Wine Advertising Regulations

FIGURE 16.9   Provincial Legislation Affecting Advertising

Unfortunately, few of these questions have been answered, which reinforces the point that U.S. and Canadian advertising legislation is built on belief rather than fact.

Clearly, more advertising legislation is needed in order to prevent abuse from unscrupulous advertisers. A large body of laws is in force in Canada, but it is largely piecemeal legislation, which is not necessarily based on sound consumer and advertising research.

Protection through Industry Self-Regulation

Canadian advertising agencies and advertisers have set up codes of conduct that are designed to keep high standards of ethics in the profession. These codes have been developed through a consensus reached among advertisers, advertising agencies, the media, government departments, and the Consumers' Association of Canada. Although these codes are adhered to on a voluntary basis, once they are endorsed by the various industry bodies, they take on a different status. Because all national media association subscribe to these codes, they agree that if the Advertising Standards Council finds an advertisement that does not conform to the code, and if the advertiser refuses to withdraw or amend this advertisement, the media are notified and must stop its distribution. Figure 16.10 lists the main self-regulatory codes in force in Canada.

One of the most important self-regulation codes is the Canadian Code of Advertising Standards (Figure 16.11). The code is written in clear and concise language and avoids legal jargon. In fifteen articles, it covers such important issues as false or misleading advertising, subliminal advertising, false price claims, testimonials, bait and switch, unfair disparagement, guarantees, imitation, safety, superstition and fears, and advertising to children.

Concerning the efficacy of such self-regulation, Robert Oliver, President of the Advertising Standards Council wrote:

> . . . . Because members of the business community, whether signatories of the code or not, are generally supportive of the self-regulatory concept, this "weapon of last resort" is rarely needed—in my memory, over the last fifteen years less than a half-dozen times with a national advertiser, and no more than twice a year with retail advertisers or advertisers from abroad. But without this resource, we could be helpless to cope with the out-and-out fraud artist or those advertisers who were firmly convinced that because their advertising was perhaps legal it was therefore necessarily ethical. . . . [82]

Protection through Consumer Action

Consumers should practice self-protection against forms of advertising that for any reason they feel are dishonest or in bad taste. Consumer groups can also influence new legislation.[83] Consumers can take an active part in consumer associations by reporting offenders. Other actions include:

1. avoiding any advertising that is considered offensive. Consumers can stop watching a commercial, do something else during the time certain commercials are aired, or turn the page of the magazine in the case of a print advertisement;
2. failing to buy products the advertising of which they do not approve. Because advertisers generally do not want to lose customers, even a small drop in market share or sales volume may produce a change in advertising messages if advertisers have been made

---

Industry Codes

Broadcast Code for Advertising to Children
Canadian Code of Advertising Standards
Code of Consumer Advertising Practices for
 Cosmetics, Toiletries, and Fragrances
Code of Consumer Advertising Practices for
 Non-Prescription Medicines
Pharmaceutical Advertising Advisory Board Code of
 Advertising Acceptance
Telecaster Committee of Canada Guidelines
Television Code of Standards for the Advertising of
 Feminine Sanitary Protection Products
CBC Commercial Acceptance Criteria

The Advertising Standards Councils are independent, autonomous bodies, founded and funded by advertisers, advertising agencies, and media through the Canadian Advertising Advisory Board.

FIGURE 16.10   Industry Codes Regulating Advertising
Courtesy Canadian Advertising Standards Council

aware that their message offends a small portion of their audience;
3. comparing sources of information, i.e., not only watching competitive advertisements but also consulting social sources (peers, neighbours, and family members);
4. contacting the advertiser directly and protesting. In the case of collective actions, this form of protest can even go as far as publishing research results that disprove the advertiser's claim or that denies the claim, in the case of an outright lie.

In a free market society consumers generally have their way, because they can select the goods they want. They decide the success or failure of all the products in the marketplace. Consequently, responsible advertisers have a vested interest in helping consumers make responsible and well-informed choices.

Background

In adopting this Canadian Code of Advertising Standards, the participating organizations are fully conscious of the dynamic role advertising plays in the Canadian economy.

Advertising is a communication channel that benefits both the buyer and the seller. Consumers benefit through easy access to low-cost information on the availability of prices of goods and services and news of improved or new products and services; sellers through advertising expand their markets and find new ones.

In an agro-industrial economy such as ours, advertising also contributes very directly to the country's economic well-being. By stimulating sales it helps to provide jobs and to pay wages, taxes and dividends; by helping sustain and level out the mass production process it often contributes to lower unit costs and stability of employment.

As advertising volume increases, so does the responsibility of the industry to the Canadian consumer and the community. The average citizen is now daily exposed to an estimated several hundred advertising messages. It is therefore important that advertising be prepared in ways that respect the taste and values of the public at large. In a society that recognizes the equality of the sexes, advertising should also reflect an awareness of and a sensitivity to this reality and to other human rights issues.

Through the adoption of this Code of Advertising Standards, the participating organizations undertake to apply high ethical standards to the preparation and execution of Canadian advertising. It is their desire and intention to make advertising more effective by continuing to raise the standard of advertising excellence and by ensuring integrity in advertising content.

This Code is no way replaces any existing Standard which have been framed to meet the individual needs of media and association groups in Canada. It is complementary to them, just as it is complementary to government regulations, both federal and provincial. Communications regarding the interpretation and application of the Code should be addressed to Advertising Standards Council, 1240 Bay Street, Suite 302, Toronto, Ontario, M5R 2A7.

The Code

Public confidence exerts an important influence upon the effectiveness of advertising, just as it affects any other communication process in a democratic environment. So directing advertising practices toward meriting and enhancing such confidence is both socially responsible and an act of practical self-interest.

This Code in no way replaces any existing Standards which have been framed to meet the individual needs of media and association groups in Canada. It is complementary to them, just as it is complementary to government regulations, both federal and provincial.

Communications regarding the interpretation and application of the Code should be addressed to Advertising Standards Council, 1240 Bay Street, Suite 302, Toronto, Ontario, M5R 2A7.

1. Accuracy, Clarity

Advertisements may not contain inaccurate or deceptive claims or statements, either direct or implied, with regard to price, availability or performance of a product or service. Advertisers and advertising agencies must be prepared to substantiate their claims promptly to the Council. Note that in assessing the truthfulness of a message, the Council's concern is not with the intent of the sender or the precise legality of the phrasing. Rather the focus is on the message as received or perceived, that is, the general impression conveyed by the advertisement.

2. Disguised Advertising Techniques

No advertisement shall be presented in a format which conceals its commercial intent. Advertising content, for example, should be clearly distinguished from editorial or program content. Similarly advertisements are not acceptable if they attempt to use images or sounds of very brief duration or physically weak visual or aural techniques to convey messages below the threshold of normal human awareness. (Such messages are sometimes referred to as subliminal.)

3. Price Claims

No advertisement shall include deceptive price claims, unrealistic price comparisons or exaggerated claims as to worth or value. "List price", "suggested retail price", "manufacturer's list price", and "fair market value" are misleading terms when used to imply a savings unless they represent prices at which a reasonable number of the items were actually sold within the preceding six months in the market area where the advertisement appears.

4. Testimonials

Testimonials must reflect the genuine, reasonably current opinion of the endorser and should be based upon adequate information about or experience with the product or service advertised. This is not meant to preclude, however, an actor or actress presenting the true experience of an actual number of users or pre-

FIGURE 16.11   The Canadian Code of Advertising Standards

senting technical information about the manufacture or testing of the product.

5. Bait and Switch
The consumer must be given a fair opportunity to purchase the goods or services offered at the terms presented. If supply of the sales item is limited, this should be mentioned in the advertisement. Refusal to show or demonstrate the product, disparagement of the advertised product by sales personnel, or demonstration of a product of superior quality are all illustrations of the "bait and switch" technique which is a contravention of the Code.

6. Comparative Advertising
Advertisements must not discredit or attack unfairly other products, services or advertisements, or exaggerate the nature or importance of competitive differences. When comparisons are made with competing products or services, the advertiser must make substantiation available promptly upon the request from the Council.

7. Professional or Scientific Claims
Advertisements must not distort the true meaning of statements made by professionals or scientific authorities. Advertising claims must not imply they have a scientific basis they do not truly possess. Scientific terms, technical terms, etc., should be used in general advertising only with a full sense of responsibility to the lay public.

8. Slimming, Weight Loss
Advertisements shall not state or imply that foods, food substitutes, appetite depressants or special devices will enable a person to lose weight or girth except in conjunction with a balanced, calorie-controlled diet; and the part played by such a diet shall be given due prominence in the advertisement.

9. Guarantees
No advertisement shall offer a guarantee or warranty, unless the guarantee or warranty is fully explained as to conditions and limits and the name of the guarantor or warrantor, or it is indicated where such information may be obtained.

10. Imitation
No advertiser shall deliberately imitate the copy, slogans, or illustrations of another advertiser in such a manner as to mislead the consumer. The accidental or unintentional use of similar or like general slogans

or themes shall not be considered a contravention of this Code, but advertisers, media, and advertising agencies should be alert to the confusion that can result from such coincidences and should seek to eliminate them when discovered.

11. Safety
Advertisements shall not display a disregard for public safety or depict situations which might encourage inappropriate, unsafe or dangerous practices.

12. Exploitation of Human Misery
Advertisements may not hold out false hope in the form of a cure or relief for the mentally or physically handicapped, either on a temporary or permanant basis.

13. Superstition and Fears
Advertisements must not exploit the superstitious, or play upon fears to mislead the consumer into purchasing the advertised product or service.

14. Advertising to Children
Advertisements to children impose a special responsibility upon the advertiser and the media. Such advertisements should not exploit their credulity, lack of experience, or their sense of loyalty, and should not present information or illustrations which might result in their physical, mental or moral harm. (See also Broadcast Code for Advertising to Children and the Quebec Consumer Protection Act, Bill 72.)

15. Taste, Opinion, Public Decency
(a) As a public communication process, advertising should not present demeaning or derogatory portrayals of individuals or groups and should not contain anything likely, in the light of generally prevailing standards, to cause deep or widespread offence. It is recognized, of course, that standards of taste are subjective and vary widely from person to person and community to community, and are, indeed, subject to constant change.

(b) The authority of the Code and the jurisdiction of the Council are over the content of advertisements. The Code is not meant to impede in any way the sale of products which some people, for one reason or another, may find offensive—provided, of course, that the advertisements for such products do not contravene section (a) of this Clause.

Advertising's Self-Regulatory Processes
The Canadian Code of Advertising Standards was originally sponsored and published by the Association of

Canadian Advertisers and the Institute of Canadian Advertising. It was revised and republished by the Canadian Advertising Advisory Board in 1967.

This latest edition was produced by the Advertising Standards Council and Le Conseil des Normes de la Publicité in 1982.

Since 1967, this Code has been supplemented by several other industry codes, an on-going process. These Codes are administered by the Advertising Standards Councils and Le Conseil des Normes de la Publicité. The Council in Toronto handles all national advertising complaints and complaints from the Ontario region, when these concern English language advertising; French language complaints, national and from the Quebec region, are handled by Le Conseil in Montreal.

Across the country Regional Councils—in the Atlantic Provinces (Halifax), Manitoba (Winnipeg), Saskatchewan (Regina), Alberta (Calgary and Edmonton), and British Columbia (Vancouver)—handle local advertising complaints in their respective areas. All councils include representatives from all three sectors—advertiser, media, and advertising agency—as well as public representatives, many of whom are nominees of the Consumers' Association of Canada.

How to Complain

If you see or hear advertising carried by Canadian media that you feel contravenes one of the industry Codes, write to the Advertising Standards Council nearest you. (The Councils, of course, have no control over advertising carried by non-Canadian media.) If it is a print advertisement, it helps if you can enclose a copy of the advertisement; with a broadcast message, give the station, approximate time, the name of the product, etc. If you have a complaint form or coupon to fill out, fine; if not, just say why you think the message contravenes the Code.

What Will Happen?

Your complaint will be acknowledged and reviewed. If it appears the Code has been violated, Council staff will get in touch with the advertiser directly. In most cases corrective action follows. Where the advertiser disagrees with staff findings, the matter is referred to the full Council. If Council sustains the complaint, the advertiser is notified, and asked to amend or withdraw the advertising. Generally, this closes the matter. Regardless of whether the complaint has been sustained or not, you will be notified of the outcome.

Occasionally an advertiser will refuse to take corrective action. The Council then notifies the media involved, or will sometimes ask that a bulletin be sent to all association members of those media, indicating that this message, in Council's judgment, contravenes the Code. In effect, this means media will not accept the message in its existing form.

Summary

Advertising has always been an area of disagreement among economists, marketers, sociologists, and the public. There is little empirical evidence to support the various arguments that advertising has positive or negative economic and social effects. It has been claimed that advertising affects a consumer's load of information or the new product development process, increases the distribution costs of goods, alters the market structure, affects consumer prices or business cycles, and has a negative impact on the mass media. Part of the controversy between proponents and critics of advertising can be traced to the underlying views of what constitutes relevant information to be given to consumers and to the acceptance of a policy of product differentiation. As for the effect of advertising on consumer prices, no definite conclusion can be safely drawn given present research. Nevertheless, advertising fulfills a function in our economy that no other communication tool presently can.

Among the social criticisms of advertising are charges of consumer manipulation (need creation, the use of emotional appeals, or of special techniques working at the subconscious levels), of affecting social values and lifestyles by enhancing consumer discontent and materialism, or by promoting undesirable stereotypes, and of polluting consumers' environment with misleading or bad taste advertisements. Critics have a tendency to overestimate the power of advertising. Although negative social effects can sometimes be attributed to advertising, critics often indirectly attack the economic system of free enterprise and/or the society of mass consumption that is promoted by this economic institution.

Various protections are available to Canadian consumers, in particular the federal and provincial regulations, industry self-regulations, and the protection that consumers can secure through their actions and behaviour.

Questions for Study

1. Take a recent issue of a magazine or newspaper and find some advertisements that you think are deceptive. Explain why and in what way they are deceptive. Propose some corrective actions that could be taken by the advertisers.

2. Answer question 1, using advertisements that you think are in bad taste.

3. Take a sample of about ten advertisements from a recent issue of a magazine and analyze what kind of stereotypes they promote. Are they desirable or undesirable stereotypes? Speculate what they might be considered 10-20 years from now.

4. Take some advertisements from a few recent issues of a magazine. Analyze the type of information provided about an advertised product or service. How much information is objective and how much is emotional appeal? Can you find a pattern according to the type of product being advertised? In your opinion, can these emotional appeals be justified for some or all of these advertisements?

5. Try to imagine and describe our society, if for some reason, all kinds of advertising were suddenly banned.

6. Should advertisers try to improve consumers' tastes or change their general attitudes by promoting more desirable images of minority groups? Justify your answer.

7. In what way is it possible to say that a country has the kind of advertising it deserves?

8. Is advertising moral, immoral, or amoral? What should advertising be? Explain.

9. Does advertising increase or decrease consumer prices? Explain in detail.

10. Is the role of advertising to inform or to persuade consumers? Why? Be specific.

Problems

1. Select one current issue of a national magazine and an issue of the same magazine published twenty years ago. Make a comparative analysis of the advertisements in both issues with respect to

 • role stereotyping
 • comparative advertising
 • the use of testimonials
 • the use of emotional appeal advertising
 • deceptive/bad taste advertisements

 What may explain the changes you have observed (if any)? Up to what point can the results you have obtained be generalized? Why?

2. Using library research, try to estimate the role advertising should/could play in a:
 (a) capitalistic economy
 (b) socialist economy
 (c) developing economy

Notes

1. Richard Caves, *American Industry: Structure, Conduct, Performance* (Englewood Cliffs, N.J.: Prentice-Hall, 1964), p. 102.

2. Roger Leroy Miller, *Economic Issues for Consumers* (St. Paul, Minn.: West Publishing Company, 1975), p. 35.

3. Ivan Preston, *The Great American Blowup* (Madison, Wis.: University of Wisconsin Press, 1975), p. 281.

4. Shelby D. Hunt, "Information vs. Persuasive Advertising: An Appraisal," *Journal of Advertising*, 5, no. 3 (Summer 1976), 5-8.

5. Ibid., p. 6.

6. Raymond A. Bauer and Stephen A. Greyser, "The Dialogue That Never Happens," *Harvard Business Review*, 50 (January-February 1969), 122-28.

7. Neil H. Borden, *The Economic Effects of Advertising* (Chicago: Richard D. Irwin, 1942), p. 609.

8. See, for instance, Frank M. Bass, "The Theory of Stochastic Preference and Brand Switching," *Journal of Marketing Research*, 11 (February 1974), 1-20.

9. Lester G. Telser, "Advertising and Competition," *Journal of Political Economy* (December 1964), pp. 537-62.

10. Ibid.

11. See, for instance, Jules Backman, *Advertising and Competition* (New York: New York University Press, 1967), pp. 90-94.

12. See, for instance, H.M. Mann, J.A. Henning, and J.W. Meehan, Jr., "Advertising and Concentration: An Empirical Investigation," *Journal of Industrial Economics* (November 1967), pp. 34-45; Lee E. Preston, "Advertising Effects and Public Policy," *Proceedings of the AMA 1968 Fall Conference* (Chicago: American Marketing Association, 1968), pp. 563-64.

13. Paul D. Scanlon, "Oligopoly and 'Deceptive' Advertising: The Cereal Industry Affair," *Antitrust Law & Economic Review*, 3 (Spring 1970), 100.

14. John K. Galbraith, *American Capitalism: The Concept of Countervailing Power* (Boston: Houghton Mifflin, 1956), p. 117.

15. William S. Comanor and Thomas A. Wilson, "Advertising, Market Structure and Performance," *Review of Economics and Statistics*, 49 (November 1967), 423-40.

16. Ibid., p. 440.

17. Paul W. Farris and Mark S. Albion, "The Impact of Advertising on the Price of Consumer Products," *Journal of Marketing*, 44 (Summer 1980), 17-35; see also James M. Ferguson, "Comments on 'The Impact of Advertising on the Price of Consumer Products'," *Journal of Marketing*, 46 (Winter 1982), 102-5; Paul W. Farris and Mark S. Albion, "Reply to 'Comments on "The Impact of Advertising on the Price of Consumer Products"'," *Journal of Marketing*, 46 (Winter 1982), 106-7.

18. D.R. Wittink, "Advertising Increases Sensitivity to Price," *Journal of Advertising Research*, 17 (April 1977), 39-42; G.J. Eskin, "A Case for Test Marketing Experiments," *Journal of Advertising Research*, 15 (April 1975), 27-33; G.J. Eskin and P.H. Baron, "Effect of Price and Advertising in Test-Market Experiments," *Journal of Marketing Research*, 14 (November 1977), 499-508; V.K. Prasad and L.W. Ring, "Measuring Sales Effects of Some Marketing Mix Variables and Their Interactions," *Journal of Marketing Research*, 13 (November 1976), 391-96.

19. Comanor and Wilson; J.J. Lambin, *Advertising Competition and Market Conduct in Oligopoly Over Time* (Amsterdam: North-Holland Publishing Co., 1976) p. 425.

20. R.D. Buzzell and P.W. Farris, "Marketing Costs in Consumer Goods Industries," Marketing Science Institute, Report No. 76-111 (August 1976); P.W. Farris and D.J. Reibstein, "How Prices, Ad Expenditures, and Profits are Linked," *Harvard Business Review*, 57 (November-December 1979), 173-84.

21. L. Benham, "The Effect of Advertising on the Price of Eyeglasses," *Journal of Law and Economics*, 15 (October 1972), 337-52; J. Cady,

"Advertising Restrictions and Retail Prices," *Journal of Advertising Research*, 16 (October 16), 27-30; R.L. Steiner, "Does Advertising Lower Consumer Prices?" *Journal of Marketing*, 37 (October 1973), 19-26; R.L. Steiner, "Learning from the Past-Brand Advertising and the Great Bicycle Craze of the 1980s," *Advances in Advertising Research and Management*, Proceedings of the annual conference of the American Academy of Advertising, ed. Steven E. Permut (1978), pp. 35-40; R.L. Steiner, "A Dual Stage Approach to the Effects of Brand Advertising on Competition and Price," *Marketing and the Public Interest*, ed. John F. Cady, Marketing Science Institute Report No. 78-105 (Boston, 1978), pp. 127-50.

22. Benham p. 340.

23. R.L. Steiner, "Toward a New Theory of Brand Advertising and Price" (Paper presented at the annual meeting of the American Academy of Advertising, March 1977); Steiner, "Does Advertising Lower Consumer Prices?" and "A Dual Stage Approach." p. 148.

24. P.W. Farris, "Advertising's Link with Retail Price Competition," *Harvard Business Review* (January-February 1981), pp. 40-44.

25. Mark S. Albion and Paul W. Farris, "The Effect of Manufacturer Advertising on Retail Pricing," Marketing Science Institute Report No. 81-105 (December 1981), p. 3.

26. Julian L. Simon, *Issues in the Economics of Advertising* (Urbana, Ill.: University of Illinois Press, 1970).

27. Fritz Machlup, *The Production and Distribution of Knowledge in the United States* (Princeton, N.J.: Princeton University Press, 1962), p. 265.

28. *The Financial Post*, November 1978, Section 5.

29. David M. Blank, "Television Advertising: The Great Discount Illusion, or Tony Panda Revisited," *Journal of Business* (January 1968), pp. 10-38.

30. *Management of New Products,* 4th ed. (New York: Booz, Allen and Hamilton, 1968), p. 8

31. Harold Kassarjian and Joel B. Cohen, "Cognitive Dissonance and Consumer Behavior," *California Management Review* (Fall 1965), pp. 55-64.

32. L. Edward Scriven, "Rationality and Irrationality in Motivation Research," *Motivation and Marketing Behaviour*, ed. Robert Ferber and Hugh G. Wales (Homewood, Ill.: Richard D. Irwin, 1958), pp. 67-70.

33. Vance Packard, *The Hidden Persuaders* (New York: Pocket Books, 1957), p. 30.

34. Timothy E. Moore, "Subliminal Advertising: What You See Is What You Get," *Journal of Advertising*, 46 (Spring 1982), 27-47.

35. James G. Barnes, "Television Viewing Patterns of Children and Adolescents in Cable and Non-Cable Households" (Paper presented at the European Marketing Academy Conference, Grenoble, France, 1983).

36. Thomas S. Robertson and John R. Rossiter, "Short-Run Advertising Effects on Children: A Field Study," *Journal of Marketing Research*, 13 (February 1976), 68-70.

37. Scott Ward, Daniel Wackman, and Ellen Wartella, *Children Learning to Buy: The Development of Consumer Information Processing Skills* (Cambridge, Mass.: Marketing Science Institute, 1975).

38. Thomas S. Robertson and John R. Rossiter, "Children and Commercial Persuasion: An Attribution Theory Analysis," *Journal of Consumer Research*, 1 (June 1974), 13-20.

39. Jean Piaget, *The Psychology of the Child* (New York: Basic Books, 1969).

40. Marvin E. Goldberg and Gerald J. Gorn, "Children's Reactions to Television Advertising: An Experimental Approach," *Journal of Consumer Research*, 1 (September 1974), 69-75.

41. Gerald J. Gorn and Marvin E. Goldberg, "Children's Television Commercials: Do Child Viewers Become Satiated Too?" (McGill working paper, 1976).

42. Scott Ward and Daniel Wackman, "Children's Purchase Influence Attempts and Parental Yielding," *Journal of Marketing Research*, 9 (August 1972), 316-19.

43. W.D. Wells, "Children As Consumers," *On Knowing the Consumer*, ed. J.W. Newman (New York: John Wiley and Sons, 1966).

44. L.A. Berey and R.W. Pollay, "Influencing Role of

the Child in Family Decision Making," *Journal of Marketing Research*, 5 (February 1968), 70-72.

45. Mark Lowell, "Advertising to Children: An Issue Where Emotion is Getting in the Way of Objectivity," *Marketing,* 4 June 1976.

46. Charles J. Dicksen, Arthur Kroeger, and Franco M. Nicosia, *Advertising: Principles and Management Cases*, 6th ed. (Homewood, Ill.: Richard D. Irwin, 1983), p. 569.

47. D. Kurnin, "Iz Opyta Sovetskoi Torgovloi Reklamy," *Sovetskaia Torgovlia* (February 1958), pp. 46-47, quoted in Marshall I. Goldman, "Product Differentiation and Advertising: Some Lessons from the Soviet Experience," *Speaking of Advertising* (Toronto: McGraw-Hill, 1963), pp. 352-53.

48. Prairie Provinces Royal Commission, *Report on Consumer Problems and Inflation* (1968), p. 254.

49. Thomas F. Pettigrew, "Complexity and Change in American Racial Patterns: A Social Psychological View," *Daedalus* (Fall 1965), p. 974.

50. *Women and Advertising: Today's Messages— Yesterday's Images*, Report of the Task Force on Women and Advertising (Toronto: Canadian Advertising Advisory Board, November 1977), p. 2.

51. Alice E. Courtney and Sarah Wernick Lockeretz, "A Woman's Place: An Analysis of the Roles Portrayed by Women in Magazine Advertisements," *Journal of Marketing Research*, 8 (February 1971), 92-95.

52. Ibid.

53. Louis C. Wagner and Janis B. Banos, "A Woman's Place: A Follow-up Analysis of the Roles Portrayed by Women in Magazine Advertisements," *Journal of Marketing Research*, 10 (May 1973), 213-14.

54. M. Vankatesan and Jean Losco, "Women in Magazine Ads: 1959-71," *Journal of Advertising Research*, 15 (October 1975), 49-54.

55. Ahmed Belkaoui and Janice Balkaoui, "A Comparative Analysis of the Roles Portrayed by Women in Print Advertisements: 1958, 1970, 1972," *Journal of Marketing Research*, 13 (May 1976), 168-72.

56. Peter W. Pasold, "Role Stereotyping in Magazine Advertising of Different Countries," *ASAC Pro-*

ceedings, ed. J.R. Brent Ritchie and Pierre Filiatrault (1976), pp. 41-50.

57. Gurprit S. Kindra, "Comparative Study of the Roles Portrayed by Women in Print Advertising," *Marketing,* ed. Michel Laroche, vol. 3 (Administrative Sciences Association of Canada, 1982), pp. 109-18.

58. *Women and Advertising*, p. 5.

59. John V. Petrof, Elie Sayegh, and Pandelis I. Vlahopoulos, "Publicité et Stéréotypes des Femmes," *Marketing,* ed. Michel Laroche, vol. 3 (Administrative Sciences Association of Canada, 1982), pp. 238-46. See also Robert G. Wyckham, "Female Stereotyping in Advertising," *Linking Knowledge and Action*, ed. James D. Forbes, vol. 4 (Administrative Sciences Association of Canada, 1983), pp. 371-82.

60. James Stafford, Al Birdwell, and Charles Van Tassel, "Integrated Advertising – White Blacklash," *Journal of Advertising Research*, 10 (April 1970), 15-20.

61. *Women and Advertising*, p. 17.

62. See, for instance, Philip H. Love, "Entertainment in the Midland," *Omaha World Herald*, 24 November 1968, p. 11; E.S. Turner, *The Shocking History of Advertising* (Baltimore: Penguin Books, 1965).

63. Ronald R. Gist, *Marketing and Society: A Conceptual Introduction* (New York: Holt, Rinehart and Winston, 1971), pp. 401-2.

64. Ibid., p. 402.

65. John Treasure and Timothy Joyce, *As Others See Us* (London: Institute of Practitioners in Advertising, 1967).

66. Prairie Provinces Royal Commission, Report on Consumer Problems, pp. 266-67.

67. Ralph S. Engle, "Advertising and the Law," *Advertising in Canada*, ed. Peter T. Zarry and Robert D. Wilson (Toronto: McGraw-Hill Ryerson, 1981), pp. 369-442.

68. Ibid., p. 369.

69. Reproduced from the Canadian Advertising Advisory Board, "Laws and Regulations Package" (Toronto, February 1980).

70. "Laws and Regulations Package," (Toronto: Canadian Advertising Advisory Board, 1980).

71. Ibid., p. 2.

72. D. Alyluia, "The Regulation of Commercial Advertising in Canada," *Manitoba Law Journal*, 5 (1972-73), 97-200.

73. Robert W. Sweitzer, Paul Temple, and John H. Barnett, "Political Dimensions of Canadian Advertising Regulation," *The Canadian Marketer*, 10 (Fall 1979), 3-8.

74. W.L. Wilkie and Paul W. Farris, "Comparison Advertising: Problems and Potential," *Journal of Marketing*, 30 (October 1975), 7-15.

75. T.E. Barry and R.L. Tremblay, "Comparative Advertising: Perspectives and Issues," *Journal of Advertising*, 4 (1975), 15-20; P. Levine, "Commercials That Name Competing Brands," *Journal of Advertising Research,* 16 (December 1976), 7-14; V.K. Prasad, "Communications Effectiveness of Comparative Advertising: A Laboratory Analysis," *Journal of Marketing Research*, 13 (May 1976), 128-37; R.D. Wilson, "An Empirical Evaluation of Comparative Advertising Messages: Subjects' Responses on Perceptual Dimensions," *Proceedings*, Fall Conference, Association of Consumer Research (1975), pp. 53-57.

76. See, for instance, Gordon H.G. McDougall, *Comparative Advertising in Canada*, Monograph (Ottawa: Consumer Research Council, 1976); Gordon M.G. McDougall, "Comparative Advertising: Consumer Issues and Attitudes," *Proceedings*, Fall Conferencel, American Marketing Association (1977), pp. 286-91; Gordon M.G. McDougall, "Comparative Advertising in Canada: Practices and Consumer Reactions," *The Canadian Marketer*, 9 (1978), 14-20.

77. See Robert G. Wyckham, "Corrective Advertising," *The Canadian Marketer*, 10 (1979), 24-28.

78. Ibid., p. 25.

79. See, for instance, Robert F. Dyer and Philip G. Kuehl, "The Corrective Advertising Remedy of the FTC: An Experimental Evaluation," *Journal of Marketing* (January 1974), pp. 48-54; Michael B. Mazis, "An Experimental Evaluation of a Proposed Corrective Advertising Remedy," *Journal of Marketing Research* (May 1976), pp. 178-83. See also A.J. Faria and Pete Mateja, "Consumer Attitudes Towards Corrective Advertising," *Linking Knowledge and Action*, ed. James D. Forbes, vol. 4 (Administrative Sciences Association of Canada, 1983), pp. 102-12.

80. H. Keith Hunt, "Effects of Corrective Advertising," *Journal of Advertising Research* (October 1973), pp. 15-22.

81. Wyckham, p. 26.

82. R.E. Oliver, letter dated July 21, 1983 to the authors.

83. J.D. Forbes, "Influence Groups in Canadian Consumer Policy Formulation," *The Canadian Marketer*, 10 (Fall 1979), 27-32.

CAMPAIGN HISTORY FOR PART 5

1. Cadbury's Thick Dairy Milk 1979-1981 Campaign

CAMPAIGN HISTORY

CADBURY'S THICK DAIRY MILK 1979—1981 CAMPAIGN
Launch of a New, Thicker Chocolate Bar

ADVERTISER: Cadbury
AGENCY: Scali, McCabe, Sloves (Canada) Ltd.

Situation Summary

In the mid-to-late 1970s, the Canadian chocolate bar market showed little vitality. Pure chocolate ("moulded") bars had become increasingly smaller and thinner in an attempt by manufacturers to compensate for rising sugar and production costs. As a consequence, these wafer thin chocolate bar products became less satisfying to consumers. Pure milk chocolate bars were therefore not a major component of chocolate bar market sales. Candy bars made with various ingredients covered in chocolate ("countline" bars), such as Coffee Crisp, Oh Henry, and Kit Kat, were the most popular brands.

In 1979, Cadbury research identified an opportunity for a "thick" baton-shaped moulded chocolate bar. Consequently, the Cadbury Dairy Milk bar was produced in a thick configuration. It was introduced in a British Columbia test market in the fall of 1979. Due to very positive test market results (share of market increased by 60 per cent over the first year), the Cadbury's "Thick" Dairy Milk brand was introduced to English Canada in 1980 and to Quebec in 1981. The launch was supported by television and transit advertising.

The launch of Cadbury's "Thick" Dairy Milk revolutionized the chocolate bar category. Competitive chocolate bar manufacturers introduced their own "thick" bars. As a consequence, chocolate bars have recently become bigger and thicker, and advertising expenditures for the category have more than doubled.

Advertising Objectives

The objectives of the launch were as follows:
1. *television*: to persuade countline bar users to try Cadbury's "Thick" Dairy Milk by positioning it as the first countline-shaped bar made of pure milk chocolate.
2. *transit*: to build awareness of Cadbury's "Thick" Dairy Milk and inextricably link the word "Thick" with Cadbury's Dairy Milk to pre-empt competitive entries; to build a distinctive personality for Cadbury's "Thick" Dairy Milk versus all other chocolate bar advertising.

Positioning Statement (theme)

Cadbury's "Thick" Dairy Milk is the ultimate chocolate bar because it provides more chocolate satisfaction than any other bar, moulded or countline. This is because it is made from Cadbury's Dairy Milk, the best quality pure milk chocolate available, and because its thick chunks of chocolate provide a highly satisfying eat appeal.

Timing for Launch Campaign

Two-year launch period.

Target Audience

Male and female moulded and countline users of all ages, but particularly those between the ages of 18 and 34.

Advertising Strategy

Cadbury's "Thick" Dairy Milk delivers a surprisingly thick mouthful of real creamy chocolate (more than any other bar available). It is the first thick chocolate bar made of six chunks of pure Cadbury's Dairy Milk chocolate.

Brand Character

Cadbury's "Thick" Dairy Milk is made from the best milk chocolate money can buy. It will have a popular, warm, human, and light-hearted personality.

Launch Creative

1. *Television*:
  • "Daryl Wells" (storyboard attached)
2. *Transit*:
  • Gymnasthicks
  • The Plot Thickens
  • Birds of a Feather Thick Together
  • Chop Thicks
  • Beware of Thickpockets
  • I Thick, Therefore I mmm . . .
  • Great Minds Thick Alike
  • Thick Joke

Media Objective

To build broad awareness for Cadbury's "Thick" Dairy Milk and maximize reach against the target group.

Media Strategy

The media objectives will be met by utilizing television as the primary vehicle to generate the most cost-efficient broadscale reach of the target group. Transit will be overlaid as a secondary medium to further expand reach and, more importantly, to build frequency in major and minor markets. This is due to the impulse nature of chocolate bar purchases.

Media Budget Summary

Television	90%
Transit	10%
Total	*100%*

ADVERTISING SCHEDULE

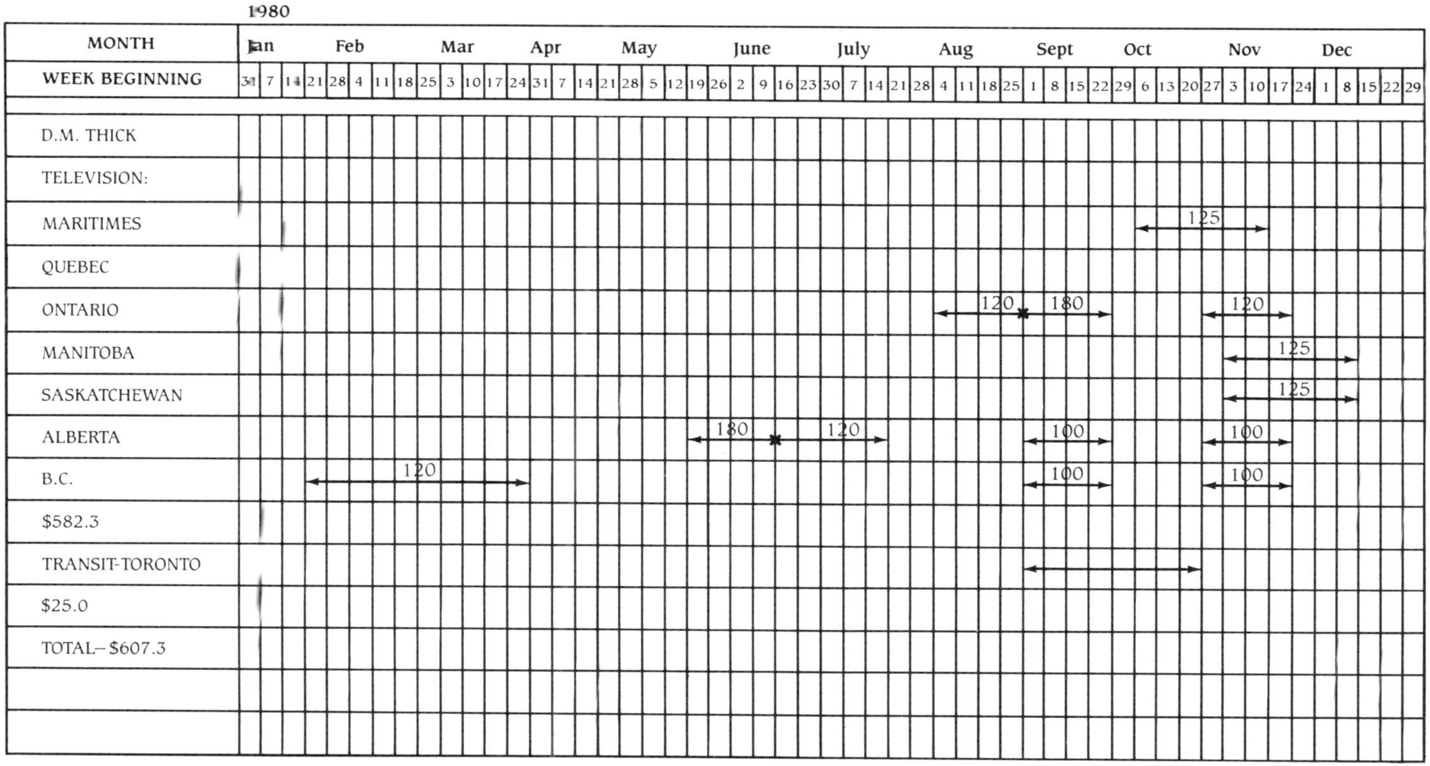

1980

MONTH	Jan	Feb	Mar	Apr	May	June	July	Aug	Sept	Oct	Nov	Dec
WEEK BEGINNING	30 7 14 21 28	4 11 18 25	3 10 17 24 31	7 14 21 28	5 12 19 26	2 9 16 23 30	7 14 21 28	4 11 18 25	1 8 15 22 29	6 13 20 27	3 10 17 24	1 8 15 22 29

D.M. THICK

TELEVISION:

- MARITIMES — 125
- QUEBEC
- ONTARIO — 180 / 120 / 120
- MANITOBA — 125
- SASKATCHEWAN — 125
- ALBERTA — 100 / 100
- B.C. — 120 / 180 / 120 / 100 / 100

$582.3

TRANSIT-TORONTO

$25.0

TOTAL—$607.3

EXHIBIT 1

Cadbury's

Cadbury, Schweppes, Powell
Thick
30 second Television Commercial
"Daryl II"

(SFX) WRAPPER TEARING
ANNCR VO: "There's a thick bar
from Cadbury that's going to
affect you like no other bar
ever has."

DARYL: "They're running along
head to head..."

DARYL: "...and coming to the
top of the stretch..."

DARYL: "...Captain Billy
takes the lead..."

DARYL: "...Dream Away challenging
on the outside..."

DARYL: "...and through the
stretch, Captain Billy and
Dream Away...Dream Away and
Captain Billy."

DARYL: "...and the winner is..."

(SFX) COMING OVER P.A. SYSTEM:
"mmm, mmm, mmm..."

DARYL: "mmm, mmm, mmm...the
winner is...mmm, mmm, mmm..."

ANNCR VO: "Cadbury's Thick
Dairy Milk. Never before,
such thick chunks of creamy
milk chocolate..."

ANNCR VO: "...never before a
taste that is so..."

The Mouth Stopper.

ANNCR VO: "...mmm, mmm, mmm..."

EXHIBIT 2

EXHIBIT 3

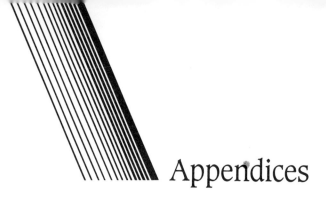

Appendices

Appendix 1

Broadcasting Regulations and Radio Advertising

Courtesy Radio Bureau of Canada. See Chapter 6.

The Broadcasting Act directs the CRTC to regulate and supervise all aspects of the Canadian broadcasting system with a view to implementing the broadcasting policy for Canada declared in Section 3 of the Act. The act empowers the CRTC to make regulations applicable to persons holding broadcasting licences respecting the character of advertising and amount of time that may be devoted to advertising.

The Broadcasting Regulations presently require the pre-clearance of commercials promoting beer, wine, cider, food, drugs, cosmetics and medical devices. In addition, the Commision has placed conditions on the licences of broadcasters requiring adherence to the Broadcast Code for Advertising to Children, which in turn require pre-clearance by the Children's Section of the Advertising Standards Council and le Conseil des Normes de la Publicité, of all broadcast advertising directed to children. The CRTC has a representative in each of these bodies.

The following sections of the CRTC Broadcasting Regulations pertain to advertising on radio:

	Section AM	(FM)
Program logs	4	(5)
Newscasts	5	(9)
Political broadcasts	6	(7)
Commercial messages	7	(8)
Insurance, financial and mining advertising	8	(10)
Liquor, beer, wine and cider advertising	10	(12)
Food and drug advertising	11	(13)

Section 4(5)

Program logs

Each station shall maintain a program log, and shall cause to be entered therein each day the following information:

(a) the date,

(b) the call letter, location and frequency of the station,

(c) the times at which station identification announcements were made;

(d) the title and a brief description of each program broadcast, the name of the sponsors, if any, the time at which the program commenced and concluded and the appropriate code work or letter set out in Schedule 1 indicating the language or origin of the program.

(e) the time and duration of each commercial announcement broadcast, the total commercial time in each sponsored program and the name of the sponsor of each such announcement and program;

(f) the name of the speaker of any talk program and the auspices, if any, under which the talk was given;

(g) the name of any candidate for public office speaking on a political broadcast and his political affiliation, if any;

(h) the name of every person speaking on a political broadcast on behalf of a political party or candidate together with the name of the party or candidate on whose behalf the talk was given; and

(i) in the case of FM stations, the time of the commencement and conclusion of any time segment in which the matter being broadcast is in a foreground format and the code letters set out in Schedule 1 indicating that format.

Section 5(9)

Newcasts

AM

No station or network operator shall broadcast any advertising content in the body of a news broadcast and for the purposes of this section, a summary is deemed to be part of the body of the news broadcast.

FM

1. The first 10 minutes of any newscast shall not be interrupted by a commercial message or public service announcement.

2. For the purposes of this section "newscast" includes headlines, reports of news events and summaries of the news but does not include an announcement that mentions only the place or origin of the news items, the title of the newscasts and the name of the news reader.

Section 6(7)

Political broadcasts

Each station or network operator shall allocate time for the broadcasting of programs, advertising or announcements of a partisan political character on an equitable basis to all parties and rival candidates.

Political programs, advertisements or announcements shall be broadcast by stations or network operators in accordance with such directions as the Commission may issue from time to time.

Section 7(8)

Commercial messages

AM

1. No station shall broadcast commercial messages the total time of which exceeds 250 minutes during the period between six o'clock in the forenoon and twelve o'clock midnight, and the total time of commercial messages in a week shall not exceed 1,500 minutes.

2. No station that is by a condition of licence to broadcasting between the hours of sunrise and sunset only shall broadcast commercial messages the total time of which exceeds 200 minutes during the period between sunrise and sunset in any day and the total time of commercial messages in any week shall not exceed 1,000 minutes.

FM

1. Between six a.m. and twelve midnight of any day

(a) no station operated by the holder of a joint FM licence shall broadcast commercial messages the aggregate time of which exceed 120 minutes, and

(b) no station operated by the holder of an independent FM licence shall broadcast commercial messages the aggregate time of which exceeds 150 minutes.

2. No station operated by the holder of a joint FM licence or an independent FM licence shall, during any clock hour between six a.m. and twelve midnight of any day, broadcast more than ten minutes of commercial messages.

Section 8(10)

Insurance, financial and mining advertising

1. No station or network operator shall broadcast any program or any flash announcement sponsored by any person for the purpose of promoting:

 (a) any act or thing prohibited by the law of Canada or of the province in which the station is located;

 (b) any insurance corporation not authorized by law to carry on business in Canada;

 (c) the investment in bonds, shares or other securities except:

   (i) securities of the Government of Canada or any province, municipality or other public authority

   (ii) certificates issued by any recognized trust company incorporated in Canada as evidence of a term deposit with such trust company, and

   (iii) debentures of any mortgage loan company incorporated in Canada that are insured or guaranteed by a federal or provincial deposit insurance corporation;

or **(d)** the sale of mining, oil or natural gas property or any interest in any mining, oil or natural gas property.

2. Subsection (1) does not apply to the broadcasting of a sponsored program of general quotations of market prices presented without comment.

Offensive or objectionable advertising

3. The Commission may, by notice in writing to any station or network operator, require that station or network operator to modify the character of any advertisement broadcast by that station where, in the opinion of a representative of the Commission, the advertisement is of an offensive or objectionable nature.

Good taste

Since broadcast messages are received in the privacy of the home, reaching old and young alike, there are certain subjects which are unsuitable for this intimate medium and others, which, if they are introduced, must be treated with restraint. Personal hygiene is an example of a topic that must be dealt with discreetly.

Only those commercial messages should be broadcast which can freely be introduced into any gathering in the home as a subject of ordinary conversation.

In the past, certain words, phrases or categories of products have been designated as unacceptable. This is no longer the case. This does not imply any less concern for good taste but does reflect the view that the decision concerning good taste of a commercial is best made by the broadcast licensee, who is responsible for all material broadcast by his station.

The CRTC relies on the licensee to exercise appropriate care in accepting commercial messages for broadcast, and in deciding the suitable time of day or night for the scheduling of certain commercials.

However, in reviewing scripts, the CRTC may ask for the deletion or substitution of certain words, expressions or may reject complete scripts which it may, in the context, consider not to be in good taste.

Section 10(12)

Spirituous liquors, beer, wine and cider

1. Subject to subsection (2), no station or network operator shall broadcast any commercial message:

(a) advertising, directly or indirectly, any spirituous liquor or any beer, wine or cider; or

(b) sponsored by or on behalf of any person whose principal business is the manufacture or sale of spirituous liquor, beer, wine or cider.

2. Where in any province the advertising of beer, wine or cider is permitted, a commercial message sponsored by a brewery, winery or cider-house may be broadcast in the provinces subject to the following conditions:

(a) the advertising shall not be designed to promote the general use of beer, wine or cider, but this prohibition shall not be construed so as to prevent industry, institutional, public service or brand preference advertising;

(b) no commercial message shall exceed sixty seconds in duration;

(c) no device and no commercial message, other than a commercial message allowed under this subsection, shall be used to advertise, directly or indirectly, the sponsor or his product; and

(d) no commercial message shall be broadcast unless it is approved by a representative of the Commission prior to broadcast.

3. For the purpose of determining whether a commercial message may be broadcast in a province pursuant to subsection (2), "cider" means that is considered to be an alcoholic beverage by the law of the province relating to the advertising of cider.

Beer, wine and cider advertising—CRTC procedures

A The main criterion in the approval of scripts is adherence to standards of good taste.

B Advertising shall not

(a) Encourage the general consumption of the product, nor should it attempt to influence non-drinkers to drink;

(b) be associated with youth or youth symbols;

(c) attempt to establish a certain product as a status symbol, a necessity for the enjoyment of life, or an escape from life's problems;

(d) show persons engaged in any activity in which the consumption of alcohol is prohibited.

C Six copies of each commercial must be submitted and received by the Continuity Section of the CRTC at least two weeks prior to the meeting. The name of the province where the commercial is to be broadcast must be mentioned.

D Scripts are examined on scheduled dates (usually every second Wednesday). Any modification to a previously approved script must be indicated. The schedule of meetings may be obtained from the CRTC.

E The advertisers or their agents who so desire, may make personal representations concerning their copy when their commercials are examined.

The Department of Consumer and Corporate Affairs has deemed that, since beer, wine and cider are considered "food" under the Food and Drug Act, the regulations pertaining to that act will be enforced as they apply to those products. Accordingly, all radio commercials for these products will be reviewed by a representative of the Department of Consumer and Corporate Affairs. The Commission will review such commercials in accordance with Sections 10 and 11 of its Radio and Television Broadcasting Regulations.

It should be noted that these commercials will now receive a continuity clearance number which will be valid for a period of one year from the date of approval.

A summary of the provincial regulations concerning the advertising of beer, wine and cider on radio

The advertising of beer, wine or cider is prohibited on radio in the following provinces:
British Columbia
Saskatchewan
New Brunswick
Prince Edward Island

In all provinces where the advertising of beer and wine is allowed, the advertisers must adhere to the CRTC regulations. In addition, each province has specific regulations relating to such advertising.

Guidelines for advertisers are available from the Head Office of the Liquor Boards in each province. The regulations relating to the content of commercial messages as they apply to Radio are essentially the same.

Ontario regulations pertaining to the content of beer, wine and cider commercial messages

(a) Beer, wine and cider advertising must be within the limits of good taste and propriety, having regard at all times to the need for discouraging abusive drinking patterns and encouraging the legal, moderate and safe consumption of alcoholic beverages.

(b) Beer, wine and cider advertisers must take into account at all times the likelihood of minors and adult non-users being exposed to their advertising. The probable audience or readership for an advertisement must consist primarily of drinking age adults.

Advertisers are required to prepare at the Board's request an annual report to the Board containing data on the ages of those exposed to their advertising in the previous one year period, based upon independent qualified sources such as the Bureau of Broadcast Measurement and the Print Measurement Bureau.

(c) There shall be no endorsement, personally or by implication, either directly or indirectly of beer, wine or cider products, by any person or group of persons who may be generally known or recognized either by reason of their exposure in the mass media, or by reputation or achievement, and whose exposure, fame or prestige is a result of activities, work or endeavour in an area other than the production of beer, wine or cider products. Actors or musicians employed in the production of advertising shall not imply that their talent or ability is dependent on the use of the Company's product.

(d) All such advertisements, commercials and endorsements shall be directed towards, and emphasize, the nature and quality of the product being advertised, and shall not imply, directly or indirectly, that social acceptance, personal success, business or athletic achievement may be acquired or result from the use of the product being advertised. All such advertisements shall be directed to the merits of the particular brand being advertised so as to promote brand preference and the responsible use of the product and not the merits of consumption or the encouragement of excessive consumption of beer, wine or cider products.

(e) Advertisements must not suggest that the consumption of alcoholic beverages per se, or of a particular category of alcoholic beverage may be a significant factor in the realization of any lifestyle or the enjoyment of any activity.

(f) Advertisements must not suggest that participants in work, sports, hobby, recreation and other similar activities should consume alcoholic beverages per se, or a particular category of alcoholic beverage or a particular brand of alcoholic beverages whilst engaging in their work or other activity. Nor may advertising suggest that consumption of alcohol in any way enhances performance or enjoyment of these activities.

(g) Advertisements shall not make any claim, direct or implied, of healthful, nutritive, curative, dietetic, stimulative or sedative qualities or properties attributable to beer, wine or cider or to any product mixed with beer, wine or cider.

(h) No media advertisement shall refer to the price at which the product may be purchased, nor to the brand number, nor that it is available in a particular licensed establishment.

(i) Except for advertisements under 2(a) and (b), no corporate name or the name of an organization other than the company displaying the advertisement or on whose behalf the advertisement is displayed shall appear in the advertisement.

(j) Advertisements shall not contain scenes in which the product is actually being consumed. Nor shall the face or figure of any person be unduly exploited as the central theme of the advertisement.

(k) Advertisements shall not appear to suggest or recommend the consumption of beer, wine or cider prior to the driving of a motorized vehicle, or participation in any sort of activity in which the participant's safety is dependent upon normal levels of alertness, physical co-ordination or speed of response, except in authorized messages of moderation. Nor shall any advertisement depict or suggest any activity which is a breach of the Liquor Licence Act or any other Provincial Statute.

(l) Advertisements shall not be directed to, or appear to be directed to, consumption by minors. Pictures of minors or persons who could reasonably be mistaken for minors are not permitted.

SOURCE: Directives on Advertising and Sales Promotions for Beer, Wine and Cider Industries, Liquor Licence Board of Ontario.

Provincial regulations limiting the frequency of beer, wine or cider commercial messages on radio

Alberta: No brewery or winery shall be permitted to purchase more than seven announcements per day, each not to exceed 60 seconds in duration.

Manitoba: Permitted only between 10:00 p.m. each evening and 7:00 a.m. the following morning.

Ontario: In any calendar year, no company shall average more than 55 commercial minutes of broadcast per week on any radio station, with a maximum in any calendar week of 75 commercial minutes.

The weekly time limitations may be extended upon application to the LCBO in the case of special cultural or sporting events but in no case shall the maximum weekly average be exceeded in any calendar year.

No company may broadcast commercials during periods when half or more of the audience is, or is likely to be, under the age of majority, as determined by the Bureau of Broadcast Measurement.

Quebec: No specific regulations on frequency.

Nova Scotia: No company shall sponsor more than three hours of radio programming on any radio station in any calendar week, with a maximum of 78 hours in any calendar year. This time limitation may be extended in the case of cultural or sporting events to cover the entire broadcast of such event.

Newfoundland: No Newfoundland regulations. Subject to CRTC regulations.

Section 11(13)

Food and Drugs

1. No station or network operator shall broadcast any advertisement or testimonial for an article to which the Proprietary or Patent Medicine Act* applies or for a drug, cosmetic or device to which the Food and Drugs Act applies unless the continuity of the advertisement or testimonial has been

---

*The Proprietary or Patent Medicine Act was revoked 1 April 1977, and has been incorporated into the Food and Drug Regulations.

approved by the Department of National Health and Welfare and by a representative of the Commission and bears the registration number (continuity clearance number) assigned by the Commission.

(a) No station or network operator shall broadcast any advertisement or testimonial for a food to which the Food and Drugs Act applies unless the continuity of the advertisement or testimonial has been approved by the Department of Consumer and Corporate Affairs and by a representative of the Commission and bears the registration number assigned by the Commission.

2. No station shall broadcast any recommendation for the prevention, treatment or cure of a disease or ailment unless the continuity thereof has been approved by the Department of National Health and Welfare and by a representative of the Commission and bears the registration number (continuity clearance number) assigned by the Commission.

The procedure for obtaining approval for broadcast commercials for products or services covered by Section 11

Prior to review by the CRTC, the appropriate government branch of either the Department of National Health and Welfare Canada or the Department of Consumer and Corporate Affairs reviews the commercial.

Continuities submitted for approval should be forwarded to the commission in triplicate at least two weeks in advance of intended use.

1. All commercials for food products must be reviewed by:
Food Division
Consumer Fraud Protection Branch
Consumer Standards Directorate Department of Consumer and Corporate Affairs
Place du Portage, Phase 1
68 Victoria Street
Hull, Quebec K1A 0C9

Restaurant commercials

Commercials for food dispensed to consumers from restaurant facilities (including drive-ins) need not be submitted for approval under Regulation 11 if they meet all of the following conditions:

(a) They are local advertisements, specially prepared for a city or metropolitan area;

(b) They are in good taste;

(c) They contain no direct or implied nutritional claims;

(d) They make no negative or derogatory statements;

(e) They make no reference to the safety of the food;

(f) Standard foods should be stated by their common name.

Perishable food products

In the case of perishable food products, temporary clearance may be obtained from the Local Inspector of the Department of Consumer and Corporate Affairs when an emergency arises.

Perishables consist of fresh produce in season, such as fruit, vegetables, fish and bakery products of a variety that cannot be stored without spoilage. It does not include any manufactured or processed products, either preserved or frozen, which may be stored in a refrigerator.

To obtain temporary clearance, a total of five (5) copies of the commercial should be prepared, of which two (2) copies should be submitted to the Local Inspector, and three (3) copies mailed to the CRTC and marked to indicate that temporary approval has been obtained.

Stock commercials

The problem of submitting commercials two weeks in advance of broadcast, where the small dealer or local merchant may wish to publicize specials on a particular day, may be met by preparing stock commercials. These may be submitted for approval, then placed on the agency or station file for emergency use.

1. All commercials for drugs or cosmetics must be previewed by:
   Drugs & Cosmetics,
   Product Regulation Division,
   Bureau of Drug Surveillance,
   Drug Directorate,
   Health Protection Branch,
   Health & Welfare Canada,
   Place Vanier, Tower B,
   355 River Road,
   Vanier, Ontario,
   K1A 1B8

It is not permitted to advertise prescription or therapeutic vitamin preparations, and drugs for human use which carry a recommended single or daily dosage or a statement of concentration in excess of the limits provided by Section C.01.021 of the Food and Drug Regulations.

The offer of drugs as samples by Radio is not allowed.

3. All commercials for "device products" must be reviewed by:
   Bureau of Medical Devices
   Health Protection Branch
   Environmental Health Directorate
   Health and Welfare Canada
   Tunney's Pasture
   Ottawa, Ontario K1A 0I.2

Section 19 of the Food and Drugs Act states:
No person shall sell any device that, when used according to directions or under such conditions as are customary or usual, may cause injury to the health of the purchaser of user thereof.

Some examples of device products are:
Health studios or reducing salons, contraceptives, optical supplies (i.e., contact lenses), hearing devices, anti-smoking devices or methods, etc.

CRTC approval
Six scripts are initially submitted to the CRTC at least two weeks in advance of intended use. The CRTC then passes them on to the appropriate department for review. If the proposed commercials are approved by the department concerned and the CRTC, they are assigned continuity clearance numbers which are valid for a period of one year.

The CRTC may make a correction to the commercial while reviewing it. So long as that correction is made in the final script and nothing else is changed, the commercial is considered approved.

Advertisers may appeal modifications, deletions or rejections of food and drug copy. With supporting evidence for claims made, appeals should be addressed to:
Chairman
Canadian Radio-Television and
Telecommunications Commission
Ottawa, Ontario K1A 0N2

Commercials must be broadcast exactly as cleared. Where any revision in words or visual material is made, the revised commercial must be forwarded for approval prior to broadcast.

Single phrases or claims cannot be cleared. Commercials must be submitted in their entirety, in the form in which they are to be broadcast.

Since the regulations may change from year to year, yearly approvals are necessary. If circumstances warrant, the copy may be requested for review within that one year period. Prior to expiration of the one year period, commercials may be submitted for approval for an additional one year period.

Although a commercial announcement may be provided with a continuity clearance number, this does not imply any obligation on the part of the broadcaster to broadcast the announcement. Final discretion as to whether an approved commercial shall be broadcast or not rests with the licensee.

Appendix 2
Advertising Production

This technical appendix provides an overview of the most common tools and techniques used to produce print and broadcast advertisements.

Print Production

Typography

To someone not familiar with the field of typography, the selection of a type style for a print advertisement may seem like a trivial task. However, there are hundreds of styles to chose from, and these come in myriad sizes and weights.

Different Type Groups

ROMAN. Roman characters are the most familiar and widely used. They are formed with a succession of broad and thin strokes and contain serifs, which are thin lines on the end of unconnected strokes. Roman faces are easy to read, which explains their popularity and frequent use in the body text of print advertisements. Roman characters are generally classified into two subgroups: Old Style and Modern. Modern roman characters are more formal and precise, have less contrast between thick and thin strokes, and have straight, horizontal serifs. These differences can be observed by comparing a popular Old Style face, such as Garamond, with a commonly used Modern face, such as Bodoni (Figure A1). Some Roman styles,

like Baskerville, do not fall clearly into either of the preceding categories, but borrow characteristics from both. Such typefaces are considered to form a transitional group between Old Style and Modern Roman characters.

SANS SERIF OR BLOCK. After Roman styles, sans serif characters are the most widely used in advertising. Their design is a straightforward and contemporary; the letters do not have serifs, and the strokes have a uniform thickness. The typeface Helvetica belongs to this category (Figure A1).

SQUARE SERIF OR EGYPTIAN. These typefaces represent a mixture of Roman and sans serif, as they take the latter's formality of design and uniformity of strokes, but nevertheless contain thick, square serifs. This type is especially appropriate for display material.

SCRIPT AND CURSIVE. This lettering very much resembles handwriting. It is almost never used in the body text of an advertisement but can be used for headlines when a special effect is desired.

BLACKLETTER. This style is rarely used because its ornamented characters are not very legible (Figure A1). However, it conveys antiquity and can be used for products or product lines for which such a connotation would be desirable.

This classification is by no means exhaustive. A multitude of typefaces borrow characteristics

Garamond

abcdefghijklmnopqrstuvwxyz
ABCDEFGHIJKLMNO
PQRSTUVWXYZ
12345678910 1234567890
★ ✔ –® • □ %ſ__ 1234567890
$]?)½;'⅓*,. ¼ $[&(/:'⅔¢¾

Commercial Script

abcdefghijklmnopqrstuvwxyz
ABCDEFGHIJKLMNO
PQRSTUVWXYZ
12345678910   – ± ÷ × = †‡§@ – °
★ ✔ #® ©□•% ●__   ☆{}|¶■◄►'"
$]?)½;'⅓*,.¼   +[&(/:'⅔–¾

Souvenir Medium

abcdefghijklmnopqrstuvwxyz
ABCDEFGHIJKLMNO
PQRSTUVWXYZ
12345678910 – ± ÷ × = †‡-@°
¡/*¢©˜©Ç%__ !ºª#®˜ç«»
$é?);'^,. ‡ &¿(:`

Park Avenue

abcdefghijklmnopqrstuvwxyz
ABCDEFGHIJKLMNO
PQRSTUVWXYZ
12345678910   – ± ÷ × = †‡§@ – °
★ ✔ #® ©□•% ●__   ☆{}| ¶ ■◄►'"
$]?)½;'⅓*,.¼   +[&(/:'⅔–¾

Old English

abcdefghijklmnopqrstuvwxyz
ABCDEFGHIJKLMNO
PQRSTUVWXYZ
12345678910   – ± ÷ × = †‡§@ – °
★ ✔ #® ©□•‰ ●__   ☆{}|¶■◄►'"
$]?)½;'⅓*,.¼   +[&(/:'⅔–¾

FIGURE A1   Examples of Character Types

from the categories outlined above and are therefore unclassifiable. Some other styles are so original as to form a distinct group. Such styles are frequently used in advertising headlines to capture readers' attention and some are designed exclusively for use in one advertisement.

Type Measurement

A special system of measurement is used in typography. Letter height is measured in points. Each point represents about 0.35 millimetres, so there are about 28.5 points to a centimetre. The most commonly used character sizes are: 6, 7, 8, 9, 10, 12, 14, 18, 24, 30, 36, 42, 48, 60, 72, 84, 96, and 120 points. A height of 12 points is called a *pica*.

The *em* is the unit used to measure both height and width. A character that is ten points high and ten points wide measures ten ems. A 12-point em is generally referred to as a *pica em*.

Principles of Good Typography

Type plays an important role in enhancing an advertisement's effectiveness by making the message more attractive, capturing the reader's attention, and/or conveying extra information about the product or product line. To make the best use of type, a typographer must obey some basic rules, and also use imagination and creativity. In this, one can say that typography is an art as well as a science. Like any art form, it is subject to certain fundamental constraints.

One of the most important standards of good typography is *legibility*. If an advertisement is difficult to read, the potential consumer in the target audience will not go through the trouble of deciphering it. Among the factors that increase or decrease readability are:

• *size of letters*. In body text, letter sizes between 8 and 12 points should generally be used. Large-sized headings are more likely to attract attention, but spacing should be proportional to the size of type.

• *spacing*. Words and letters should not be too close together, nor separated by too much blank space because reading becomes more difficult. Readers do not move their eyes in a continuous movement along the page but shift them from one group of words to the next. These shifts are the most time-consuming aspect of reading. To reduce them to a minimum, the distance between words should not be too great. For the same reason, lines should not be too long.

The space between lines—the leading—should ideally be equal to the space between words. There should also be more space between paragraphs than between lines.

• *length of lines*. It is often necessary to break headings into several lines. Each line should contain a word or group of words that makes sense by itself, so that readers can understand the heading at a glance. Such headings as the following should be avoided:

THE NEW XEROX COPIER: A
BREAKTHROUGH IN OFFICE
AUTOMATION

A more effective heading is:

THE NEW XEROX COPIER:
A BREAKTHROUGH
IN OFFICE AUTOMATION

Uppercase letters are less legible than lower case characters but their appearance is more striking. In the same way, even though italics are useful for emphasizing a word or a group of words, they are less readable and should therefore be avoided for entire body texts.

A good type style should not clash with the mood of the advertisement or the message. For instance, Blackletter characters would be incongruous in a commercial for a state-of-the-art IBM microcomputer. A delicate, ornamental script would be appropriate for advertising women's perfume but not after-shave lotion. Type styles carry important connotations for consumers, and advertisers should be careful to avoid using lettering that might weaken the effectiveness of their advertising message.

Typesetting

Once the character style and text format have been selected, the advertisement must be set in type. Many techniques are available for this task.

Metal Typesetting

Until recently, the most widespread techniques of typesetting relied on movable metal characters.

HAND SETTING. Hand setting has largely been replaced by more efficient, less expensive methods. It is now mainly used for display material. With hand typesetting, an operator selects the needed characters from a box divided into compartments containing the letters, numbers, punctuation, and various symbols. These are inserted into a composition stick, which is a tray that holds the characters for one line of text. Once a line has been completed, the characters are cast and the resulting mould is placed on a galley tray. The movable characters are then returned to their respective compartments or job cases in the type font, ready to be used again.

Although this method allows for a greater flexibility than mechanical techniques, it is tedious and expensive, and more practical methods have been perfected.

MACHINE SETTING. Machine setting covers two types of processes: linotype and monotype.

Linotype. A linotype machine somewhat resembles a massive and very complex typewriter. When the operator punches the keyboard, brass characters or matrices are released from the magazine of the machine and form words on the operator's right. Narrow triangular wedges or space bands are inserted between each word. Once a line is completed, the space bands are pushed up, increasing the space between words until the line is just the right length to justify the right- and left-hand margins. After this has been done, the line is cast. The resulting cast (or slug) is deposited onto a galley tray. The matrices are then returned to the magazine, ready to be re-used. Linotype is a very efficient way to set type and is therefore widely used for newspapers. Corrections may be somewhat onerous, since changing an individual character involves resetting the whole line.

Monotype. Monotype avoids the inconvenience of linotype. Letters are cast individually, and individual corrections can thus be made without destroying a whole line. Monotype machines usually comprise two units—a keyboard and a caster. The operator punches words onto the keyboard. The text is then stored in the form of perforations on a paper ribbon. At the end of each line, a calculator integrated with the keyboard indicates the amount of space that must be inserted between words in order to justify the right- and left-hand margins. The operator punches this amount at the end of the line. The ribbon is then fed to the caster, which automatically casts individual letters and places the mouldings on a galley tray. The caster "reads" the ribbon backwards, so that it knows the amount to insert between each word before composing the line. This system is more expensive than linotype and therefore is less commonly used for the body text of advertisements, but it is useful for printing display material.

Phototypography

Printing by using plates composed of movable metal characters has been almost completely replaced by more efficient methods. The technique of phototypography involves exposing text onto photosensitive paper or film. Phototypography has many advantages, because it allows for more aesthetic lettering, a wider array of letter styles, increased sharpness and quality of detail, and greater versatility.

Photodisplay

This method enables an operator to compose a display manually and then expose it onto photosensitive paper or film. This allows for great flexibility, since an artist can compose almost any kind of display or headline without the constraints or costs of metal typography. Semi-automatic photodisplay allows the operator to see each character before it is exposed individually, set the right letter size through lenses incorporated into the photodisplay machine, and adjust the spacing.

PHOTOTEXT. One example of the phototext process is monophoto, which is based on the same principle as the monotype machine except that the metal matrices are replaced by negatives of letters that are exposed on film. Operators use a keyboard that resembles a monotype keyboard and produces a paper ribbon or magnetic tape onto which the text is coded. The lines are automatically adjusted to the right length, because a calculator incorporated into the machine tells the operator how much extra space must be inserted between words. The paper ribbon or tape is then fed into a photo-processing unit that uses negative film fonts to expose the words on film or photosensitive paper. For advertisements, film is more common.

Other machines are more sophisticated and have electronic features. Such machines are the most widely used in advertising, and include the Alphatype and Linofilm. In an age in which computers are rapidly taking over in all walks of life, typesetting is no exception to this rule. As computers increase in cost-effectiveness and versatility, their use will become even more widespread.

It is possible to print display material with any kind of automatic phototext equipment, but the results are generally inferior to photodisplay equipment.

Phototext equipment for advertising does not develop the film. This must be executed separately, either by hand or through an automatic film processor. Film allows more flexibility than metal type, and trademarks or logotypes can easily be included. Once the film is obtained, it must be transferred onto a printing plate before the actual printing.

Printing

Generally, in the case of newspaper or magazine advertisements, advertisers have no control over the printing technique which is used, as this depends solely on the newspaper that is carrying the advertisement. With other print advertisements, such as catalogues or posters, advertisers must base their choice on such considerations as cost effectiveness and quality of print. The most common techniques for printing advertisements are letterpress, gravure, and offset.

LETTERPRESS. Letterpress has traditionally been the most popular technique and is based on the principle of relief printing. It involves taking a printing plate on which the letters are raised above the non-printing surface, inking the entire surface, and then pressing the plate onto the paper. Three kinds of printing presses rely on this process: the platen or job press, gravure or intaglio, and offset lithography.

With the *platen* or the job press paper is placed on a flat surface and the printing plate is pressed on top of it (Figure A2). This technique is slow and rather impractical for printing large runs. A more convenient method is the *cylinder press*, in which paper is placed on a cylinder that rolls over the printing surface. The most practical and popular method is the *rotary press*, because of its high printing speed. Both the printing surface and the printing plate are cylindrical, and the paper is fed between the two rolls, either in the form of individual sheets or in the form of a roll. By using several cylinders, it is easy to print in colour or print on both sides of one page simultaneously. Of course, rotary printing involves the additional task of putting the printing plate onto a curved surface, either by using stereotypes or electrotypes or flexible plastic printing plates.

GRAVURE OR INTAGLIO. This process involves printing from a depressed surface. It is the reverse of letterpress, since the printing surface

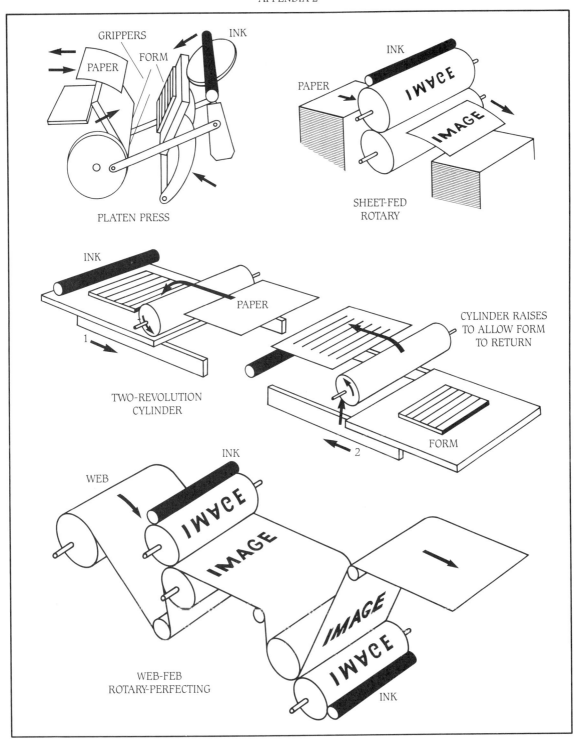

FIGURE A2   Types of Letterpress Presses

is etched into the plate (Figure A3). The ink is deposited on the printing plate by a roller, and then a knife clears the non-printing surface of ink so that ink remains only in the tiny wells etched into the plate. Once this is done, the printing plate is pressed onto a sheet of paper, which absorbs the excess ink.

OFFSET LITHOGRAPHY. Offset lithography uses a smooth surface to print the material (Figure A4). The first phase of offset printing requires the preparation of a special photographic plate made of aluminum or copper. This cylindrical plate is wet, and because of its chemical properties, water remains on the non-printing surface. Next, a greasy ink is applied on the plate. It cannot mix with water, so it adheres only to those parts of the cylinder that are not wet (the printing surface). Next, the printing cylinder is pressed onto a smooth surface or a blanket cylinder. The text is transferred onto the paper by the cylinder, which serves as an intermediary between the actual printing plate and the paper. Offset lithography is relatively inexpensive and easy to carry out.

Photoengraving

Most print advertisements also contain illustrations. Photoengraving is the process of creating special printing plates for reproducing illustrations. There are two main types of photoengraving; line and half-tone.

LINE ENGRAVING. Line engravings are generally used for drawings or diagrams that do not contain any shading. First a picture of the drawing is taken in order to obtain a negative. Then light is projected through the negative onto a metallic plate covered with a light-sensitive emulsion. This emulsion hardens on the areas that have been exposed to light. The soft emulsion that coincides with the non-printing surface is then removed. Next, an acid is applied to the plate. The acid eats away at the metal but does not attack the emulsion. Therefore, the surface that is to be printed is raised relative to the non-

printing surface. This last phase is etching. Finally, the plate is routed to remove more metal from the non-printing surface and increase the precision and contrast of the drawing.

HALF-TONE ENGRAVING. The process of reproducing pictures containing different shades of black and white is slightly more complicated than line engraving, although it is similar in principle. The main difference is that the film is exposed through a grid. The light coming from the picture is decomposed into dots that appear on the negative. The size of each dot is proportional to the intensity of the light. A printing plate is created from the negative in much the same way as in line engraving. Although only black and white is used in half-tone, the illusion of different shades of gray can be created by increasing or decreasing the size of the dots. The concentration of black therefore determines an infinity of shades of gray even though only two discrete colours are used.

COLOUR PHOTOENGRAVING. The three primary colours—yellow, red, and blue—are mixed with black to obtain a colour photoengraving. Four half-tone plates are produced, one for each of the three primary colours and for black. The plates are obtained by making four distinct negatives, using light filters so that only the desired colour is transferred to each negative. The four half-tones are then reproduced on a sheet of paper. A superimposition of two or more colours can create the illusion of any colour in the spectrum. (See Plate X1.)

Duplicating the Advertisement

If an advertisement is to be carried by several newspapers or magazines, an advertising agency must send duplicates of the original printing plates to all the newspaper publishers on its media list. These duplicates can be made by stereotype or electrotype.

STEREOTYPES. Stereotypes are obtained by pressing the original printing plate onto a mat,

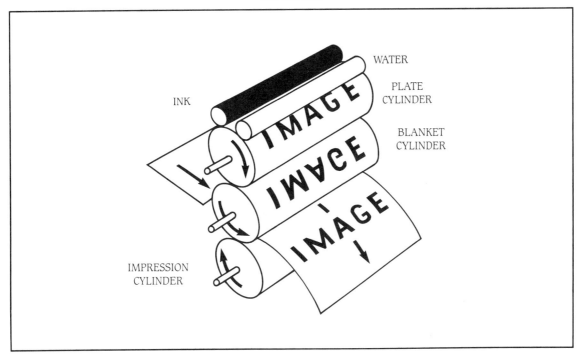

FIGURE A3   The Offset Lithographic Press

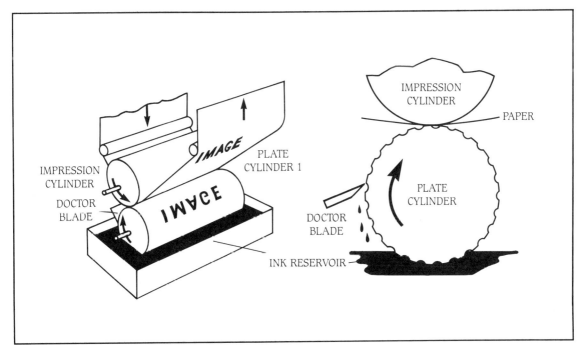

FIGURE A4   A Gravure Press

which is made of a soft, cardboard-like substance. The mat then takes the shape of the advertisement. It is sent to the newspaper, which can make the stereotype by casting the mats into molten lead. Plastic rather than cardboard can also be used for the mats.

ELECTROTYPES. Electrotypes are more expensive to produce but allow for sharper detail. A mould of the original plate is made with wax or lead. This mould is then plunged into a electrolytic substance, where it is covered with a very thin layer of copper or aluminum. This thin coat is removed from the wax or vinylite, routed, and mounted.

Telecast Production

Choosing the Medium for the Commercial

The two types of media for producing a television commercial are film and videotape. Producers who rely on the former may use 35-mm film or the less expensive, lower quality 16-mm film. If a commercial is intended for extensive national airing, it would be unwise to use anything but the very best quality film. Local advertisers, however, may prefer the cheaper 16-mm film. Taped commercials use one of three standard sizes: 2 inch, 1 inch, and 3/4 inch, although 2-inch tapes are most commonly relied on for good quality pictures.

One of the first decisions a producer must make is whether to use film or videotape. Although film has traditionally enjoyed widespread use, tape is considered by many to be the medium of the future.

In many respects tape is an improvement over film. First and foremost, tape offers the advantage of immediate feedback; editors can see how the commercial will look on TV while it is being taped in the studio. In addition, new computerized techniques have greatly enhanced the speed and effectiveness of editing on tape.

All these improvements have reduced the production time from several weeks for a filmed commercial to one or two days. Furthermore, tape is usually less expensive and more durable—a taped commercial can run indefinitely, while film will show signs of wear after about 25 runs. Finally, tape can lend a commercial a more live mood. However, there are drawbacks: tape is considered a cheap medium, whereas film projects a higher quality image. Film also makes for more flexibility than tape and is therefore advised for shooting in remote places. This difference is disappearing rapidly, however, with the advent of less cumbersome portable videotape recorders. Thus there is no clear-cut advantage to using one medium rather than the other. The producer must evaluate each situation individually and decide which means is more appropriate for the mood, circumstances, and technical constraints of the commercial.

After the Commercial Is Shot

Once a commercial has been shot, the producer has several yards of film or tape containing numerous versions of each scene. This material, called the *dailies* or *rushes*, is sent to the editor, who selects the best scenes and assembles them into a rough version of the commercial. This work print or rough cut is then submitted to the client for tentative approval. Next, the editor prepares the sound track on a separate reel and installs the opticals, which are the special effects intended to provide a smooth transition from one scene to the next. The most commonly used opticals are:

- the *cut*: this is the simplest technique, since one scene simply replaces the next;
- the *matte*: one scene is placed over another so that two or more scenes occupy the screen;
- the *wipe*: the next scene just slides over the previous one, from any direction, or according to some geometric pattern;
- the *dissolve*: as one scene fades out, the next picture gradually appears, so that the two scenes briefly overlap;

- the *zoom*: the camera suddenly focuses on one element of a scene or moves from a closeup to a long shot.

Next, the sound track and the film are synchronized on the same reel, yielding the composite, or optical print. Once this composite print has been approved by the client, it becomes an answer print and is ready for the final stages of production, when the editor puts in the finishing touches, correcting the colour and perfecting the synchronization. From the final print, duplicates (dupes or release prints) are made, and sent to the various stations to be aired.

GLOSSARY

(English/French)

Account *(compte-client).* A term designating a current client of an advertising agency.

Account Executive *(chargé de compte).* A member of the advertising agency's account service group.

Account Service Group *(service de comptes clients).* Group of specialists provided by a full-service advertising agency to ensure a liaison between the client and the agency and to supervise the planning and execution of the client's advertising campaign.

Advertiser *(publicitaire).* A firm or organization that uses advertising with or without the use of an advertising agency.

Advertising *(publicité).* A marketing communication process that directs messages to prospects through the mass media as a means of meeting marketing objectives.

Advertising Agency *(agence de publicité).* An organization providing advertising services to advertisers.

Advertising Appropriation *(allocation publicitaire).* The total sum of money to be spent on advertising within a planning period.

Advertising Budget *(budget de publicité).* A detailed plan specifying how the total amount of money allocated to advertising is to be spent within a planning period.

Advertising Campaign *(campagne de publicité).* A co-ordinated advertising effort conducted over a specified period of time, using messages placed in selected media in order to reach specific objectives.

Advertising Information *(information publicitaire).* The bulk of information that potential buyers receive through the usual advertising media.

Advertising Plan *(plan de publicité).* A plan that describes in some detail the entire advertising program to be followed over a specified period of time.

Advertising Standards Council *(Conseil des normes de la publicité).* A national association of public and business organizations responsible for providing voluntary guidelines to the Canadian advertising industry.

Advertising Strategy *(stratégie de publicité).* An advertising program for the target market segment(s) designed to achieve the campaign's communication objectives within a specified budget and time period.

Affective Attitude Components *(composantes affectives de l'attitude).* Components of the attitude structure that include the feelings and affective reactions provoked by a message.

Affiliate *(membre).* A television or radio station that has a contractual agreement with one network and that must carry specific programs, including commercials.

Agate Line *(ligne d'agate).* A unit of space measurement for newspapers that is one column wide and 1.8 mm (¼″) deep.

Agency Charges *(frais d'agence).* Additional costs, chargeable to the client, incurred by the agency in developing the advertising campaign.

Agency Commission *(commission d'agence).* Compensation (usually 15 per cent) paid to an advertising agency by the advertising medium for time and space bought by an agency on a client's behalf.

Agency of Record *(agence de coordination).* A client that deals with several advertising agencies may select one agency (of record) to assume the co-ordination of media use by the various agencies involved and to qualify for media discounts.

Aided Recall *(rappel assisté).* Percentage of individuals indicating that they know of a brand when presented with that brand name.

A-la-Carte Agency *(agence à-la-carte).* A full service advertising agency that allows clients to choose unbundled services tailored to their needs.

Argumentative Advertisement *(annonce argumentative).* An advertisement that gives potential buyers specific and explicit reasons to buy a product or a particular brand.

Artist *(artiste).* Individual in an agency responsible for developing the visual or audio component of the advertising creative strategy.

Attitude *(attitude).* A hypothetical construct that intervenes between buyers' perception formation process and actual behaviour as they are exposed to stimuli and communications from the marketing environment.

Attitude Structure *(structure des attitudes).* A system of cognitions, positive or negative evaluations, emotional feelings, and pro or con action tendencies regarding social objects.

Audience *(auditoire).* An individual or group of individuals for whom a communicator's message is intended.

Audience Duplication *(duplication d'auditoire).* The number of people or households reached by two media vehicles.

Audience Fragmentation *(fragmentation de l'auditoire).* A situation of reduced reach and higher costs due to the increasing number of vehicles at any given time.

Audio *(audio).* Sound portion of a broadcast commercial.

Audit Bureau of Circulation (ABC). An association of advertisers, agencies, and publishers that conducts audits of reported paid circulation of various periodicals.

Availability *(disponibilité).* Unsold commercial time that is available for purchase by an advertiser.

Background Music *(musique de fond).* Live or recorded music used in a commercial in order to convey a certain mood or atmosphere.

Backlight *(affiche illuminée de l'arrière).* An outdoor advertisement printed on reinforced translucent plastic and illuminated from the rear.

Bait (and Switch) Advertising *(publicité appât et substitution).* Low price offer to induce buyers to come to a store where it is difficult or impossible to buy the product at the advertised price.

Behavioural Segmentation *(segmentation selon les réactions comportementales).* Segmentation of markets by finding "natural". groupings of consumers with the same consumer needs and problems and similar lifestyles.

Benefit Segmentation *(segmentation selon les bénéfices que les consommateurs retirent des produits).* Segmentation of markets according to the benefits that users seek from products.

Billing *(facturation).* A term used by an advertising agency to refer to the total amount an advertiser spends through the agency.

Bleed Advertisement *(annonce à franc bord).* An advertisement printed to the very edge of a page, thus having no margin.

Blocking Chart *(tableau des périodes).* A document summarizing the media schedule.

Blow-Up *(agrandissement).* Enlarged reproduction of print artwork.

Body Copy *(texte descriptif d'une annonce).* The main copy blocks of an advertisement.

Borrowed Interest *(attention par utilisation d'un intermédiaire).* A technique that uses someone (e.g., a baby) or something (e.g., a cat or parrot) to attract attention to the advertised product.

Boutique Agency *(agence de création).* See CREATIVE BOUTIQUE.

Brand *(marque).* The name, term, symbol, design, or any combination of these elements, that distinguish a firm's products from competing products.

Brand Awareness *(connaissance de la marque).* Refers to the level of brand knowledge that customers have acquired.

Brand Development Index *(indice de développement du marché).* An index of per capita sales of a brand in a given market compared to the national figure.

Brand Image *(image de marque).* The set of attributes that consumers perceive as belonging to a brand.

Brand Image Value *(valeur de l'image de marque).* A comparison of the brand image against the traits that buyers in the market segment would consider positive or negative for a brand in that product category.

Brand Loyalty *(loyauté à la marque).* Loyalty of a customer to a particular brand.

Brand Manager *(chef de marque).* In many large packaged goods companies, this is the individual responsible for planning, executing, and controlling the advertising campaign for one (or a few) brand(s) and for co-ordinating the advertising between the agency and the company.

Brand Name *(nom commercial).* Name of a product offering or service. It refers to the verbal element of a brand.

Brand Preference *(préférence de marque).* The degree to which prospects consider a brand acceptable or unacceptable, especially in relation to competitive brands.

Broadsheet *(journal grand format).* A full-size newspaper approximately 380 mm wide and 560 mm deep (15″ by 22″).

Broadside or Bedsheet *(in-plano).* A large sheet with full colour illustrations that are folded for direct-mail distribution and used to create high impact.

Brochure *(dépliant publicitaire).* A high quality booklet used in direct mail advertising.

Bureau of Broadcast Measurement (BBM). A non-profit organization of advertisers, agencies, and broadcasters that provides estimates of radio and television audiences.

Buy *(achat).* The purchase of time or space.

Buyer *(acheteur).* The individual(s) in the advertising agency responsible for purchasing radio time, and/or television time, and/or space in print media.

Buying Service *(service d'achats média).* See MEDIA BUYING SERVICE

Campaign Reach *(couverture de la compagne).* See REACH

Canadian Advertising Rates and Data (CARD). A monthly catalogue of advertising media rates and other related information.

Canadian Advertising Research Foundation (CARF). A non-profit organization supported by advertisers, advertising agencies, and media to improve the effectiveness of advertising through the use of proper research methods.

Canadian Association of Broadcasters (CAB). A national organization of broadcasters that manages a credit rating system of advertising agencies.

Canadian Broadcasting Corporation (CBC) *(Société Radio Canada).* A Crown corporation established in 1936 to provide national broadcasting service. The CBC's Commercial Acceptance Committee must approve all commercials to be aired on its stations.

Canadian Circulation Audit Board (CCAB). An association of advertisers, agencies, and publishers that conducts audits of reported circulations of business publications and some controlled-circulation consumer magazines.

Canadian Community Newspapers Association (CCNP). A national organization of Canadian community newspapers that manages a credit rating system of advertising agencies.

Canadian Daily Newspaper Publishers Association (CDNPA). A national organization founded in 1925 whose membership consists of most major daily newspaper publishers. The association manages a credit rating system of advertising agencies.

Canadian Radio-Television and Telecommunications Commission (CRTC) *(Conseil de la Radiodiffusion et des Télécommunications Canadiennes).* Commission established by the Broadcasting Act of 1968 to regulate and supervise all aspects of the Canadian broadcasting system.

Caption *(légende).* Text accompanying an illustration.

Car Card Advertising *(publicité dans les voitures de transport en commun).* An advertisement placed inside transit vehicles.

CARD. See CANADIAN ADVERTISING RATES and DATA

Carry-Over Effect of Advertising *(effet différé de l'action publicitaire).* Advertising expenses for one year may affect subsequent periods but may yield diminishing results as time elapses.

Cents-Off Deal *(offre de réduction promotionnelle).* A sales promotion technique that consists of offering a temporary price reduction to entice consumers to try or repurchase a brand.

Circular *(prospectus).* An advertisement printed on one page and used in direct-mail advertising.

Circulation *(circulation).* The number of copies of a publication that are sold or distributed. Also used for outdoor advertising to refer to the number of people exposed to a poster during a given time period.

Classified Advertising *(annonce classée).* A form of media advertising in which the message may be very short and falls into specific categories grouped together without editorial matter around it.

Closing Date *(date de clôture ou date limite).* The date when advertising material must arrive at a publication to appear in the next issue.

Clucas Method *(méthode Clucas).* A theatre test conducted by J.E. Clucas and Associates.

Clutter *(méli-mélo).* A situation in which an advertisement must compete for attention with many other messages, thus reducing its effectiveness.

Cognitive Attitude Components *(composantes cognitives des attitudes).* Components of the attitude structure that include the knowledge an individual has acquired as well as the evaluation of the importance of information.

Cognitive Dissonance *(dissonance cognitive).* The psychological tension that develops when an individual is exposed to information that contradicts some information already assimilated or that constitutes the personal beliefs of the individual.

Colour Separation *(séparation des couleurs).* Separation of colour copy into primary colours using colour filters.

Commercial *(message publicitaire).* An advertising message in the broadcast media.

Commission *(commission).* See AGENCY COMMISSION

Communication Channels *(canaux de communication).* The media used to convey a message to an audience.

Communication Task *(tâche de communication).* The intended effect(s) of the advertising campaign on the target audience.

Communicator *(émetteur).* An individual or organization initiating the communication.

Community Antenna Television (CATV). A system for distributing any television signal directly to homes by means of a cable.

Comparative Advertising *(publicité comparative).* A technique for showing how an advertised brand is superior to competitive brands.

Composition *(composition).* Setting of type for printing.

Conative Attitude Components *(composantes conatives des attitudes).* The components of the attitude structure that refer to an individual's tendency to act toward the attitude object.

Concentrated Marketing *(marketing concentré).* The selection of a small segment of the total market in order to concentrate all a firm's marketing resources to satisfying this single segment.

Conceptual Segmentation Criterion *(critère conceptuel de segmentation).* The defining of various consumer groups on the basis of consumers' needs and desires.

Consumer Advertising *(publicité grand public)*. Advertising directed toward the ultimate consumer of products or services.

Consumer Protection Act (Quebec) *(Loi sur la protection du consommateur)*. A legislative act passed in April 1980. The Committee for the Application of Articles 248 and 249 decides whether a commercial is directed toward children under 13 years, which is unlawful under this Act.

Contests *(concours)*. A sales promotion technique similar to sweepstakes, except that the consumer must demonstrate some skills in answering a question or performing a task.

Continuity of Campaign *(continuité de la campagne)*. The overall pattern of advertising exposures over the time horizon of the campaign.

Co-operative Advertising *(publicité à frais partagés)*. Joint advertising between a manufacturer and a retailer whereby the manufacturer covers part of the costs of advertising a brand in the retailer's advertising.

Copy *(texte de l'annonce)*. Original material for a print advertisement, such as text, illustration, or photographs that are put into final form for printing. Also refers to the advertisement's body copy.

Copy Testing *(tests de messages publicitaires)*. Verifying whether an advertisement or a commercial has had the intended effect on consumers. May be done before (pre-test) or after (post-test) the start of the campaign.

Copywriter *(concepteur-rédacteur)*. The individual responsible for developing the verbal or written communication of the advertising creative strategy.

Corporate Advertising *(publicité institutionnelle)*. Advertising aimed at enhancing a company's image among selected target groups or the overall population.

Corrective Advertising *(publicité correctrice)*. Advertising run (voluntarily or as a result of a court order) to correct a misleading or false advertisement.

Cost per Rating Point *(coût unitaire de couverture brute)*. The cost of a schedule divided by the GRPs delivered by that schedule.

Cost per Thousand *(coût par mille)*. The cost of reaching one thousand units of the audience of one particular vehicle, calculated as the unit cost of a message in the vehicle divided by its audience size (in thousands).

Coupons *(bons de réduction)*. A sales promotion technique consisting of granting price reductions in the form of certificates to encourage consumers to buy or try a certain product.

Coverage *(couverture)*. Per cent of the members of a target audience who are reached by one print vehicle.

CPM *(CPM)*. See COST PER THOUSAND

CPRP *(CUCB)*. See COST PER RATING POINT

Creative Boutique *(agence de création, studio créateur)*. Agency specializing only in creative work for advertisements or commercials.

Creative Plan *(programme créatif)*. A plan to address the problem of translating the communication tasks specified in the advertising campaign's objectives into effective advertisements.

Creative Services *(création publicitaire)*. Copy, art, and production services offered by an advertising agency.

Cumulative Audience *(auditoire accumulé)*. The number of different units reached by successive vehicles.

Dadson Compare Test *(test Dadson de messages publicitaires)*. A mall test using a test group and a control group.

Day-After-Recall *(mesure de la mémorisation différée)*. A form of copy testing a commercial the day after it was aired.

Dayparts *(intervalles de temps)*. Segments of a broadcast day specified by a station as a basis for setting rates.

Demand Elasticity *(élasticité de la demande)*. A measure of the percentage change in demand brought about by a one per cent change in a variable.

Depth Interview *(entrevue en profondeur)*. A technique using trained interviewers to probe respondents' reactions to a product, a brand, or a message.

Diary Method *(méthode utilisant un journal).* A technique of asking respondents to accurately record in a diary their purchasing of products or the broadcast programs they viewed during a specified period of time.

Direct Mail Advertising *(publicité directe).* Advertising sent by mail to a pre-selected audience.

Direct Personal Information *(information directe).* Buyers receive this information through physical contact with the product.

Disaggregative Process *(processus de desagrégation).* The recognition of the existence of an overall market, various demand schedules, or demand functions within this market as various groups of consumers experience different needs and wants.

Distinctive Brand Attributes *(attributs distinctifs de la marque).* The attributes through which a consumer distinguishes among different brands.

Double-Page Spread *(double page).* An advertising space covering two pages facing each other.

Duplication *(duplication).* The number of individuals or homes exposed to two or more vehicles.

Durable (or Hard) Goods *(biens durables).* High-priced products, such as automobiles and appliances, that require a long search process.

Editorial Matter *(texte de fond).* Material other than advertising that is contributed to a publication or a broadcast station.

Electroencephalograph (EEG). An instrument used to measure brain waves.

Evoked Set *(ensemble évoqué).* All the brands that a potential buyer considers as possible purchase alternatives to satisfy the same general need or desire.

Exposure *(exposition).* A contact between one individual (or family) and one vehicle.

Extensive Problem Solving *(résolution longue du problème).* Displayed when a consumer does not know either the product category or the brand.

Fact Book *(classeur regroupant des informations de base sur une marque ou un produit).* Compilation of relevant information concerning a product or brand for advertising purposes.

Fear Appeal Advertising *(publicité véhiculant une peur).* Advertising in which the rationale is to show consumers the negative consequences that may result from non-usage of a product or brand.

Feedback *(retour d'information).* The effect of advertising results on the firm.

Fees *(honoraires).* A type of compensation negotiated between the advertising agency and the advertiser to cover all the services rendered by the agency.

Fixed Position *(position fixe).* In broadcast media, this term refers to contracting the same period for the commercial to be aired.

Flat Rate *(taux uniforme).* Unit rate charged irrespective of volume or frequency of purchase.

Flexform *(annonce de format flexible ou libre).* Any advertising shape that does not conform to the normal rectangular format of print media.

Flight *(vague publicitaire).* The concentrated use of one medium followed by a period of inactivity.

Flighting *(publicité par vague).* A scheduling method of alternating periods of heavy advertising with periods of inactivity.

Focus Group *(groupe d'entretien en profondeur).* A small group of consumers assembled to discuss a given advertising topic by a trained moderator.

Freeform *(annonce de format libre).* See FLEXFORM

Frequency *(fréquence).* The number of times one member of a target audience is reached by a media vehicle or a media schedule.

Full-Service Agency *(agence à services complets).* An agency that provides clients with a complete range of advertising services.

Gatefold *(encart à volets).* Pages that fold out from a two-page spread advertisement.

General Advertising *(publicité nationale).* Advertising placed by a manufacturer or a wholesaler.

Gross Impressions *(impressions brutes).* The sum of all the audiences of the selected media vehicles, including duplications.

Gross Rating Points *(indice de couverture brute).* The number of messages delivered to the target audience, irrespective of the number of messages received by each individual, expressed as a percentage of the target audience.

GRP *(ICB).* See GROSS RATING POINTS

Headline *(gros titre).* The most conspicuous verbal element of a print advertisement.

Hi-Fi Colour *(couleur hi-fi).* The process of pre-printing rolls of high quality colour advertisements that appear in a continuous pattern, bleeding off the top and bottom of the page.

Horizontal Publication *(publication horizontale).* An industrial publication that reaches similar readers across all industries.

Ideal Brand *(marque idéale).* The brand that, if technically and economically feasible, would have all the features and characteristics desired by consumers.

Image Clarity *(clarté de l'image).* The degree to which a brand image is perceived clearly by consumers.

Image Content *(contenu de l'image de marque).* The personality traits characterizing the brand image.

Image Proximity *(proximité de l'image).* How present a brand is in the buyer's mind.

Impact of the Campaign *(impact de la campagne).* All selected physical characteristics (media options) of messages that may increase their effectiveness given a basic creative execution.

Impression *(impression).* A count of every time a message is received by a member of the audience of the media schedule.

Impulse Purchase *(achat par impulsion).* An unplanned consumer purchase.

Independent Station *(station indépendante).* A broadcast station not affiliated with any network.

Industrial Advertising *(publicité de produits industriels).* Advertising directed toward a professional audience responsible for evaluating the products a company uses.

In-House Agency *(agence-maison).* Advertising agency owned and operated by an advertiser.

Insert *(encart).* An advertisement printed in advance by an advertiser and bound in or inserted into a newspaper.

Institute of Canadian Advertisers (ICA). A national organization of advertisers.

Instrumental Relation Hypothesis *(hypothèse de la relation instrumentale).* The hypothesis that an attitude toward any object or situation is related to the end to which the object serves, i.e., to its consequences.

Intended Effect *(effect visé).* The precise objective of a message.

Intensity of Campaign *(intensité de la campagne).* Level of average effort (measured in monthly GRPs) over the time horizon of an advertising campaign.

Interpersonal Information *(information interpersonnelle).* Information flowing through interpersonal channels as people interact with social groups.

Irregular Purchase Cycle Markets *(marchés à cycle d'achat irrégulier).* Markets characterized by products that are purchased irregularly.

Isopreference Curve *(courbe d'isopréférence).* According to the vector model, all the brand points that are on the same perpendicular to a vector and thus equally liked by the consumer represented by this vector.

Jingle *("jingle" or refrain publicitaire).* A musical commercial with a short lyric stressing the product.

Layout *(maquette).* A rough draft of a print advertisement.

Lewin's Field Theory *(théorie du champ psychologique de Lewin).* An individual's behaviour is the result of a number of motives and forces in this individual's life-space.

Limited Problem Solving *(résolution courte du problème).* Displayed when a consumer knows a product category well but not a particular brand.

Line Rate *(taux d'une ligne).* The cost of using one agate line in a publication.

Line *(Ligne).* See AGATE LINE

Local Advertising *(publicité de détail).* Advertising placed by a retailer at a lower rate than for a national advertiser.

Logotype *(logotype).* A non-verbal symbol used to identify a brand.

Long or Unpredictable Purchase Cycle Markets *(marchés à cycle d'achat long ou imprédictible).* Markets characterized by products for which purchase decisions cannot be predicted.

Loss Leader *(article sacrifié).* Items sold at cost and used to attract attention to a store and/or its advertisements.

Mall Test *(test dans un lieu public).* A form of copy testing conducted with respondents intercepted in shopping malls and plazas.

Market Aggregation *(aggrégation des marchés).* A strategy that consists of a firm selling its product to as many customers as possible with a single marketing program.

Market Concentration *(concentration du marché).* The share of market enjoyed collectively by the four leading firms in an industry.

Market Development *(développement du marché).* A strategy of adapting existing products to other consumers or other markets.

Market Penetration *(pénétration du marché).* A strategy aimed at increasing the frequency of use of a brand (or product) and its rate of use by a potential market.

Market Segment *(segment de marché).* An identifiable subgroup of purchasers or consumers within a market who share a common characteristic or a special need.

Market Segmentation *(segmentation du marché).* A strategy that accounts for changes in intensity of demand within the same market and thus adjusts the products and their marketing programs accordingly.

Market Share *(part de marché).* One firm's proportion of an industry's total actual volume.

Marketing Macroenvironment *(environnement macro du marketing).* The marketing environment whereby the forces that influence a market are absolutely uncontrollable by the marketing manager (e.g., legal environment).

Marketing Microenvironment *(environnement micro du marketing).* The marketing environment characterized by forces over which marketers have no direct control but which they may attempt to manipulate by means of promotional actions.

Marketing Mix *(marketing mix, ou mix marketing).* The combination of elements of the marketing operation that are within a firm's control. These variables are classified into four groups: product, place, promotion, and price.

Marketing Plan *(plan marketing).* A plan that comprises all the elements of the marketing program and is designed to respond to the expectation of the target market(s) over a specified period of time

Marketing Planning *(planification marketing).* A process for working out a detailed account (most frequently in writing) of a company's self-image, objectives, the market program designed to achieve the objectives, and the methods used to measure the success of the planning effort.

Marketing Program *(programme marketing).* An action program formulated by a firm to respond as much as possible to the needs of a selected target market.

Marketing Strategy *(stratégie marketing).* The general term used to describe the overall program for selecting a particular market segment and then satisfying the customers in that segment through the careful use of the elements of the marketing mix

Maslow's Hierarchy of Needs *(hiérarchie des besoins de Maslow).* According to this theory there are five levels of human needs: (1) psychological; (2) safety; (3) love and affection; (4) self-esteem and respect; (5) self-actualization.

Matrices (or Mats) *(flans).* Moulds made of papier mâché used by newspapers to make stereotypes of clients' advertisements.

Media Buying Service *(service d'achat de médias ou service d'achat média).* An agency that specializes in purchasing media time or space for advertisers.

Media Plan *(plan-média).* A planning document that outlines and explains the decisions concerning media objectives, selection, schedule, budget, and research.

Media Schedule *(calendrier d'insertions).* A document listing all the selected media vehicles and describing when and for how long a message is to run.

Media Services *(service de médias).* Service provided by a full-service advertising agency. It comprises the development of a media plan and a media strategy, and the purchase of space and time for advertisers.

Media Strategy *(stratégie-média).* A set of decisions concerning the selection of media and the timing of the media placements.

Media Vehicle *(support publicitaire).* A single advertising medium, like a specific newspaper, magazine, radio or television program, or type of outdoor.

Message *(message).* The set of words, sounds, and images used by a communicator to convey an idea to an audience.

Milline Rate *(coût par mille lignes).* The cost of one thousand lines of newspaper space for each thousand of circulation.

Motivation *(motivation).* The underlying force of any action. This force reduces the state of psychological tension generally aroused by an unsatisfied need or desire, whether physiological or psychological.

Multiplexity *(multiplexité).* A characteristic of the components of attitude based on the number of elements involved.

Multi-Segment Marketing *(marketing à segments multiples).* The process of approaching several or all of the defined market segments.

National Advertising *(publicité nationale).* See GENERAL ADVERTISING

Negative Motivations *(motivations négatives).* Motivations that prevent the performance of certain acts through fear, aversion, or inhibition.

Negative Publicity *(publicité négative).* Editorial matter that reports problems encountered by a product, a service, or a company.

Net Unduplicated Audience *(auditoire sans duplication).* The number of different individuals reached by several vehicles during a given time period.

Net Unduplicated Reach *(couverture nette sans duplication).* The number of different individuals or families reached by single issues of several publications.

Network *(réseau).* A group of broadcast stations that carry the same signal at the same time periods.

Newspaper Marketing Bureau (NMB). An industry organization that promotes newspapers as viable national advertising vehicles.

Nielsen of Canada, A.C. A privately owned company providing television audience estimates and program ratings. The Nielsen Television Index (NTI) reports on network audiences. The Nielsen Broadcast Index (NBI) reports on local audiences.

Noted *(côte notée).* The percentage of individuals who have noticed a specific advertisement in a specific publication as measured by Starch ratings.

O & O Station *(station appartenant à un réseau).* A television or radio station owned and operated by a network.

Out-of-Home Media *(média hors domicile).* Mainly advertising media that can be viewed only outside the home.

Outdoor Advertising Association of Canada (OAAC). A national association of outdoor advertising companies that manages a credit rating system of advertising agencies.

Package Inserts *(encarts).* A sales promotion technique that consists of including in the package a promotional piece about the product, the product line, or a related product manufactured or distributed by a firm.

Packaged Goods *(produits emballés).* A convenience non-durable item characterized by frequent purchases and extensive distribution.

Pass-Along Circulation *(lecteurs secondaires).* The number of persons who read a newspaper or a magazine that was not purchased by a member of the household.

Pay-TV *(télévision à péage).* Television programs transmitted through cable and paid for by subscribers.

Perception *(perception).* A mental configuration that an individual has of a stimulus.

Periodical *(périodique).* A newspaper, magazine, or other publication that appears at regular intervals.

Periodical Press Association (PPA). A national organization of publishers of periodicals that manages a credit rating system of advertising agencies.

Personal Selling *(vente personnelle).* A personal rather than a mass communication (like advertising) directed to a prospect as a means of meeting marketing objectives.

Pica *(pica).* A unit of measure equal to 4.2 mm (1/6″) and 12 points.

Place *(canaux de distribution).* One of the four elements of the marketing mix. It refers to the distribution channels through which products flow from producers to consumers.

Plans Board *(réunion spéciale des chefs de service d'une agence, pour la mise au point d'une campagne).* A board usually composed of the chief executives of a full-service agency, whose responsibility is to approve the advertising strategy developed by the agency before it is submitted to the client.

Pleasant Appeal Advertising *(publicité utilisant un effet agréable).* Advertising that associates a product or brand with pleasant events, objects, or feelings so that buyers might make the association in the future.

Point *(point).* A unit of measure of the height of type equal to 0.35 mm (1/72″).

Point of Purchase Advertising *(publicité au point de vente).* Signs and displays at the point of final sale.

Position *(position).* The place where an advertisement appears or the spot where a commercial is inserted.

Positive Motivations *(motivations positives).* Needs or desires that cause an individual to favour certain acts.

Positive Valence/Negative Valence *(valence positive ou négative).* In terms of Lewin's theory, the forces inducing buyers to purchase or preventing them from making a purchase can be represented by vectors that characterize an individual's motivations.

Poster *(affiche).* An outdoor advertisement printed on paper and placed on a standardized panel.

Pre-emptible Rate *(taux avec possibilité de préemption).* A lower rate given to an advertiser who agrees to give priority to any advertiser paying a higher rate.

Preferred Position *(position préférée).* A specific position requested by an advertiser, who pays a premium for it.

Premium *(prime).* A sales promotion technique that consists of offering consumers, free of charge or sold at or below cost, a product different from the one they purchased.

Price *(prix).* One of the four elements of the marketing mix. It refers to all those aspects of the marketing program relating to the terms of the transaction.

Price Deal *(offre à prix spéciaux).* An offer to sell a product at a lower price (for example, "Buy ten, get one free").

Primary Audience *(auditoire primaire).* The main group(s) targeted by an advertising campaign or primary readers, listeners, or viewers.

Primary Circulation *(lecteurs primaires).* Household members who read a publication through subscription or purchase.

Primary Readership *(lecteurs primaires).* See PRIMARY CIRCULATION.

Prime Time *(heures de pointe).* A period of several consecutive hours in the evening for television or during the morning or afternoon rush hours for radio (also called drive time), when the audience size is the greatest.

Print Measurement Bureau (PMB). A nonprofit organization of advertisers, agencies, and magazine publishers that provides readership data on consumer magazines.

Product *(produit).* One of the four elements of the marketing mix. It represents a material offering (tangible) or a service (intangible).

Product Class *(classe de produits).* A group of products or services that share common attributes and compete directly for the same market.

Product Development *(développement du produit).* A strategy of developing a product with new characteristics that is aimed at a present target market.

Product Differentiation *(différentiation des produits).* The degree to which a product has succeeded in establishing an image as unique, especially when this uniqueness is perceived as beneficial.

Product Life-Cycle *(cycle de vie du produit).* The history of a product from its introduction to its demise, in terms of sales and profits. It is customarily divided into four stages: introduction, growth, maturity, and decline.

Product Positioning *(positionnement du produit).* Determination of the position of a product relative to the level of its attributes and its life-cycle.

Product Segmentation Strategy *(stratégie de segmentation des produits).* Strategy consisting of designing and marketing products based on the characteristics of the products as perceived by consumers in various market segments.

Product Variety *(variété de la gamme des produits).* A strategy of marketing a variety of products to an entire market, rather than catering to specific market segments.

Production *(production).* Translation of an advertising idea into a print advertisement or a broadcast commercial.

Profile *(profil).* A description of the characteristics of the users of a product or the audience of a medium.

Profile-Matching Strategy *(stratégie d'assortiment des profils).* A media strategy by which the profile of potential users of a product are matched with the audiences of the various print and broadcast media.

Projective Technique *(technique projective).* A research technique whereby respondents are asked to interpret and find meaning in an ambiguous stimulus in order to reveal hidden feelings and opinions.

Promotion *(promotion).* One of the four elements of the marketing mix. It refers to activities initiated by the seller, through communication tools and vehicles, in order to sell a product, service, or idea.

Promotional Mix *(mix promotionnel).* The combination of all the communication means used to affect sales.

Propaganda *(propagande).* A type of mass communication, whose source is not identified and which generally has an exclusively political rather than an economic purpose.

Psychogalvanometer *(psychogalvanomètre).* An instrument that measures the conductivity of the skin, which is affected by perspiration, which in turn is affected by an individual's emotional reactions.

Psychographics *(psychographie).* The characterization of an individual according to various lifestyle dimensions.

Public Relations *(relations publiques).* Communications designed to enhance the image of an individual or an organization.

Publicity *(publicité à titre gracieux).* Promotional activities originated by an advertiser that aim at obtaining free media space or time. Such activities include articles, editorials, and press releases, which are reproduced free of charge by the media.

Pull *(aspiration).* The degree of demand for a product or service from purchasers.

Pull Strategy *(stratégie d'aspiration).* A marketing strategy aimed at building interest in the market for a brand so that consumers recognize it or request it from retailers, thus creating a demand through the distribution channels.

Push Strategy *(stratégie de pression).* A marketing strategy aimed at convincing wholesalers and retailers to purchase a product.

Radio Bureau of Canada (RBC). A non-profit industry organization that promotes the use of radio as an advertising medium.

Rate Card *(carte de tarifs).* A document published by a particular medium that lists prices and other information related to placing messages in a medium.

Rating *(côte).* The percent of TV (or radio) households that are tuned, on the average, to one time period in a particular program.

Reach *(couverture).* The percentage of a target audience reached once by a media vehicle or a media schedule.

Readership *(lecteurs).* The audience of a publication; equal to circulation multiplied by readers per copy.

Read Most *(lu en majeure partie).* The percentage of people who state they have read more than 50 per cent of the copy in an advertisement, as measured by Starch ratings.

Rebate *(remboursement).* The additional amount paid by a medium to an advertiser who qualifies for a lower rate because of heavier use of the medium than originally contracted.

Recognized Agency *(agence agréée).* An advertising agency entitled to the standard commission based on a credit check by the various media.

Reference Group *(groupe de référence).* A social group to which an individual may belong or aspire to belong.

Refund Offers *(offre de remboursement).* A sales promotion technique by which cash refunds are offered to consumers who buy a given number of items of the same brand.

Regional Edition *(édition régionale).* An edition of a national magazine distributed with some changes in advertising in a specific geographic area.

Reminder Advertising *(publicité de rappel).* An attempt to influence a consumer's memory by reminding him of the existence of the product and of the brand.

Retail Advertising *(publicité/détaillants).* See LOCAL ADVERTISING

Retailer or Seller's Information *(information fournie par le détaillant ou le vendeur).* Product or brand information from retailers or from people in the distribution channels.

ROB *(EOCR).* See RUN-OF-BOOK

ROP *(EOCJ).* See RUN-OF-PRESS

ROS *(MPCS).* See RUN-OF-SCHEDULE

Routinized Response Behaviour *(comportement routinier).* Displayed when a consumer is very familiar with a product category and knows the characteristics of competing brands.

Run-of-Book *(emplacement ordinaire, au choix de la revue).* A magazine term indicating that an advertisement will be placed at the discretion of the publisher.

Run-of-Press *(emplacement ordinaire, au choix du journal).* A newspaper term indicating that an advertisement is to be printed on standard newsprint paper along with editorial matter, at the discretion of the publisher.

Run-of-Schedule *(messages placés au choix de la station).* A broadcast term indicating that the commercial is to be scheduled at the discretion of the station during a given time period.

Sales Promotion *(promotion des ventes).* Promotional activities other than publicity, advertising, and personal selling that are used to promote products and/or services.

Salient Attributes *(attributs importants).* Buyers tend to perceive only those attributes that are important to them.

Sampling *(distribution d'échantillons gratuits).* A sales promotion technique consisting of providing consumers with a sample of a product, at no cost, to induce trial.

Saturation Phase *(phase de saturation).* The part of the maturity stage of a product's life-cycle when all potential buyers have tried the product and sales are only replacement sales.

Selective Attention *(attention sélective).* Individuals filter the stimuli to which they are exposed and perceive only a small proportion of them.

Selective Distortion *(déformation sélective).* Individuals distort the messages filtered through selective attention so that the meanings are congruent with their need patterns.

Selective Retention *(mémoire sélective).* The propensity of a person to remember informative stimuli that support prior beliefs or feelings and to forget the stimuli that are at odds.

Semantic Differential Scale *(échelle sémantique différentielle).* A type of scale using a pair of opposites, such as dislike/like, or not believable/believable, often with seven points.

Share-of-Mind Recall *(rappel de la part de la mémoire).* Recall of a brand as a percentage of all brands mentioned unaided.

Short Purchase Cycle Markets *(marché à cycle d'achat court).* Markets characterized by routine purchase decision processes, or by limited problem solving when a new brand is introduced into a market.

Short Rate *(tarif réajusté).* The additional amount paid to a medium by an advertiser who has not met the quantity requirement of the contract. It is the difference between the earned rate and the contracted rate.

Simulcasting *(émission simultanée).* The practice of scheduling the same episode of the same program at the same time as for a U.S. station. Cable companies may be required to substitute the Canadian signal for the U.S. signal.

Sleeper Effect *(effet d'indolence).* Psychological phenomenon which suggests that as time elapses, individuals who are submitted to persuasive communications tend to dissociate the communication content from the source.

Slogan *(slogan).* A set of words associated with a brand, which embodies an advertising theme. It may last for years.

Soft Goods *(produits "doux" ou articles de consommation intermédiaire).* Shopping non-durable items, moderately priced, featuring a selected distribution. Includes such products as clothing, carpeting, and linens.

Source *(source).* See COMMUNICATOR

Source Credibility *(crédibilité de l'émetteur).* Before any communication takes place, a source is perceived by an audience as having expertise, trustworthiness, and attractiveness.

Spectacolour *(spectacouleur).* The process of pre-printing rolls of four-colour advertisements with the dimensions of the newspaper page and cutting and incorporating the advertisements into the newspaper as full pages.

Spectacular *(panneau géant spécial).* An outdoor advertisement designed to be conspicuous.

Speculative Presentation *(présentation spéculative).* An advertising campaign proposal for a product submitted by an agency to a client.

Split-Run *(tirage partagé).* A service offered by some newspapers or magazines whereby the advertiser can run different advertisements in alternate copies of the same publication at the same time.

Sponsor, To *(parrainer un programme).* An advertiser buys all the commercial time available in a given program or segment.

Spot Time *(temps publicitaire).* Commercial time available from local stations and purchased by advertisers on a market-by-market basis.

Storyboard *("storyboard" ou scénario du message publicitaire).* Sequence of drawings designed to portray copy, dialogue, and action for a television commercial.

Subliminal Advertising *(publicité subliminale).* A communication received by a subject at such a high speed that it falls below the subject's perceptual threshold.

Suggestive Advertising *(publicité suggestive).* Advertising that appeals directly to consumers' emotions and feelings and conveys a certain product or brand image.

Superboard *(panneau géant).* Hand-painted or printed designs on structures larger than posters.

Starch Method. A recognition method of testing print advertisements conducted by Daniel Starch (Canada) Ltd.

Sweepstakes *(loterie publicitaire, ou "sweepstakes").* A sales promotion technique that consists of asking consumers to provide their names and addresses to the advertiser who, at a fixed date, selects the winners by random drawing from all entries.

Tabloid *(journal petit format).* A small-size newspaper approximately 254 mm wide and 356 mm deep (10″ by 14″).

Tachitoscope *(tachistoscope).* An instrument that measures the attention levels of various executions by varying the time of exposure to an advertisement.

Target Audience *(cible).* Group(s) of individuals to whom a communication is directed.

Target Market *(marché-cible).* A specific group of consumers selected by the firm and to which it directs one or several of its products (or services).

Telecaster Committee (TC). A committee formed in 1972 that approves all commercials to be aired on a group of CTV affiliated stations plus one independent outlet, using similar criteria.

Television Bureau of Canada (TVB). A non-profit industry organization that promotes the use of television as an advertising medium.

Testimonial Advertising *(publicité avec témoignage).* Advertising that uses a credible source to testify for the product claim.

Theatre Test *(test d'annonces en salles de cinéma).* A form of copy testing conducted with subjects who preview a program at a theatre.

Theme *(thème).* The basic idea on which an advertising campaign is built.

Top-of-Mind Recall *(test première marque à l'esprit).* The percentage of individuals mentioning a brand as the first one that comes to mind.

Trade Advertising *(publicité destinée au réseau).* Advertising aimed at wholesalers and/or retailers.

Trade Deals *(promotion/réseau, ou offres spéciales).* Price reduction by a company to an intermediary for a limited period of time to encourage the intermediary to carry the promoted brand.

Trading Stamps *(timbres de réduction).* Technique that consists of offering consumers a set of products in exchange for receipts totalling a given amount or a cumulative number of points.

Traffic Manager *(surveillant de la production).* The individual in an advertising agency who is responsible for co-ordinating and ensuring the timely completion of the work of the various specialists within the agency.

Two-Step Flow of Communication *(communication en deux étapes).* The concept according to which ideas are transmitted through the mass media to opinion leaders and then from these opinion leaders to less active segments of the population.

Ultra-High Frequency Channels (UHF) *(canaux à fréquences ultra-hautes).* Television channels 14 and higher.

Unaided Recall *(souvenir spontané).* The percentage of individuals mentioning a brand when asked to name all brands that come to mind.

Unique Selling Proposition (USP) *(proposition exclusive de vente).* An advertising technique according to which an advertisement should stress an exclusive selling argument.

Valence *(valence).* The intensity of various attitude components.

Vehicle *(support).* See MEDIA VEHICLE

Vertical Publication *(publication verticale).* A business publication aimed at readers in a specific industry.

Very High Frequency Channels (VHF) *(canaux à très hautes fréquences).* Television channels 2 through 13.

Video *(vidéo).* The visual part of a commercial.

Volume Discount *(réduction de quantités).* A discount to advertisers that is based on the dollar amount spent for advertising.

Wear-Out *(usure).* TV commercials' loss in effectiveness after several viewings.

INDICES

Subject Index

Author Index